Mac OS X

THE MISSING MANUAL

*The book that
should have been
in the box*

From the Reviewers

Mac OS X: The Missing Manual is honest, thorough, and to the point. It really does cover aspects of using OS X that are essential but may not be obvious—even to experienced Mac users, such as how to change the background color of Finder folders and what accounts in Unix are all about.

—Mark Sealey, thinksecret.com

I can't think of a better Mac author working right now than David Pogue, and this book is one of his best. An excellent price, and an excellent book by an excellent writer. Nuff said.

—John Manzione, www.macnet2.com

With characteristic humility, author/publisher David Pogue describes this as "the book that should have been in the box"—and, well, yeah, he's right. To quote Dizzy Dean, it ain't braggin' if you done it.

—Jamie McCormack, About This Particular Macintosh (atpm.com)

Befitting his musical background, Pogue's prose is equal parts lyrical and percussive—with a sometimes wry, sometimes silly humor that never gets in the way of the point he is making. It's a style Pogue has honed to an art; no one else can take a subject as dry as a computer operating system and make it seem so completely accessible, and even fun.

—Chuck la Tournous, NJ MUG Reviews

A fact-packed romp through the operating system and the extras that come with it, made resoundingly more readable by the depth of Pogue's knowledge, his familiarity with Mac history, and his eagerness to engage novices as members of the Mac user community.

—David Wall, amazon.com

Pogue is consistently funny, and has a clear, concise prose style as well as Mac chops to spare.

—boingboing.net

Detailed without becoming dense, [with] just the right touch of folksy humor to put tech newbies at ease.

—Julio Ojeda-Zapata, Writer's Digest

O'Reilly seems to have tapped into the current state of consumer/commercial software angst with its Missing Manual series. The titles tend to be well-written, attractively designed, and liberally illustrated, and they're not shy about pointing out flaws in a product—a feature you're not likely to find in a vendor's official documentation.

—Shirl Kennedy, Information Today

Mac OS X: The Missing Manual presents a huge (HUGE) subject with clarity, wit, and delightfully useful tips that any (ANY) user of Mac OS X will find helpful, time-saving, and wicked cool. David Pogue didn't give us the first manual for OS X... but he has delivered the best. I wish all technical writing were this good.

—Russ Harlan, Augusta, GA

Mac OS X
THE MISSING MANUAL

David Pogue

POGUE PRESS™
O'REILLY®

Beijing • Cambridge • Farnham • Köln • Paris • Sebastopol • Taipei • Tokyo

Mac OS X: The Missing Manual
by David Pogue

Copyright © 2002 Pogue Press, LLC. All rights reserved.
Printed in the United States of America.

Published by Pogue Press/O'Reilly & Associates, Inc., 101 Morris Street,
Sebastopol, CA 95472.

January 2002:	First Edition
February 2002:	Second Printing
Februray 2002:	Third Printing
February 2002:	Fourth Printing
March 2002:	Fifth Printing
March 2002:	Sixth Printing
March 2002:	Seventh Printing
March 2002:	Eighth Printing
April 2002:	Ninth Printing
June 2002:	Tenth Printing
June 2002:	Eleventh Printing
July 2002:	Twelfth Printing

ISBN: 0-596-00082-0

Table of Contents

Part Four: The Technologies of Mac OS X

Part Six: Appendixes

The Missing Credits

About the Author

David Pogue, computer columnist for the *New York Times* and former *Macworld* columnist, is the creator of the Missing Manual series. He's the author or co-author of 20 books, including five titles in the Missing Manual series (*Mac OS 9, iMovie 2, Windows Me, Windows XP,* and this one*); six books in the *...for Dummies* series (*Macs, The iMac, The iBook, Magic, Opera,* and *Classical Music*); *PalmPilot: The Ultimate Guide;* and *Macworld Mac Secrets,* 6th Edition.

In his other life, David is a former Broadway show conductor, a magician, and an incorrigible pianist. He lives in Connecticut (photos at *www.davidpogue.com*).

He welcomes feedback about this book and others in the Missing Manual series by email: *david@pogueman.com.* (If you're seeking technical help, however, please refer to the help sources listed in Appendix E.)

About the Creative Team

Nan Barber (copy editor) co-authored *Office 2001 for the Macintosh: The Missing Manual.* She's the principal copy editor for the Missing Manual series, having edited the titles on Mac OS 9, AppleWorks 6, iMovie, and Windows Me. She's also managing editor for *Salamander (www.salamandermag.org)* and contributing copy editor for *www.thespook.com.* Email: *nanbarber@mac.com.*

Rose Cassano (cover sailboat illustration) has been an independent designer and illustrator for 20 years. Assignments have ranged from the nonprofit sector to corporate clientele. She lives in beautiful Southern Oregon, grateful for the miracles of modern technology that make living and working there a reality. Email: *cassano@cdsnet.net.* Web: *www.rosecassano.com.*

Dennis Cohen (technical reviewer) has served as the technical reviewer for many bestselling Mac books, including several editions of *Macworld Mac Secrets* and most Missing Manual titles. He's the co-author of *AppleWorks 6 for Dummies, Macworld AppleWorks 6 Bible, Macworld Microsoft Office 2001 Bible,* and *Macworld Mac OS X Bible.* Email: *drcohen@mac.com.*

Alan Graham (research and testing) is an author for the O'Reilly Network, where he writes the column "Designing for Aqua," and an editor for VisorCentral.com. A design consultant for 3D, video, Web, user-interface, and FileMaker Pro, he has appeared in *Wired, The London Observer,* CNET Radio's *Mac Show Live,* and *The NewsHour with Jim Lehrer* on PBS. He also appears in Po Bronson's bestselling book, *Nudist on the Late Shift.* (He is not the nudist.)

Joseph Schorr (author, Chapters 8 and 9) senior product manager for Extensis, began collaborating with David Pogue in 1982—on musicals at Yale. Since then, Joe co-wrote six editions of *Macworld Mac Secrets,* wrote *Macworld's* "Secrets" column for many years, and founded the Schorr Family of Portland, OR.

Phil Simpson (book design and layout) works out of his office in Stamford, CT *(pmsimpson@earthlink .net),* where he has had his graphic design business for 20 years. He is experienced in many facets of graphic design, including corporate identity, publication design, and corporate and medical communications.

Chris Stone (author, Chapters 15 and 16) is the Senior Macintosh Systems Administrator at O'Reilly & Associates. Though at times it might appear otherwise, he really does love his wife Miho, and sons Andy and J.J., (much) more than Macs and the San Francisco Giants. Email: *cjstone@mac.com.*

Acknowledgments

The Missing Manual series is a joint venture between Pogue Press (the dream team introduced on these pages) and O'Reilly & Associates (a dream publishing partner). I'm indebted, as always, to Tim O'Reilly, Cathy Record, and the rest of the gang.

AppleScript genius Bill Briggs overhauled my AppleScript chapter for Mac OS X compliance. Patrick Gerrity, Bruce O'Leary, and Apple's Ken Bereskin and Bill Evans also helped with special favors. I'm also grateful to proofreaders John Cacciatore and Danny Marcus; to this book's beta readers, Jim Elferdink and Elizabeth "Eagle Eye" Tonis, who spent a holiday weekend stomping typos out of existence; and to David Rogelberg for believing in the idea. And above all, thanks to Jennifer, Kelly, and Tia, who make these books—and everything else—possible.

The Missing Manual Series

Missing Manual books are superbly written guides to computer products that don't come with printed manuals (which is just about all of them). Each book features a handcrafted index; cross-references to specific page numbers (not just "See Chapter 14"); and a promise never to use an apostrophe in the possessive word *its.* Recent and upcoming titles include:

- *Office X for Macintosh: The Missing Manual* by Nan Barber & David Reynolds

- *DreamWeaver 4: The Missing Manual* by David Sawyer McFarland

- *Mac OS 9: The Missing Manual* by David Pogue

- *AppleWorks 6: The Missing Manual* by Jim Elferdink & David Reynolds

- *iMovie 2: The Missing Manual* by David Pogue

- *Office 2001 for Macintosh: The Missing Manual* by Nan Barber & David Reynolds

- *Windows Me: The Missing Manual* by David Pogue

- *Windows 2000 Pro: The Missing Manual* by Sharon Crawford

- *Windows XP Home Edition: The Missing Manual* by David Pogue

Introduction

W ithout a doubt, Mac OS X is a stunning technical achievement. In fact, it may be the most advanced personal-computer operating system on earth. But beware of its name.

The X is meant to be a Roman numeral, pronounced "ten." Unfortunately, many people see "Mac OS X" and say "Mac O.S. Ex." That's a sure way to get funny looks in public.

Then there's the "Mac OS" part—what a misnomer! Mac OS X is not, in fact, the Mac OS. Under the hood, it bears no resemblance whatsoever to the traditional Mac operating system. Apple designed Mac OS X to *look* something like the old Mac system software, and certain features have been written to *work* like they used to. But all of that is just an elaborate fake-out. Mac OS X is utterly new, written from scratch. It's not so much Mac OS X, in other words, as Steve Jobs 1.0.

If you've never used a Macintosh before, none of this matters. You have nothing to unlearn. You'll find an extremely simple, beautifully designed desktop waiting for you.

But if you're one of the 25 million people who have grown accustomed to the traditional Mac OS, then Mac OS X may come as a bit of a shock. Hundreds of features you thought you knew have been removed, replaced, or relocated. (If you ever find yourself groping for an old, favorite feature, see Appendix A, the "Where'd it go?" dictionary.)

Why did Apple throw out the operating system that made it famous to begin with? Through the years, Apple kept on piling new features onto a software foundation originally poured in 1984, doing its best to perform nips and tucks to the ancient software to make it resemble something modern. But underneath, the original foundation was beginning to creak, and programmers complained of the "spaghetti code" that the Mac OS had become.

Apple felt that there wasn't much point in undertaking a dramatic system-software overhaul if they couldn't nail every key feature of modern computer technology in the process, especially crash-proofness. Starting from scratch—and jettisoning the system software we'd come to know over the years—was the only way to do it.

The result is an operating system that provides a liberating sense of freedom and stability—but one that, for existing Mac fans, requires a good deal of learning (and forgetting).

Most people eventually conclude that the trade-off is well worth making. But in fact, you have little choice. Apple is switching to Mac OS X, and if you expect to remain a Mac user, sooner or later, you will, too.

What Mac OS X Gives You

The main thing you gain by moving to Mac OS X is stability. You and your Mac may go for years without ever witnessing a system crash. Oh, it's technically possible for Mac OS X to crash—but few have actually witnessed such an event. Rumors of such crashes circulate on the Internet like Bigfoot sightings.

Underneath the gorgeous, shimmering, translucent desktop of Mac OS X is Unix, the industrial-strength, rock-solid OS that drives many a Web site and university. It's not new by any means; in fact, it's decades old, and has been polished by genera-tions of programmers. That's precisely why Steve Jobs and his team chose it as the basis for the NeXT operating system (Jobs's project during his twelve years away from Apple), which Apple bought in 1997 to turn into Mac OS X.

But crash resistance is only the big-ticket item. Mac OS X also brings you goodies like these:

- **New Finder features.** In addition to the familiar list and icon views, a Mac OS X Finder offers something called column view, which lets you burrow deeply into nested folders without leaving a trail of open windows behind you. This view even lets you look at pictures, view movies, and play sounds right there in the Finder window, without having to launch a program to do so.

  At your option, every Finder window can also display a button-studded toolbar, exactly as in a Web browser. You can install and remove buttons there (frequently used files or programs, for example) just by dragging.

  The new Finder even offers an Undo command that really works—a first for the Macintosh. It can restore to its original folder an icon that you just dragged, for example.

- **The Dock.** At the bottom of the screen, you'll find a row of beautiful, photorealistic icons. This is the Dock, the single most controversial and important new feature in Mac OS X. It combines elements of the menu, the Launcher, pop-up win-dows, the old Application menu, and even the Windows taskbar. All at once, it's a launcher, a status display, and an organizational tool. Chapter 3 covers the Dock in astounding detail.

- **Advanced graphics.** What the programmers get excited about is the set of advanced graphics technologies called things like *Quartz* (for two-dimensional graphics) and *OpenGL* (for three-dimensional graphics). For the rest of us, these technologies translate into a beautiful, translucent look for the desktop (a design scheme Apple calls Aqua); smooth looking *(antialiased)* lettering everywhere on the screen; and the ability to turn any document on the screen into an Adobe Acrobat (PDF) file.

   (The beauty of PDF files, of course, is that anyone else, on virtually any kind of computer, can open them; they'll see all the original fonts and graphics used when preparing it, even if they don't have the same programs or fonts on their machines.)

- **Advanced networking.** When it comes to hooking up your Mac to other computers, including those on the Internet, the old Mac operating system can't touch the new one. As you can read in Chapter 12, Mac OS X's networking software is light-years more polished and advanced than what came before. The result is not only fewer settings to change—only one networking control panel instead of four—but advanced features like *multihoming,* which lets your laptop switch automatically and invisibly from its cable modem settings to its dial-up modem settings when you take it on the road. And in Mac OS X version 10.1 and later, you can view and open folders from a networked Windows machine exactly as though it were a Mac.

- **Lots of accessory programs.** Mac OS X comes with a broad array of interesting software. Some, like Mail, you may wind up using every day; others, like the 3-D, voice-activated Chess program, are designed primarily to let you and Apple show off Mac OS X to flabbergasted onlookers.

- **Simpler everything.** Most applications in Mac OS X show up as a single icon. Behind the scenes, they may have dozens of individual software crumbs, just like the programs of Mac OS 9—but Mac OS X treats that single icon as though it's a folder. All the support files are hidden away inside, where you don't have to look at them. In other words, to remove a program from your Mac, you just drag the application's single icon to the Trash, without having to worry that you're leaving scraps behind.

- **More keyboard control.** Beginning in Mac OS X version 10.1, you can operate every menu in every program entirely from the keyboard—a terrific timesaver for efficiency freaks. See page 106.

- **Tighter Internet integration.** Mac OS X makes your Mac more a part of the Internet than it ever has been before. Not only can you treat your iDisk (Chapter 18) as though it's an external hard drive, available all the time, but Mac OS X includes the famous and popular Apache Web server. That's Unix software that lets your Mac *be* a Web site, dishing out Web pages to all comers (Chapter 21).

- **A command-line interface.** In general, Apple has completely hidden from you every trace of the Unix operating system that lurks beneath Mac OS X's beautiful skin. For the benefit of programmers and other technically oriented fans, however, Apple left uncovered a couple of tiny passageways into that far more complex realm.

Chapters 15 and 16 cover Mac OS X's Unix underpinnings in more depth. For now, it's enough to note that, if you like, you can capitalize on the *command-line*

POWER USERS' CLINIC

Mac OS X: the Buzzword-Compliant Operating System

You can't read an article about Mac OS X without hearing certain technical buzzwords that were once exclusively the domain of computer engineers. Apple is understandably proud that Mac OS X offers all of these sophisticated, state-of-the-art operating system features; unfortunately, publicizing them means exposing the rest of us to a lot of fairly unnecessary geek terms. Here's what they mean:

Preemptive multitasking. Most people know that multitasking means "doing more than one thing at once." The Mac has always been capable of making a printout, downloading a file, and letting you type away in a word processor, all at the same time.

Unfortunately, the Mac OS 7/8/9 version of multitasking works by the rule of the playground: the bully gets what he wants. If one of your programs insists on hogging the attention of your Mac's processor (because it's crashing, for example), it leaves the other programs gasping for breath. This arrangement is called *cooperative* multitasking. Clearly, it works only if your programs are in fact cooperating with each other.

Mac OS X's *preemptive* multitasking system brings a teacher to the playground to make sure that every program get a fair amount of time from the Mac's processor. The result is that the programs get along much better, and a poorly written or crashing program isn't permitted to send the other ones home crying.

Multithreading. Multithreading means "doing more than one thing at once," too, but in this case it's referring to a single program. Even while iMovie is exporting your movie, for example, it lets you continue editing at the same time. Not all Mac OS 9 programs offer this feature, but all programs written especially for Mac OS X do. (Note, however,

that programs that are simply adapted for Mac OS X— "Carbonized" software, as described on page 116—don't necessarily offer this feature.)

Symmetrical multiprocessing. Macs containing more than one processor chip are nothing new. But before Mac OS X, only specially written programs—Adobe Photoshop filters, for example—benefited from the speed boost.

But no more. Mac OS X automatically capitalizes on multiple processors, sharing the workload of multiple programs (or even multithreaded tasks within a single program), meaning that every Mac OS X program gets accelerated. Mac OS X is smart enough to dole out processing tasks evenly, so that both (or all) of your processors are being put to productive use.

Dynamic memory allocation. As noted below, Mac OS X programs no longer have fixed RAM allotments. The operating system giveth and taketh away your programs' memory in real time, so that no RAM is wasted. For you, this system means better stability, less hassle.

Memory protection. In Mac OS X, every program runs in its own indestructible memory bubble—another reason Mac OS X is so much more stable than its predecessors. If one program crashes, it isn't allowed to poison the well of RAM that other programs might want to use, as in Mac OS 9. Programs may still freeze or quit unexpectedly; the world will never be entirely free of sloppy programmers. But in Mac OS 9, you would have seen a message that says, "Save open documents and restart." In Mac OS X, you'll be delighted to find that the message says, "The application 'Bomber' has unexpectedly quit. The system and other applications have not been affected."

---

interface of Mac OS X. That simply means that you can type out cryptic commands, which the Mac executes instantly and efficiently, in an all-text window.

If you're splurting your orange juice, outraged at the irony, well, you wouldn't be the first. Apple is, after all, the company that put itself on the map by establishing the superiority of the *graphic* interface—mouse, icons, menus, and windows. The requirement to type out memorized commands, Apple led us to believe, should die a quick and ugly death. Yet here it is again, in what's supposed to be the world's most modern and advanced operating system.

Still, there's not much harm in it. The command line is completely hidden until you ask for it. It's very useful for programmers, network administrators, and other people for whom the computer is not just an adventure—it's a job.

What Mac OS X Takes Away

Getting used to the new features is very easy. What's much harder is unlearning what you had once worked so hard to master in the old Mac operating system. You'll find yourself especially alarmed at how few troubleshooting steps are required—or even possible—in Mac OS X. For example:

• **Extension conflicts.** The number one destabilizing factor of the traditional Macintosh has been banished forever: Mac OS X doesn't use system extensions and control panels. It's time to forget all of the troubleshooting routines Mac fans have had to learn over the years, including pressing the Shift key at startup, using Extensions Manager, and buying Conflict Catcher. You will never again perform an extension conflict test, trying to figure out which extension is making your Mac freeze. None of those habitual routines has any meaning in Mac OS X.

Software companies can still add new features to your Mac, just as they once did using extensions—but now they'll do it by writing startup applications, which is a much safer, more organized method that can't destabilize your Mac.

• **Memory controls.** There's no Memory control panel in Mac OS X. Nor will you find a Get Info window for each application that lets you change its memory allotment. This is *great* news.

Mac OS X manages memory quickly, intelligently, and constantly. The reason you don't allot a certain amount of your Mac's memory to a program, as you had to do in Mac OS 9, is that Mac OS X simply gives each running program *as much memory as it needs*. And if you undertake some task that requires more memory, Mac OS X instantly *gives* that program more memory—on the fly.

So what happens if you're running 125 programs at once? Mac OS X uses *virtual memory*, a scheme by which it lays down pieces of the programs running in the background onto your hard drive, so that it may devote your actual RAM to the programs in front. But this virtual memory scheme bears very little relationship to the relatively crude, slow virtual memory of the old Mac OS. In Mac OS X, this shuffling happens almost instantaneously, and virtual memory is called in only to park *pieces* of applications as necessary.

The bottom line: You can forget everything you knew about concepts like virtual memory, the Disk Cache, the Get Info window's memory boxes for applications, and the panic of getting out-of-memory messages. For the most part, they're gone forever.

- **Rebuilding the desktop.** If you don't remember having to perform this arcane procedure on your Mac, you don't know how lucky you are. Unlike Mac OS 9, Mac OS X doesn't have the unfortunate habit of holding in its internal database the icons of programs long since deleted from your hard drive. As a result, you never have to rebuild that desktop, and you'll never see the symptoms that suggest that it's time for desktop rebuilding (a general slowdown and generic icons replacing the usual custom ones).

- **The clean install.** When troubleshooting the pre–Mac OS X Mac, the last resort was the *clean install.* This time-consuming procedure involved installing a second, factory-fresh System Folder onto your hard drive. It almost always worked in solving random system glitches, but it really did a number on your Saturday afternoon. For example, the new System Folder didn't have any of the preference files, Internet settings, fonts, extensions, control panels, and other components that you had carefully built up over the years.

  In Mac OS X, preferences and fonts are no longer in the System folder. And, as noted above, neither are extensions and control panels. What's left in the System folder, therefore, is the real Mac OS X, which never changes. As you install new programs, they're not permitted to touch the actual System folder, which remains as virginal and fresh as the day it was installed, sealed under clear acrylic.

  In short, you'll never need to perform a clean install.

- **The menu and Application menu.** The menus at the upper corners of the screen, which used to anchor the Mac desktop experience, have been eliminated or changed in Mac OS X. As noted above, the Dock takes on their functions.

  You'll still find an menu in Mac OS X, but it's no longer a place to store aliases of your favorite files and folders. Instead, it lists commands, such as Restart and Shut Down, that are relevant no matter what program you're using.

- **The Control Strip.** This handy floating strip of tiles is gone, too. In Mac OS X 10.1 and later, you'll find its replacement in the upper-right corner of the screen, on the menu bar; see page 87 for details. This is now where you make quick control panel settings, like adjusting the volume, checking your laptop battery charge, and so on. (In versions of Mac OS X before 10.1, special tiles on the Dock fulfilled this function.)

- **Icon labels, pop-up windows, spring-loaded folders, password protection, Put Away, sound recording, randomized desktop pictures.** As you explore Mac OS X, you'll continue to find—or, rather, not find—Mac OS 9 features that no longer exist. Some are gone for good; for example, there hasn't been much outcry that Button view and Simple Finder are gone for good.

On the other hand, some of the absent features will return. Apple continues to restore old standby features with every successive version of Mac OS X. Version 10.1, for example, restored several big-ticket features (such as CD burning and DVD playback) and many other smaller ones (such as accessibility features for the disabled).

Finally, remember that some features aren't actually gone—they've just been moved. Before you panic, consult Appendix A for a neat, alphabetical list of every traditional Mac feature and its status in the new operating system.

Three OSes in One

Despite the fact that many individual aspects of the new operating system have been revisited and redesigned to make them simpler, the big Mac OS X picture is actually more complex than the old Mac OS picture. For the next few years, at least, you'll have to contend with elements of *three different* operating systems that Apple fused together to make Mac OS X: Something old, something new (and blue), and something borrowed.

- **Unix.** As noted above, the very old portion is Unix. (You may also hear the terms Darwin, OpenStep, and NextStep; these are all variations of Unix. NextStep, later renamed OpenStep, was the version adapted by Steve Jobs during his years at NeXT. Much of Mac OS X, in fact, is based on the work done by Jobs and his team at NeXT.)

Unix is beloved by programmers, it's rock-solid, and it eliminates almost all of the troubleshooting headaches Mac fans once endured. But it couldn't be much more user-hostile—it's the very antithesis of Macintosh simplicity. Unix requires you to type out cryptic commands. The mouse is pretty much irrelevant.

Fortunately, as noted above, you may never even see it. Apple has almost completely hidden Mac OS X's Unix personality from you, leaving only a few tiny keyholes through which you can peek at it (see Chapter 15).

- **Aqua.** What covers up Mac OS X's technical underpinnings is an extremely clean, beautiful operating-system overlay called Aqua. (That's the new and blue part.) This is the look of Mac OS X, in which buttons look like glistening globs of Colgate Very Berry Gel, menus are translucent, and tiny animations seem to make your screen live and breathe.

- **Mac OS 9 (Classic).** Only software programs especially written or adapted for Mac OS X benefit from many of Mac OS X's new features, including its stability. This is the bad news about Mac OS X: you need all-new *programs* to run on it. That's right—you'll have to get upgrades to the new, Mac OS X-tailored versions of Word, Excel, FreeHand, Photoshop, FileMaker, Quicken, and whatever other programs you use.

That doesn't mean that you *can't* use the 18,000 existing Macintosh applications, however. The first time you double-click the icon of one these pre–Mac OS X programs each day, you wait about a minute as a special Mac OS 9 emulation program called *Classic* starts up. In effect, you're running one operating system within another. Your old programs then open, work, and look just as they did in Mac OS 9, but they don't enjoy any of the new Mac OS X features. If a Classic program crashes, for example, the whole Classic bubble crashes (but you still don't have to restart the Mac—just Classic).

Chapter 5 contains full details about using Classic. For now, resign yourself to the fact that using Mac OS X, at least for the next couple of years, generally means having to master *two different* operating systems—the old and the new.

Despite the fact that elements of three different operating systems power Mac OS X, there's no reason to panic. You can safely ignore the Unix part. And even the Classic mode is transitional; years from now, when nobody makes anything but Mac OS X-savvy applications, you won't even have to think about the Classic mode.

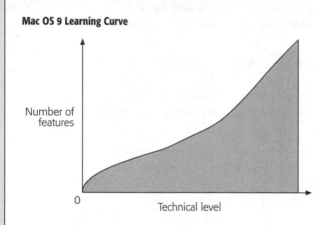

Mac OS 9 Learning Curve

Number of features

0

Technical level

Mac OS X Learning Curve

Number of features

0

Technical level

Figure I-1:
Top: In Mac OS 9, there's nothing fancy about the learning curve. You're a beginner, then you're intermediate, and then you're advanced.

Bottom: In Mac OS X, the basics are very easy to learn—but the amount of advanced stuff is considerable. This book is dedicated to helping you along both curves.

About this Book

Because Mac OS X is such a unique hybrid operating system, you may well find that learning it follows the graph illustrated at bottom in Figure I-1. That is, whereas the old Mac OS offered a steady learning curve, Mac OS X presents two *different* learning curves. The basics are very easy to learn, and the advanced topics are very technical.

Unfortunately, Mac OS X comes with little more than a pamphlet in the way of printed instructions. To find your way around, you're expected to use Apple's online help system. (Balloon Help and Apple Guide are gone.) And as you'll quickly discover, these help pages are tersely written, offer very little technical depth, lack useful examples, and provide no tutorials whatsoever. You can't even mark your place, underline, or read it in the bathroom. And there's not a word about the powerful Unix underpinnings of Mac OS X.

The purpose of this book, then, is to serve as the manual that should have accompanied Mac OS X. In this book's pages, you'll find step-by-step instructions for using every Mac OS X feature, including those you may not even have quite understood, let alone mastered: networking, CD burning, AppleScript, and even the basics of tapping into the Unix operating system that beats within the chest of Mac OS X.

Mac OS X: The Missing Manual is designed to accommodate readers at every technical level. The primary discussions are written for advanced-beginner or intermediate Mac users. But if you're a first-time Mac user, miniature sidebar articles called Up To Speed provide the introductory information you need to understand the topic at hand. If you're an advanced Mac user, on the other hand, keep your eye out for similar shaded boxes called Power Users' Clinic. They offer more technical tips, tricks, and shortcuts for the more experienced Mac fan.

About Mac OS X Version 10.1 and Later

The earliest versions of Mac OS X—numbered 10.0 through 10.0.4—were very slow and relatively incomplete. A few thousand hard-core, red-blooded Mac fans tried out these versions, but relatively few actually used them for day-to-day work.

Mac OS X version 10.1, which Apple released in September 2001, is the real thing. It's dramatically faster, much more polished, and better organized. AppleScript has been beefed up; AirPort wireless network tools are restored; the columns in the Finder list views are resizable; and a row of tiny menu icons provide quick access to settings like volume and battery charge. Version 10.1 introduced the freedom to position the Dock vertically on the sides of your screen, if you like. It was also the first version that could burn CDs from the desktop and play DVD movies.

Note: A series of minor, no-new-features updates followed, including 10.1.1 (improvements in USB and FireWire, printing, camera compatibility, CD burning, etc.), 10.1.2 (better DVD playback, USB and FireWire compatibility, and so on), and 10.1.3 (still more hardware compatibility updates and bug fixes). The Software Update feature (page 203) is designed to notify you automatically when they become available.

In retrospect, versions before 10.1 look like nothing more than a dress rehearsal for the real Mac OS X show.

You'll find this book useful no matter which version you have, but it describes and illustrates version 10.1 and later. If you're still working with one of the earlier versions, proceed immediately to the Apple Web site (or an Apple store) to order the upgrade to the latest version.

About the Outline

Mac OS X: The Missing Manual is divided into six parts:

- The chapters in Part 1, **The Mac OS X Desktop,** cover everything you see on the screen when you turn on a Mac OS X computer: the Dock, icons, windows, menus, scroll bars, the Trash, aliases, the menu, and so on.

- Part 2, **Applications in Mac OS X,** is dedicated to the proposition that an operating system is little more than a launch pad for *programs*—the actual applications you use in your everyday work, such as email programs, Web browsers, word processors, graphics suites, and so on. These chapters describe how to work with applications in Mac OS X: how to launch them, switch among them, swap data between them, use them to create and open files, and control them using the AppleScript automation software. This is also where you can find out about using your old, pre–Mac OS X programs (by running the Classic program).

- Part 3, **The Components of Mac OS X,** is an item-by-item discussion of the individual software nuggets that make up this operating system. These chapters include a guided tour of the hundreds of icons in the System and Applications folders on your hard drive.

- Part 4, **The Technologies of Mac OS X,** treads in more advanced topics. Networking, dialing into your Mac from the road, and setting up private accounts for people who share a single Mac are, of course, tasks Mac OS X was born to do—and these chapters show you how to do it. Other chapters cover the prodigious visual talents of Mac OS X (fonts, printing, graphics), its multimedia gifts (sound, speech, movies), and the Unix beneath.

- Part 5, **Mac OS X Online,** covers all the special Internet-related features of Mac OS X, including the built-in Mail email program, the Sherlock Web-searching program, Web sharing, and Apple's online iTools services (which include free email accounts, secure file-backup features, Web-site hosting, and so on). If you're feeling particularly advanced, you'll also find instructions on riding Mac OS X's Unix underpinnings for connecting to, and controlling, your Mac from across the wires—FTP, SSH, Telnet, and so on.

At the end of the book, you'll find several appendixes. They include a "Where'd it go?" listing of traditional Mac features that have been moved or removed in Mac OS X; a menu-by-menu explanation of the Mac OS X Finder commands; guidance in installing this operating system; a troubleshooting handbook; and a list of resources for further study.

About→These→Arrows

Throughout this book, and throughout the Missing Manual series, you'll find sentences like this one: "Open the System folder→Libraries→Fonts folder." That's shorthand for a much longer instruction that directs you to open three nested folders in sequence, like this: "On your hard drive, you'll find a folder called System. Open that. Inside the System folder window is a folder called Libraries; double-click it to open it. Inside *that* folder is yet another one called Fonts. Double-click to open it, too."

Similarly, this kind of arrow shorthand helps to simplify the business of choosing commands in menus, such as →Dock→Position on Left, as shown in Figure I-2.

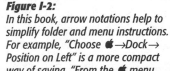

Figure I-2:
In this book, arrow notations help to simplify folder and menu instructions. For example, "Choose →Dock→ Position on Left" is a more compact way of saying, "From the menu, choose Dock ; from the submenu that then appears, choose Position on Left," as shown here.

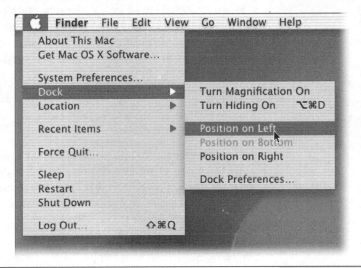

About MissingManuals.com

If you have an Internet account, visit *www.missingmanuals.com*. Click the "Missing CD-ROM" link to reveal a neat, organized, chapter-by-chapter list of every piece of shareware and freeware mentioned in this book. (As noted on the inside back cover, having the software online instead of on a CD-ROM saved you $5 on the cost of the book.)

But the Web site also offers corrections and updates to the book (to see them, click the book's title, then click Errata). In fact, you're invited and encouraged to submit such corrections and updates yourself. In an effort to keep the book as up-to-date and accurate as possible, each time we print more copies of this book, we'll make any confirmed corrections you've suggested. We'll also note such changes on the Web site, so that you can mark important corrections into your own copy of the book, if you like.

In the meantime, we'd love to hear your own suggestions for new books in the Missing Manual line. There's a place for that on the Web site, too, as well as a place to sign up for free email notification of new titles in the series.

The Very Basics

To use this book, and indeed to use a Macintosh computer, you need to know a few basics. This book assumes that you're familiar with a few terms and concepts:

- **Clicking.** This book gives you three kinds of instructions that require you to use the mouse that's attached to your Mac. To *click* means to point the arrow cursor at something on the screen and then—without moving the cursor at all—to press and release the clicker button on the mouse (or your laptop trackpad). To *double-click,* of course, means to click twice in rapid succession, again without moving the cursor at all. And to *drag* means to move the cursor while pressing the button.

  When you're told to ⌘-*click* something, you click while pressing the ⌘ key (which is next to the Space bar). Such related procedures as *Shift-clicking, Option-clicking,* and *Control-clicking* work the same way—just click while pressing the corresponding key at the bottom of your keyboard.

- **Menus.** The *menus* are the words at the top of your screen: File, Edit, and so on. (The menu at the top left corner of your screen is a menu, too.) Click one to make a list of commands appear, as though they're written on a window shade you've just pulled down.

  Some people click to open a menu and then release the mouse button; after reading the menu command choices, they click again on the one they want. Other people like to press the mouse button continuously after the initial click on the menu title, drag down the list to the desired command, and only then release the mouse button. Either method works fine.

- **Keyboard shortcuts.** If you're typing along in a burst of creative energy, it's sometimes disruptive to have to take your hand off the keyboard, grab the mouse, and then use a menu (for example, to use the Bold command). That's why many experienced Mac fans prefer to trigger menu commands by pressing certain combinations on the keyboard. For example, in most word processors, you can press ⌘-B to produce a **boldface** word. When you read an instruction like "press ⌘-B," start by pressing the ⌘ key; while it's down, type the letter B, and then release both keys.

- **Icons.** The colorful inch-tall pictures that appear in your various desktop folders are the *icons*—graphic symbols that represent each program, disk, and document on your computer. If you click an icon one time, it darkens; you've just *highlighted* or *selected* it, in readiness to manipulate it by using, for example, a menu command.

If you've mastered this much information, you have all the technical background you need to enjoy *Mac OS X: The Missing Manual.*

Part One:
The Mac OS X Desktop

1

Folders and Windows

Getting into Mac OS X

When you turn on a Mac OS X computer, you may think at first that you're simply seeing a newer, bluer version of the traditional Mac startup process. There's a tiny happy-Mac icon, a Mac OS X logo, and then a progress bar that shimmers its way across the screen as Mac OS X loads. Only the absence of a system-extension icon parade at the bottom of the screen lets you know that you're not in Kansas anymore.

Logging In

What happens next depends on whether you are the Mac's sole proprietor or have to share it with other people in an office, school, or household.

- **If it's your own Mac,** and you've already been through the Mac OS X setup process described in Appendix C, no big deal. You arrive at the Mac OS X desktop.

- **If it's a shared Mac,** you may encounter the Login dialog box, shown in Figure 1-1. Click your name in the list (or type it, if there's no list); type your password if you're asked for it, and click Log In (or press Return). You arrive at the desktop. (See Chapter 11 for much more on this business of user accounts and logging in.)

The Elements of the Mac OS X Desktop

Upon first starting up Mac OS X, most people emit (or manage to suppress) two successive gasps. The first is one of amazement, as the shimmering, three-dimensional Mac OS X desktop appears—a new world on an old machine (see Figure 1-2).

The second is one of dismay, which comes upon closer examination of the strangely named folders and icons in the main hard drive window. Don't panic; if you can accept that Mac OS X imposes an unfamiliar folder structure, the rest is easy. (Page 49 explains these folders in more detail.)

Figure 1-1:
Left: On Macs that have been configured to accommodate different people at different times, the first thing you see upon turning on the computer is this dialog box. Click your name. (You may have to scroll to find your name—or just type the first couple of letters of it—if the list is long.)

Right: At this point, you're asked to type in your password. Type it and then click Log In (or press Return or Enter; pressing these keys always "clicks" the blue, pulsing button in a dialog box).

If you've typed the wrong password, the entire dialog box vibrates, in effect shaking its little dialog-box head, suggesting that you guess again. See page 286 for details and solutions.

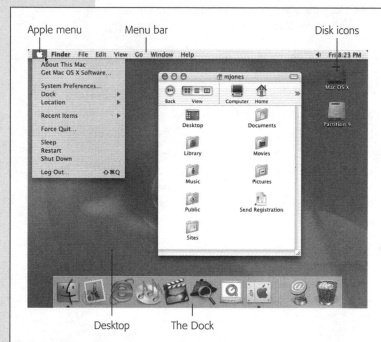

Figure 1-2:
The Mac OS X landscape looks like a futuristic version of Windows or the Mac OS. This is just a starting point, however. You can dress it up with a different background picture, adjust your windows in a million ways, and of course fill the Dock with only the programs, disks, folders, and files you care about.

For example, most of the objects on your screen are nothing more than updated versions of the elements made famous by the older Mac OS or even Windows. Here's a quick tour (see Figure 1-2).

Disk icons

Here they are, just where they've always been: the icons of your hard drive and any other disks attached to your Mac at the moment. Double-click to open one, as always.

You may notice that icons and Mac OS X are much larger than they were in previous operating systems. You can make them any size you like (see page 29), but Apple made them bigger for two reasons. First, in this era of monitors with ever larger resolution, the icons on our screens were getting ever smaller and harder to see.

Second, Apple thinks its Mac OS X icons look really cool.

Note: The desktop also includes a folder alias called "Desktop (Mac OS 9)." It's a side effect of the fact that you may be doing a lot of switching back and forth between Mac OS 9 and Mac OS X, at least at first. This folder contains whatever you left sitting out on the desktop when you were working in Mac OS 9. (If you're sure there's nothing important inside, you can throw it away.)

The Dock

This row of translucent, almost photographic icons is a launcher for programs, files, folders, and disks you use often.

In principle, the Dock is very simple:

- Programs go on the left side; everything else goes on the right, including documents, folders, and disks. (Figure 1-2 shows the fine white dividing line.)

- You can add a new icon to the Dock by dragging it there. Rearrange Dock icons by dragging them like tiles on a puzzle. Remove a Dock icon by dragging it away from the Dock, and enjoy the animated puff of smoke that appears when you release the mouse button. (You can't remove the icon of a program that's currently open, however.)

- Click something *once* to open it. A tiny triangle underneath a program's icon lets you know that it's open.

- Each Dock icon sprouts a pop-up menu; a folder can show you what's inside, for example. To see the menu, hold the mouse button down on a Dock icon, or Control-click it, or (if you have a two-button mouse) right-click it.

Because the Dock is such a critical component of Mac OS X, Apple has decked it out with enough customization controls to keep you busy experimenting for months. You can change its size, move it to the sides of your screen, hide it entirely, and so on. Chapter 3 contains complete instructions for using and understanding the Dock.

The menu

Though stripped of its stripes, you might say that the menu has finally *earned* its stripes: it houses important Mac-wide commands that used to be scattered—sometimes illogically—in other menus. For example, the Sleep, Restart, and Shut Down commands now appear here, where they're always available.

Some of the elements you'll find here are familiar menu items, including System Preferences (formerly Control Panels), Recent Items, and About This Mac. Others are new to Mac OS X, including Dock, Location, and Log Out. You'll learn the functions of these commands later in the book; for now, the point is that you can no longer add your own icons to the menu. In Mac OS X, this menu never changes. It looks the same on every Mac OS X computer in the land.

The menu bar

Aside from the new typeface (Lucida Grande), the menu bar looks and works much like it has on Macs past. But you'll note a few new nuances in Mac OS X menus:

- **They're translucent.** You'll notice that you can actually see through an open menu to whatever window is beneath. This feature doesn't particularly help you—in fact, critics claim that it makes the commands in the menu harder to read. But only an operating system with graphics software as powerful as Mac OS X's could even pull off such a sophisticated graphics treat; consider translucent menus a bit of showoff-ware.

- **They stay down.** For years, Macintosh menus remained open for only 15 seconds before snapping closed again. That's because when a menu was open, all other Macintosh activity stopped.

  Mac OS X, however, is *multithreaded*, as noted on page 4, which means that it's perfectly capable of carrying on with its background activities while you study its open, translucent menus. Therefore, Mac OS X menus stay open until you click, press a key, or buy a new computer, whichever comes first.

- **They've been rearranged.** The first menu in every program is no longer called File. Like the Application menu that used to appear at the right end of the menu bar, its name tells you at a glance what program you're in (now in boldface type); the commands in it include About (which tells you what version of the program you're using), Preferences, Quit, and commands like Hide Others and Show All (which help you control window clutter, as described on page 97).

Tip: Mac OS X, for the first time, offers a keystroke for hiding the windows of the program you're currently using: ⌘-H. That's a great tip when, for example, you're browsing the Web but want to duck back to the desktop for some quick administrative task.

In short, the Application menu finally makes sense. All of its commands actually pertain to the application you're using.

The File and Edit menus come next. As in the past, the *File* menu contains commands for opening, saving, and closing *files* (see the logic?); the Edit menu contains the Cut, Copy, and Paste commands.

The last menu is almost always Help. As in the past, it opens a miniature Web browser that lets you search the online Mac Help files for explanatory text (see page 47).

- **You can operate them from the keyboard.** For the first time in Macintosh history, you can now operate every menu in every program *entirely from the keyboard*. You'll find the details on page 106.

Windows and How to Work Them

In designing Mac OS X, one of Apple's key goals was to address the window-proliferation problem. As you create more files, stash them in more folders, and launch more programs, it's easy to wind up paralyzed before a screen awash with cluttered, overlapping rectangles. Mac OS X offers some clever new tools for retaining control.

Title Bar

The title bar has several functions. First, when several windows are open, the darkened window name and light pinstripes tell you which window is *active* (in front); windows in the background appear dimmed, with translucent, slightly darker-striped title bars. Second, the pinstripes act as a *handle* that let you move the entire window around on the screen. That's a critical tool in Mac OS X, because you can no longer drag the other three edges of a window to move it.

Figure 1-3:
Press ⌘ and click a window's title bar (top) to summon the hidden folder-hierarchy menu (bottom). The Finder isn't the only program that offers this trick, by the way; it also works in most other Mac OS X-compatible programs, and even many Mac OS 9 programs.

After you've opened one folder that's inside another, the title bar's secret *folder hierarchy menu* is an efficient way to backtrack—to return to the enclosing window. Figure 1-3 reveals everything about the process after this key move: press the ⌘ key as you click the name of the window. (You can release the ⌘ key immediately after clicking.)

By choosing the name of a folder from this menu, you open the corresponding window. When browsing the contents of the Users folder, for example, you can return to the main hard drive window by ⌘-clicking the folder name Users and choosing Macintosh HD from the menu.

Tip: Keyboard lovers, take note. Instead of using this title bar menu, you can also jump to the enclosing window by pressing ⌘-up arrow. Add the Option key if you want to switch into "Old Finder Mode" in the process (see page 25).

Pressing ⌘-down arrow takes you back into the folder you started in, assuming that it's still highlighted. (This makes a lot more sense when you try it than when you read it.)

Once you've mastered simple dragging, you're ready for these three terrific title bar tips:

- Just as in Mac OS 9, pressing the ⌘ key lets you drag the title-bar area of an *inactive* window—one that's partly covered by a window in front—without bringing it to the front.

    As a matter of fact, Mac OS X takes this concept much farther. Now, depending on the program you're clicking into, you can operate *any* control in a background window without bringing it to the front—its resize box, buttons, pop-up menus, and even scroll bars. In fact, you can even *drag through text* without bringing a window forward. In every case, just keeping ⌘ pressed as you click or drag is the secret. (*Cocoa* programs, as described on page 116, offer all of these ⌘-clickable controls; programs that have simply been *Carbonized* respond only when you ⌘-click title-bar elements.)

    (Note, by the way, that you don't need the ⌘ key to *close* a background window. Just click its close button normally. Mac OS X closes the window without taking you out of your current window or program.)

- The title bar does one other trick: by double-clicking the stripes, you *minimize* the window, making it collapse into the Dock exactly as though you had clicked the minimize button (described on page 22).

- The Option key means "apply this action to all windows." For example, Option-double-clicking any title bar minimizes all desktop windows, sending them flying to the Dock.

Close Button

As the tip of your cursor crosses the three buttons at the upper-left corner of a window, tiny symbols appear inside them: x, -, and +. Ignore the gossip that these symbols were added to help colorblind people who can't distinguish the colors red, yellow, and green; colorblind people are perfectly capable of distinguishing the buttons by their positions, just as they do with traffic lights.

Instead, these cues appear to distinguish the buttons when all three are identical *gray,* as they are when you use Graphite mode (page 87). They also signal you when it's time to click. For example, it's perfectly possible to close a window that's not the frontmost one, as described in the previous section; the appearance of those tiny symbols in the background window lets you know that such a thing is possible.

The most important window gadget is the close button, the red, droplet-like button in the upper-left corner (see Figure 1-4). Clicking it closes the window, which collapses back into the icon from which it came.

Tip: If, while working on a document, you see a tiny dot in the center of the close button, Mac OS X is trying to tell you that you haven't yet saved your work. The dot goes away when you save the document.

Figure 1-4:
When Steve Jobs unveiled Mac OS X at a Macworld Expo in 1999, he said that his goal was to oversee the creation of an interface so attractive, "you just want to lick it." Desktop windows, with their juicy, fruit-flavored controls, are a good starting point.

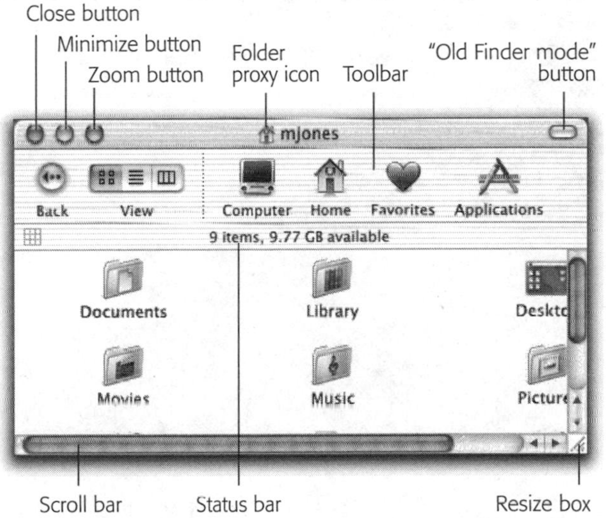

Close button
Minimize button
Zoom button
Folder proxy icon
Toolbar
"Old Finder mode" button

Back   View   Computer   Home   Favorites   Applications

9 items, 9.77 GB available

Documents   Library   Desktc

Movies   Music   Picture

Scroll bar   Status bar   Resize box

The universal keyboard equivalent of the close button is ⌘-W (for *window*)—a keystroke well worth memorizing. If you get into the habit of dismissing windows with that deft flex of your left hand, you'll find it far easier to close several windows in a row, because you don't have to aim for successive close buttons.

In many programs, something special happens if you're pressing the Option key when using the close button or its ⌘-W equivalent: You close *all* open windows. This trick is especially useful in the Finder, where a quest for a particular document may have left your screen plastered with open windows for which you have no further use. Option-clicking the close button of any *one* window closes all of them—or just press ⌘-Option-W.

On the other hand, the Option-key trick doesn't close all windows in every program—only those in the current program. Option-closing an AppleWorks document closes all *AppleWorks* windows—but your Finder windows remain open. Moreover, Option-closing works only in enlightened applications, such as AppleWorks, Quicken, and the Finder. (In this department, Microsoft is not yet enlightened.)

Minimize Button

Click this yellow drop of gel to *minimize* (hide) any Mac window, sending it shrinking, with a genie-like animated effect, into the right end of the Dock, where it now appears as an icon. The window isn't gone; it hasn't actually closed. It's just out of your way for the moment, as though you've set it down on a shelf. To bring it back, click the newly created Dock icon (see Figure 1-5, and see Chapter 3 for more on the Dock).

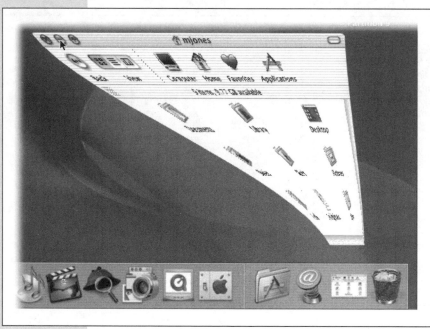

Figure 1-5:
Clicking the minimize button sends a window scurrying down to the Dock, collapsing in on itself as though being forced through a tiny, invisible funnel.

Minimizing a window in this way is a great window-management tool. In the Finder, doing so lets you see whatever icons are covered by a window. In a word processor, this technique lets you type up a memo that requires frequent consultation of a spreadsheet behind it.

Tip: If you enjoy the ability to roll up your windows in this way, remember that you actually have a bigger target than the tiny minimize button. The entire striped title bar is a giant minimize button; just double-click anywhere on it.

Better yet, you can also minimize a window from the keyboard by pressing ⌘-M. That's a keystroke worth memorizing on Day One.

The minimize button harbors only one hidden feature, but it's very entertaining. If you Option-click it, *all* windows in the current program shrink away simultaneously—great when you've got several Web browser windows open, for example, or word-processor documents. (Unfortunately, there's no one-click method for un-minimizing all of the windows in that program. You have to click them one at a time on the Dock.)

Tip: Mac OS X's high-horsepower graphics engine can even change menu commands *as* you press modifier keys. For example, open a couple of Finder windows and then click the Window menu. Focus your eyes on the Minimize Window command. Now, when you press Option, you can see that both the wording and the listed keyboard equivalent change instantly to Minimize All Windows (Option-⌘-M).

Zoom Button

A click on this green geltab (see Figure 1-4) makes a desktop window just large enough to show you all of the icons inside it. If your monitor isn't big enough to show all the icons in a window, the zoom box resizes the window to show as many as

---

GEM IN THE ROUGH

Speeding Up the Genie

Apple has a name for the animation you see when you minimize a window: the *genie effect,* because it so closely resembles the way Barbara Eden, Robin Williams, and other TV and movie genies entered and exited their magic lamps and bottles.

But you don't have to watch the "genie" animation precisely the same way, day in and day out. You can slow it down or speed it up like this:

Slow it down. Whenever Steve Jobs does a Mac OS X demo, one of his favorite bits is slowing down the animation so that we can see it in all its graceful, slow motion. How does he do that?

If you *Shift*-click a window's minimize button, it collapses into the Dock at about 1/4 speed. Press Control *and* Shift to slow it down even more—about 1/8 speed (cancel your appointments for the day). The Shift key also slows down the un-minimizing animation, the one you see when you click a window icon in the dock to restore it to full size.

Speed it up. There's no secret keystroke for making the animation go faster. You can, however, replace the genie animation with a faster *style* of animation.

To do so, choose ⌘→Dock→Dock Preferences. From the "Minimize using" pop-up menu, choose Scale Effect, and then close the window. Now, instead of collapsing through an invisible funnel, minimized windows simply shrink as they fly down to the dock, remaining rectangular, requiring less computing by Mac OS X and therefore taking less than a second to disappear.

---

possible. In either case, a second click on the zoom button restores the window to its original size. (The Window→Zoom Window command does the same thing as clicking the zoom button.)

Tip: Option-clicking this button doesn't make a Finder window fill the entire screen, as it did in Mac OS 9. But Option-clicking it still works in many Mac OS X *applications;* a few, such as OmniWeb, require Shift-clicking it instead.

The Folder Proxy Icon

Each Finder-window title bar features a small icon next to the window's name (Figure 1-6), representing the folder or disk from which this window was opened. By dragging this tiny icon, you can move or copy the folder to a different folder or disk, to the Trash, or into the Dock, without having to first close the window. (If this feature strikes you as unimpressive, you probably never witnessed a hapless Mac novice making repeated attempts to drag an *open window* into the Trash in, say, System 7.5.)

Tip: When clicking this proxy icon, hold down the mouse button for a full half second, or until the icon darkens. Only then are you allowed to drag it.

When dragging this proxy icon to a different place on the same disk, the usual folder-dragging rules apply: hold down the Option key if you want to *copy* the original disk or folder. Without the Option key, you *move* the original folder. (You'll find details on moving and copying icons in the next chapter.)

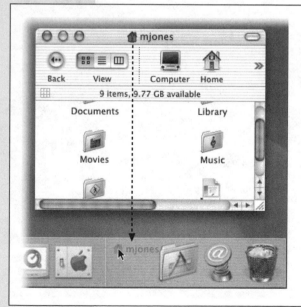

Figure 1-6:
When you find yourself confronting a Finder window that contains useful stuff, consider dragging its proxy icon to the Dock. You wind up installing its folder or disk icon there for future use.

That's not the same thing as minimizing the window, which puts the window *icon into the Dock, and only temporarily.*

Most Mac OS X document windows offer the same feature, but produce only an alias when dragged to a different folder or disk.

The Finder Toolbar

Chapter 3 describes this fascinating new Mac OS X desktop-window element in great detail.

"Old Finder Mode" (Toolbar Disclosure) Button

In the old days, double-clicking any folder opened it into a new window. Double-click three folders, you get three windows. But Mac OS X doesn't work that way, as shown in Figure 1-7.

Tip: If you *Option*-double-click a folder, you don't simply replace the contents of a fixed window that remains on the screen; you actually *switch* windows, as evidenced by their changing sizes and shapes.

Figure 1-7:
In an effort to help you avoid window clutter, Apple has designed Mac OS X windows so that double-clicking a folder in a window (top) doesn't actually open another window (bottom). Every time you double-click a folder in an open window, its contents replace *whatever was previously in the window. If you double-click three folders in succession, you still wind up with just one open window.*

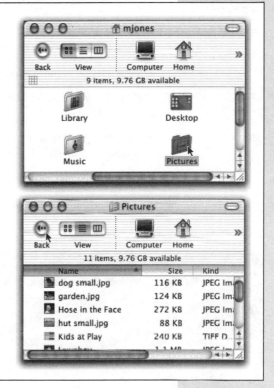

So what if you've now opened inner folder B, and you want to backtrack to outer folder A? In that case, just click the tiny left-arrow button labeled Back, shown in Figure 1-7, or use one of these alternatives:

• Choose Go→Back.

• Press ⌘-[(left bracket).

• Press ⌘-up arrow.

None of that will help you, however, if you want to copy a file from one folder into another, or to compare the contents of two windows. In that case, you'll probably want to see both windows open at the same time.

In such situations, you can open a second window using any of these techniques:

- Choose File→New Finder Window (⌘-N).

Tip: The window that appears when you do this is the Computer window, which isn't especially helpful most of the time. Fortunately, you can change this setting. Choose Finder→Preferences and click the Home button instead. Now every new Finder window shows you your Home folder (page 49), which contains all your files—a much more useful arrangement.

- ⌘-double-click a disk or folder icon.

- Double-click a folder or disk icon on your desktop.

- Click the Finder icon on the Dock (versions before 10.1 only).

- Switch to Old Finder Mode, described next.

"Old Finder Mode," of course, isn't the technical Apple term, but it should be. Here's how it works.

The upper-right corner of every Finder window contains a little button that looks like a half-inch squirt of Crest toothpaste. When you click it, you enter Old Finder Mode.

Tip: You can also enter Old Finder Mode by pressing ⌘-B, the equivalent for the View→Hide Toolbar command.

Multiple Views, Same Folder

If you've read this section carefully, you may have discovered a peculiar new quirk of the Mac OS X Finder: By choosing File→New Finder Window (or ⌘-double-clicking a disk or folder icon), you open a second, completely independent Finder window. If you stop to think about it, therefore, there's nothing to stop you from opening a second, third, or fourth copy of *the same folder window*. Once they're open, you can even switch them into different views.

Try this, for example: Choose Go→Applications. Choose File→New Finder Window (⌘-N), and then choose Go→Applications *again*. Using the View menu or the con-

trols in the toolbar, put one of these windows into list view, and the other into icon view.

This phenomenon has its advantages. For example, you might decide to open the same window twice while doing some hard-drive housekeeping; by keeping a list view open, you can check the Size column as you move your files into different folders (so you can make sure the folders fit onto a blank CD, for example)—but by keeping a column view open, you gain quicker navigational access to the stuff on your drive.

In this mode, the two biggest behavioral differences between Mac OS X and its predecessor disappear. First, the Finder-window toolbar, shown in Figure 1-4, slides out of sight, to the relief of many Mac old-timers.

The second big change in Old Finder Mode is that double-clicking a folder now works like it used to. Every time you double-click a folder, you open a new corresponding window, just as in Mac OS 9.

When you've had enough of Old Finder Mode, you can return to regular Mac OS X mode by clicking the Toolbar Disclosure button again, by pressing ⌘-B again, or by choosing View→Show Toolbar.

Note: You'll find this little white toolbar-control nubbin in a number of toolbar-endowed programs, including Mail, Internet Explorer, System Preferences, and others. Clicking it always makes the toolbar go away.

Scroll Bars

Scroll bars appear automatically in any window that isn't big enough to show all of its contents. Without scroll bars in word processors, for example, you'd never be able to write a letter that's taller than your screen. You can manipulate a scroll bar in three ways, as shown in Figure 1-8.

Figure 1-8:
Three ways to control a scroll. The scroll bar arrows (right end) appear nestled together when you first install Mac OS X, as shown here; if you're an old-timer who prefers these arrows to appear on opposite ends of the scroll bar, visit the General panel of System Preferences, described on page 185.

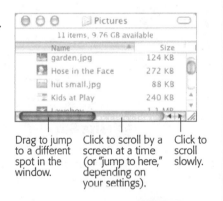

Drag to jump to a different spot in the window.

Click to scroll by a screen at a time (or "jump to here," depending on your settings).

Click to scroll slowly.

Mac OS X introduces a new scroll bar option called "Jump to here." Ordinarily, when you click into scroll bar track above or below the gelatinous handle, the window scrolls by one screenful. But if you visit the General panel of your System Preferences (see page 185), you can turn on "Jump to here" mode. Now when you click into scroll bar track, the Mac considers the entire scroll bar a proportional map of the document, and scrolls precisely to the spot you clicked. That is, if you click at the very bottom of the scroll bar track, you see the very last page. (As of Mac OS X 10.1.5, you have to quit and re-launch your program, or log out and back in, to see the change in behavior.)

Tip: No matter which scrolling option you choose in the General panel, you can always override your decision on a case-by-case basis by *Option*-clicking in the scroll bar track. In other words, if you've selected the "Scroll to here" option, you can produce a "jump to next page" scroll by Option-clicking in the scroll bar track.

It's worth noting, however, that the true speed expert eschews scroll bars altogether. Using your Page Up and Page Down keys lets you scroll up and down, one screen at a time, without having to take your hands off the keyboard to grab the mouse. The Home and End keys, meanwhile, are generally useful for jumping directly to the top or bottom of your document (or Finder window).

At first glance, you might assume that scroll bars are an extremely inefficient mechanism when you want to scroll a window *diagonally*—and you'd be right. Fortunately, Mac OS X includes an alternate scrolling system for such situations. Position your mouse inside a Finder window; while pressing ⌘ and Option, you can drag—and scroll—in any direction, as shown in Figure 1-9.

Figure 1-9:
Position your mouse inside a Finder window (list views not included) or even an Internet Explorer window; while pressing ⌘ and Option, you can drag–and scroll–in any direction. As you drag, the cursor changes in shape, becoming a white-gloved butler's hand. Where can you get that kind of service these days? (Note that this keystroke was ⌘ by itself in Mac OS 9.)

Resize Box

The lower-right corner of every standard Mac OS X window is ribbed, a design that's meant to imply that you can grip it by dragging. Doing so lets you resize and reshape the window (see Figure 1-4).

Status Bar

In Mac OS 9 days, an information strip appeared in every Finder window, just beneath the title bar. It told you how many icons are in the window ("14 items," for example) and the amount of free space remaining on the disk.

When you first run Mac OS X, this information strip is missing. If you miss it, choose View→Show Status Bar. This strip now appears in every Finder window (see Figure 1-4)—at least until you hide it again by choosing View→Hide Status Bar.

Tip: If the window is very narrow, the status bar shows only the number of icons in the window (such as "1 item"). To see how much free space is on the disk, *click* the "1 item" text; Mac OS X changes it to show you the remaining free-space statistic. Click again to return to the item count.

Icon View, List View, and Column View

You can view the files and folders in a desktop window in any of three ways: as icons; as a single, tidy list; or in a series of neat columns. (Figure 1-10 shows the three different views.) Every window remembers its view settings independently. You might prefer to look over your Applications folder in list view (because it's crammed with files and folders), but you may prefer to view the less populated Control Panels folder in icon view, where the larger icons are easier to double-click.

To switch a window from one view to another, just click one of the three corresponding icons in the window's toolbar, as shown in Figure 1-10.

If you've hidden the toolbar, you can also switch views by choosing View→as Icons (or View→as Columns, or View→as List).

Icon View Notes

In an icon view, each file, folder, and disk is represented by a small picture—an *icon*. This humble image, a visual representation of electronic bits and bytes, is the cornerstone of the entire Macintosh religion. (Maybe that's why it's called an icon.)

Tip: As in Mac OS 9, you can highlight an icon in icon view—or list view, for that matter—by typing the first couple letters of its name. You can also press Tab to highlight the next icon (in alphabetical order), or Shift-Tab to highlight the previous one.

Choosing icon sizes

For years, Mac fans had to live with a choice of two icon sizes. But Mac OS X draws the little pictures that represent your icons using sophisticated graphics software; you (or the Mac) can scale them to almost any size without losing any quality or smoothness. You can specify a new icon size either for a single window, or for every icon view window on your machine.

WORKAROUND WORKSHOP

How Much is That Doggie in the Window?

The status bar shows you disk-space information for the entire disk, but not how much disk space *this particular window's* contents occupy.

To find out *that* piece of information, make sure that no icon in the window is highlighted. Then choose File→Show Info (or press ⌘-I). The resulting Info window, which is described in more detail at the end of the next chapter, shows the size of the folder or disk whose window you're browsing, along with other useful statistics.

Try this experiment. Open a window that's filled with icons (double-click the hard-drive icon on your desktop, for example). Put it into icon view, if necessary.

Now choose View→Show View Options (⌘-J). The floating window shown in Figure 1-11 appears, complete with an Icon Size slider. Click one of the buttons at the top of the window, either "This window only" or "Global," to indicate whether you want to change the icon sizes in just the frontmost window or everywhere on the Mac. Finally, drag the Icon Size slider back and forth until you find an icon size you like. (For added fun, make little cartoon sounds with your mouth.)

Keeping your icons neat and sorted

In general, you can drag icons anywhere within a window. For example, some people like to keep current project icons at the top of the window, and move older stuff to the bottom.

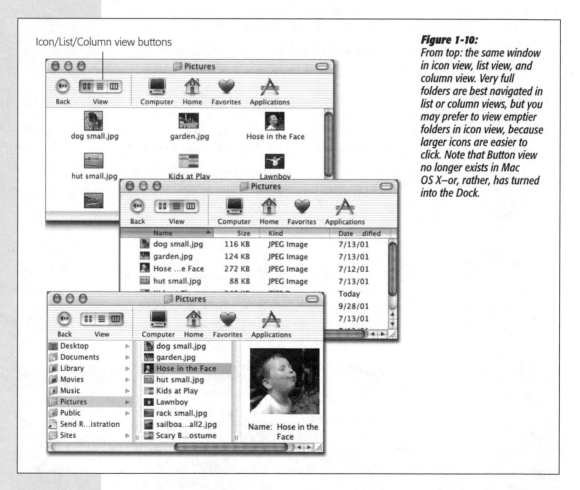

Icon/List/Column view buttons

Figure 1-10:
From top: the same window in icon view, list view, and column view. Very full folders are best navigated in list or column views, but you may prefer to view emptier folders in icon view, because larger icons are easier to click. Note that Button view no longer exists in Mac OS X—or, rather, has turned into the Dock.

If you'd like Mac OS X to impose a little discipline on you, however, it's easy enough to request a visit from an electronic housekeeper who tidies up your icons, aligning them neatly to an invisible grid.

Note: As of Mac OS X 10.1.5f, you can't specify how tight or loose this invisible grid is.

Figure 1-11:
Mac OS X lets you choose an icon size to suit your personality. As shown at left, dragging the slider all the way to the Small setting puts the icon names to the right of their icons, rather than beneath them, emulating the Small Icon view of Mac OS 9. You now have all the handy, freely draggable convenience of an icon view, along with the compact spacing of a list view.

Mac OS X offers an enormous number of variations on the "snap icons to the underlying grid" theme:

- **Aligning individual icons to the grid.** Press the ⌘ key while dragging an icon or several highlighted icons. (Don't push down the key until after you've begun to drag.) When you release the mouse, you'll find the icons you've moved all jump into neatly aligned positions.

- **Aligning all icons to the grid.** Choose View→Clean Up. Now *all* icons in the window jump to the closest positions on the invisible underlying grid.

  This is a temporary status, however—as soon as you drag icons around, or add more icons to the window, the newly moved icons wind up just as sloppily positioned as before you used the command.

  If you'd rather have icons snap to the nearest underlying grid positions *whenever* you move them, choose View→Show View Options. In the resulting dialog box, turn on "Always snap to grid." Make sure the proper button is selected at the top of the window ("This window only" or "Global"), and then close the window.

Note: You can't override the grid by pressing the ⌘ key when you drag. In other words, when grid-snapping is turned *off,* ⌘ overrides that setting. But when grid-snapping is turned *on,* ⌘ doesn't let you drag an icon freely.

Note, by the way, that neither of these grid-snapping commands—View→Clean Up and the "Always snap to grid" option—moves icons into the most compact possible arrangement. If one or two icons have wandered off from the herd to the lower-right corner of the window, they're merely nudged to the closest grid points to their present locations. They aren't moved all the way back to the crowd of icons elsewhere in the window. To make them jump back to the primary cluster, read on.

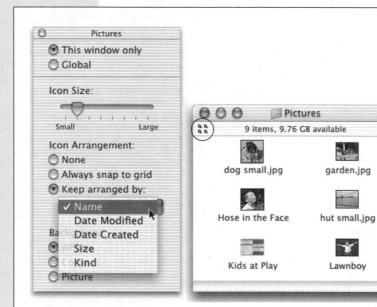

Figure 1-12:
Use the View Options dialog box (left) to turn on permanent-cleanliness mode (right). A tiny four-square icon (circled) appears just below the window's close button. That symbol is supposed to remind you that you've turned on the Mac's spatial lockjaw feature, so that you don't get frustrated when you try to drag an icon into a new position and discover that it won't budge.

- **Sorting all icons for the moment.** If you choose View→Arrange→by Name, all icons in the window snap to the invisible grid *and* sort themselves alphabetically. Use this method to place the icons as close as possible to each other within the window, rounding up any strays. (There are no equivalent commands for arranging icons by size, date modified, and so on, as in Mac OS 9.)

As with the Clean Up command, View→Arrange serves only to reorganize the icons in the window at this moment. Moving or adding icons in the window means you'll wind up with icons out of order. If you'd rather have all icons remain sorted *and* clustered, try this:

- **Sorting all icons permanently.** This arrangement is the ideal solution for neat freaks who can't stand seeing icons out of place. It maintains sorting and alignment of all icons in the window, present and future—if you add more icons to the window, they jump into correct alphabetical position. If you remove icons, the remaining ones slide over to fill in the resulting gap.

  To make it happen, choose View→Show View Options. In the resulting dialog box, click the "Keep arranged by" button. From the pop-up menu, specify what order you want your icons to snap into, as shown in Figure 1-12. Close the window. As shown at right in Figure 1-12, your icons are now locked into sorted position, as compactly as possible.

Although it doesn't occur to most Mac users, you can also apply any of the commands described in this section—Clean Up, Arrange, Keep Arranged, and so on—to icons lying loose on your *desktop*. Even though they're not technically in any window at all, you can specify small or large icons, automatic alphabetical arrangement, and so on. Just click the desktop before using the commands in the View menu.

Note: There's only one View Options dialog box. Once it's open on the screen, you can adjust the icon sizes or arrangement options of other windows just by clicking them. Each time you click inside a window, the View Options dialog box remains in front, changing to reflect the settings of the window you clicked. This handy feature may, at first, confuse diehard Mac OS 9 users, who are accustomed to opening a separate View Options dialog box for every Finder window.

List View Notes

In windows that contain a lot of icons, the list view is a powerful weapon in the battle against chaos. It shows you a tidy table of your files' names, dates, sizes, and so on.

All of the usual file-manipulation tips apply in list view. For example, double-clicking a folder doesn't open a new window (unless you're also pressing the ⌘ key); instead, the contents of the folder you double-clicked replace the contents of the window, as described on page 25.

You have complete control over your columns: how wide they should be, which of them should appear, and in which order (except that Name is always the first column). Here's how to master these columns:

Specifying how the icons are sorted

Most of the world's list view fans like their files listed alphabetically. It's occasionally useful, however, to view the oldest files first, largest first, and so on.

When a desktop window displays its icons in a list view, a convenient new strip of controls appears: the column headings (Figure 1-10). The column headings aren't just signposts; they're also buttons. Click Name for alphabetical order, Date Modified to view newest first, Size to view largest files at the top, and so on. (You can no longer perform the same function using commands in the View menu or by Control-clicking inside a window.)

It's especially important to note the tiny, dark gray triangle that appears in the column you've most recently clicked (Figure 1-13). It shows you *which way* the list is being sorted. Unlike Mac OS 9, Mac OS X has no tiny sort-order pyramid button over the scroll bar for this purpose.

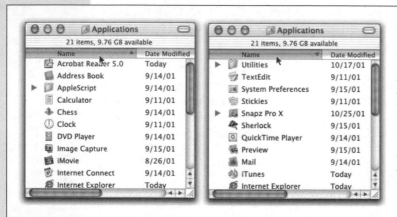

Figure 1-13:
You control the sorting order of a list view by clicking the column headings (left). Click a second time to reverse the sorting order (right). You'll find the identical triangle, indicating the identical information, in email programs, in Sherlock (Chapter 20), and anywhere else where reversing the sorting order of the list can be useful.

When the triangle points upward, oldest files, smallest files, or files beginning with numbers (or the letter A) appear at the top of the list, depending on which sorting criterion you have selected.

Tip: It may help you to remember that when the *smallest* portion of the triangle is at the top, the *smallest* files are listed first when viewed in size order. (That's a welcome change from the reversed logic of Mac OS 9 and earlier.)

To reverse the sorting order, just click the column heading a second time. Now newest files, largest files, or files beginning with the letter Z appear at the top of the list. The tiny triangle turns upside-down, as shown in Figure 1-13.

Flippy triangles in list view

One of the Mac's most attractive features is the tiny triangle that appears to the left of a folder's name in a list view. In its official occurrences, Apple calls these triangle buttons *disclosure triangles;* internally, the programmers call them *flippy triangles.*

Either way, these triangles are very useful: When you click one, you turn the list view into an outline, in which the contents of the folder are displayed in an indented list, as shown in Figure 1-14. Click the triangle again to collapse the folder listing. You're saved the trouble and clutter of having to open a new window just to view the folder's contents.

By selectively clicking flippy triangles, you can, in effect, peer inside of two folders simultaneously, all within a single list view window, as shown in Figure 1-14. You can move files around by dragging them onto the tiny folder icons you see here.

Tip: Once you've expanded a folder by clicking its flippy triangle, you can even drag a file icon out of its folder, so that it's now loose in the list view window. To do so, drag it directly upward onto the *column headings* (where it says Name, for example). When you release the mouse, you'll see that the file is no longer inside the expanded folder.

Figure 1-14:
Click a "flippy triangle" (left) to see the listing of the folders and files inside that folder (right). Or press the equivalent keystrokes: ⌘-right arrow (to open) and ⌘-left arrow (to close).

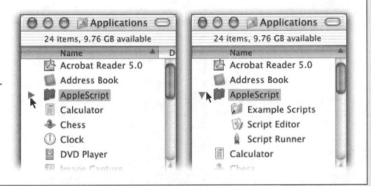

POWER USERS' CLINIC

Flippy Triangle Keystrokes

The keystrokes that let you open and close flippy triangles in a list view are worth committing to memory.

First, pressing the Option key when you click a flippy triangle lets you view a folder's contents *and* the contents of any folders inside it. The result, in other words, is a longer list that may involve several levels of indentation.

If you prefer to use the keyboard, substitute the right-arrow key (to expand a selected folder's flippy triangle) and left-arrow key (to collapse the folder listing again). Here again, adding the Option key expands all levels of folders within the selected one.

Suppose, for example, that you want to find out how many files are in your Pictures folder. The trouble is, you have organized your graphics files within that folder in several category folders. And you realize that the "how many items" statistic in the status bar shows you how many icons are *visible* in the window. In other words, you won't know your

total photo count until you've *expanded* all the folders within the Pictures folder.

You could perform the entire routine from the keyboard like this: Get to your own Home folder (see page 49) by pressing Option-⌘-H. Select the Pictures folder by typing the letter P. Open it by pressing ⌘-O (the shortcut for File→Open) or ⌘-down arrow. Highlight the entire contents by pressing ⌘-A (the shortcut for Edit→Select All).

Now that all folders are highlighted, press Option-right arrow. You may have to wait a moment for the Mac to open every subfolder of every subfolder. But eventually, the massive list appears, complete with many levels of indentation. At last, the "items" statistic in the status bar (see page 28) gives you a complete, updated tally of how many files are in all of those folders added together.

Finally, press Option-left arrow to close every flippy triangle in the Pictures folder.

Determining which columns appear

Choose View→Show View Options. In the dialog box that appears, you're offered on/off checkboxes for the different columns of information Mac OS X can show you, as shown in Figure 1-15.

Figure 1-15:
You can add up to six columns of file information to a list view. The checkboxes you turn on here, in the View Options dialog box, determine which columns of information appear in a list view window.

Most people live full and satisfying lives with only the three default columns—Date Modified, Kind, and Size—turned on. But the other columns can be helpful in special circumstances; the trick is knowing what information appears there.

- **Date Modified.** This date-and-time stamp indicates when a document was last saved. Its accuracy, of course, depends on the accuracy of your Mac's built-in clock (see page 201).

Note: Many an up-to-date file has been lost because a Mac user spotted a very old date on a folder and assumed that the files inside were equally old. That's because the modification date shown for a folder doesn't reflect the age of its *contents*. Instead, the date on a folder indicates only when items were last *moved* into or out of that folder. The actual files inside may be much older, or much more recent.

- **Date Created.** This date-and-time stamp shows you when a document was *first* saved.

- **Size.** With a glance, you can tell from this column how much disk space each of your files and folders is taking up in kilobytes or megabytes—whichever the Mac thinks you'll find most helpful. (There are 1,024 kilobytes in a megabyte.)

- **Kind.** In this column, you can read what *kind* of icon each item represents. You may see, for example, Folder, JPEG document, Application, and so on.

- **Version.** This column displays the version numbers of your programs. For folders and documents, you just see a dash.

- **Comments.** This rarely seen column can actually be among the most useful. Suppose that you're a person who uses the Comments feature (highlight an icon, choose File→Show Info, type notes about that item into the Comments box). The option to view the first line of comments about each icon can be very helpful, especially when tracking multiple versions of your documents, as shown in Figure 1-16.

Note: Unfortunately, the systems for storing comments are different in Mac OS 9 and Mac OS X. When you run Mac OS X, you won't see the icon comments you added in Mac OS 9, and vice versa.

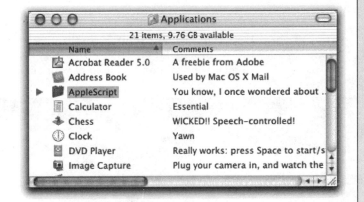

Figure 1-16:
The Comments column is often worth making visible. If your monitor is big enough, you can make the Comments column wide enough to show several paragraphs of text, all in a single line—enough to reveal the full life history of each icon. Or you can simply use the Comments window as you once used Labels in Mac OS 9.

Other view options

The dialog box that appears when you choose View→Show View Options for a list view contains several other useful settings. As always, be sure to click either "Global" or "This window only" before closing the window, so that your changes will have the scope of effect that you intended.

- **Use relative dates.** In a list view, the Date Modified and Date Created columns generally display information in a format like this: "Saturday, February 2, 2002." (As noted on page 39, the Mac uses shorter date formats as the column gets narrower.) But when the "Use relative dates" option is turned on, the Mac substitutes the word "Yesterday" or "Today" where appropriate, making recent files much easier to spot.

- **Calculate all sizes (list view only).** The sidebar box on the next page describes this option for showing the disk-space totals for folders.

- **Show columns (list views only).** Turn on the columns you'd like to appear in the current window's list view, as described in the previous section.

• **Icon Size.** These two buttons offer you a choice of standard icon size for the current window. You can choose standard size or tiny size; unlike icon view, list view doesn't give you a size slider.

Even so, Mac OS X improves on Mac OS 9 in this regard: Thanks to the much more powerful graphics software, the tiny icons aren't so small that they show up blank. You still get a general idea of what they're supposed to look like.

Rearranging the columns

You're stuck with the Name column at the far left of a window. But you can rearrange the other columns just by dragging their gray column headers horizontally. If the Mac thinks you intend to drop a column, say, to the left of the column it overlaps, you'll actually see an animated movement even before you release the mouse button, as the Mac reshuffles the columns.

Adjusting column widths

Place your cursor carefully on the dividing line between two column headings. When the cursor sprouts horizontal arrows from each side, you can drag horizontally. Doing so makes the column to the *left* of your cursor wider or narrower.

FREQUENTLY ASKED QUESTION

Calculate All Sizes

When I sort my list view by size, I see only dashes for folder sizes. What am I doing wrong?

Nothing at all; that's normal. When viewing a Finder window, you see a Size statistic for each *document.* For *folders,* however, you're shown only an uninformative dash.

Most Mac fans study this anomaly only momentarily, scratch their chins, and then get back to their work. (Former Windows users don't even scratch their chins. Windows PCs *never* show folder-size information in a list view.)

The explanation: It can take a computer a long time to add up the sizes of all files inside a folder. Your System→Library folder alone, for example, contains over 1,500 files. So that you don't have to wait while the Mac does all of this addition, Mac OS X simply shows you a dash in the Size column for a folder.

On occasion, however, you really *do* want to see how big your folders are. In such cases, choose View→Show View Options, turn on "Calculate all sizes," and close the dialog box. You'll see the folder sizes slowly begin to pop onto the screen, from the top of the window downward, as the

Mac crunches the numbers of the files within. (In Mac OS X, you can even turn on the "Calculate all sizes" option globally—that is, for all windows. In the Mac operating systems of days gone by, this act would have resulted in a massive slowdown of the entire computer. But remember that Mac OS X is *multithreaded*—that is, it has exactly the opposite of a one-track mind. It's perfectly capable of devoting all of its attention to calculating your folder sizes *and* all of its attention to whatever work you're doing in the foreground.)

But now consider this anomaly: Suppose you've opted to sort a particular window by folder size (in other words, you've clicked the word Size at the top of the column). Turning on "Calculate all sizes" bewilders the unprepared, as folders arbitrarily begin leaping out of order, forcing the list to rearrange itself a couple of times per second.

What's happening, of course, is that all folders *begin* at the bottom of the list, showing only dashes in the Size column. Then, as the Mac computes the size of your folders' contents, they jump into their correct sorted order at what may seem to be random intervals.

What's especially delightful about this activity is watching Mac OS X scramble to rewrite its information to fit the space you give it. For example, as you make the Date Modified (or Created) column narrower, "Saturday, February 2, 2002, 2:22 PM" shrinks first to "Sat, Feb 2, 2002, 2:22 PM," to "2/2/02, 2:22 PM," and finally to the terse "2/2/02."

If you make a column too narrow, Mac OS X shortens the file names, dates, or whatever by removing text from the *middle*. An ellipsis (…) appears to show you where the missing text would have appeared. (Apple reasoned that truncating the *ends* of file names, as in previous versions of the Mac OS, would hide useful information like the number at the end of "Letter to Marge 1," "Letter to Marge 2," and so on. It would also hide the three-letter *extensions*, such as Thesis.*doc*, that may appear on file names in Mac OS X.)

For example, suppose you've named a Word document called "Madonna—A Major Force for Humanization and Cure for Depression, Acne, and Migraine Headache." (Yes, file names can really be that long in Mac OS X.) If the Name column is too narrow, you might see only "Madonna—A Major… Migraine Headache."

Tip: You don't have to make the column mega-wide just to read the full text of a file whose name has been shortened. Just point to the icon's name without clicking. After a moment, a yellow, floating balloon appears—something like a tooltip in Microsoft programs—to identify the full name.

And if you don't feel like waiting, hold down the Option key. As you whip your mouse over truncated file names, their tooltip balloons appear instantaneously. (Both of these tricks work in any view—icon, list, or column.)

DON'T PANIC

Pop-Up Windows, Spring-Loaded Folders

Help! How do I make pop-up windows in Mac OS X? You know, those little folder tabs that peek up from the bottom of the screen?

Apple figured you wouldn't need them. After all, you can achieve much the same purpose by dragging folders *into the Dock* (Chapter 3); once there, you can click a folder icon to open it, or view a pop-up list of its contents by Control-clicking it, right-clicking it (if you have a two-button mouse), or just holding the mouse button down on it.

If you really want little tabs along the bottom, you can download PopupX, a shareware program that restores this feature (available at *www.missingmanuals.com,* among other places).

Spring-loaded folders, that peculiar feature where you hold the cursor down on a disk or folder until its window pops open (so that you can, without releasing the button, continue "drilling down" into other nested folders), is also gone. But column view, described on these pages, achieves much the same purpose.

Column View Notes

Icon view and list view should certainly be familiar to anyone who's used a personal computer before. But for most Mac fans, *column* view is something new—and welcome.

The goal is simple: To create a means of burrowing down through nested folders without leaving a trail of messy, overlapping windows in your wake.

The solution is shown in Figure 1-17. It's a list view that's divided into several vertical panes. The first pane shows all the icons of your disks, including your main hard drive. (The Network icon gives you access to other computers on your office network, if you have one.)

When you click a disk (once), the second pane shows a list of all the folders on it. Each time you click a folder in one pane, the pane to its right shows what's inside; the other panes slide to the left, sometimes out of view. (Use the horizontal scroll bar or the Shift-Tab keystroke to bring them back.) You can keep clicking until you're actually looking at the file icons inside the most deeply nested folder.

Figure 1-17:
If the rightmost folder contains pictures, sounds, or movies, Mac OS X even lets you look at them or play them, right there in the Finder. If it's a certain kind of text document (AppleWorks, PDF, and so on), you actually see a tiny image of the first page. If it's any other kind of document, you see a blowup of its icon and a few file statistics. You can drag this jumbo icon anywhere that fine icons get dragged—into another folder, for example.

If you discover that your hunt for a particular file has taken you down a blind alley, it's not a big deal to backtrack; the trail of folders you've followed to get here is still sitting there before you on the screen. As soon as you click a different folder in one of the earlier panes, the panes to its right suddenly change, so that you can now burrow down a different rabbit hole.

The beauty of column view is, first of all, that it keeps your screen tidy. It effectively shows you several simultaneous folder levels, but contains them within a single window. With a quick ⌘-W, you can close the entire window, panes and all. Second, column view provides an excellent sense of where you are. Because your trail is visible at all times, it's much harder to get lost, wondering what folder you're in and how you got there, than in any other window view.

Note: Column view is always alphabetical. There's no way to sort the lists by date, for example, as you can in list view.

Column view by keyboard

You can operate this entire process by keyboard alone, a great timesaver for keyboard fans. For example:

- You can jump from one pane to the next by pressing Tab (move to the right) or Shift-Tab (to the left). When you reach the far edge of the window, Tab or Shift-Tab wraps around the other side. (One day when you have nothing better to do, try holding down the Tab key continuously. You'll see the closest thing Apple has ever built to a merry-go-round.)

- Pressing the right or left arrow key is very similar, but highlights the closest *icon* in the next or previous pane instead of simply highlighting the pane itself.

- You can use any of the commands in the Go menu, or their keyboard equivalents (see page 535), to fill your columns with the contents of the corresponding folder—Home, Favorites, Applications, and so on. (See page 49 for more on these important folders.)

Figure 1-18:
You can make all the columns wider or narrower simultaneously by dragging any of the small handles (circled) at the bottom of the columns. To make a single *column wider or narrower, Option-drag the column handle at the bottom of its right edge.*

- The Back command (clicking the Back button on the toolbar, pressing ⌘-[, or choosing Go→Back) works just as it would in a Web browser: it lets you retrace your steps backward. You can use this command over and over again until you return to the column setup that first appeared when you switched to column view.

- Within a pane, press the up or down arrow keys to highlight successive icons in the list. Or type the first couple of letters of an icon's name to jump directly to it.

- When you finally highlight the icon you've been looking for, press ⌘-O or ⌘-down arrow to open it (or double-click it, of course). You're welcome to open anything in any column; you don't have to wait until you've pinpointed a file in the rightmost column.

Manipulating the columns

The number of columns you can see without scrolling depends on the width of the window. In no other view is the zoom button (page 23) or the resize box (page 28) so important.

That's not to say, however, that you're limited to four columns (or whatever fits on your monitor). You can make the columns wider or narrower—either individually or all at once—to suit the situation. Figure 1-18 shows the details.

UP TO SPEED

Everything Old Is New Again

For many observers, Mac OS X's column view is one of the most radical new features of the operating system. The truth is, however, that it's not new at all.

In fact, column view's most recent ancestor appeared in the NeXT operating system, which Apple bought (along with Steve Jobs, its CEO) in 1997. But column view is even older than that.

As you can see in this sketch from May 1980, the idea of a single-window, multiple-column view has been kicking around at Apple long before the Macintosh debuted.

In the end, this view was deemed too complex for the original Mac, which finally appeared (with only list and icon views) in 1984; it took 17 more years to find its way into the standard Mac OS.

Folder Genetics

Every folder window can have different view settings. Maybe you like your Pictures folder to use very narrow columns, your Public folder to use a neat list, and your Music folder to use small icons.

That's great if you like every window to have independent settings. But sooner or later, you may find yourself wishing that every window looked the same—even just for a moment. Maybe you're doing some housecleaning, opening folder after folder and deleting or backing up the really old files. Maybe you're just on a frantic search for some document. Either way, list view is the obvious candidate for what you're doing. But because every folder opens with its own independent view settings, you quickly develop Desktop Rage, growing tired of switching every window back to list view, list view, list view.

Precisely for such situations, Mac OS X offers a new feature that preserves the view selection for every new folder you open. You can make it so that, if you begin in an icon view, then every folder you double-click will also open into icon view. If you start out in list view, you'll stay in list view as you open more folders. And so on. In other words, every "child" folder will open with the inherited characteristics of its "parent."

To set this up, choose Finder→Preferences. In the Finder Preferences window, turn on "Keep a window's view the same when opening other folders in the window." Close the dialog box.

Some people leave this feature on permanently, on the assumption that whatever view they're using at the moment will be relevant for the next few folders they open.

Window Backgrounds

Here's another Mac OS X luxury that other operating-system fans can only dream about: You can fill the background of any window on your Mac with a certain color— or even a photo. Color-coordinating or "wallpapering" certain windows is more than just a gimmick; it can actually serve as a time-saving psychological cue. Once you've gotten used to the fact that your main Documents folder has a sky-blue background, you can pick it out like a sharpshooter from a screen filled with open windows. (Color-coded Finder windows are also especially easy to distinguish at a glance when you've minimized them to the Dock.)

Note: The background color or picture you choose is visible only in icon view. It disappears in list or column view.

Once a window is open, choose View→View Options (⌘-J). The bottom of the resulting dialog box (Figure 1-19) offers three choices:

- **White.** This is the standard option.

Figure 1-19:
The View Options dialog box (left) for an icon view window offers the chance to create colored backgrounds for certain windows (top right) or even to use photos as window wallpaper (lower right). Using a photo may have a soothing, annoying, or comic effect.

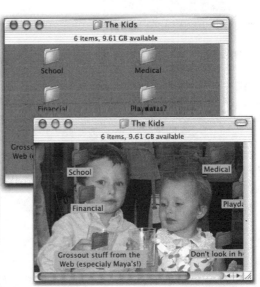

- **Color.** When you click this button, you see a small rectangular button beside the word Color. Click it to open the Color Picker (see page 115), which you can use to choose a new background color for the window. (Unless it's April Fool's day, pick a light color; if you choose a dark one—like black—you won't be able to make out the lettering of the icons' names.)

- **Picture.** If you choose this option, a Select button appears. Click it to open the Select a Picture dialog box, already open to your Library→Desktop Pictures folder. Choose a graphics file (one of Apple's—in the Desktop Pictures folder—or one

---

POWER USERS' CLINIC

The Go to Folder Command

Every now and then, a Unix tentacle pokes through the user-friendly Aqua interface. Every now and then, you find a place where you can use Unix shortcuts instead of the mouse.

One classic example is the Go→Go to Folder command (⌘-~). It brings up a box like the one shown here.

The purpose of this box is to let you jump to a certain folder on your Mac directly by typing its Unix *folder path.* Depending on your point of view, this special box is either a shortcut or a detour.

For example, if you want to see what's in the Documents folder of your Home folder, you could choose Go→Go to Folder, type this—

/Users/mjones/Documents

—and then click Go or press Return. (In this example, of course, *mjones* is your short account name.)

In other words, you're telling the Mac to open the Users folder in your main hard drive window, then your Home folder inside that, and then the Documents folder inside *that.* Each slash means, "and then open." (Leaving off the name of your hard drive is optional.) When you press Enter, the folder you specified pops open immediately.

Of course, if you really wanted to jump to your Documents folder, you'd be wasting your time by typing all that. Unix (and therefore Mac OS X) offers a handy shortcut that means, "my home folder." It's the tilde character (~) at

the upper-left corner of your keyboard. To see what's in your Home folder, then, you could type just that ~ symbol into the Go To box and then press Return. Or you could add some slashes to it to specify a folder inside your Home folder, like this:

~/Documents

If you get into this sort of thing, here's another shortcut worth noting: If you type nothing but a slash (/) and then press Return, you jump immediately to the Computer window, which provides an overview of all your disks, plus a Network icon.

Go to the folder:

`/Users/mjones/Movies/`

Cancel   Go

Note, too, that you don't have to type out the full path—only the part that drills down from the *window you're in.* If your Home folder window is already open, for example, you can open the Pictures folder just by typing *Pictures.*

But the Go to Folder trick *really* turns into a high-octane time-saver if you use *tab completion.* After each slash, you can type only enough letters of a folder's name to give Mac OS X the idea—*de* instead of *desktop,* for example—and then press the Tab key. Mac OS X instantly and automatically fills in the rest of the folder's name.

For example, instead of typing */applications/Microsoft Office X/clipart/standard,* you could type nothing more than */ap/mi/cl/st,* remembering to press Tab after each pair of letters. Now *that's* how to feel like a Unix programmer.

---

of your own). When you click Select, you'll see that Mac OS X has superimposed the window's icons on the photo (see Figure 1-19).

Logging Out, Shutting Down

If you're the only person who uses your Mac, finishing up a work session is the same as it always has been: You can either turn off the machine or simply let it go to sleep—in any of several ways.

Bring up the Shut Down dialog box

Many of these methods bring up the dialog box shown in Figure 1-20, which brings you to a crossroads: You can restart the machine, make it sleep, shut it down, or cancel (that is, go back to whatever you were doing). Here are two ways to bring up that dialog box:

- Press the keyboard power button, if your Mac has one.

- Press Control-Eject on current Apple keyboards.

Note: If you have a flat-panel Apple screen, pressing the power button doesn't summon the "Are you sure you want to shut down?" box; it simply puts the Mac to sleep.

Figure 1-20:
Once the Shut Down dialog box appears, you can press the S key instead of clicking Sleep, R for Restart, Esc for Cancel, or Enter for Shut Down.

Are you sure you want to shut down your computer now?

Restart   Sleep   Cancel   Shut Down

Shutting down or restarting immediately

If you're a more decisive sort, you can save yourself a step by bypassing the Shut Down dialog box altogether:

- Use the Sleep, Restart, or Shut Down commands in the menu.

- Press Control-⌘-Eject (F12) for a quick restart.

- Press Control-Option-⌘-Eject for a quick shutdown. (It's not as complex as it looks—the first three keys are all in a tidy row to the left of the Space bar.)

- If you decide to let it sleep, just walk away, confident that the Energy Saver system preference described on page 195 will send the machine off to dreamland automatically at the specified time.

Logging out

If you share your Mac, on the other hand, you should *log out* when you're done. Doing so ensures that your stuff is safe from the evil and the clueless even when you're away from the room.

Logging out is described in much more detail in Chapter 11; for now, all you have to do is choose →Log Out (Shift-⌘-Q); in the confirmation dialog box, click Log Out (or press Enter). The Mac hides your world from view and displays the Sign In dialog box, ready for the next victim.

Getting Help in Mac OS X

It's a good thing you've got a book about Mac OS X in your hands, because you certainly won't get much help from Apple. Balloon Help is gone from Mac OS X. So is Apple Guide. What's left is the standard Help→Mac Help command, which you can also summon by pressing ⌘-?. You get a Web-browser-like program that reads help files in your System folder→Libraries folder (see Figure 1-21).

Figure 1-21:
When you choose Help→Mac Help, you're shown a welcome screen for the Mac's collection of Mac OS X help topics. Note that the Back button at the bottom of the screen is active and clickable. If you click it, you're taken to the master list of help topics—AirPort Help, AppleScript Help, and so on—of which Mac Help is only one category. In other words, you can actually read the help screens for a program that you haven't yet launched.

You're expected to find the topic you want in one of these two ways:

- **Use the Ask blank.** Type the phrase you want, such as *printing* or *switching applications,* into the blank at the top of the window, and then click Ask (or press Return).

  The Mac responds by showing you a list of help-screen topics that may pertain to what you're seeking (see Figure 1-22).

- **Drill down.** The starting screen offers several "quick click" topics that may interest you. If so, keep clicking blue underlined links until you find a topic you want to read.

As with the Search method, you can backtrack by clicking the Back (left-arrow) button at the bottom of the "browser" window.

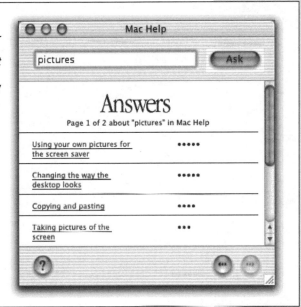

Figure 1-22:
The black dots indicate the Mac's "relevance" rating—how well it thinks each help page matches your search. Click one to read the corresponding topic; if it isn't as helpful as you hoped, click the Back button (the left-pointing arrow) at the bottom of the window to return to the list of relevant topics. Click the little question-mark button to return to the master Help Center.

Organizing Your Stuff

The Mac OS X Folder Structure

If you're used to older versions of the Mac OS, switching to Mac OS X means having to unlearn one deeply ingrained habit right away: double-clicking your hard drive icon to get started for the day.

If you do, you'll find a disorienting collection of folders in the Macintosh HD window—folders that you didn't put there—called things like Applications, Library, and Users. (If you upgraded an existing Mac to Mac OS X, you'll also see all your original hard-drive folders nestled among them.)

Most of these new folders aren't very useful to you, the Mac's human companion. They're there for Mac OS X's own use. Think of your main hard drive window the way you used to think of the System folder: as storage for the operating system itself, to be accessed only occasionally for administrative purposes. (No wonder that in early versions of Mac OS X, Apple didn't put your hard drive icon on the desktop at all. The truth is, double-clicking it gains you absolutely nothing.)

Your Home Folder

Instead of setting up your nest—your files, folders, aliases, and so on—in the hard drive window, from now on, you'll set it up in your *Home folder*. That's a folder bearing your name (or whatever name you typed when you installed Mac OS X).

One way to find it is to double-click the Users folder, and then double-click the folder inside it that bears your name and looks like a house (see Figure 2-1). Here, at last, is the window that you'll eventually fill with new folders, organize, back up, and so on.

Mac OS X is rife with shortcuts for getting to this all-important folder:

- Choose Go→Home.

- Press Option-⌘-H.

- Click the Home icon on the toolbar (page 81).

- Click the Home icon on the Dock. (If you don't see one, see page 80 for instructions on how to put one there.)

All of these steps open your Home folder directly.

So why has Apple demoted your files to a folder three levels deep? The answer may send you through the five stages of grief—Denial, Anger, Bargaining, Depression, and finally Acceptance—but if you're willing to go through it, much of the mystery of Mac OS X will fall away.

Mac OS X has been designed from the ground up for *computer sharing*. It's ideal for any situation where different family members, students, or workers share the same Mac. (In Mac OS 9, the Multiple Users control panel offered much the same feature—but in Mac OS X, the feature is much more deeply ingrained, more secure, and more effective.)

In fact, in Mac OS X, every person who uses the computer will turn on the machine to find his own separate, secure desktop picture, set of files, Web bookmarks, font collection, and preference settings. (Much more about this feature in Chapter 11.)

Like it or not, Mac OS X considers you one of these people. If you're the only one who uses this Mac, fine—you can simply ignore the sharing features. (You can also ignore all that business at the beginning of Chapter 1 about logging in.) But in its little software head, Mac OS X still considers you an account holder, and stands ready to accommodate any others who should come along.

Note: Some Mac fans have noted with dismay that Mac OS X lacks an Encrypt command for protecting individual files. Now you know why: you don't need it. Why would you want to protect individual files when *your entire machine environment* is protected by Unix-standard security? That's like wondering why you can't tie down a single gold bar in the vault at Fort Knox.

In any case, now you should be seeing the importance of the Users folder in the main hard drive window. Inside are folders—the Home folders—named for the different people who use this Mac. In general, nobody is allowed to open what's inside anybody else's folder.

If you're the sole proprietor of the machine, of course, there's only one Home folder in the Users folder—named for you. (You can ignore the Shared folder; it's described on page 287.)

This is only the first of many examples in which Mac OS X imposes a fairly rigid folder structure. Old-time Mac fans may miss the freedom of being able to put files and folders wherever they like, but the Mac OS X approach has its advantages. For example, you're not the only one who must live by its rules; software installers are equally regulated. By keeping such tight control over which files go where, Mac OS X keeps itself pure—and very, very stable. (Other operating systems known for their stability, such as Windows 2000 and Windows XP, work the same way.)

Furthermore, keeping all of your stuff in a single folder will make it very easy for you to back up your work. It also makes life easier when you try to connect with your machine from elsewhere in the office (over the network) or elsewhere in the world (over the Internet), as described in Chapter 21.

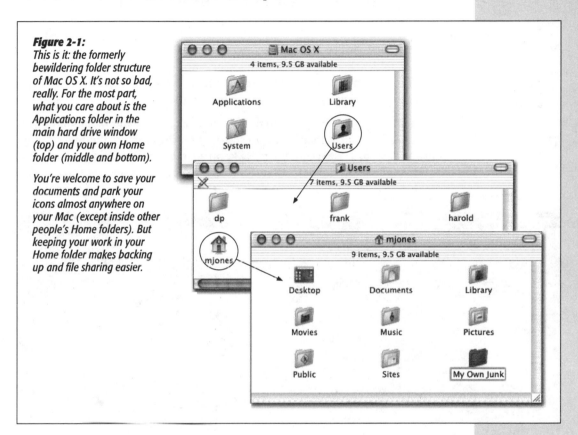

Figure 2-1:
This is it: the formerly bewildering folder structure of Mac OS X. It's not so bad, really. For the most part, what you care about is the Applications folder in the main hard drive window (top) and your own Home folder (middle and bottom).

You're welcome to save your documents and park your icons almost anywhere on your Mac (except inside other people's Home folders). But keeping your work in your Home folder makes backing up and file sharing easier.

What's in Your Hard Drive Window

When you first run Mac OS X, you'll find these folders in the main hard drive window:

• **Applications.** The Applications folder, of course, contains the complete collection of Mac OS X programs on your Mac. (Even so, you'll rarely launch programs by opening this folder; the Dock is a far more efficient launcher, as described in the next chapter.)

• **Developer.** You'll find this folder only if you bothered to install the *second* CD in the Mac OS X box, the one called Developer Tools (page 246).

- **Library.** This folder bears more than a passing resemblance to the System Folder sub-folders of Mac OSes gone by. It stores components for the operating system and your programs (sounds, fonts, preferences, help files, printer drivers, modem scripts, and so on).

- **System.** This is Unix, baby. This is the actual code that turns on your Mac and controls its operations. You'll rarely have any business messing with this folder, which is why Apple made almost all of its contents invisible.

- **Users.** As noted above, this folder stores the Home folders for everyone who uses this machine.

What's in Your Home Folder

Within the folder that bears your name, you'll find another set of standard Mac OS X folders. Except as noted, you're free to rename or delete them; Mac OS X creates these folders solely as a convenience. For example:

- **Desktop.** When you drag an icon out of a folder or disk window and onto your Mac OS X desktop, it may *appear* to show up on the desktop. But that's just an optical illusion, a visual convenience, like an alias; in truth, nothing in Mac OS X is ever *really* on the desktop. It's just in this Desktop *folder*, and mirrored on the desktop area.

UP TO SPEED

The Computer Window

As noted in this chapter, the hard drive icon in the upper right doesn't actually do you much good. Opening it reveals only a handful of folders that you can't do anything with.

Another dramatic change is the Computer window. Exactly as in Microsoft Windows, it holds the icons for all the disks connected to your machine—the hard drive, a CD that you've inserted, an iPod, another external hard drive, and so on—as well as an icon called Network. (The Network icon shows up even if you're not, in fact, on a network.) You can open the Computer window either by clicking the Computer icon on the Finder toolbar or by choosing Go→Computer (Option-⌘-C).

This is the topmost level of your Mac, the one Unix fiends call the *root level*. This is the stuff that can't be put into any folder at all.

So what's it for? In some ways, the Computer window is redundant. After all, Mac OS X automatically puts disk icons at the right side of your screen, just as in Mac OS 9.

But some people, particularly Windows refugees, don't care for that icons-on-the-desktop feature. In the interests of creating a neater, cleaner desktop, they turn it off, in fact (by choosing Finder→Preferences and turning off the three checkboxes under "Show these items on the Desktop"). In that case, the Computer window still gives you access to all of your disks.

If you prefer the icons-on-the-desktop scheme (because you've been using a Mac for years, for example), you'll probably never need the Computer window. You've got your disks on the desktop, and you can access the network from the Go menu (see page 299). In that case, you may as well remove the Computer icon from the Finder toolbar to save space; instructions are on page 252.

The reason is simple enough: Remember that everyone who shares your machine will, upon logging in, see her own stuff sitting out on the desktop. Now you know how Mac OS X does it: There's a separate Desktop folder in every person's Home folder.

You can entertain yourself for hours by proving this yourself. If you drag something out of your Desktop folder, it also disappears from the actual desktop. And vice versa. (You're not allowed to delete or rename this folder.)

Tip: The desktop is actually a folder in your Home folder. That's handy, because it gives you a quick and sneaky way to jump to your Home folder from anywhere: Click the desktop (the colored one, not the folder) and then press ⌘-up arrow. Because that keystroke always means "open whatever folder *contains* the one I'm examining," it instantly opens your Home folder. (Your Home folder is, of course, the "parent" of your Desktop folder.)

- **Documents.** Apple suggests that you keep your actual work files in this folder. Sure enough, whenever you save a new document (when you're working in, for example, AppleWorks or Word), the Save As box proposes storing the new file in this folder, as described in Chapter 4. (Annoyingly enough, some programs— notably AppleWorks—store their preferences here instead of in the Library folder.)

- **Library.** As noted above, the *main* Library folder (the one in your main hard drive window) contains folders for fonts, preferences, help files, and so on.

  But you have your *own* Library folder, too, right there in your Home folder. It stores exactly the same kinds of things—but they're *your* fonts, *your* preferences, and so on.

  Once again, this setup may seem redundant if you're the only person who uses your Mac. But it makes perfect sense in the context of families, schools, or offices where people share a single machine. Because you have your own Library folder, you can have a font collection that's "installed" on the Mac only when *you're* using it. Each person's program preference files are stored independently, too (the files that determine where Photoshop's palettes appear, and so on). And each person, of course, sees his own email when launching Mac OS X's Mail program (Chapter 19)—because your mail, too, is stored in your own Library folder.

  Other Library folders store your Favorites (page 64), Internet Search Sites (page 496), Web browser plug-ins and cached Web pages, keyboard layouts, sound files, and so on. (It's best not to move or rename this folder.)

- **Movies, Music, Pictures.** These folders, of course, are designed to store multimedia files. The various Mac OS X programs that deal with movies, music, and pictures will propose these specialized folders as storage locations. For example, when you plug a digital camera into a Mac OS X computer, Mac OS X automatically begins to download the photos on it—and stores them in the Pictures folder. Similarly, iMovie is programmed to look for the Movies folder when saving its files.

- **Public.** If you are on a network, or if others use the same Mac when you're not around, this folder can be handy: it's the "Any of you guys can look at these files" folder. Other people on your network, and other people who sit down at this machine, are allowed to see whatever you've put in here, even if they don't have your password. (If your Mac isn't on an office network and isn't shared, you can throw away this folder.) Details on sharing the Mac are in Chapter 11, and on networking in Chapter 12.

- **Sites.** Mac OS X has a built-in *Web server*—software that turns your Mac into an Internet Web site that people all over the world can connect to. (This feature is practical only if your Mac is connected to the Internet all the time, via cable modem or DSL, for example.) This Mac OS X feature relies on a program called the Apache Web server, which is so highly regarded in the Unix community that programmers lower their voices when they mention it.

  Details are in Chapter 21. For now, note that this is the folder where you will put the actual Web pages you want to make available to the Internet at large.

Icon Names

Every document, program, folder, and disk on your Mac is represented by an *icon:* a colorful little picture that you can move, copy, or double-click to open. In Mac OS X, icons look more like photos than cartoons, and you can scale them to any size (page 29).

A Mac OS X icon's name can have up to 256 letters and spaces. If you're accustomed to the 31-character limit of Mac OS 9, that's quite a luxurious ceiling.

You can use letters, numbers, punctuation—in fact, any symbol you want except for the colon (:), which the Mac uses behind the scenes for its own folder-hierarchy designation purposes. (If you type a colon when renaming an icon, Mac OS X automatically substitutes a hyphen—a much more considerate behavior than showing you some rude error message.)

Note: You can't use a period or a slash, either, if it *begins* a file's name.

To rename a file, begin with one of these two methods:

- Click once on the icon, and then press Return or Enter.

- Click once squarely on the icon's name. (If the window is in icon view, this method works only if the icon is already selected.)

Either way, a rectangle now appears around the name (see Figure 2-2). At this point, the existing name is highlighted; just begin typing to replace it. If you type a very long name, the rectangle grows vertically to accommodate new lines of text—a first on the Macintosh.

Tip: If you simply want to add letters to the beginning or ending of the file's existing name, press the left or right arrow key immediately after pressing Return or Enter. The insertion point jumps to the corresponding end of the file name.

Figure 2-2:
Click an icon's name (top left) to produce the renaming rectangle (top right), in which you can edit the file's name. At this point, the existing name is highlighted; just begin typing to replace it (bottom left). When you're finished typing, press Return, Enter, or Tab to seal the deal, or just click somewhere else.

Drivers

Drivers

Vehicular Operation Engineers

Vehicular Operation Engineers

When you're finished typing, press Return, Enter, or Tab—or just click somewhere else—to make the renaming rectangle disappear.

You can give more than one file or folder the same name, as long as they're not in the same folder. For example, you can have as many files named "Chocolate Cake Recipe" as you like, as long as each is in a different folder.

As you edit a file's name, remember that you can use the Cut, Copy, and Paste commands in the Edit menu to move selected bits of text around, exactly as though you were word processing. The Paste command can be useful when, for instance, you're

---

DON'T PANIC

Long and Short File Names

Hey, what's this deal about long file names? I tried saving an AppleWorks document, and it didn't let me use more than 31 letters!

It's true that you can give a file a very long name in the Finder. But you may soon discover that pre–Mac OS X programs, and even programs that have been rewritten (*Carbonized*) to run in Mac OS X, still limit you to 31 letters when you get down to naming a new document in the Save As dialog box.

Over time, software companies may get with the program and rejigger their software to overcome this anachronistic glitch. For now, though, all is not lost.

Even though you can use only 31 letters when saving a new document from, say, AppleWorks or Internet Explorer, you're welcome to *rename* the file in the Finder, using all 255 characters Mac OS X permits. When you reopen the document in the original program, you'll see an abbreviated name in the title bar (a file that, at the desktop, is called *My Visit to Bill Gates's House, and Why I'll Take the Apple Bumper Sticker Off my Car Next Time* opens into AppleWorks as *My Visit to Bill Gates's H#B6C5*).

The good news is that behind the scenes, Mac OS X still remembers its long name. Even if you edit and re-save the document, you'll still find its long file name intact when you view its icon at the desktop.

---

renaming many icons in sequence (*Quarterly Estimate 1, Quarterly Estimate 2,* and so on).

Remember, too, that when the Finder sorts files, a space is considered alphabetically *before* the letter A. To force a particular folder to appear at the top of a list view window, precede its name with a space.

Selecting Icons

To highlight a single icon in preparation for printing, opening, duplicating, or deleting, click the icon once with the mouse. (In a list or column view, as described in Chapter 1, you can also click on any visible piece of information about that file—its size, kind, date modified, and so on.)

That much may seem obvious. But most first-time Mac users have no idea how to manipulate *more* than one icon at a time—an essential survival skill in a graphic interface like the Mac's.

To highlight multiple files in preparation for moving or copying, use one of these techniques:

- **To highlight all the icons.** To select all the icons in a window, press ⌘-A (the equivalent of the Edit→Select All command).

- **To highlight several icons by dragging.** You can drag diagonally to highlight a group of nearby icons, as shown in Figure 2-3. In a list view, in fact, you don't even have to drag over the icons themselves—your cursor can touch any part of any file's row, such as its modification date or file size.

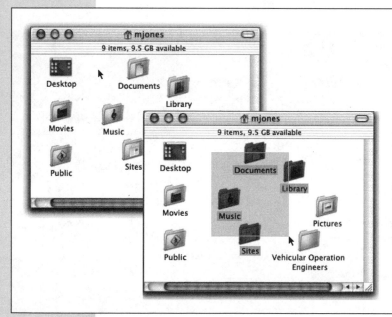

Figure 2-3:
You can highlight several icons simultaneously by dragging a box around them. To do so, drag from outside of the target icons (left) diagonally across them (right), creating a transparent gray rectangle as you go. Any icons touched by this rectangle are selected when you release the mouse. If you press the Shift or ⌘ key as you do this, any previously highlighted icons remain selected.

Tip: If you include a particular icon in your diagonally dragged group by mistake, ⌘-click it to remove it from the selected cluster.

- **To highlight consecutive icons in a list.** If you're looking at the contents of a window in list or column view, you can drag vertically over the file and folder names to highlight a group of consecutive icons, as described above.

  But Mac OS X offers a new, faster way to do the same thing: Click the first icon you want to highlight, and then Shift-click the last file. All the files in between are automatically selected, along with the two icons you clicked. Figure 2-4 shows the idea.

  This technique is a change from the Mac operating system of years gone by. But it makes perfect sense. It mirrors the way Shift-clicking works in a word processor and in many other kinds of programs.

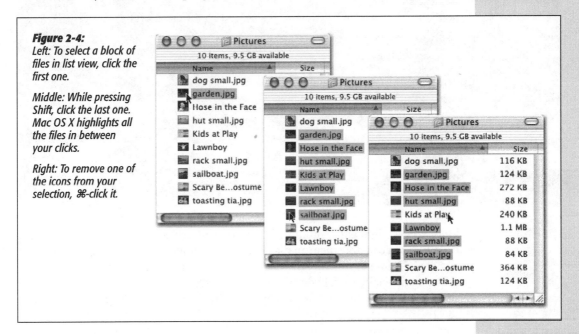

Figure 2-4:
Left: To select a block of files in list view, click the first one.

Middle: While pressing Shift, click the last one. Mac OS X highlights all the files in between your clicks.

Right: To remove one of the icons from your selection, ⌘-click it.

- **To highlight random icons.** If you want to highlight only, for example, the first, third, and seventh icons in a window, start by clicking icon No. 1. Then ⌘-click each of the others (or ⌘-drag new rectangles around them). Each icon darkens to show that you've selected it.

  If you're highlighting a long string of icons and then click one by mistake, you don't have to start over. Instead, just ⌘-click it again; the dark highlighting disappears. (If you do want to start over from the beginning, you can deselect all selected icons by clicking any empty part of the window.)

The ⌘ key trick is especially handy if you want to select *almost* all the icons in a window. Press ⌘-A to select everything in the folder, then ⌘-click any unwanted icons to deselect them.

Tip: In icon views, you can also *Shift*-click (rather than ⌘-click) to select multiple individual icons, just as in Mac OS 9. But because Shift-clicking has a different purpose in list and column views, as described above, you may as well just learn to use the ⌘ key when selecting individual icons. That way, you won't have to remember to use a different key in each view.

Selecting Icons from the Keyboard

For the speed fanatic, using the mouse to click an icon is a hopeless waste of time. Fortunately, you can also select an icon by typing the first couple letters of its name.

When looking at your home window, for example, you can type *M* to highlight the Movies folder. And if you actually intended to highlight the *Music* folder instead, press the Tab key to highlight the next icon in the window alphabetically. (Shift-Tab highlights the previous icon alphabetically.) You can use the arrow keys, too, to highlight a neighboring icon. (Pressing Tab has a different effect in column view; see page 41.)

After having highlighted an icon in this way, you can ma-nipulate it using the commands in the File menu—or their keyboard equivalents: open (⌘-O), put it into the Trash (⌘-Delete), show information (⌘-I), duplicate (⌘-D), or make an alias, as described later in this chapter (⌘-L). If you turn on the special disability features described on page 191, you can even *move* the highlighted icon using only the keyboard.

If you're a first-time Mac user, you may find it excessively nerdy to memorize keystrokes for functions the mouse does perfectly well. If you make your living using the Mac, however, the speed and efficiency of these keystrokes will reward you for memorizing them many times over.

Once you've highlighted multiple icons, you can manipulate them all at once. For example, you can drag them en masse to another folder or disk by dragging any *one* of the highlighted icons; all other highlighted icons go along for the ride. This technique is especially useful when you want to back up a bunch of files by dragging them onto a different disk, or when you want to delete them all by dragging them to the Trash.

Dragging to Copy a Disk

Help! I'm trying to copy a CD onto my hard drive. But when I drag it onto the hard drive icon, I get only an alias—not a copy of the CD. I used to do this all the time in Mac OS 9, but I can't make it work now.

Apple switched some things around in Mac OS X; sure enough, dragging a disk onto a disk creates an alias now.

But producing a copy of the dragged icon is easy enough: Just press Option as you drag.

When multiple icons are selected, furthermore, the commands in the File and Edit menus—such as Duplicate, Open, and Make Alias—apply to all of them simultaneously.

Tip: Don't forget that you can instantly highlight all the files in an open window by choosing Edit→Select All (or by pressing ⌘-A)—no icon clicking required.

Moving and Copying Icons

In Mac OS X, it's easier than ever to move or copy icons from one place to another. In fact, there are two ways to do it: by dragging icons, or by using the Copy and Paste commands.

Copying by Dragging

You can drag icons from one folder to another, from one drive to another, from a drive to a folder on another drive, and so on. (When you've selected several icons, drag any *one* of them; the others tag along.) While the Mac is copying an icon, you can cancel the copying process by pressing either ⌘-period or the Esc key.

POWER USERS' CLINIC

Designing Your Own Icons

You don't have to be content with the icons provided by Microsoft, Apple, and whoever else wrote your software. Exactly as in Mac OS 9, you can paste new icons onto your file, disk, and folder icons to help you pick them out at a glance.

The easiest way to replace an icon is to copy it from *another* icon. To do so, highlight the icon, choose File→Show Info, click the existing icon in the resulting window, and then choose Edit→Copy. Now click the icon to which you want the copied picture transferred, and choose Edit→Paste. (Because Mac OS X maintains only a single Show Info window, you don't even have to close it and then reopen it for the target icon.)

If you'd rather introduce all-new icons, you're welcome to steal some of the beautifully designed ones at *www.iconfactory.com* and the icon sites linked to it. Once you've downloaded these special icon files, you can copy their icon images from the Show Info window exactly as you would any icon.

To design a Mac OS X icon from scratch, you could, of course, use a graphics program like Photoshop, the painting module of AppleWorks, or shareware like GraphicConverter; remember to make your new icons 128 pixels square. But sooner or later, you'll want to finish up in Iconographer (available at *www.missingmanuals.com*), which saves the result in the *.icns* format required by Mac OS X.

Once you've saved your icon file this way, select it, choose File→Show Info, click the existing icon in the resulting window, choose Edit→Copy, click the icon you want to replace, and paste into its Show Info window.

Note that you can't change certain folder icons that Mac OS X considers important, such as Applications or System. (You can, however, change the special Mac OS X folder icons in your Home folder—Pictures, Documents, and so on. As of Mac OS X 10.1.1, you can also replace your hard drive icon.) You're also not allowed to change icons that belong to other people who share this Mac and sign in under a different name (Chapter 11).

Tip: If you're copying files into a disk or folder that already contains items with the same names, Mac OS X asks you individually about each one. ("An item named "Fiddlesticks" with extension '.doc' already exists in this location.") Unfortunately, Mac OS X no longer tells you whether or not the version you're replacing is *older* or *newer* than the one you're moving.

Click Replace or Don't Replace, as you see fit (or Stop to call off the whole copying business).

Understanding when the Mac copies a dragged icon and when it just *moves* the icon bewilders many a beginner. However, the scheme is fairly simple (see Figure 2-5):

- Dragging from a folder to another folder on the same disk *moves* the icon.

- Option-dragging it *copies* the icon instead of moving it. If you do so within a single window, you get a duplicate of the file called "[Whatever its name was] copy."

- Dragging from a disk to another disk *copies* the folder or file.

Tip: You can drag icons either into an open window or directly onto a disk or folder *icon*.

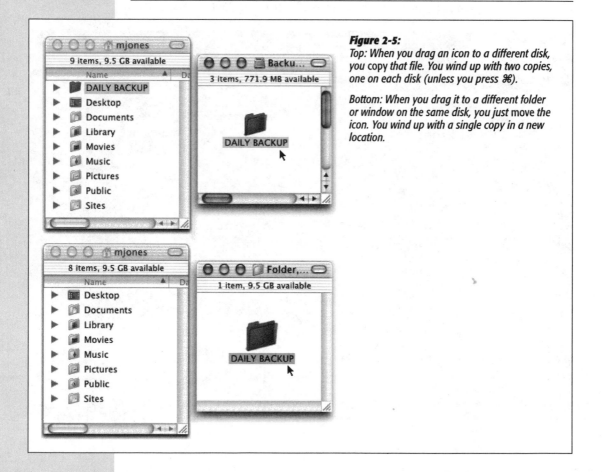

Figure 2-5:
Top: When you drag an icon to a different disk, you copy that file. You wind up with two copies, one on each disk (unless you press ⌘).

Bottom: When you drag it to a different folder or window on the same disk, you just move the icon. You wind up with a single copy in a new location.

- Dragging an icon from one disk to another while pressing ⌘ *moves* the file or folder, in the process deleting it from the original disk.

This last trick is a dramatic change from the Mac OS 9 era, where you could never *move* an icon to a different disk. You had no choice but to manually delete the original from your hard drive after dragging it to the second disk.

Mac OS X frees you from this kind of housekeeping task forever.

Copying by Using Copy and Paste

Dragging icons to copy or move them may feel good, because it's so direct: You actually see your arrow cursor pushing the icons into the new location.

But you pay a price for this satisfying illusion: You may have to spend a moment or two fiddling with your windows so that you have a clear "line of drag" between the icon to be moved and the destination folder.

There's a better way in Mac OS X 10.1 and later: For the first time on the Macintosh, you can use the Copy and Paste commands to move icons from one window into another. (Apple borrowed this idea from Windows, but that's OK; it's irresistible.) The routine goes like this:

1. **Highlight the icon or icons you want to move.**

   You can use any of the techniques described on page 56.

2. **Choose Edit→Copy.**

   Or press the keyboard shortcut: ⌘-C.

DON'T PANIC

The Undo (Put Away) Command

Hey! Where's the Put Away command?

For years, expert Macaholics have known that the File→Put Away command has two functions. One is ejecting a disk. The other is moving icons on the desktop or in the Trash back to their previous folder locations.

For example, suppose you've double-clicked your Trash icon. You discover two icons waiting in the Trash window that shouldn't be deleted. Rather than trying to figure out what folder they originally came from, and shuffling windows around to receive them, you could just highlight the icons and then choose File→Put Away (or press ⌘-Y). Before your eyes, those icons disappear from the Trash window; not only that, Mac OS 9 would put them safely

back in the folder from which they were dragged to the Trash.

Put Away has been, well, put away; it's no longer in Mac OS X.

You should note, however, that Mac OS X has a new feature that can sometimes get you out of the same scrapes: a true, working Undo command. (It's the first command on the Edit menu, or press ⌘-Z.) It can undo all kinds of things you've done on the desktop, including dragging an icon into a different folder or to the Trash. Unfortunately, it can only take back the most recent action you've taken, so you'd be well advised to realize your mistakes soon after making them.

Tip: You can combine steps 1 and 2 by Control-clicking an icon and choosing the Copy command from the contextual menu that appears. (If you've selected several icons, the command says "Copy 5 items," or whatever.)

3. **Open the window where you want to put the icons. Choose Edit→Paste.**

   Once again, you may prefer to use the keyboard equivalent: ⌘-V. And once again, you can also Control-click inside the window and then choose Paste from the contextual menu that appears.

A progress bar may appear as Mac OS X copies the files or folders; press Esc or ⌘-. to interrupt the process. When the progress bar goes away, you've successfully transferred the icons, which now appear in the new window.

Aliases: Icons in Two Places at Once

By highlighting an icon and then choosing File→Make Alias (or pressing ⌘-L), you generate an *alias,* a specially branded duplicate of the original icon (see Figure 2-6). It's not a duplicate of the *file*—just of the *icon,* requiring negligible storage space. When you double-click the alias, the original file opens. Because you can create as many aliases as you want of a single file, aliases let you, in effect, stash that file in many different folder locations simultaneously. Double-click any one of them, and you open the original icon, wherever it may be on your system.

Tip: You can also create an alias of an icon by Option-⌘-dragging it out of its window. (Aliases you create this way lack the word *alias* on the filename—a distinct delight to those who find the suffix redundant and annoying.) You can also create an alias by Control-clicking a normal icon and choosing Make Alias from the contextual menu that appears.

Applications

Applications alias

Figure 2-6:
You can identify an alias by the tiny arrow badge on the lower-left corner. Alias names are no longer italicized, as they were in Mac OS 9.

What's Good About Aliases

An alias takes up almost no disk space, even if the original file is enormous. Aliases are smart, too: Even if you rename the alias, rename the original file, move the alias, and move the original, double-clicking the alias still opens the original icon.

And that's just the beginning of alias intelligence. Suppose you move the original icon to a removable disk, such as a Zip disk. When you double-click the alias on your hard drive, the Mac requests that particular disk by name. And if you copy the original to a different machine on the network, your Mac attempts to connect to the appropriate machine, prompting you for a password (see Chapter 12)—even if the other machine is thousands of miles away and your Mac must dial the modem to connect.

In Mac OS X, aliases aren't nearly as important as they once were. There's less call for creating aliases of programs you use frequently, for example, because now you can just drag those programs' icons onto your Dock or Finder toolbar, as described in the next chapter. The Mac OS X versions of the Recent Items, Recent Folders, and Startup Items features no longer depend on aliases, either.

Still, aliases can be handy in Mac OS X. For example:

- You still may want to file a document you're working on in several different folders, or to place a particular folder in several different locations.

- The Favorites command (see page 64) still relies on aliases. By choosing Go→Favorites, you open a window that reveals the aliases of every icon you've ever designated as a Favorite, so that you can delete them, move or rename them, and so on.

- You can use the alias feature to save you some of the steps required to access another hard drive on the network. Details on this trick in Chapter 12.

- Put an alias of your Documents folder (which is inside your Home folder) on the desktop. After all, this is the folder most people spend the most time in. It's very silly to have to burrow four folders deep every time you want to find it. (You may as well put your Home folder itself on the Dock, too.)

- It's extremely useful to put aliases of your *Mac OS 9* programs into the Applications folder, so that they appear listed among the Mac OS X programs. Otherwise, you'll have to maintain your programs in two separate folders, arbitrarily separated by whether they're old or new.

Tip: Mac OS X makes it easy to find the file to which an alias "points" without actually having to open it. Just highlight the alias and then choose File→Show Original (⌘-R); Mac OS X immediately shows you the actual, original file, sitting patiently in its folder, wherever that may be.

Broken Aliases

An alias doesn't contain any of the information you've typed or composed in the original. Don't burn an *alias* of your slide show onto a CD and then depart for the airport, hoping to give the presentation in your arrival city. When you double-click the alias, now separated from its original, you'll be shown the dialog box in Figure 2-7.

If you're on a plane 3,000 miles away from the hard drive on which the original file resides, click Delete Alias (to get rid of the orphan alias you just double-clicked) or OK (to do nothing, leaving the orphaned alias where it is).

In certain circumstances, however, the third button—Fix Alias—is the most useful of all. Click it to summon the Fix Alias dialog box, which you can use to navigate your entire Mac. When you click a new icon and then click Choose, you associate the orphaned alias with a different original icon.

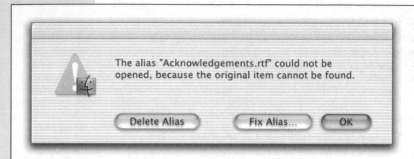

Figure 2-7:
If the alias can't find the original file, you're offered the chance to associate it with a different file.

The alias "Acknowledgements.rtf" could not be opened, because the original item cannot be found.

Delete Alias   Fix Alias...   OK

Such techniques become handy when, for example, you click your novel manuscript's alias on the desktop, forgetting that you recently saved it under a new name and deleted the older draft. Instead of simply showing you an error message that says "'Revenge of the Deltoids' can't be found," the Mac shows you the box that contains the Fix Alias button. By clicking it, thus re-associating it with the new document, you can save yourself the trouble of creating a new alias. From now on, double-clicking your manuscript's alias on the desktop opens the new draft.

_____

Tip: You don't have to wait until the original file no longer exists before choosing a new original for an alias; you can perform alias reassignment surgery any time you like. Just highlight the alias icon and then choose File→Show Info. In the Show Info dialog box, click Select New Original. In the resulting window, find and double-click the file you'd like to open from now on whenever you double-click the alias.

_____

Favorites

After years of watching Microsoft pilfer great ideas from the Mac OS, Apple decided that two could play that game—and it stole a feature right back. The File→Add to Favorites command (⌘-T) places the names of icons you've highlighted into the Go→Favorites command, as shown in Figure 2-8. The Favorites scheme, therefore, is yet another mechanism that lists your favorite files, folders, programs, disks, and even network-accessible folders for quick access—much like the Dock.

Nor is the Go menu the only place Favorites are listed. You'll also see your personal Favorites list show up whenever you open or save a file (page 109) or click the Favorites icon on your Finder toolbar.

This feature relies on a special folder inside your Home→Library folder called, reasonably enough, Favorites. Every time you use the Add to Favorites command, the Mac puts an alias of the highlighted icon into this Favorites folder. (If you share your Mac, nobody else sees your Favorites. Mac OS X keeps track of each person's Favorites folder independently.)

This behind-the-scenes transaction is worth knowing about, if only because it offers the sole method of *removing or renaming* something from the Go→Favorites listing. That is, choose Go→Favorites→Go To Favorites (or press Option-⌘-F) to open the Favorites window; throw away or rename any of the aliases in it; and then close the window. The Go→Favorites submenu updates itself instantly.

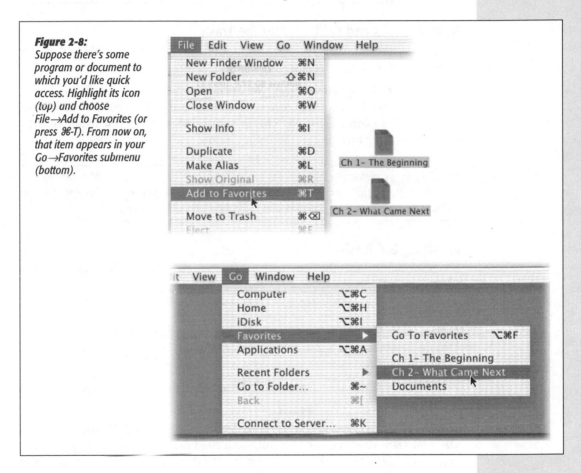

Figure 2-8:
Suppose there's some program or document to which you'd like quick access. Highlight its icon (top) and choose File→Add to Favorites (or press ⌘-T). From now on, that item appears in your Go→Favorites submenu (bottom).

The Trash

No single element of the Macintosh interface is as recognizable or famous as the Trash can, which now appears at the right end of the Dock.

You can discard almost any icon by dragging it onto the Trash icon (which now looks more like a wastebasket than a trash can, but let's not quibble). When the tip of your arrow cursor touches the Trash icon, the little wastebasket turns black. When you release the mouse, you're well on your way to discarding whatever it was you dragged. As a convenience, Mac OS X even replaces the empty-wastebasket icon with a wastebasket-filled-with-crumpled-up-papers icon, to let you know there's something in there.

Tip: Learn the keyboard alternative to dragging something to the Trash: highlight the icon and then press ⌘-Delete. This technique is not only far faster than dragging, but requires far less precision, especially if you have a large screen. Mac OS X does all the Trash-targeting for you.

Rescuing Files and Folders from the Trash

Icons that represent folders and files sit in the Trash forever—or until you choose Finder→Empty Trash, whichever comes first.

If you haven't yet emptied the Trash, you can open its window by clicking the waste-basket icon once. Now you can review its contents: icons that you've placed on the waiting list for extinction. If you change your mind, you can rescue any of these items by dragging them out of the Trash window.

Tip: If dragging something to the Trash was the last thing you did, you can press ⌘-Z—the keyboard shortcut of the Edit→Undo command—which not only removes it from the Trash, but also puts it back into the folder from whence it came. This trick works even if the Trash window isn't open.

Emptying the Trash

If you're confident that the items in the Trash window are worth deleting, use any of these three options:

• Choose Finder→Empty Trash.

• Press Shift-⌘-Delete. It's not as hard to remember as it looks, because it's the same keystroke you use to throw an icon into the Trash—⌘-Delete—with the Shift key added.

• Control-click the wastebasket icon; choose Empty Trash from the contextual menu.

The Macintosh asks you to confirm your decision (see Figure 2-9). When you click OK, Mac OS X deletes those files from your hard drive. In cases of desperation, a program like Micromat Drive X can resurrect deleted files, if used promptly after the deletion. In even more dire cases, DriveSavers (*www.drivesavers.com)* and similar companies can use sophisticated clean-room techniques to recover crucial information—for several hundred dollars.

Locked Files: The Next Generation

By highlighting a file or folder, choosing File→Show Info, and turning on the Locked checkbox, you protect that file or folder from accidental deletion (see Figure 2-9). But that much is old news to Mac veterans.

What's new is that the Locked checkbox is smarter in Mac OS X than it once was. Mac OS X doesn't even let you put a locked icon *into* the Trash. (In the old days, it only objected if you tried to *empty* the Trash.) You can't put the icon of an open program into the Trash, either, as the error message will tell you if you try.

If something that's already *in* the Trash turns out to be locked, simply pressing the Option key as you choose Finder→Empty Trash is no longer the solution, as it was in Mac OS 9.

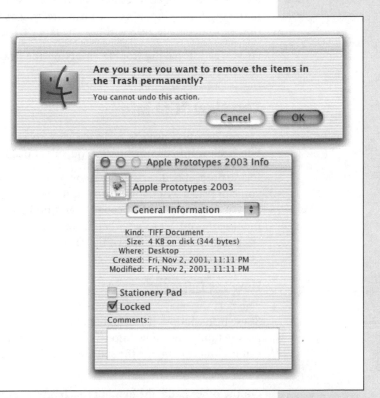

Figure 2-9:
Top: Your last warning. As of Mac OS X 10.1.2, you're no longer told how many items are in the Trash or how much disk space they take up.

Bottom: The Show Info window for a locked file. Locking a file in this way isn't military-level security by any stretch—any passing evildoer can unlock the file in the same way. But it does trigger a "You do not have sufficient privileges" warning when you try to put into the Trash, giving you at least one layer of protection against mistakes.

POWER USERS' CLINIC

Turning Off the Trash Warning

The "Are you sure?" message that appears whenever you try to empty the Trash is, for the novice, a useful safety net. But after you've become a proficient Mac user, you'd probably just as soon have the Trash empty promptly at your command, without bothering you for confirmation.

By pressing Option as you choose Finder→Empty Trash, you can suppress this confirmation box each time you

empty the Trash. But even that trick is one step too many for the power user.

Fortunately, you can also instruct Mac OS X to suppress its confirmation box permanently (version 10.1 and later). To do so, choose Finder→Preferences. In the dialog box, turn off "Show warning before emptying the Trash." Close the window and savor the resulting time savings.

Instead, you must now press Option *as you click and hold on the Trash itself.* Now, when you choose Empty Trash from its pop-up menu, Mac OS X empties the Trash without warnings, locked files and all.

Of course, the other alternative is to unlock what's in the Trash. Fortunately, there's a quick way to do so. Click the Trash icon to open its window. Highlight the icons you want to unlock (or choose Edit→Select All).

Now press ⌘-I (or choose File→Show Info). When you turn off the Locked checkbox in the resulting window, you're un-protecting *all* of the selected files, which you can now send to data heaven without any fancy tricks.

(If you're still having trouble emptying the Trash, see Chapter 16 for some Unix commands that can help.)

The New "Get Info"

One of the first aspects of Mac OS X to stymie veteran Mac users is the new File→Show Info command, the equivalent of the old File→Get Info command.

Its purpose, of course, is to open a window like the one shown in Figure 2-10, where you can read a wealth of information about an icon. If you click a disk icon, you're shown statistics about its capacity and how much of it is full. If you click a document icon, you get to see when it was created and modified, and what programs it "belongs" to. If it's an alias, the Show Info window identifies the location of the actual icon it refers to.

How It's Different

The part that may confuse veteran Mac users is that in Mac OS X, there's only one Show Info window. If you highlight five icons and then choose File→Show Info, you now get only one Show Info window, not five, as you would have in Mac OS 9. You can no longer compare the statistics for the Get Info windows of two or three folders side-by-side.

On the other hand, the new approach offers several benefits:

- You no longer have to highlight an icon *before* you invoke the Show Info command. No matter what you're doing on the desktop, you can hit ⌘-I (the equivalent for File→Show Info) at any time. Once the Show Info window appears, *then* you can click the icon you'd like to investigate.

Tip: Better yet, if you open the Show Info window when *nothing* is selected, you get something you could never get before: information about the desktop itself, including the amount of disk space consumed by everything sitting on it.

- Getting info on another icon is incredibly easy—just click it. The original Show Info window remains on the screen exactly where it was, but its contents change instantly to give you the details on whatever icon you've just clicked.

- The new scheme makes it a snap to summarize information about a group of highlighted icons. For example, if you highlight a gaggle of icons on the desktop all at once, the Show Info window shows you precisely how many you highlighted and adds up the total of their file sizes for you.

The Show Info Pop-up Menu

You use the pop-up menu at the top of the window to summon different screens full of information. Depending on whether you clicked a document, program, disk, alias, or whatever, this pop-up menu's commands may include:

- **General Information.** Here's where you can view (and edit) the name of the icon, and also see its size, creation date, most recent change date, comments, and so on. If you click a disk, this info window shows you its capacity and how full it is. If you click the Trash, you see how much stuff is in it.

  Here, too, you can type in random comments for your own reference, as shown in Figure 2-10. And by pasting over the icon picture in the upper-left corner of the window, you can replace the picture itself used for this icon (page 59).

- **Name & Extension.** On this screen, you can read and edit the name of the icon in question. The "Hide extension" checkbox refers to the suffix on Mac OS X file names (the last three letters of *Letter to Congress.doc,* for example).

  As described on page 103, many Mac OS X documents, behind the scenes, have file name extensions of this kind—but Mac OS X comes factory set to hide them. By turning off this checkbox, you can make the suffix reappear for an individual file. (Conversely, if you've elected to have Mac OS X *show* all file name suffixes, this checkbox lets you hide file name extensions on individual icons.)

- **Memory.** You'll see this option only when showing info for Classic programs (those that haven't been updated for Mac OS X). You see three different memory statistics: Suggested Size (the software company's official recommendation), Minimum Size (below which the program won't even run—a number you shouldn't change), and Preferred Size. This final number is the one you should feel free to adjust, giving the program more memory if it seems unstable in your Classic world (Chapter 5).

- **Open with application.** Available for documents only. Use the controls on this screen to specify which program will open when you double-click this document, or all documents of this type. (Details on page 104.)

- **Preview.** Available for documents. On this panel, you see a handsome, very large thumbnail image. In the case of spreadsheets, word processing documents, HTML documents, and so on, this is nothing to write home about—you see only a magnified version of the generic document icon.

But when you're examining pictures, text files, PDF files, sounds, clippings, and movies, this feature can be extremely useful. As you click each icon, you see a magnified-thumbnail version of what's actually *in* that document. A controller lets you play sounds and movies, where appropriate.

- **Privileges.** Available for all kinds of icons. If other people have access to your Mac (either from across the network or when logging in, in person), this window lets you specify who is allowed to open this particular icon. See Chapter 12 for complete details on setting up folder or disk network privileges.

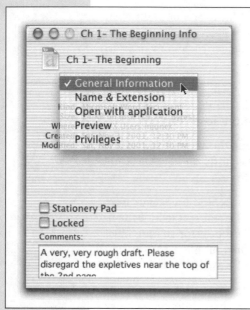

Figure 2-10:
The pop-up menu in the middle of this window takes you to various panels of information. The Comments box at the bottom is yours to edit.

Dock, Desktop, and Toolbar

I f you've used a Macintosh before, some of the Mac OS X landscape should look immediately familiar. There's the Macintosh HD icon in the upper-right corner. There's the menu. There's the menu-bar clock.

After only another moment, however, you discover several unfamiliar elements: the Dock at the bottom edge of the screen; the toolbar at the top of every Finder window; and the shimmering, sometimes animated backdrop of the desktop itself. This chapter shows you how to use and control these most dramatic new elements of Mac OS X.

The Dock

In the old days, the optimists saw the doughnut, and the pessimists saw the hole.

If you're a Mac fan, the debate doesn't concern the doughnut so much as the Dock. This strip of icons at the bottom of the Mac OS X desktop combines the functions of what Mac fans once knew as the Application menu, menu, Launcher, Control Strip, pop-up windows, and spring-loaded folders—all in a single new onscreen gadget.

The pessimist thinks that's ridiculous. "You've just combined the *Launcher* function, which stores unopened programs until you need them, with the *Application menu* function, which is supposed to show you which programs are currently running."

The optimist says: "Well, yeah—isn't that great?"

Apple's thinking goes like this: Why should we have to know whether or not a program is already running? That's the computer's problem, not ours. In an ideal world, this distinction should be irrelevant. A program should appear when we click its icon, whether it's open or not—just as on a PalmPilot, for example.

"Which programs are open" already approaches unimportance in Mac OS X, where sophisticated memory-management features make it hard to run out of memory. You can open dozens of programs at once in Mac OS X; the limiting factor is no longer how much memory you have, but how much unused hard drive space.

And *that's* why the Dock combines the launcher and status functions of a modern operating system. Only a tiny triangle beneath a program's icon tells you that it's open. Icons no longer appear dark and hollow in Mac OS X when they're running, as they did in previous systems.

In any case, the Dock is a core element of Mac OS X, and it's here to stay. Whether or not you agree with Apple's philosophy, Apple has made it as easy as possible to learn to like the Dock. You can customize the thing to within an inch of its life, or even get rid of it completely. This section tells you everything you need to know.

Setting Up the Dock

Apple starts off the Dock with a few icons it thinks you'll enjoy: QuickTime Player, iTunes, Sherlock, and so on. But using your Mac without putting your *own* favorite icons on the Dock is like buying an expensive suit and turning down the free alteration service. At the first opportunity, you should make the Dock your own.

The concept of the Dock is simple: Any icon you drag onto it, shown in Figure 3-1, is installed there as a large, square button. A single click, not a double-click, opens the corresponding icon. In other words, the Dock is an ideal parking lot for the icons of disks, folders, documents, and programs you frequently access.

Tip: You can install batches of icons onto the Dock all at once—just drag them as a group.

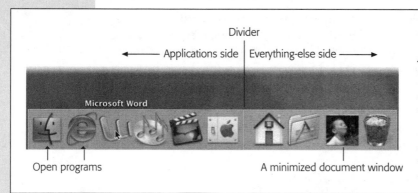

Divider

← Applications side | Everything-else side →

Microsoft Word

Open programs

A minimized document window

Figure 3-1:
To add an icon to the Dock, just drag it there. Note that you haven't actually moved the original file. When you release the mouse, it remains exactly where it was. What you've actually done is to install a copy of its icon—like an alias, you might say—of that file onto your Dock.

Here are a few aspects of the Dock that may throw you at first:

- **It has two sides.** See the fine white line running down the Dock in Figure 3-1? That's the divider. Everything on the left side is an application—a program. Everything else goes on the right side: files, documents, folders, and disks.

  It's important to understand this division. If you try to drag an application to the right of the white line, for example, Mac OS X will teasingly refuse to accept it. (Even aliases observe that distinction; aliases of applications can go only on the left side, for example.)

- **Its icon names are hidden.** To see the name of a Dock icon, just point to it without clicking. You'll see the name appear just above the icon.

  When you're trying to find a certain icon on the Dock, you can run your cursor slowly across the icons without clicking; the icon labels appear as you go. Better yet, you can sometimes tell documents apart just by looking at their icons alone, as shown in the box on page 75.

- **Folders and disks are hierarchical.** If you remember nothing else in this chapter, remember this one: If you click a folder or disk icon on the right side of the Dock and *hold down* the mouse button, a list of its contents sprouts from the icon. It's a hierarchical list, meaning that you can burrow into folders within folders this way. See Figure 3-2 for an illustration.

Tip: To make the pop-up menu appear instantly, just Control-click the Dock icon, or (if you have a two-button mouse) right-click it.

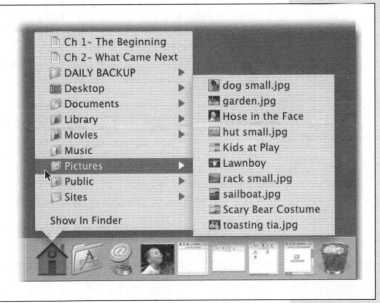

Figure 3-2:
As long as you keep the mouse button pressed, you can burrow into folders within folders—either with the intention of opening a file or folder (by releasing the mouse button as you point), or just to see what's inside.

• **Programs appear there unsolicited.** Nobody but you can put icons on the *right* side of the Dock. But program icons appear on the left side of the Dock automatically whenever you open a program (even one that's not listed in the Dock). Its icon remains there for as long as it's running.

Tip: The Dock is already extremely cool looking, but you haven't seen the end of its tricks. Using Tinker-Tool, you can make it translucent (see-through) to a degree that you specify–a great way to show off at user-group meetings. See page 420 for details.

TROUBLESHOOTING MOMENT

Curse of the Missing Files

Oh my God! I stuck a folder into my Dock like you said. But when I click and hold on it, half of my files are gone!

They're not gone, just hidden. As of version 10.1, a Dock icon's pop-up menu can list only 96 files. Even fewer fit on most screens–a tiny "more this way!" triangle appears at the top and bottom of pop-up lists that require scrolling–

but even if you scroll, you'll find that files beyond 96 aren't accessible this way.

The only solution is a more disciplined approach to your filing system–creating enough folders-in-folders for filing your files, for example, to bring the total items inside any one folder to 96 or fewer.

Organizing and Removing Dock Icons

You can move the tiles of the Dock around just by dragging them horizontally. As you drag, the other icons scoot aside to make room. Drop the icon you've just dragged when you're satisfied with its new position.

To remove a Dock icon, just drag it away. Once your cursor has cleared the Dock, let go of the mouse button. The icon disappears; its passing is marked by a charming little puff of animated cartoon smoke. The other Dock icons slide together to close the gap. (Mac OS X won't let you remove the Finder, the Trash, or the Dock icon of a program or document that's currently open.)

Tip: You can replace the "puff of smoke" animation with one of your own, as described on page 425.

Weirdly enough, this technique (removing a Dock program's icon by dragging it away) works even while a program is still running. You won't see any change immediately, because the program is still open. But when you ultimately quit the program, you'll see that its previously installed icon is no longer on the Dock.

Three Ways to Get the Dock out of Your Hair

It occurred to more than one Mac fan that the bottom of the screen isn't the ideal location for the Dock. Because most screens are wider than they are tall, the Dock eats into your limited vertical screen space. Worse, a bottom-feeding Dock can actually overlap your document windows, getting directly in your way as you work.

In these situations, you have three ways out. You can hide the Dock, shrink it, or rotate it 90 degrees.

Auto-hiding the Dock

To turn on the Dock's auto-hiding feature, choose →Dock→Turn Hiding On (or press Option-⌘-D).

Tip: You can also find this on/off switch when you choose →Dock→Dock Preferences (Figure 3-3), or when you click the System Preferences icon on the Dock, then Show All, and then the Dock icon. (Chapter 8 contains much more about the System Preferences program.)

When the Dock is hidden, it doesn't slide into view until you move the cursor to the Dock's edge of the screen. When you move the cursor back to the middle of the screen, the Dock slithers out of view once again. (Individual Dock icons may occasionally shoot upward into Desktop territory when a program needs your attention—cute, very cute—but otherwise, the Dock lies low until you summon it.)

On paper, an auto-hiding Dock is ideal—it's there only when you summon it. In practice, however, you may find that the extra half-second the Dock takes to appear and disappear makes this feature slightly less appealing.

For many Mac fans, then, the solution is to hide and show the Dock at will by pressing the hide/show keystroke, Option-⌘-D. This method makes the Dock pop on and off the screen without requiring you to move the cursor.

GEM IN THE ROUGH

Living Icons

Mac OS X brings to life a terrific idea, a new concept in mainstream operating systems: icons that *tell* you something. As shown here, for example, you can often tell documents apart just by looking at their icons.

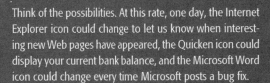

Some program icons, furthermore, actually change over time. The Clock program (in your Applications folder), for example, is a living icon that actually ticks away the time, right there in the Dock. The Mail icon (see Chapter 19) displays a live counter that indicates how many new email messages are waiting for you. (After all, why should you launch the Mail program if you'll only be dis-

appointed?) The America Online icon sprouts a flag to let you know if an instant message is waiting. You can make your CPU Monitor graph (page 235) show up right on its icon. And if you minimize a QuickTime movie while it's playing, it shrinks down and continues playing right there in the Dock.

Think of the possibilities. At this rate, one day, the Internet Explorer icon could change to let us know when interesting new Web pages have appeared, the Quicken icon could display your current bank balance, and the Microsoft Word icon could change every time Microsoft posts a bug fix.

Shrinking and Enlarging the Dock

Depending on your screen's size, you may prefer smaller or larger Dock buttons. Fortunately, Mac OS X's sophisticated graphics technology, called Quartz, can display Mac OS X icons at almost any size; you're not limited to some feeble choice of Small, Medium, or Large settings.

The official way to resize Dock icons goes like this: Choose ■→Dock→Dock Preferences. In the resulting dialog box, drag the Dock Size slider, as shown in Figure 3-4.

There's a much faster way to resize the Dock, however: just position your cursor carefully on the Dock's white divider line, so that it turns into a double-headed arrow (shown in Figure 3-3). Now you can simply drag up or down to make the Dock larger or smaller.

Tip: If you press Option as you drag, the Dock snaps to certain canned icon sizes—those that the programmer actually drew. You won't see the in-between sizes that Mac OS X generally calculates on the fly.

Figure 3-3:
Look closely—you can see the secret cursor that resizes the Dock. If you don't see any change in the Dock size as you drag upward, you've reached the size limit; Mac OS X won't make your Dock icons so big that they burst through the sides of your screen (there's nothing worse than a bunch of broken glass and pixels all over your desk).

As noted in Figure 3-3, you may not be able to *enlarge* the Dock, especially if it contains a lot of icons. But you can make it almost infinitely *smaller*. Which begs the question: How can you distinguish the icons if they're the size of molecules?

The answer lies in the ■→Dock→Turn Magnification On command. What you've just done is to trigger the swelling effect shown in Figure 3-4; now your Dock icons balloon to a much larger size as your cursor passes over them. It's a weird, rippling, magnetic sort of animated effect that takes some getting used to. But it's yet another spectacular demonstration of the graphics technology in Mac OS X—you'd never find a feature like this in Windows, for example—and it can actually come in handy when you find your icons otherwise shrinking away to nothing.

Moving the Dock to the sides of the screen

Yet another approach to getting the Dock out of your way is to rotate it, so that it sits vertically against a side of your screen. From the ■→Dock submenu, choose "Position on Left," "Position on Right," or "Position on Bottom," as you see fit. (Although Apple doesn't like to admit it, you can even put the Dock across the *top* of your screen—a weird and interesting effect. See page 420.)

You'll probably find that the right side of your screen works better than the left; most Mac OS X programs put their document windows against the left edge of the screen, where the Dock and its labels might get in the way.

Note: When you position your Dock vertically, the "right" side of the Dock becomes the bottom. In other words, the Trash now appears at the bottom of the vertical Dock. As you read references to the Dock in this book, mentally substitute the phrase "bottom part of the Dock" when you read references to the "right side of the Dock."

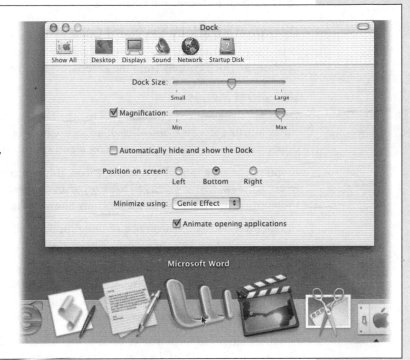

Figure 3-4:
*To find a comfortable setting for the Magnification slider, choose *→Dock→Dock Preferences. Leave the Dock Preferences window open on the screen, as shown here. After each adjustment of the Dock Size slider, try out the Dock (which still works when the Dock Preferences window is open) to test your new settings.*

Using the Dock

Most of the time, you'll use the Dock as either a launcher (click an icon once to open the corresponding program, file, folder, or disk) or as a status indicator (the tiny black triangles, identified in Figure 3-1, show you which programs are running).

But the Dock has more tricks than that up its sleeve. You can use it, for example, to pull off any of the following stunts.

Switch Applications

In some ways, the Dock is exactly like the torn-off Application menu of Mac OS 9. For example, it lets you:

• Jump among the programs you've opened by clicking their icons.

• Jump among the programs you've opened by pressing ⌘-Tab.

• Drag a document (such as the text file) onto a Dock application button (such as the Microsoft Word icon) to open the former with the latter.

• Hide all windows of the program you're in by Option-clicking another Dock icon.

This is just a quick summary of the application-management functions of the Dock; you'll find the full details in Chapter 4.

Operate the Dock by Keyboard Control

If you turn on the amazing Mac OS X feature called *full keyboard access,* you can operate the Dock entirely from the keyboard; see page 106.

Use Secret Menus

Don't get so enamored of single-clicking the Dock icons that you miss this one. It turns out that if you Control-click a Dock icon—or, if you're in no hurry, hold down the mouse button on it—a secret menu sprouts out of it (Figure 3-5).

If you've clicked a minimized window icon, this shortcut menu says only the name of the window. If you've clicked the icon of an application that's not running at the moment (or an alias), the menu says only Show In Finder.

But if you've clicked the icon of a *running* application, you get some incredibly useful commands that have never before been available in the Mac OS. For example:

• **[Window names.]** At the top of the shortcut menus of most running-application Dock icons, you'll find at least one tiny, neatly labeled window icon, as shown in Figure 3-5. This useful new Mac OS X feature means that you can jump directly not just to a certain program, but to a certain *open window* in that program.

  For example, suppose you've been using Word to edit three different chapters. You can use its Dock icon as a Window menu to pull forward one particular chapter—even from within a different program.

Tip: The Finder tile that's always at the left (or top) of the Dock is, in effect, its own Window menu. By holding the mouse down on this icon for a moment, you produce a menu that lists all open desktop windows. Of course, the Window menu at the top of the screen does the same thing. But it's often faster to use the Dock icon for switching windows because it doesn't list all the other Window-menu commands (Zoom Window, Minimize Window, and so on).

• **Keep In Dock.** Whenever you launch a program, Mac OS X puts its icon in the Dock—marked with a little black triangle—even if you don't normally keep its icon there. As soon as you quit the program, its icon disappears again from the Dock.

If you understand that much, then the Keep In Dock command makes a lot of sense. It means, "Hello, I'm this program's icon. I know you don't normally keep me on your Dock, but I'd be happy to stay here even after you quit my program; just say the word." If you find that you've been using, for example, Terminal (Chapter 15) a lot more often than you thought you would, this command may be just the ticket.

Tip: Actually, there's a faster way to tell a running application to remain on the Dock from now on: Just drag its icon up off the Dock and then right back onto it—yes, while the program is running. You have to try it to believe it.

- **Show In Finder.** Choose this command to highlight the actual icon, in whatever folder window it happens to sit, of the application, alias, folder, or document you've clicked. You might want to do this when, for example, you're using a program that you can't quite figure out, and you want to jump to its desktop folder in hopes of finding a Read Me file there.

Tip: If you really want to reveal an icon in the Finder, there's a much faster way: Just ⌘-click its Dock icon. You jump right to it. (You can even ⌘-click an item that's listed in one of the Dock's pop-up menus, illustrated in Figure 3-5, to highlight *its* icon.)

- **Quit.** You can quit any program directly from its Dock shortcut menu. No longer must you actually switch into a program in order to access its Quit command.

  Of course, thanks to Mac OS X's state-of-the-art memory management features, there's less need these days to quit programs at all. Still, you might be thankful for this quick-quitting feature when, for example, your boss is coming down the hallway and the Dilbert Web site is on your screen where a spreadsheet is supposed to be.

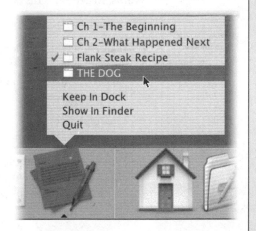

Figure 3-5:
Control-click a Dock icon, or click and hold on it, to open the secret menu. The names at the top of this shortcut menu are the names of the windows currently open in that program. The checkmark next to a window's name tells you that it's the frontmost window of that program (even if that program is in the background).

Tip: If you hold down Option—even after you've opened the pop-up menu—the Quit command changes to say Force Quit. That's your emergency hatch for jettisoning a locked-up program.

- **Conduct speed tests.** When you click an application icon on the Dock, its icon jumps up and down a few times as the program launches, as though with excitement at having been selected. The longer a program takes to start up, the more bounces you see, which has given birth to a hilarious phenomenon: the counting of these bounces as a casual speed benchmark for application-launching times. "Internet Explorer took twelve bouncemarks to open in Mac OS X 10.0.4," you might read online, "but only three bouncemarks in version 10.1."

Tip: If you find the icon bouncing a bit over the top, try this: Choose →Dock→Dock Preferences. In the Dock dialog box (shown in Figure 3-3), turn off "Animate opening applications." From now on, your icons won't actually bounce—instead, the little triangle underneath it simply *pulses* as the application opens. (You can still use it to see how long programs take to open, but now you have to call them pulsemarks.)

- **Do your filing.** Once you've tried stashing a few important folders on the right side of your Dock, there's no going back; you can mostly forget all the other navigation tricks you've had to learn in Mac OS X. After all, the folders you care about are always there, ready for opening with a single click.

  Better yet, they're easily accessible for *putting away* files; you can drag them directly into the Dock's folder icons as though they're regular folders. In fact, if you press ⌘ just before releasing the mouse, docked folder icons don't even scoot out of the way, as they usually do to make room for something you're adding to the Dock. The folder icon you want just sits there, a sitting duck for the file you're filing.

Great Things to Put on Your Dock

Now that you know what the Dock's about, it's time to set up shop. Install the programs, folders, and disks you'll be using often.

They can be whatever you want, of course, but don't miss these opportunities:

- **Your Home folder.** Many Mac fans immediately drag their hard drive icons onto the right side of the Dock—or, perhaps more practically, their Home folders (see page 49). Now they have quick access to every single file in every single folder they'll ever use.

- **The Applications folder.** Here's a no-brainer: Stash the Applications folder here, so you'll have quick pop-up menu access to any program on your machine.

- *Your* **Applications folder.** As an even more efficient corollary, create a new folder of your own. Fill it with the aliases of *just* the programs you use often and park it on the Dock. Now you've got an even more useful Applications folder.

- **The Documents folder.** The Documents folder in your Home folder is another primary center for your Mac activity. Stash it here for quick access.

- **The System Preferences.** Once you stash a folder full of the System Preferences (Chapter 8) onto your Dock, you'll never again miss the hierarchical →Control Panels folder in Mac OS 9. Want to adjust one of your Mac's settings? Leap directly to it from your Dock. (Instructions on page 204.)

The Finder Toolbar

At the top of every Finder window is a row of navigation and function icons. One click on any of these icons takes you directly to the corresponding disk or folder, or triggers the corresponding command.

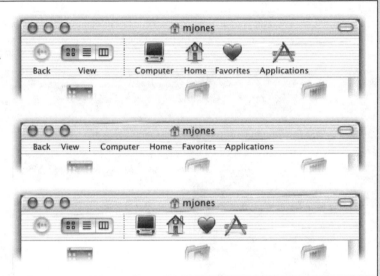

Figure 3-6:
The Finder toolbar starts out with both picture and text buttons (top). But you may prefer to see only text (middle) for greater vertical compactness or only pictures (bottom) for greater horizontal compactness.

The first time you run Mac OS X, for example, you'll find these icons on the toolbar (Figure 3-6):

- **Back.** As you've probably noticed, the Mac OS X Finder works something like a Web browser. Only a single window remains open as you navigate the various folders on your hard drive.

  This button takes you back to whatever folder you were just looking at. (Instead of clicking Back, you can also press ⌘-[, or choose Go→Back—which is particularly handy to remember if the toolbar is *hidden*, as described on page 25.)

  There's no Forward button. If you really want to return to a certain folder, you'll have to double-click your way there by opening folders.

- **View controls.** The three tiny buttons next to the Back button switch the current window into icon, list, or column view, respectively. See page 29 for details, and remember that if the toolbar is hidden, you can get by with the equivalent View menu commands.

- **Computer.** Click this button to open a window that contains icons for all your disks. Page 52 has the details.

- **Home.** As noted on page 49, this may be the single most important button on your Mac in Mac OS X. It takes you to *your* folder, the one that contains all of your documents, preference files, personal programs, and so on.

- **Favorites.** This folder contains aliases of the documents, files, disks, and folders you've designated as Favorites (page 64).

- **Applications.** This button takes you directly to the folder that contains most of the programs on your machine.

Tip: The Go menu lists the same folders itemized above (among others), for use when you have hidden the toolbar. The Go menu also shows you the keyboard equivalents for summoning these folders.

FREQUENTLY ASKED QUESTION

Putting the Trash on the Finder Toolbar

I've got the mother of all Frequently Asked Questions for you. Can I put the Trash on my Finder toolbar? It would really be a lot handier to have it right there above the icons I'm trying to get rid of, instead of having to drag them all the way to the lower-right corner of the Dock.

The Web is filled with complex recipes for adding the Trash to your toolbar. Some require hacking; others require add-on shareware utilities.

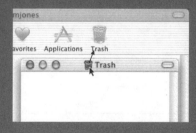

Forget all of that unauthorized rigamarole; the answer is right under your nose. Open the Trash window (by clicking the Trash icon on the Dock). Then drag its *folder proxy icon,* shown here, directly onto the toolbar, where it's now ready for action. (Click and hold the folder proxy icon for a moment, until it darkens, before dragging.)

Wasn't that easy?

Removing or Shrinking the Toolbar

For many grizzled Mac veterans, the Finder toolbar is a disconcerting new element. Most people who dislike it cite two complaints. First, it takes up even more screen space; between the toolbar, the Dock, and the unusually large icons of Mac OS X, it almost seems like an Apple conspiracy to sell big screens. Second, Apple seems to presume it knows which folders you'll want frequent access to; if you like your disk icons on the desktop, for example, the Computer icon on the toolbar seems like a waste of space.

Never fear. There are simple solutions to both problems.

First of all, you can eliminate the toolbar with one click—on the white, oval "Old Finder Mode" button (see page 25). You can also hide the toolbar by choosing View→Hide toolbar, or just by pressing ⌘-B. (The same keystroke, or choosing View→Show toolbar, brings it back.)

But you don't have to do without the toolbar altogether. If its consumption of screen space is your main concern, you may prefer to simply collapse it—to get rid of the pictures but preserve the text buttons.

To make it so, choose View→Customize toolbar. As shown in Figure 3-7, the dialog box that appears offers a Show pop-up menu at the bottom. It lets you choose picture-buttons, with Icon Only, or, for the greatest space conservation, Text Only. (In Text Only mode, the three View buttons become a little pop-up menu.) You can see the results without even closing the dialog box.

Click Done or press Enter to make your changes stick.

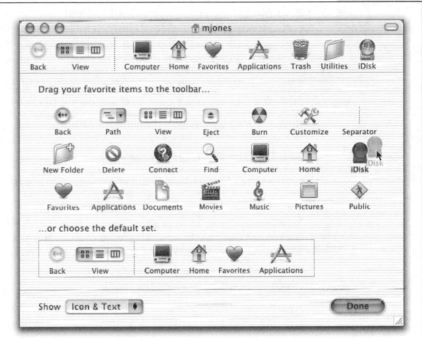

Figure 3-7:
While this window is open, you can add additional icons to the toolbar by dragging them into place from the gallery before you. You can also remove icons from the toolbar by dragging them up or down off the toolbar, or rearrange them by dragging them horizontally.

Adding Your Own Icons to the Toolbar

As it turns out, Apple *doesn't* presume to know what icons you want on your Finder toolbar. Mac OS X not only offers a collection of beautifully designed icons for alternate (or additional) toolbar buttons, but makes it easy for you to add *anything* to the toolbar, turning it into a supplementary Dock.

Apple's toolbar-icon collection

To see the optional toolbar icons that Apple has prepared for you, choose View→Customize Toolbar. The window shown in Figure 3-7 appears.

Tip: There's a great secret shortcut for opening the Customize Toolbar window: *Shift-click* the "Old Finder Mode" button (the white capsule in the upper-right corner of every Finder window).

This is your chance to rearrange the existing toolbar icons, or to get rid of the ones you don't use. You can also add any of Apple's buttons to the toolbar simply by dragging them from the "gallery" upward to the toolbar itself. The existing icons scoot out of your cursor's way, if necessary.

Most of the options listed in the gallery represent shortcuts to certain folders, or duplicate the functions of menu commands. Here are a few of the options that don't appear on the standard toolbar:

- **Path.** Most of the gallery elements are buttons, but this one creates a *pop-up menu* on the toolbar. When clicked, it shows (and lets you navigate) the hierarchy—the *path*—of folders that you open to reach whatever window is open. (*Equivalent:* ⌘-clicking a window's title bar, as described on page 19.)

- **Eject.** This button ejects whatever disk is currently highlighted. (*Equivalent:* The File→Eject command, or the Eject key on your keyboard.)

- **Burn.** If your Mac has a compatible CD burner (see Chapter 10), this button "burns" a blank CD with whatever folders and files you've dragged onto it. (*Equivalent:* The File→Burn CD command.)

- **Customize.** Opens this toolbar-customizing window. (*Equivalent:* The View→Customize Toolbar command.)

- **Separator.** This is the only gallery icon that doesn't actually do anything when clicked. It's designed to set apart *groups* of toolbar icons. (For example, you might want to segregate your *folder* buttons, such as Documents and Applications, from your *function* buttons, such as Delete and Connect.) Drag this dotted line between two existing icons on the toolbar.

- **New Folder.** Creates a new folder in whatever window you're looking at. (*Equivalent:* the File→New Folder command, or the Shift-⌘-N keystroke. But millions of Mac fans spend their first weeks with Mac OS X hitting the old keystroke, ⌘-N, when they want a new folder, little realizing that ⌘-N triggers the New Finder Window command now. Adding the New Folder "command" to the toolbar is a quick solution.)

- **Delete.** Puts the highlighted file or folder icons into the Trash. (*Equivalent:* the File→Move to Trash command, or the ⌘-Delete keystroke.)

Tip: The New Folder and Delete icons are among the most valuable ones to put on your toolbar. They represent functions you'll probably use often.

- **Connect.** If you're on an office network, opens the Connect to Server dialog box (see page 299) so that you can tap into another computer. (*Equivalent:* The Go→Connect to Server command, or the ⌘-K keystroke.)

- **Find.** Opens Sherlock (see Chapter 20), which you can use to search your hard drive or the Internet.

- **iDisk.** The iDisk is your own personal 20 MB virtual hard drive on the Internet. It's your private backup disk, stashed at Apple, safe from whatever fire, flood, or locusts may destroy your office.

  In Mac OS X, your iDisk is more useful than ever, because it's so well integrated into the operating system itself. For example, you can connect to the Internet and bring your iDisk's icon onto the screen just by clicking this toolbar icon. Chapter 18 contains more information about your iDisk.

- **Documents, Movies, Music, Pictures, Public.** These buttons open the corresponding folders in your Home folder, as described on page 52.

- **Default set.** If you've made a mess of your toolbar, you can always reinstate its original, factory-installed arrangement just by dragging this rectangular strip directly upward onto your toolbar.

Note: If a window is too narrow to show all the icons on the toolbar, you see, at the right end of the toolbar, a >> symbol. Click it for a pop-up menu that names whatever icons don't fit at the moment. (You'll find this toolbar behavior in many Mac OS X programs—System Preferences, Mail, Address Book, and so on—not just the Finder.)

Adding your own stuff

As useful as some of Apple's toolbar-gallery icons may be, the toolbar really takes off only when you add your own icons. You can drag *any icons at all* onto the toolbar— files, folders, disks, programs, or whatever—to turn them into one-click buttons.

In short, you can think of the Finder toolbar as a secondary Dock. Together, the Dock and the toolbar offer so many parking places for icons, you may never pine for the old menu again.

Note: You don't have to choose View→Customize Toolbar to add your own icons to the toolbar. Just drag them from the desktop or any folder window directly onto the toolbar, at any time.

Here are a few possibilities:

- Install toolbar icons of the three or four *programs* you use the most (or a few documents you work on every day). Sure, the Dock can also serve this purpose, but only the toolbar keeps their names in view.

- Install toolbar icons for other Macs on the network, which saves you several steps when you want to connect to them (see Chapter 12).

• Install toolbar icons of Web sites you visit often (see page 452), so that you can jump directly to them when you sit down in front of your Mac each morning.

Remember that toolbar icons work exactly like Dock or desktop icons. You can even drag things *onto* them: For example, you can drag a document onto a folder icon to file it there, drag a downloaded *.sit* file onto the StuffIt Expander icon there, and so on.

Tip: Ordinarily, you can't edit a toolbar icon's name (or its icon, if you're into that). The sneaky workaround: Make an alias of whatever you'd like to put there, rename or change its icon, and *then* drag it aboard.

Rearranging Toolbar Icons

You can drag toolbar icons around, rearranging them horizontally, by pressing ⌘ as you drag. (You can also do so after choosing View→Customize Toolbar, of course.)

Removing Toolbar Icons

Taking an icon off the toolbar is almost as easy as putting it on: While the Customize window is open, just drag them clear away from the toolbar—or when the Customize window *isn't* open, just ⌘-drag icons clear away from the toolbar at any time. (Watch your Trash on the Dock turn into a pair of snipping scissors as you do it. Cute!)

Designing Your Desktop

From the day it was born, the Macintosh was the computer for the individualist. To this day, corporations purchase thousands of Windows PCs—but when they go home at night, the executives often keep Macs for their own personal use.

In other words, buying a Macintosh was a dramatic act of self-expression in itself. But that's only the beginning. Now it's time to bend the computer screen itself to your personal sense of design and fashion.

FREQUENTLY ASKED QUESTION

Desktop Fonts, Desktop Sounds

How do I change the fonts used by the Mac OS X Finder?

In Mac OS versions gone by, you could choose any font you liked for your icon labels. You even had a choice of several fonts for use in your menus.

At least in Mac OS X 10.1, that flexibility is gone. You get Lucida Grande in your menus and as icon labels, love it or leave it.

Nor do desktop *sounds* remain in Mac OS X—the little squeaks, whooshes, and burps that accompanied the operation of scroll bars, buttons, and icons, which you could turn on to keep yourself awake. (For people who work in libraries and churches, this feature isn't such a big loss.)

For now, Apple intends to remain conservative with the look of Mac OS X—both for "branding" reasons (to make Mac OS X instantly recognizable) and for technical ones (to make sure that it doesn't open a Pandora's box of interface hacks that wind up destabilizing the machine).

System Preferences

Cosmetically speaking, Mac OS X offers two dramatic full-screen features: desktop backgrounds and screen savers. (That's not counting the pictures and colors you can apply to individual folder windows, as described on page 43—and not counting the replacement startup screens and login screens described in Chapter 17.)

The command center for both of these functions is the System Preferences program (which longtime Mac fans may recognize as the former Control Panels). Open it by clicking the System Preferences icon on the Dock, or by choosing its name from the menu.

When the System Preferences program opens, click Show All. From here, you can choose a desktop picture by clicking the Desktop button, or a screen saver by clicking the Screen Saver button. For further details on these System Preferences modules, see Chapter 8.

Graphic Designers' Corner: The Gray Look

One of the earliest objections to the lively, brightly colored look of Mac OS X came from Apple's core constituency: artists and graphic designers. Some complained that Mac OS X's bright blues (of scroll-bar handles, progress bars, the menu, pulsing OK buttons, highlighted menu names and commands), along with the red, green, and yellow window-corner buttons, threw off their color judgment.

UP TO SPEED

Menulets: The Missing Manual

Apple calls them Menu Extras, but Mac fans on the Internet have named the little menu-bar icons shown here *menulets*. These menu-bar icons are the direct descendants of the controls once found on the Mac OS 9 Control Strip— that is, each is both an indicator and a menu that gives you direct access to some settings in System Preferences. One lets you adjust your Mac's speaker volume; another lets you change the screen resolution; another shows you the remaining power in your laptop battery; and so on. (They replace the very similar gizmos called *docklings* that were on the Dock in Mac OS X versions 10.0.4 and earlier.)

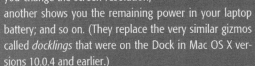

The Menu Extras pictured here, for example, adjust your network settings, dial-up Internet connection, monitor settings, speaker volume, laptop battery, and clock.

You can adjust and fiddle with menulets in a number of different ways:

- You install one by turning on the representative checkbox in System Preferences. You'll find such checkboxes in the Date & Time, Display, Sound, and other panels (see Chapter 8).

- You can remove one just by ⌘-dragging it off of your menu bar (or by turning off the corresponding checkbox in System Preferences).

- You can rearrange menulets by ⌘-dragging them horizontally.

These little guys are useful, good-looking, and respectful of our screen space. The world could use more inventions like menulets.

In response, Apple created what it calls the Graphite look for Mac OS X, which turns all of those interface elements gray instead of blue. To try out this look, click the System Preferences icon on the Dock (or choose System Preferences from the menu); click Show All; click General; and then choose Graphite from the Appearance pop-up menu.

Tip: The Highlight Color pop-up menu does exactly what it did in previous versions of the Mac OS: it lets you choose a different accent color. You'll see this color in several very subtle spots; for example, this is the background color of highlighted text (and icon names). It's also the color that lines the inside of a window as you drag an icon into it.

Startup Screens, Login Screens, "Poof" Animations

You can substitute graphics of your own for the "Welcome to Mac OS X" and Login screens, and you can even replace the "poof" animation (which appears when you drag something off the Dock) with animations of your own. Chapter 17 has full details on these and other sneaky hacks.

Part Two:
Applications in Mac OS X

2

Programs and Documents

From the day Apple first announced Mac OS X, the company made clear that Mac OS X offered a lot of advantages, particularly in stability—but that you would need all-new versions of your programs to take advantage of these benefits. Most software companies announced that they would get to work Mac OS X-izing their programs, but Mac fans still kept reading the same advice: don't switch to Mac OS X until most or all of the programs you use every day have been adapted to run on it.

For most people, that time is here, or near. One by one, the Mac OS X versions of big-name programs were ready (or nearly ready): Microsoft Office, AppleWorks, iMovie, iTunes, Photoshop, Illustrator, Freehand, Quicken, FileMaker, QuarkXPress, Internet Explorer, America Online, and so on, with thousands more soon to come.

The time has also come, therefore, to grow accustomed to the way programs and documents relate in Mac OS X—which, as this chapter makes clear, differs in several substantial ways from the Mac OS that came before.

Note: Within Mac OS X, you can run two different categories of programs, known by the geeks as *Carbon* and *Cocoa* programs (see page 116). This chapter describes how Carbon and Cocoa programs work.

You can also run older, Mac OS 9-compatible programs that haven't yet been updated for Mac OS X–but when you launch one of these, your Mac automatically opens a Mac OS 9 simulator called Classic. For details on running the older, Mac OS 9-specific programs in this way, see Chapter 5.

Launching Mac OS X Programs

You can launch (open) a program in any of several ways:

- Double-click an application's icon in the Finder.

- Click a program's icon on the Dock or Finder toolbar (Chapter 3).

- Highlight an application icon and then press ⌘-O (short for File→Open) or ⌘-down arrow.

- Use the submenus of the menu's Recent→Applications command. (You control *how many* programs this feature tracks using the System Preferences panel described on page 185.)

Note: Mac OS X stores a list of your recently used programs in a text file called *com.apple.recentitems.plist* in your Home folder→Library→Preferences folder. And with about $1.00, that information will buy you a cup of coffee in most restaurants.

- Use your Go→Favorites command.

- Open a *document* icon in any of these ways, or drag a document onto the icon of a program that can open it (whether in the Dock, the Finder toolbar, or in a folder window).

Tip: If you press Option as you open an application in the Finder, you automatically close the window that contains its icon. Later, when you return to the Finder, you'll find a neat, clean desktop—no loitering windows.

When you launch a program, the Mac reads its computer code, which lies on your hard drive surface, and feeds it quickly into RAM (memory). During this brief interval, the icon of the opening program jumps up and down eagerly in your Dock. (You can turn off this bouncing, as noted on page 80.)

Tip: Want to see *multithreading* in action? Launch some program that takes a long time to open—that is, its icon on the Dock does a lot of bouncing. Multithreading simply means that Mac OS X can crunch more than one process at a time.

In this case, you don't have to wait for the application to finish bouncing—you're wasting perfectly good computing time. Just switch to another program and get to work, as the newly opened program keeps right on launching in the background.

What happens next depends on the program you're using. Most present you with a new, blank, untitled document. Some, such as FileMaker and PowerPoint, welcome you instead with a question: Do you want to open an existing document or create a new one? In AppleWorks, the welcome screen generally asks you to specify what *kind* of new document you want to create. And a few oddball programs don't open any window at all when first launched.

FREQUENTLY ASKED QUESTIONS

Virtual Memory and Memory Allotments

I'm completely at sea when it comes to using memory in Mac OS X. There's no Memory control panel. There's no box to set the memory allotment in the Get Info dialog box of any program. There's no on/off switch for virtual memory. There isn't even an About This Macintosh box that shows where all my RAM is going. What on earth is going on?

Mac OS X handles memory with light-years more sophistication and skill than anything you've used before—so much so, in fact, that these controls no longer even exist.

In the old days, each program claimed for itself a fixed amount of RAM as soon as you launched it. You could see this number for yourself—or even change it—in the program's Get Info box. When you launched a program, it instantly claimed for itself 20 MB of memory, or whatever its programmers thought it might need.

But in Mac OS X, memory allotments are *dynamic* (changing). When you launch a program, it might not use very much RAM at all. But when you then use that program to open a huge, complex document, the system gives it more memory automatically. Then, when you close that document, Mac OS X automatically returns the RAM it was using to the "pot," so that it's available for use by other programs and functions.

It's true that the About This Mac command no longer opens a little graph showing how much RAM each program is using. There's no longer much point; the answer is, "exactly as much as it needs, and it's changing minute by minute."

Still, if you're desperate to know how much memory each of your running programs is using at this instant, open your Applications→Utilities folder. Open the program called Process Viewer. It presents a little table showing what percentage of your Mac's memory each running program is using (see page 246).

Then there's the matter of virtual memory, which is a computer scheme that helps you open more programs simultaneously than should fit into the amount of RAM (electronic memory) your computer has. It works by using a chunk of *hard drive space* as temporary overflow RAM when necessary. Of course, real memory delivers information to your Mac's brain about 100 times faster than the hard drive, which is why virtual memory gained a reputation, in the old Mac OS, for slowing down your machine.

In Mac OS X, virtual memory is turned on all the time. But these days, virtual memory is far less likely to slow down your machine—first, because each program uses only as much RAM as it needs to begin with, so far less is wasted; second, because virtual memory puts only *pieces* of your programs onto the hard drive. In any case, even if you have 50 programs open, Mac OS X devotes your Mac's actual RAM to whatever program is frontmost, so the active program doesn't grow sluggish. You'll notice the sluggishness kicking in only when *switching* programs. (Want to see how much virtual memory has kicked in? Mac OS X can show you. See page 412 for instructions.)

Therefore, if you find yourself actually getting "out of memory" messages, which are otherwise unheard of in Mac OS X, it's probably because your hard drive is running out of space, therefore thwarting the efforts of Mac OS X's virtual memory scheme. Make more room—or install more RAM.

The Application Menu

In every case, however, you'll notice a few changes to your menu bar. The File, Edit, and other application menus are still there—but they're no longer immediately to the right of the menu. The very first menu shows up with bold lettering, and it identifies the program you're using. It might say Internet Explorer, or Microsoft Word, or Stickies.

This Application menu (Figure 4-1) consolidates a number of commands that used to be scattered among several different menus in Mac OS 9, including About, Quit, and Hide.

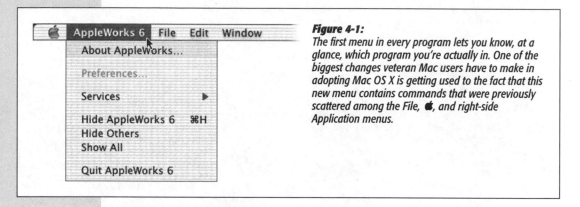

Figure 4-1:
The first menu in every program lets you know, at a glance, which program you're actually in. One of the biggest changes veteran Mac users have to make in adopting Mac OS X is getting used to the fact that this new menu contains commands that were previously scattered among the File, , and right-side Application menus.

Quitting Programs

You quit programs in Mac OS X just as you did in previous versions of the Mac: by pressing ⌘-Q, which is the keyboard equivalent for choosing the Quit command. The only tricky part here is that the Quit command is no longer in the File menu—it's now at the bottom of the Application menu.

But Mac OS X offers two much more fun ways to do it:

- Control-click a program's Dock icon and choose Quit from the pop-up menu.
- When you've highlighted a Dock icon by pressing ⌘-Tab to rotate through the running programs, type the letter Q. The program quits instantly.

Force Quitting Programs

Everybody knows that Mac OS X is a rock-solid operating system, but that doesn't mean that *programs* never screw up. Individual programs are as likely as ever to freeze or lock up. In such cases, you have no choice but to *force quit* the program—to terminate it with a blunt instrument, just as in Mac OS 9.

The big Mac OS X difference is that doing so doesn't destabilize your Mac. You don't have to restart it. In fact, you can usually reopen exactly the same program and get on with your life.

You can force quit a stuck program in any of several ways. First, you can Control-click its Dock icon (or just hold your mouse down on it); once the pop-up menu appears, press Option so that the Quit command now says Force Quit (see Figure 4-2). Bingo: that program is outta here.

Second, you can press Option-⌘-Esc, the traditional Mac "force quit" keystroke. Third you can choose →Force Quit. Either way, proceed as shown in Figure 4-2.

Again, force quitting is no longer bad for your Mac. Dire warnings no longer appear. The only downside to force quitting a program is that you lose any unsaved changes to your open documents.

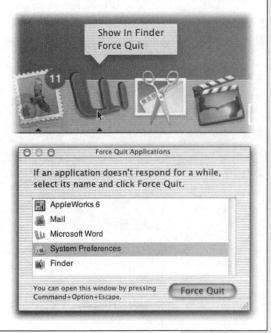

Figure 4-2:
Top: You can force quit a program from the Dock, thanks to the Option key.

Bottom: When you press Option-⌘-Esc or choose Force Quit from the menu, you get a tidy box listing all open programs. Just click the one you want to abort, click Force Quit, and click Force Quit again in the confirmation box. (Using more technical tools, there are other ways to jettison programs—see pages 247 and 507—but this is by far the most convenient.)

Juggling Programs with the Dock

Mac OS X includes an elegant solution to tracking the programs you've opened: the Dock.

Chapter 3 describes the navigational features of this multi-purpose icon row—but once you've actually opened a program or two, it takes on a whole new purpose in life.

Switching Programs

One primary purpose of the Dock is simple: it lets you know which programs are running. Only one can be in front, or *active*, at a time. (It's the program whose name appears at the upper-left corner of your screen, next to the menu.)

To make a different program active, you can repeat whatever technique you used to launch the program to begin with. Click its Dock icon, double-click a document icon, or whatever.

Most people, however, switch to a different program by clicking its icon on the Dock. Doing so makes the program, along with any of its open windows and toolbars, pop to the front.

Tip: You can also press ⌘-Tab repeatedly to cycle through all open programs, in left-to-right Dock order, until you arrive at the one you want. (Watch the current application's icon get highlighted, and its name appear, as you press ⌘-Tab.) When you release the keys, Mac OS X brings the corresponding program to the front.

To move backward through the open programs, press Shift-⌘-Tab.

When Programs Are Actually Folders

You may have noticed that OS X programs don't seem to have 50,000 support files strewn across your hard drive. To open Internet Explorer, you no longer have to first open an Internet Explorer folder; you can just double-click the Internet Explorer icon itself. That's a much better arrangement than in Mac OS 9, where many programs had to remain in special folders, surrounded by libraries, dictionaries, foreign language components, and other support files and folders.

The question is: Where did all those support files go?

Mac OS X features something called *packages* or *bundles,* which are *folders that behave like single files.* Every well-behaved Mac OS X program looks like a single, double-clickable application icon. Yet to the Mac, it's actually a folder that contains both the actual application icon *and* all of its support files, which are hidden for your convenience.

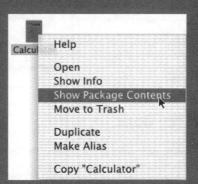

If you'd like to prove this to yourself, try this experiment. Choose Go→Applications. Switch the window to icon view.

See the Calculator program in the list? Control-click it. From the contextual menu, choose Show Package Contents. You're asking Mac OS X to show you what's inside the Calculator "application icon" folder.

The Calculator package window opens, revealing a Con-

tents folder that you've never seen before. If you open this folder, you'll find a handful of strange-looking, Unix-named folders and files that, behind the scenes, are pieces of the Calculator program itself.

The application-as-folder trick is convenient for you, of course, because it means that you're free to move the application to a different window without worrying that you're leaving behind its entourage of support files. It's also convenient for programmers, because they can update certain aspects of their applications just by replacing one of these component files, without having to rewrite the entire program.

You can even try out this programmery benefit for yourself. In the case of the Calculator and many other Mac OS X programs, the Resources folder contains individual graphics file—PDF or TIFF files—that serve as the graphic elements that you see when you're using the program. For example, the file *lcd.tif* in the calculator's Resources folder contains the image of the calculator's "screen"—where the numbers appear as you punch the calculator number buttons. Using a graphics program, you can change the background of this light yellow calculator screen to, say, light blue. The next time you double-click the Calculator—which you now realize is, behind the scenes, actually a folder—you'll see your modified calculator design.

Hiding Programs

If the open programs on your Mac are like overlapping sheets of paper on a messy desk, then *hiding* a program makes its sheet of paper transparent. When a program is hidden, all of its windows, tool palettes, and button bars disappear. You can bring them back only by bringing the program to the front again (by clicking its Dock icon again, for example).

If your aim is to hide only the program you're using at this moment, Mac OS X offers a whole raft of approaches to the same problem. Many of them involve the Option key, exactly as in Mac OS 9:

- Option-click any visible portion of the desktop. The program you were in vanishes.

- Option-click any other program's icon on the Dock. You open that program (or bring all of its windows to the front) *and* hide all the windows of the one you were using.

- Option-click any visible portion of another program's windows. Once again, you switch programs, hiding the one you were using at the time.

- From the Application menu (the boldfaced menu that bears the program's name), choose Hide [Program Name].

- When you've highlighted a Dock icon by pressing ⌘-Tab to rotate through the running programs, press the letter H key. The program hides itself instantly. (Leave the ⌘ key down the whole time, and after pressing the H, press Tab again to move on to the next program. If you release the keys while "stopped" on the program instead, you'll bring it forward instead of hiding it.)

- Press ⌘-H. This may be the easiest and most useful trick of all. When you do this, you hide the program you're in and "fall down" into the next running program.

Tip: Some Mac OS X fans *never quit* the programs they use frequently. Instead, they simply hit ⌘-H whenever they're finished working in a program. That way, the next time they need it, that program launches with zero wait time. Because Mac OS X's virtual-memory scheme is so good, there's almost no downside to leaving all your programs open all the time.

To un-hide a program and its windows, click its Dock icon again, or choose the Show All command in the Application menu.

Tip: The Dock continues to display the icons of all running programs without any indication that you've hidden them. Fortunately, that's easy enough to fix. All you need is the shareware program TinkerTool, which is described on page 420. It offers a simple checkbox that makes hidden programs show up with transparent Dock icons.

Hiding All Other Programs

Choosing Hide Others from your program's Application menu means, of course, "hide the windows of every program but this one." It even hides your Finder (desktop) windows, although desktop icons remain visible.

If this trick interests you, you might also enjoy its Mac OS X-only corollary, described next:

The Bring-Forward, Hide-All-Others Trick

Here's a brand-new Mac OS X secret that has no precursor in Mac OS 9. It's a terrific technique that lets you bring one program to the front (along with all of its open windows), and hide all other windows of all *other* open programs, all with one click. You might think of it as Hero mode, or Front-and-Center mode, or Clear My Calendar mode.

In any case, the trick is to Option-⌘-click the lucky program's icon on the Dock. It jumps to the fore, and all other windows on your Mac are instantly hidden. (You can bring them back, of course, by clicking the appropriate Dock icons.)

Hiding (Minimizing) Individual Windows

In Mac OS X, there's more to managing your window clutter than simply hiding entire programs. Now you can hide or show *individual windows* of a single program. In fact, Apple must believe that hiding a window will become one of your favorite activities, because it gives you at least four ways to do so:

- Click the Minimize button on its title bar, as shown in Figure 4-3.

- Double-click the window's title bar.

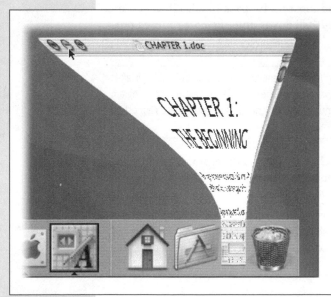

Figure 4-3:
When you click the center button on a window title bar, you minimize that window, getting it out of your way and off your screen. It's now represented by a window icon on your Dock—which you can click to reopen the window. (All this should sound familiar to people who have used Microsoft Windows.)

- Choose Window→Minimize Window, if your program offers such a command.
- Press ⌘-M.

Tip: If you press the Option key as you perform any of these techniques, you minimize *all* of your program's open windows to the Dock. (If you had several document windows open, they turn into side-by-side document icons on the Dock.) This isn't the same thing as hiding the entire program, as described above—you remain in the same program, but now all of its windows are hidden.

Unfortunately, there's no way to bring them all back at once. You simply have to click their Dock icons one at a time.

In any case, the affected window shrinks down until it becomes a new icon on the right side of the Dock. Click that icon to bring the window back.

Window Layering

Steel yourself for one big difference between Mac OS X and what came before. In Mac OS 9, bringing a program to the foreground also brought *all of its windows* to the foreground. If you were working in Internet Explorer, but Word was running in the background with six open documents, all six windows would pop to the front when you switched to Word.

As shown in Figure 4-4, however, Mac OS X takes a much more layered approach; it's entirely possible to wind up with the windows of different programs sandwiched and layered, front to back.

Figure 4-4:
Suppose you have Microsoft Excel in the foreground, but Word in the background. If you click within a visible portion of a background window, you bring only that window of Word to the front—a sandwiched effect that never would have been possible in Mac OS 9.

The remedy for this situation, if it bothers you, is the Window→Bring All to Front command, which appears in the Finder and many other programs. It brings all of a program's windows to the front.

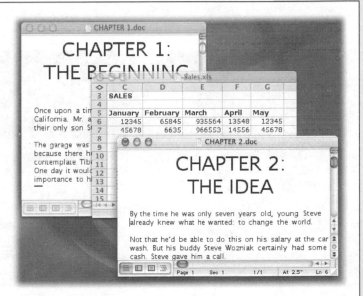

If you click a visible portion of a background program's window, or if you use the Dock's pop-up menus to choose a single document window (as shown in Figure 3-5), that layered, sandwiched effect is what you get. To make Mac OS X work like it did in the Mac OS 9 days, just click the Dock *icon* of a background program. Mac OS X brings all of its windows to the front, just as in Mac OS 9.

Using the Dock for Drag-and-Drop

As described on the next page, the Mac is smart about the relationship between documents and applications. If you double-click an AppleWorks document icon, for example, the AppleWorks program launches automatically and shows you the document.

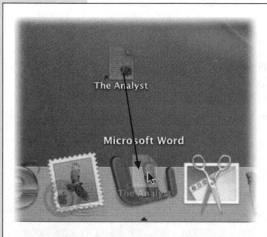

Figure 4-5:
To open a document using a program that didn't create it, drag the document icon onto the corresponding tile of the Dock. This technique is ideal for opening a downloaded graphics file into your favorite graphics program (such as AppleWorks or GraphicConverter). It's also useful when you want to open a Read Me file into your word processor, such as Word, instead of the usual TextEdit program.

GEM IN THE ROUGH

Beyond the Dock

The Dock is one way to manage, launch, and arrange your applications, but it isn't the only way. Mac OS X early adopters long ago abandoned it in favor of DragThing, a Dock-like shareware program that's far more flexible.

cursor passes over them). You can create as many different ent docks as you like, one for each project or function. You can even create multiple Dock tabs, as shown here, which are great for organizing large numbers of icons.

For example, unlike the Dock, DragThing can show the names of all of your docked icons (and not just when your

You can download DragThing from *www.missingmanuals .com,* among other places.

But these days, it's occasionally useful to open a document using a program *other* than the one that created it. Perhaps, as is often the case with downloaded Internet graphics, you don't *have* the program that created it, or you don't know which one was used.

In such cases, the Dock is handy: just drag the mystery document onto one of the Dock's tiles, as shown in Figure 4-5. Doing so forces the program to open the document, if it can.

Tip: Only Dock icons of programs that can, in fact, open the file you're dragging become highlighted. The others just shrug indifferently or even scoot aside, thinking you're trying to drag the file *into* the dock.

You can force them to be more tolerant by pressing Option-⌘ as you drag—now *all* Dock program icons "light up" as your document touches them, indicating that they'll *try* to open your file. Even so, a "could not be opened" error message may still result. As they say in Cupertino, sometimes what a can really needs is a can opener.

How Documents Know Their Parents

Every operating system needs a mechanism to associate documents with the applications that created them. When you double-click a Microsoft Word document icon, for example, you want Microsoft Word to launch and open the document.

In Windows, every document bears a three-letter file-name suffix. If you double-click something called *memo.doc,* it opens in Microsoft Word; if you double-click *memo.wri,* it opens in Microsoft Write; and so on.

Mac OS 9 uses a similar system, except that you never see the identifying codes. Instead, it relies on invisible, four-letter *creator codes* and *type codes,* as they're known. Apple carefully monitors and tracks these four-letter codes, in conjunction with the various Mac software companies, so that no two codes are alike.

As a Macintosh/Unix hybrid, Mac OS X uses *both* creator codes (like Mac OS 9) *and* filename suffixes (like Windows).

It's possible to live a long and happy life without knowing anything about these codes and suffixes. Indeed, the vast majority of Mac fans may never even encounter them. But if you're prepared for a little bit of technical bushwhacking, you may discover that understanding creator/type codes and file name suffixes can be useful in troubleshooting, keeping your files private, and appreciating how Mac OS X actually works.

Type and Creator Codes

The four-letter creator code of a Macintosh document identifies the program that will open it.

If you're feeling especially inquisitive, restart your Mac in Mac OS 9 and open Sherlock (⌘-F). (Or, if you're running in Classic, choose →Sherlock.) Click the Edit button, and then drag the icon in question anywhere onto the Sherlock screen, as shown in Figure 4-6. As a little experimentation will soon show you, the creator code for a program and the documents it creates are identical—MSWD for Microsoft Word, FMP3 for FileMaker Pro, and so on. That's the entire point: the creator code tells the Mac which program to open when you double-click a particular document.

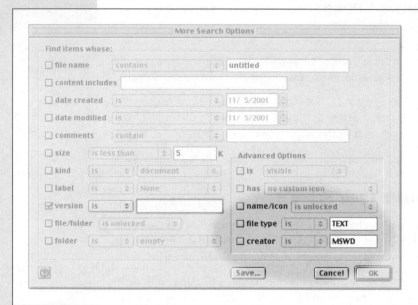

Figure 4-6:
Drag any icon from the desktop directly into Sherlock's More Search Options screen to view the icon's creator code, highlighted here at lower right. (Unfortunately, this feature doesn't work in the Mac OS X version of Sherlock.) Capitalization and spaces count. If you see a creator code that appears to have only three letters, then a space is also part of the code.

Sherlock also reveals the *second* four-letter code in the DNA of most Macintosh icons: the *type code*. This code specifies the document's file format. Photoshop, for example, can create graphics in any of dozens of different formats: GIF, JPEG, TIFF, and so on. If you inspect your Photoshop documents, you'll discover that they all share the same creator code, but have a wide variety of type codes.

Tip: If the type code is supposed to identify the file format of a document, does a standard application have a type code?

It does: APPL.

When you double-click a document, Mac OS X checks to see if it has a creator code. If so, it then consults an invisible database of icons and codes. This database is the master index that lists the correspondence between creator codes and the applications that generate them. Together, the type and creator codes also specify what *picture* appears on a particular icon.

If the desktop file discovers a match—if, say, you double-clicked a document with creator code BOBO, which corresponds to the AppleWorks entry in your desktop database—then the corresponding program opens the document, which now appears on your screen.

File Name Extensions

In Mac OS 9, it was easy to spot a document whose type and creator codes had somehow become muddled. Its icon resembled a plain white piece of paper with a dog-eared corner. That was your cue that the Macintosh couldn't find an entry for its type and creator codes in your desktop database, or that your desktop database had become corrupted.

In Mac OS X, however, plenty of documents don't have type and creator codes. Documents created by *Cocoa* applications (see page 116), for example, generally don't.

That's because Mac OS X is a Unix operating system. In Unix, type and creator codes are unheard of. Instead, what determines which programs opens when you double-click a document is its *file name extension*, just as in Windows—a suffix following a period in the file's name, as in *Letter to Mom.doc*.

In Mac OS X, the file name extension can be much longer. It can even identify the name of the program that will open when you double-click something; the file called Registration.setup, when double-clicked, launches the Mac OS X Setup application.

The bottom line is that Mac OS X offers *two different* mechanisms that associate documents with the programs that created them. Mac OS X looks for type/creator codes first. Where they're absent, the file name suffixes kick in.

Hiding and Showing File Name Extensions

Mac OS X comes set to hide most file name extensions, on the premise that they make the operating system look more technical and threatening. If you'd like to see them, however, choose Finder→Preferences and turn on "Always show file name extensions." Now examine a few of your documents—you'll see that their names now display the previously hidden suffixes.

POWER USERS' CLINIC

The Trouble with Hidden Extensions

In general, the file name extension system of Mac OS X 10.1 and later is very effective. You get to see normal file names without those "dot suffixes" (because Mac OS X comes factory set to hide them). Yet if you send your files by email to Windows people, your documents will open just fine.

Occasionally, however, this business of hidden extensions can get hairy. For example, you may see what looks like several icons in the same folder, *all having the same name.* We all know that's impossible. They're not actually named identically, of course, but the difference lurks in the file name extensions that you can't see.

Furthermore, it's sometimes possible to get into a mess where you think you're adding a file name extension to a document that lacks one—but actually, you're adding a *second* extension, winding up with a name like *Essay.rtf.txt.*

Until subsequent Mac OS X versions get smarter about invisible-suffix handling, one solution is to make your Mac show you all extensions, all the time, which eliminates this kind of confusion. In the Finder, choose Finder→ Preferences and turn on "Always show file extensions."

Your Mac will look a lot more like Windows, but at least you won't trip up on your extensions.

You can hide or show these suffixes on an icon-at-a-time basis, too (or a clump-at-a-time basis). Just highlight the icon or icons you want to affect and then choose File→Show Info. In the resulting Info window, proceed as shown in Figure 4-7.

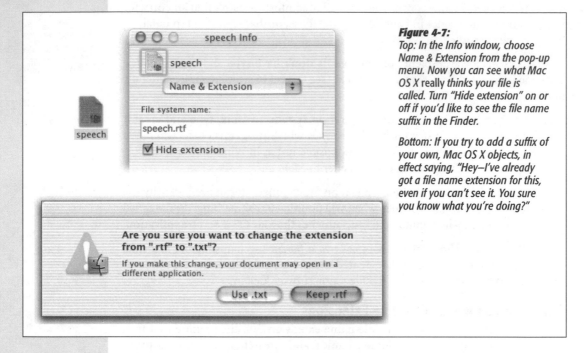

Figure 4-7:
Top: In the Info window, choose Name & Extension from the pop-up menu. Now you can see what Mac OS X really thinks your file is called. Turn "Hide extension" on or off if you'd like to see the file name suffix in the Finder.

Bottom: If you try to add a suffix of your own, Mac OS X objects, in effect saying, "Hey—I've already got a file name extension for this, even if you can't see it. You sure you know what you're doing?"

Reassigning Documents to Programs

Unfortunately, type and creator codes aren't of much use when you encounter a document created by a program you don't have. If I email you a MIDI file (a generic exchange file for music, like a text file for word processors) that I exported from my Finale sheet-music program, you won't be able to double-click it to open it unless you, too, have Finale installed. Even if you have a different sheet music program on your hard drive, just double-clicking the MIDI file won't, by itself, open it.

The file name extension system, meanwhile, has problems of its own. File name extensions are even less likely to pinpoint which parent program should open a particular document. Suppose you've downloaded a graphic called Sunset.JPEG. Well, almost any program these days can open a JPEG graphic—AppleWorks, Word, Preview, Internet Explorer, and so on. How does Mac OS X know which of these programs to open when you double-click the file?

The solution is simple. You can *reassign* a document to a specific program (or all documents of its type). Here's the rundown:

Reassigning a single document
Double-clicking a downloaded graphics file generally opens it in Preview, the graphics viewer included with Mac OS X (see page 216). Most of the time, that's a perfectly

good arrangement. But Preview can only *display* graphics—it can't edit them. What if you decide you want to edit a graphics file? You'd want it to open, just this once, into a different program—GraphicConverter, for example.

To do so, highlight the file's icon and then choose File→Show Info (or press ⌘-I). The Show Info window for that file appears, as shown in Figure 4-7.

From the pop-up menu, choose "Open with application." The "icon pop-up menu" just beneath it (see Figure 4-8) tells you what program *usually* opens this kind of document. From this pop-up menu, choose the name of the program you'd rather open this particular file.

Tip: You can perform this parent-reassignment procedure to a whole flock of selected icons at once. Once you've selected them, just choose File→Show Info as usual and use the "icon pop-up menu" as described above. The message at the top of the window—"22 items are selected," for example—reminds you that you're changing the whole batch at once.

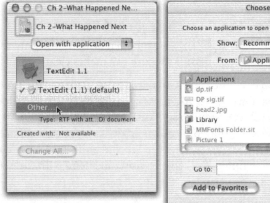

Figure 4-8:
Left: The "icon pop-up menu" offers a list of programs that can open an icon.

Right: If the program you want to open this document isn't listed, choose Other. You'll be prompted to choose a different program from those on your hard drive (Mac OS X dims all but the ones that can actually open the document).

Reassigning all documents of this type

So much for the one-shot, one-document procedure. What if you're writing, say, a book about Mac OS X, and you've been taking a lot of screenshots (see page 343)? Mac OS X saves each captured screen illustration as a graphics file in TIFF format. That's all fine, except that every time you double-click one of these, it opens into Preview, where you can't edit—you can only look.

Sure, you could reassign all of these files, one at a time, to a different program, but your grandchildren would be retired before you'd finished. In this case, you want to tell Mac OS X, "For heaven's sake, make *all* TIFF files open in Photoshop from now on!"

To bring this about, highlight any one of the TIFF files in question, and then choose File→Show Info (or press ⌘-I).

Once again, the Show Info window for that file appears, as shown in Figure 4-8. And once again, you begin by choosing a new "parent" program from the "icon pop-up menu" shown in Figure 4-8. But this time, follow up by clicking Change All at the bottom of the window. (This button is dimmed until you've actually selected a different program from the pop-up menu.) Mac OS X asks you to confirm (by clicking Continue or pressing Enter).

From now on, double-clicking any similar kind of document opens the newly selected program.

Controlling Menus from the Keyboard

Mac OS X 10.1 and later offers a fantastic new feature for anyone who believes that life is too short: keyboard-controllable menus, dialog boxes, pop-up menus, and even Dock pop-up menus. For the first time in Macintosh history, you can operate every menu in every program without the mouse or add-on software.

What You Can Do with Keyboard Control

Once you're in keyboard control, menus aren't the only thing you'll be able to control from the keyboard. As Figure 4-9 makes clear, the possibilities include:

- **Menu bar.** Once Full Keyboard Access is turned on, the first menu on your screen drops down when you press a Control-key combination of your choice (such as Control-M). At this point, you can highlight individual commands on that menu by pressing the up or down arrow keys; open a different menu by pressing the right and left arrow keys (or Tab and Shift-Tab); and "click" a menu command by pressing Enter. You can also close the menu without making a selection by pressing Esc, ⌘-period, or the Space bar.

  Over time, as you learn precisely how many Tabs and arrow keys you need to trigger certain commands, you can get very good at this technique.

- **Dock.** Operate the Dock by keyboard alone? Sure, that's easy enough: just press ⌘-Tab to cycle through the open programs. Everybody knows that.

  But ⌘-Tab just highlights successive icons of *open programs* on the Dock. It skips over the icons of folders, disks, documents, and programs that aren't yet running.

  If you turn on Full Keyboard Access, you get much more flexibility. Once you've pressed the "highlight the Dock" Control-key stroke of your choice, you can highlight *any* icon on the Dock by pressing the right or left arrow keys (or, once again, Tab and Shift-Tab).

  Once you've highlighted a Dock icon, you "click it" by pressing Enter. If you change your mind, once again, press Esc, ⌘-period, or the Space bar.

Tip: Once you've highlighted a disk or folder icon, you can press the up arrow to make the list of its contents appear. Using the arrow keys, you can now highlight and open virtually anything in any disk or folder on the Dock. Similarly, once you've highlighted the icon of an application that has several windows open, you can press the up and down arrows to highlight the name of an individual window; when you press Enter, that window pops to the front.

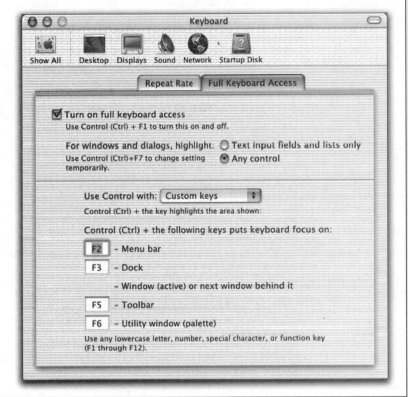

Figure 4-9:
The Full Keyboard Access panel of the Keyboard control panel lets you specify how you'd like to control your menus and other Mac OS X interface elements without even using the mouse.

- **Window (active) or next window behind it.** This command lets you switch windows using keyboard control. Each time you press Control-F4, you bring the next window forward. (At least that's Apple's intention. Due to a last-minute programming glitch, this feature is turned off—and even the F4 assignment is missing—in Mac OS X 10.1.1.)

- **Toolbar.** This one works in any Cocoa program that displays a Mac OS X-style toolbar (Mail, Finder, Address Book, and so on). When you press Control-F5, you highlight the first button on that toolbar. Move the "focus" by pressing the arrow keys or Tab and Shift-Tab. Then just tap the Space bar to "click" the highlighted button.

• **Utility window (palette).** In a few programs that feature floating tool palettes, Ctrl-F6 highlights the frontmost palette. At this point, you can use the arrow keys to highlight the various buttons on the palette.

Note: As noted above, these final three functions are quirky, to say the least, in Mac OS X 10.1; in most programs, they don't do anything at all. But the menu-bar and Dock commands are solid, and work in any program.

Turning on Full Keyboard Access

Apple made sure that this feature was turned off by default, to avoid freaking out people who sometimes set their sandwiches down on the keyboard between bites. But it's easy enough—and well worthwhile—to turn on.

Start by opening System Preferences, as described on page 181. Click Keyboard, and then click the Full Keyboard Access tab (see Figure 4-9). Turn on "Turn on full keyboard access."

You've just powered up one of Mac OS X's most useful timesavers.

Tip: In the future, you can skip all of these steps. You can turn keyboard control on or off just by pressing Control-F1.

The choices at the top of the screen are designed to let you navigate dialog boxes from the keyboard. When "Text input fields" is selected, pressing the Tab key does just what it's always done: moves your insertion point from one text box to the next within a dialog box. But when you turn on "Any control," pressing Tab highlights the next control of *any* type—radio button, pop-up menu, and so on.

The good stuff is at the bottom of the dialog box. Using the "Use Control with" pop-up menu, tell the Mac how you'll be triggering commands. You have three choices:

• **Function keys.** In any program, no matter what you're doing, you'll be able to seize control of the menus by pressing Control-F2 (that is, the F2 key at the top of your keyboard). Similarly, you'll activate the Dock, toolbars, palettes, and other elements by pressing Control-Fkey combinations, as illustrated in Figure 4-9.

• **Letter keys.** This option will probably gave you a lot less trouble remembering how to operate the various keyboard-controllable elements of your Mac. Just press Control-M to highlight the menu bar, Control-D to highlight the Dock, and so on.

• **Custom keys.** This option lets you define your *own* keystrokes for operating the various keyboard-controllable elements. Just remember that the Control key is always required, along with any letter, number, or function key you want to trigger the five options displayed in the dialog box.

Note: In Microsoft Office programs and several others, these key combinations may already come assigned to certain functions. Mac OS X will intercept these keystrokes.

The Save and Open Dialog Boxes

For years, the least satisfying part of using a Macintosh was saving a newly typed document. When you used File→Save, a dialog box appeared, in which you were supposed to type a name for, and specify the file format for, the new file you were saving.

To the beginner, these specifications are confusing and unnatural. They bear no resemblance to any real-world process. Nobody asks you to name cookies you've just baked, or what file format you'd like them to assume as they come out of the oven.

Figure 4-10:
Top: The old Save dialog box, an inevitable part of Mac computing, displays a list of the folders on your hard drive–but where are you? What folder is this one inside of?

Bottom: In Mac OS X, you can see a familiar column display that matches the Finder, making it much easier to figure out what you're doing and how you got here.

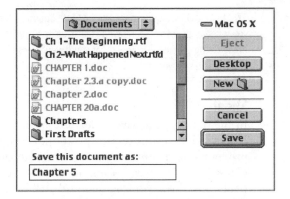

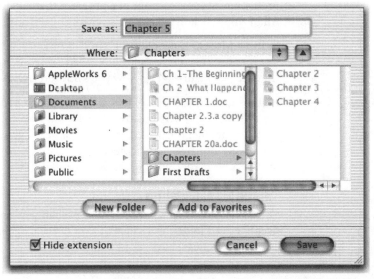

But it gets worse. In the Save dialog box, you're also asked where you want the new document stored on your hard drive. Filing a document away in a folder *does* have a real-world equivalent; that's why it's so easy to understand the folder icons on the Mac desktop. Unfortunately, compared with the Finder's self-explanatory folder display, the old Save dialog box's presentation of your hard drive's contents was about as friendly as a tax form, as Figure 4-10 illustrates. All of these factors conspired to make the old Save dialog box—and its sibling, the Open file dialog box—among the most challenging parts of the Mac operating system.

All of this explanation is necessary to understand why Apple, and specifically Steve Jobs in his stage presentations, gets so excited about the way Mac OS X's Save and Open Dialog boxes work.

To give it a try, launch almost any program that has a Save or Export command in the File menu—a word processor or TextEdit, for example. Type a couple of words and then choose File→Save. The Save *sheet* appears.

Tip: In Mac OS X, a quick glance at the Close button in the upper-left corner of a document window tells you whether or not it's been saved (see Figure 4-10). When a small dot appears in the red button, you've made changes to the document that you haven't yet saved (time to press ⌘-S!). The dot disappears as soon as you save your work.

Sheets

In the old days, the Save dialog box appeared dead center on the screen, where it commandeered your entire operation. You weren't allowed to switch to any other program—or do anything else—until you had clicked Save or Cancel to close the dialog box. Moreover, because it seemed stuck to your *screen* rather than to a particular *document,* you couldn't really tell which document you were saving—a real problem when you quit out of a program that had three unsaved documents open. All of this struck Mac OS X's designers as user-hostile and unnecessarily rigid.

In most Mac OS X programs, there's no mystery as to which document you're saving, because a little Save dialog box called a *sheet* slides directly out of the document's title bar (see Figure 4-11). Now you know precisely which document you're saving.

Better still, you can think of this little Save box as a sticky note attached to the document. It will stay there, neatly attached and waiting, even if you switch to another program, another document within the same program, the desktop, and so on. When you finally return to the document, the Save sheet will still be there, waiting for you to type a file name and save the document.

Simplified Navigation

Of course, *you,* O savvy reader, have probably never saved a document into some deeply nested folder by accident, never to see it again. But millions of novices (and even a few experts) have fallen into this trap.

When the Save sheet appears, however, a pop-up menu shows you precisely where Mac OS X proposes putting your newly created document: in the Documents folder of your own Home folder. For many people, this is an excellent suggestion. If you keep everything in your Documents folder, it will be extremely easy to find, and you'll be able to back up your work just by dragging a single folder (the Documents folder) to a backup disk.

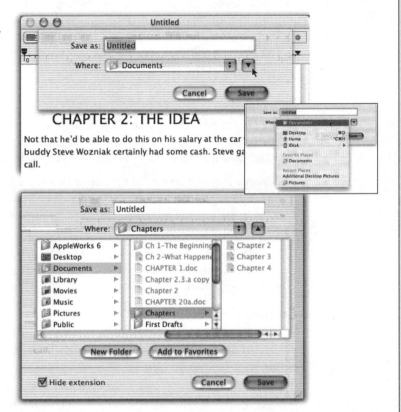

Figure 4-11:
Top: The new Save dialog box, or sheet, initially appears in a compact view.

Inset: To spare you from having to navigate your hard drive every time you save a file, your most frequently accessed folders are listed in the Where pop-up menu.

Bottom: If you want to choose a different folder, create a new folder, or designate a Favorite folder, click the Column-view triangle to open this Finder-like navigation view.

But the Where pop-up menu gives you direct access to some other places you might want to save a newly created file:

- **Desktop.** Just type a name for the file, choose Desktop from this pop-up menu, and then click Save. (You can also simply press ⌘-D, exactly as in the Mac OS of days gone by.)

  You've just made sure that your file won't fall accidentally into some random folder. Instead, the newly minted document will be waiting for you on the desktop itself when you quit your program or close its window. From there, you can drag it manually into any folder you like.

Tip: To open the Where pop-up menu—or any pop-up menu, for that matter—you don't have to click the tiny, blue, double-headed triangle button at the right end. You can click anywhere on the pop-up menu, such as where it says Documents.

• **Home.** Choosing this item from the pop-up menu (or pressing Option-⌘-H) takes you directly to your Home folder, which is described on page 49.

• **iDisk.** Apple's free Internet-based backup hard drive is better integrated with Mac OS X than ever before. You can now save documents directly onto it just by choosing this command. (Actually, you can't save icons into your iDisk window— you must save them into a folder *within* your iDisk. That's why the submenu of this iDisk command lists the various folders on your iDisk, as described in Chapter 18.)

When you do so, your Mac will dial and connect to the Internet, if you're not already online, and pull your iDisk onto the screen so that you can save your new document there. All of this takes a considerable amount of time, even if you have a high-speed connection like a cable modem or DSL connection.

• **Favorite Places.** This part of the pop-up list is a duplicate of the Favorites menu in the Finder, which is described in Chapter 2. Its purpose is to list the disks, servers, folders, and other items you use frequently, so that you don't have to go burrowing through your folders every time you want access.

• **Recent Places.** This part of the menu lists folders and disks you've accessed recently. Once again, the idea is to give you quick access to folder locations on your hard drive that matter to you, without making you do any navigation.

Column-View Navigation

When you save a file, the options in the Where pop-up menu have you covered 90 percent of the time. Most people work with a limited set of folders for active documents.

But when you want to save a new document into a new folder, or when you want to navigate to a folder that isn't listed in the Where pop-up menu, all is not lost. Click the large black triangle shown in Figure 4-11.

After a moment, a familiar scene appears: a compact version of a Finder-window column view, exactly as described on page 40.

Tip: Your first instinct should be to widen this window, making more columns available. Do so by carefully dragging the lower-right corner of the dialog box. Mac OS X will remember the size you like for this Save sheet independently in each program.

Click a column, or press Tab, to highlight the column view itself. Now, using exactly the same techniques described on page 40, you can navigate your entire Mac system. Most of the usual keystrokes and mouse clicks work here. For example, you can press the arrow keys to navigate the columns, or type the first letters of disk or folder names to highlight them. (You just can't press Tab to highlight successive columns, because pressing Tab again highlights the Save As box, where you type the name of your new file.)

Highlight the name of the folder in which you want to save your newly created document, or use these options:

• **New Folder.** Click this button to create a new folder *inside* whatever folder is highlighted in the column view. You'll be asked to type the new name for the folder. After you've done so, click Create (or press Enter). The new folder appears in the rightmost panel of the column view. You can now proceed with saving your new document into it, if you like.

Note: The keystroke ⌘-N no longer triggers the New Folder button. Remember that in Mac OS X, the Save sheet is nothing more than an attachment to your document window. Keystrokes like ⌘-N go right "past" the sheet to the program you're using. In Microsoft Word or TextEdit, for example, pressing ⌘-N produces a new, untitled Word or TextEdit document, which appears right in front of the Save sheet.

• **Add to Favorites.** In addition to the methods described on page 64, the Save sheet gives you a quick way to add a particular folder to your list of Favorites. Just highlight the folder in the column view and then click Add to Favorites. The favorite folder appears instantly in the Where pop-up menu—in the Favorites section, of course.

The point is that the *next* time you save a new document, you won't even have to bother with the column view. You'll be able to jump quickly to the favorite folder you've just specified.

The next time you save a new document, the Save sheet will reappear in whatever condition you left it—that is, if you used column view the last time, it will still be in column view. At any time, you can collapse it into simplified view shown at top in Figure 4-11 by again clicking the fat black triangle to the right of the Where pop-up menu.

Insta-Jumping to a Folder Location

Whether you're using the mini-sheet or the column view, you can drag the icon of any folder or disk *from your desktop* directly into the Save or Open sheet, as shown in Figure 4-12. Mac OS X instantly shows you what's in that folder or disk.

This shortcut can save you time when you want to save a file into, or open a file from, a deeply nested folder that's already visible in the Finder. This feature is totally undocumented—but well worth learning.

The File Format Pop-up Menu

Although it's by no means universal, the Save dialog box in many programs offers a pop-up menu of file formats below the Save As box. Use this menu when you want to prepare a document for use by somebody else—somebody whose computer doesn't have the same software. For example, if you've used a graphics program to prepare a photograph for use on the Web, this menu is where you specify JPEG format (the standard Web format for photos).

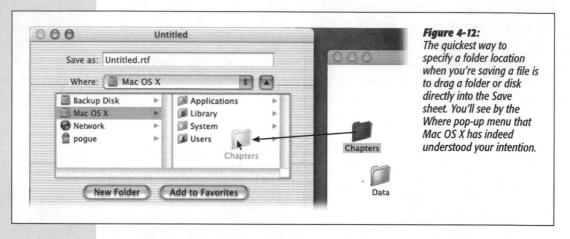

Figure 4-12:
The quickest way to specify a folder location when you're saving a file is to drag a folder or disk directly into the Save sheet. You'll see by the Where pop-up menu that Mac OS X has indeed understood your intention.

The Open File Dialog Box

The dialog box that appears when you choose File→Open is almost identical to the Save File sheet, except that it offers *both* the Where list of frequently used folders *and* the column view (see Figure 4-13). Because you encounter it only when you're opening an existing file, this dialog box lacks the New Folder button, Save button, file name field, and so on.

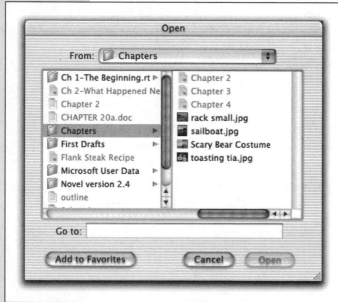

Figure 4-13:
Mac OS X's Open dialog box shows you only icons for disks, folders, and documents that you can actually open at this moment. For example, when using Preview as shown here, Word and TextEdit documents appear dimmed and unavailable, but picture files show up fine.

Most of the other Save File dialog box controls, however, are equally useful here. Once again, you can begin your navigation by seeing what's on the desktop (press ⌘-D) or in your Home folder (press Option-⌘-H). Once again, you can open a folder or disk by double-clicking its name in the column-view list, or navigate the list by pressing the left, right, up, and down arrow keys. And once again, you can drag a folder or disk off of your desktop directly into the dialog box to specify where you want to look.

When you've finally located the file you want to open, do so by double-clicking it or by highlighting it (which you can do from the keyboard) and then pressing Return, Enter, or ⌘-O.

In general, most people don't encounter the Open File dialog box nearly as often as they do the Save File dialog box. That's because the Mac offers many more convenient ways to *open* a file—double-clicking its icon in the Finder, choosing its name from the →Recent Items command, and so on—but only a single way to *save* a new file.

The Color Picker

Here and there—in System Preferences, Finder Preferences, Microsoft Office, and many other programs—Mac OS X offers you the opportunity to choose a *color* for some element: for your desktop background, a window, and so on.

The dialog box that appears offers a miniature color lab that lets you dial in any color in the Mac's rainbow. *Several* color labs, actually, each designed to make color-choosing easier in certain circumstances:

CMYK. The acronym stands for *cyan, magenta, yellow,* and *black.* People in the printing industry will feel immediately at home, because these four colors are the component inks for color printing. (These people may also be able to explain why *K* stands for *black.*)

Crayon. Now *this* is a good user interface. You can click each crayon to see its color name: "Lemon," "Sea Foam," "Maraschino," and so on. (Some interior decorator in Cupertino had a field day naming these crayons.)

HSV. Stands for Hue, Saturation, and Value—a favorite color-specifying scheme in scientific circles.

Name. This one's for you, Web designers. You can choose color by their *hex codes,* just as Web-design programs like Dreamweaver and GoLive do.

RGB. This is how a TV or computer monitor thinks of colors: as proportions of red, green, and blue.

In most of these color pickers, you can drag the sliders around to pinpoint a color, or type in percentages of component colors. But you can also "sample" a color that's *outside* the dialog box—a color you found on a Web page, for example—just by pressing Option as you move your cursor around the screen. You'll see the sliders and numbers change inside the dialog box automatically.

(And if you've selected the Crayon picker, you'll be told Apple's name for any color you Option-click, even when it gets ridiculous: "Melon-ish" and "Asparagus-ish," for example.)

Tip: Instead of using the column view to specify a folder, you can also use the Go To box at the bottom of the Open sheet. That is, you can type a folder path (such as *~/pictures* or *~/pi* and a Tab) right into the blank. And if you have no idea what these codes refer to, see the box on page 378.

Three Kinds of Programs: Cocoa, Carbon, Classic

Mac OS X was supposed to make life simpler. It was supposed to do away with the confusion and complexity that the old Mac OS had accumulated over the years—and replace it with a smooth, simple, solid system.

Five or ten years from now, that's exactly what Mac OS X will be. For the moment, however, you'll be stuck with running three different kinds of programs, each with different characteristics: *Cocoa, Carbon,* and *Classic.*

The explanation involves a little bit of history and a little bit of logic. To take full advantage of Mac OS X's considerable technical benefits, software companies have to write new programs for it from scratch. So what should Apple do—send out an email to the authors of the 18,000 existing Mac programs, suggesting that they throw out their programs and rewrite them from the bottom up?

At big companies like Microsoft and Adobe, such a suggestion would wind up on the Joke of the Week bulletin board.

Instead, Apple gave software companies a break. It wrote Mac OS X to let programmers and software companies choose precisely how much work they wanted to put into compatibility with the new system:

- **Do nothing at all (Classic).** Let's face it: Software companies go out of business, unprofitable product lines are dropped, and shareware authors go off to law school. All of them leave behind orphaned programs that run only on the old Mac OS.

  Your Mac OS X machine can still run this entire library of older software. When you try to open one of these older programs, Mac OS X launches a Mac OS 9 *simulator* called the Classic environment. Suddenly your screen is taken over by the ghost of Mac OS 9. You leave behind all the trappings (and benefits) of Mac OS X—its new look, the Dock, crash protection, and so on—but at least you're still running your favorite programs.

  See Chapter 5 for much more detail on the Classic environment; the point here is that Mac OS X doesn't relieve you of having to know Mac OS 9. Like it or not, until a huge library of Mac OS X programs is available, most people wind up having to master *both* Mac OS X and certain elements of Mac OS 9.

- **Update the existing programs (Carbon).** If software companies and programmers are willing to put *some* effort into getting with the Mac OS X program, they can simply adapt, or update, their existing software so that it works with Mac OS X. The resulting software looks and feels almost every bit like a true Mac OS

X program—you get the crash protection, the good looks, the cool-looking graphics, the Save sheets, and so on—but behind the scenes, the bulk of the computer programming is the same as it was in Mac OS 9. These are what Apple calls *Carbonized* programs, named for the technology (Carbon) that permits them to run on Mac OS X.

Carbonized programs don't offer all of the features available to Mac OS X, however. In the following pages, you'll find out what Mac OS X goodies you sacrifice when you use programs that have been adapted in this way.

On the other hand, such software offers a spectacular feature that software companies like a *lot:* a single Carbonized program can run on *both* Mac OS 9 and Mac OS X. (Not all do—Microsoft Office X doesn't run on Mac OS 9—but they all *can,* if their programmers choose to make it so.) For the next few years, most of the big-name software companies will produce nothing but Carbonized programs.

Other examples of Carbonized programs include AppleWorks, iMovie, iTunes, Photoshop, FileMaker, Internet Explorer, and, believe it or not, the Finder itself.

- **Write new programs from scratch (Cocoa).** If Mac OS X is a hit, more and more programmers and software companies will create new programs exclusively for it. The geeks call such programs *Cocoa* applications—and they're the best of all. Although they look exactly like Carbonized programs, they feel a little bit more smooth and solid. More important, they offer a number of special features that you don't get with Carbonized programs.

Many of the programs that come with Mac OS X are true Cocoa applications, including TextEdit, Stickies, Mail, Address Book, and so on.

Tip: Having trouble keeping straight the definitions of Carbon and Cocoa? You wouldn't be alone; it's like reading a novel where two characters' names start with the same letter. Here's one way to remember: *Carbon* programs are generally the *older* ones, those for which you might need Carbon-dating techniques to calculate their ages.

Telling Cocoa from Carbon

How can I tell whether a program is Carbonized or a true-blue, fully Cocoa effort?

Here's the surest way: In icon view, Control-click the program's icon and choose Show Package Contents. Open the Contents→Resources folder that appears.

Is there a file inside the Resources folder that ends with the letters *.nib?* If so, you've got Cocoa. If not, you're working with a Carbonized program.

The Cocoa Difference

Here are some of the advantages offered by Cocoa programs. It's worth reading, not to make you drool about a future when *all* Mac programs will fall into this category, but to help clear up any confusion you may have about why certain features seem to be only sometimes present.

Note: The following features show up in almost all Cocoa programs. That's not to say that you'll *never* see these features in Carbonized programs; the occasional Carbon program may offer one of these features or another. That's because programmers have to do quite a bit of work to bring them into Carbon applications—and almost none to include them in Cocoa.

The Fonts Panel

The Mac has always been the designer's preferred computer, and Mac OS X only strengthens its position. For one thing, Mac OS X comes with about 100 absolutely beautiful fonts that Apple licensed from commercial type companies—about $1,000 worth, according to Apple.

When you use a Carbon program, you usually get at these fonts the same way you always did: using a Font menu. But when you use a Cocoa program, you get the Fonts panel, which makes it far easier to organize, search, and use your font collection (see Figure 4-13).

See Chapter 13 for much more on fonts—and using the Fonts panel.

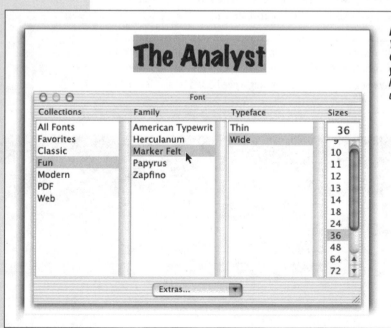

Figure 4-14:
You'll find the Fonts panel only in Cocoa programs. As you adjust your font selections, you see the highlighted text in your program updated instantly.

Title Bar Tricks

You may remember from Chapter 1 (Figure 1-3) that the title bar of every Finder window harbors a secret pop-up menu. When you ⌘-click it, you're shown a little folder ladder that tells you precisely where you are in your folder hierarchy. You may also remember that the tiny icon just to the left of the window's name is actually a handle, which you can drag to move a folder into a different window.

In Cocoa programs, you get the same features in *document* windows, as shown in Figure 4-15. (This feature is available in some Carbonized programs, but it isn't a sure thing.) By dragging the tiny document icon next to the document's name, you can perform two interesting stunts:

- **Drag to the desktop.** By dragging this icon to the desktop, or onto a folder or disk icon, you create an instant alias of the document you're working on—a useful feature when, for example, you're about to knock off for the night, and want easy access to whatever you've been working on when you return the next day.

- **Drag to the Dock.** If you drag this title-bar icon onto the *Dock* icon of an appropriate program, you open your document in that other program. For example, if you're in TextEdit working on a memo, and you decide that you'll need the full strength of Microsoft Word to dress it up, you can drag its title-bar icon directly onto the Word icon in the Dock. Word launches and opens up the TextEdit document, ready for editing.

Unfortunately, you can't drag an open document directly into the Trash—a technique that could come in handy for writers who struggle with first drafts.

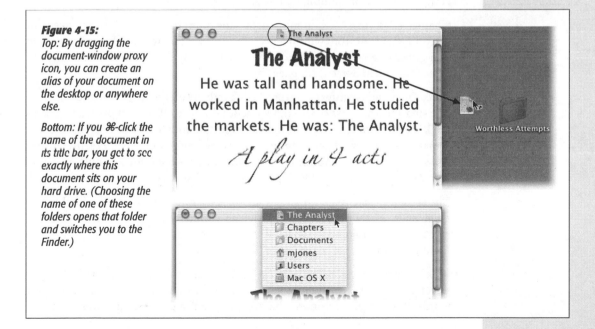

Figure 4-15:
Top: By dragging the document-window proxy icon, you can create an alias of your document on the desktop or anywhere else.

Bottom: If you ⌘-click the name of the document in its title bar, you get to see exactly where this document sits on your hard drive. (Choosing the name of one of these folders opens that folder and switches you to the Finder.)

Services

Apple has always dreamed of a software architecture that would let you mix and match features from different programs—using the AppleWorks spelling checker in Microsoft Word, the drawing tools of PowerPoint in your email program, and so on. (Remember something called OpenDoc? Neither does anybody else.)

In Mac OS X, Apple's dream has finally become a reality. Nestled in the Application menu of every Mac OS X program is a command called Services. Its submenu lists several functions that technically belong to other programs, as described below.

As of Mac OS X 10.1, however, these commands are dimmed when you use most Carbonized programs (like AppleWorks, Microsoft Office, and Internet Explorer). They become available only when you use Cocoa programs (like TextEdit, Mail, and OmniWeb). Here's a rundown of what they do.

Note: Not all of these Services work in all programs—even Cocoa programs. Implementing them is left to the discretion of the programmers. In these early days of Mac OS X, a little unpredictability along these lines is par for the course.

- **Disk Copy→Mount Image.** If you've downloaded a disk image, as described on page 125, and it's highlighted on the desktop, this command *mounts* it (turns it into a simulated CD inserted on your Mac).

- **Grab.** Grab is a screen-capture program in your Applications→Utilities folder. You use it to turn what you see on the screen into graphics files, for use in writing computer books or training manuals.

  Chapter 9 describes Grab in more detail; the point here is that you can take your software snapshot from within any Cocoa application, without having to go find and launch Grab separately. You'll find details on its submenu commands (Screen, Selection, Timed Screen) on page 240.

- **Mail.** This handy command springs to life only if you highlight some text first. In one step, the Mail Text command launches the Mac OS X Mail program (Chapter 19) and pastes the highlighted text into the body of a new, outgoing email message. You're saved the trouble of copying, launching Mail, creating a new message, and pasting. You might use this feature when, for example, you find something interesting on a Web page that you'd like to send to someone by email.

  The second submenu command, Mail To, is useful only if you've highlighted an email *address* in some text document. This command, too, switches to Mail and creates a new, outgoing message—but this time, Mac OS X pastes the text you've highlighted into the "To" field.

- **Make Sticky.** Although "make sticky" sounds like this command will cover the selected object with melted ice cream, it really means "Make *a* Sticky." In other words, this command copies whatever text you've got highlighted, switches to

your Stickies program (page 217), creates a new sticky note, and pastes your selected material in it. If you're the kind of person who keeps your life—lists, passwords, favorite URLs, to do list, notes—in Stickies, this one can save you considerable hassle over the months.

• **Summarize.** Talk about intriguing: When you choose this command after highlighting some text in a Cocoa application, the Mac analyzes the sentences you've
highlighted. After a moment, it launches Summary Service, a little program you
probably never even knew you had, which displays a greatly shortened version of
the original text. (Summary Service doesn't actually do any creative rewriting;
instead, it chooses the most statistically significant sentences to include in the
summary.) Figure 4-16 offers details.

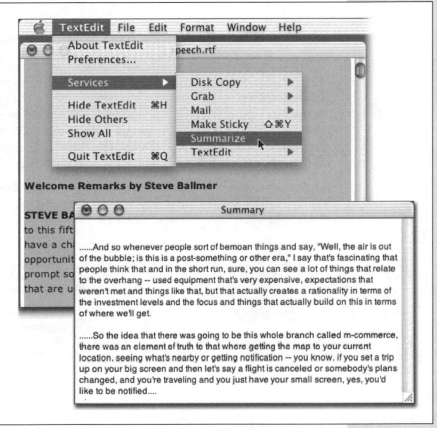

Figure 4-16:
*Use the Summarize
command to create a
one-paragraph
summary (right) of a
longer passage (left).
For even more fun,
you can even
summarize the
summary—once in
Summary Service,
simply choose
Summary Service→
Services→Summarize
again, and then
again, ad infinitum.*

• **TextEdit.** This pair of commands, too, requires that you first highlight some text
in the Cocoa application. If the text you've highlighted happens to match the
precise name of the TextEdit document on your hard drive (including its *folder
path*, like *~/Documents/essay.txt*), you can choose Services→TextEdit→Open File
to find and open that document in TextEdit. (If what you've highlighted *isn't* the

name of a document, you'll get only an error message.) If you've highlighted any other blob of text, choose Services→TextEdit→Open Selection; Mac OS X automatically launches TextEdit, creates a new untitled document, and pastes the highlighted text.

These are the commands that come built into a fresh installation of Mac OS X, but that's not the end of it. The real beauty of Services is that, as new, clever Cocoa applications come along, they can add their own commands to this menu for your data-manipulation pleasure.

Tip: InstantLinks, a piece of $5 shareware from Subsume Technologies, offers a useful look ahead to the future of Services. It adds to your Services menu commands that send your highlighted text to various services on the Web.

For example, you can choose Dictionary Lookup (looks up the selected text in an online dictionary), Map Location (looks up the selected address at MapQuest.com—great when somebody emails you an invitation), Open URL, Search Web, and Thesaurus Lookup. You can download it from *www.missingmanuals.com*.

Toolbar Tricks

The toolbar is an increasingly common sight at the top of modern application windows. In any thoughtfully written program, the Preferences command lets you indicate how you want this toolbar to show up—with icons, icons with text labels beneath them, or text labels alone, which saves window space.

But in many Cocoa programs, including OmniWeb, Mail, Address Book, and Project Builder, there's a much faster way to switch among these three toolbar styles: ⌘-click the white button shown in Figure 4-17.

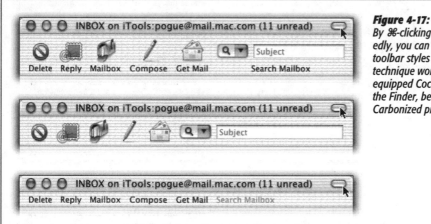

Figure 4-17:
By ⌘-clicking this button repeatedly, you can cycle among the three toolbar styles shown here. This technique works in most toolbar-equipped Cocoa programs (but not the Finder, because it's actually a Carbonized program).

Secret Keyboard Shortcuts

The Cocoa
Difference

For the most part, it's possible to ignore the Unix that beats within the heart of Mac OS X. But every now and then, a refreshing reminder pokes its head up through the waves of Aqua—and here's one of them.

Although you'll never see it mentioned in the user manuals for Cocoa applications (if there even were such thing as user manuals anymore), all of them respond to certain keystrokes left over from the NeXT operating system (which was Mac OS X's ancestor). If you're a card-carrying number of KIAFTMA (the Keyboard Is Always Faster Than the Mouse Association), you'll love these additional keyboard navigation strokes:

- **Control-A.** Moves your insertion point to the beginning of the paragraph. (*Mnemonic:* A = beginning of the alphabet.)

- **Control-E.** Deposits your insertion point at the end of the paragraph. (*Mnemonic:* E = *end.*)

- **Control-D.** Forward delete (deletes the letter to the *right* of the insertion point).

- **Control-K.** Instantly deletes all text from the insertion point to the right end of the line. (*Mnemonic:* K = kills the rest of the line.)

- **Control-O.** Inserts a paragraph break, much like Return, but leaves the insertion point where it was, above the break. This is the ideal trick for breaking a paragraph in half when you've just thought of a better ending for the first part.

- **Control-T.** Moves the insertion point one letter to the right—and along with it, drags whatever letter was to its left. (*Mnemonic:* T = *transpose* letters.)

- **Option-Delete.** Deletes the entire word to the left of the insertion point. When you're typing along in a hurry, and you discover that you've just made a typo, this is the keystroke you want. It's much faster to nuke the previous word and retype it than to fiddle around with the mouse and the insertion point trying to fix one letter.

Four additional keystrokes duplicate the functions of the arrow keys. Still, as long as you've got your pinky on that Control key:

- **Control-B, Control-F.** Moves the insertion point one character to the left or right, just like the left and right arrow keys. (*Mnemonic:* Back, Forward).

- **Control-N, Control-P.** Moves the insertion point one row down or up, like the down and up arrow keys. (*Mnemonic:* Next, Previous).

Background Window Control

As hinted in Chapter 1, the ⌘ key unlocks a slick trick in Cocoa programs: It lets you operate the buttons and controls of an inactive, background window without bringing it to the front. You can operate a background window's resize box, buttons, pop-up menus, and scroll bars, all while another window is in front of it. In fact, you can even *drag through text* in a background window—and then drag-and-drop it into the foreground window. (Freaky!)

In every case, the secret is simply to keep ⌘ pressed as you click or drag.

Installing Mac OS X programs

Learning to live with Mac OS X also involves learning some new tricks for installing software.

.tar and .gz

Programs you download from the Internet may no longer arrive on your machine as .sit (StuffIt) files. Instead, many of them come compressed using the Unix equivalent of StuffIt. You'll know that you're dealing with such a file if its name ends in *.tar* or *.gz*.

.Tar is short for *tape archive,* an ancient Unix utility that combines (but doesn't compress) several files into a single icon, for simplicity in sending. Meanwhile, *.gz* is short for *gzip,* the standard Unix compression program. You may even find files whose names end with *.tar.gz,* which represents one compressed archive containing several files.

The only thing you need to know about these new compression and archiving formats is that StuffIt Expander can turn them back into human form, just as it does with .sit files. StuffIt Expander, a program in your Applications→Utilities folder, kicks in automatically when you double-click a downloaded compressed file, so there's really not much to learn about the new Mac OS X formats.

FREQUENTLY ASKED QUESTION

Where Have You Gone, Drag-and-Drop?

I'm devastated: Drag-and-drop doesn't work anymore! I used to love editing by dragging some highlighted text to a new position, or even to the desktop as a clipping. But it doesn't seem to work anymore in Mac OS X! Is there a support group?

Drag-and-drop is alive and well in Mac OS X. It just requires a different technique in Cocoa programs.

After highlighting some text, you can't simply drag it; if you try, you'll succeed only in highlighting a different blob of text. Instead, the trick is to click inside the highlighted area and then *hold down* the mouse button for about half a second. *Now* you can drag.

In Carbonized programs, drag-and-drop works the same way it always did. You can drag highlighted text immediately, without having to pause first.

If it's any consolation, you get a spectacular visual effect in both Carbonized and Cocoa programs under Mac OS X: Instead of just seeing a dotted-line outline of the text you're dragging, as in Mac OS 9, you see the *actual* letters, ghostly and transparent, move along with your cursor.

Disk Images

Once you've unstuffed (or untarred) a downloaded program, it often takes the form of a disk image, whose name ends with the letters *.dmg* (see page 237). Disk images have been around for years on the Mac, but they're even more common in Mac OS X. All you have to do is double-click the .dmg icon. After a moment, it magically turns into a disk icon on your desktop, which you can work with just as though it's a real disk. For example:

- Double-click it to open it. The software you downloaded is right inside.

- Get it off your desktop by pressing the Eject button at the upper-right corner of your keyboard (if you have a modern Apple keyboard), dragging it to the Trash (whose icon turns into a big silver Eject key as you drag), or highlighting it and pressing ⌘-E (the shortcut for File→Eject). (You've still got the original .dmg file you downloaded, so you're not really saying goodbye to the disk image forever.)

Performing the Installation

Working with .tar, .gz, and .dmg files are all skills unique to downloading Mac OS X programs from the Internet. Installing software from a CD is much more straightforward.

In either case, once you've got a disk icon on your desktop (either a pseudo-disk from a disk image or a CD you've inserted), you're ready to install the software. You can install many Mac OS X programs just by dragging their icons or folders to your hard drive. Others offer a traditional installer program that requires you to double-click, read and accept a license agreement, and so on.

In both cases, *where* you decide to install the new program is suddenly a big issue. You have two alternatives:

- **In the Applications folder.** Most programs, of course, sit in your Applications folder, as described on page 51. Most of the time, this is where you'll want to install new programs. Putting them in the Applications folder makes it available to anyone who uses the Mac.

- **In your Home folder.** This option is valuable only if you share your Mac with other people, as described in Chapter 11. If that's your situation, you may occasionally want to install a program privately, reserving it for your own use only. In that case, all you have to do is install or drag it into your Home folder (see page 49). When other people log onto the machine, they won't even know that you've installed that new program, because it doesn't show up in the Applications folder.

Back to
Mac OS 9

I f only we could move into Mac OS X and live there! Unfortunately, *software* makes the world go 'round, and it will be a long time before every program you'll ever want to use has been written or rewritten for Mac OS X.

That doesn't mean you can't use them at all. You can certainly run your old favorites within Mac OS X—by flipping back into Mac OS 9. There are two ways you can do that, as described in this chapter.

The bad news is that now you've got *two different* operating systems to learn. The landscape, features, and locations of favorite commands are different in each one.

If you've got the old Mac OS in your blood, you're way ahead of the game. But pity the novice who's picking up the Mac for the first time and discovers a shiny blue menu one moment, and a striped one with completely different commands the next, as the machine flips back and forth between the two OSes.

There's no solution to this dilemma except to wait until every program you'll ever want to use is available in a Mac OS X version. Fortunately, most of the biggies are already available for Mac OS X. The sooner you can stop using the Mac OS 9 tricks described in this chapter, the better.

Two Roads to Mac OS 9

You can return to Mac OS 9 in either of two ways. Here's a summary that outlines the pros and cons of each method:

• **Run Classic.** The program called Classic is one of the crowning achievements of Mac OS X. You can think of it as a Mac OS 9 simulator or emulator. It runs automatically whenever you double-click the icon of a pre–Mac OS X program.

At that point, the Classic (Mac OS 9) world takes over your screen, looking exactly like the old Mac OS 9 you used to know (or not know) is starting up. There's the old startup logo, the parade of extensions across the screen, your old menu, the non-striped menu bar, and so on. Once it's running, you can run almost all of your older Mac OS 9 programs without a hitch.

Classic is the reason Apple recommends that you install Mac OS X only on Macs with at least 128 MB of memory. When you run it, your Mac is running two operating systems at once, which takes quite a bit of memory.

For most people, most of the time, Classic is the easiest, quickest, and most effective way to run older Mac programs.

Note: For Mac OS X 10.1, Classic requires Mac OS 9.2 or later. The most recent version of Mac OS 9 is almost always the best.

• **Restart the Mac in Mac OS 9.** Unfortunately, Classic isn't always the solution. Remember that it's only a simulator. It isn't your operating system at the time—it isn't actually controlling your Mac. (Mac OS X continues to run beneath it.)

Whenever a certain program "reaches for" a particular piece of circuitry on your Mac, such as the FireWire or USB jack, it comes up empty-handed. That's why many scanners, digitizing tablets, and even printers don't work when you run programs in the Classic mode.

Fortunately, you can also restart your Mac in Mac OS 9, just as though you didn't have Mac OS X installed at all. At this point, you've got just a regular Mac OS 9 machine, just as it was before you ever got Mac OS X, and all your old gear works just as it always did. Of course, you don't get any of the benefits of Mac OS X, such as its stability and multitasking prowess.

Classic: Mac OS 9 on Mac OS X

If you still harbor the notion, propagated by certain Macintosh books in the 80s, that it's bad form to have two System folders on the same hard drive, welcome to the 21st century. When you use Mac OS X, it's not only a good idea to have two System folders—it's almost a requirement. You should have one of each: Mac OS 9 and Mac OS X. (Appendix C describes various ways to set all this up.)

It's easy to spot the Mac OS 9 System folder on your hard drive, as shown in Figure 5-1.

How to Start Classic

You can start up your Classic program in any of several ways.

Double-click a Mac OS 9 program

The most common method of launching Classic is simply double-clicking the icon of a pre–Mac OS X program. Your Mac instantly concludes: "Well, this program won't run in Mac OS X, so I'll just go ahead and launch your Mac OS 9 simulator."

Figure 5-1:
When you're running Mac OS X, the System Folder that contains Mac OS 9 is clearly marked by the big golden 9. Only one System Folder per disk may bear this logo, which indicates that it's the only one officially recognized by the Mac. (As the programmers say, it's the "blessed" System Folder.)

At this point, several things happen. The very first time you ever run Classic, you may see a message that says, "Some Classic-specific resources need to be added to or updated in your System Folder." Mac OS X is telling you that your Mac OS 9 System Folder requires a couple of extensions and other system files (listed later on this chapter) in order to run within Mac OS X, and that it's offering to put them in the right place. Click OK.

Now a progress bar appears in a floating window, as shown in Figure 5-2. Classic takes a minute or so to start up—unless you streamline it using the tricks described in the following pages. During the startup process, you'll see a little Classic (numeral 9) icon bouncing up and down in your Dock, just to help you understand what's going on.

Tip: If you haven't got the time to wait, or you suddenly change your mind, you can cancel the Classic startup process by clicking the Stop button. In the confirmation box, click Stop Classic. You return to the desktop, no harm done.

When all the bouncing stops, you'll see a number of changes on your screen. Your Apple menu is now rainbow-striped, as it was in the days before Mac OS X, and it lists whatever programs, documents, and other icons you've put there. The menu bar is light gray, its fonts are smaller, and its menus and commands are different. In short, you've now gone back in time to Mac OS 9.

Note: As an entire operating system, Mac OS 9 could well be the subject of an entire book unto itself—like *Mac OS 9: The Missing Manual.* The rest of this book assumes that you either know Mac OS 9 already or have a good source of information to help you with it.

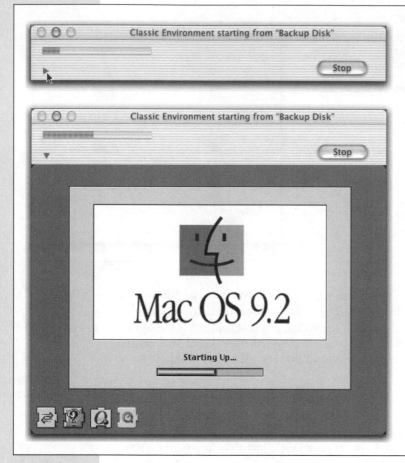

Figure 5-2:
Top: Starting up Classic involves waiting for the progress bar to fill up.

Bottom: If you click the flippy triangle to the left of the progress bar, you summon what looks like the full screen of a Macintosh floating within your own Mac's monitor, showing the standard extensions and control panel icons, the Mac OS 9 logo, and other landmarks of the traditional Mac OS 9 startup process.

Launch it manually

You can also start up Classic manually, although you'll rarely have much need to do so. The master control panel for controlling Classic is in System Preferences, and it works like this:

1. **Open System Preferences.**

   You can choose →System Preferences, or click the System Preferences icon in the Dock. Either way, in a moment, the System Preferences window appears (see Chapter 8).

2. **Click the Classic icon.**

   Now the Classic preference panel appears, as shown in Figure 5-3.

At this point, you'll see a list of every disk that contains a Mac OS 9 System Folder, also shown in Figure 5-3. Any one of them can serve as the System Folder that runs when you enter the world of Classic. Make sure the right one is selected; more on this topic later in this chapter.

3. **To start Classic manually, click Start.**

   Water appears to flow into the progress bar, exactly as shown in Figure 5-2. (If the Start button is dimmed, check the boldface message above the list of disks. It may be that Classic is already running.)

Tip: You can also add the icon of Classic to your Dock, creating a quick and easy way to launch it without having to burrow into System Preferences. Open your hard drive→System→Library→CoreServices folder. Inside this folder, you'll find an icon called Classic Startup. Drag it onto your Dock, where it will remain for easy access.

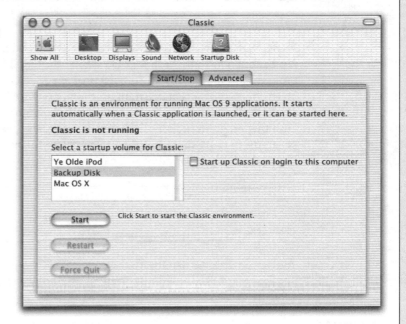

Figure 5-3:
This preference panel lets you specify which Mac OS 9 System Folder takes over when you launch the Classic mode.

Start up Classic automatically

If you find yourself using Classic every day, you'll have by far the best time with Mac OS X if you instruct it to start up Classic *automatically* when the computer turns on (or, if you share your Mac with others, when you log in). It's true that your Mac will now take an extra minute or so to start up each day, as it loads first one operating system (Mac OS X), and then another (Mac OS 9). But you won't care. You'll be reading the paper and drinking coffee. And when you do need to run a Mac OS 9 program, you won't have to wait while Classic starts up. The environment will already be waiting for you.

Getting Classic to start up automatically is extremely easy. Follow steps 1 and 2 in the preceding instructions—but at step 3, turn on "Startup Classic on login to this computer." Close the System Preferences window.

From now on, Classic will automatically launch when you turn on, or log into, your Mac.

What to Expect from Classic

Once Classic is running, you're free to use the Mac OS 9 program you originally double-clicked—or any other Mac OS 9 programs, for that matter. You'll probably find, in fact, that Mac OS 9 programs launch even faster in Classic than they would on an actual Mac OS 9 computer.

Tip: The "soundtrack" feature of the Appearance control panel (⌘ menu→Control Panels) can slow down some Classic operations quite a bit, especially scrolling. Leave it off for best speed.

Remember, you're running two operating systems simultaneously. You can freely flip back and forth between Mac OS 9 and Mac OS X: When you click a Mac OS X program's icon on the Dock (or click inside a Mac OS X program's window), you bring forward *both* that program and Mac OS X. When you double-click a Mac OS 9's Dock icon (or click inside a Mac OS 9 program's window), you bring forward both that program and Mac OS 9. You can copy and paste information between the programs you have running in these two worlds—or even drag-and-drop highlighted material, exactly as described in Chapter 6.

Note: If you can't seem to paste something into Mac OS X that you just copied from a Classic program, wait a moment and try again. Classic requires a moment of silence before it passes the copied material into the future.

You'll soon discover that the icons of open Mac OS 9 programs appear on the Dock, just like Mac OS X programs. (Well, maybe not *exactly* like them: pre–Mac OS X

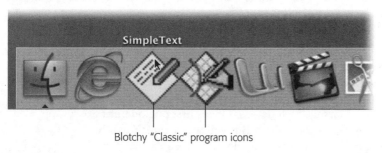

Figure 5-4:
Most pre–Mac OS X programs exhibit ragged icons on the Dock—a side effect of being enlarged to Mac OS X size. There are some exceptions: For example, Microsoft knew about Mac OS X in time to design Mac OS X-style icons for Office 2001.

SimpleText

Blotchy "Classic" program icons

programs generally show up with blotchy, ragged program icons on the Dock, as shown in Figure 5-4.)

It's important to note, however, that Mac OS 9 is no more stable now than it ever was. It doesn't offer Mac OS X's memory protection, multithreading, preemptive multitasking, and other goodies. The bottom line is that one buggy program can still freeze or crash the entire Classic bubble. At that point, you may have to exit the entire Mac OS 9 portion of your machine, losing unsaved changes in any of your Mac OS 9 programs, just as though it were a Mac OS 9 machine that had locked up.

On the other hand, even when your Classic world goes down, you won't have to restart the actual computer. Mac OS X soldiers on, unaffected, and all your Mac OS X programs remain safe, open, and running.

POWER USERS' CLINIC

Dr. Jekyll and Mr. Carbon

You may recall from the previous chapter that Mac OS X-compatible programs come in two flavors: Cocoa (that is, written expressly for Mac OS X) and Carbon (usually those that have adapted for Mac OS X from a previous version). Carbonized programs generally offer a unique feature: they can run in either Mac OS 9 or Mac OS X, unmodified.

But you probably have both Mac OS 9 and Mac OS X installed on your Mac. Maybe you even have Classic running, ready to open any Mac OS 9 program you happen to double-click. What happens, then, when you click the icon of a Carbonized program, such as Internet Explorer? Will it open in Mac OS X or the Classic environment? And can you control what happens?

The answer is: yes, it's all up to you. You can specify whether a particular Carbon program will open in Mac OS 9 (Classic) or Mac OS X by highlighting its application icon and then choosing File→Show Info. In the Show Info window, you'll find the checkbox illustrated here: "Open in the Classic environment." If you turn that box on, double-clicking that program's icon opens it in Classic instead of Mac OS X.

That's good to know for winning a bar bet or running an old AppleScript applet, perhaps, but otherwise rarely useful, since almost every program runs better in Mac OS X than in Mac OS 9.

Getting Out of Classic

There's really no good reason to quit the Classic simulator, ever. Because Classic is a genuine Mac OS X program, it doesn't consume any memory or horsepower to speak of when it's in the background. You may as well leave it open so that you won't have to wait for the startup process the next time you want to use a Mac OS 9 program.

In fact, Classic doesn't even distract you by putting its icon on the Dock. Apple hoped to make the Classic experience seamless by hiding its Dock icon once Classic is running. The idea was that you shouldn't really care whether one program or another is running in Mac OS 9 or Mac OS X. All application icons—whether in

Classic or not—show up on the Dock, and clicking one switches to it, whether in Mac OS 9 or Mac OS X. (Of course, this theory falls apart somewhat when you consider the changes in the menu, menu bar, window design, and so on, but let's not quibble.)

There are a few situations when you might want to quit Classic manually, however. For example, you might want to close it following a system crash or lockup within Classic, or you might want to restart Classic after making changes to its extensions, control panels, drivers, or other System Folder elements.

You can exit Classic in any of several ways:

- In the System Preferences panel shown in Figure 5-3, click Stop or Restart. The Mac invites you to save the changes to any open documents, if necessary.

- If your Classic environment has frozen or crashed, it may be too late for clicking the Stop button, saving your unsaved changes, and so on. In that case, you may have to *force quit* your Classic program—that is, shut it down with the subtlety of a sledgehammer. You lose any unsaved changes in any Classic programs, but at least you escape the freeze or crash.

  You can force quit Classic just as you would any program, by pressing Option-⌘-Esc and then proceeding as described on page 94. (In the list that appears, click Classic Environment and then click Force Quit.) And if you can't remember that keystroke, remember that you can always accomplish the same thing by clicking Force Quit in the System Preferences window shown in Figure 5-3.

POWER USERS' CLINIC

Preserving Bookmarks Across the Switch

If you browse the Web using Internet Explorer in both Mac OS X and in Classic, you may have cursed the inconvenience of having to maintain two separate lists of favorite Web sites—and of having to lose your history trail every time you switch from one browser to the other. Fortunately, you don't have to.

All you have to do is replace your Mac OS X Favorites and History files with *aliases* of your Mac OS 9 Favorites and History files.

That's the short version: here's the full story.

Open your Mac OS 9 System Folder (the one you've selected for use in the Classic mode—see Figure 5-3). Open its Preferences→Explorer folder. Inside are two critical files: *Favorites.html* (your bookmarks) and *History.html* (the list

of Web sites you've visited recently). Create aliases of them on the desktop; the easiest way is to Option-⌘-drag them there.

The next task is to put them in the right place in your Mac OS X world. Start by opening your own Home folder (choose Go→Home or press Option-⌘-H). In it, open the Library→Preferences folder. Drag your two aliases, Favorites.html and History.html, onto the Explorer folder icon. Mac OS X asks you if you're sure you want to replace the existing files of the same names. You are.

That's all there is to it. Whenever you use Internet Explorer, whether in Mac OS X or in Classic, you'll see the same, up-to-date set of favorites (bookmarks), and your history list will always be current.

Tip: In some cases, force quitting a frozen Classic isn't enough. You may also need to quit *TruBlue-Environment,* an invisible program that also runs when Classic does. TruBlue doesn't show up in the Force Quit dialog box. It does, however, show up in Process Viewer (page 246). If you double-click its name there, you can force quit it (if, indeed, it's still running).

Specifying a Classic System Folder

Classic doesn't operate at all unless you have a Mac OS 9 System Folder on your Mac somewhere. (See Appendix C for instructions on installing Mac OS 9 and Mac OS X.)

On the other hand, it's perfectly legal, in the world of Mac OS X, to have *more* than one Mac OS 9 System Folder on board—and many people do. You may want to designate one of them exclusively for use in Classic. (You might want to use a second one for *dual booting,* as described at the end of this chapter.) Note, however, that for Classic purposes, each Mac OS 9 System Folder must sit on a different disk or disk partition (see Appendix C).

To choose which Mac OS 9 System Folder you want Classic to use, open the Classic panel of System Preferences, as described on page 130. You'll find a tidy list of every disk, hard drive, and drive partition that contains a working Mac OS 9 System Folder; as shown in Figure 5-3, you can simply click the one you'll want to take control when you enter the Classic environment.

Why does it matter? Because the System Folder you select here affects how much time it takes Classic to start up, which extensions and control panels it has (and therefore how stable it is), what preference settings are taken for your various programs, what Web-browser bookmarks are available, and so on.

Controlling Classic Startup

If you're smart or lucky, you'll eventually figure out a way to eliminate the Classic startup delay altogether. For example, you can set up Classic so that it opens automatically at startup or login. Or maybe you'll get into the habit of never shutting down your computer at all, allowing it simply to sleep when not in use, so that Classic remains running essentially forever. Or you may eventually move almost all your operations into Mac OS X programs, rendering Classic obsolete—the dream of everyone who uses Mac OS X.

But if you find yourself having to open—and wait for—Classic every day, you might find it valuable to shave down the amount of time it takes to get going. The best way to do that is to turn off as many extensions and control panels as possible. That's just one of the ways you can control the Classic startup process, as described in the following section.

Summoning Extensions Manager

By the time Mac OS X arrived on the scene, the System Folder of its predecessor, Mac OS 9, was caked solid with extensions and control panels (self-launching software that loads into memory at startup time). Each controls some function of the

Mac, but taken together, they account for much of the standard Mac OS 9's propensity to freeze, crash, and otherwise act up.

Within the Classic world, you don't need many of these extensions anymore. Remember that Classic is a workaround, not your main operating system; Mac OS X now duplicates many of its functions (and in a much superior way). Turning off as many Mac OS 9 extensions as possible, therefore, makes using your Classic environment a much smoother and more stable experience, and makes Classic start up much faster.

The key to controlling which extensions load is to press and hold the Space bar *just* after the progress bar begins filling up, as shown in Figure 5-5. Release the Space bar only after you see the appearance of the Extensions Manager window.

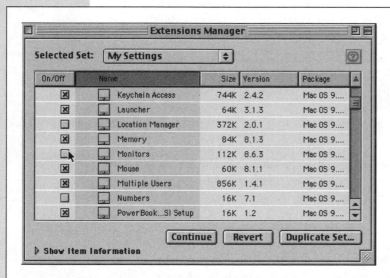

Figure 5-5:
Pressing the Space bar while Classic is starting up opens Extensions Manager, just as though you pressed Space while starting up a Mac OS 9 computer.

Extensions Manager, of course, is the Mac OS 9 program that lets you turn certain extensions or control panels on and off. One of its most useful features is its ability to create canned *sets* that permit you to switch among sets of preselected extension combinations with a single mouse click. You use the Selected Set pop-up menu at the top to switch among them.

To begin setting up your winnowed-down extension set, click Duplicate Set in the lower-right corner of the window. In the dialog box that appears, type a name for the set you're about to create (such as *Classic Speedy Startup*), and then click OK.

Extensions to turn off

Now you're ready to start paring down the extensions and control panels that make Classic take so long to start up (and so prone to crashes). Depending on what functions you need to use in Classic, you might consider turning off the extensions and control panels in these function categories (by clicking their checkboxes so that the X no longer appears):

- **Control Panels.** Many of Mac OS 9's control-panel functions are superseded by new panels in the Mac OS X System Preferences (see Chapter 8). Changing your mouse speed using Mac OS 9's Mouse control panel, for example, doesn't have much meaning if you've already set your mouse speed in Mac OS X.

  Therefore, you should turn off the following control panels immediately—they don't work in Classic and gain you nothing: Control Strip, Energy Saver, File Sharing, Infrared, Location Manager, Modem, Monitors, Mouse, Multiple Users, Password Security, PowerBook SCSI Disk Mode, Remote Access, Software Update, TCP/IP, Trackpad, and Web Sharing.

Note: These Mac OS 9 control panels work, although with limited functions, within Classic: Appearance, AppleTalk, Date & Time (for menu-bar clock control only), General Controls (some commands, like Show Desktop, are dimmed), Keyboard (duplicated functions are dimmed), Memory (Disk Cache only), Monitors, and Sound (for alert sounds only).

- **Internet.** If you've moved your Web-surfing, email, and remote dial-in operations over to Mac OS X, you may have little need for the equivalent functions in the Classic environment. If that's the case, you can safely turn off DialAssist, Internet, Location Manager Extension, Apple Modem Tool, Internet V.90 Modem (and other modem names, such as PowerBook Modem), the LDAP extensions, NBP Plugin, NetSprocketLib, Remote Only, and ShareWay IP Personal Bgnd, in addition to the control panels listed above. You may as well turn off the Software Update extensions, too, because they rely on Internet access.

- **Networking, Multi-User features.** Most of Mac OS X's networking and Mac-sharing features far outshine those in Mac OS 9. So if you won't be connecting to other computers on your office network from within Classic, you may as well turn off AppleTalk, any AirPort extensions, Keychain Access, IrDA Tool and IrDALib, Apple Enet, Apple Enet DLPI Support, AppleShare, EnetShimLib, File Sharing Extension, File Sharing Library, Multi-User Startup, OpenTpt Remote Access, Network Setup Extension, and SLPPlugin

- **Printing.** If you don't plan to print from within Classic programs, you can turn off anything containing the words Print, Printer, Printing, or ColorSync, as well as the extensions bearing specific printer names (Color SW 1500, Color SW 2500, LaserWriter, and so on).

- **DVD.** The old, Mac OS 9-style DVD Player program doesn't even work in Classic. Turn off everything containing DVD in its name.

- **CD burning.** Here again, Mac OS X does a far better job of burning CDs than Mac OS 9 does. For example, Mac OS X can even burn data *DVDs,* which hold a delightful 4.7 GB per disc. By all means, turn off the Disc Burner Extension.

- **Video games.** A few video games require the OpenGL, QuickDraw 3D, NVIDIA, and ATI extensions. If you're a gamer, you'll experience the best game play by *restarting* your Mac in Mac OS 9 (see page 140) rather than trying to play Mac OS 9 games in the Classic mode. If you agree, turn off all extensions that contain the words QuickDraw 3D, OpenGL, NVIDIA, and ATI.

- **FireWire.** Even if you have a digital camcorder for use with iMovie, you may as well turn off the FireWire extensions, because the Mac OS X version of iMovie is better than the Mac OS 9 version. Leave the FireWire extensions on only if you have FireWire gadgets like external hard drives that you want to access from within Mac OS 9.

Once your pruning session is complete, click Continue. You should find that the Classic mode now starts up dramatically faster than before.

Note: These are only suggestions. If, after turning off some of these extensions and control panels, you find that certain familiar Mac OS 9 functions are no longer available, exit Classic, restart it with the Space bar pressed again, and experiment with restoring some of the things you turned off. And if you don't have the time to fiddle with individual extension settings, you can always turn on the entire Apple-authorized original set by choosing Mac OS 9 All (or Mac OS 9.2.1 All, or whatever) from the Selected Set pop-up menu.

Extensions to leave on

You can't go totally hog-wild turning off System Folder elements. Classic expects to find certain System Folder items when it launches. If you turn them off, an error message will explain that "Some Classic-specific resources need to be added to or updated in your System Folder on [Disk Name]." If you click OK, Mac OS X copies them into the Mac OS 9 System Folder. Here's a list, current as of Mac OS 9.2.1:

- *Control Panels:* General, Startup Disk.

- *Extensions:* Apple Guide, CarbonLib, Classic RAVE, Open Transport, Open Transport ASLM Modules.

- *Loose in the System Folder:* Classic Support, Classic Support UI, ProxyApp.

"Holding down keys" during startup

On a Mac OS 9 machine, holding down certain keys during the startup process triggers certain utility functions. Pressing Shift, for example, turns off all extensions and control panels. Holding down Option and ⌘ eventually rebuilds the desktop database file, a Mac OS 9 troubleshooting technique that can cure general slowdowns as well as the "generic," blank-icon problem. If you've installed Conflict Catcher, a commercial extensions manager, a wide range of startup-process keystrokes is available: ⌘-P for pause, ⌘-R for restart, and so on.

As Classic is starting up, these keystrokes work exactly as they do when a Mac OS 9 Mac is starting up. That is, if you press Shift immediately after the Classic progress bar appears on the screen, you'll see the usual "Extensions Off" message in the middle of the simulated Mac OS 9 startup screen. Similarly, if you hold down the Option and ⌘ keys as the extension-loading process comes to an end, you'll eventually be offered the opportunity to rebuild the desktop. (Well, sort of. After Classic has finished loading, click the blank-document icon that appears in your Dock with the name Classic Support UI, to bring forward the "Are you sure you want to rebuild the desktop?" dialog box.)

Still, Apple's engineers worried that you might find it difficult to gauge when the right moment is to hold down these various startup keys, so they offer you an alternative method of holding them down.

To see it, open the Advanced tab of the Classic preference panel (see Figure 5-6).

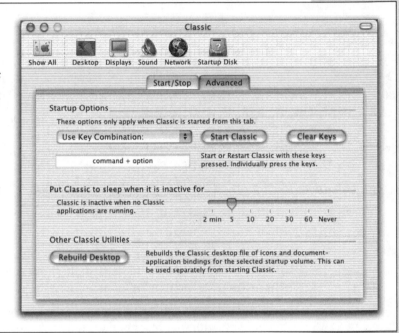

Figure 5-6:
The Advanced tab of the Classic panel lets you specify what keys you want "held down" for you as Classic starts up. It also lets you specify when Classic can "sleep"—that is, to slip down into virtual memory, returning the RAM (and processor attention) it was claiming to the general pool. Once it's sleeping, Classic programs take slightly longer to open—but not nearly as much as when you start Classic for the first time.

On this tab, you'll find a pop-up menu that helps you control the startup process:

- **Turn Off Extensions.** If you choose this command and then click the Start Classic (or Restart Classic) button next to it, you'll launch the Classic emulator with all extensions turned off, just as though you had held down the Shift key during its startup.

- **Open Extensions Manager.** If you choose this command and then click Start Classic (or Restart Classic), the Mac behaves as though you had pressed the Space bar while Classic was starting up. As a result, the Extensions Manager window opens, just as described on page 135.

- **Use Key Combination.** This option is designed to accommodate all other startup keys, such as those available in Conflict Catcher. Start by clicking in the <press up to five keys> box. Now you can press up to five different keys (one at a time, please) that the Mac will "hold down" when you start Classic by clicking the Start Classic (or Restart Classic) button in this dialog box. As you press the keys, you'll see them recorded in the text box.

Note that whatever option you choose from the pop-up menu will apply only to the next Classic startup you trigger *from within this dialog box*. These options don't affect Classic when you start it up in any of the usual ways.

Tip: You don't have to press Option-⌘ when Classic is starting up if you want to rebuild the Desktop file. The Rebuild Desktop button in this dialog box does the trick automatically, without your even having to launch Classic at all.

Restarting in Mac OS 9

Classic mode is a terrific technical achievement. If you're lucky, it's the only trace of Mac OS 9 you'll ever see once you've taken the Mac OS X plunge.

Unfortunately, Classic can only get you so far. Sure enough, it fakes out your older software fairly well—but your Mac is not *actually* running Mac OS 9. Anytime a piece of software tries to communicate with some physical component of your Mac, such as the SCSI, USB, FireWire, or serial ports, it will bruise its knuckles on the stainless-steel dome of Mac OS X, which is *really* in charge of your ports. That's why a lot of add-on equipment, including USB-to-serial adapters, certain printers, SCSI cards, scanners, and so on may not run properly when you're running programs in the Classic environment.

What this kind of equipment really needs, of course, is Mac OS X-specific driver software. If drivers exist (check the manufacturer's Web site), you can once again use your gear.

Otherwise, you have only one alternative when you want your external gadgets to work properly with your Mac just the way they did when it ran Mac OS 9: restart the Mac *in* Mac OS 9.

Oh yes, you can do that. Anytime you like, you can flip back into Mac OS 9 and return to complete compatibility with all your old gadgets and all your old programs. When you're finished, you can restart the Mac again, this time with Mac OS X "in charge." This ability to switch back and forth between two radically different operating systems on the same computer is called *dual booting*.

Dual Booting the Long Way

The key to switching back and forth between Mac OS 9 and Mac OS X is the Startup Disk control panel (or System Preferences panel).

Switching from Mac OS X to Mac OS 9

Suppose you're running Mac OS X, and you need to duck back into Mac OS 9 to use, say, your scanner. The routine goes like this.

1. **Open System Preferences.**

   As always, you can do it by clicking the System Preferences icon on the Dock or by choosing menu→System Preferences. The System Preferences screen appears.

2. **Click Startup Disk.**

   You now see the panel shown at top in Figure 5-7. The icons here represent the various System folders, both Mac OS 9 and Mac OS X flavors, that your Mac has found on all disks currently attached to your Mac.

   You may see several system folders displayed here. If you're wise, you'll have deliberately set up at least two of them: one for use by Classic, and another, more complete one for use when restarting the Mac. Details on this thinking are on page 143.

Figure 5-7:
Top: If you're running Mac OS X, you can indicate that you'd like Mac OS 9 to seize control at the next startup by using the Startup Disk system-preference panel. If you're having trouble telling the System Folders apart (because, after all, System Preferences shows you only their System versions and disk names, not their folder names), point to the folder icon until the identifying yellow balloon appears.

Bottom: If you're running Mac OS 9, you use the Startup Disk control panel to specify that you want Mac OS X to be in charge at the next startup.

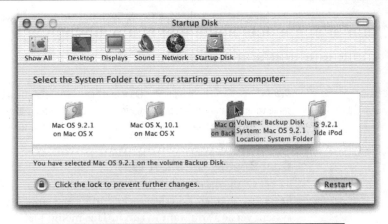

3. **Click the Mac OS 9 System Folder you'll want to be in charge, and then click Restart.**

   The Mac asks you: "Are you sure you want to set the Startup disk and restart the computer?"

4. **Click "Save and Restart" (or press Enter).**

   Your Mac restarts, and you'll feel like it's 1999 all over again. There go the parade of extension icons, the Mac OS 9 logo, and all the other trappings of the traditional, pre–Mac OS X startup process. You're now fully back in Mac OS 9, ready to use all your old add-on equipment and software (but without the benefit of Mac OS X's stability, good looks, and other features).

Switching from Mac OS 9 to Mac OS X

The process of returning to Mac OS X is very similar.

1. **Choose →Control Panels→Startup Disk.**

   The Startup Disk control panel appears, as shown in Figure 5-7. Click the "flippy triangle" next to a disk's name, if necessary, to see the list of System folders on it.

2. **Click the specific Mac OS X System folder you'll want to be in charge, and then click Restart.**

   Mac OS X starts up.

Big fat tip: If you have both Mac OS 9 and Mac OS X installed on the same hard drive (technically, the same volume), and you last started up from Mac OS 9, you can skip these steps. Use this shortcut instead: Just hold down the letter X key while the Mac is starting up. You'll go straight to Mac OS X.

Dual Booting the Short Way

There's a sneaky shortcut that lets you forget about all the preceding steps—a single keystroke that lets you decide, each time the computer turns on, which operating-system version you want to run it. This method lets you postpone making the decision until the moment you actually turn the thing on, instead of having to make the switch after the computer has already started up.

Note, however, that this technique works only if you've installed Mac OS 9 and Mac OS X on different disks or different *partitions* of a single disk. You'll find instructions for setting up multiple partitions—and installing different operating system versions on them—in Appendix C.

Now you're ready. Turn on the Mac. Just as it's lighting up, hold down the Option key. Hold it down until you see the display illustrated in Figure 5-8.

This screen, known inside Apple as the Startup Manager, offers icons for every disk, CD, or partition containing a working System folder (either Mac OS 9 or Mac OS X).

Just click the one you'll want to start up the Mac and then click the "continue" button. Without missing a beat, your Mac continues to start up using the operating system you selected.

Clearly, this technique requires a bit of preparation and planning—not just because it requires different disks or partitions, but also because it limits you to having one System folder on each. The display shown in Figure 5-8 offers a list of startup *disks,* not System *folders.* (The Startup Disk method described above, by contrast, lets you choose from among several System folders on the same disk.)

Still, if you find that switching between Mac OS 9 and Mac OS X is a daily feature of your work routine, you may decide to bite the bullet and partition your hard drive (or buy a second, external one) just to gain the convenience of this switching-at-startup feature.

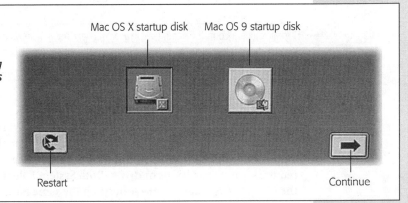

Mac OS X startup disk   *Mac OS 9 startup disk*

Figure 5-8:
This display, known as the Startup Manager, appears when you press Option during startup. It shows you the icons of all the disks, or disk partitions, that contain working System folders. Just click the icon you want, and then click the arrow button at the lower right.

Restart   Continue

Separate System Folders for Classic and Rebooting

If you've really thought this through, it may have dawned on you that the ideal Mac OS 9 System Folder for use in the Classic emulator program makes a lousy System Folder for restarting your Mac, and vice versa.

The Mac OS 9 System Folder you want for Classic is a slimmed-down, streamlined System Folder with as few extensions and drivers as possible. Here, your aim is to make Mac OS 9 launch as quickly, and to be as stable, as possible. When you restart the Mac in Mac OS 9, on the other hand, you want maximum compatibility. You want all your Mac's features intact, especially the drivers that will operate your external equipment.

Maintaining a single Mac OS 9 System Folder

You *can* maintain a single Mac OS 9 System Folder on your Mac, of course. You can simply use Extensions Manager (or Conflict Catcher, if you have it) to create two different sets of extensions: one for use in Classic and one for use when restarting the Mac. You can use the Select Set pop-up menu (see Figure 5-5) to switch sets.

Obviously, this method presents one massive inconvenience: You have to remember to press the Space bar every time Mac OS 9 starts up (either in Classic or when dual booting) in order to summon Extensions Manager to make the switch. (Technically, you wouldn't have to open Extensions Manager *every* time—only when switching the function of your Mac OS 9 System Folder [Classic or dual booting].)

This option can work just fine if:

- you do most of your Mac OS 9 work in Classic, and you find yourself rebooting in Mac OS 9 only occasionally, or

- you do most of your Mac OS 9 work by restarting the Mac into Mac OS 9, and you rely on Classic only occasionally.

In other words, the only inconvenient aspect of this setup is switching the function of your single Mac OS 9 System Folder.

Tip: If you have Conflict Catcher (*www.casadyg.com*), this single-System Folder business is much simpler. Its auto-detect feature can load one set of extensions when Classic is starting up, and a different set when you restart the Mac into Mac OS 9–all automatically.

Maintaining two different Mac OS 9 System Folders

Some people maintain *two separate* Mac OS 9 System Folders: one that's trimmed down for use in Classic (see Figure 5-3), and another that loads a complete set of extensions and drivers for use in restarting the Mac (Figure 5-8). This method doesn't require separate partitions or drives. Both System Folders—or all three, if you count the Mac OS X System folder—can sit on the same hard drive.

This arrangement frees you from the inconvenience of having to switch extension sets when switching a single System folder's function. But it comes with a hassle of its own: You're now maintaining duplicate sets of preference settings, Web bookmarks, and the like.

Suppose you bookmark a Web site when running a Classic Web browser. The next day, when you reboot into Mac OS 9, your Web browser no longer lists that bookmark—because Mac OS 9 stores its bookmark lists, like its preference files, inside the System Folder that's "in charge" at the time.

Fortunately, this inconvenience, too, may turn out to be a red herring, depending on your purpose in using Mac OS 9. The Web bookmark example really isn't a good one, for example, because you probably wouldn't want to use *any* version of Mac OS 9 for Web browsing—excellent Web browsers are available right in Mac OS X. In real life, most people reboot into Mac OS 9 only for special purposes like scanning or using an old CD burner that doesn't work in Mac OS X or Classic. In these cases, the fact that each Mac OS 9 System Folder is maintaining a duplicate set of preference files will probably have little impact on your life, if you even notice it at all.

Exchanging Data

The original 1984 Mac didn't make jaws drop because of its speed, price, or sleek looks. What amazed people most was the simplicity and elegance of the user interface. At some point in every Apple demo, the presenter copied a graphic drawn in a painting program (MacPaint) and pasted it directly into a word processor (MacWrite), where it appeared neatly nestled between typed paragraphs of text.

We take this example of data exchange for granted today; but in those days, that simple act struck people like a thunderbolt. After all, if this little computer let you copy and paste between different programs, it could probably do anything.

Today, the Mac is even better at helping you move and share your hard-won data. Mac OS X offers several different ways to move information within a single document, between documents, between different programs, and even between the Mac and Windows computers. This chapter leads you through this broad range of data-exchange mechanisms.

Moving Data Between Documents

You can't paste a picture into your Web browser, and you can't paste MIDI music information into your word processor. But you can put graphics into your word processor, paste movies into your database, insert text into GraphicConverter, and combine a surprising variety of seemingly dissimilar kinds of data.

Cut, Copy, and Paste

The original copy-and-paste procedure of 1984—putting a graphic into a word processor—has come a long way. Most experienced Mac users have learned to trigger the Cut, Copy, and Paste commands from the keyboard, quickly and without even thinking. Here's how the process works:

1. **Highlight some material in the document before you.**

   In most cases, this means highlighting some text (by dragging through it) in a word processor, layout program, Web-design program, or even a Web page in your browser. You can also highlight graphics, music, movie, database, and spreadsheet information, depending on the program you're using.

2. **Use the Cut or Copy command.**

   You can either choose the Cut and Copy commands found in the Edit menu of almost every Mac program, or press the keyboard shortcuts ⌘-X (for Cut—think of the X as representing a pair of scissors) or ⌘-C (for Copy). When you do so, the Macintosh memorizes the highlighted material, socking it away on an invisible storage pad called the Clipboard. (If you chose Copy, nothing visible happens. If you chose Cut, the highlighted material disappears from the original document.)

   At this point, most Mac fans take it on faith that the Cut or Copy command actually worked—but if you're in doubt, switch to the Finder (by clicking its Dock icon, for example), and then choose Edit→Show Clipboard. The Clipboard window appears, showing whatever you've copied.

3. **Click the cursor to indicate where you want the material to reappear.**

   This may entail switching to a different program, a different document in the same program, a program running in Classic mode, or simply a different place in the same document. (Using the Cut and Paste commands within a single document may be these commands' most popular function; it lets you rearrange sentences or paragraphs in your word processor.)

GEM IN THE ROUGH

Styled Text

When you copy text from, for example, Word X, and then paste it into another program, such as Mail, you may be pleasantly surprised to note that the formatting of that text—bold, italic, your choice of font, size, and color, and so on—appears intact in Mail. You're witnessing one of the Mac's most useful but under-publicized features: its support for *styled text* on the Clipboard.

Not every Mac program on earth transfers the formatting along with the copied text, but almost all Mac OS X-compatible programs do. Every time you paste text copied from one of these programs, the pasted material appears with the same typographical characteristics it had in the original program. Over time, this tiny time-saver spares us years' worth of cumulative reformatting effort—yet another tiny favor the noble Macintosh does mankind.

4. Choose the Paste command.

Here again, you can do so either from a menu (choose Edit→Paste) or from the keyboard (press ⌘-V)—and in many programs, even by clicking a toolbar button. The copy of the material you had originally highlighted now appears at your insertion point—that is, if you're pasting into a program that can accept that kind of information. (You won't have much luck pasting, say, a paragraph of text into Quicken.)

The most recently cut or copied material remains on your Clipboard even after you paste, making it possible to paste the same blob repeatedly. Such a trick can be useful when, for example, you've designed a business card in your drawing program and want to duplicate it enough times to fill a letter-sized printout. On the other hand, whenever you next copy or cut something, whatever was already on the Clipboard is lost forever.

Drag-and-Drop

As useful and popular as it is, the Copy/Paste routine doesn't win any awards for speed; after all, it requires four steps. In many cases, you can replace that routine with the far more direct (and enjoyable) drag-and-drop method. Figure 6-1 shows how it works.

Note: As noted in Chapter 4, some Mac OS X programs (*Cocoa* programs) require you to press the mouse button for half a second before beginning to drag.

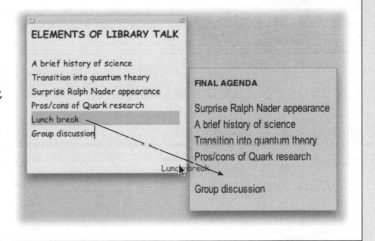

Figure 6-1:
To use drag-and-drop, highlight some material. Click in the middle of the highlighted area; press the mouse button for about half a second. Now, with the button pressed continuously, drag to another place in the document, into a different window, or into a different application. As your cursor enters the target window, a shaded outline appears inside the window's boundaries—the Mac's way of letting you know that it understands your intention. When you release the mouse, the highlighted material appears instantly in its new location.

Virtually every Mac OS X program works with the drag-and-drop technique, including TextEdit, Stickies, Mail, Sherlock, QuickTime Player, Preview, iMovie, and Apple System Profiler, not to mention commercial programs like Microsoft applications, America Online, and so on.

When to use drag-and-drop

As shown in Figure 6-1, drag-and-drop is ideal for transferring material between windows or between programs. It's especially useful when you've already copied something valuable to your Clipboard, because drag-and-drop doesn't involve (and doesn't erase) the Clipboard.

Its most popular use, however, is rearranging the text in a single document. In Word or AppleWorks, for example, you can rearrange entire sections, paragraphs, sentences, or even individual letters, just by dragging them—a great editing technique.

Tip: When you use drag-and-drop to move text within a document, the Mac *moves* the highlighted text, deleting the highlighted material from its original location. If you press Option as you drag, however, you make a *copy* of the highlighted text.

Using drag-and-drop to the desktop

You can also use drag-and-drop in the one program you use every single day: the Finder itself. As shown in Figure 6-2, you can drag text, graphics, sounds, and even movie clips out of your document windows and directly onto the desktop. There your dragged material generally becomes an icon called a *clipping file*.

Note: Internet Explorer 5.1 and a few other programs create text files instead. Nobody's perfect.

When you drag a clipping from your desktop *back* into an application window, the material in that clipping reappears. Drag-and-drop, in other words, lets you treat your desktop itself as a giant, computer-wide pasteboard—an area where you can temporarily stash pieces of text or graphics as you work.

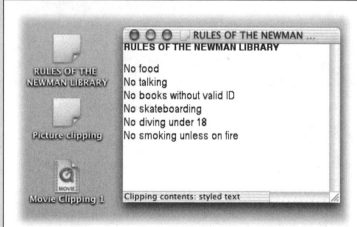

Figure 6-2:
When you drag material out of the document window and onto the desktop, you get a clipping file. Its icon depends on the kind of material contained within: from top, a text clipping, picture clipping, and movie clipping. (Mac OS X conveniently titles text clippings with the first line of the text contained inside for easy identification.) You can view a clipping just by double-clicking it, so that it opens into its own window (right).

Tip: When the material you drag to the desktop contains nothing but an Internet address, such as an email address or Web page URL, Mac OS X gives it a special icon and a special function: an *Internet location document*. See page 452 for details.

Export/Import

When it comes to transferring large chunks of information—especially address books, spreadsheet cells, and database records—from one program to another, none of the data-transfer methods described so far in this chapter do the trick. For these purposes, use the Export and Import commands found in the File menu of almost every database, spreadsheet, email, and address-book program.

These Export/Import commands aren't part of Mac OS X, so the manuals (if any) of the applications in question should be your source for instructions. For now, however, the power and convenience of this feature are worth noting—it means that your four years' worth of collected addresses in, say, your old email program can find its way into a newer program, such as Mail, in a matter of minutes.

Exchanging Data with Windows PCs

It's no surprise that the Mac is great at transferring information among Mac programs. The big news is how easy Mac OS X makes it to transfer files between Macs and Windows computers:

Documents can take one of three roads between your Mac and a Windows machine: you can transfer it on a disk (such as a CD or Zip disk), over an Ethernet cable (if you're on an office network), or as an attachment to an email message.

Preparing the Document for Transfer

Without special adapters, you can't plug an American appliance into a European power outlet, play a CD on a cassette deck, or open a Macintosh file in Windows. Before sending a document to a colleague who uses Windows, you must be able to answer "yes" to both of these questions:

Is the document in a file format Windows understands?

Most popular programs are sold in both Mac and Windows flavors, and the documents they create are freely interchangeable. For example, documents created by recent versions of Word, Excel, PowerPoint, FileMaker, FreeHand, Illustrator, Apple-Works, Photoshop, Dreamweaver, and many other Mac programs don't need any conversion. The corresponding Windows versions of those programs open such documents with nary a hiccup.

Files in one of the standard exchange formats don't need conversion, either. These formats include JPEG (the photo format used on Web pages), GIF (the cartoon/logo format used on Web pages), HTML (raw Web page documents before they're posted on the Internet), Rich Text Format (a word processor exchange format that maintains bold, italic, and other formatting), plain text (no formatting at all), QIF (Quicken Interchange Format), MIDI files (for music), and so on.

But what about documents made by Mac programs that don't exist on the typical Windows-PC hard drive, such as AppleWorks 6? It's available to educators in a Windows version, but you certainly can't count on your recipient having it.

Do your recipients the favor of first saving such documents into one of the formats listed in the previous paragraphs. In AppleWorks, for example, choose File→Save As; from the File Type pop-up menu, choose "Word Win 97, 2000"; name this special version of the document (remember the .doc suffix); and then click Save.

Does the file have the correct three-letter file name suffix?

As noted in Chapter 4, every document on your hard drive has some kind of tag to tell the computer what program is supposed to open it: either a pair of invisible four-letter codes or a filename suffix like .doc.

Microsoft Windows uses *only* the latter system for identifying documents. Here are some of the most common such codes:

Kind of document	Suffix	Example
Microsoft Word	.doc	Letter to Mom.doc
Excel	.xls	Profit Projection.xls
PowerPoint	.ppt	Slide Show.ppt
FileMaker Pro	.fp3	Recipe file.fp3
JPEG photo	.jpg	Baby Portrait.jpg
GIF graphic	.gif	Logo.gif
Web page	.htm	Index.htm

The beauty of Mac OS X (starting in 10.1) is that your Mac adds these file name suffixes *automatically* and *invisibly,* every time you save a new document from a Mac OS X program. You and your Windows comrades can freely exchange documents without ever having to worry about this former snag in the Macintosh/Windows relationship.

By Disk

Once you've created a document destined for a Windows machine, your next challenge is to get it *onto* that machine. One way is to put the file on a disk—a CD you've burned, a floppy, or a Zip disk, for example—which you then hand to the Windows user. (Modern Macs don't have built-in floppy drives, of course, but millions of older Macs do, and any Mac can be equipped with an external, add-on drive. Most Windows PCs still have built-in floppy drives.)

In theory, this kind of exchange shouldn't be possible, because Macs and PCs format disks differently. When you insert a Mac floppy disk into a PC, for example, an error message declares it to be unreadable—and Windows offers to "correct" the problem by erasing the disk.

How the Mac reads Windows disks

Fortunately, although Windows can't read Mac disks, the Mac can read Windows disks. When you insert a Windows-formatted floppy, Zip, or CD into your Mac, its icon shows up on the screen just like a Mac disk. You can drag files to and from this disk (or its window), rename files, delete files, and so on, exactly as though you're working with a Mac disk. (It doesn't operate nearly as quickly as a Mac disk, though.)

Creating a Windows disk on the Mac

You can even *create* a Windows disk on your Macintosh, as long as you're willing to erase it in the process. Launch Disk Utility (in your Applications→Utilities folder), click the Erase tab, and then insert the floppy disk. Its icon should show up in the list at the left side of the window. Click it, and then use the pop-up menu to specify MS-DOS File System format—and then click Erase. After the erasing process is over, you can insert the floppy into both Macs and PCs with equal success.

By Network

Here's one of the best new features of Mac OS X: it can "see" shared disks and folders on Windows PCs. Yes, you gain more features and flexibility using a program like Dave (*www.thursby.com*), but this one is built-in and free. It's even easy. Here, for example, is how it might work in Windows XP (although the same feature works in Windows Me, Windows 2000, and other recent editions):

1. **On your Windows PC, share a folder.**

   You have to specify which folders you want to make available on the network, if some administrator hasn't already done so. In Windows XP, for example, you right-click a folder, choose Properties from the shortcut menu, click the Sharing tab, and turn on "Share this folder on the network" (Figure 6-3, top left). In the "Share name" box, type a name for the folder as it will appear on the network (no spaces are allowed).

2. **On the Mac, choose Go→Connect to Server (⌘-K).**

   The Connect to Server dialog box appears, as shown at top right in Figure 6-3.

3. **Type *smb://*, followed by the Windows machine's name or IP address. Add a slash (/) and then type the name of the shared folder.**

   In other words, what you type into the Connect box might look like this: *smb://Dell4100/drafts* or *smb://192.168.1.45/documents*.

Tip: You may have to insert your network's *workgroup name* into this address, as described in Figure 6-3 on the next page.

This isn't as much gibberish as you might think—here's how it breaks down.

SMB is the networking protocol that made its Mac debut in Mac OS X 10.1.

The next segment specifies which PC on the network you're connecting to; you can type either its name or IP address. To find out its network name, right-click the My Computer icon (in XP, choose Start→My Computer and then right-click a blank spot in the window). Choose Properties from the shortcut menu. In the resulting box, click Computer Name. (What you want is the "Full computer name," *not* the "Computer description." Capitalization counts. This is also where you find out its *workgroup name,* which you may need—see Figure 6-3.)

Finding out the IP address is trickier. In XP, choose Start→Control Panel→ Network Connections. Right-click the Local Area Connection icon, choose Properties from its shortcut menu, and double-click the Internet Protocol (TCP/IP) listing. The resulting window shows your machine's IP address.

The final part of the address is the name of the shared folder.

4. **Click Connect.**

Now the Authentication dialog box appears, as shown at bottom left in Figure 6-3.

5. **Type your name and password, if necessary, and then click OK.**

If you have an account on the Windows PC, great—use that name and password. If the PC isn't in a corporation where somebody administers access to each machine, you may be able to leave the password blank.

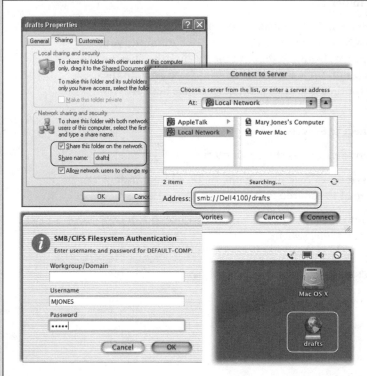

Figure 6-3:
Top left: Begin by sharing certain folders on the Windows machine.

Top right: In the Connect to Server box, type out the network address of the folder you want to access from the Mac. If the shared folder name contains spaces (My Documents), leave them out (MyDocuments).

Bottom left: Specify your name and password, if necessary. If you just get an error message, then you may need to add the PC's workgroup name, such as MSHOME, followed by a semicolon, to the address you typed in the second dialog box. The full address might look like this: smb://MSHOME;Dell4100/Drafts.

Bottom right: Like magic, the Windows folder shows up on your Mac screen, ready to use!

Now the shared folder on the Windows machine appears on your desktop with a network-drive icon (Figure 6-3, lower right), just as though you've tapped into another Mac. From there, it's a simple matter to drag files from one machine's icon to another, exactly as described in Chapter 12.

By Email Attachment

Among the most popular means of transferring files between Mac and Windows is plain old email. When using Mail, for example, you can drag any icon from your desktop directly into the email message window. The file you dragged will shortly arrive in the email box of your lucky recipient.

For many people, however, the email-attachment route is fraught with frustration. At times, it seems as though half of all attachment files arrive at the other end in unopenable condition.

In most cases, the problem is either that you're sending a document that Windows can't open, or your email program is making the attachment incompatible when it shrinks and encodes it for sending. Compression and encoding are necessary parts of the email process, as explained below; the idea is to use the proper settings so that as many people as possible will be able to open your attachments.

File compression and encoding

The technology behind email attachments is somewhat technical, but extremely useful in understanding why some attachments don't make it through the Internet alive.

When you send an email attachment, your email program does two things. First, it may *compress* the attached file so that it takes less time to send and receive.

The second process is more technical. Surprising as it may seem, the Internet cannot, in fact, transmit files—only pure text. Your email program, therefore, takes an additional moment to *encode* your file attachment, converting it into a stream of text codes that will be reconstructed by your recipient's email program.

Each of these processes can foul up file attachments.

- **File compression problems:** Some Mac email programs compress outgoing files using the StuffIt method—but Windows recipients can't open StuffIt files. When sending files to Windows computers, therefore, you can turn off the StuffIt compression option in your email program. (Alternatively, you can ask your recipient to download StuffIt Expander for Windows, available at *www.aladdinsys.com*, which can indeed open StuffIt attachments. But unless your correspondent is related to you by blood, don't expect a warm reception to this suggestion.)

  America Online is a particular problem. When you attach multiple files to a single email message, AOL uses StuffIt compression automatically—and you can't override this behavior. When sending files to Windows friends from AOL, therefore, attach only a single file per email message.

- **File encoding problems:** Most email programs offer a choice of encoding schemes, which bear such unfriendly names as MIME/Base64 (the only option in the Mail program that comes with Mac OS X), UUEncode, and AppleDouble. If you have a choice in your particular email program, use MIME/Base 64 or AppleDouble. File attachments encoded this way arrive intact on both Mac and Windows machines.

Problems receiving Windows files

When your Mac receives Windows files by email, the problems aren't so severe. Most email programs, including Mail and Entourage, decompress and decode file attachments automatically. When they don't, you can drag the downloaded file onto the icon of the free utility program StuffIt Expander (which comes with Mac OS X, in your Applications→Utilities folder). StuffIt Expander can convert almost any Internet file in existence back into human form.

It's worth noting once again, however, that not every file that came from Windows *can* be opened on a Macintosh, and vice versa. A file whose name ends in *.exe*, for example, is a double-clickable Windows application, which doesn't run on the Mac (at least, not unless you've gone to the expense and trouble of installing a Windows emulator program like Virtual PC). See the table on page 150 for some examples of files that transfer well from Windows to Mac and don't need conversion or adapters of any kind.

An Introduction to AppleScript

Y ou can think of AppleScript programs (called *scripts*) as software robots. A simple AppleScript might perform some simple daily task for you: backing up your Documents folder, for example.

A more complex script can be pages long. In professional printing and publishing, where AppleScript enjoys its greatest popularity, a script might connect to a photographer's hard drive elsewhere on the Internet, download a photo from a pre-determined folder, color-correct it in Photoshop, import it into a specified page-layout document, print a proof copy, and send a notification email to the editor—automatically.

Even if you're not aware of it, you use technology that underlies AppleScript all the time. Behind the scenes, numerous components of your Mac communicate with each other by sending *Apple Events,* which are messages bearing instructions or data that your programs send to each other. When you use the Show Original command for an alias, or the Show Info command for a file or folder, an Apple Event tells the Finder how to respond. Many of the files in the Speakable Items folder (page 369), furthermore, are AppleScripts that quit your programs, open AppleWorks, switch a window into list view, and so on.

Running Ready-Made AppleScripts

You don't have to *create* AppleScripts to get some mileage of out this technology. Mac OS X comes with several dozen prewritten scripts that are genuinely useful—and all you have to do is choose their names from a menu. "Playing back" an AppleScript in this way requires about as much technical skill as pressing an elevator button.

To sample some of these cool starter scripts, open your Applications→AppleScript folder and double-click the program called Script Runner. As shown in Figure 7-1, Script Runner is nothing more than a tiny floating palette with a pop-up menu, whose commands list all of the canned scripts that come installed with Mac OS X. (They reflect the contents of your Home folder→Library→Scripts folder, and the main Library folder→Scripts folder.)

Tip: These scripts aren't just for running like the little software slaves they are. They're also ideal for opening up in Script Editor (just by double-clicking each) and analyzing line by line, to learn how they work. After you've understood the syntax, you can then copy bits of the code to modify and use in your own scripts.

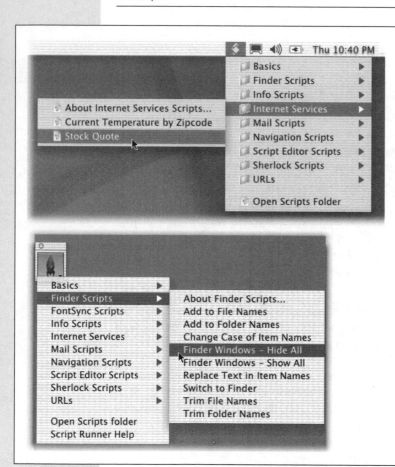

Figure 7-1:
Mac OS X comes with an assortment of useful scripts to try—and two easy ways to trigger them.

Top: Script Menu (which you download from the Apple Web site) lets you launch Perl, Shell, and AppleScript scripts, just by choosing their names, from within any application. To install it, just drag it onto your menu bar.

Bottom: This palette, called Script Runner, is available no matter what application is active. To make it appear, just double-click the Script Runner icon in your Applications→ AppleScript folder.

Some of the scripts operate on familiar components of the Mac OS, like the Finder; others show off new applications or features that weren't part of Mac OS 9. Here's what they do:

Basics

In this folder, you'll find a few simple scripts:

- **AppleScript Help** opens the Help Viewer, brings it to the front, and searches for the word *AppleScript* to bring up a list of links to the AppleScript topics available in Help.

- **AppleScript Website** simply opens the AppleScript Web page in your Web browser.

- **Open Script Editor** launches the Script Editor application, which you can use to edit and write your own AppleScript programs.

Finder Scripts

All of these scripts have to do with work in the Finder: manipulating files and windows, for example. Several are designed to change file or folder names en masse, which can be a huge timesaver.

- **About Finder Scripts** opens a dialog box that tells you how the *other* Finder scripts operate—that is, they affect whatever is in the frontmost window.

- **Add to File Names, Add to Folder Names.** These scripts tack on a prefix or suffix to the name of every file or folder in the frontmost Finder window (or, if no windows are open, on the desktop). Now you're starting to see the power of AppleScript: You can use this script to add the word *draft* or *final* or *old* to all of the files in a certain folder, for example.

- **Change Case of Item Names** offers to capitalize, or un-capitalize, all the letters of the file names in the window before you.

- **Finder Windows - Hide All** minimizes all open Finder windows to the Dock. **Finder Windows - Show All**, of course, brings them back from the Dock.

- **Replace Text in Item Names** lets you do a search-and-replace of text bits inside file names, folder names, or both. When one publisher rejects your 45-chapter book proposal, you can use this script to change all 45 chapter files from, for example, "A History of Mouse Pads—A Proposal for Random House, Chapter 1" to "A History of Mouse Pads—A Proposal for Simon & Schuster, Chapter 1."

- **Switch to Finder** is a great one. It brings the Finder to the front *and* hides all of the other running applications.

- **Trim File Names, Trim Folder Names.** If you made a mistake in using the Add to File Names script, you can always use Trim File Names script to undo the damage. This one *removes* file extensions, suffixes, or prefixes of your choosing.

  For example, suppose you've just made a lot of new folders at once. Mac OS X calls them "untitled folder," "untitled folder 2," and so on. But what if you'd rather have them just called "folder 1," "folder 2," and so on? Run the Trim Folder Names script; when the dialog box asks you what you want trimmed, type *untitled* and click OK.

FontSync Scripts

FontSync is a noble Apple attempt to solve an old problem for desktop publishers. You finish designing some beautiful newsletter, take it to the local printing shop for printing on a high-quality press, and then have to throw out the entire batch—all because the fonts didn't come out right. The printing shop didn't have exactly the same fonts you had when you prepared the document. Or, worse, it did have the same font—but from a different font company, with the same name but slightly different type characteristics.

FontSync is designed to give you early warning for such disasters. When you run the Create FontSync Profile script, several minutes elapse—and then the Mac generates a FontSync Profile document. This file contains staggering amounts of information about the design, spacing, and curlicues of every font installed in your system. When you hand that profile over to your print shop, they can drop it onto the accompanying script, called Match FontSync Profile; it will tell them precisely what fonts are different on their Macs and yours.

The wishful-thinking aspect of this technology is, of course, that it assumes a lot: that your print shop uses Mac OS 9 or Mac OS X, that the print shop knows how to use FontSync, and that you remember to create the profile and submit it.

Info Scripts

These two scripts offer minor usefulness:

- **Current Date & Time** displays the current date and time in a dialog box, which contains a Clipboard button that, needless to say, puts that information on the invisible Macintosh Clipboard, ready for pasting.

- **Font Sampler** is designed to show you what all your fonts look like (see Figure 7-2).

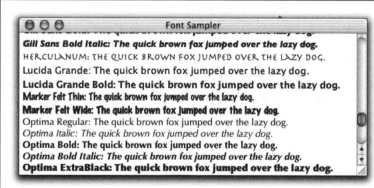

Figure 7-2:
The Font Sampler script launches TextEdit, opens a new TextEdit document, and fills it with dozens of copies of the classic "What does this font look like?" test sentence: The quick brown fox jumped over the lazy dog. *Then, as you watch, it formats each line with a different font—a good page to print out and keep as a reference.*

Internet Services

These scripts are designed to show off the power of *XML-RPC* and *SOAP*, two new Internet-query technologies that debuted in Mac OS X 10.1.

- **About Internet Services Scripts** tells you what the other two scripts in this folder are all about. The dialog box offers a "Visit Web site" button that takes you to *www.xmethods.com,* where you can find out more about creating Internet service scripts.

- The **Stock Quote** and **Current Temperature by Zipcode** fetch those respective bits of information, popping them into a dialog box *without* having to use your Web browser, thanks to the power of SOAP (Simple Object Access Protocol).

Mail Scripts

These scripts both communicate with Mail (see Chapter 19).

- **Crazy Message Text** is Apple at its wackiest. When you run it, a dialog box asks you what message you want to send ("Happy Birthday," for example). Mail then creates a colorful, zany, outgoing formatted message in which each letter has a random typeface, style, color, and size. It's ideal for making people think you spent a long time with your Format menu for their entertainment.

- **Quick Mail** prompts you for an address and a subject line, and then launches the Mail application and sets up a new message for you with those attributes. With a little analysis of this script, you should be able to see how it could save you time in generating canned, regularly scheduled outgoing mail messages.

Navigation Scripts

Four of these scripts—**New Applications Window, New Home Window, New Documents Window,** and **New Favorites Window**—all open the corresponding windows, just as though you'd used the Go menu to choose their names. (As for the word "New"—it's a red herring. These scripts do not, in fact, open a new window if one is already open.)

The **Open Special Folder** script presents a list of Mac OS X's special folders: Applications, Favorites, Movies, Sites, Utilities, and so on. Double-click the one you want to open—a straight shot to some of Mac OS X's most important folders.

Tip: If you're game to edit this script in Script Editor, you can modify the script so that it will let you choose and open more than one folder simultaneously. Just type *multiple selections allowed true* right after the text *Choose folder to open:* (which appears at the end of a line about a third of the way down the script). Save your changes.

Sherlock Scripts

The sole script here, Search Internet, prompts you for a *search string* (the words you want to search the Web for). When you click Search, the script opens Sherlock and proceeds to execute your search. All of this saves you a few mouse clicks, but this script was likely designed to serve primarily as an example for study by scripting hopefuls.

Script Editor Scripts

These are AppleScript tools for people who make AppleScripts.

- **About these scripts** lets you know that these scripts put canned chunks of Apple-Script code onto the Clipboard, ready for pasting into a program you're writing in Script Editor. If you begin scripting in earnest, these scripts-to-go can help you write faster and more accurate scripts, because the code chunks are free of typos and syntax errors.

- **Error Handlers** are mini-routines that advanced scripters can use to handle situations when a script runs into trouble. One displays an error message with an OK button, another with a Cancel button, and so on.

- **Repeat Routines** let you create loops within your script, so that, for example, you can process every file in a folder the same way.

URLs

All of the scripts in this folder simply open your browser, connect to the Internet if necessary, and then open the specified Mac-fan Web pages (the stock quote for Apple on Yahoo, the Apple Store, CNN, MacWeek [now defunct], and Macintouch). The last script, Download Weather Map, is much cooler; in a flash, it downloads the current U.S. weather-map image and then opens the file in the Preview program for viewing.

The AppleScript Related Sites scripts in this folder open the most popular and useful AppleScript sites: Bill Cheeseman's AppleScript Sourcebook, MacScripter.net, and Apple's own AppleScript Web site. Each offers a wealth of information and links to even more great AppleScript sites.

Writing Your Own AppleScripts

If you ask a crowd of Mac users how many of them write AppleScripts, few hands are likely to go up. That's too bad, because as programming languages go, AppleScript is easy to understand. It takes only a few weeks, not years, to become comfortable with AppleScript. And the power AppleScript places in your hands is well worth the effort you'll expend learning it.

For example, here's a fragment of actual AppleScript code:

```
open folder "AppleScript" of folder "Applications" of startup
disk
```

You probably don't need a manual to tell you what this line from an AppleScript program does. It opens the Applications→AppleScript folder on your hard drive. (That's the folder that contains Script Editor, the Mac OS X program that lets you write your own AppleScripts.)

If you have no interest in learning to program, you're forgiven; you're not alone. But almost every Mac user can benefit by understanding what AppleScript can do, why it's important in certain industries, and how it may be useful in special situations. Even skimming this section will give you an appreciation of AppleScript's power—and yet another reason to relish being a Mac user: Windows has no equivalent of AppleScript.

What's New in Mac OS X

Some of the new features in Mac OS X (10.1 and later) include:

- **Toolbar Scripts.** In Mac OS X, you can turn scripts into standard, double-clickable programs that you can stash on your Dock, in a Finder-window toolbar, or anywhere else fine applications are stashed. Several dozen come with Mac OS X (see page 157), and many more are available for downloading from *www.apple.com/applescript/macosx.*

- **Script Runner** is the quick-access palette for your scripts shown in Figure 7-1.

- **Script Menu** adds a Scripts menu to your menu bar (Figure 7-1), offering a secondary way to trigger your scripts. (Veteran scripters may recognize it as the Mac OS X equivalent of the venerable OSA Menu for pre–Mac OS X systems.) Script Menu isn't part of the standard installation—you have to download it from Apple's Web site (at this writing, it's at *www.apple.com/applescript/macosx/script_menu*).

UP TO SPEED

AppleScript in Mac OS X: Starting from Scratch

In Mac OS 9, after many system updates, AppleScript had become a solid, feature-rich, mature tool. Unfortunately, adapting AppleScript to Mac OS X hasn't been completely painless.

A lot of the great old scripting tools (such as scripting additions), Web sites, and Internet discussion are all relevant only to AppleScript in Mac OS 9 and earlier. Scripts that expect the Finder to work the old way—of which there are thousands—flounder when asked to do their work in the Mac OS X Finder, which works differently. And although Apple has added a number of new and more powerful tools to the AppleScript kit bag, some great features of the Mac OS 9 AppleScript have disappeared—folder actions, for example, and Finder recordability (the ability to write scripts just by *doing* something as the Mac records your actions in "watch me" mode). As a result, few people who depend on AppleScript have made the switch to Mac OS X.

Until power users' applications have all been adapted for Mac OS X, bugs have all been squashed, and the scripting additions have begun to appear in serious numbers for Mac OS X, people who want to learn scripting have to live in three worlds. You have to master AppleScript as it works in Mac OS 9, as it works in Classic (Chapter 5), *and* as it works in Mac OS X. AppleScript is different in each of these three environments.

In order to ease the transition, Apple has made it possible for scripts written in Mac OS X to control applications running in Classic, and vice versa. If you're still obligated to run certain programs in the Classic world, this feature may turn out to be very handy.

Nonetheless, Apple has made huge strides in restoring AppleScript to health in Mac OS X. In each version, more of what's broken gets fixed, and more of what's missing returns. This chapter, then, takes you through AppleScript in all three worlds—Mac OS 9, Mac OS X, and Classic. You'll be a better-armed scripter for knowing all three systems during the migration period.

Note: if you put a new script into one of your Mac's two Scripts folders, it immediately shows up in the Scripts menu. To see it in Script Runner, however, you have to quit Script Runner and restart it.

- **Unicode** is a system designed to replace ASCII as the data format for representing text, and now Mac OS X understands it. (Unicode can describe a much larger "alphabet" than ASCII, making it possible to incorporate all the symbols of languages like Greek, Chinese, and Japanese into a single font file.)

- **Support for XML-RPC and SOAP.** As noted earlier, these new protocols let certain Web sites serve up almost any kind of data imaginable to your script for further processing. Even at this early stage, you can write AppleScripts that pull down word definitions, jokes of the day, currency exchange rates, and so on, right to your Mac; a script query of a SOAP server is much faster than loading a Web page.

- **Scriptable Terminal.** Not only can you run scripts from the command line in Terminal (Chapter 15), now you can script the Terminal application itself so that it runs other scripts.

- **AppleScript Studio** (ASS for short—how did this one get past marketing?). When you get really serious about creating AppleScripts, you'll want to check out this new programming kit from Apple. Technically, it's an integrated development environment that combines a Project Builder and an Interface Builder, making AppleScript a peer language of Java and Objective C. In plain language, this new tool allows you to put a real Aqua user interface on your scripts, complete with dialog boxes, text boxes, buttons, slide controls, and much more.

Recording Scripts in "Watch Me" Mode

You can, if you wish, create a script by typing out the computer commands one at a time, just as computer programmers do the world over. Details on this process later in the chapter.

But if the task you want it to handle isn't especially complex, you can create a script just by doing the job manually—using menu commands, dragging icons, opening windows, and so on—as Script Editor watches and writes out the necessary lines of code automatically. Recording an action and watching the Mac turn your movements into lines of AppleScript code is a fantastic way to learn how AppleScript works.

Unfortunately, as noted earlier, one of the biggest disappointments in Mac OS X version 10.1 is that the Finder is no longer *recordable*; that is, you can no longer create an AppleScript by performing certain actions as the Mac writes down what you're doing.

Apple may well restore recordability to later versions of the Mac OS X Finder. But in the meantime, you can try out recordability either in a Mac OS X program that *is* recordable, such as AppleWorks, or by restarting your Mac in Mac OS 9, where the

Finder *is* recordable. Because not everyone has AppleWorks, the following tutorial takes the second approach.

A Simple Auto-Recorded Script

Try this experiment in Mac OS 9 (or earlier). It's a script that creates a brightly colored, can't-miss-it folder into which you can stuff your newly created documents each day for backup. In the following section, you'll find a line-by-line analysis of the result.

1. **Open Script Editor.**

   Script Editor, the heart of the AppleScript suite, is in your Apple Extras→AppleScript folder. It looks like Figure 7-3 (except that the window appears empty when it first opens). If you don't see an open window like the one illustrated, choose File→New Script.

2. **Click Record.**

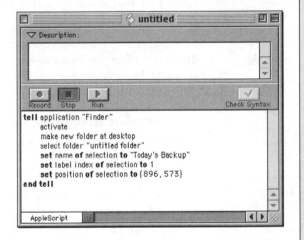

Figure 7-3:
The Script Editor in action. Type a short description into the top window, if you like—or eliminate the top window by collapsing the "flippy triangle" button beside it. This script appears already formatted with boldface and indents since it was created using "watch-me" mode.

   Script Editor is about to write out the code that describes each mouse movement, click, and menu command from now on. In this experiment, you'll create a new folder, name it, label it, and then move it to a convenient position on the desktop.

3. **Click your desktop. Choose File→New Folder. Type *Today's Backup* and then press Return.**

   You've just made a new folder on your desktop. If you sneak a peek at your Script Editor window, you'll see that it has begun to notate the computer commands that represent what you've done so far.

So that you can't miss it when it's time to back up your work for the day, apply a label to your new folder:

4. **Choose File→Label→Essential (or whichever label you prefer).**

   Finally, you should move this backup folder away from your hard drive, where it's too easy to get lost.

5. **Drag the Today's Backup folder to a new position on the screen—just above the Trash, for example.**

   That's all this modest AppleScript will do: Create a new folder, name and label it, and then drag it to a new spot.

6. **Click in the Script Editor window, and then click Stop.**

   Your newly created script is complete, as shown in Figure 7-3.

To try out this masterful automation sequence, click your desktop and then throw away the Today's Backup folder, so that you can start fresh. Once again, return to Script Editor—but this time, click Run.

In rapid, ghost-driven sequence, you'll see AppleScript create *another* Today's Backup folder, label it with a color, and drag it to precisely the spot on the screen where you dragged the first one by hand—all in a fraction of a second. The script you've created isn't the world's most useful, but it illustrates how powerful and fast AppleScript can be.

Understanding AppleScript Commands

Eventually, you'll discover that scripts you create in "watch me" mode are fairly limited. If you want to write scripts for non-recordable programs—like the Mac OS X Finder—you'll eventually have to learn to type out AppleScript code for yourself.

As a first step in understanding the AppleScript language, study the code written by Script Editor in the previous example. As it turns out, much of this script consists of standard AppleScript jargon that appears in almost every script. Here's a line-by-line analysis of the little folder-creating script you just made.

```
tell application "Finder"
    activate
    make new folder at desktop
    select folder "untitled folder"
    set name of selection to "Today's Backup"
    set label index of selection to 1
    set position of selection to {896, 573}
end tell
```

tell application "Finder"

Every recorded script begins with a line like this. It specifies which Mac program or window this section of your script will control. If you were writing a script for Mac OS X's Finder, you'd begin by typing this line.

Complex scripts can involve *several* programs—grabbing information from File-Maker and pasting it into QuarkXPress, for example. In those longer scripts, you'd see *tell application "FileMaker Pro"* at the beginning of the steps that involve the first program, and then *tell application "QuarkXPress"* later in the script, where the steps pertain to QuarkXPress.

activate

This command means, "Bring the abovementioned program to the front." Technically, you don't have to make the Finder the active program to perform the simple folder-creation steps in this script—AppleScript could create, name, label, and move your Today's Backup folder even while the Finder is in the background. But Script Editor inserted this step automatically because, when recording your actions, *you* made the Finder the active program (by clicking the desktop). You're welcome to delete this step from your Script Editor window. (The *activate* command works exactly the same way in Mac OS X, but isn't necessary if you're typing out this script by hand.)

This is only the first of many examples you'll find in which Script Editor records wordier scripts than necessary. Hand-typed scripts, like those described later in this chapter, are typically more compact and faster in execution.

Tip: A program you're controlling with a script doesn't have to be the frontmost program. Still, most scripts in Mac OS 9 or Classic work faster and better if their subjects *are* frontmost. But Mac OS X's superior multitasking eliminates that consideration. There's no longer any advantage to bringing an application to the front before controlling it.

WORKAROUND WORKSHOP

Rejiggering in Mac OS X

If you're following along by typing out the script in Mac OS X, you'll discover that a number of the commands in the "Today's Backup" script don't work in Mac OS X. The line *set name of selection to "Today's Backup,"* for example, brings you smack into a bug: AppleScript in Mac OS X has problems manipulating selected objects, and this step produces only an error message.

Here's a prime example of the kind of script-rejiggering that people have to do to make Mac OS 9 scripts work in Mac OS X. To work around this limitation, for example, you can simply replace these three auto-generated commands—

```
make new folder at desktop
select folder "untitled folder"
```

```
set name of selection to "Today's
Backup"
```

—with this single command:

```
set name of (select folder
"untitled folder") to "Today's
Backup"
```

AppleScript processes the expression in parentheses first, just as in mathematics, and uses its *result* to evaluate that part outside of the parentheses. Either way, the result is a renamed folder.

Better yet, now the same script works in both Mac OS 9 and Mac OS X. In other words, Mac OS X workarounds like this are not only easy, they're backward compatible.

make new folder at desktop

This command, of course, tells the Finder to create a new folder at the desktop level. If you had made the new folder in your hard drive window, this command would say, "make new folder at startup disk."

In Mac OS 9, this command creates a new folder on your desktop called "untitled folder." If you have only one drive (or one partition), then there's only one place it can go: right there on the desktop (technically, it's in the Desktop folder of your hard drive).

select folder "untitled folder"

This step highlights the new folder, making it the selected item ("the selection"). (Script Editor leaves out words like "the," but if inserting such articles would make AppleScript easier for you to understand, you're welcome to use them.)

set name of selection to "Today's Backup"

This step renames the new folder.

set label index of selection to 1

The *label index* just refers to the *label,* as it appears in your File→Label menu. The Mac doesn't refer to these labels as Essential, Hot, In Progress, and so on, because you might change the names of these labels at any time. Instead, it refers to them by number, 1 through 7, as they're listed in the File→Label menu.

If you wanted your script to apply the second label (Hot, for example) to your icon instead, you could change the 1 in your script to a 2 (or some other number less than 8).

set position of selection to {896, 573}

This is the script step that actually moves your icon to the specified position. In Mac OS 9, the numbers represent coordinates as measured in pixels (screen dots) from the upper-left corner of your screen (horizontally and vertically, respectively). (The icon's position is measured from its own upper-left corner—the corner you'd see if the icon filled its entire imaginary 32-pixel square.)

Note: In Mac OS X, this command doesn't work as it did in Mac OS 9. Among other differences, the numbers in the brackets now represent coordinates from the upper-left corner of the *window,* not the screen. Furthermore, because icons in Mac OS X can be almost any size, they specify the icon's position as measured from its *center.*

---

end tell

This command tells the Finder that it can stop paying attention to AppleScript, which is finished having its way. *End tell* always accompanies the *tell application* command that begins a script; they form the bookends that delineate the instructions to the program in question. (AppleScripters call the entire chunk, beginning with *tell* and ending with *end tell,* a *tell block.*) Tell blocks are the same in both Mac OS 9 and Mac OS X.

Tip: You can change the fonts and formatting Script Editor uses to write out your scripts. Choose Edit→AppleScript Formatting, click a category of formatting, and then use Script Editor's Font and Style menus to choose new type specs. Experienced scripters change the formatting to *color code* their scripts, making the scripts easier to read and debug.

FREQUENTLY ASKED QUESTION

Boldface Words in Scripts

Why does Script Editor put random words in bold type?

They're not actually random.

The words in boldface type are AppleScript *reserved words,* terms that have a special meaning for AppleScript and therefore can't be used in your script for other purposes (like variable names).

Some reserved words are commands, like *get,* or *set,* and

some define the beginning and the end of control statements like *repeat…end repeat,* or *tell … end tell.* Others, like *the,* do nothing but improve the readability of the script commands.

Some reserved words always appear in pairs in commands. For example, a set command always has the reserved word *to* later in the same line (*set myAge to 17,* for example).

Saving a Script

Before you save a script, let Script Editor check its *syntax.* Do that by clicking the Check Syntax button at the right side of the window. If you don't perform a syntax check manually before trying to save, Script Editor will automatically do it for you as soon as you try to save.

Note: The Check Syntax button won't find any errors if you created a script using the "watch me" system; after all, Script Editor itself wrote the script, so *of course* it's perfect. But when you write scripts by hand, as described later in this chapter, you'll find the Check Syntax button a useful tool for cleaning stray errors out of your scripts.

If Script Editor finds the syntax of your script to be correct, you'll get no reaction from Script Editor except to see your script formatted, as shown in Figure 7-4. If it does find a problem with the syntax, you'll be limited to saving your script file in only one format: plain text.

At this point, you're ready to save your script. You start as you would in any Mac program, by choosing File→Save. Name your script and choose a location for it, by all means—but the important step to take here is to choose a *format* for your completed script (see Figure 7-5). Your choices depend on whether you're working in the Mac OS 9 or Mac OS X version of Script Editor:

- **Text.** You can't actually run an AppleScript that's saved as a text file, but saving it this way provides a good way to exchange scripts with other people or to save an unfinished script you want to work on later. (Available in both Mac OS 9 and Mac OS X.)

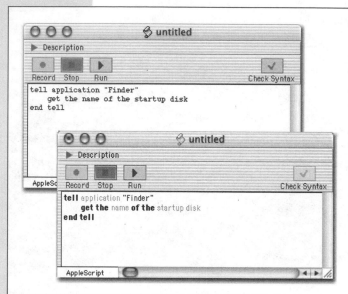

Figure 7-4:
If you type an AppleScript manually, it appears just as it would in a word processor (top left): in Courier type with no special formatting. When you click the Check Syntax button, however, Script Editor indents the tell *block and changes all type to Geneva (bottom right), with AppleScript's reserved words in bold type and comments in italics. Congratulations: You've got the Script Editor seal of approval.*

- **Compiled script.** You can't double-click a compiled script to run it. Nonetheless, compiled scripts are required by a number of *programs* that launch AppleScripts, including Script Runner and Script Menu (see Figure 7-1) or programs that themselves can run AppleScripts (FileMaker Pro, Outlook Express, Eudora, and Palm Desktop, among others). (Available in both Mac OS 9 and Mac OS X.)

- **Classic applet.** Choose this option (available in Mac OS 9 only) if you want to create a stand-alone, double-clickable application script. You can put the resulting script into your menu, for example, so that you can trigger it whenever you like, just by choosing its name. Or you can put the finished script into, say, your Startup Items folder to run automatically at startup (to search the Web for news of your industry and save the Web pages in a new folder, for example).

When you choose this option, you're offered two additional checkboxes. If you choose Stay Open, the applet you've created remains running after it's launched—just what you'd want for scripts that monitor some activity on your computer and then act when some particular condition is satisfied.

In general, you'll want to leave Never Show Startup Screen on, so the startup message never appears. If you turn this off, then whatever description you provided for your script appears whenever the script runs. You, or whoever is using your script, must then click either Run or Quit.

- **Mac OS X applet.** This option (Mac OS 9 only) creates a double-clickable, self-running script application that can run on Mac OS X machines *or* Mac OS 9 Macs that have the Carbon Lib system extension installed.

Figure 7-5:
When you save a script, use the Format pop-up menu to specify its format, which will have a lot to do with determining how useful your script is. (In Mac OS 9, use one of the Applet choices to create a double-clickable application. In Mac OS X, the Application option creates Apple-Scripts that work in all systems: Mac OS X, Mac OS 9, and the Classic environment.)

- **Application.** This option (Mac OS X only) creates a double-clickable, self-running script application that can run on Macs in any system: Mac OS X, Mac OS 9, or the Classic environment. (You're offered the same two checkboxes described in the Classic Applet description above.)

- **Stationery Options.** Use this option (Mac OS 9 only) if you plan to create several similar scripts, all of which are variations on a single script. Create your example script, then choose this command and click Stationery. Thereafter, you can open this template script and use it as a starting point for all the different variations.

Tip: You can create stationery scripts in Mac OS X, but it's a two-step process. First, save the script as described above. Then, at the desktop, highlight its icon, choose File→Show Info, and turn on the Stationery Pad checkbox.

Writing Commands by Hand

Using the "watch me" mode described earlier in this chapter, you can create only very simple scripts. If you want to create anything more elaborate—or anything at *all* in Mac OS X—you must type out the script steps one by one, testing your work, debugging it, reworking it, and so on.

Scriptable Programs

Most of the introductory articles you'll read about AppleScript discuss scripts that perform useful tasks *in the Finder*—that is, scripts that manipulate your files, folders, disks, and so on. That's because the Finder is an extraordinarily *scriptable* program; AppleScript can control almost every element of it.

But AppleScript can also control and communicate with almost every popular Mac program: FileMaker, AppleWorks, Adobe and Microsoft applications, and so on. Among the built-in Mac OS X programs that you can control with AppleScript scripts are Sherlock, Terminal, Text Edit, Print Center, Mail, Internet Connect, and Image Capture—a list that will grow with subsequent Mac OS X updates.

Almost every Mac program understands four AppleScript commands: Open, Print, Quit, and Run. These commands constitute part of what Apple has designated the Required Suite of commands. Even so, some programs don't understand any of them, and some understand many other commands.

But before you can write a script that manipulates, say, Eudora, you need to learn which commands Eudora can understand. To do that, you need to look at the application's *dictionary*—the list of AppleScript commands a program understands.

To do so, open Script Editor. Choose File→Open Dictionary. You'll be offered a list of all scriptable applications available on your Mac (see Figure 7-6), including any Scripting Additions (page 178). Double-click the name of the program you want to check out.

Tip: You can also open a dictionary by dragging a program's icon onto the Script Editor icon—a good argument for parking Script Editor's icon on the Dock.

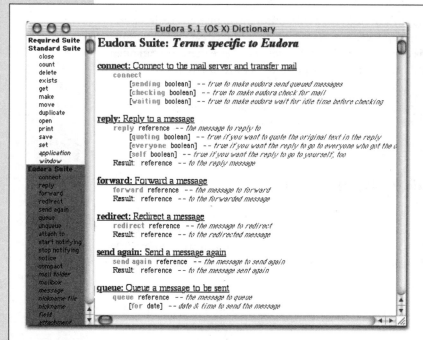

Figure 7-6:
The dictionary for a program lists the AppleScript commands and objects it knows about. If you click one of the commands on the left side of the window, you see an explanation of how to use it on the right. Unfortunately, you don't get any examples; it's up to you to try each command to see how it works. If you're having trouble making sense of the dictionary, contact the software company by phone or email and ask for a list of its AppleScript features.

That's not to say, of course, that these commands make much sense to someone who's never written an AppleScript before. These commands, and scripts that incorporate them, still require study and experimentation. But a glance at a program's AppleScript dictionary is a good way to assess its scriptability—and therefore how much the software company has embraced the Macintosh Way.

Two Sample Scripts

In the following hand-typed examples, you'll encounter new kinds of *tell blocks,* scripts that control more than one program at a time, and scripts that do things you can't even do manually. If you look over these examples carefully—and type them up for yourself in Script Editor—you'll begin to see how similar to English AppleScript can be. You may also wind up with some useful scripts that can make your Macintosh life easier.

Auto-backup before shutting down

Suppose you'd like to use your new iPod (Apple's MP3 player/FireWire hard drive) as a backup disk. You want to be able to back up your Home→Documents folder each day without having to burrow through folders, drag and drop, click OK, and so on. AppleScript can do the job automatically.

In Script Editor, choose File→New Script, and then type this:

```
tell application "Finder"
duplicate folder "Documents" of folder "chris" of folder
"Users" of startup disk to disk "Ye Olde iPod" with replacing
end tell
```

Here's how the key command breaks down:

- *duplicate.* AppleScript also offers commands called *move* and *copy.* So why *duplicate?*

  As it turns out, the *copy* command isn't smart enough to *replace* an existing folder of the same name. Because you probably plan to run this auto-backup script every day, you'll want it to wipe out *yesterday's* Documents backup each time you run it.

  The *move* command—in conjunction with its optional modifier phrase "with replacing"—is a better bet, in Mac OS 9, anyway. It makes the Mac copy the Documents folder to the iPod, *replacing* the Documents folder that's already there, without asking for confirmation or showing an error message. Unfortunately, the *move* command also produces an error message in Mac OS X.

  Fortunately, the *duplicate* command works smoothly *and* understands the *with replacing* modifier—and therefore does exactly what you want.

- *folder "Documents" of folder "chris" of folder "Users" of startup disk.* All of that "folder of folder" business simply reflects the location of your Documents folder. It's in your Users→Home folder, of course, which bears your name. In this example, substitute your actual Home folder's name for "chris." (If you're one of those highly mobile people who put the Home folder on a different disk [see page 282], substitute its name for "startup disk." And change "Ye Olde iPod," of course, to the actual name of your backup disk.)

After you've run your script a couple times from within Script Editor (by clicking the Run button) and enjoyed the mad, brain-shocking power, add a little finesse by adding the new commands shown here in italics:

```
tell application "Finder"
duplicate folder "Documents" of folder "chris" of folder
"Users" of startup disk to disk "Ye Olde iPod" with replacing
  activate
  beep
  display dialog "Backup Successful!" buttons "Cool!"
end tell
```

The additional commands make the Mac beep and report, in a little dialog box, "Backup Successful!" after it makes the copy. It even gives you a button ("Cool!") with which to dismiss the dialog box; of course, you can make the button say anything you like ("OK," "Get on with it," "Good boy!" or whatever).

Once you've created this little script, save it as an application and put it in the Dock or on your Finder toolbar. Or save it as a compiled script and put it in your Home folder→Library→Scripts folder, so that you'll be able to trigger your backup from Script Runner or the Scripts menu (page 156).

Universal shutdown

Every now and then, you might find it useful to quit all running programs (except the Finder). Unfortunately, there's no one-step command that quits all of your open programs—but you can create one yourself.

Nearly every Mac program on earth understands the Quit command when sent by AppleScript. All you have to do, then, is to send that command to each of the programs you're likely to have open. If you spend most of your time in AppleWorks, Mail, and Internet Explorer, for example, your script might look like this:

```
tell application "AppleWorks"
  quit
end tell
tell application "Mail"
  quit
end tell
tell application "Internet Explorer"
  quit
end tell
```

In time, after hanging out on AppleScript mailing lists and studying a few other scripts, you'd realize that you could shorten those tell blocks like this:

```
    tell application "Mail" to quit
    tell application "AppleWorks" to quit
    tell application "Internet Explorer" to quit
    end tell
```

Even so, this script is doomed. If some of these programs aren't actually running, the script will dutifully *launch* each application and *then* quit it, which takes away a good bit of this script's usefulness. Fortunately, there's a better way.

Specifically, you want a script that briskly exits every running program, but is smart enough *not* to disturb the important system processes that run in the background. (Note that *process,* in computer-speak, refers to any running program, including both the applications you're using and the secret background ones that the Mac runs all the time.) So you'd want this:

```
    tell application "Finder"
        set quitList to the name of every application process whose
    file type is "APPL"
    end tell
    repeat with i from 1 to count of quitList
        tell application (item i of quitList) to quit
    end repeat
```

Here's how some of these unfamiliar lines break down:

- *set quitList to the name of every application process whose file type is "APPL."* You're defining a new variable, a stunt double, called *quitList.* It's a list of every program whose file type (page 101) is APPL—that is, every double-clickable program. By limiting it to processes whose file type is APPL, you avoid quitting all of Mac OS X's important background programs (see page 246).

- *repeat with i from 1 to count of quitList.* This is a loop. You're saying, "run through the quitList list, exiting each program until you're at the end of the list."

If you actually try this script (hint: save it first), you'll discover that it's the neutron bomb of scripts: It quits *everything in sight,* including the Dock and Script Editor itself. By adding a few more lines, however, you can specify a few process names that you want untouched:

```
    set excludedOnes to {"Script Editor", "loginwindow", "Dock",
    "SystemUIServer"}
    tell application "Finder"
        set quitList to the name of every application process whose
    file type is "APPL"
    end tell
    repeat with i from 1 to count of quitList
    set aProcess to item i of quitList
    if aProcess is not in excludedOnes then
        tell application aProcess to quit
```

```
end if
end repeat
```

This script gives you an even greater degree of control, because you can add to the list of processes excluded from the execution. Just add them to the bracketed list in the first line, always in quotes and followed by a comma.

Advanced AppleScript

No single chapter—in fact, no entire book—can make you a master AppleScript programmer. Gaining that kind of skill requires weeks of experimentation and study, during which you'll gain a lot of appreciation for what full-time software programmers endure every day. AppleScript, despite its friendly appearance and abundance of normal English words, uses many of the same structures and conventions as more advanced programming languages.

By far the best way to learn AppleScript is to study existing scripts (like those in the Library→Scripts folder) and to take the free online training courses listed at the end of this chapter. And there are thousands of examples available all over the Web. Trying to figure out these scripts—running them after making small changes here and there, and emailing the authors when you get stuck—is one of the best ways to understand AppleScript.

Figure 7-7, for example, is a script called Add to File Names.scpt. It's one of the professionally written sample scripts that come with Mac OS X. To open it, navigate to your Library→Scripts→Finder Scripts folder and double-click Add to File Names.scpt. A quick glance can tell you a lot about the tricks of professional scripters:

- **Description.** Careful script writers *document* their work; they add lots of notes and explanatory comments for the benefit of whoever might want to study or amend the script later (which is often themselves). Adding a description of the script's function in the Description box (at the top of the Script Editor window) is a good first step.

  (Whoever wrote this particular description didn't know the difference between *effect* and *affect,* but it's the thought that counts.)

- **Variables.** Ever seen a legal contract? It often begins, "This contract is between John F. Grisham, Esquire, of 2234 Mission Bell Lane, New Orleans, LA ('AUTHOR'), and Time Warner Publishing, Inc., 23 Avenue of the Americas, New York, NY ('PUBLISHER')." The names John Grisham and Time Warner never appear again in the contract—instead, the lawyers refer only to AUTHOR and PUBLISHER.

  Those lawyers are using *variables*—made-up terms that serve as stand-ins for more complicated ideas, which help to simplify the script, clarify its purpose, and save typing. In AppleScript, as in other programming or scripting languages, you can define your own variables.

  In the one line of the Add to File Names script, for example, you can see the command *set this_item to item i of the item_list.* That common command tells

AppleScript that you're defining your own variable called *this_item*, which will henceforth mean "a reference to the ith item in the list of items called *item_list*." In this case, "i" is a counter that refers to the item's position in the list.

Note: For some reason, AppleScripters tend to use variable names where the first letter is lowercase, but subsequent words appear with no spaces and capital letters, *somethingLikeThis,* or with underlines, *like_this.* Scripters also like to use *i, j,* and *k* as variables instead of, say, *n* or *x.)*

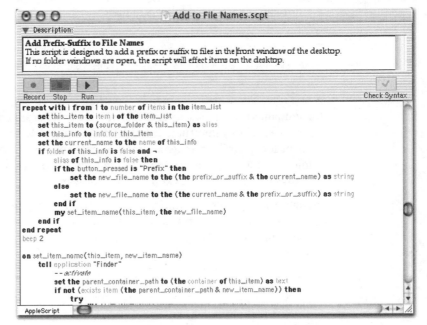

Figure 7-7:
The Add to File Names script is a classic AppleScript example. It contains variables, subroutines, nested "if" statements, and many other common elements of professionally written scripts. (After typing a description into the box at the top of the window, you can click the flippy triangle to the left of the Description box to hide the entire thing, thus maximizing your script-writing space.)

- **Subroutines.** About a third of the way into the script, you'll find a line that says, *my set_item_name(this_item, the new_item_name).* That step tells the script *not* to proceed down the list of commands in sequence, like the scripts described so far in this chapter, but instead to jump to a *subroutine*—a group of commands that's been separated from the first batch. Subroutines allow groups of commands to be more easily reused in different parts of the script. In this case, the subroutine begins four lines later (*'my set_item_name(this_item, new_item_name)'*).

- **Nested "if" statements.** You might tell an underling, "If you have time this afternoon, would you please run to the store? If the steaks are still on sale, buy three pounds; otherwise, buy just one pound." That, believe it or not, is a *nested "if" statement.* In other words, the steak-buying will take place only if the underling has time this afternoon.

The Add to File Names script has a few nested "if" statements. For example, the sixth line says, in essence, "If this thing is neither a folder nor an alias"; the next line says, "…and if whoever's operating this thing clicks the Prefix button." The script proceeds only if both of those conditions are true.

- **Comments.** Do you see the italicized comment, "*--the suggested name is too long*"? That's the programmer's note to anyone who studies the script. It's a *comment*, an annotation to make clear what the code is supposed to be doing. When the Mac runs AppleScript programs, it ignores the comments. You create one by typing two hyphens (--); when you click the Check Syntax button, Script Editor automatically sets what follows in italics.

Tip: If you want to type a out a longer comment—a whole paragraph between commands in your script, for example—just precede and follow it with a parenthesis and asterisk (*like this*).

- **Looping.** The paired commands *repeat* and *end repeat* create a loop—a set of commands that AppleScript repeats over and over again until something (which you've specified) interrupts it. In the case of the Add to File Names script, the script loops until it's added a prefix or suffix to all of the files in the specified folder—at which point it's supposed to beep twice. (It actually beeps only once, thanks to a quirk of Mac OS X's sound software.)

- **Dialog boxes and buttons.** If you ever want to play programmer for a day, open Script Editor and try creating dialog boxes and buttons of your own. The script command *display dialog* (followed, in quotes, by whatever message you want to appear on the screen) is all you need, as shown in Figure 7-8.

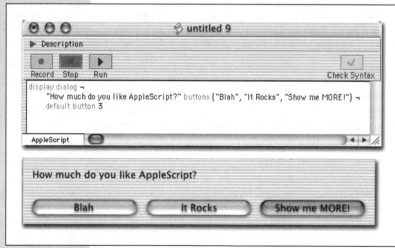

Figure 7-8:
The script shown here at top produces the dialog box shown at bottom. The buttons *command lets you create your own buttons (up to three, punctuated exactly as shown here). The* default button *command tells the script which button should be the default, the pulsing or outlined one that you can "click" just by pressing the Return key. Default button 3 means that the third button is the default button.*

Tip: Instead of a dialog box, you can also interact with the person using the computer by making the Mac *speak*. (See Chapter 14 for more on speech.) Just use the *Say* command. If your AppleScript contains the line, *say "Hey! Pay some attention to me!" using "Zarvox,"* then the Mac speaks that line using the voice called Zarvox. In addition to being fun, audio feedback can be useful when debugging scripts.

- **Line breaks.** When a line of AppleScript code gets too long, it's hard to read—especially if it's wider than the Script Editor window itself. AppleScript pros, therefore, insert a special *continuation symbol* that makes the text wrap to the next line, which causes AppleScript to treat both lines as a single command. You create this line-break symbol by pressing Option-Return. (Some of these characters appear in the scripts shown in Figures 7-6 and 7-7.)

Note: Don't use a line-break character in the middle of text that appears inside quotation marks; commands that you break up like this won't work. You can, however, put Returns in a text string.

- *Try...On error...End try.* This suite of three commands appears frequently in polished AppleScript scripts—including the one shown in Figure 7-8. In essence, it tells the Macintosh: "Try to do this. If it doesn't work out, show this error message." Here's an example:

```
tell application "Finder"
    try
        make new folder at startup disk with properties
{name:"Backup Folder"}
    on error
        display dialog "A folder already has that name."
    end try
end tell
```

This script tries to make a new folder named Backup Folder on the startup disk. But if there's already a folder there by that name, then AppleScript generates an error—and shows the error message you specify.

What Else AppleScript Can Do

Mac OS X comes with almost no online help at all for AppleScript. But if you fire up Mac OS 9, you'll find that its AppleScript Help screens are full of useful examples—and copious enough to serve as a detailed overview of AppleScript's powers. There you'll find out, for example, that simple scripts can:

- Manipulate specific files and folders (copy, delete, rename or label them, and so on).

- Read, copy, or insert text into the Comments field of a certain icon's Get Info window.

- Use artificial intelligence to create a summarized version of a longer text document.

Where to Learn More

As noted earlier, AppleScript isn't something you can master in a day or two. Fortunately, few Mac technologies have more ardent fans than AppleScript, and free beginners' (and experts') tutorials are available all over the Web. It may be a while before this material is updated for Mac OS X, but in the meantime, you can study the Mac OS 9 material; much of it is directly applicable in Mac OS X.

Begin your quest at Apple's AppleScript Web site, *www.apple.com/AppleScript*. There you'll find the link to an excellent, step-by-step tutorial in hand-coding scripts, as well as links to these outstanding online AppleScript guides:

- **Bill Briggs' AppleScript Primers.** Read dozens of articulate, thoughtful tutorials for the beginning scripter. A good exercise might be to restart your Mac in Mac OS 9, work through the tutorials, then go back to Mac OS X and, as homework, try to figure out how to modify the featured scripts to run in Mac OS X.

- **AppleScript Guidebooks.** Download and install these additions to the Help→Help Center menu (Mac OS 9 only). Each adds, to your built-in Mac help system, detailed instructions on various specialized AppleScript topics: Open Transport, subroutines, speech, program linking, and so on. Each includes several dozen sample scripts for you to dissect. It's worth booting into Mac OS 9 to study them.

- **AppleScript mailing lists.** Sign up for one of these free, email-based discussion lists whose members are all AppleScript fans. Apple runs one; the MacScript list is independent. Given the shortage of specific tutorials based on Mac OS X, these lists are possibly the best source of solutions for the new scripter.

Other links on this page take you to commercial AppleScript training course offerings, technical encyclopedias that describe every single AppleScript command in detail, AppleScript news sites, and so on.

POWER USERS' CLINIC

Scripting Additions

Much of AppleScript's power comes in the form of add-on files called *scripting additions*. You can think of them as plug-ins, each of which adds a particular new feature to AppleScript's repertoire. In Mac OS 9, they sit in your System Folder→Scripting Additions folder.

In Mac OS X, you may find scripting additions in any of three different places. The standard additions are in the System→Library→Scripting Additions folder of the Mac's hard drive. As with fonts, sounds, or other settings, you can also install scripting additions that only you can access by making a Scripting Additions folder in your Home→Library folder. Similarly, if you're an administra-

tor, you can make a Scripting Additions folder in the main Library folder (in the hard drive window); everyone with an account will be able to use the scripting additions you file there.

Like a scriptable application, each of these scripting additions has its own *dictionary*—its own specialized AppleScript commands that you can use in your scripts. You view these new commands just as you would when studying the vocabulary of a program: by opening Script Editor, choosing File→Open Dictionary, and then navigating to and opening the scripting addition you want.

3

Part Three:
The Components of
Mac OS X

System
Preferences

T he hub of Mac customization is System Preferences, the modern-day successor to the old Control Panels of the older Mac OS. Some of its panels are
extremely important; their settings determine whether or not you can connect to a network or go online to exchange email. Others handle the more cosmetic
aspects of customizing Mac OS X. This chapter guides you through all of the System
Preferences program, panel by panel.

Tip: Only a system administrator (see page 275) can change some of the preference settings described in
this chapter. These are the settings that affect everyone who shares a certain machine: its Internet settings,
Energy Saver settings, and so on.

The tiny padlock in the lower-left corner of a panel (see Figure 8-9, for example) is the telltale sign. If you,
a non-administrator, would like to edit some settings, call an administrator over to your Mac and ask him
to click the lock, input his password, and supervise your tweaks.

The System Preferences Window

You open System Preferences either by choosing its name from the menu, clicking its icon in the Dock, or double-clicking its icon in the Applications folder. Notice the rows of icons grouped according to function: Personal, Hardware, and so
on. (That's how they're organized in this chapter, too.)

When you click one of the icons, the corresponding controls appear in the main
System Preferences window, and the other icons vanish. To go to a different preference pane, you have a number of options:

• *Fast:* Click the Show All icon in the upper-left corner of the window (or press
⌘-L, a shortcut worth learning). Then click the icon of the new panel you want.

• *Faster:* Choose any panel's name from the View menu.

• *Fastest:* Click the icon you want, if it's there, on the System Preferences toolbar.
And why shouldn't it be there? By all means, stash the panels you use frequently
up there, as shown in Figure 8-1.

Tip: You can rearrange toolbar icons by dragging horizontally, or remove one by dragging it directly away
from the toolbar. On the other hand, you can hide the toolbar altogether (to maximize your screen space)
by clicking the white oval button in the window's upper-right title-bar corner. At that point, you can still
switch among different System Preferences panes by using the View menu.

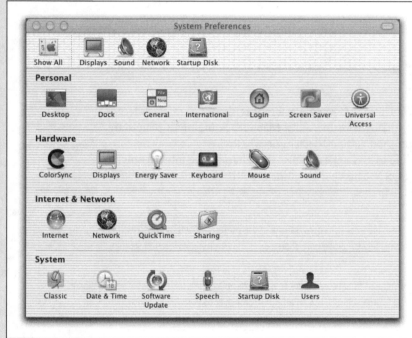

Figure 8-1:
Like a Finder window,
System Preference has a
toolbar across the top of its
window. By all means, drag
the icons of the System
Preferences panels you use
the most to the toolbar so
you can get to them more
easily. With your most
frequently-used icons
ensconced on the toolbar,
you can jump from panel to
panel—from Screensaver to
Startup Disk, for example—
without having to hit the
Show All icon first.

Personal Settings

The first set of seven panels in System Preferences lets you bend the Mac OS X environment to your personal sense of design and fashion. The changes you make with
these panels are what make your Mac uniquely yours.

Desktop

Desktop is the command center for dressing up your Desktop with the background
image of your choice. You can choose from one of the several dozen background
pictures that come with Mac OS X, or use your own pictures.

Using a canned Mac OS X picture

Mac OS X comes with four collections of Desktop pictures, ranging from National Geographic-style nature photos to plain solid colors. To install a new background picture, first choose one of the four image categories from the Collections pop-up menu—Apple Background Images (muted, soft-focused swishes and swirls), Nature (plants, bugs, water), Abstract (swishes and swirls with wild colors), or Solid Colors (boring grays, blues, and greens). Now click the thumbnail of any available picture to apply it immediately to the Desktop. (There's no need to remove the previously installed picture; picking a new picture automatically replaces the old one.)

Note: Several of Apple's ready-to-use Desktop pictures come in two sizes. The elongated versions (with the flatter, squashed-down thumbnails) are designed to perfectly fill the extra-wide screens on Titanium PowerBooks, Apple Cinema Displays, and other unusually wide screens.

Using your own pictures

Decorating your Mac desktop is much more fun if you use one of your own pictures. You can use any digital photo, scanned image, or graphic you want in almost any graphics format (JPEG, PICT, GIF, TIFF, PDF, or Photoshop).

Just drag the image file itself onto the mini-desktop displayed in the Desktop panel. A thumbnail of your picture instantly appears on the mini-desktop and, a moment later, your picture is plastered across your monitor.

If the picture is larger than your monitor (in pixels), Mac OS X scales it down to fit on the screen, sometimes clipping it vertically or horizontally in the process. If the picture is *smaller* than your screen, one of two things happens.

POWER USERS' CLINIC

How They Work

The entire System Preferences program is nothing more than a series of graphical front ends for underlying Unix settings. (If you know Unix and feel so inclined, in fact, you can bypass the System Preferences panel completely. Using the *defaults* command, you can make any of the changes described in this chapter from within Mac OS X's Terminal program.)

The individual preference panels are represented by "package" icons in your various Library folders. For example, icons in the basic Mac OS X set are in System→Library→PreferencePanes. Mac OS X also checks the Network→Library→PreferencePanes folder, if there is one, when it decides which icons it should show in System Preferences.

You can easily expand System Preferences, however, just by dropping new pane modules into your Home folder→Library→PreferencePanes folder. Or, if you're an administrator, you can create a PreferencePanes folder in the Mac's main Library folder, so that everyone with an account on the Mac (Chapter 11) will be able to access your newly added System Preferences panels. (TinkerTool 2, for example, which is described at the beginning of Chapter 17, takes the form of one of these add-on control panels.)

Any new panes you add in this way show up in System Preferences in a new row of icons labeled Other. The beauty of this arrangement, of course, is that everyone who shares a Mac can see a different assortment of customized preference panes.

• If the graphic is a perfect square, or taller than it is wide, your Mac *tiles* the picture across the screen, repeating it until the images fill the entire monitor.

• If the graphic is wider than it is tall, Mac OS X enlarges it until the left and right edges of the picture stretch to the edges of your monitor, even if it chops off the top and bottom edges.

Tip: For the best results, use a program like Adobe Photoshop, AppleWorks, or GraphicConverter to make your desktop images the exact size and shape of your screen. If your monitor displays 1024 by 768 pixels, create a picture that's exactly 1024 by 768 pixels, so that your Mac doesn't have to scale, crop, or distort the image. As a rule, smallish images that have to be scaled up to fill the desktop end up looking very bad.

Figure 8-2:
Using the Collections pop-up menu, you can preview an entire folder of your own images before installing any one of them as your new Desktop picture. Just use the Choose Folder command from the pop-up menu to select a folder to see thumbnails of all the images it contains, as shown in this example. Clicking one of the thumbnails installs the corresponding picture on the desktop.

DON'T PANIC

Desktop Pictures—Now with Fewer Features!

Adorning the Mac OS X Desktop with your own pictures is easy—*too* easy, some veteran Mac users might think.

In the old days, you could control *how* the Mac displayed your picture—tiling it in a repeating pattern, plastering it dead center, or stretching it across the whole monitor—using commands like Center on Screen or Scale to Screen.

Not any more. Now the Mac just does what *it* considers to be the best thing for your picture: Large pictures get centered and cropped. Square pictures get tiled. Period.

The solution is easy enough: Install TinkerTool 2, as described at the beginning of Chapter 17. It offers all of the old placement options for your desktop pictures.

You may also notice that the randomizing feature is gone. In Mac OS 9, you could drag a *folder* of pictures on to the Appearance control panel's mini-desktop to activate them. The Mac would switch randomly to a different desktop picture from that folder each time you restarted your Mac. This time, alas, there's no freeware solution—randomizing is simply gone from Mac OS X 10.1.

Dock

See Chapter 3 for details on the Dock and its System Preferences pane.

General

The General panel puts you in control of the look and behavior of windows, menus, buttons, scroll bars, and fonts in Mac OS X. Nothing you find here lets you do any *radical* surgery on the Aqua interface—the overall Mac OS X look stays the same— but you can tweak several settings to match your personal style.

Changing colors

Two pop-up menus let you crank up or tone down Mac OS X's overall colorfulness:

- **Appearance.** Choose between Blue or Graphite. Blue refers to the Mac OS X default bright, candy-colored scroll-bar handles, progress bars, ● menu, and pulsing OK buttons—and shiny red, yellow, and green buttons in the corner of every window. If you, like some graphics professionals, find all of this circus-poster coloring a bit distracting, you can choose Graphite, which renders all of those interface elements in various shades of gray.

- **Highlight color.** When you drag your cursor across text, its background changes color to indicate that you've selected it. Exactly what color the background becomes is up to you—just choose the shade you want using the pop-up menu. (The Highlight color also affects the color that lines the inside of a window as you drag an icon into it and a few other subtle spots.)

  If you choose Other, the Color Picker palette appears, from which you can choose any color your Mac is capable of displaying (page 115).

Tweaking the scroll bars

These radio buttons control the scroll-bar arrow buttons of all your windows. You can keep these arrows together at one end of the scroll bar, or you can split them up so that the "up" arrow sits at the top of the scroll bar, and the "down" arrow is at the bottom. (Horizontal scroll bars are similarly affected.) For details on the "Jump to next page" and "Scroll to here" options, see page 27.

DON'T PANIC

The Evolution of Control Panels

The really old-time Mac veterans, the ones who still remember the different musical notes the original Mac floppy drive made as it spun, laughed their heads off when they first saw System Preferences in Mac OS X. In System 7 through Mac OS 9, every control panel was a different program with its own window. But in System 6, there was a single control panel window, lined with icons. You'd click an icon to make the main control-panel window show the corresponding controls.

In Mac OS X, the various control panels have once again been merged into a single application. Instead of having to launch two dozen different programs to adjust your Mac's settings, you launch *one:* System Preferences. It contains a series of panels, each represented in the main System Preferences screen by an icon.

Limiting the number of Recent Items

Just how many of your recently opened documents and applications do you want the Mac to show using the Recent Items command in the menu? Pick a number from the pop-up menus. (You'll probably find that 5 is too few; 30 is more useful.)

Turning off text-smoothing on tiny fonts

Generally, the Mac's built in text-smoothing (*antialiasing*) feature works beautifully, producing smoother, more commercial-looking text anywhere it appears on your Mac: in word processing documents, email messages, Web pages, and so on.

But at smaller type sizes, such as 10-point and smaller, you might find that text is actually *less* readable with font smoothing turned on, as shown in Figure 8-3. For that reason, the Size pop-up menu lets you choose a cutoff point for font smoothing. If you choose 12 from this pop-up menu, for example, then 12-point (and smaller) type still appears crisp and sharp; only larger type, such as headlines, displays the graceful edge smoothing. (These settings have no effect on your *printouts*—only on screen display.)

International

The International panel lets you set up your Mac to work in other languages. If you bought your Mac with a *localized* operating system—a version that already runs in your own language—and you're already using the only language, number format, and keyboard layout you plan on using, then you can ignore the International panel.

But at least check it out; when it comes to showing off Mac OS X to your friends and loved ones, the "Wow" factor on the Mac's polyglot features is huge.

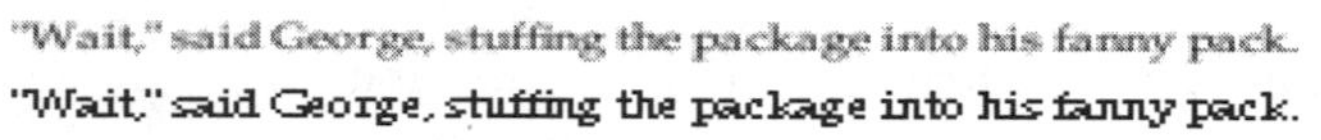

Figure 8-3:
The same 9-point type with text smoothing turned on (top) and off.

Teach your Mac another language—instantly

The Mac has always been able to run software in multiple languages—if you installed the correct fonts, keyboard layouts, and localized software (a French copy of the Mac OS, a French version of Outlook Express, and so on). But in Mac OS X, you can shift from language to language in certain programs on the fly, without reinstalling the operating system or even restarting the computer.

Open the International panel and click the Language tab. The Language list shows the seven different languages the Mac can switch into—French, German, Spanish, and a few others. Just drag one of the languages to the top of the list to select it as the target language, as shown in Figure 8-4. (You can also choose a different *script*—not just a different language, but an entirely different alphabet representation, such as one of the Asian character sets you see listed.)

Now launch Internet Explorer, or TextEdit, or Stickies. Every menu, button, and dialog box is now in the new language you selected! If you log out and back in (or just restart) at this point, the entire Finder will be in the new language, too.

Figure 8-4:
Feel like working in Dutch? Just drag Nederlands to the top of the Language list, log out and back in, and you're ready to start. Programs like TextEdit and Internet Explorer show up in Dutch. To switch back, simply return to System Preferences→International, and drag your own language back up to the top of the list. (You have to relaunch any programs that are running to switch them to a different language.)

Of course, if you're *really* French (for example), you'll also want to make these changes:

- Choose French from the Behaviors pop-up menu (also on the Language pane) so that sorting, capitalization, and word definitions also conform to French rules.

- Choose the French *keyboard layout* from the Keyboard layouts pane, explained below.

- Know French. The Mac doesn't do any translating.

Note: Not all programs are language-switching aware. Also note that, while you can add other languages to the Language list using the Edit button, they don't actually work unless you install additional language kit software.

International dates, times, numbers, and prices

The Date, Time, and Numbers panes let you set up Mac OS X to display the date, time, currency, and other numbers in a format appropriate for the language:

- **Date pane.** Controls how dates are displayed in list view Finder windows. If you think that 7/4 means July 4, skip this section. But if, as a European, you interpret it as April 7, you can use this pane to rearrange the sequence of date elements. The Region pop-up menu lists 20 ready-made settings for countries where the Mac is popular. If none of those suit your fancy, use the Long Date pop-up menus to specify some radical new order for the elements of your dates.

- **Time pane.** Some people prefer a 12-hour clock (3:05 PM), and others prefer a military or European-style, 24-hour clock (15:05). As with the Date pane, you can select a country from the Region pop-up menu to fill in the proper settings.

- **Numbers pane.** You specify the decimal and thousands separator characters for displaying large numbers, because these, too, differ from country to country. (The number 25,600.99, for example, would be written as 25 600,99 in France, and as 25.600,99 in Spanish.) The Numbers pane also lets you pick an appropriate currency symbol ($, F, £, and so on) and has the same pop-up list of Regions.

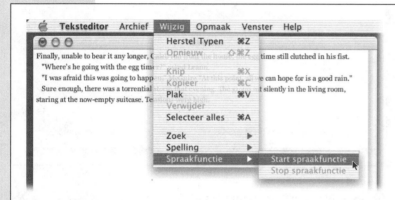

Figure 8-5:
Here's TextEdit running in Dutch. Actually understanding Dutch would be useful at a time like this—but even if you don't, it can't help but brighten up your work day to choose commands like Spraakfunctie *or* Knip.

The Keyboard Menu pane

While the Mac can display many different languages at the same time, *typing* in those languages is another matter. The symbols you use when you're typing Swedish aren't the same as when you're typing English. Apple solved this problem by creating different *keyboard layouts,* one for each language. Each rearranges the letters that appear when you press the keys.

For example, when you use the Swedish layout and press the semicolon key, you don't get a semicolon (;)—you get an ö. (Apple even includes a Dvorak layout—a scientific rearrangement of the standard layout that puts the most common letters directly under your fingertips on the home row. Fans of the Dvorak layout claim greater accuracy, better speed, and less fatigue.)

Use the list in the Keyboard Menu pane to indicate which keyboard layout you want to use. (To see what your new keyboard arrangement looks like, launch the Key

Caps program described in the next chapter.) If you check off more than one keyboard layout, a tiny flag icon appears near the right end of your menu bar—a keyboard *menu* that lets you switch from one layout to another just by choosing its
name.

Tip: Instead of using the keyboard menu, you can rotate through the different keyboard layouts you've
selected by pressing ⌘-Space bar. If this keystroke conflicts with one of the programs you already use,
open the Keyboard control panel, click Options, and turn on the Use Command+Option+Space checkbox
to substitute this less-common keystroke.

Login

The settings in the Login panel determine what you see in the Login window that
pops up each time you start up your Mac. It also controls which programs launch
automatically at startup time. Details in Chapter 11.

Screen Saver

You don't technically *need* a screen saver to protect your monitor from burn-in.
Today's energy-efficient monitors wouldn't burn an image into the screen unless
you left them on continuously—unused—for two years, according to the people
who actually design and build them.

No, screen savers are mostly about entertainment, pure and simple—and Mac OS X's
built-in screen saver, the first in Mac history, is certainly entertaining.

In the Screen Saver panel, you can choose from six different screen saver modules—
most of them beautifully designed. Aqua Icons sends a meteor shower of Mac OS X
icons hurling through space, zooming past you as they fade into oblivion. The Abstract one features psychedelic swirls of modern art melting into each other. In the
Beach, Cosmos, and Forest screen savers, you see a series of gorgeous photos—tropical
ocean scenes, deep space objects, lush rain forests. Each image slowly zooms in or
out as it softly dissolves into the next, creating an amazingly dramatic, almost cin-
ematic experience, worthy of setting up to "play" during dinner parties like the lava
lamps of the '70s.

Tip: If you can't decide which one of the modules to use, click Random. The Mac will choose a module
each time your screen saver kicks in.

When you click a module's name in the Screen Savers list, you see a mini-version of
it playing back in the Preview screen. Click Test to give the module a dry run on
your full screen.

When you've had enough of the preview, just move the mouse or press any key. You
return to the Screen Saver panel.

Creating your own screen saver

One of the coolest Screen Saver modules is Slide Show, which lets you turn your *own* collection of pictures into a self-playing slide show (Figure 8-6). Once you've rounded up the photos you want to use, click Slide Show in the Screen Savers module list, then click Configure; navigate to your folder of pictures and select it.

The slide show featuring your images, complete with spectacular zooming and dissolving effects, appears on the Preview screen in the Screen Saver panel.

Tip: For best results, use photos that are large enough to fill the screen, so that Mac OS X doesn't scale and distort your pictures beyond recognition.

Activating the screen saver

You can control when your screen saver takes over your monitor in any of several ways:

- In the **Activation** pane, you can set the amount of time that has to pass without keyboard or mouse activity before the screen saver starts. The duration can be as short as five minutes or as long as an hour, or you can drag the slider to Never to turn the screen saver off completely.

Tip: The Activation pane also gives you the option of requiring you to enter your user password (page 278) in order to disengage the screen saver. If you turn this feature on, you can use the screen saver as a sort of lock for your Mac. You can walk away from your desk at work, knowing that once the screen saver takes over, no one will be able to read the email on your screen or rifle through your files.

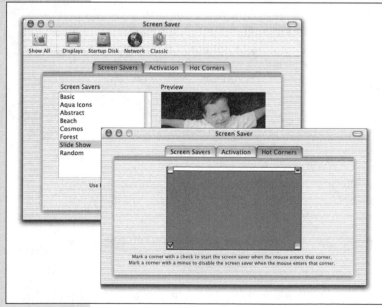

Figure 8-6:
Left: Create your own slide shows—an absolute must if you have a G4 Cube, an Apple Cinema Display, and a cool Manhattan loft apartment.

Right: Setting up screen saver hot corners: Click once to put a checkmark in any one of the corners, designating it an instant-activation spot; sliding the mouse to that corner turns on your screen saver right away. To disable the screen saver, drag the mouse into a corner that you've marked with a minus sign (by clicking twice on the checkbox).

- On the **Hot Corners** pane, you can turn each corner of your monitor into a *hot spot* (Figure 8-6). Whenever you roll your cursor into that corner, the screen saver can either turn on instantly (great for those times when you happen to be shopping on eBay at the moment your boss walks by) or stay off permanently (for times when you're reading on screen or watching a movie).

Tip: You can find dozens more screen saver modules at *www.epicware.com*.

Universal Access

The Universal Access panel is designed for people who type with one hand or find it difficult to use a mouse.

- **Keyboard tab (Sticky Keys).** This feature, designed for people who have trouble pressing more than one key at a time, lets you press modifier keys like ⌘, Shift, Option, and Control in *succession*, rather than in combination. In other words, with Sticky Keys turned on, you could use the Empty Trash shortcut (⌘-Shift-Delete) by pressing the ⌘ key, then the Shift key, and then the Delete key, one at a time.

  Once you've turned on the master switch at the top of the Universal Access screen, you can turn Sticky Keys on from the keyboard by pressing the Shift key five times in a row. Several seconds (or even several minutes) can separate the five keystrokes, as long as the mouse doesn't move. You hear a neat little starting-up chirp as confirmation that Sticky Keys is on (see Figure 8-7). (Pressing Shift five times again turns Sticky Keys off.)

- **Mouse tab (Mouse Keys).** Mouse Keys lets you convert the numeric keypad on your keyboard into cursor keys that move the pointer. The 5 key becomes the mouse button; the number keys surrounding it move the pointer up, down, diagonally, and so on. Sliders in the Mouse pane of the Universal Access panel let you control the speed of the pointer (Maximum Speed) and the length of the delay before the pointer starts moving (Initial Delay).

Tip: Mac OS X no longer comes with CloseView, the screen-magnification program for people who'd prefer a larger screen display. Of course, setting a low resolution (see the next page) is one solution.

But if you prefer the CloseView approach, install the Developer Tools (page 246). There, in your Developer→Applications folder, you'll find a program called Pixie that is a close approximation of CloseView's effect (a floating window showing a magnified view of the cursor's neighborhood). Its Preferences command lets you choose the degree of magnification you want, up to 12x natural size.

Figure 8-7:
When Sticky Keys is turned on, huge symbols representing the modifier keys (Shift, Option, and Command, in this example) float over the upper-right corner of your desktop to remind you they've been pressed. Once a keyboard shortcut is completed, the symbols disappear. If you change your mind, press the same modifier key again to cancel the keystroke and make the symbol go away.

Hardware Settings

The panels in the Hardware category control the various gadgets that are attached to your Mac: your monitor, keyboard, mouse, and speakers, as well as certain hardware components of the Mac itself.

ColorSync

This control panel is part of the software suite that attempts to maintain color fidelity throughout the life of a scanned image or digital photo—from scanner or camera to monitor, and finally to color printout. You can find a full description on page 338.

Displays

Displays is the center of operations for all your monitor settings. Here, you set your monitor's *resolution*, determine how many colors get displayed onscreen, and cali-

---

FREQUENTLY ASKED QUESTION

Blurry Flat-Panel Screens

Yucko! I tried the 800 x 600 setting on my 2001 iBook, and everything got all blurry and fuzzy! How do I fix it?

On any flat-panel screen—not just laptop screens—only one resolution setting looks really great: the maximum one. That's what geeks call the *native* resolution of that screen.

At lower resolutions, the Mac does what it can to blur together adjacent pixels, but the effect is fuzzy and unsatisfying. (On a traditional bulky monitor, the electron gun can actually make the pixels larger or smaller, but on flat-panel screens, every pixel is a fixed size.)

---

brate color balance and brightness. The specific controls you'll see here depend on the kind of monitor you're using, but here are the ones you'll most likely see:

Display tab

This tab is the main headquarters for your screen controls. It governs these settings:

- **Resolution.** All Mac desktop and laptop screens today can make the screen picture larger or smaller, thus accommodating different kinds of work. You do this magnification or reduction by switching among different *resolutions* (measurements of the number of dots that compose the screen). The Resolutions list shows the various resolution settings your monitor can accommodate: 800 x 600, 1024 x 768, and so on.

  When you use a low resolution setting, such as 800 x 600, the dots that make up your screen image get larger, thus enlarging (zooming in on) the picture—but showing a smaller slice of the page. Use this setting when, for example, playing a small QuickTime movie, so that it fills more of the screen. At higher resolutions (such as 1024 x 768), the screen dots get smaller, making your windows and icons smaller, but showing more overall area. Use this kind of setting when you want to see as much screen area as possible—when working on two-page spreads in your page-layout program, for example.

- **Colors.** Today's Mac monitors offer different *color depth* settings, each of which permits the screen to display a different number of colors simultaneously. The Colors pop-up menu generally offers only two choices: Thousands and Millions. (The 256-color choices is dimmed on most Macs unless you turn off the "Show modes recommended" checkbox, as described in Figure 8-8.)

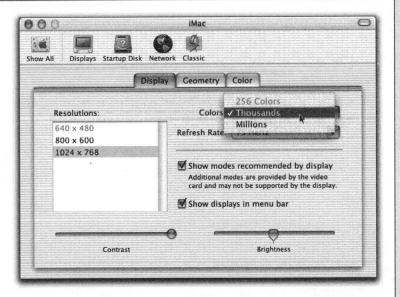

Figure 8-8:
If some of these settings are dimmed, as shown here, turn off "Show modes recommended by display." These "unauthorized" settings now become available; when you choose one, the Mac may ask you to confirm that you can see the effect. If it does something wacky to your screen, on the other hand, the Mac restores the previous setting in 15 seconds.

In the early days of Macintosh, higher color settings required a sacrifice in speed; the Mac took time to compute the color for each of thousands of individual dots that make up the screen image. Today, however, there's very little downside to leaving your screen at its maximum depth setting ("Millions of Colors"). Photos, in particular, look best when your monitor is set to higher depth settings.

Tip: If Mac OS X doesn't seem to recognize a second monitor that you attached while the Mac was asleep, try switching this pop-up menu–to Thousands and then back to Millions, for example. That often forces the Mac to notice its new screen.

• **Refresh Rate.** If you have a choice here at all, this pop-up menu lets you adjust how many times per second your screen image is repainted by your monitor's electron gun. (You don't see this pop-up menu if you have a flat-panel screen.) Choose a setting that minimizes flicker.

• **Brightness, Contrast.** Use these sliders to make the screen look good in the prevailing lighting conditions. You'll usually want Contrast control—if you have it at all (flat-panel screens usually don't)—all the way up, and Brightness near the middle.

Of course, all Mac laptops, most Apple monitors, and Apple keyboards have their own brightness controls, so these software controls are included just for completeness' sake. (Many current Apple keyboards have dedicated brightness controls. If you have an older keyboard, the F14 and F15 usually work as brightness controls.)

Tip: You can adjust the color depth and resolution of your monitor without having to open System Preferences. Just turn on "Show Displays in menu bar," which adds a Monitors pop-up menu (a *menulet*–page 87) to the right end of your menu bar for quick adjustments.

Geometry tab

This pane appears only on Macs with built-in, non-flat screens—for the most part, that means iMacs. It lets you adjust the position, size, and angle of the screen image on the glass itself—controls that can be useful in counteracting distortion in aging monitors.

Tip: Don't miss the opportunity to eliminate the black borders around your screen perimeter! That's just wasted space. Click the Height/Width button. Then click the "expand vertical" and "expand horizontal" buttons at the lower-right corner of the miniature monitor image until you've eliminated the black borders around the screen.

The Color pane

The Color pane lets you calibrate your monitor to create an accurate Color Sync profile for it. See page 338 for details.

Energy Saver

The Energy Saver program is good for you and your Mac in a number of ways. By blacking out the screen after a period of inactivity, it prolongs the life of your monitor. By putting the Mac to sleep a half an hour after you've stopped using it, Energy Saver cuts down electricity costs and pollution. And if your Mac is a laptop, Energy Saver extends the length of the battery charge by controlling the activity of the hard drive and screen.

Sleep settings

When you first open Energy Saver, you're shown a trio of sliders (two of which start out dimmed). The top slider controls when the Mac will automatically go to sleep—anywhere from five minutes to an hour after your last activity. (Activity can be mouse movement, keyboard action, or Internet data transfer; Energy Saver never turns off your Mac in the middle of a download.)

At that time, the screen goes dark, the hard drive stops spinning, and your processor chip slows to a crawl. Your Mac is now in *sleep* mode, using only a fraction of its usual electricity consumption. To wake it up when you return to your desk, press any key; everything you were working on, including open programs and documents, is still on the screen, exactly as it was. (To turn off this automatic sleep feature entirely, drag the slider to Never.)

For more control over the sleeping process, activate the two other sliders by turning on the "Separate timing" checkboxes, as shown in Figure 8-9.

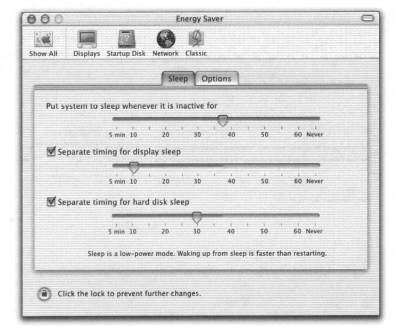

Figure 8-9:
When you turn on the two "Separate timing" sliders, you can specify independent sleep settings for the screen and the hard drive. As shown here, you can have the screen go black after just ten minutes, but keep the hard drive spinning for 30 minutes.

Note: Energy Saver no longer offers automatic scheduled startup and shutdown. There is, however, a workaround: Start up the Mac in Mac OS 9. Use its Energy Saver control panel to schedule a startup. Open the Startup Disk control panel to select Mac OS X as the startup disk, and shut down the Mac. At the appointed time, the machine will start up automatically—in Mac OS X.

Tip: On Macs of old, the beauty of setting the monitor to sleep sooner than the Mac itself was that it put your Mac into *light sleep.* The screen would go dark after its specified period, but awaken *instantly* when you touch a key or click the mouse. This setup didn't save as much electricity as regular sleep, but protected the screen equally well and spared you those ten-second wakeup periods.

In Mac OS X, the Mac *always* wakes almost instantly from sleep—one of the great payoffs of Mac OS X. In short, there's very little reason to set the screen to sleep independently of the Mac itself.

Waking and other options

Click the Options tab in the Energy Saver panel to summon a few more checkboxes:

- **Wake when the modem detects a ring.** This checkbox can be useful in two circumstances: first, if you use your Mac as a fax machine that accepts incoming faxes, and second, if you dial into your Mac from the road. In either case, when a phone call reaches the laptop's modem, the computer wakes up and accepts the call—if this option is turned on.

- **Wake for network administrative access.** This option exists exclusively for the purchasers of the software suite called Mac OS X Server, which lets the network guru in an office control (and, with this checkbox, even wake up) sleeping Macs on the network.

- **Restart automatically after a power failure.** This is a good option to turn on if you leave your Mac unattended and access it remotely, or if you use it as a network file server or a Web server. It ensures that, if there's even a momentary blackout that shuts down your Mac, it will start itself right back up again when the juice returns.

- **Show battery status in menu bar.** You see this one only on a laptop. It puts a handy status indicator in the menu bar—a menulet (page 87)—that keeps you informed of your battery's life, as shown in Figure 8-10.

Figure 8-10:
The battery-status indicator in the menu bar is actually a menu, as shown here. Use the Show command to choose between displaying the actual number of minutes left until a battery is depleted (or recharged, if plugged in) or the percentage of battery life that has been discharged/ recharged.

Keyboard

The Keyboard panel lets you do some frivolous fine-tuning of your keyboard. It also unlocks Mac OS X's strange and remarkable Full Keyboard Access feature, which lets you control your Mac's menus, windows, dialog boxes, buttons, the Dock, and the toolbar, all from the keyboard.

Repeat Rate tab

You're probably too young to remember the antique once known as a *typewriter*. On some electric versions of this machine, you could hold down the letter X key to type a series of XXXXXXXs—ideal for crossing something out in a contract, for example.

On the Mac, *every* key behaves this way. Hold down any key long enough, and it starts spitting out repetitions, making it easy to type, for example, "No WAAAAAAY!" or "You go, girrrrrrrrl!" The two sliders in the Repeat Rate pane of the Keyboard panel govern this behavior. On the right: a slider that determines how long you must hold down the key before it starts repeating (to prevent triggering repetitions accidentally, in other words). On the left: a slider that governs how fast each key spits out letters once the spitting has begun.

Full Keyboard Access tab

For a full discussion of the options on the pane, see page 106.

Mouse

It may surprise you that the cursor on the screen doesn't move five inches when you move the mouse five inches on the desk. Instead, the cursor moves farther when you move the mouse faster.

How *much* farther depends on how you set the first slider in the Mouse panel. The Fast setting is nice if you have an enormous monitor, because you don't need an equally large mouse pad to get from one corner to another. The Very Slow setting, on the other hand, forces you to pick up and put down the mouse a lot as you scoot across the screen. It offers no acceleration at all, but it can be great for highly detailed work like pixel-by-pixel editing in Photoshop. Experimentation is the key.

The Double-Click Speed setting specifies how much time you have to complete a double-click. If you click too slowly—beyond the time you've allotted yourself with this slider—the Mac "hears" two *single* clicks instead.

Trackpad pane

On laptops, the Mouse panel also has a Trackpad pane, whose Tracking Speed and Double-Click Speed controls correspond to the same controls on the Mouse tab.

Much more interesting are the "Use Trackpad for" controls. Under normal circumstances, you touch your laptop's trackpad exclusively to move the cursor. For clicking and dragging, you're supposed to use the clicking button beneath the trackpad.

Many people find, however, that it's more direct to tap and drag directly on the trackpad—using the same finger that's been moving the cursor. That's the purpose of these four checkboxes:

- **Clicking.** When this box is turned on, you can tap the trackpad surface to register a mouse click at the location of the cursor. Double-tap to double-click.

- **Dragging.** Turn on this option if you want to be able to move icons, highlight text, or pull down menus—in other words, to be able to drag, not just click—

using the trackpad. Start by tapping twice on the trackpad—but *immediately* after the second tap, begin dragging your finger. (If you don't start moving promptly, the laptop assumes that you were double-clicking, which could wind up opening some icon you didn't intend to open.) You can stroke the trackpad repeatedly to continue your movement, as long as your finger never leaves the trackpad surface for more than about one second. When you finally stop touching the pad, you "let go," and the drag is considered complete. (All of this is much easier to do than to describe.)

• **Drag lock.** If the dragging maneuver described above makes you too nervous that you're going to "drop" what you're dragging if you stop moving your finger for a fraction of a second, turn on this option instead. Once again, begin your drag by double-clicking. Once again, begin moving your finger immediately after the second click.

When this option is on, however, you can take your sweet time about continuing the movement. In between strokes of the trackpad, you can take your finger off the laptop for as long as you like. You can take a phone call, a shower, or a vacation; the Mac still thinks that you're in the middle of a drag. Only when you tap *again* does the laptop consider the drag a done deal.

• **Ignore Trackpad while typing.** This last option is a huge Mac OS X perk. It addresses a chronic syndrome of laptop owners who turn on the Clicking option of Apple trackpads: As you type along, a finger accidentally brushes the trackpad, sending the insertion point onto a different line of text. Before you even notice, you've typed over, or typed into, some random part of your document.

This glorious option locks out the click-and-drag trackpad functions when you're actually typing on the keyboard—a sweet and simple solution.

Sound

Mac OS X's sound options are a little on the lean side (page 348), but a visit to the Sound panel is still worthwhile. Using the two panes of the Sound panel, you can configure the sound system of your Mac in the following ways:

Alerts

"Alerts" means *error beeps*—the sound you hear when the Mac wants your attention, or when you click someplace you shouldn't.

Mac OS X has introduced a mostly new set of choices in the list of thirteen alert sounds. Only one of the classic old favorites remains—the famous Sosumi (named, the legend goes, when Apple Records threatened to sue Apple Computer for adding sound-recording features to the Mac years ago). The newcomers, including Basso, Frog, Funk, Ping, Pop, and Tink, are funny and clever, yet subdued enough to be of practical value as alert sounds. Just click the sound of your choice to make it your default system beep.

Tip: See the Alert Volume slider in the Alerts pane? Some Mac users are confused by the fact that even when they drag this slider all the way to the left, the sound from games and music CDs still plays at full volume.

The actual *Main Volume* slider for your Mac is at the bottom of the Sound panel. The slider on the Alert Sounds panel is *just* for error beeps; Apple was kind enough to let you adjust the volume of these error beeps independently.

Output tab

"Output" means speakers. For 99 percent of the Mac-using community, this panel offers nothing useful except the Balance slider, with which you can set the balance between your Mac's left and right stereo speakers. The "Choose a device" wording seems to imply that you can choose which speakers you want to use for playback. But Built-in is generally the only choice, even if you have external speakers. (The Mac uses your external speakers automatically when they're plugged in.)

Tip: This System Preferences is another one that offers a "Show in menu bar" option at the bottom. It installs a volume control right in your menu bar, making the volume control instantly accessible from any program.

Internet & Network

The four panels in this section control your Mac's communications with the outside world, whether that means hooking up to the Mac in the next cubicle or a Web site thousands of miles away.

Internet

In the dark and time-consuming days of the early 1990s, the worst aspect of using the Internet was having to set up the Internet programs you used: your email program, Web browser, FTP client, and so on. Each required you to input several pounds of information about you, your Internet connection, and so on.

This control panel neatly solves the problem. It provides a central location where you can record all of this information *once*. After you've done so, you don't need to type these settings into your Internet programs; most can retrieve the information they need from the Internet control panel.

The Internet control panel has five tabs. For most purposes, you don't need to fill in all of these fields, but filling in a few choice ones can save you a lot of time down the road:

- **iTools.** This is where you fill in your member name and password for your free iTools account, if you have one. (See Chapter 18 for a full discussion of iTools.) If you don't have an iTools account, click the Sign Up button to get started.

• **E-mail.** Fill in all blanks; if you're not sure what to type, contact your Internet access company (or its Web page) for help. The most important setting is the Default E-mail Reader pop-up menu, which tells the Mac which email program you use (Mail, Entourage, or whatever). From now on, whenever you click a "Click here to send email" link on a Web page, your that program opens automatically.

• **Web.** Almost all of the settings on this panel are important. Fill in the Home Page (the page you want to open when you first launch your Web browser) and the Search Page (the page you want to open when you click Search in your browser; try *www.google.com*). Next, click Select to specify a Downloads folder—files you download from the Internet will be stored here. (Mac OS X proposes the desktop itself, which is a good idea. The point is to eliminate the frustration of not being able to find something that you downloaded.)

Use the Default Web Browser pop-up menu to indicate which browser—say, Internet Explorer or OmniWeb—you prefer. This is the browser that will open automatically whenever you double-click an Internet location file or a Sherlock Internet-search result, for example.

• **News.** If you're a fan of Internet *newsgroups* (electronic bulletin boards), you can use this panel to specify your server, name, and preferred newsreader program.

Network

The Network panel is the brain of your Mac's Internet and local networking connections. See Chapters 12 and 18 for the rundown of settings you need to plug in.

QuickTime

The settings in the QuickTime panel affect the way movies get played back on your Mac, including movies that stream to you from a Web page and movies stored on your own system that you watch using QuickTime Player (Chapter 14).

You don't even have to touch most of these settings, but a few are worth tweaking to improve your Mac movie-watching experience:

• **Plug-in.** The settings in this pane control the way your Web browser's QuickTime plug-in works with streaming video. The "Play movies automatically" option, for example, tells the plug-in to start playing streaming movies as soon as they begin downloading (rather than waiting for an entire movie to download before starting).

• **Connection.** The only important setting here is Connection Speed. Set it to match the actual speed and type of your Internet connection. Some streaming QuickTime Web sites are set up with multiple versions of the same movie, each saved at a different size and frame rate. Based on your connection speed setting, the QuickTime plug-in can automatically request the appropriately sized version of a movie for the best possible playback.

• **Music.** Nothing to see here, folks. You're supposed to choose a music synthesizer for playing back MIDI music files—but you have only one choice.

- **Media Keys.** Media keys are supposed to be special passwords supported by Quick-Time that unlock movies so you can watch them. As it turns out, nobody uses them.

- **Update.** These controls provide an easy way to download the latest QuickTime software from Apple.

Sharing

Details on how to use the Sharing panel are in Chapter 11.

System Settings

"System" might just as well have been labeled "Misc"; the System Preferences panels in this last row let you configure a jumble of miscellaneous settings.

Classic

Pre–Mac OS X programs can still run under Mac OS X, thanks to a program called Classic. This panel lets you start, stop, and restart Classic (see Chapter 5).

Date & Time

Your Mac's conception of what time it is can be very important. Every file you create or save is stamped with this time; every email you send or receive is marked with this time. As you might expect, setting your Mac's clock is what the Date & Time panel is all about.

Date & Time tab

Go to the Date & Time pane. Select the correct month and year under Today's Date by clicking the little arrow buttons next to the month and year labels. Then specify the *day* of the month by clicking a date on the mini-calendar. Click Save.

To set your clock, start by clicking one of the numbers in the time field under the Current Time label. Then adjust the corresponding number, either by typing the numbers or by clicking the tiny up or down arrow buttons. To jump to the next

---

GEM IN THE ROUGH

Your Free Time-Difference Calculator

You can use the Time Zone pane of the Date &Time panel to calculate the exact time difference between any two points on earth. To do this, you need to have the Time Zone pane open and your *menu bar clock* turned on—set to View as Text, with a digital readout (see the discussion of the menu bar clock in this chapter).

To calculate a time difference, make a note of the current time shown in the menu bar, with the Time Zone correctly set to your own zone. Now drag across the Time Zone map, moving the pointer to a different part of the world. As you drag, notice that the time in the menu bar changes, updating itself as you cross from time zone to time zone. By comparing the *original time* on your menu bar with the *new time* that appears when you've finished dragging, you can easily figure out what the time difference is between any two locations.

---

number for setting, press the Tab key. Alternatively, you can set the time by dragging the hour, minute, or second hands on the analog clock. Finally, click Save. (If you get carried away with dragging the clock hands around and lose track of the *real* time, just click the Revert button to restore the panel settings.)

Tip: You don't have to set the date, time, or time zone on your Mac manually if you use the Network Time option, described below.

Time Zone tab

You'd be surprised how important it is to set the Time Zone for your Mac. If you don't do so, the email and documents you send out—and the Mac's conception of what documents are older and newer—could be hopelessly skewed. Teach your Mac where it lives using the Time Zone map, as shown in Figure 8-11.

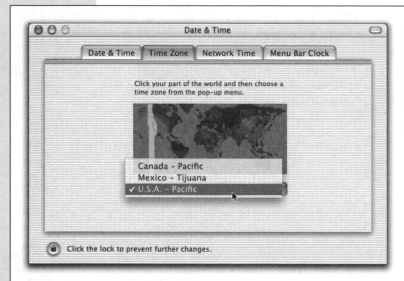

Figure 8-11:
Setting the Time Zone is a two-step process. In the Time Zone pane, first click on a section of the map to select a general region of the world, then use the pop-up menu to specify your country within that region.

Network Time tab

With the network time server option turned on, your Mac sets its own clock by consulting a highly accurate scientific clock on the Internet. Turn on the "Use a network time server" checkbox, select one of the time servers listed in the pop-up window, and then click Set Time Now. (No need to worry about Daylight Savings Time, either; the time servers take that into account.)

Menu Bar Clock tab

In the Menu Bar Clock pane, you can specify whether or not you want the current time to appear, at all times, at the top of your screen. If you turn on the "Show the clock" checkbox, you can choose between two different clock styles from the Options pop-up menu—digital (View as Text) or analog (View as Icon). If you go the View as Text route, you get several other options that govern this digital clock display: whether or not you want to include designations for AM and PM, the display of seconds, the day the week, and a blinking colon.

And by the way: your menu bar clock always shows the current *time*. When you need to know today's *date*, just click the clock. A menu drops down showing the complete date. The menu also lets you switch between digital and analog clock types and provides a shortcut to the Date & Time panel in System Preferences.

Tip: Attention Unix geeks: You can also set the date and time from within Terminal (Chapter 15). Use *sudo* (page 403), type *date yyyymmddhhmm.ss,* and press Enter. (Of course, replace that code with the actual date and time you want, such as *200204051755.00* for April 5, 2002, 5:55 p.m.) You might find this method faster than the Date & Time System Preferences method.

Software Update

Few operating-system ideas are simpler or better than this one: whenever Apple improves or fixes one of the innumerable software pieces that make up Mac OS X, the Software Update program can notify you, download the update, and install it into your System automatically.

Software Update doesn't run rampant through your system software, however; it's quietly respectful. For example, in the beginning, you must manually click the Update Now button when you want the program to dial the Internet for updates. Fur-

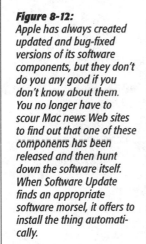

Figure 8-12:
Apple has always created updated and bug-fixed versions of its software components, but they don't do you any good if you don't know about them. You no longer have to scour Mac news Web sites to find out that one of these components has been released and then hunt down the software itself. When Software Update finds an appropriate software morsel, it offers to install the thing automatically.

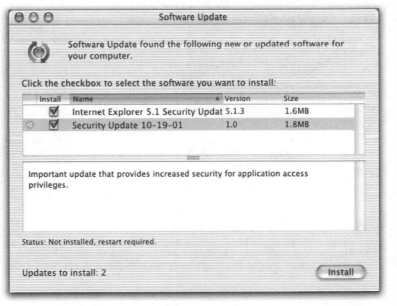

thermore, Software Update doesn't actually download the new software without asking your permission first and explicitly telling you what it plans to install, as shown in Figure 8-12.

For maximum effortlessness, turn on the Automatically radio button and then select a frequency from the "Check for updates" pop-up menu—daily, weekly, or monthly.

Software Update also keeps a meticulous log of everything it drops into your system. You can read this log by clicking the Show Log button.

Speech

Your Mac's ability to speak—and be spoken to—is described starting on page 364.

Startup Disk

Use this panel to pick the System Folder your Mac will use the next time you start your Mac, swapping between Mac OS X and Mac OS 9.2, for example. Check out the details in Chapter 5.

Users

The Users panel contains the tools for creating and setting up new password-protected user accounts on your Mac (see Chapter 11).

Direct System Preferences Access from the Dock

Pining for the days of Mac OS 9, when all control panels were only a click away (in the ⌘ menu)? Pine no more; within one minute, you can have yourself a tidy pop-up menu of System Preferences panels right there in your Dock.

Make a new folder (in your Home folder, for example). Name it whatever you'll want the Dock icon to say—SysPrefs or Control Panels, for example.

Now open your System→Library→ PreferencePanes folder, which contains the icons for the various System Preferences panes. Select all of them—or only the ones you actually use.

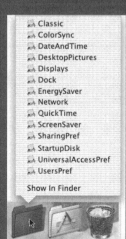

While pressing Option-⌘, drag them into your SysPrefs folder. (Option-⌘-dragging makes aliases of them.) If the .prefPane suffix on the aliases bugs you, select all of the aliases, press ⌘-I, choose Name & Extension from the pop-up menu, and turn on "Hide extension."

Finally, drag the SysPrefs folder onto the right side of your Dock. Now, whenever you want to open a particular panel, just Control-click (or hold the mouse button down on) this SysPrefs Dock icon. You get a handy pop-up list, as shown here.

The Free Programs
of Mac OS X

I n the end, Mac OS X's success or failure will depend on applications. If every
program on earth were available in a Mac OS X version, this clearly superior
operating system would be a runaway hit. We'll get there in time.

In the meantime, Apple has jump-started your software collection by including over
30 freebies: applications for sending email, writing documents, doing math, even
playing games. If you've used earlier incarnations of the Mac OS, several of these
programs will look very familiar. Apple has punched them up with 3-D graphics
and tweaked them to work under Mac OS X, but otherwise they're simply new versions of programs that have been around for years.

Some of the other goodies, however, are totally new programs that not only show
off some of Mac OS X's most dramatic new technologies but let you get real work
done—without having to invest in additional software.

Your Free Mac OS X Programs

You've got a broad assortment of programs in the Applications folder in the main
hard drive window. The Applications→Utilities folder holds another couple dozen
mini-programs that handle such workaday jobs as setting up printers and network
connections, fixing problems on your hard disk, and monitoring the behind-the-
scenes processing that your Mac does whenever you launch and run programs.

All of these programs have been either written expressly for Mac OS X (Cocoa applications) or adapted for it ("Carbonized"—see page 116). This chapter guides you
through every piece of your new software library, one program at a time.

Tip: A reminder: you can jump straight to the Applications folder in the Finder by pressing Option-⌘-A, or by clicking the Applications button in the Finder window toolbar (it's the button that looks like an *A*). You might consider adding the Application folder's icon to the right side of your Dock, too, so that you can get to it no matter what program you're in.

Acrobat Reader 5.0

Just about every computer on earth comes with a copy of Acrobat Reader, the free Adobe program that lets you open and read PDF (Portable Document Format) files (see page 330). As its name implies, Acrobat Reader lets you open and read PDF files—a useful task since, as you've probably noticed, software manuals, product brochures, tax forms, and many other documents get distributed as PDFs these days.

Tip: Here's the most important thing to remember about reading PDF files in Acrobat: *press the Enter key.* With each press, you "turn the page" (or, if you're looking at only part of a page, brings the next portion into view). Press Shift-Enter to go *up* the page (or back a page).

At first glance, the inclusion of Acrobat Reader with Mac OS X may seem a little redundant. After all, Mac OS X comes with its *own* free PDF-reading utility: Preview (described later in this section). Why do you need Acrobat Reader if you already have Preview?

Don't be fooled. Preview can open and display PDFs, but that's about it. Here are some of the features in Acrobat Reader that are missing in Preview:

- **The toolbar.** Reader has a full-blown toolbar that makes it easy to navigate multipage documents, zoom in at any magnification, and trigger other Reader commands with a single click.

- **Full screen mode.** With Reader, you can fill the entire screen with the contents of a PDF, turning it into a cheapo alternative to PowerPoint for making presentations (just press ⌘-L, or choose View→Full Screen).

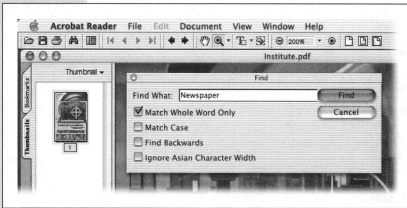

Figure 9-1:
Preview does an admirable job of displaying PDF files, but only Acrobat Reader can let you search for text within a document—a valuable feature considering the vast number of user guides, instruction manuals, product brochures, and business forms that come in PDF form nowadays.

- **Zoom tool.** Lets you zero in on one specific portion of a document. Just click the magnifying-glass tool and then drag diagonally across the section of the page you want to fill your screen.

- **Interactivity.** A PDF can contain form fields that you fill in, or bookmarks and hyperlinks that allow you to jump quickly to various parts of the document, or even to other documents or a Web site. But a PDF's interactive features are lost in Preview, which displays a PDF as if it were only a static picture.

- **Search tools.** Only Acrobat lets you search for text within a PDF, as shown in Figure 9-1.

Adobe has done a surprisingly good job of documenting its additional features within the program itself. Just choose Help→Reader Help in Acrobat (or press ⌘-?) for the details.

Address Book

The Address Book is a database that stores names, addresses, email addresses, phone numbers, and other contact information. It works seamlessly with Mail; both Mail and Address Book are described in Chapter 19.

AppleScript

This folder contains all of the scripts and tools described in Chapter 7.

Calculator

Many features of Mac OS X may take your breath away. You'll keep right on breathing, however, when you encounter the humble Calculator, which lets you do only the most basic math—addition, subtraction, multiplication, and division—using a small onscreen keypad with clickable buttons.

This Calculator isn't wildly different from the one that shipped with Mac OS 9. In fact, it's not wildly different from the *original* Mac calculator that shipped with System 1.0 back in 1984. You won't find memory keys, a percentage key, or any other advanced functions. There's not even a CE key to clear your last entry; if you make a mistake while entering a series of numbers, you have no choice but to hit the Clear key and start over.

Despite its lack of sophistication, the Calculator can be useful for doing quick arithmetic without having to open a spreadsheet. Here's everything you need to know:

- You can operate the Calculator by clicking the onscreen buttons, but it's much easier to press the corresponding number and symbol keys on your keyboard.

Tip: If you have a recent Mac laptop, don't miss the *embedded* numeric keypad, superimposed on the right side of the keyboard, labeled on the keys in a different color ink. When you press the Fn key in the lower-left corner of the keyboard, typing these keys produces the numbers instead of the letters.

- Press the C key to clear the calculator display.

• Once you've calculated a result, you can copy it (using File→Copy, or ⌘-C) and paste your answer directly into another program.

Note: The most shocking thing about the Calculator isn't its lack of new features; it's that it is actually more archaic than the Calculators that came with Mac systems gone by. Apple *removed* one of the coolest features of the old Calculator: you can no longer paste equations from other programs into the Calculator to have them automatically computed for you.

Chess

Mac OS X comes with only one game, but it's a beauty. Chess is a traditional chess game played on a gorgeously rendered board with a set of realistic 3-D style pieces. The program is actually a 15-year-old Unix-based chess program, Gnu Chess, that Apple packaged up in a new wrapper.

Figure 9-2:
Chess isn't just another computerized chess game; it's also one of the more visually striking programs you get with Mac OS X. You don't have to be terribly exact about grabbing the chess pieces when it's time to make your move. You can click anywhere within a piece's current square to drag it into a new position on the board.

Playing a game of Chess

When you launch Chess, you're presented with a fresh, new game that's set up in Human vs. Computer mode—meaning that you (the Human, with the white pieces) get to play against the Computer (your Mac, on the black side). Drag the chess piece of your choice into position on the board, and the game is underway.

Choose Chess→Preferences to find some useful controls like these:

• **Level.** Use this slider to determine how frustrated you want to get when trying to win at Chess. The further you drag the slider toward the Hard side, the more calculations the computer runs before making its next move (and, thus, the harder it gets for you to outthink it). At the easiest setting, Chess won't spend more than five seconds ruminating over possible moves. Drag the slider all the way to the left, however, and the program may analyze *each move* for as long as 10 fun-filled hours. This hardest setting, of course, makes it all but impossible to win a game (which may stretch on for a week or more anyway).

Choosing the Easy setting makes it only mildly impossible.

- **Game.** When you switch the pop-up menu to Computer vs. Human, you and your Mac trade places; the Mac takes the white side of the board and opens the game with the first move, and you play the black side.

On some night when the video store is closed and you're desperate for entertainment, you might also want to try the Computer vs. Computer option, which pits your Mac against itself. To kick off a Computer vs. Computer game, you first have to choose the appropriate Game option in the Preferences dialog box, and then have to open Game→Controls and click the Start Computer vs. Computer Game button. Pour yourself a beer, open a bag of chips, and settle in to watch until someone—either the Mac or the Mac—gains victory.

- **Speech.** This checkbox lets you play Chess using the Mac's built-in voice-recognition features, *telling* your chess pieces where to go instead of dragging them. Page 372 has the details.

Tip: If your Chess-playing skills are less than optimal, the Move menu will become your fast friend. The three commands tucked away there let you undo your last move (great for recovering from a stupid mistake), show your opponent's previous move (in case you failed to notice what the computer just did), or get hints (when you don't have a clue what to do next).

Saving your games

If you want to save your chess games for posterity, Chess gives you three different ways to do so. First, as you might expect, you can choose Game→Save (or Save As) to save a game in progress, so that you can resume it at a later time.

FREQUENTLY ASKED QUESTION

Human vs. Human

Chess has a Computer vs. Human option, a Human vs. Computer option, and even a Computer vs. Computer option. What happened to Human vs. Human? Can't two people play a round of chess on that cool 3-D game board?

Surprisingly, there is no such option. The circa-1986 chess-playing engine on which Apple's Chess game is built was originally developed to demonstrate a computer's remarkable ability to crunch through massive amounts of data when analyzing possible chess moves—not to simply provide a virtual game board. So there's no provision for running a game in which the computer isn't at least one of the players.

If you and a friend want to play chess, break out a real chess set and play in three dimensions. And don't complain...it's good for you.

To archive the moves making up an entire game instead, use the List command, which creates a TextEdit file documenting every move in your game. It lists the moves according to the board coordinates displayed on the game board. A typical move would be recorded as "f8b4," meaning that a piece was moved from the f8 square to the b4 square. Equipped with a Chess list document, you could re-create an entire game, move by move.

Finally, the Print command lets you print full-color "snapshots" of your game-in-progress at any point.

Pink Knight Takes Mauve Bishop

There isn't much you can do to customize the appearance of Chess. You can't choose between different style chess pieces, game boards, or backgrounds, as you can with some other commercial chess software. You can, however, easily change the colors of the chess pieces. What better way to have, say, Pink vs. Green battle it out instead of the usual White and Black?

To colorize, choose Game→Controls. Click one of the rectangular color swatches that appear next to each of the chess pieces to open the standard

Mac OS X color picker.

Pick a color using any of the Color Picker options (see page 115).

Click the Set Piece Color button to apply the color to the selected chess pieces.

These colors *don't* appear, by the way, when you pop Chess into ugly, boring two-dimensional mode (View→2 Dimensional), which displays an unimpressively flat, 1985-ish 2-D version of the game board.

Clock

Launching Clock puts a digital or analog clock in a floating window right on your desktop, or in the Dock. This was a big deal in the Public Beta version of Mac OS X, which lacked a menu-bar clock. Today, of course, you can use the Date & Time pane in System Preferences to plant a clock (digital or analog) right in your menu bar, just as in earlier versions of the Mac OS.

Still, a visit to Clock→Preferences gives you all sorts of options as to how you want this clock to look and act.

- **Analog vs. digital.** You can choose between two different formats for the clock: either traditional analog (with or without a second hand) or digital, which also displays the month, day, and day of the week. The analog version is more elegant, but the digital display is more informative.

- **Location.** You can put the Clock in its own free-floating window on the desktop or permanently park it in the Dock as a living icon that ticks away right there in its docked location.

- **Transparency.** Transparency effects—made possible by the powerful Quartz graphics engine—look dazzling in the Clock program. The Transparency slider has six settings that let you control the degree to which you can see through the clock face itself when you display it in its own window (see Figure 9-3).

Tip: Why order custom-made clocks (logo clocks, comedy clocks) from cheap mail-order catalogs? Deface your *own* clock! Page 426 has the details for making Clock use a face design of your very own.

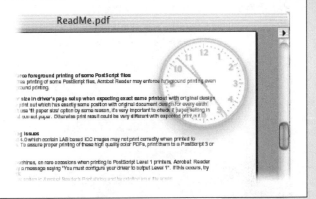

Figure 9-3:
The ghosted, semi-transparent image of the Clock can float over the desktop, hover above Finder windows, or even superimpose itself over open documents windows, as shown here. If it gets in your way, you can always banish the Clock to the Dock. Open Clock Preferences and change the Display setting from "In a floating window" to "In the Dock."

TROUBLESHOOTING MOMENT

Clock Problems

I can't get to my Clock Preferences anymore! The Clock program is running—it's out there on my desktop, hovering translucently over my windows—and Clock is listed as the active program in the menu bar. But when I go to pull down the Clock menu, I get nothing. The menus have disappeared!

This can happen when the Clock is in floating-window mode and you switch back to it after working in other programs. To restore the menus, make Clock the active program (by either clicking on the clock itself or on its icon in the Dock), and then press ⌘-H to hide it. Now click the clock icon in the Dock again. The Clock reappears, and the menus are back.

DVD Player

DVD Player, your Mac's built-in movie projector, didn't appear in Mac OS X until version 10.1. See complete details starting on page 265.

Image Capture

This powerful (and unsung) little program makes it easy to download pictures from a USB digital camera and process them automatically (turning them into a Web page, scaling them to email-able size, and so on).

Image Capture works only with USB cameras that are designed to be auto-recognized in this way. Most recent Canon, HP, Olympus, Epson, Nikon, Sony, Kodak, and Fuji cameras work this way, but check Apple's Web site for a partial list of compatible models.

If you have one of the lucky cameras, though, the system is beautiful; just switch on the camera and hook it up to your Mac. Image Capture pops open automatically (see Figure 9-4).

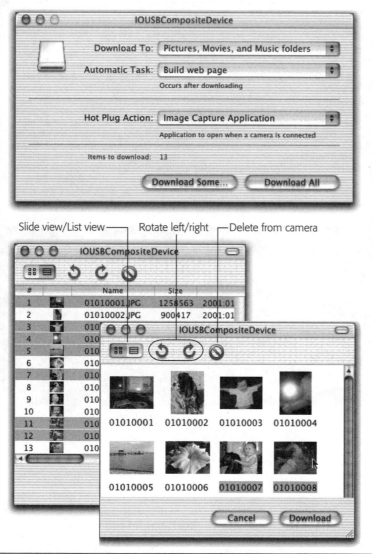

Slide view/List view — Rotate left/right — Delete from camera

Figure 9-4:
Top: Image Capture opens automatically when you attach a USB camera to your Mac. One click (on Download All) transfers its pictures to your hard drive.

Bottom: If you click Download Some, you get this "slide-sorter" window, where you can choose the individual pictures you want to download, or use the buttons at the top to rotate or delete (from the camera) selected shots. In slide-sorter view, Shift-click or ⌘-click the thumbnails of the pictures you want. In list view, Shift-click or ⌘-click as though they're Finder list-view files (see page 57 for details).

Tip: Sure, Image Capture *opens* automatically when you plug in your camera. But you still have to click the Download button to transfer the pictures—you call that automatic?

Yes, if you visit Image Capture→Preferences and turn on "Automatically download all items." From now on, just plugging in the camera both opens Image Camera *and* downloads its photos!

Here, you can use these pop-up menus:

Download To

Use this pop-up menu to choose a destination folder for the pictures. Image Capture proposes putting them into your home folder's Pictures folder. (Most cameras these days can also record sound and short video clips, which Image Capture proposes storing in your Music and Movies folders.)

That's as good a place as any. When the downloading process is complete, Mac OS X opens this folder automatically, saving you the trouble or confusion of finding it.

Automatic Task

Download, schmownload—Image Capture is just warming up. It comes equipped to process the downloaded photos in several useful ways. For example:

- **None.** Translation: "Just download the pictures, please."

- **Web page.** Creates an actual, and very attractive, Web page of your downloaded shots. Against a black background, you get thumbnail (small) images of the pictures in a Web page document called index.html. (You'll find it in your home folder→Pictures→Index folder, which also contains the graphics files incorporated into this HTML document.) Image Capture automatically opens up this page in your Web browser, proud of its work.

  Just click one of the small images to view it at full size, exactly as your Web site visitors will be able to do once this page is actually on the Web. (Getting it online is up to you, although Apple's free HomePage feature is one of the easiest methods; see page 449.)

- **Format 3 x 5, Format 8 x 10....** These options also create Web-page photo galleries, but not for displaying on the Web. Instead, these are designed for printing out. Each offers neatly arranged photos in the dimensions you've selected—3 x 5, 4 x 6, and so on—ready to print out (and then, presumably, to cut apart with scissors or a paper cutter).

  After the download, the first of these pages opens automatically in your Web browser. The page itself is called *5x7index01.html* (for example), and it sits in your designated Pictures folder along with the downloaded pictures themselves. (If you downloaded too many pictures to fit on one sheet, you'll also find Web page documents called *5x7index02.html*, *5x7index03.html*, and so on.)

  Alongside these HTML documents, however, you'll find an important file called *5x7tips.html*. It's a half-page instruction sheet that explains how to set up your

Web browser for correctly printing these photo sheets (for example, turn off headers and footers, turn on "Print Wide Pages," and so on).

Once you've read these instructions and turned on your printer, you're ready to choose File→Print and pretend you're a one-hour photo shop.

Note: These "Format" commands never touch the actual downloaded photos. The downloaded image files themselves retain their full size and resolution.

- **Other.** The beauty of the Image Capture system is that these post-processing commands are ordinary AppleScripts (Chapter 7). People can write additional processing scripts—and, in fact, have already done so (by downloading new scripts from the Apple Web site). Once you've downloaded them, drop them into your Library→Image Capture→Scripts folder, and then enjoy their presence in the newly enhanced Automatic Task pop-up menu.

Hot Plug Actions

This pop-up menu specifies what program should open automatically when you connect the camera to the Mac. Usually you'll want Image Capture itself to open, or better yet, iPhoto (Apple's free downloading/organizing/printing program). But if your camera came with a specialized downloading application, you can identify it using this pop-up menu.

Download All, Download Some

Clicking Download All, of course, begins the process of downloading the photos to the folder you've selected. A progress dialog box appears, showing you thumbnail images of each picture that flies down the wire.

Clicking Download Some, however, opens the picture browser shown at bottom in Figure 9-4. In either a list view or a slide-sorter view, you can Shift- or ⌘-click the photos you want to download, rotate, or delete from the camera.

GEM IN THE ROUGH

Image Capture Super-Prefs

Apple spared no expense on this baby. Lurking in Image Capture→Preferences are, of course, some preference settings you can change. But in Image Capture's case, these aren't just little tweakers. They're very powerful options, and well worth exploring.

The Download Options tab, for example, is where you can set the downloading to happen automatically when you plug in the camera, saving you a click on the Download button. Here's where you specify, too, that you want to delete the photos from the camera after they've been downloaded to the Mac—a step-saving option.

The View Options tab controls the displays you see at bottom in Figure 9-4: how big the icons appear in "slide-sorter" view, and which columns of information appear in the list view—date, height and width, resolution (DPI), aperture, and so on.

Internet Connect

If you have a full-time Internet connection (cable modem, DSL, or corporate network, for example), skip this section.

Internet Connect is just for dial-up modems. It shows your current dial-up status and settings (as configured in the Network pane of your System Preferences) and provides a Connect/Disconnect button for opening or closing a connection. Here's what you can accomplish with Internet Connect:

- Click Connect to dial out using your current modem settings.

- Once you're hooked up, check the status display to confirm whether or not your modem successfully connected to your ISP—or if you've been disconnected.

- You can also see your connection *speed,* to find out if you really connected up at 56 K (ha!), or if your modem was only able to negotiate a 28 K connection.

- A timer shows how long you've been connected.

- Internet Connect keeps a neat log of your connection activity (choose Window→ Connection Log). Reading this log is about as exciting as reading random entries from the White Pages. But if you're having serious connection problems, it can be a useful troubleshooting tool.

- The "Show modem status in menu bar" checkbox lets you use a menu-bar icon to dial and observe your connections—without using Internet Connect at all.

Of course, even then, you don't really need Internet Connect to get online. If your dial-up settings are configured correctly (see page 434), your Mac will automatically dial whenever you launch a program that requires one (such as Internet Explorer).

Internet Explorer

The OS X version of Microsoft's Web browser is almost identical to its predecessor, except for the new window style, buttons, and other Aqua interface features.

iPhoto

This remarkable (and free) new "i" program debuted in January 2002 as a worthy member of the iMovie/iTunes family. When you connect a USB camera and click Import, the program automatically sucks the pictures in to your Mac, whereupon you can rotate, crop, organize, sort and print them. The best part may be the Book feature, which lets you design and order a hardbound, linen-covered, professionally printed picture book for as little as $30. It comes to you by mail in about a week.

iTunes

iTunes is Apple's beloved digital music-library program. (Chapter 10 tells all.)

Mail

For the first time in Macintosh history, Apple has written its own email program. See Chapter 19 for the whole story on Mac OS X Mail.

Preview

Preview is Mac OS X's native graphics viewer—a more powerful version of Picture-Viewer, the graphics viewer that came with earlier versions of the Mac OS. Whenever you take a screenshot in Mac OS X, grab an image from a Web page, make a picture clipping, or use the Preview button in a Print dialog box, Preview takes over. It does the work of opening and displaying the image on screen.

Preview's hallmark is its surprising versatility. It works with pictures saved in a wide variety of formats, including not just the typical JPEG, TIFF, GIF, and PICT images, but also less commonly used formats like BMP, PNG, SGI, TGA, and MacPaint. In addition, Preview can open Photoshop files and multipage PDF documents.

Converting images with Preview

Preview doesn't just open all these file formats—it can also convert between most of them (see Figure 9-5). You can pop open some old Mac PICT files and turn them into BMP files for a Windows user, pry open some SGI files created on a Silicon Graphics workstation and turn them into JPEGs for use on your Web site, and so on.

All you have to do is open the file you want to convert and choose File→Export. In the Save As dialog box that appears, choose the new format for the image using the Format pop-up menu. (For each format, the Options button may be available. When exporting to JPEG, for example, you can choose a Quality setting. When saving TIFF files, you can choose to turn built-in compression on or off. If the Options button is active, click it and choose the settings you want.)

Finally, click OK to dismiss the Options dialog box, and then click Save to export the file.

Figure 9-5:
One of Preview's most powerful features is its Export command, which lets you save documents in ten different file formats. While Preview understands many of the most common formats, there are a few notable exceptions. You can't open, save, or export EPS files using Preview. And while you can open GIFs, Preview can't convert files in other formats into GIF (you can thank the lawyers for that; see page 342).

Flipping your view with Preview

Preview isn't Photoshop. It's not even AppleWorks; you won't find a single drawing or painting tool. But the Display menu does let you do some image manipulation of the most basic kind. You can rotate most images (but not PDF files) in 90-degree increments and flip them vertically or horizontally.

Preview and PDF

You can open and read PDF files with Preview, but you won't be able to use any of the interactive features built into some PDF files—things like bookmarks, hyperlinks, forms, and so on. For those functions, you need to use Acrobat Reader, described earlier in this chapter.

Here's what you *can* do with a PDF file using Preview:

- Save out a single page from a PDF as a TIFF file, so that you can use it in other graphics, word processing, or page layout programs—some of which might not directly support PDF. Microsoft Word, for example, can accept TIFF graphics, but not PDFs.

- Use ⌘-left arrow and ⌘-right arrow to page through a document.

- Zoom in and out using ⌘-Up Arrow and ⌘-Down Arrow. You can also fit a page to the size of the window (⌘-=), and display the PDF at actual size (⌘-Option-=).

- Turn antialiasing (font smoothing) on or off to improve readability. (Though antialiased text generally looks great, it's sometimes easier to read very small type with antialiasing turned off. It's a little jaggy, but clearer.)

- Turn on Continuous Scrolling, so that you can scroll through multipage PDF documents in one long continuous stream instead of jumping from page to page when you use the scroll bars.

QuickTime Player

There is a lot to say about Apple's new QuickTime player, but it's in Chapter 14.

Sherlock

Sherlock, another carryover from earlier Mac operating systems, is a search program designed to help you track down files on your own system and on the Internet. Read all about it in Chapter 20.

Stickies

Stickies lets you create virtual Post-it notes that you can stick anywhere on your screen—a triumphant software answer to the thousands of people who stick notes to themselves on the edges of their *actual* monitors.

You can use Stickies to type quick notes and to-do items, paste in Web addresses or phone numbers you need to remember, or store any other little scraps and snippets of text you come across. Your electronic Post-its show up whenever the Stickies program is running.

These sticky notes have been a feature of the Mac OS since the days of System 7—but they've taken a quantum leap forward in Mac OS X. In the old days, the notes you created with Stickies were text-only, single-font deals (which, when you think about it, was all you really needed to type effective little notes like "don't forget to buy cabbage" or "acupuncturist @ 3 pm").

With the Mac OS X version of Stickies, however, you can use a mix of fonts, text colors, and styles within each note. You can even copy and paste *pictures, movies and sounds* into your notes; by dropping PICT, GIF, JPEG, QuickTime, AIFF, whole PDF files, and other files into your notes, you can create the world's most elaborate reminders and to-do lists (Figure 9-6).

In a more practical vein, you can now spell-check your notes. And the Find command can search and replace text across multiple notes, which is great for tracking down stray morsels of information without having to scan through your notes one at a time.

Figure 9-6:
Stickies never looked like this *before. Thanks to full text formatting features and support for graphics and multimedia, even the humble "to-do item" can display a certain graphic sophistication in Mac OS X. No wonder Apple killed off the Scrapbook—who needs it anymore?*

Creating sticky notes

The first time you launch Stickies, a few sample notes show up automatically, describing some of the program's features. You can quickly dispose of each sample by clicking the close box in the upper-right corner of each note or by choosing

File→Close (⌘-W). Each time you close a note, a dialog box asks if you want to save the note. If you click Don't Save, the note disappears permanently.

To create a new note, choose File→New Note (⌘-N) and start typing. Besides the obvious click-and-type method, there are at least a few other interesting ways you can add information to a note:

- Drag text in from any other program, such as TextEdit, AppleWorks, or Microsoft Word.

- Drag text clippings from the desktop directly into notes to add their entire contents.

- Drag the icon of a single-page PDF file into a note. (Stickies can't accept multipage PDF files.)

- Choose File→Import and select any plain text file or RTF (Rich Text Format) document to bring into a note.

- Drag a PICT, GIF, JPEG, or TIFF file into a note to add a picture. Or drag a sound or movie in. (A message will ask if you're sure you want to copy the whole whomping QuickTime movie into a little Stickies note.)

- Drag URLs into a note directly from Internet Explorer's Address Bar.

- In TextEdit, Mail, or other Carbon applications, select a chunk of text and then choose TextEdit→Services→Make Sticky. This command launches Stickies, creates a new note, and fills it with your selected text, all in one step.

Tip: Have a favorite style for your Stickies notes? First create a new note, choosing the color and text style that you like and setting it to the size you prefer. Then choose Note→Use as Default. All new notes you create will now appear in the size, font, and color of your choice.

Growing and shrinking notes

Once you start plastering your Mac with notes, it doesn't take long to find yourself plagued with desktop clutter. Fortunately, Stickies includes a few built-in tricks for managing a deskful of notes:

- There's a small resize handle on the lower-right corner of each note. Drag it to make notes larger or smaller on screen.

- Use the small triangle in the upper-left corner of each note to zoom and shrink note windows with a single click. The first click collapses a note down to a more compact size. Another click pops the note back open to normal size.

- The best option: Double-click anywhere along the dark strip at the top of each note to miniaturize it into a compact one-line mini-note, as shown in Figure 9-7. You also can miniaturize a selected note by choosing Window→Miniaturize Window (⌘-M).

- If you have notes scattered randomly across the desktop, you can line them all up in a neatly ordered cascading stack by choosing Window→Arrange in Front. This works especially well if you keep your notes minimized, as suggested in the previous paragraph. The Arrange in Front command gathers up the minimized notes and stacks them at the center of the screen.

Tip: The most efficient way to use Stickies is to keep them in their miniaturized state, as shown in Figure 9-7. When a note is miniaturized, the first line of text shows up in tiny type right in the collapsed title bar of the note, so you don't have to expand the note to remember what's in it. And since many—if not most—of your notes can probably be summed up in a couple of words ("pick up dry cleaning," "call mom,") it's perfectly possible to keep your sticky notes in their miniaturized state permanently.

Figure 9-7:
If the first line of text gets truncated, as in the third note shown here, you can tug the right corner of the note and drag it wider without deminiaturizing it.

Formatting notes

Stickies has several word-processor-like commands for creating designer sticky notes, with any combination of fonts, colors, and styles. (You can also choose from six different background colors from the Color menu.) For the full scoop on Mac OS X's Font panel, choosing colors, and using the Copy Font command, see page 334.

Saving sticky notes

The notes you create in Stickies last only as long as you keep them open. If you close a note to get it out of the way, it vanishes permanently.

Tip: If you accidentally close a note that contains information you need, you have one chance to recover it: promptly choose Edit→Undo Close Window. It brings the recently closed note back from oblivion.

If you want to preserve the information you've stuffed into your notes in a more permanent form, you can use File→Export Text to save each note as a stand-alone TextEdit document. When you use the Export Text command, you have several options:

- **Plain Text.** This option saves the contents of your note as a plain text file, with no formatting and no pictures.

- **RTF** stands for Rich Text Format, a special format recognized by most word processors (including AppleWorks and Microsoft Word) that preserves most formatting, including font, style, and color choices. You'll be able to open the resulting RTF file in just about any word processor with all of your formatting still intact.

- **RTFD.** RTFD, a strange and powerful variant of RTF, is a Rich Text Format document *with attachments*. How do you "attach" items to an RTFD file? There's only one way using Stickies: Drag the icon of an actual application (such as Clock or Calculator, or whatever), or a multipage PDF file, into a sticky note. The icon for the program or document appears in the note, but double-clicking on the icon doesn't do anything. When you export the note as an RTFD file, the result is a TextEdit document that has embedded within it the *entire* program or document that you dragged in. The program icon appears just as it did in the sticky note, but if you double-click it, the program now actually launches. (For more about RTFD files, see the "Files within Files within Files" sidebar on page 228.)

  If you don't have embedded programs or documents in your notes, then exported RTFD files are exactly the same as their RTF counterparts.

- **Save as Stationery.** This checkbox, available whenever you export a note, lets you save a note that can serve as a template, complete with formatting and even text or graphics, for new notes in the future. So, for example, if you wanted to regularly post a note that had the heading "This Week's Shopping List," you could create a stationery document and save yourself from having to type those words into a new note each week.

  Mac OS X saves Stickies stationery with a *.tpl* file name extension. To use the template, choose File→Import Text, and then choose the .tpl file. (You can't double-click on a Stickies stationery document to create a new note.) You get a

Kenneth, Where are the Stickies?

In the days of Mac OS 9, it was easy to find the file that actually stores the text of your Stickies—it was called Stickies File, and it sat right there in your System Folder→ Preferences folder. Because you could see it, you could back it up, copy it when you bought a new Mac, email it to other people, or whatever.

In Mac OS X, the Stickies note database is in your Home folder→Library, but don't bother looking; it's invisible, thanks to the period that begins its name (.StickiesDatabase).

In other words, you'll have to use Terminal (Chapter 15) to copy it. You can read that chapter for a full explanation of the commands you'll need to type. Here, however, is all you have to do:

At the % symbol, type *cd ~/Library* and press Return. (You've just shifted the Mac's attention on your home folder→Library folder.)

Now type *cp .StickiesDatabase ['the folder path where you want to copy it']*—and press Enter again. Replace the phrase in brackets (including the brackets) with the *path* of the folder or disk where you want to move the Stickies database—a backup disk or another Mac, for example. (You have to use slashes to separate the names of folders-in-folders, and you have to surround the whole path with single quotes if any of the folder names include spaces.) Full details on paths on page 378.

In any case, this command copies your Stickies database to its new home.

fresh, new note containing whatever was in the template. (Unfortunately, a Stickies stationery document stores a note's text and font style, but not its color, size, or shape.)

Tip: You can import your old Stickies file from your old Mac OS 9 System Folder. Just choose File→Import Classic Stickies. In the Open File dialog box, navigate to the old System Folder→Preferences→Stickies File document and open it.

Stickies Services

Several of Mac OS X's *Services*—basic features that can be shared by any Mac OS X program, as described on page 120—have special relevance in Stickies:

- **Grab.** Using the various Grab commands, you can capture a screenshot (either the whole screen, or a selected portion of it) and plug it directly into a note in one step. (For details on creating these screenshots, see page 343.)

- **Mail.** This command launches the Mail program, creates a new email message, and then pastes whatever text you had selected in a sticky note directly into the Message box.

  Or, if you'd highlighted an email address in a sticky note, use the Mail To command; watch as your Mac automatically creates a new email message in Mail and fills in the "To" field with the selected address.

Note: You must have some sticky-note text *selected* to use the Mail, Summarize, and TextEdit services listed in the Stickies menu. Otherwise, those commands are dimmed out.

The Hidden Stickies Commands

The casual Stickies user may miss some of the program's more interesting commands, which are accessible only through the contextual menus that pop up when you Control-click a sticky note. Here's what you'll find *only* in the contextual pop-up menus:

Check Spelling As You Type. Turning this spell-check option on flags misspelled words the moment you type them. You have to turn this option on or off for each individual *note*—not for the Stickies program in general.

Font underlining. For some reason, you can format text with underlining using only the contextual pop-up menu,

not the regular Note menu. (Bold and italic, however, are available from *both* menus.)

Speech. Don't just read your notes—*listen* to them. You can use the Mac's Text-to-Speech feature to hear your notes read aloud. Choose Speech→Start Speaking to hear the Mac read a selected portion of a note, or use the command with nothing selected to hear the entire contents of a note. The only way to stop the speech is to Control-click again and choose Speech→Stop Speaking.

(To pick the voice and speed of the reader, go to the Speech pane of System Preferences, as described on page 370).

- **Summarize.** Select text in a note and choose Summarize; you get a new text document containing a condensed, summarized version of your note, created by a program called Summary Service (see page 120). To save the summarized document as a TextEdit document, choose File→Save As.

- **TextEdit.** Here's the easiest way to turn a sticky note into a real double-clickable document. Select the contents of the note and then choose Stickies→Services→TextEdit→Open Selection. Mac OS X instantly turns your selection into a new TextEdit document ready to be saved.

Tip: Earlier versions of Stickies had a useful preference setting called "Launch at system startup." Turning on this checkbox caused Stickies to launch every time you started your Mac, so that your sticky notes automatically appeared on your desktop. (What's the point of writing yourself reminders, after all, if you then forget to launch the program that displays them?)

The "Launch at system startup" checkbox is conspicuously absent from the Mac OS X version of Stickies—but you can accomplish precisely the same arrangement by using the Login tab of System Preferences, as described on page 279.

System Preferences

This program opens the door to the very nerve center of Mac OS X's various user preferences, settings, and options. Chapter 8 covers every option in detail.

TextEdit

The Mac has always come with some kind of basic word processor. In the old days there was TeachText, a stone-tools-level program that could open only one text file at a time. Then came SimpleText, which opened multiple documents and offered a few more formatting options, but still couldn't handle anything more than a 32 K file.

TextEdit, however, qualifies as a real word processor—a basic one, to be sure, but capable of creating real documents with real formatting. (There's even a multiple-level Undo command.) If you had to, you could write a novel in TextEdit and it would look pretty decent.

Plain Text vs. Rich Text

TextEdit can create documents of two types: rich text and plain text. It's important to understand the difference.

Plain text is just what it sounds like: plain, unformatted text. In a plain text document, there are no font attributes, no bold or italic styles, no margins, no hanging indents, no formatting of any kind—just plain text. A text file usually has a three-letter .txt file name extension.

In *rich text* mode, TextEdit saves documents as RTF (Rich Text Format) files, complete with font, style, color, paragraph alignment, and other formatting. Any word processor can open the resulting file (which is saved with an extension of ".rtf" at the end of its name).

TextEdit also has some surprising hidden power. For example, you can open up HTML documents with TextEdit in two different modes. In one mode, TextEdit interprets the HTML and displays it just like a Web browser; in the other, it opens the file as plain text so that you can edit the source code.

Tip: TextEdit recognizes some of the very same keyboard shortcuts found in Microsoft Word. For example, you can advance through documents one word at a time by pressing Option-left arrow or Option-right arrow. Adding the Shift key to those key combinations lets you *select* one whole word at a time. You can also use the Control or ⌘ key in conjunction with the right and left arrow keys to jump to the beginning or end of a line.

Setting up TextEdit

When you first launch TextEdit, it's not very impressive. You see a blank, untitled document with no toolbar, no margins, and no rulers. It looks like a nearly useless text editor. It looks like TeachText.

To unleash the program's full potential as a word processor, you have to do some setting up:

- **Choose Format→Wrap to Page.** Now you'll see the actual width of your page, with visible margins—just as in a real word processor. (The default Wrap to Window mode is a marginless view in which your text reflows to fill the width of the window.) Wrap to Page view also gets you a Zoom menu in the lower-right corner of each window with ten different levels of magnification.

- **Turn on the text ruler.** Choose Format→Text→Show Ruler (⌘-R). Now you've got a ruler across the top of the window, with all the standard tools for setting margins, indents, tabs, line spacing, and paragraph alignment. It works almost exactly like the rulers you'd find in Microsoft Word or AppleWorks (Figure 9-8).

- **Fire up the spell-checker.** Go to Edit→Spelling→Check Spelling As You Type, if you like, to turn on interactive spell-checking. It works just as it does in Microsoft Word and other word processors: misspelled words get flagged with a dashed red line the moment you type them.

Now you've got something that's starting to look and act like a real word processor. But before you start typing away, pay a visit to TextEdit→Preferences to set up some other important TextEdit options.

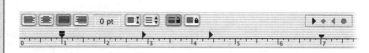

Figure 9-8:
The Text Ruler is always hidden when you create a new document. Pressing ⌘-R makes it appear and disappear.

Tip: To open and work with a Microsoft Word or AppleWorks document in TextEdit, with formatting intact, export it from Word or AppleWorks as a Rich Text Format file. This will keep all your formatting intact.

The TextEdit Preferences

The settings in the TextEdit Preferences window have no effect on already open documents—only to documents you open or create from now on. Most of the settings are self-explanatory, but here are a few that may not be immediately clear:

- **New Document Font.** If Helvetica 12 doesn't especially float your boat, you can change TextEdit's starting font. Note that you can set *two* default fonts—one for Rich Text documents and another one for Plain Text files.

- **New Document Format.** Change this to Rich Text, with the Wrap to Page checkbox turned on, so that any new documents you create will appear in page-layout view.

- **New Window Size.** These settings have no effect unless you're in Wrap to Window mode. If you *are* in Wrap to Window mode, then these dimensions determine the size of the window that appears each time you create a new TextEdit document.

- **Saving.** Feel free to ignore the backup and read-write preferences; they have no effect on TextEdit. However, it's a good idea to keep the last option turned on, so that text files you create with TextEdit are automatically saved with a ".txt" extension, which makes it easier to exchange files with Windows users.

- **Plain Text Encoding.** These settings reconcile the slightly different character sets (alphabets) that may be used by different operating systems to represent plain text. Keep these settings on Automatic and forget about them. In almost every case, TextEdit will select the right encoding system based on the contents of the file.

- **Rich text processing.** When you keep these settings turned off, TextEdit opens and displays HTML documents as though it's a Web browser, interpreting the tags to render a fully formatted page. It handles RTF documents the same way, interpreting the behind-the-scenes tags that indicate the font faces, colors, styles,

---

TROUBLESHOOTING MOMENT

Case of the Disappearing Ruler

It could happen to you. All of a sudden, your whole document switches to an ugly font, you can't change any of the formatting, and the Show Ruler command is dimmed out. What's gone wrong?

You've accidentally thrown yourself into Plain Text mode, which ignores all that formatting stuff. Font styles, paragraph attributes, and the text ruler are only available when

you create a rich text document. In all likelihood, you inadvertently hit Shift-⌘-T, the keystroke that toggles between Plain Text and Rich Text modes.

You can remedy the situation by pressing ⌘-Shift-T again, or by choosing Format→Make Rich Text. You might also want to double-check the TextEdit Preferences to make sure the New Document Format is set to Rich Text, too.

---

and so on. But if you turn on the Ignore checkboxes, TextEdit *doesn't* interpret the HTML or RTF tags; instead, it opens these files as plain text, so that you can view the raw "source" inside them (see Figure 9-9).

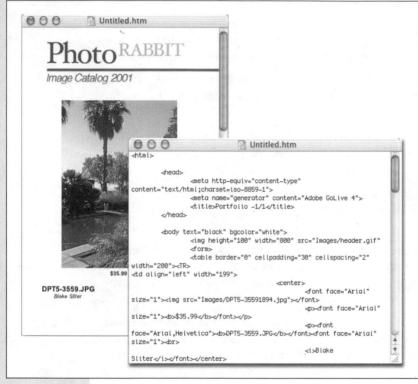

Figure 9-9:
Here's the same Web page as seen by TextEdit in its default mode (left), and in its "Ignore rich text commands" mode, which lets you edit the raw source code. You can choose the mode you want on the fly each time you open a file: Just turn on or off the "Ignore rich text commands" option right in the Open dialog box.

Formatting documents in TextEdit

For a free program that Apple tossed in primarily for opening Read Me files, TextEdit has a surprisingly good selection of real formatting tools:

- In the Format→Font submenu are the standard commands for applying Bold, Italic, and Underline styles to selected text.

- To change a font, or font size, press ⌘-T or choose Format→Font→Font Panel to open up the standard Mac OS X Font Panel (page 334).

- Common paragraph-alignment options—Align Left, Align Right, Center, Justify—are all available in Format→Text submenu.

Tip: In the old days, you could add pictures to a SimpleText document, but not by simple pasting or dragging. Fortunately, you can easily add graphics to TextEdit files by dragging or pasting pictures directly into a document. The program understands TIFF, PICT, JPG, and GIF formats.

TextEdit's other writing tools

TextEdit includes a couple of other very useful document-editing tools:

- **Allow Hyphenation.** When you select this command from the Format menu, TextEdit breaks up words by syllable and inserts hyphens when necessary in order to create more visually pleasing line breaks.

POWER USERS' CLINIC

Advanced Typography in TextEdit

If you just sprayed your coffee upon reading the heading of this sidebar, you're to be forgiven. *Advanced typography* in TextEdit? Isn't that a little bit like saying, "page layout in SimpleText"?

Not at all. Apple designed humble TextEdit to be more than a Read Me file-opening machine. It's also a showcase for Mac OS X's typographical smarts.

Most of the commands in the Format→Font submenu should be familiar to you: Bold, Italic, Underline, and so on. But a few were once found only in expensive page-layout programs like PageMaker and QuarkXPress. For example:

Kern. Use these commands, such as Tighten and Loosen, to nudge the letters of the selected text closer together or farther apart—an especially useful feature when you're fiddling with headlines and headings.

There are no controls to set *how much* you want to kern the text, but you can apply these commands repeatedly to the same text selection to intensify them. If you want your text to be very tight, for example, just keep choosing the Tighten command; the characters will creep closer and closer together until they crash into each other.

Ligature. Ligatures are letter pairs, such as fl and ff, that, in fancy typesetting, are often conjoined into special combination characters, as shown here. If you choose Format→Font→Ligature→Use Default (or Use All) TextEdit will display these letter pairs with the appropriate ligatures. (This works only if the font you're using has those ligatures built into it. New York, Charcoal, Apple Chancery,

and Adobe Expert fonts do, for example, but many other fonts don't.)

Baseline. The baseline is the imaginary "floor" that text characters rest on in a line of type. You can push text above this line or sink it below the baseline using the Raise and Lower commands in the Baseline submenu. The Superscript and Subscript commands shift characters far above or below the baseline, so you can write stuff like H_2O^5.

Character Shape. In a few fonts, such as Adobe Expert fonts, this submenu offers a choice between Traditional Form and specialized type treatments like Small Caps.

fluffy fluffy

Copy Font/Paste Font. Once you've formatted some text using all these elaborate formatting controls, it would be a shame to have to spend time formatting another passage the same way. Fortunately, these commands let you copy and paste just the font formatting to other text in your document—the font, color, style, and size, but none of the actual text or paragraph attributes, such as alignment. This process is especially quick and easy if you use the keyboard shortcuts: ⌘-3 to copy selected font attributes and ⌘-4 to paste them.

Copy Ruler/Paste Ruler. Just like the Copy Font and Paste Font commands, these transfer attributes from one paragraph to the next. But the attributes they transfer are the margins, indents, tab stops, and line-spacing settings indicated on TextEdit's text ruler. Font, color, and style settings are unaffected. (To speed things up, you can press ⌘-1 to copy ruler settings and ⌘-2 to paste them.)

Tip: It's especially important to turn this feature on if your paragraph alignment is set to Justify, or if you create narrow columns of text. If hyphenation is turned off, TextEdit won't break up whole words at the end of a line, even if it leaves big, ugly white gaps between words.

- **Make Read Only.** When you turn this option on (again, in the Format menu), you're locked out. You can select and copy text to your heart's content, but you can't change anything. Read Only mode can be useful if you want to prevent yourself from making accidental changes to a file, but it's not much of a security feature. (All anyone has to do is choose Format→Make Editable to regain full editing privileges.)

- **Spell Checking.** As mentioned earlier, TextEdit can check spelling as you type, flagging questionable words with red underlining. To open the full Spelling panel at any time, choose Edit→Spelling→Spelling (or press Shift-⌘-;). Using the panel, you can correct errors (choosing from the suggestions generated by Apple's built-in spelling dictionary) or tell TextEdit to learn or ignore other suspected misspellings.

However, quickest way to handle spelling corrections is shown in Figure 9-10.

Files within Files within Files

It's no surprise that you can include formatted text and pictures in a TextEdit document, but here's a shocker: You can also embed an entire *program or document* within a TextEdit file.

Try this experiment: Create a new TextEdit document in Rich Text mode. Drag the icons from a couple of programs into the TextEdit document. Do the same with some *documents* that were created using native Mac OS X programs (another TextEdit document, for example).

When you save the file, Mac OS X saves embedded copies of the applications and documents you dragged into the TextEdit document itself. (The TextEdit file is saved in a format called RTFD, which is a Rich Text Format document *with attachments*.)

Once you've saved the file, you can double-click any of the icons in the file to launch the embedded items. In the TextEdit document shown here, you could launch the Clock, Chess, DVD Player, and Mail programs—all right from within the file.

To make things even wilder, it's possible to drag a TextEdit file containing embedded items into *another* TextEdit file, saving a file within a file within a file.

One important point to keep in mind: The double-clickable icons you create in TextEdit using this method are *not* aliases or links to your original documents and programs. They're actual, full copies. If you make changes in the original document, they won't be reflected in the copies embedded in the TextEdit file. And if you embed a 10 MB program into a TextEdit document, you'll end up with a 10 MB TextEdit file!

- **Find and Replace.** No self-respecting word processor would be complete without a good find and replace command. Choose Edit→Find→Find Panel (⌘-F) to search for and replace text in TextEdit documents.

Tip: One command worth learning is Edit→Find→Use Selection for Find (or ⌘-E). Instead of having to type words into the Find field, this command searches for the next occurrence of whatever text you've already selected *in your document,* without even opening the Find Panel. Select one occurrence of the word you want to look for. Press ⌘-E, and then press ⌘-G to jump to each new occurrence of that word.

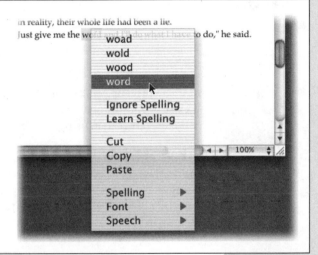

Figure 9-10:
You're never more than a Control-click away from better spelling in TextEdit. Control-click on a questionable word; the suggestions of Apple's built-in dictionary appear right in the contextual pop-up menu, along with the Learn and Ignore commands.

POWER USERS' CLINIC

Documentation Writers Rejoice!

The combination of TextEdit and Grab (the Mac's built-in screen capture utility) are a dream come true for people who write computer books and manuals—especially because these two programs are tied together as *services* (page 120) under Mac OS X. You can drop screenshots directly into a TextEdit document without having to switch between multiple programs.

To add a screen capture to a TextEdit document, choose

TextEdit→Services→Grab and then select one of the three menu options: Screen (for a full screen capture), Selection (to capture a rectangular region), or Timed Screen (a full screen capture snapped ten seconds after you choose the command). After the Grab utility snaps your picture, it will automatically place the image right in your current TextEdit document, so you can drop in the needed screenshot and then keep on typing.

Utilities: Your Mac OS X Toolbox

The Utilities folder (inside your Applications folder) is home to another batch of freebies: a set of 23 tools for monitoring, tuning, tweaking, and troubleshooting your Mac.

The truth is, though, that you're likely to use only about six of these utilities. The rest are very specialized gizmos primarily of interest only to network administrators or Unix geeks who are obsessed with knowing what kind of computer-code gibberish is going on behind the scenes.

AirPort Admin Utility

Don't even think about this program unless you've equipped your Mac with the hardware necessary for Apple's wireless AirPort networking technology. (That entails installing a $100 AirPort card in your Mac and a base station, as described in Chapter 12.)

Even then, you don't use the AirPort Admin Utility to set up AirPort connections for the first time. For that task, you use the AirPort Setup Assistant described below, which takes you gently by the hand and guides you through the steps of hooking up a wireless network connection.

After you're set up, you can use AirPort Admin Utility to monitor the connections in an existing AirPort network. (You can also use this utility to set up new connections manually, rather than using the step-by-step approach offered by the Assistant.)

AirPort Setup Assistant

An Assistant, in Apple-ese, is an interview program. It presents a series of screens, posing one question at a time; after answering each question, you're supposed to click the right-arrow (or Next) button. At the end of the interview, the Assistant program incorporates your answers into some finished product—such as configuring numerous System Preferences all at once.

The AirPort Setup Assistant is the screen-by-screen guide that walks you through the steps needed to set up and use AirPort wireless networking. You'll be asked to name your network, provide a password for accessing it, and so on. When you've followed the steps and answered the questions, your AirPort hardware will be properly configured and ready to use.

Apple System Profiler

ASP is a great tool for finding out exactly what's installed on your Mac and what's not—in terms of both hardware and software. Does your PowerBook's G3 chip run at 400 MHz or 500 MHz? Does your G4 tower have any open slots for extra RAM? What percentage of your external hard drive is filled up? Want a comprehensive list of every program installed on your Mac, with version numbers?

The Apple System Profile (ASP) answers all those questions. It combs through your Mac OS X System folder, performing a quick analysis of every piece of hardware plugged into your machine and every program installed, and produces a neat, printable report about what it finds.

Note: The people who answer the phones on Apple's tech-support line are particularly fond of Apple System Profiler; the detailed information it reports can be very useful for troubleshooting nasty problems. If you call for tech support, be ready to run it.

When you launch Apple System Profiler, it reports information about your Mac on a series of five tabbed panels:

- The **System Profile** screen shows the exact Mac model you have, its serial number, how much RAM it has, and its processor chip and speed. It also reports which memory slots are filled, the size of the memory module in each slot, and the amount of Level 2 cache memory installed—incredibly useful details that save you from having to stick your fingers into your Mac's case to find out what's in there.

    On the software side, the System Profile screen shows the exact version of Mac OS X you're running. The Network overview section shows what kind of network your Mac is on and which printer is selected.

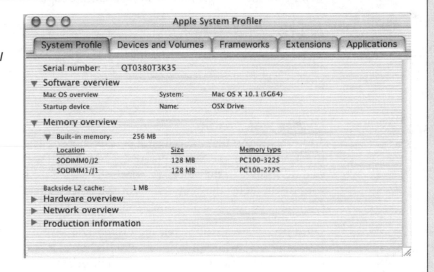

Figure 9-11:
ASP is listed hierarchically. You can click the flippy triangles to reveal more or less detail. When the triangle is "closed," you only see the name of a device. Flip it down to see manufacturer, version number, and other details.

- The **Devices and Volumes** panel shows every disk (including every *partition* of each disk) attached to your Mac: hard drive, CD-ROM, Zip drive, and so on, along with its SCSI, USB, FireWire, or ATA connection, size, and other specs.

- The next panel, **Frameworks**, reveals the core technologies that drive your Mac and that are shared by the various programs you run. (The software chunks that actually provides these services is stored on your hard drive in System→ Library→Frameworks. They resemble the interchangeable software parts known as *shared libraries* in the old Mac OS.)

For example, you'll see frameworks listed here for AudioToolbox, Speech Recognition, Navigation Services, CoreGraphics, and other software modules that your applications may need.

- Similar information shows up in the **Extensions** panel. In this sense, "extensions" doesn't mean *system* extensions of the type that made life a living hell in Mac OS 9 and earlier. In Mac OS X, the term *extensions* refers to a different kind of add-on component to the core system software—generally drivers for the Mac's various components, which sit in the System→Library→Extensions folder. The contents of the Extensions folder is what you see listed in this panel.

Tip: Take note of the column called "Is Apple." It shows which of these software components came from Apple (marked "Yes") and which didn't. In times of trouble, this can be valuable information, since problems are often traced to the software that didn't come with your Mac.

- The **Applications** screen shows you a list of every program on your system, with version information in parentheses—a quick inventory of what you have installed on your Mac. It's great for spotting duplicate copies of programs.

Note: Don't freak out when you see the astronomical number of applications on the list. Only a fraction of them are regular, double-clickable *programs*. The rest are little applications, scripts, and utilities that you never touch, like ScreenSaverEngine or DisplayAlert, that do their important (or unimportant) work behind the scenes.

Creating printed reports

To create a report that you can print or save, choose File→New Report, and then use the checkboxes in the New Report dialog box to choose the type of information you want to include in the report. Be selective, because it can take ASP a while to scan your drive and list the items it finds. If you don't really care about Frameworks, for example (and you probably don't), turn off the Frameworks checkbox.

Once you create a report, you can display and save it as a native ASP document (openable only with Apple System Profiler) or as a Text document that any word processor or text editor can open. Radio buttons at the top of the report window let you toggle between the two different modes.

Extracting information from an ASP report

Sometimes you don't need a whole report. You need just a bit of information about one particular item—maybe just your RAM configuration or the specs for your DVD drive, for example.

In that situation, open ASP to the panel containing the information you want. Move the mouse over the chunk of info you want; the pointer turns into a "hand grabber" icon; now you can drag that information right out of ASP onto the desktop (or into a folder, or another drag-and-drop-aware program) to create a text clipping containing all the information you dragged.

Search options

By default, ASP searches for extensions, frameworks, and applications only on your startup disk. If you want to include other drives attached to your Mac, choose Commands→Search options (⌘-F), and turn on the checkboxes for any of the drives that you want to have included in searches. After changing the search options, you have to force ASP to update its reports by choosing Commands→Update all information (⌘-U), or Commands→Update Applications (or Update Extensions, or Update Frameworks, depending on which tab you have open in ASP).

Applet Launcher

An *applet* is a little program written in the Java computer language—and Applet Launcher is a program that lets you launch and run such applets as stand-alone programs on your Mac. If you don't need or want to run Java applets, you can ignore this one.

Usually you encounter Java applets while Web browsing. Programmers use Java to create small programs that they then embed into Web pages—animated effects, clocks, calculators, stock tickers, and so on. Your browser automatically downloads and runs such applets (assuming that you have "Enable Java" turned on in your browser; it's a preference you can turn on or off).

But applets are really just *programs*. So what if you want to run one without going through a Web site and launching your Web browser? That's what Apple Launcher is for: to open and launch Java applets without relying on a Web browser.

The Applet Launcher window contains only two buttons: Open and Launch. To run an Applet, first select it using the Open command, then click Launch and you're in business: An Applet Viewer window opens containing the applet you want to use.

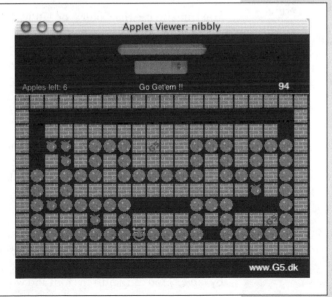

Figure 9-12:
Thanks to the Applet Viewer, you can use your Mac to run hundreds of free Java applets available for download over the Internet, such as this vintage Commodore 64-era game.

The pop-up menu in the Applet Launcher window remembers the applets you've opened most recently, so that you can run them later by choosing them from the menu. (To erase the list of remembered applets, choose Edit→Preferences and click the Clear History button.)

Tip: You might wonder—where do you *find* Java applets to run with Applet Launcher? Just launch your browser and type *free Java applets* into any search engine. You'll find Web sites galore containing hundreds of applets—games, utilities, animations, and more—that you can download immediately. Once you've downloaded them, use Apple Launcher to open the *.html* file associated with each applet (see Figure 9-12).

Applet Viewer

Once you're running an applet in the Applet Viewer, an Applet menu appears in the menu bar, containing a few useful (and mostly self-explanatory) commands, such as Stop, Start, Restart, and Reload. If an applet locks up, the Restart command can generally get it going again.

ColorSync Utility

This "bet-you'll-never-touch-it" utility performs a fairly esoteric task: repairing ColorSync profiles that may be "broken" because they don't strictly conform to the *ICC profile* specification. (ICC [International Color Consortium] profiles are part of Apple's ColorSync color management system, as described on page 338.)

If you happen to use ColorSync (because you're in the high-end color printing business, for example), and a profile for your specific monitor or printer doesn't show up in the ColorSync panel of System Preferences when it should, this is the tool you need to fix it. (See page 338 for a full explanation of ColorSync profiles.)

You can also use the ColorSync Utility to see and review all the ColorSync profiles installed on your system. In the main ColorSync Utility window, click the Profiles icon at the top of the window to see a list of all available profiles, or the Devices icon for profiles associated with specific printers, scanners, and so on. The area on the right side of the window shows information about each ColorSync profile you select from the list on the left.

Console

Console is a magic window that peels back the layers of the Mac OS X interface and shows you what's happening under the hood of your Mac as you go about your business. Its function is to record a text log of all the internal status messages being passed between the Mac OS X and other applications as they interact with each other.

Opening the Console log is a bit like stepping into an operating room during a complex surgery; you're exposed to stuff the average person just isn't supposed to see. (Typical Console entries: "kCGErrorCannotComplete" or "doGetDisplayTransfer ByTable.") You can adjust the font and word wrapping using Console's Format menu, but the fact is that the phrase "CGXGetWindowType: Invalid window –1" looks ugly in just about *any* font.

Console isn't useless, however. These messages can be of great value to programmers who are debugging software or troubleshooting a messy problem.

CPU Monitor

CPU Monitor, another techie tool, lets you see how much of your Mac's available processing power is being tapped at any given moment. Think of it as an electrocardiogram for your Mac.

Launch CPU Monitor so that the thermometer-like Monitor window is open. Then go about your usual Mac business: launch a few programs, drag a playing Quick-Time movie across the screen, or play a game. You'll see the level on the monitor rise and fall, depending on how busy you're keeping the CPU. On multiple-processor Macs, you see a different bar for each chip, and you can see how efficiently Mac OS X is distributing the work among them.

CPU Monitor actually gives you three different ways of displaying the monitor read-out, as explained in Figure 9-13. If you choose CPU Monitor→Preferences, you can customize the various monitor panels in a number of ways, changing the colors and other attributes of the various monitor panels.

Tip: If you want to keep your eye on your Mac's activity without taking up additional space on the screen, open CPU Monitor→Preferences→Application Icon, and turn on one of the first two radio buttons. This replaces the icon that appears in the Dock when CPU Monitor is running with a live readout showing the CPU load as you work.

Figure 9-13:
Top: The three faces of CPU Monitor. The unobtrusive floating view (left) hovers over your desktop and can be turned semi-transparent in the Preferences window. The Standard view (middle) provides a single level indicator. The Extended view (right) uses different colors to represent different processes and can be stretched to any size.

Bottom: The CPU Monitor icon can be set to display moment-by-moment CPU activity right in the Dock.

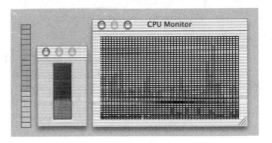

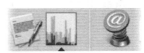

DigitalColor Meter

With the DigitalColor Meter, you can grab the exact color value of any pixel on your screen, which can be helpful when matching colors in Web page construction or other design work. After launching the DigitalColor Meter, just point to whatever pixel you want to measure, anywhere on your screen; a magnified view appears in the meter window, and the RGB color value of the pixels appears in the meter window. You can display the color values as RGB percentages or absolute values, or in Hex form (which is how colors are defined in HTML; white is represented as #FFFFFF, for example).

Here are some tips for using the DigitalColor Meter to capture color information from your screen:

- To home in on the exact pixel (and color) you want to measure, drag the Aperture Size slider to the smallest size—one pixel. Then use the *arrow keys* to move the aperture to the precise location you want.

- Press ⌘-C to put the numeric value of the color you're pointing to on the Clipboard.

- Press Shift-⌘-H (Hold Color) to "freeze" the color meter on the color you're pointing to—a handy stunt when you're comparing two colors on screen. You can point to one color, hold it using ⌘-Shift-H, then move your mouse to the second color. Pressing Shift-⌘-H again releases the hold on the color.

- When the Aperture Size slider is set to view more than one pixel, DigitalColor Meter measures the *average* value of the pixels being examined.

Directory Setup

If you use your Mac at home, or if it's not connected to a network, you'll never have to touch Directory Setup. Even if you *are* connected to a network, there's only a remote chance you'll ever have to open Directory Setup unless you happen to be a network administrator.

This administrative utility controls the access that each individual Mac on a network has to Mac OS X's *directory services*—special databases that store information about users and servers. Directory Setup also governs access to *LDAP directories* (Internet- or intranet-based "white pages" for Internet addresses).

A network administrator can use Directory Setup to do things like select *NetInfo domains,* set up *search policies,* and define *attribute mappings.* If those terms don't mean anything to you, just pretend you never read this paragraph and get on with your life.

If you *are* a network administrator, download "Understanding and Using NetInfo" from Apple's Web site. You can get it at *www.apple.com/macosx/server/pdf/ UnderstandingUsingNetInfo.pdf.* It tells you how to use Directory Setup to configure various user privileges on a Mac OS X network.

Disk Copy

This program creates and manages *disk images,* electronic versions of disks or folders that you can send electronically to somebody else.

The world's largest disk image fan is Apple itself; the company often releases new software in disk image form. A lot of Mac OS X add-on software arrives from your Web download in disk image form, too, as described on page 125.

When you download a disk image and double-click its icon, Disk Copy re-creates the original disk icon on your screen (although most people never realize that Disk Copy was involved). Figure 9-14 shows the routine.

Tip: You can click Skip in the verification box that appears when you double-click a disk image. If something truly got scrambled during the download, you'll know about it right away (your file won't decompress correctly, it will show the wrong icon, and so on).

In fact, you can make Disk Copy *always* skip that verification business, which is a relic from the floppy-disk days. To do so, choose Disk Copy→Preferences, click the Verifying tab, and turn off Verify Checksums.

You can also use Disk Copy to create disk images of your own. To make a disk image from an actual disk (such as a Zip or a CD), choose Image→New Image from Device. To make an image from a folder, choose Image→New Blank Image. Select a name, size and format for the disk image and click Create. Disk Copy creates the image and then mounts it, so that it appears just like a real disk on your desktop. Now just copy the folders and files you want onto the "disk."

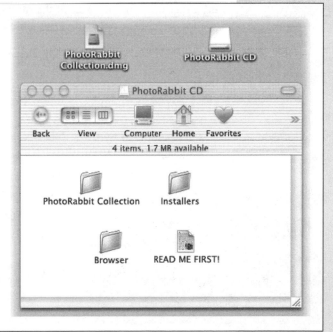

Figure 9-14:
The usual life cycle of a disk image file: First, you download it from the Internet. The result is an icon whose name usually ends in .img or .dmg (upper left). (Files that end with .smi are also disk images, but self-mounting ones that don't require Disk Copy.) When you double-click this icon, Disk Copy creates an icon that simulates a new disk (upper right). When you double-click this icon, you see exactly what the original creator of the image wanted you to see (bottom).

Disk Utility

Disk Utility fuses together two older Mac OS applications: Disk First Aid (for repairing damaged disks, mangled directories, and other glitches) and Drive Setup (for initializing and partitioning hard drives). You'll rarely need to run Disk Utility, but keep it in mind, just in case you ever find yourself facing a serious disk problem.

Here are some of the tasks you can perform with Disk Utility:

- Get size and type information about any disks attached to your Mac (but with less detail than you get with Apple System Profiler).

- Fix disks that won't mount on your desktop or behave properly.

- Completely erase disks—including rewritable CDs (CD-RW).

- Partition a disk into multiple *volumes* (that is, subdivide a drive so that its segments show up on the desktop with separate disk icons).

- Set up a *RAID array* (a cluster of separate disks that act as a single volume).

Note: Disk Utility can't verify, repair, erase, or partition your *startup disk*—the disk on which your system software is currently running. That would be like having a surgeon perform an appendectomy on himself—not a great idea.

If you want to use Disk Utility to fix or reformat your startup disk, you must start up your Mac from a different system disk, such as the Mac OS X Install CD.

The left Disk Utility panel displays a list of all available disks—your hard drive and any other disks in your Mac at the moment. On the right is a panel with five tabs, one for each of the five main Disk Utility functions:

- **Information.** Click the icon of a disk to read size, type, and partition information.

- **First Aid.** This is the disk-repair part of Disk Utility. You're supposed to click the icon of a disk and then click either Verify (to get a report on the disk's health) or Repair (which fixes whatever problems the program finds). In other words, First Aid attempts to perform the same healing effects on a sick hard drive as, say, a program like Norton Utilities. It does a great job at fixing many disk problems; when you're troubleshooting, Disk Utility should always be your first resort.

DON'T PANIC

Where's My Erase Disk Command?

Erasing a disk on a Mac used to be easy. All you had to do was select the disk in the Finder and choose Special→Erase Disk. But in Mac OS X, there's no Special menu, and the Erase Disk command is nowhere to be found.

That's because the Disk Utility program now handles your disk-erasing needs. Launch it, click the Erase tab, and blow away the data on the disk of your choice, whether it's a floppy, hard drive, or CD-RW.

If Disk First Aid reports that it's unable to fix the problem, *then* it's time to invest in Norton Utilities (if a Mac OS X version is available) or its rival, Drive 10 (*www.micromat.com*).

Tip: If Disk First Aid finds nothing wrong with a disk, it reports: "The volume appears to be OK." Don't be alarmed at the wishy-washy, not-very-confident wording of that message–that's the strongest vote of confidence Disk First Aid can give. Even a brand-new, perfectly healthy hard drive only *appears* to be OK to Disk First Aid.

• **Erase.** Select a disk, choose a format (*always* Mac OS Extended, unless you're formatting a disk for use on an ancient Mac running Mac OS 8.1 or earlier), give it a name, and click Erase to wipe a disk clean.

• **Partition.** This is the part of Disk Utility that used to be called Drive Setup in the Mac's earlier days. With the Partition tools, you can erase a hard drive in such a way that you subdivide its surface. Each chunk is represented on your screen by two (or more) different hard drive icons. (See Figure 9-15.)

There are some very good reasons *not* to partition a drive these days: A partitioned hard drive is more difficult to resurrect after a serious crash, requires more navigation when you want to open a particular file, and offers no speed or safety benefits.

But there's one very good reason *to* do it, too: to keep Mac OS 9 and Mac OS X on different "disks," as described on page 142.

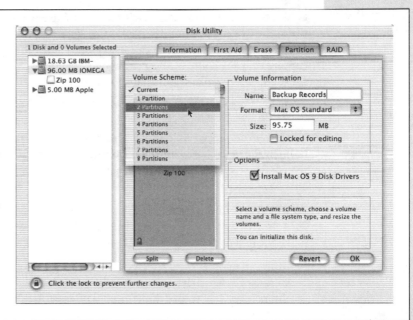

Figure 9-15:
To partition your drive– which involves erasing it completely–launch Disk Utility, switch to the Partition pane, and select the hard drive you want to partition from the list on the left. From the Volume Scheme pop-up menu, choose the number of partitions you want, as shown in this figure. Now drag the horizontal lines in the Volumes map to specify the relative sizes of the partitions you want to create. Assign a name and format for each partition in the Volume Information area, and then click OK.

• **RAID.** RAID stands for Redundant Arrays of Independent Disks, and refers to a special formatting scheme in which a group of separate disks are configured to work together as one very large, very fast drive. In a RAID array, multiple disks share the job of storing data—a setup that can improve speed and reliability.

Most Mac users don't use or set up RAID arrays, but this panel makes it possible to turn a group of disks connected to your Mac into a RAID system.

Display Calibrator

The Display Calibrator is another of the Mac's Assistant programs, designed to help you adjust your monitor's color settings. It walks you through a series of six screens, presenting various brightness and color balance settings in each screen. You pick the settings that look best to you; at the end of the process, you save your monitor tweaks as a *ColorSync profile* (page 338) that can be used by ColorSync-savvy programs to adjust the display of colors on your screen for improved color accuracy.

Note: You don't need Display Calibrator to adjust your monitor's brightness and contrast; to do that, just use the hardware controls on your monitor or the Display panel of System Preferences.

Without realizing it, you may end up launching the Display Calibrator when you use the Displays panel in System Preferences. Clicking the Calibrate button in the Color pane of the Displays panel automatically turns on Display Calibrator. (For more on the Displays panel in System Preferences, see page 192.)

Grab

Grab takes pictures of your Mac's screen, for use when you're writing up instructions, illustrating a computer book, or collecting proof of some secret screen you found buried in a game. You can take pictures of the entire screen (press ⌘-Z) or capture only the contents of a rectangular selection (press Shift-⌘-A). When you're finished, Grab displays your snapshot in a new window, which you can print, close without saving, or save as a TIFF file, ready for emailing, posting on a Web page, or inserting into a manuscript.

Now, as experienced Mac users already know, the Mac OS has long had its *own* built-in shortcuts for capturing screenshots: You press Shift-⌘-3 to take a picture of the whole screen, and Shift-⌘-4 to make capture a rectangular selection. These shortcuts have been around for years—and they still work in Mac OS X 10.1 and later.

So why use Grab instead? In many cases, you shouldn't. The Shift-⌘-3 and Shift-⌘-4 shortcuts work like a dream. But there are three specific cases in which it might make more sense to opt for Grab:

• Grab can make a *timed* screen capture (choose Capture→Timed Screen, or press Shift-⌘-Z), which lets you enjoy a 10-second delay before the screenshot is actually taken. After you click the Start Timer button, you have an opportunity to activate windows, pull down menus, drag items around, and otherwise set up the shot before Grab shoots the picture.

Note: As of Mac OS X 10.1, the Capture→Window command in Grab still doesn't work. If you want to neatly capture a Mac OS X window without having to crop out the rest of the screen, use Snapz Pro X, as described in the next tip.

- When you capture a screenshot using Grab's Selection command, the *size* of your selection is displayed, in pixels, right under the pointer as you drag. If you need to capture a 256-pixel-wide square, for example, you can do so with pinpoint accuracy. (The Image Inspector window, which you can open by choosing Edit→Inspector or by pressing ⌘-1, shows the dimensions of each screenshot *after* you capture it.)

- With Grab, you have the option of including the cursor in the picture, which is extremely useful when you're showing a menu being pulled down or a button being clicked. (Mac OS X's screenshot keystrokes, by contrast, always eliminate the pointer.) Use the technique described in Figure 9-16 to add the pointer style of your choice to a Grab screenshot.

Tip: Actually, if you're going to write a book or manual about Mac OS X, the program you really need is Snapz Pro (available for download from *www.missingmanuals.com,* among other places). It offers far more flexibility than any of Mac OS X's own screenshot features: For example, you have a choice of file format, you can neatly snip out just one dialog box or window with a single click, and you can even capture movies of screen activity.

Figure 9-16:
One of the advantages Grab offers over simply snapping screenshots with Shift-⌘-3 or Shift-⌘-4 is that it lets you include the pointer/cursor in the picture—or hide it. Choose Capture→Preferences and pick one of the nine different point styles, or choose to keep it hidden by picking the blank button in the upper-left corner.

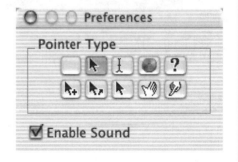

Installer

You'll never launch this. It's the engine that drives the Mac OS X installer program and other software installers. There's nothing for you to double-click, configure, or set up.

Java Web Start

Java Web Start isn't an Apple product—it's a free program from Sun Microsystems designed to streamline the process of downloading and running Java-based programs on your Mac.

If you want to see what this is all about, launch Internet Explorer and go to *http:// java.sun.com/products/javawebstart/demos.html* to access a page of demo programs. When you click one of the demo Launch buttons, Java Web Start (JWS) kicks in to do its thing, as shown in Figure 9-17.

JWS downloads all the necessary files and starts running the program you select— all with one click, and without relying on the Web browser. In fact, JWS doesn't just *run* Java programs; it also stores them on your system so you can launch them again later, either by double-clicking their icons or from within the JWS application itself (choose View→Downloaded Applications). You don't have to use a Web browser or reconnect to a Web site.

The catch is that Java Web Start is a fledgling technology and only a handful of (mostly lame) demo programs are available that actually make use of JWS.

Ultimately, Sun is hoping that JWS will become an important software distribution tool, enabling people to connect to a Web site, click a button, and start using whatever program they need, without having to hassle with manual installation at all. It's a great concept—but at this point, mostly *just* a concept.

Figure 9-17:
This is Java Web Start in the process of downloading and activating a Java program from the Sun Microsystems Web site. If you want to poke around on Java Web Start without downloading the demo programs from Sun, launch JWS and go to the Application Manager window. Click Welcome to Java Web Start, and then click the Start button on the right side of the screen. A small Java program from Apple starts running that briefly describes this technology and includes some meaningless demos.

Key Caps

Key Caps, a part of the Mac since its earliest days, consists of a single window containing a tiny onscreen keyboard (Figure 9-18). When you hold down any of the various modifier keys on your keyboard (such as ⌘, Option, Shift, or Control), you can see exactly which keys produce which characters. The point, of course, is to help you learn which keys to press when you need special symbols or non–English characters, such as © or ¢, in each font.

If you want to see the effect of typing while pressing the modifier keys, you can either click the onscreen keys or type on your actual keyboard. The corresponding keys on the onscreen keyboard light up as they're pressed.

Tip: If the A key on your PowerBook stops working, or you accidentally spill an entire Snapple onto your keyboard and the whole thing gives out, remember: You can *type* using Key Caps. Use the mouse to click the onscreen keyboard characters, typing into the one-line display in the Key Caps window. Then copy and paste what you've typed into your other documents. Agonizingly slow? Yes, but in a pinch, it's good to know there's a way to type without a keyboard.

Change the Key Caps font

Different fonts contain different hidden characters. For example, Palatino contains a character (produced by pressing Shift-Option-K), but Adobe Garamond does not.

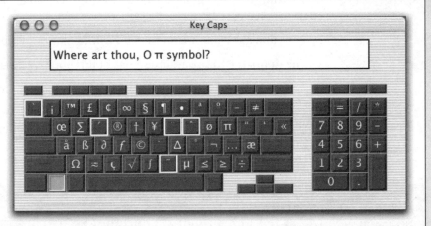

Figure 9-18:
How do you make a π? Key Caps reveals the answer. When you press the Option key, the Key Caps keyboard shows that the pi character (π) is mapped to the P key. Once you've found and typed the character in Key Caps, you can copy and paste it into any other program.

Where art thou, O π symbol?

UP TO SPEED

Bringing Dead Keys to Life

If you press Option while the Key Caps window is open, you see little white outlines around certain keys (shown in Figure 9-18, for example). These rectangles identify the Mac's five *dead keys*—keys that, when pressed once, type *nothing* onscreen. However, when you type *another* key—

a normal letter, for example—it appears with the dead key's displayed marking over it. To type the ñ in *jalapeño,* you have to press Option-N and *then* type an *n*. This same two-step approach lets you type characters like ö and é.

Fortunately, Key Caps lets you see the characters lurking within *any* installed font; just choose a font's name from the Font menu to see all of its modifier-key characters.

Tip: You're not stuck viewing all characters in 12-point size—a good thing, because some of them are hard to read when displayed that small. Just "zoom" the Key Caps window (by clicking the green gel-button near the top-left corner) to magnify the Key Caps window and its font, as shown in Figure 9-18.

Keychain Access

Keychain Access manages all your secret information—passwords for network access, file servers, FTP sites, Web pages, and other secure items. For instructions on how to use Keychain Access, see Chapter 12.

NetInfo Manager

NetInfo is the central Mac OS X database that keeps track of user and group accounts, passwords, access privileges, email configurations, printers, computers, and just about anything else network related. NetInfo Manager is where a network administrator (or a technically inclined Mac guru) can go to view and edit these various settings.

You can find more information about NetInfo in these places:

- The tutorials in the relevant sections of this book, such as on pages 244 and 291

- Article #106416 ("NetInfo: What is it? How to Set Up NetInfo") at *http://kbase.info.apple.com*

- "Understanding and Using NetInfo," an Apple user manual for network administrators. Launch your Web browser and go to *www.apple.com/macosx/server/pdf/UnderstandingUsingNetInfo.pdf*

UP TO SPEED

Sleuthing around with NetInfo Manager

While most of NetInfo Manager is of little use to a typical Mac user, a few parts of this utility can be valuable even to a non–system administrator.

To dive into NetInfo Manager, start by clicking the padlock button at the bottom of the main window and enter an administrator's password. Then examine the various parameters in the top-left Directory Browser list. As you'll quickly discover, most of these settings are written in Unix techno-speak.

A few, however, are easy enough to figure out. If you click *users* in the left-side list, you'll see, in the next column, a list of accounts you've created. Click one of the user names there, and you'll see, in the properties pane at the bottom of the screen, some parameters that may come in handy—such as each person's name, password, and password hint. By double-clicking one of these info items, you can edit it, which can come in genuinely handy if someone on your school or office network forgets their password.

Network Utility

The Network Utility gathers information about Web sites and network users. It offers a suite of industry standard Internet tools such as NetStat, Ping, Traceroute, Finger, and WhoIs—advanced tools, to be sure, but ones that even novice Mac users may be asked to fire up when calling a technician for Internet help.

Otherwise, you probably won't need to use Network Utility to get your work done. But Network Utility can be useful when you're performing Internet detective work:

• Use **WhoIs** to gather an amazing amount of information about the owners of any particular domain (such as *www.apple.com*), including name and address info, telephone numbers, and administrative contacts, using the technique shown in Figure 9-19.

• Use **Ping** to enter a Web address (such as *www.google.com*), and then "ping" (send out a "sonar" signal to) the server to see how long it takes for it to respond to your request. Network Utility reports the response time in milliseconds—a useful test when you're trying to find out whether or not a remote server (a Web site, for example) is up and running.

• **Traceroute** lets you track how many "hops" are required for your Mac to communicate with a certain Web server. Just type in the network address then click Trace. You'll see that your request actually jumps from one *trunk* of the Internet to another, from router to router, as it makes its way to its destination. You'll find that a message sometimes crisscrosses the entire country before it arrives at its destination. You can also see how long each leg of the journey took, in milliseconds.

Figure 9-19:
The WhoIs tool is a powerful part of Network Utility. First enter a domain that you want information about, then choose a WhoIs server from the pop-up menu (you might try whois.networksolutions.com). When you click the WhoIs button, you'll get a surprisingly revealing report about the owner of the domain: phone numbers, fax numbers, contact names, and so on.

Print Center

This is the hub of your Mac's printing operations. You can use the Print Center to set up and configure new printers, and to check on the status of print jobs, as described in Chapter 13.

Process Viewer

Even when you're only running a program or two on your Mac, dozens of computational tasks *(processes)* are going on in the background. Process Viewer lets you see all the different processes—foreground and background—that your Mac is handling at the moment.

If you want to get a peek at just how busy your Mac is, even when you're not doing anything but staring at the desktop, launch the Process Viewer. Check out how many items appear in the Process Listing Window. Some are easily recognizable programs (such as Finder), while others are background system-level operations you don't normally see. For each item, you can see the percentage of CPU being used, who's using it (either your account name or *root,* meaning the Mac itself), and the percentage of memory it's using.

Process Viewer, in other words, is the closest Mac OS X comes to offering the kind of memory graphs that once appeared under the menu in the About This Computer window.

The Developer CD Extras

Not everyone installs the *second* Mac OS X CD in the boxed, store-bought version of Mac OS X, the one called Developer. It's intended, of course, for developers (programmers) who write software that runs in Mac OS X.

But it offers some interesting extra programs that aren't included with the regular Mac OS X installation. (After you install the developer tools—by double-clicking Developer.pkg in the CD window—you'll find a new folder called Developer on your hard drive. The goodies are in the Developer→Applications→Extras folder.)

For example, **Sketch** is a simple drawing program; if you're a Mac old-timer, you might describe it as something along

the lines of the old MacDraw. It makes smooth lines, circles, and text boxes.

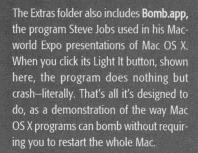

The Extras folder also includes **Bomb.app,** the program Steve Jobs used in his Macworld Expo presentations of Mac OS X. When you click its Light It button, shown here, the program does nothing but crash—literally. That's all it's designed to do, as a demonstration of the way Mac OS X programs can bomb without requiring you to restart the whole Mac.

Finally, there's **WorldText.app,** which is a lot like TextEdit but with more features, including proper Font, Size, and Style menus, a Sound menu whose Speak command can read your text back to you, and more.

Tip: When one of your programs freezes or crashes, double-click its name in Process Viewer. You'll be offered the Quit Process dialog box, which you can use to exit the stuck program as safely as possible. This technique often works to jettison the troublemaker when all else fails.

StuffIt Expander

StuffIt Expander, a free program from Aladdin Systems, is an indispensable utility for decompressing and decoding files, especially those that you download from the Internet or receive as email attachments. It automatically restores all kinds of compressed files into usable form, including StuffIt files (whose names end with .sit), Zip files (.zip), BinHex files (.hqx), UUEncoded files (.uu), MIME or Base64 files (.mime), and—especially important in Mac OS X—.tar and .gzip files, which were once found only on Unix machines. (Now your Mac *is* a Unix machine.)

Usually, you don't have to *do* anything with StuffIt Expander. It just does its thing, automatically and unbidden, whenever you download a compressed file. That's because most Web browsers come configured to treat StuffIt Expander as a *helper application;* the browsers summon Expander the moment they recognize that you've downloaded a compressed file (see Figure 9-20).

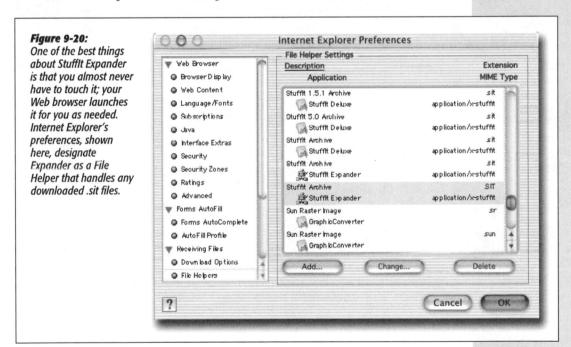

Figure 9-20:
One of the best things about StuffIt Expander is that you almost never have to touch it; your Web browser launches it for you as needed. Internet Explorer's preferences, shown here, designate Expander as a File Helper that handles any downloaded .sit files.

If you end up with a .sit or .zip file on your Mac that needs decompressing—and StuffIt Expander hasn't been launched automatically—just drag the file onto the StuffIt Expander icon to expand it.

Terminal

Terminal opens a terminal window with a *command line interface,* taking you deep into the world of Unix, the operating system on which Mac OS X is based. Chapters 15 and 16 offer a crash course in this powerful window into the Mac's shadow operating system.

CDs, DVDs, and iTunes 2

How the Mac Does Disks

Apple shocked the world when, in 1997, it introduced the iMac without a floppy-disk drive—and proceeded to eliminate the floppy drive from all subsequent Mac models in the following years. Apple argues that the floppy disk is dead—it's too small to serve as a backup disk, and, in this day of the Internet, it's a redundant method of exchanging files with other computers.

Disks Today

But the floppy disk didn't disappear entirely. Millions of older Macs still have floppy drives, and many modern-Mac owners buy add-on floppy drives. In fact, you can insert all kinds of disks into a Mac these days (see Figure 10-1). Here are the most popular examples:

Hard drives and the iPod

Thanks to the Mac's FireWire jack, it's easier than ever to attach an external hard drive for extra storage. In Mac OS X, having such a spare disk around is especially useful for *dual-booting* purposes: you can keep Mac OS X on one hard drive, and Mac OS 9 on another (page 140).

It would be hard to imagine a more convenient second hard drive than, for example, Apple's iPod, which is not only an outstanding MP3 music player but doubles as a self-powered, extremely compact, bootable, five-gigabyte hard drive.

Zip disks, Peerless drives

Whether your Zip drive is built into the front panel of your Power Mac or attached via the USB port, you wind up with an inexpensive system for backing up and transferring files: each $10 Zip disk holds 100 or 250 megabytes (depending on the model you buy)—that's 70 to 178 times as much as a floppy.

For some people, the Iomega Peerless drive is a better value. You buy a single drive, which you leave connected to your Mac, and then as many interchangeable hard-drive cartridges—holding 10 or 20 GB apiece—as you need.

Fortunately, the necessary driver software for both of these drive systems is built into Mac OS X.

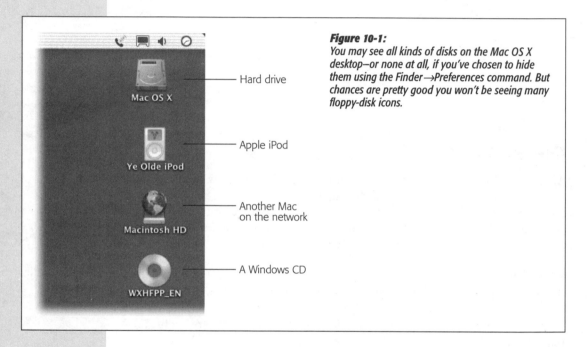

Figure 10-1:
You may see all kinds of disks on the Mac OS X desktop—or none at all, if you've chosen to hide them using the Finder→Preferences command. But chances are pretty good you won't be seeing many floppy-disk icons.

Hard drive

Apple iPod

Another Mac
on the network

A Windows CD

SuperDisks

A SuperDisk drive, another gadget you can plug into your Mac's USB connector (not to be confused with Apple's *SuperDrive,* a DVD burner), poses a fascinating alternative to the Zip drive. Its disks look exactly like floppies, but hold about 85 times as much. The real advantage of a SuperDisk drive, though, is that it *also* accepts standard floppy disks. The only downsides: (1) SuperDisk drives are slow, and (2) it's up to you to figure out how to tell a SuperDisk disk apart from a floppy disk.

The driver software for this kind of drive, too, is built right into Mac OS X.

Floppy drives

Despite Apple's conviction that the era of floppy disks is over, millions of floppies continue to populate the earth. In Chapter 12, you can find out how to connect

Macs by network wires, and you can always transmit your files by the world's best file transfer system: the Internet. But if you still crave the hands-on, in-your-pocket solidity of the good old floppy disk, about $80 buys an external floppy-disk drive for your floppy-less Mac. (This device, too, connects to your USB jack, and once again exploits the built-in Mac OS X drivers.)

CD-ROMs

You wouldn't get far in today's computer world without a CD-ROM drive. Most commercial software comes on CD—not to mention the music CDs that the Mac can play so expertly (see page 257).

DVDs

Many a Mac laptop and desktop includes a built-in DVD drive. You use it primarily for playing back DVD movies that you've rented or bought, but you may also occasionally encounter data DVDs—that is, DVDs that contain Mac files or software installers.

Recordable CDs and DVDs

CD-ROM stands for "compact disc, *read-only* memory"—in other words, you can't ever put your own files on them. Read-only means you can't write (save files) onto them.

Yet some of the most popular Mac add-ons these days are various kinds of *CD burners*—special CD drives that can record onto special blank discs. All of these discs look like normal CDs, but they (and the drives that accommodate them) may fall into any of these categories:

- **CD-R.** You can fill such a disc with your own files—once. The disk can't be changed thereafter. CD-R burners are quickly going out of fashion, thanks to the flexibility of CD-RW, described next.

- **CD-RW.** The initials stand for *rewritable;* you can record such discs over and over again. Of course, both the recorders that do this and the blank discs are somewhat more expensive than the one-shot kind. (CD-RW drives can read both CD-R and CD-RW discs.)

- **DVD-RAM** is just like a CD-rewritable, but holds eight times as much, thanks to the DVD format. Note, however, that this format is incompatible with regular DVDs, and is quickly dying out. (At one time, Apple offered a built-in DVD-RAM drive in some Power Macs sold on its Web site.)

- **DVD-RW.** The latest—and definitely the greatest—is the Apple SuperDrive, which can play *and* record CDs *and* DVDs. If your Mac came with a SuperDrive built in, you can take advantage of a Mac OS X feature that neither Windows nor any previous version of the Mac OS offers: you can use blank DVDs (which Apple sells for $5 each in a five pack of what are technically called DVD-R discs) as massive backup disks that hold 4.7 GB each.

If you've used iMovie to edit your home camcorder footage, you can also save them onto one of these DVDs for playback in standard home DVD players—the perfect way to distribute your masterpiece to friends and family without sacrificing any of the pristine video quality. (Both editing movies and saving them onto a DVD using Apple's iDVD software are described in *iMovie 2: The Missing Manual*.)

Disks In, Disks Out

Yes, you can insert all kinds of different disks into a Mac. But as far as the Mac is concerned, they're all just disks. (Actually, the Mac thinks of them as *volumes*—you can tell because that's how your Apple System Profiler describes them, for example.)

When you insert a disk, its icon shows up on the right side of the screen. If you've used only Windows computers, this behavior may throw you at first; you don't have to go hunting for the inserted disk's icon in some My Computer icon, as you do on a PC. To see what's on a disk you've inserted, just double-click its icon.

Note: You *can* use Mac OS X like Windows if you want to. To open a single window containing icons of all currently inserted disks, choose Go→Computer. To complete the illusion that you're running Windows, you can even tell Mac OS X not to put disk icons on the desktop at all. Just choose Finder→Preferences and turn off the three top checkboxes—"Hard disks," "Removable media (such as CDs)," and "Connected servers." They'll no longer appear on the desktop—only in your Computer window.

To get a disk out of your Mac, use one of these methods:

- **Drag its icon onto the Trash icon.** For years, this technique has confused and frightened first-time computer users; doesn't the *Trash* mean *delete*? Well, yes, but only when you drag document or folder icons there—not disk icons. Dragging disk icons onto the Trash (at the right end of the Dock) makes the Mac spit them out.

  Actually, all you can really do is *intend* to drag it onto the Trash can. The instant you begin dragging a disk icon, the Trash icon on the Dock changes form, as

---

When Good Disks Go Bad

Any disk can go bad. When this happens, you may get an error message that reports the disk as being "damaged" or "unusable."

If it happens to you, run the Disk Utility program in your Applications→Utilities folder. Use its First Aid tab. Click the broken disk, and then click Repair. Sometimes running the Repair function several times in a row can correct a disk problem that's too stubborn for a single pass.

Note that unlike its predecessor Disk First Aid, Disk Utility can't repair the disk it's *on*. To repair a disk, therefore, you must either restart the Mac from the Mac OS X CD or use the built-in Unix version of Disk Utility, which is called *fsck* (see page 559).

And, if after several times you don't succeed, try running a program like Micromat's Drive 10 (which you can think of as a more powerful, commercial version of Disk Utility).

---

though to reassure the novice that dragging a disk icon there will only eject, not erase it. As you drag, the wastebasket icon turns into a giant-sized Eject logo (which matches the symbol on the upper-right key of current Mac keyboards).

- **Press the Eject key on your keyboard.** Recent Mac keyboards, both on laptops and desktops, have a special Eject key in the upper-right corner. Hold it down for a moment to make a CD or DVD pop out. (If it's any other kind of disk, highlight the icon first.)

- **Highlight the disk icon, and then choose File→Eject (⌘-E).** The disk now pops out. (Alternatively, you can Control-click the disk's icon and then choose Eject from the pop-up menu that appears.)

FREQUENTLY ASKED QUESTION

The Eject Button That Doesn't

When I push the Eject button on my keyboard (or on my CD-ROM drawer), how come the CD doesn't come out?

There might be two things going on. First of all, to prevent accidental pushings, the Eject key on the modern Mac keyboard is designed not to work unless you hold it down steadily for a second or two. Just tapping it doesn't work.

Second, remember that once you've inserted a CD, DVD, or Zip disk, the Mac won't let go unless you eject it in one of the official ways. On Mac models with a CD tray, pushing the button on the CD-ROM door opens the drawer only when it's *empty*. If there's a disk in it, you can push that button till doomsday; the Mac will simply ignore you.

That behavior especially confuses people who are used to using Windows. (On a Windows PC, pushing the CD but- ton does indeed eject the disc.) But on the Mac, pushing the CD-door button ejects an inserted disk only when the disc wasn't seated properly (or when the disk drive's driver software isn't installed), and the disk's icon never did show up on the screen.

The Eject key on the modern Mac keyboard, however, isn't so fussy. It pops out whatever CD or DVD is in the drive.

Oh—and if a CD or DVD won't come out at all (and its icon doesn't show up on the desktop), restart the Mac. When it "comes to," it will either recognize the disc now or give you an error message containing an Eject button. (Most drives also feature a tiny pinhole in or around the slot. Inserting a straightened paper clip, slowly and firmly, will also make the disc pop out.)

Startup Disks

When you turn the Mac on, it hunts for a *startup disk*—that is, a disk containing a System folder. If you've ever seen the dispiriting blinking-question-mark icon on a Mac's screen, you know what happens when the Mac *can't* find a startup disk. It blinks like that forever, or until you find and insert a disk with a viable System folder on it.

Creating a startup disk
By installing the Mac OS onto a disk—be it a hard drive or rewritable CD or DVD—you can create a startup disk. Not all disks are capable of starting up the Mac, however. Among those that can't are RAM disks and a few, older external FireWire disks. Even if they have a System folder installed, these kinds of disks can't start up the Mac.

Selecting a startup disk

It's perfectly possible to have more than one startup disk attached to your Mac simultaneously. That's the deal, for example, whenever you've inserted the Mac OS X CD into your Mac—now you've got both it and your hard drive. Each contains a System folder, and each is a startup disk. Some veteran Mac fans deliberately create other startup disks—on burnable CDs, for example—so that they'll easily be able to start the Mac up from a backup startup disk, or a different version of the OS.

Only one System folder can be operational at a time. So how does the Mac know which to use as its startup disk? You make your selection in the Startup Disk panel of System Preferences (Figure 10-2). Use it to specify which disk you want the Mac to start up from the next time it starts up.

Tip: If you're in a hurry to start the machine up from a different disk, just click the disk icon you want and then click the Restart button in the System Preferences window. You don't have to close the System Preferences window first.

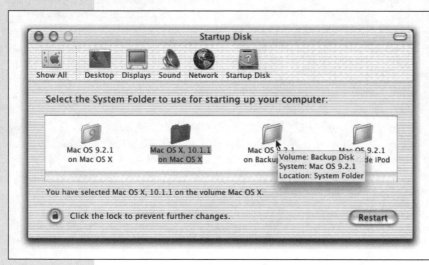

Figure 10-2:
In the Startup Disk panel of System Preferences, the currently selected disk—the one that will be "in force" the next time the machine starts up—is always highlighted. You see the System folder's version and the name of the drive it's on, but not its actual name—until you point to an icon without clicking.

Erasing, Formatting, and Initializing

Mac OS X no longer includes an Erase Disk command. When you want to erase a disk (such as a CD-RW disc), therefore, you have to use Disk Utility, which is in your Applications→Utilities folder.

As described on page 238, you can use this program to erase, repair, or subdivide (*partition*) a hard drive. You can also use it to lock a hard drive or cartridge so that it behaves like a CD-ROM: people can look at what's on it, but they can't store anything new on it.

To erase a CD, launch Disk Utility, click the Erase tab, click the name of the CD (in the left side list), and click the Erase button.

You won't be able to do so, though, if:

- The disk is a standard CD-ROM, DVD, or previously recorded CD-R (CD-recordable) disc, which can't be erased. (The only shiny silver discs you can re-record are *CD-RW* [rewritable] discs, which are slightly more expensive than standard blank CD-R discs.)

- You're trying to erase the startup disk. You can't wipe out the disk that contains the currently running System folder any more than you can paint the floor directly beneath your feet. You can only erase a disk that's *not* the one you started up from. (To erase your built-in hard drive, for example, you must start up from the Mac OS X CD-ROM.)

How the Mac
Does Disks

UP TO SPEED

Mac OS Extended Formatting

Whether you use Disk Utility to erase a disk (or when you first install Mac OS X and elect to erase the hard drive in the process), you'll be confronted with a choice between formatting options called *Mac OS Extended* and *UNIX File System (UFS)*. (When you erase a floppy disk, you also get an option to create a DOS-formatted disk for use in Windows machines.)

Mac OS Extended refers to the HFS Plus filing system, a disk format that has been proudly maximizing disk space

for Mac fans since Mac OS 8.1.

Mac OS X still accepts disks that were prepared using the older, *Mac OS Standard* formatting—the ancient *HFS* (hierarchical filing system) format—but you can't use one as your startup disk.

As for the UNIX File System option, it's exclusively for use on computers that run Unix (the pure variety, not the dressed-up version that is Mac OS X).

Burning CDs and DVDs

If your Mac has a CD-RW drive or an Apple SuperDrive in it, you've got yourself the world's most convenient and elegant backup system. It's just like having a floppy disk drive, really—except that a blank CD holds about 450 times as many files, and a blank DVD holds about 3,350 times as many!

You can buy blank CDs very inexpensively in bulk ($50 for 100 discs, for example) via the Web. (To find the best prices, visit *www.shopper.com* and search for *blank CD-R.*) Blank DVDs are much more expensive, but not ridiculously so considering their capacity. At this writing, the Apple Web site sells them, for example, at $30 for five; prices are sure to come down.

To use one for backup, transporting files, or mailing files, insert a blank CD-R, CD-RW, or DVD-R disc into your Mac. (If you have a slot-loading Mac, simply slip the disc into the slot. If your Mac has a sliding CD/DVD tray instead, press the button on the tray—or, if you have an Eject key in the upper-right corner of your keyboard, press it for about one second—to make the CD/DVD tray open.)

CHAPTER 10: CDS, DVDS, AND ITUNES 2

Tip: Once you've inserted a CD or DVD into your tray, you can close it either by pushing gently on the tray or, if your keyboard has an Eject key, by pressing the Eject key again.

After a moment, the Mac notices the blank disc and displays the dialog box shown in Figure 10-3. Type a name for the new disc, if you like, and then click Prepare. (For the purposes of copying files and folders, leave the Format pop-up menu set to Standard.)

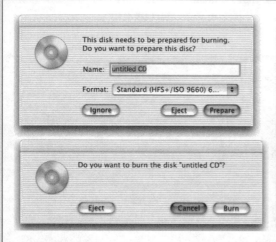 

Figure 10-3:
Top left: Choose Standard *if you plan to copy regular Mac files onto the CD;* iTunes Audio *if you plan to burn a standard music CD using iTunes; or* MP3 CD *if you'll be using iTunes 2 to burn an MP3 music CD (lower quality than standard CDs, less compatibility with players, but longer play time).*

Right: Drag the fully "loaded" CD or DVD onto the Burn icon on the Dock.

Lower left: Confirm your choice in this box.

After another moment, you'll see the disc's icon show up on the desktop. At this point, you can begin dragging files and folders onto it, exactly as though it were a particularly well-endowed floppy disk. You can add, remove, reorganize, and re-name the files on it just as you would in any standard Finder window. You can even rename the CD or DVD itself just as you would a file or folder (page 54).

Tip: Behind the scenes, the Mac is creating a *disk image* of the CD-to-be, as described on page 125. If your hard drive is very full—too full to set aside a 650-megabyte loading area for your files, that is—you'll get an error message.

When the disk contains the files and folders you want to immortalize, do one of these things:

- Choose File→Burn Disc.

- Drag the disc's icon toward the Trash icon on the Dock. As soon as you begin to drag, the Trash icon turns into what looks like a bright yellow fallout-shelter logo (also shown in Figure 10-3). Drop the disc's icon onto it.

- Control-click the disc's icon on the Dock and choose Burn Disc from the contextual menu that appears.

Tip: If you do a lot of CD burning, consider adding a Burn button right to your Finder toolbar. It's one of the canned options available in Mac OS X, as described on page 84.

In any case, the dialog box shown at bottom left in Figure 10-3 now appears. Click Burn. The Mac's laser proceeds to record the CD or DVD, which can take some time. Fortunately, because this is Mac OS X, you're free to switch into another program and keep using your Mac.

When the recording process is over, you'll have yourself a newly minted DVD or CD that you can insert into any other appropriately equipped Mac. It will show up on that Mac's desktop complete with all the files and folders you put onto it.

Here are a few final notes on burning CDs and DVDs at the desktop:

- Not sure whether your Mac even *has* a CD-burning drive? Launch Apple System Profiler (which is in your Applications→Utilities folder). Click the Devices and Volumes tab. Near the bottom of the display, you'll see, next to a gray triangle, an indication of the kind of drive your Mac has. It might say "DVD-ROM drive," for example (meaning you can't record anything), or "CD-RW" (meaning you can burn CDs).

- The procedure described above works very well if your recordable CD or DVD drive came built into your Mac. It also works on many external USB or FireWire CD burners. It probably won't work, however, on older burners that connect to the Mac using the SCSI port.

- You can only do the most basic recording right in the Finder—convenient as all get-out, but very basic. For example, you can only record an entire CD at once. You can't add any more files or folders to it once it's been burned (unless it's a CD-RW, in which case you must erase the entire disc and then rerecord the whole thing).

  If you'd like to be able to add more to a previously recorded CD-R or CD-RW (technically, to create a *multisession* disc), to make a copy of a CD, to turn a disk image (page 125) into a CD, and so on, you'll need a full-fledged CD-burning program like Toast Titanium *(www.roxio.com)*.

- When you insert a CD-RW disc that you've previously recorded, the box shown at top left in Figure 10-3 doesn't appear. Instead, the disc's icon simply appears on the desktop as though it's any ordinary CD. Before you can copy new files onto it, you must erase it using Disk Utility as described in the previous section.

iTunes 2: The CD and MP3 Jukebox

iTunes, in your Applications folder, is the ultimate software jukebox (Figure 10-4). It can play music CDs, tune in to Internet radio stations, and play back *MP3 files* (sound files in a popular, highly compressed format that stores CD-quality music in remarkably small files) and AIFF files (the sound files on standard audio CDs). It can also turn selected tracks from your music CDs *into* MP3 files, so that you can store favorite songs on your hard drive for anytime playback without having to dig up the original CDs. In fact, iTunes can even load your MP3 files onto certain portable MP3 players. And if your Mac can burn CDs, iTunes even lets you burn your own custom audio CDs that contain only the good songs.

If iTunes 2 didn't come with your copy of Mac OS X, you can—and should—download it from Apple's Web site. This newer version adds a handful of useful new features, including a graphic equalizer and synchronization of your music library with an Apple iPod. iTunes 2 can also burn *MP3 CDs:* music CDs that fit much more than the usual 74 minutes of music onto a disc (because they store songs in MP3 format instead of AIFF format). Not all CD players can play MP3 discs, however, and the sound quality is lower than standard CDs.

The first time you run iTunes, you're treated to the appearance of the iTunes Setup Assistant: a series of interview screens that lets you specify (a) whether or not you want iTunes to be the program your Mac uses for playing MP3 files from the Internet, (b) whether or not you want it to ask your permission every time it connects to the Internet, and (c) if you want the program to scan your hard drive for all MP3 files already on it. (If you decline to have your hard drive scanned at this time, you can always do so later just by dragging your hard drive icon directly into the iTunes window.)

Tip: Some new Mac models come with hundreds of MP3 files already on board. If yours isn't among them, it's possible that this hard drive scan won't find any MP3 files at all. In that case, consider visiting a Web site like *www.mp3.com* to download a few free MP3 music files so you'll have something to work with, or turn some of your own CDs into MP3 files following the instructions later in this chapter.

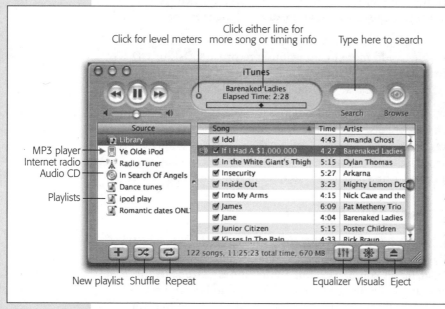

Figure 10-4:
The Shuffle button plays the selected songs in a random order, so that you don't have to listen to them in the same order every time. The Loop button behaves like the one on a CD player: when you've clicked it, your playlist will play to the end and then repeat. If you see a tiny digit 1 superimposed on this button, your playlist will loop only once.

MP3 Files

The iTunes screen itself is set up to be a list—a database—of every song you've got in MP3 or AIFF format. iTunes automatically finds, recognizes, and lists all the MP3 files in your Home folder→Documents→iTunes Music folder.

Tip: You can tell it to show you the contents of other folders, too, by choosing File→Add to Library. But as a warning lets you know, iTunes can only "point to," not actually track, these files. If you move or rename a folder that you add in this way, iTunes will no longer list the MP3 files inside.

FREQUENTLY ASKED QUESTION

Mac OS 9 and Mac OS X in Glorious iTunes Harmony

Is there any way to synchronize my music libraries between the Mac OS 9 and Mac OS X copies of iTunes?

Here's another one of these situations where you may get real headaches when you switch between Mac OS 9 and Mac OS X. Fortunately, it's easy to solve.

The Mac OS X version of iTunes tracks the MP3 files in your Home folder→Documents→iTunes→iTunes Music

Library folder. But by choosing iTunes→Preferences and clicking the Advanced tab, you'll see that you can change the Music Folder Location.

If you change it to the same folder that contains your Mac OS 9 iTunes files (usually Documents→iTunes→iTunes Music folder), you'll be able to keep a single iTunes music folder no matter which operating system you're using at the moment.

Audio CDs

If you're not into collecting MP3 files—and, if you're not a college student or teenager, you may not be—you can also populate the main list here simply by inserting a music CD. The songs on it immediately show up in the list.

FREQUENTLY ASKED QUESTION

Auto-Playing Music CDs

In Mac OS 9, you can set the QuickTime Settings control panel to play music CDs automatically when they're inserted into the Mac. Can Mac OS X do that?

There's no feature to autoplay music CDs. But iTunes can automatically begin playing CDs: Choose iTunes→Preferences, click the General tab, and from the On CD Insert pop-up menu, choose Begin Playing, and click OK.

Now you just have to make iTunes launch itself and hide itself automatically when your Mac starts up. Remember, in Mac OS X, there's almost no downside to having pro-

grams like this lurking in the background. When they're not in use, they aren't using much memory or horsepower.

Page 279 offers the details on setting up a program to run automatically at startup time, but here's a summary: Open System Preferences, click Login, click Add, and then navigate to, and select, the iTunes icon in your Applications folder. Turn on the Hide checkbox.

From now on, iTunes will launch in the background, invisibly, automatically when you turn the Mac on or sign in, waiting and ready to begin playing any music CD you insert.

At first, they may show up with the exciting names "Track 01," "Track 02," and so on. Similarly, the CD itself shows up in the list at the left side of the window with the uninspiring name Audio CD.

Fortunately, iTunes immediately attempts to connect to the Internet and compare your CD with the listings at cddb.com, a global database of music CDs and their contents. If it finds a match among the thousands of CDs there, it copies the album and song names right into iTunes, where they reappear every time you use this particular music CD.

Tip: If you connect an iTunes-compatible portable MP3 player to your Mac, its name, too, shows up in the left-side Source list. This is your opportunity to make your Mac the "hub for the digital lifestyle," exactly as Apple advertises: You can add or remove songs on your player (by dragging them onto its icon), rename or reorder them, and so on.

The iPod

The iPod is a beautiful, tiny, white-and-chrome Apple MP3 player containing a five-gigabyte hard drive—enough to hold about 1,200 songs. It's designed to integrate seamlessly with iTunes 2.

All you have to do is connect the iPod to the Mac via its FireWire cable. You'll see the iPod's icon show up on your desktop as though it's a hard drive (which it is). You'll also see an iPod icon show up in the iTunes "folder list." Click its icon to see what's on it.

GEM IN THE ROUGH

Turning Off Auto-Synchronization

Out of the box, the iPod and iTunes come set for automatic synchronization. That is, as soon as you hook them together, iTunes sends your complete music library (the contents of your Library "folder" in iTunes) to the iPod. The iPod's songs and playlists always match the Mac's.

It doesn't have to be that way. You can maintain a completely different set of playlists and songs on the iPod, as long as you understand that there's no easy way to get songs *from* the iPod *to* the Mac.

To restore the iPod's independence, click the iPod button (which appears at the bottom edge of the screen whenever you highlight the iPod icon in the source list). In the iPod Preferences dialog box, select "Manually manage songs and playlists" and then click OK.

Now, back at the main iTunes window, choose Advanced→Show Device Playlists. You're ready to create new playlists on the iPod itself: Just click the iPod in the source list (shown here) and then click the + button at the lower-left corner of the window. You've just made a new playlist, which you can name and then, by dragging, load up with songs from your Library or other playlists.

By switching to manual mode in this way, you also assure yourself that iTunes will never *delete* songs from the iPod after they've been deleted from iTunes.

Playing Music

To turn your Mac into a music player, click the triangular Play button (or press the Space bar). The Mac immediately begins to play the songs whose names are checked in the main list. Check Figure 10-4 to see what the various onscreen buttons do.

Tip: The central display of the top of the window shows not only the name of the song and album, but also where you are in the song, as represented by the diamond in the horizontal strip. You can drag this diamond, or click elsewhere in the strip, to jump around in the song.

Or just click in this display to see a dancing VU meter that pulses to show the current music's sound levels at various frequencies.

Fun Things to Do During Playback

As music plays, you can control and manipulate the music and the visuals of your Mac in all kinds of interesting ways. Some people don't move from their Macs for months at a time.

Turning on visuals

Visuals is the iTunes term for an onscreen laser-light show that pulses, beats, and dances in perfect sync to the music you're listening to. The effect is hypnotic and wild. (For real party fun, invite some people who grew up in the '60s to your house to watch.)

To summon this psychedelic display, click the flower-power icon in the lower right corner of the window (see Figure 10-4). The show begins immediately, although it's much more fun if you choose Visuals→Full Screen so that the movie takes over your whole monitor. True, you won't get a lot of work done. But when it comes to stress relief, visuals are a lot cheaper than a hot tub.

Once the screen is alive with visuals, you can turn it into your personal biofeedback screen by experimenting with these keys:

Key	Function
?	Displays a cheat sheet of secret keystrokes. (Press it repeatedly to see the other shortcut keys.)
F	Displays, in the upper-left corner of your screen, how many frames per second iTunes' animation is managing—a quick, easy way to test the power of your graphics circuitry.
T	Turns *frame rate capping* on or off—a feature that limits the frame rate to 30 frames per second, to avoid sapping your Mac's horsepower when you have work to do in other programs (not really much of an issue in Mac OS X, of course).
I	Shows/hides info about the current song.
C	Shows/hides the current Visuals configuration (the name of the current waveform, style, and color scheme) in the upper-right corner of the screen.

M	Turns slideshow mode on or off. In slideshow mode, the Visuals keep changing color and waveform as they play. (Otherwise, the visuals stick with one style and color.)
B	Turns on an Apple logo in the center of the Visuals screen.
R	Chooses a new waveform/style/color at random.
Q or W	Cycles through the various waveform styles stored in iTunes.
A or S	Cycles though *variations* on the currently selected waveform.
Z or X	Cycles through color schemes.
Number keys	Cycles through the ten different preset, preprogrammed waveform/color/style configurations.
D	Restores the default waveform settings.

Keyboard control

You can control iTunes' music playback using its menus, of course, but the keyboard can be far more efficient. Here are a few of the control keystrokes worth noting:

Function	Keystroke
Play, Pause	Space bar
next song/previous song	right arrow, left arrow
next source/previous source	down arrow, up arrow
louder	⌘-up arrow
quieter	⌘-down arrow
mute	⌘-M
fast-forward, rewind	Option-⌘-right arrow, -left arrow
eject	⌘-E
Turn Visuals on	⌘-T
Turn Visuals off	⌘-T or mouse click
Full-Screen Visuals	⌘-F
Exit full-screen visuals	⌘-T, ⌘-F, or mouse click

Tip: You can also control CD playback from the Dock. Just Control-click the iTunes icon (or click and hold on it) to produce a pop-up menu offering playback commands like Pause, Next Song, and Previous Song, along with a display that identifies the currently playing song.

Figure 10-5:
Drag the sliders (bass on the left, treble on the right) to accommodate the strengths and weaknesses of your speakers or headphones (and listening tastes). Or save yourself the trouble— use the pop-up menu above the sliders to choose a canned set of slider positions for Classical, Dance, Jazz, Latin, and so on. Unfortunately, these settings don't transfer to the iPod.

Playing with the graphic equalizer

If you click the Graphic Equalizer button (identified back in Figure 10-4), you get a handsome, "brushed-aluminum" control console that lets you adjust the strength of each musical frequency independently (see Figure 10-5).

Copying (Ripping) CD Songs to Your Hard Drive

iTunes lets you convert your favorite songs from audio CDs into MP3 files on your hard drive. Once they've been transferred to your Mac, you can play them whenever you like, without even requiring the original CD.

To *rip* a CD in this way (as aficionados would say), make sure that only the songs you want to capture have checkmarks in the main list. (The bottom of the window shows you how many songs are on the CD, their total playback time, and how many megabytes of disk space it would take to copy them to your hard drive.) Then click the Import button at the upper-right corner of the window (see Figure 10-6).

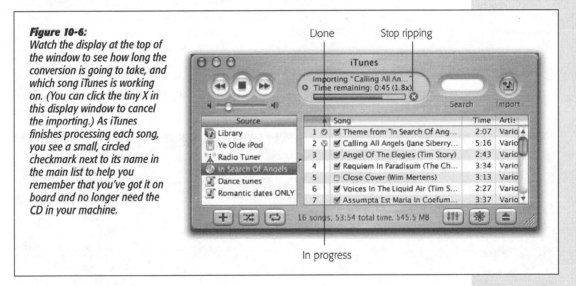

Figure 10-6:
Watch the display at the top of the window to see how long the conversion is going to take, and which song iTunes is working on. (You can click the tiny X in this display window to cancel the importing.) As iTunes finishes processing each song, you see a small, circled checkmark next to its name in the main list to help you remember that you've got it on board and no longer need the CD in your machine.

When it's all over, you'll find the imported songs listed in your Library (click the Library icon in the left-side Source list). From there, you can drag them into any other "folder" (playlist), as described next.

Building Playlists

When you click the Library icon in the left-side Source list, you see, in the main part of the screen, every MP3 file iTunes knows about. It's organized much like a Finder window, with columns indicating the song length, singer or band, album, and so on. As always, you can rearrange these columns by dragging their headings, sort your list by one of these criteria by clicking the heading, reverse the sorting order by clicking the heading a second time, and so on. And here's the best part: To find a particular song, just type a few letters into the Search blank above the list. iTunes hides all but the ones that match.

But Apple recognizes that you may not want to listen to *all* your songs every time you need some tunes. That's why iTunes lets you create *playlists*—folders in the Source list that contain only certain songs, like albums of your own devising. You might create one called Party Tunes, another called Blind Date Music, and so on.

To create a new playlist, click the New Playlist button in the lower-left corner of the window, or choose File→New Playlist (⌘-N). (Alternatively, if you've already highlighted certain songs—by ⌘-clicking them or Shift-clicking them, exactly as though they were files in a Finder list—you can choose File→New Playlist From Selection. iTunes creates a new playlist that contains only the songs you had highlighted.)

A new playlist shows up as an icon in the list at the left side of the screen. You can rename one by clicking and add songs to one by dragging them out of the main list.

Tip: Songs in the Playlist are like aliases to the contents of your Library. That is, deleting a song from a playlist doesn't delete it from the Library (or your hard drive). Similarly, it's fine to add the same song to as many different playlists as you like; you're not actually increasing the size of your Library.

---

iTunes: Burning Music CDs

If your Mac has a CD burner, Mac OS X can be your own private record label. iTunes can record selected sets of songs, no matter what the original sources, onto a blank CD. When it's all over, you can play the burned CD on any standard CD player, just

---

GEM IN THE ROUGH

Internet Radio

Audio CDs and MP3 files aren't the only sources of musical and spoken sound you can listen to as you work. iTunes also lets you tune in to any of hundreds of Internet-based radio stations, which may turn out to be the most convenient music source of all. They're free, they play 24 hours a day, and their music collections make yours look like a drop in the bucket.

Click Radio Tuner in the left-side Source list. In the main list, you'll see categories like Blues, Classic Rock, Classical, and so on, as shown here. Click the flippy triangle to see a list of Internet radio stations in that category.

When you see one that looks interesting, click it and then click the Play button. (The higher the number in the Bit Rate column, the better the sound quality.) Wait a moment for your Mac to connect to the appropriate Internet site, and then let the music begin!

Unfortunately, there's no easy way to capture Internet broadcasts or save them onto your hard drive. You can, however, drag the name of one into another "folder" in the Source List to make it easier to get to later on.

(If you find out about other Internet radio stations that sound interesting, choose Advanced→Open Stream, type in the Web address [URL] of the station, and press Return.)

like the ones from Tower Records—but this time, you hear only the songs you like, in the order you like, with all of the annoying ones eliminated.

Tip: Use CD-R discs. CD-RW discs are not only more expensive, but may not work in standard CD players. (Not all players recognize CD-R discs either, but the odds are better.)

Start by creating a playlist for the CD you're about to create. Drag the songs you want onto its "folder icon" (out of your Library list, for example). Click its icon in the left-side Source list to see the list you've built. Take a moment to drag them up or down in the list to reflect their playback order. Keep an eye on the readout at the bottom of the list, which tells you how much time the songs will take (about 74 minutes is the limit for a CD).

Tip: You can control how many seconds of silence iTunes leaves between tracks on your custom CD. Choose iTunes→Preferences, click the CD Burning tab, and make a selection from the Gap Between Tracks pop-up menu. This is also where you specify whether you want to make a standard audio CD or a CD in the newer, less compatible MP3 CD format (which holds much more music per disc).

When everything is set up, click the Burn CD button in the playlist window. Insert a blank CD into the Mac and then click Burn CD again.

The burning process takes some time—you can always cancel by clicking the tiny X button in the progress bar—but you should feel free to work in other programs while iTunes chugs away.

Tip: iTunes can Burn CDs using any built-in CD burner or those from most major manufacturers. If your drive isn't on Apple's list, you'll need the help of a program like Toast Titanium (*www.roxio.com*). Launch Toast and prepare to burn a new CD, choosing Audio CD as the Format. Then drag and drop selections from an iTunes playlist directly to the Toast window and click Burn. Toast burns your custom CD using the files you encoded, organized, and ordered in iTunes.

Playing DVD Movies

If your Mac has a DVD drive (or a combo DVD/CD-RW drive or SuperDrive), you're in for a treat. Your Mac can play rented or purchased Hollywood movies on DVD as though it was born to do so. The initial releases of Mac OS X didn't include DVD-playing abilities, but version 10.1 and later certainly does.

Watching movies on your Mac screen couldn't be simpler: just insert the DVD. The Mac automatically detects that it's a video DVD—as opposed to, say, one that's just filled with files—and launches the DVD Player program (Figure 10-7).

Note: As of Mac OS X 10.1, DVD Player works (and gets installed) only on recent Macs. Bronze-keyboard PowerBook G3 (Lombards) and most blue-and-white Power Macs, for example, are deprived of this pleasure.

Figure 10-7:
Top: DVDs on your screen!

Bottom: You can orient this controller either horizontally or vertically on your screen by choosing one of the commands in the Controls→Select Controller Type submenu. You can also do without this remote control altogether, because all of its buttons have keyboard equivalents.

If DVD Player doesn't start up automatically when you insert a DVD movie, you can open it yourself. It's sitting there in your Applications folder.

DVD Player starts out playing your movie in a relatively small window—but you didn't come this far and pay this much just to watch movies on a *slice* of your screen. Your first act, therefore, should be to choose one of the commands from the Video menu to enlarge the picture. Maximum Size is better, except that it leaves the Dock and the menu bar exposed.

For best results, choose Video→Enter Full Screen (⌘-0). At this point, the movie screen fills your entire monitor, and even the menu bar disappears. (To make it reappear, just move your cursor close to the top of the screen.)

At this point, you're ready to start the movie playing. By far the easiest way is to just press the Space bar—once to start, again to pause, again to start again.

You can also use the "remote control," which is deconstructed in Figure 10-7. Its buttons include:

- **Menu.** Most DVD movies offer a main-menu screen that lists its various segments, extra features, setup screen, and so on. Click this button to summon the menu. (You have to click Play before you can use this button or the next.)

- **Title.** Takes you directly to the feature presentation: the movie itself.

Note: Not all DVDs have been programmed to respond to these buttons. If it's any consolation, these DVDs wouldn't respond to the Menu and Title buttons on a physical DVD player's remote control, either.

- **Eject.** Ejects the DVD.

- **Play/Pause, Stop, Rewind, Fast Forward.** These controls do just what you'd expect. Only the Rewind and Fast Forward buttons need explanation: you have to hold the mouse button down on one of these buttons to scan forward or backward through the movie. You control the speed of this rewinding or fast-forwarding by choosing from the Controls→Scan Rate submenu.

Tip: For maximum control, don't even bother with the Rewind and Fast Forward buttons. Instead, control these functions from the keyboard. Press ⌘-right arrow to fast-forward; press that combination repeatedly to cycle from twice to four or eight times normal speed. Similarly, press ⌘-left arrow to scan backwards, rewinding at two, four, or eight times normal speed by pressing it repeatedly. Click Play (or press the Space bar) to resume normal playback.

- **[Arrow buttons], Enter.** You use these control keys to choose the various menu options and buttons on your movie DVD's screens. (Clicking the red pills on the credits screens of *The Matrix*, for example, unlocks special, secret extra features—DVD Easter eggs.)

- **Volume slider.** You can make the movie louder or quieter either by dragging the slider or by repeatedly tapping ⌘-up or -down arrow. That's a good keystroke to remember when you've hidden the remote control itself.

If you click the tiny handle identified in Figure 10-7 while the movie is playing, the remote control sprouts an added bank of controls. They include:

- **Slow motion.** You can click this button repeatedly to slow down the movie more, more, and more. One more click restores original speed.

- **Frame advance.** Plays one frame of the movie at a time, of course. Ideal for spotting the director's foot in a shot, the piece of spinach in Julia Roberts's teeth, the "hanging Munchkin" in the Wizard of Oz, and so on.

- **Return.** If you leave the movie to visit the DVD's menu, this button takes you back to the spot in the movie where you stopped.

- **Subtitle.** Most Hollywood DVDs have been programmed with onscreen subtitles to help those with hearing impairments and people sitting in noisy bars. Click this button to turn on the subtitles, again to hide them. (You can specify the language you want—English subtitles, Spanish subtitles, or whatever the DVD offers—by choosing DVD Player→Preferences, clicking the Disc tab, and choosing a language from the Subtitle pop-up menu.)

- **Language.** Each time you click this button, the soundtrack of your movie will switch to a different language (if, in fact, alternate soundtrack languages have been provided). You'll see the name of each language appear briefly on the screen.

Tip: For real fun, turn on English subtitles but switch the soundtrack to a foreign language. No matter how trashy the movie you're watching, you'll gain much more respect from your friends and family when you tell them that you're watching a foreign film.

- **Angle.** Technically, movie companies can program a DVD so that you can switch camera angles during certain scenes. You'll probably go for years without ever seeing a movie that's been programmed this way. But if you get lucky, this is the button to click to switch from one camera angle to another.

Ditching the Remote Control

There's really no reason to leave the remote control on the screen. When you're playing the movie in full-screen mode, as you should be, the remote control blocks your view every bit as effectively as a lady in the movie theater who refuses to take off her flower hat.

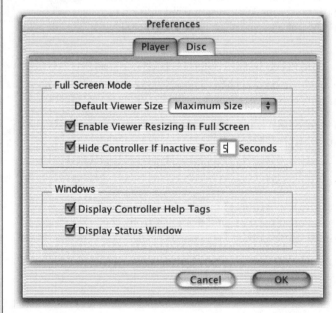

Figure 10-8:
If you also turn on Enable Viewer Resizing In Full Screen, you'll be able to use the Video menu to change the size of the "screen" on your screen even while you're in full-screen mode. (Remember to move the mouse close to the top of the monitor to make the menu bar reappear.)

Choose DVD Player→Preferences. In the Preferences dialog box shown in Figure 10-8, "Hide Controller If Inactive For __ Seconds" should be turned on. Change the number of seconds before the remote disappears automatically according to your tolerance.

Once the remote control is hidden, you can always bring it back onto the screen just by moving your mouse around. But the true DVD master would never bother with such a sissy technique. The secret keystrokes of DVD Player—some of which, mercifully, are the same as in iTunes—are all you really need to know:

Function	Keystroke
Play, Pause	Space bar
fast-forward	⌘-right arrow
rewind	⌘-left arrow
louder	⌘-up arrow
quieter	⌘-down arrow
mute	⌘-K
next/previous "chapter"	right arrow, left arrow
main menu	⌘-' (upper-left of your keyboard)
full-screen mode	⌘-0
half, normal, maximum size	⌘-1, -2, -3
eject	⌘-E
show/hide remote control	Control-C
remote-control orientation	Shift-⌘-H (horizontal), Shift-⌘-V (vertical)
show/hide "movie screen"	Control-V
show movie Info	⌘-I

Tip: Watching a movie while sitting in front of your iMac or Power Mac is not exactly the great American movie-watching dream. But remember that you can connect the video-output jacks of your Mac (most models) to your TV for a much more comfortable movie-watching experience.

Just be sure to connect the cables from the Mac's video-output jacks *directly* to the TV. If you connect to your VCR instead, you'll get a horrible, murky, color-shifting picture—the result of the built-in copy-protection circuitry of every VCR.

Part Four:
The Technologies of
Mac OS X

4

One Mac,
Many Users

For years, teachers, parents, and computer lab instructors have struggled to answer a difficult question: How do you rig one Mac so that several different people can use it throughout the day, without interfering with each others' files and settings? And how do you protect a Mac from getting fouled up by mischievous (or bumbling) students and employees?

Some schools, labs, families, and businesses just muddled through as best they could. Others installed Mac OS 9 and relied upon its Multiple Users control panel, which did a reasonable job of tacking a multiple-accounts feature onto the traditional, single-user Mac OS.

Mac OS X takes a radically different approach. Like the Unix under its skin (and also like Windows XP and Windows 2000), Mac OS X is designed from the ground up to be a multiple-user operating system. A Mac OS X machine can be set up so that everyone must *log in*—that is, you have to click or type your name and type in a password—when the computer turns on. And upon doing so, you discover the Macintosh universe just as you left it, including these elements:

• Your icons on the desktop and in the Dock

• Your desktop picture, screen saver, and language settings

• Your Dock settings (small or large icons, bottom or side of the screen, and so on)

• Your Web browser bookmarks, Web browser preferred home page, and email account

• Your personally installed programs and even fonts

• Your choice of programs that launch automatically at startup

If you're a solo operator (the only person who uses your Mac), you can safely skip this chapter. You *will* be using one of these accounts, whether you realize it or not—it's just that there won't be any other accounts on your Mac, so it will look to you as though you're using a Mac just as you always have. The Mac will never ask you for the name and password you made up when you installed Mac OS X, because Apple's installer automatically turns on something called *automatic login* (page 283).

Even so, when you're stuck in line at the Department of Motor Vehicles, you may find the concepts presented here worth skimming, because certain elements of this multiple-user operating system may intrude upon your solo activities—and the discussions in this book—from time to time.

Tip: Even if you don't share your Mac with anyone and don't create any other accounts, you might still be tempted to learn about this feature because of its ability to password-protect the entire computer. All you have to do is to turn *off* the automatic login feature described on page 283. Thereafter, your Mac is protected from unauthorized fiddling when you're away from your desk (or when your laptop is stolen). (There is a backdoor—you could start up from a Mac OS 9 disk, for example—but this step is better than nothing.)

Introducing User Accounts

When you first installed Mac OS X, as described in Appendix C, you were asked for a name and password. You may not have realized it at the time, but you were creating the first *user account* on your Macintosh. Since that fateful day, you may have made a number of changes to your desktop—adjusted the Dock settings, set up your folders and desktop the way you like them, added some favorites to your Web browser, and so on—without realizing that you were actually making these changes only to *your account*.

As noted in Chapter 2, you've probably been saving your documents into your own *Home folder,* which is the cornerstone of your own account. This folder, named after you and stashed in the Users folder on your hard drive, stores not only your own work, but also your preference settings for all the programs you use, special fonts that you've installed, programs you've installed for your own use, and so on.

Now then: If you create an account for a second person, when she turns on the computer and signs in, she'll find the desktop exactly the way it was as factory installed by Apple—blue swirling desktop picture, Dock along the bottom, the default Web browser home page, and so on. She can make the same kinds of changes to the Mac that you've made, but nothing she does will affect your environment the next time you log in. You'll still find the Mac desktop the way you left it: *Your* desktop picture fills the screen, the Web browser lists *your* bookmarks, the Dock lists *your* favorite documents, and so on.

In other words, the multiple-accounts feature has two components: first, a convenience element that hides everyone else's junk; and second, a security element that protects both the Mac's system software and other people's work.

Figure 11-1:
When you set up several accounts—something like an infinitely more stable successor to the old At Ease kid-proofing software—you don't turn on the Mac so much as sign into it. A command in the menu called Log Out also summons this sign-in screen. Click your own name, and type your password, to get past this box and into your own stuff.

Setting up Accounts

If you plan to share your Mac with at least one other person, you'll have to learn how to set up accounts for other people.

Begin by opening System Preferences (page 181). In the System Preferences window, click Show All, and then click Users.

The screen shown in Figure 11-2 appears, showing the list of everyone for whom accounts have been created. If you're new at this, there's probably just one account listed here—yours. This is the account that Mac OS X created when you first installed Mac OS X.

Administrator Accounts

It's important to understand the phrase you see in the Kind column. On your own personal Mac, it probably says *Admin* next to your name. This, as you could probably guess, stands for Administrator.

Because you're the person who installed Mac OS X to begin with, the Mac assumes that you are its administrator—the technical wizard who will be in charge of it. You're the teacher, the parent, the resident guru. You're the one who will maintain this Mac. Only an administrator is allowed to:

- Install new programs into the Applications folder.

- Add fonts (to the Library folder) that everybody can use.

- Make changes to certain System Preferences panels (including Network, Date & Time, Energy Saver, Login, and Startup Disk).

- Use the NetInfo Manager and Disk Utility programs.

- Create new folders outside of your Home folder.

- Decide who gets to have accounts on the Mac.

In the olden days, there may have been a few Mac-heads who took charge of maintaining the computers, but there was no such thing as an Administrator *account*. This is unfamiliar terrain for most Mac fans.

But the notion of administrators is an important pill to swallow. For one thing, you'll find certain settings all over Mac OS X that you can change *only* if you're an administrator—including those in the Users panel itself (see Figure 11-2). For another thing, whether or not you're an administrator plays an enormous role when you want to network your Mac to other kinds of computers, as described in the next chapter. And finally, in the bigger picture, the fact that the Mac has an industrial-strength accounts system, just like traditional Unix and Windows 2000 operating systems, gives it a fighting chance in the corporations of America.

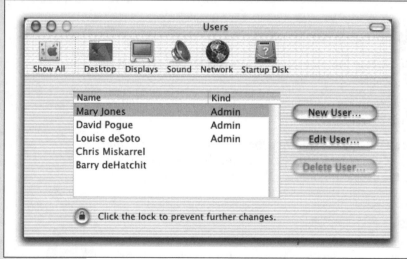

Figure 11-2:
The screen lists everyone for whom you've created an account. From here, you can create new accounts or change people's passwords. Notice the padlock icon: Whenever you see it, you're looking at settings that only administrators are allowed to change.

As you go about creating accounts for other people who will use this Mac, you'll be offered the opportunity to make each one an administrator just like you. Needless to say, use discretion. Bestow these powers only upon people as responsible and technically masterful as you.

Normal Accounts

Anyone who isn't an administrator will probably just be an ordinary, everyday Normal account holder. These people will have everyday access to their own Home folders and to some of the System Preferences, but most other areas of the Mac will be off-limits. Mac OS X won't even let them create new folders on the main hard drive except inside their own Home folders (or in the Shared folder described later).

A few of the System Preferences panels contain a padlock icon like the one in Figure 11-2. If you're a Normal account holder, you can't make changes to these settings without the assistance of an administrator. Fortunately, you won't actually have to log out so that an administrator can log in and make changes. You can just call the administrator over, click the padlock icon, and let him type in his name and password—if, indeed, he feels comfortable with you making the changes you're about to make.

Adding an Account

To create a new account, click New User. The dialog box shown in Figure 11-3 appears. This is where you fill in certain information about the new account holder:

- **Name.** If it's just the family, this could be Chris or Robyn. If it's a corporation or school, you'll probably want to use both first and last names.

- **Short Name.** Particularly if your name is, for example, Alexandra Stephanopolous, you'll quickly discover the value of having a short name—an abbreviation of your actual name. When you sign into your Mac, you can use either your long or short name—and when you access this Mac by dialing into it or connecting from across the network (as described in the next chapter), the short variation is all you need.

  As soon as you tab into this field, the Mac proposes a short name for you. You can replace the suggestion with whatever you like, as long as it's fewer than eight characters and all lowercase letters.

- **Login Picture.** The usual Mac OS X sign-in screen (Figure 11-3) displays each account holder's name, accompanied by a little picture.

  You can choose a little graphic for yourself using any of several methods. If you like the selections that Apple has provided along the bottom of the window (drag the horizontal scroll bar to see them all), just click one to select it. If there's some other graphics file somewhere on the hard drive that you'd rather use instead—a digital photo of your own head, for example—you can click the Choose button. You'll be shown a list of what's on your hard drive so that you can select it.

Tip: You can also click out of this window, find the graphics file you want (in almost any conceivable graphics format) in whatever window contains it, and drag the graphic itself onto the Login Picture box, also shown in Figure 11-3.

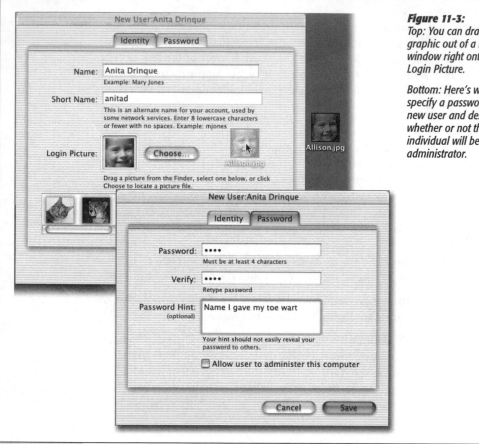

Figure 11-3:
Top: You can drag a graphic out of a Finder window right onto the Login Picture.

Bottom: Here's where you specify a password for your new user and designate whether or not this lucky individual will be an administrator.

- **Password, Verify.** If you click the Password tab of the dialog box, you'll see where you're supposed to type this new user's password (Figure 11-3, bottom). In fact, you're supposed to type it twice, to make sure you didn't introduce a typo the first time. (The Mac shows only dots as you type, to guard against the possibility that somebody is snooping by watching over your shoulder.)

Tip: Mac OS X pays attention only to the first eight characters of your password. Capitalization counts.

The usual computer book takes this opportunity to stress the importance of a long, complex password—a phrase that isn't in the dictionary, something made up of mixed letters and numbers. This is excellent advice if you create sensitive documents and work in a big corporation.

But if you share the Mac only with a spouse or a few trusted colleagues in a small office, for example, you may have nothing to hide. You may see the multiple-users feature more as a convenience (keeping your settings and files separate) than for secrecy and security. In these situations, there's no particular urgency to the mission of thwarting the world's hackers with a convoluted password. In fact, you may want to consider setting up *no* password—leaving both password blanks empty. Later, whenever you're asked for your password, just leave the Password box blank. You'll be able to log in that much faster each day.

Note: Only Normal account holders can have blank passwords. Mac OS X forces you to come up with a password for any new Administrator accounts you create here.

You have only one shot at creating an Administrator account with no password—and that's at the moment you first install Mac OS X, as described on page 545.

- **Password Hint.** If you gave yourself a password, you can give yourself a hint in this box. If your password is the middle name of the first person who ever kissed you plus your junior-year phone number, for example, your hint might be "middle name of the first person who ever kissed me plus my junior-year phone number."

  Later, if you ever forget your password, the Mac will show you this cue to jog your memory (if you've left this option turned on, as described on page 286).

- **Allow user to administer this computer.** This is the big one—this is the master switch that turns this ordinary, unsuspecting computer user into an administrator, as described previously.

When you're finished with the settings, click Save (or press Enter). After a moment, you return to the Users list, where the new person's name joins whatever names were already there. You can continue adding new accounts forever or until your hard drive is full, whichever comes first.

Editing User Accounts

Changing the settings you've just established is very easy: just double-click somebody's name in the Users list. (Or, if it's a slow day at work, click the name and then click Edit User.) You return to the dialog box shown in Figure 11-3, where you can change whatever settings you like. (*Almost* any settings: you can't change a user's short name once the account has been created.)

Setting Up Your Startup Items

You do most of your account-tweaking on the Users pane of System Preferences—or, rather, an administrator does. But one more important decision is left to the individual account holder: which programs or documents will open automatically upon login.

To specify what you'd like to auto-open, open System Preferences and click the Login icon. As shown in Figure 11-4, you can now build a list of programs or documents that will auto-launch each time you log in.

Tip: Don't bother trying to add Classic to this list, however. As noted in Chapter 5, it *is* a great idea to have Classic start up automatically upon login. But you set it up using a checkbox on the Classic pane of System Preferences, not on the Login pane.

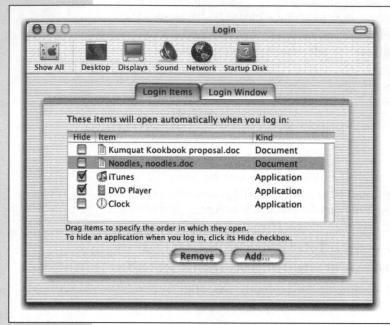

Figure 11-4:
You can add any program or document to the list of things you want to start up automatically. Click Add to summon the Open dialog box where you can find the icon, select it, and then click Choose. Better yet, if you can see the icon of whatever-it-is in a folder or disk window (or on the desktop), you can drag it directly into this list.

You can specify the order in which your startup items auto-open just by dragging them up or down in the list. To remove an item, click it in the list and then click Remove.

Longtime Mac fans may assume that this feature is the successor to the traditional Mac Startup Items folder, but it's not quite as flexible. For example, you can auto-start only programs and documents, not disks, folders, servers, and other fun icons. Furthermore, your auto-start items no longer auto-start if you rename or move them in the Finder.

Deleting User Accounts

It happens: Somebody graduates, somebody gets fired, somebody dumps you. Sooner or later, you may need to delete a user account from your Mac.

Deleting somebody's account doesn't delete all of the corresponding documents, settings, and so on. All of the dearly departed's folders remain on the Mac—but control of them gets turned over to you or an administrator of your choosing.

To delete a user account, click the appropriate name in the Users list (Figure 11-2) and then click Delete User. As shown in Figure 11-5, Mac OS X now offers a list of people who have Administrator accounts on your machine, and asks you which one should assume control of the deleted person's folders. Click the appropriate Administrator account and then click Delete.

Once you, the administrator, have deleted somebody's account, you'll discover the word Deleted tacked onto that person's folder in the Users folder (Figure 11-5, top). If, upon deleting the account, you designate yourself as the lucky recipient of that person stuff, you can see and access these "Deleted" files.

Tip: Even though you have access to open and change the left-behind files, you're not allowed to delete them. If you try to drag them to the Trash, for example, you'll be told, "The operation could not be completed because this item is owned by root."

To find out who *root* is, see page 290. In the meantime, you can get rid of one of these orphaned user folders either by typing a simple Unix command (page 400) or by restarting the Mac from your Mac OS 9 CD.

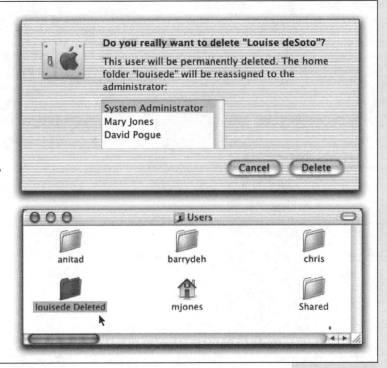

Figure 11-5:
Top: This dialog box seems to imply that you're about to delete one of these administrator accounts, but don't believe it. In fact, you're indicating which administrator account should receive the digital belongings of the person whose account you are *about to delete.*

Bottom: The files and settings of accounts you deleted live on, in the Users folder.

Do you really want to delete "Louise deSoto"?

This user will be permanently deleted. The home folder "louisede" will be reassigned to the administrator:

System Administrator
Mary Jones
David Pogue

Cancel   Delete

Users

anitad   barrydeh   chris

louisede Deleted   mjones   Shared

If you ever need to reinstate the deleted person's account, you'll discover that there's no tidy way to do it. You must create a brand new account, and then move the files and folders from the "Deleted" folder to the new account holder's Home folder→Public→Drop Box folder. At that point, she'll have to move the old files and folders into the appropriate folders (Documents, Desktop, and so on) herself.

Setting Up the Login/Logout Process

Once you've set up more than one account, the dialog box shown in Figure 11-1 appears whenever you turn on the Mac (or whenever you relinquish your turn at the Mac by choosing ▲ menu→Log Out). But a few extra controls let you, an administrator, set up either more or less security on the login screen—or, put another way, less or more convenience.

Moving Your Home Folder between Computers

Mac OS X proposes putting all of the account holders' Home folders in one special folder (Users) on the main hard drive. But being able to put somebody's Home folder–such as your own–on a different disk can have its advantages. If you travel back and forth between home and work, for example, you might find it convenient to keep your entire life on a Zip or some other portable disk that you carry back and forth.

You can do it, but you'll have to exploit the sometimes intimidating power of NetInfo Manager, a program included with Mac OS X designed to let you perform just such technical tasks.

You'll find this program in your Applications→Utilities folder. Open the program, click the lower-left padlock, and then enter an administrator's name and password.

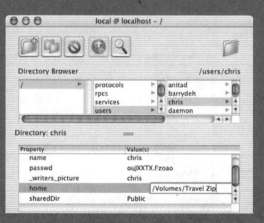

In the second column, click *users*. In the column to its right, click the name of the account whose Home folder you want to move–let's say it's *chris*.

In the bottom half of the window, scroll down until you see an entry called *home*. In the next column, you'll see its current location: /Users/chris (that is, the Home folder is called chris, and it's in the Users folder).

Double-click this notation (/Users/chris) to edit it. Change this text to */Volumes/diskname*, where *diskname* is the name of your removable disk. ("Volumes" is the name of an invisible folder on your Mac OS X machine that lists the names of all disks present.) Press Enter, and then choose Domain→Save (and click "Update this copy" in the confirmation box).

Log out and then log back in again–as Chris. You should see by the house-shaped icon on your desktop that the Zip disk is now, in effect, your Home folder, complete with all the usual Home-folder subfolders (Desktop, Documents, Library, and so on)..

You're not allowed to remove the disk from the Mac until you've logged out and logged back in under a different account. Once you've done so, eject the disk, take it to work (or wherever the other Mac OS X machine is). Insert the disk and then repeat all of these steps so far.

From now on, both Macs will expect to find your Home folder on that removable disk. (Make sure that you've inserted it and given it time to "spin up" before you try to log in.)

And by the way: The procedure described here will leave the original Chris folder on the primary hard drive–an orphaned duplicate. It's not doing any harm, but if its presence confuses you, you can always delete it by restarting your Mac in Mac OS 9, thereby bypassing Mac OS X's stringent permissions system.

Login Options

Open System Preferences, click Show All, and then click Login. On the resulting panel, click the Login Window tab (see Figure 11-6).

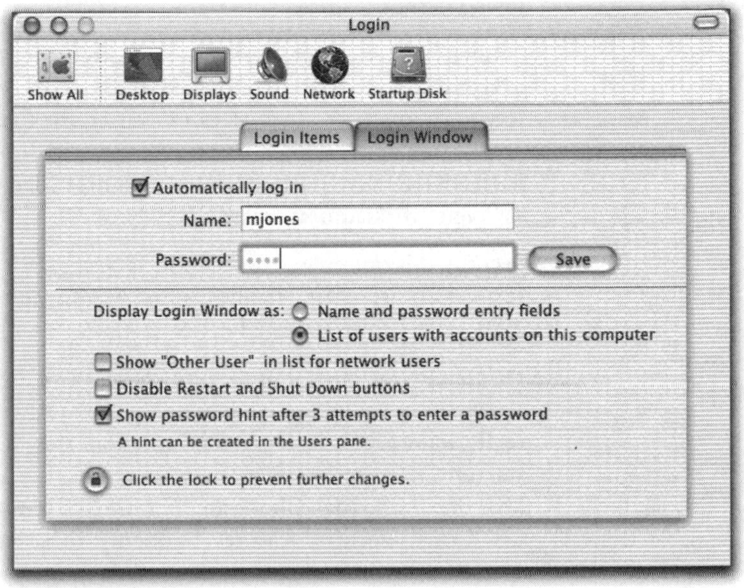

Figure 11-6:
These options make it easier or harder for people to sign in, offering various degrees of security. Only one person gets the pleasure of automatic login—and only then when turning on the Mac from a complete shutdown (or restart).

Here are some of the ways you can shape the login experience:

- **Automatically log in.** If only one person uses this Mac, or if one person uses it most of the time, don't miss this convenient option. If you turn on this checkbox and fill in your name and password, the dialog box shown in Figure 11-5 won't appear *at all* at startup time. After turning on the machine, you'll zoom straight to your desktop, precisely as you've done for years in previous versions of the Mac OS.

  Of course, only one lucky person can enjoy this streamlined entrance experience. Everybody else will still have to enter their names and passwords.

Note: Automatic login only applies when you *turn on or restart* the Mac. When you choose →Log Out, the usual login screen appears. If you want to log in this time, you'll have to type in your name and password.

- **Display Login Window as.** Under normal circumstances, the login screen presents a list of account holders when the Mac is first turned on, as shown in Figure 11-1. That's the "List of users with accounts on this computer" option in action.

  If you're especially worried about security, however, you might not even want that list to appear. If you turn on "Name and password entry fields," each person who signs in must type both his name (into a blank that appears) *and* his password—a very inconvenient, but secure, arrangement.

- **Show "Other User" in list for network users.** If you turn on this option, your login screen will show an account holder called Other; if you click it, you're allowed to type in an account name.

"Other," in this case, means "not anybody with an account on this Mac." It's relevant in any of three situations. First, this feature is the key to giving you access to your home-base Mac account (your Home folder, desktop and Dock settings, and so on) from another Mac on the network, or even from another Mac on the Internet—a very cool feature that requires Mac OS X Server and an extremely savvy network administrator.

Second, this option lets you sign in as *>console,* a troubleshooting technique described on page 560. Finally, it's one way to sign in with the *root account* (page 290), once you've activated it.

- **Disable Restart and Shut Down buttons.** The dirty little secret of the Mac OS X security system is that it's incredibly easy to bypass. If some passing evildoers really want access to everybody's files, all they have to do is insert a Mac OS 9 startup CD, restart your Mac while pressing the letter C key, and grin evilly. The Mac boots into Mac OS 9—an operating system that knows nothing about Mac OS X or its security features. Suddenly, these no-goodniks have full access to every document on the machine, blowing right past all of the safeguards you've so carefully established.

One way to thwart them is to turn on this checkbox. Now nobody can restart the Mac from a Mac OS 9 CD—in fact, they can't restart the Mac, *period.* (Even then, somebody who's especially sneaky could insert the Mac OS 9 CD and then simply pull the plug, shutting down the Mac the hard way—but let's not be picky.)

Tip: The moral of the Mac OS X security story is that your *system CDs are your keys.* For a truly secure system, lock them away as you would the master keys to a vault. Without access to startup disks, the bad guys will have a very difficult time getting into any Mac OS X accounts but their own.

- **Show password hint after 3 attempts to enter a password.** Remember the password hint you created on page 279? If you haven't been at work for a while, and you're fumbling to sign in, unable to remember your password, you'll be glad you left this option turned on. It makes your hint appear after three attempts to sign in with the wrong password.

Logout Options

As you can read later in this chapter, the usual procedure for finishing up a work session is for each person to choose →Log Out. The sign-in screen then appears, ready for the next victim.

But sometimes people forget. You might wander off to the bathroom for a minute, run into a colleague there who breathlessly begins describing last night's date, proposes finishing the conversation over pizza, and the next thing you know, you've left your Mac unattended but logged in, with all your life's secrets accessible to anyone who walks by your desk.

Fortunately, Mac OS X offers a simple but effective form of protection against this phenomenon: a password-protected screen saver that locks your Mac after a few minutes of inactivity.

In the System Preferences, click Screen Saver (described more completely on page 189). Click the Activation tab. Here you'll find a slider that lets you control how much time the Mac waits before password-protecting your screen. Turn on "Use my user account password" to seal the deal. Now, whenever somebody tries to wake up your Mac after the screen saver has appeared, the "Enter your password" dialog box will appear. No password? No access.

Signing In

Once somebody has set up your account, here's what it's like getting into, and out of, a Mac OS X machine. (For the purposes of this discussion, "you" are no longer the administrator—you're one of the students, employees, or family members for whom an account has been set up.)

Identifying Yourself

When you first turn on the Mac—or when the person who last used this computer chooses →Log Out—you get the login screen shown in Figure 11-1. At this point, you can proceed in any of several ways:

DON'T PANIC

The Case of the Forgotten Password

Help—I forgot my password! And I never told it to anybody, so even the administrator can't help me!

No problem. Your administrator can simply open up System Preferences, click Users, click the name of the person who forgot the password, and then click Edit to re-establish the password.

But you don't understand. I am the administrator! And I'm the only account!

Aha—that's a different story. Insert the Mac OS X CD. Re-

start the Mac while pressing down the letter C key, which starts up the Mac from the CD and launches the Mac OS X installer.

On the first installer screen, choose Installer→Reset Password. When the Reset Password screen appears, click the hard drive that contains Mac OS X. From the first pop-up menu, choose the name of your account. Now make up a new password and type it into both of the boxes. Click Save, close the window, click the installer, and restart. You're saved.

- **Restart.** Click if you need to restart the Mac for some reason—for example, if you decide to start up the machine from Mac OS 9. (The Restart and Shut Down buttons don't appear here if the administrator has chosen to hide them as a security precaution; see page 284.)

- **Shut Down.** Click if you're done for the day, or if sudden panic about the complexity of user accounts makes you want to run away. The computer turns off.

- **Log in.** To sign in, click your account name in the list. If you're a keyboard speed freak, you can also type the first letter or two—or press the up or down arrow keys—until your name is highlighted. Then press Return or Enter.

Either way, the password box appears now. If you accidentally click the wrong person's name on the first screen, you can click Go Back. Otherwise, type your password and then press Enter (or click Log In; see Figure 11-7).

Figure 11-7:
If your account was set up with a password, you now encounter the Password box. You can try as many times as you want to type the password in; with each incorrect guess, the entire dialog box shudders violently from side to side, as though shaking its head "No."

If you try unsuccessfully three times, your hint appears, if you had set one up.

Your World

Once you're in, the world of the Mac looks just the way you left it (or the way an administrator set up for you). As noted in Chapter 2, most of the action revolves around the Applications folder, the Dock, and your own Home folder (press Option-⌘-H to open it).

Mac OS X keeps almost everything in your Mac world separate from anybody else who uses this Mac, but a few examples are especially worth noticing:

- **Fonts.** You can install your own preferred fonts into your Home folder→Library→ Fonts folder. Only you will be able to see them and use them in your programs.

- **Programs.** Unless you're an administrator, you'll quickly discover that you're not allowed to install any new programs (or indeed, to put anything at all) into the Applications folder. That folder, after all, is a central software repository for everybody who uses the Mac, and all such universally shared folders are off-limits to everyday account holders. (You can drag things out of the Applications folder, but doing so doesn't actually move them—it just copies them.)

  That's not to say, however, that you can't install new programs of your own. You can—but you must put them somewhere in your own Home folder. (You may want to create a Programs folder there just for this purpose.) You'll be the only person with access to such programs.

- **Bookmarks.** When you browse the Web, you can freely "bookmark" your favorite Web pages, confident that nobody else who uses your Mac will be able to see where you've been or what you consider your favorite sites.

Shared Folder

Every Mac OS X machine has a Users folder in the main hard drive window. It contains the individual Home folders of everybody with an account on this machine.

If you try to open anybody else's Home folder, you'll see a tiny red "no go here" icon superimposed on almost every folder inside, telling you: "look, but don't touch." The exceptions: As shown in Figure 11-8, two folders here are designed to be distribution points for files your co-workers want you to see.

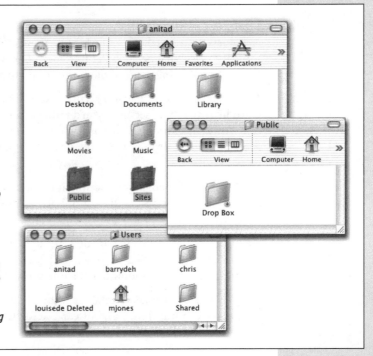

Figure 11-8:
In general, nobody is allowed to peek into anybody else's Home folders. There are three exceptions, however.

Top: In other people's Home folders, only the Public and Sites folders are available for your inspection. These two folders contain files that you're welcome to open, read, and copy to your own folders—stuff that other people have wanted to "publish" for the benefit of their co-workers.

Middle: In the Public folder is the Drop Box, which serves the opposite purpose. It lets anyone else who uses this Mac hand in files to you when you're not around.

Bottom: Inside the Users folder (to get there from a Home folder, press ⌘-up arrow) is the Shared folder, a wormhole between all accounts. Everybody has full access to everything inside.

You, too, have Public and Sites folders in your own Home folder, of course. Here again, anything you put into these folders is available for inspection—although not for changing—by anyone else who uses this Mac.

Sitting in the Users folder is one folder that doesn't correspond to any particular person: Shared. This is the one and only folder that everybody can access, freely putting in and taking out files. It's the common ground among all the account holders. It's Central Park, the farmer's market, and the grocery store bulletin board.

Changing Permissions

A factory-fresh installation of Mac OS X offers one way for you to submit files *to* somebody else (that person's Public folder), one way to accept files *from* other people (your Drop Box folder), and one community folder (the Shared folder).

This arrangement is relatively secure and relatively easy to understand. But maybe you'd like even more security; you'd rather seal off your Public folder so that people can't see what's inside. Or maybe you'd like greater convenience; you'd like to set up some additional drop box folders, or other "public" folders, for your co-workers' use.

The business of changing the permissions, or *access privileges,* for certain folders can be complex and brain-bending. A full discussion begins on page 307; in the meantime, here's a quick summary of some typical setups:

- **Full access by everybody.** If you want to turn one of your other folders into one that resembles the Shared folder (full free access by anyone with an account), set up its Show Info window like the one shown at left in Figure 11-9.

- **Give, but don't take.** To make another folder work like your Drop Box folder (people can put things in, but can't actually open the folder), set things up as shown at middle in the figure.

Tip: Remember that people can't put anything into a new Drop Box-type folder if they can't get *to* it. That is, make sure you've turned on "Read" access for whatever folder it's in. (Making a Drop Box folder in your Documents folder, for example, won't work—because nobody is allowed to *open* your Documents folder to begin with.)

- **Look, but don't touch.** You can also turn any of your folders into another Public-type, "bulletin-board" folder—that is, people can open or copy files from inside, but they can't put anything in or save any changes they make.

Figure 11-9:
Three typical configurations for folder you've created in your Home folder. Highlight the folder and then choose File→Show Info; choose Privileges from the pop-up menu at top. Then set the three pop-up menus as shown for a Shared-type folder (left), a drop-box folder (middle), and the "bulletin board"-type folder (right). Click the Apply button if you want the same settings to apply to all the folders inside this one. Finally, close the Show Info window.

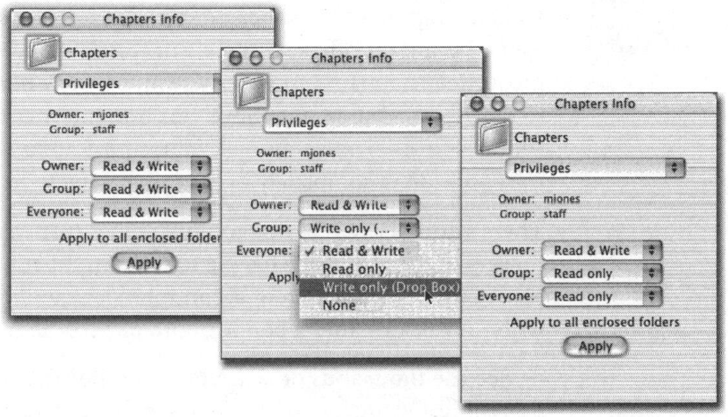

You'll realize the importance of mastering these various access permissions when you get a load of this startling fact: Unless you intervene, everybody else who uses this Mac will be able to peek into everything *in every new folder* you create (unless it's inside a folder that is, itself, off-limits). Technically speaking, every new folder springs into existence with Read-only permissions for Everyone. They're allowed to open or copy anything inside.

The bottom line: As you type the title of a new folder that you suspect might be best kept private (*Salaries 2002* or *My Spicy Dreams Journal,* let's say), remember to use the File→Show Info routine to change the new folder's Everyone and Group settings to None.

Logging Out

When you're finished using the Mac, choose →Log Out (or press Shift-⌘-Q). A confirmation message appears; if you click Cancel or press Esc, you return to whatever you were doing. If you click Log Out, or press Return, you return to the screen shown in Figure 11-1, and the entire sign-in cycle begins again.

The Root Account

An administrator's account isn't exactly a skeleton key that gives you unfettered access to every corner of the Mac. Even an administrator, for example, isn't allowed to open the files in other people's Home folders, or even to drop files into them. Nor are administrators allowed to remove files from the System folder or other files whose removal could hobble your machine.

It turns out that normal and administrator aren't the only kinds of accounts. There's one account that wields ultimate power, one person who can do anything to any file anywhere. This person is called the *superuser.*

Unix fans speak of the superuser account—also called the *root* account—in hushed tones, because it offers absolutely unrestricted power. The root account holder can move, delete, rename, or otherwise mangle any file on the machine, no matter what folder it's in. One wrong move—or one Internet hacker who manages to seize the root account—and you've got yourself a $2,500 doorstop. That's why Mac OS X's root account is completely hidden and, in fact, deactivated.

There's another reason this account comes turned off: You can enjoy most root-like powers without actually having to turn on the root account. Here, for example, are some of the things the root account holder can do—and the ways you can do them without ducking into a phone booth to become the superuser:

- **See the thousands of crucial system files that Mac OS X ordinarily renders invisible.** Of course, you can also see them extremely easily just by using the shareware program Super GetInfo (see page 314). You can also use the Terminal program as described in Chapter 15.

- **Manipulate the files within the System folder's Library folder.** First of all, you'd be nuts to try. The numero uno virtue of Mac OS X is its stability—its System folder's invulnerability to change. Sure, you can mess around with its contents, but if you really wanted a crash-prone machine, you could have stuck with Mac OS 9.

  Anyway, even if you did want to fool around with these files, there's a much easier way: Restart the Mac in Mac OS 9. You'll have full access to all Mac OS X files and folders.

- **Throw away things that no one else can.** You may have read, earlier in this chapter, that deleting a user account doesn't actually delete that person's Home folder. It sits there in your Users folder, orphaned and useless—and even an administrator can't throw it away. But what if you *want* to throw it away? The root user would certainly have no problem tossing it.

  On the other hand, a quick Unix command could do so without your having to mess around with the root user account; page 403 has the details.

- **Use powerful Unix system commands.** As you'll find out in Chapter 16, some of the Unix commands you can issue in Mac OS X require superuser powers. As you'll also find out in that chapter, however, there's a simple command—the *sudo* command—that simulates root powers without your actually having them. Details on page 403.

Treat the root account, in other words, as you would one of those "Break glass in case of fire" boxes. If you know what you're doing, and you see no alternative, you might occasionally be glad the root account is available. Programmers who compile source code, for example, may need to enable the root account.

You can turn on the root account in any of several ways. One of them involves typing a Unix command or two (they're on page 408), but the technique most people use goes like this:

1. **In your Applications→Utilities folder, open the NetInfo Manager program. Click the tiny padlock in the lower-left corner of its screen.**

   A dialog box asks you for an administrator's name and password.

2. **Type your name and password, if you're an administrator (page 275), and then click OK.**

   You're in. (If you're not an administrator, then you probably shouldn't be using the root account.)

3. **Choose Domain→Security→Enable Root User.**

   If this is the first time you've performed this particular surgery, you'll be asked to make up a password for your newly created root account—in fact, a "non-trivial" one (meaning virtually impossible for anyone to guess). Click OK and then type the password, eight characters or less. Click OK again. You're asked to retype it; do so, then click Verify.

4. **Quit NetInfo Manager.**

   You've just brought the dormant root account to life.

5. **Turn on the "Show 'Other User'" option.**

   The root account is never listed on the standard login screen. If you intend to log in as the root account holder, therefore, you must first visit the Login panel of System Preferences, click the Login Window tab, and turn on the "Show 'Other User' in list for network users" option described on page 284.

6. **Log out. Log back in again as *root*.**

   That is, when the login screen appears, click Other User. In the first text box, type *root*. In the second, type the password you made up in step 3. Click Login.

That's it—you arrive at the desktop, where no matter what you do, no error messages regarding access privileges or ownership will interrupt the proceedings. In the words of every movie hero's sidekick: Be careful out there.

When you're finished going about your business as a root user, immediately log out again. It's important to rule out the possibility that some clueless or malicious person might wander up to the Mac while you're still logged in as the superuser.

In fact, if you don't anticipate needing your superuser powers again soon, consider turning off the root account altogether. (Just repeat steps 1 and 2 on the previous page. In step 3, choose Security→Disable Root User.)

Networking in Mac OS X

Every Mac made in the last fifteen years is network-ready. Buy a few cables and adapters, and you can wire all the Macs in your office together. The process of rigging the hardware and software for a network isn't exactly rocket science, but it's somewhat more technical than, say, emptying the Trash.

Once it's done, you can copy files from one machine to another just as you'd drag files between folders on your own Mac. You can send little messages to each other's screens. Everyone on the network can consult the same database or calendar. You can play games over the network. You can share a single laser printer, cable modem, or fax modem among all the Macs in the office. You can connect to this network from wherever you are in the world, using the Internet as the world's longest extension cord back to your office. And in Mac OS X, you can even connect to Windows machines without having to buy any additional software.

Best of all, all the software you need to create such a network is built right into Mac OS X.

As you read this chapter, remember the difficulty Apple faces: It must design a networking system simple enough for the laptop owner who just wants to copy things to a desktop Mac when returning home from a trip—and yet secure and flexible enough for the network designer at a large corporation. The Mac OS X networking software contains many different layers of security, which you can apply independently to every folder on your hard drive. Fortunately, you can ignore all of this if the network is just you, your two Macs, and a printer.

Wiring the Network

The old wiring system called LocalTalk, if you remember it at all, is gone from Mac OS X. Instead, you can connect the Macs (and other computers) in your office using either of two connection systems: Ethernet or AirPort.

Ethernet Networks

These days, every Mac and every network-ready laser printer has an Ethernet jack on the back panel (see Figure 12-1). If you connect all of the Macs and Ethernet printers in your small office to a central *Ethernet hub*—a compact $25 box with jacks for five or ten computers and printers—you've got yourself a very fast, very reliable network. (Most people wind up trying to hide the Ethernet hub in the closet, and running the wiring either along the edges of the room or inside the walls.) You can buy Ethernet cables, plus the Ethernet hub, in any computer store or, less expensively, from an Internet-based mail-order house; hubs aren't Mac-specific.

Tip: If you want to connect only two Macs—say, your laptop and your desktop machine—you don't need an Ethernet hub at all. Instead, you just need an Ethernet *crossover cable*—about $8 from a computer store or online mail-order supplier. Run it directly between the Ethernet jacks of the two computers. (Better yet, if you have a PowerBook Titanium G4 or a 2001 iBook, either a crossover cable or traditional Ethernet cable will do.)

Figure 12-1:
*Every Mac OS X-compatible
Mac has an Ethernet jack (left).
It looks like an overweight
telephone jack. It connects to
an Ethernet hub (right) via
Ethernet cable (also known as
RJ-45), which looks like an
overweight telephone wire.*

Ethernet jack   Ethernet hub

Ethernet is the best networking system for most offices; it's fast, easy, and cheap.

AirPort Networks

Of course, the Mac wouldn't be the Mac if it couldn't connect to other Macs using the most exciting kind of networking connection: radio waves. You can install a $100 metal AirPort card, about the size of a Visa card, into almost any Mac OS X–compatible Mac. This card lets your machine connect to your network without any wires at all—as long as they're within about 150 feet of a *base station,* which must in turn be physically connected to your network. (If you think about it, the AirPort system is a lot like a cordless phone; the Mac is the handset.)

The base station can either be the $300 AirPort Base Station—which looks like a small, silver flying saucer—or one of the less expensive *wireless broadband routers* from, for example, MaxGate *(www.maxgate.net)* or Macsense *(www.xsense.com)*. You can plug the base station into an Ethernet hub, thus permitting 10 or 20 AirPort-equipped Macs to join an existing Ethernet network without wiring. (You may also hear the term *802.11,* the much less fun "official" name of the AirPort technology.)

In fact, you may be able to get away with not buying a base station at all. You can use instead an AirPort-equipped Mac OS 9 machine that you've configured, using the AirPort Setup Assistant, to serve as a *software-based* base station. (As of Mac OS X 10.1.2, you can't set up a Mac OS X Mac to be a software base station.) Much more on AirPort network setups in Chapter 18.

After having wired your network (or unwired it, as the case may be), your network is ready. Your Mac should "see" any Ethernet printers, in readiness to print (see Chapter 13). You can now play network games or use a network calendar. And you can now turn on *File Sharing,* one of the most useful and most sophisticated features of the Mac OS.

Mac, Meet Network

You won't get far connecting your Macs unless each one has an *IP address,* a string of four numbers separated by periods like the one illustrated in Figure 12-3.

To see if your Mac OS X machine has one, choose →System Preferences; click the Network icon (see Figure 12-3); and, from the Show pop-up menu, choose the appropriate connection: Built-in Ethernet or AirPort.

You may have established these numbers when installing Mac OS X to begin with, as described in Appendix C. If you connect to the Internet using a high-speed connec-

---

UP TO SPEED

How to Skip 10 Pages

Much of this chapter assumes that you are your own system administrator, that you are the unlucky geek who has to set up your office network. Nobody pretends that this stuff is simple.

If somebody else sets up your network, fortunately, there's a lot less to learn—in fact, everything you need to know can fit inside this sidebar box. These instructions assume that your network has been set up as described in these pages, and that File Sharing has been turned on.

To make one of your files available to everybody on the network: Copy the file into the Public folder in your own Home folder.

To "hand off" one of your files directly to a co-worker: Bring that person's hard drive onto your screen, as described on page 299. Open your co-worker's Home folder→Public→Drop Box folder. (You might want to let that person know, by email or by yelling across the office, that you've done so.)

To grab a copy of a file that someone else on the network wants you to have: If they haven't put it into your Drop Box, then you'll probably find it inside that person's Home folder→Public folder. (Of course, you have to connect to their machine, following the instructions on page 299.)

---

tion like a cable modem or DSL, you may also find a string of numbers already in the IP Address box.

If you connect to the Internet via standard dial-up modem, however, choose Using DHCP from the Configure pop-up menu and then click Apply Now. (DHCP stands for *dynamic host control protocol,* and means "issue me a new IP address every time I try to connect." You'll find much more information on setting up these controls in Chapter 18.)

Note: You can change these settings only if you're an administrator, as described in Chapter 11.

Quit the System Preferences program, if you like.

File Sharing

In File Sharing, you can summon the icon for a folder or disk attached to another computer on the network. It shows up on your screen underneath your own hard drive, as shown in Figure 12-2. At this point, you can drag files back and forth, exactly as though the other Mac's folder or disk is a gigantic CD you've inserted into your own machine.

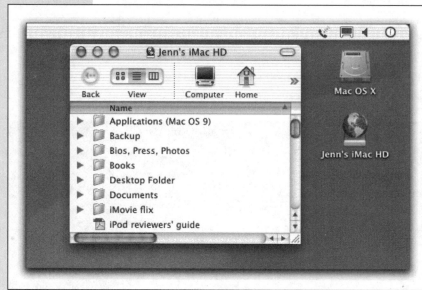

Figure 12-2:
The whole point of file sharing: to bring icons for the hard drives or folders from other Macs, such as the Jenn's iMac HD icon, onto your own screen. By dragging icons back and forth, you can transfer your work from your main Mac to your laptop; give copies of your documents to other people; create a "drop box" that collects submissions from various authors for a publication; and so on.

Phase 1: Setting up the Computers

These instructions assume that you've already wired the network together, as described at the beginning of this chapter.

Setting up a Mac OS X machine

The first thing you have to do when preparing a Mac OS X computer for invasion over the network is to set up an account—a name, password, and Home folder—for each person who might want to visit. See Chapter 11.

If you've used older versions of the Mac OS, note this important change: in Mac OS X, the name and password you use to log in when you sit down in front of the computer—as described in the previous chapter—are the *same* name and password you need to connect over the network. In other words, Mac OS X doesn't care how you try to get into your own stuff, just as long as it's sure that you're you.

Once you've established accounts for everybody who might want to access your Mac OS X computer—even if it's only you—you're ready to proceed with preparing the machine for access from elsewhere on the network.

1. **Open System Preferences.**

   You can click its icon on the Dock, for example, or choose →System Preferences. Either way, the System Preferences program (Chapter 8) opens.

2. **Click the Sharing icon.**

   The Sharing panel appears, as shown at top in Figure 12-3.

Note: Only administrators (page 275) are allowed to fool around with the settings you're about to change. If the little padlock icon in the lower-left corner of the dialog box looks locked, call an Administrator over, click the lock, and prove that you have permission to do what you're doing by entering (or asking the administrator to enter) the administrator's name and password.

---

3. **In the Computer Name blank, type a name for the computer.**

   Your Mac will appear on the network with this name. Make it nice and descriptive, such as Front Desk iMac.

4. **Click the Start button near the top of the dialog box.**

   The feature takes a moment to warm up; when File Sharing is finally on, the button says Stop. Close the window, if you like.

Tip: If you work alone, or with only a few trusted others, you can make life easier for yourself in a couple of ways. First, give yourself no password at all (see page 278). Second, give yourself a very short, easy to type name—just your initials, for example—as described on page 277.

Repeat this process on each Mac OS X machine in your office, giving each one a different computer name.

Note: If any Macs on your network run some version of the Mac OS before 9.0, also click the AppleTalk tab and turn on "make AppleTalk active." (The technical reason: All modern Macs communicate using the TCP/IP language, just as the Internet does. Older Macs spoke only the Apple-only AppleTalk protocol.)

Setting up a pre–Mac OS X machine

Setting up a Mac that's running Mac OS 8.5 through Mac OS 9-point-whatever, if there is one on your network, follows almost exactly the same steps as outlined above—but the locations of the controls are different. Here's a summary:

- **Setting up user accounts.** Use the Users & Groups tab of the File Sharing control panel.

- **Naming the computer.** Use the File Sharing control panel.

- **Clicking Start.** You do this in the File Sharing control panel, as well. But there's one additional step: Turn on the checkbox called "Enable File Sharing clients to connect over TCP/IP," if you have it (shown at the very bottom of Figure 12-3).

This TCP/IP option is available in Mac OS 9 and later. If your Mac runs Mac OS 8.5 or 8.6, be sure to turn on AppleTalk on the Mac OS X machine (see the top of this page). Without either TCP/IP or AppleTalk, you won't be able to access the

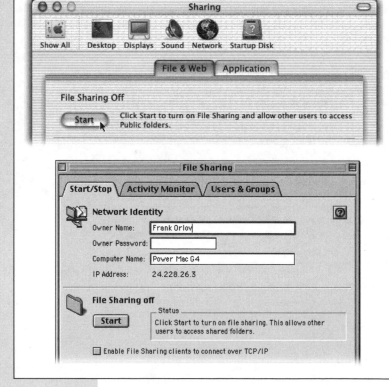

Figure 12-3:
Top: Here's the master on/off switch for file sharing over the network in Mac OS X.

Bottom: In Mac OS 9, this is the setup for a security-free, high-convenience file-sharing arrangement. You'll be able to access any Mac on the network without having to type in anything—no name, no password. If you work alone with a couple of Macs, or with co-workers you trust, this is the most efficient arrangement.

files or folders on your older computer from a Mac OS X machine. (You will, however, be able to go the other direction: you'll be able to access a Mac OS X machine on the network from your older machine.)

Phase 2: Connecting to Another Mac from Mac OS X

Suppose you're seated at your Mac OS X Power Mac, but you need a file that's on the iMac DV down the hall. (The steps are the same, no matter what version of the Mac operating system the other machine's running [as long as it's later than Mac OS 8.5].)

To bring its hard drive icon (or a shared folder's icon) onto your screen, follow these steps on the Mac OS X machine:

1. **Choose Go→Connect to Server (or press ⌘-K).**

   The Connect to Server command in Mac OS X replaces a pair of much more awkward mechanisms in previous Mac OS versions: the Chooser and the Network Browser. It opens up the window shown in Figure 12-4.

   If you've done this before, don't miss the "At" pop-up menu at the top of the dialog box. Its commands include a list of Recent Servers—computers you've accessed recently over the network. If you choose one of them from this pop-up menu, you can skip the next two steps.

Tip: If you know the IP address of the Mac you're trying to access—you geek!—you've just found another way to skip steps 2 and 3. Just type the IP address into the Address field at the bottom of the dialog box. You can also precede it with *afp://* (like this: *afp://192.168.1.2*), but that's not necessary.)

The next time you open the Connect To dialog box, Mac OS X will remember that address, as a courtesy to you, and show it pre-entered in the Address field.

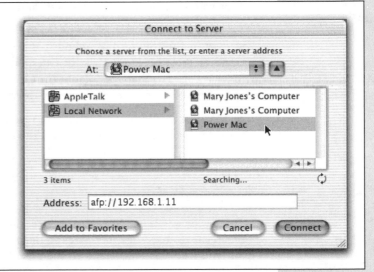

Figure 12-4:
In the unlikely event that you work in a corporation with hundreds or thousands of Macs, you may see the icons, in this left-side list, of other zones—sections of the network. In that case, you may have been instructed to click one of these zone names rather than Local Network. (Don't worry about the double computer names, and don't be freaked out by the appearance of your own Mac's name. That's all normal.)

2. **Click Local Network.**

If you're lucky enough to work in a huge, all-Mac corporation, you may see several of these Network icons, representing different limbs of the company network. Click the appropriate limb, and count yourself lucky—there aren't many huge, all-Mac corporations.

In the second column, you should now see a list of every Mac for which you turned on File Sharing. (If not, then something's wrong with your network wiring, or you haven't prepared those Macs as described in "Phase 1: Setting up the Computers," above.)

Tip: You can also access other Macs on your network directly from within the Open File dialog box described in Chapter 4. This box, too, contains a Network icon (scroll all the way to the leftmost column of the Open File box). Click it, then click Servers, and then continue with the steps outlined here.

---

3. **Double-click the name of the Mac you want to access.**

Alternatively, press the right-arrow key to highlight the second column, press the up or down arrow keys to highlight the Mac you want, and then press Enter or Return to "click" the Connect button.

Tip: If your network is a real bear to navigate, consider taking this opportunity to click the name of a Mac you plan to access frequently, and then click Add to Favorites at the bottom of the window. For now on, you'll be able to skip steps 2 and 3 by choosing the Mac's name from the At pop-up menu at the top of the window.

Now the "Connect to the file server" box appears, where you're supposed to input your name and password (Figure 12-6, center).

4. **Type your short user name, press Tab, and type your password.**

Type precisely what you would use to log into the networked computer if you were sitting in front of it. If nobody has set up an account for you on that machine, on the other hand, click the Guest button; you'll have only limited access to what's on the other Mac. And if the Guest button is dimmed, then someone has turned off Guest access altogether. You're completely out of luck.

(Not sure what your short user name is? Open System Preferences on your home-base Mac, click Users, click your name, and then click Edit to find out what it is.)

Tip: If you work alone or with a small group of trusted people, and you've left your password blank, just skip the password box here.

This, by the way, is your opportunity to perform several administrative functions that relate to accessing other Macs on the network. If you click the Options button, you get the dialog box shown and described in Figure 12-5. For example, the

Add Password to Keychain option saves you even more of these steps the next time you connect. (Visit this dialog box only if you want to turn *off* that option.) Read the discussion of the Keychain later in this chapter.

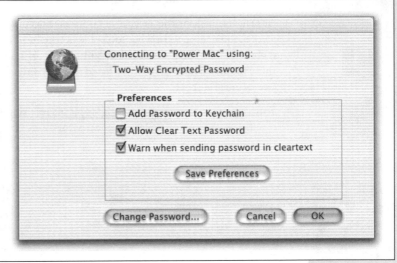

Figure 12-5:
When you're connecting to a Mac OS 9 machine, you can click Change Password; you'll be given the opportunity to change your account password. (You can't change your Mac OS X account password over the network in this way, however.) A clear text *password is one that isn't encrypted–a less secure, but more compatible, method of transmitting your password over the network.*

5. **Click Connect, or press the Return or Enter key.**

   Now a list of disks and folders on that Mac that have been *shared* for network access appears (Figure 12-6, bottom).

DON'T PANIC

Accessing Mac OS X from Mac OS 9

Suppose you're seated at a Mac that isn't running Mac OS X, but you need a file that's on the Mac OS X machine down the hall. To bring its hard drive's icon onto your screen, you can use either of two programs listed in the menu: the Chooser or the Network Browser.

Network Browser: Once the program is open, double-click the AppleTalk icon to see the list of Macs on your network, and then double-click the name of the Mac you want to access.

Chooser: Once the program is open, click the AppleShare icon to see the list of Macs, and then double-click the name of the Mac you want to access on the right side of the dialog box. (If the Mac OS X machine doesn't show up in the list, click the Server IP Address button at the bottom of the Chooser, type in the IP address of the Mac OS X machine [see page 498], and then press Enter.)

Either program: Now the "Connect as" box appears, where you're supposed to input your name and password. Type the name and password of your Mac OS X account, as it was set up for you. Click Connect.

Now you see a list of shared disks and folders connected to that Mac. Double-click the name of the disk you want to open.

At last, the disk or folder you've connected to appears on the right side of your screen. You can open this icon to open, copy, move, rename, or delete the files on it, subject to the rules of Mac OS X, as described on page 307.

6. Double-click the name of the disk or folder you want to open.

Or, if you see several disks or folders listed here that you'd like to open all at once, you can ⌘-click them to highlight several—and then click OK to bring all of their icons onto your desktop.

At last, the disk or folder you've connected to appears on the right side of your screen, illustrated with what looks like a tiny hard drive with a globe balanced on it. It usually appears just below your built-in hard drive icon. (You'll also see these mounted hard drive icons listed in the window that appears when you choose Go→Computer.)

You can open this icon to open, copy, move, rename, or delete the files on it, exactly as though the files were on your own computer—with certain limitations, described next.

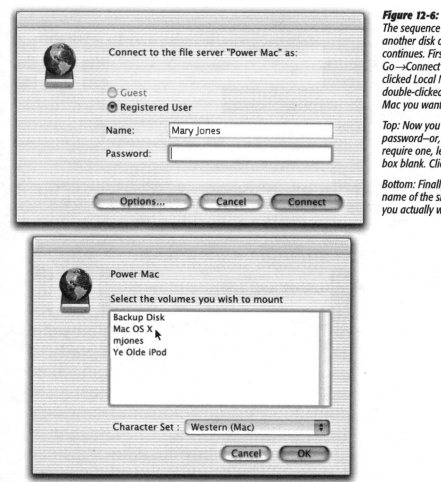

Figure 12-6:
The sequence of connecting to another disk on the network continues. First, you chose Go→Connect to Server; double-clicked Local Network; and then double-clicked the name of the Mac you want (Figure 12-4).

Top: Now you specify your password–or, if you didn't require one, leave the password box blank. Click Connect.

Bottom: Finally, double-click the name of the shared folder or disk you actually want to open.

Tip: Make an alias of the hard drive icon that you've just pulled onto your screen. The next time you want to connect to it, just double-click its icon—you'll skip all six steps of the connection process described above. The disk or folder pops open instantly (assuming you've allowed the Keychain to memorize your password).

Phase 3: What You Can Do Once You're In

When you tap into a *Mac OS 9* machine over the network, you're allowed complete freedom. Once you've brought its hard drive onto your screen, you can trash, re-name, move around, or otherwise wreak havoc with the files and folders you find there.

But when you tap into a *Mac OS X* machine, you can access only what's in certain designated folders. Precisely which folders are available depends on whether you're a *guest*, a *normal user*, or an *administrator* (see the previous chapter).

If You're a Guest

If you're just a guest—somebody for whom an account hasn't already been set up—you'll be able to:

- **Put things into** anyone's Drop Box folder. As shown in Figure 12-7, connecting to a Mac OS X machine as Guest offers you a list of everyone who has an account on it. When you double-click someone's name, you'll discover that there's nothing inside that folder except a Drop Box folder and sometimes a Public folder. (The Drop Box folder is actually inside each person's Home→Public folder.)

  You can copy files into a Drop Box, but can't open it. (Yes, Mac OS X is very secure, but even a high-security prison has a mailbox.)

- **Open** anything that people have put into their Public folders. (If no Public folders show up, then there's nothing in them for you to see.) Figure 12-8 has the details.

The rest of the Mac is invisible and off-limits to you.

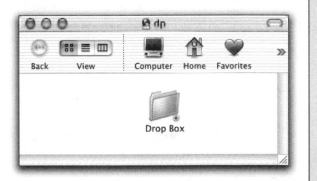

Figure 12-7:
If you connect as a guest, there's not much to see. You can deposit files into the Drop Box folder of any account holder, but not into the window that holds it—the little slashed-pencil icon in the upper-left corner tells you that you're off-limits.

If You're a Normal Account Holder

If you have a Normal account, you'll enjoy Drop Box access, Public-folder access, *and* the ability to see and manipulate what's inside your own Home folder (see page 49). You can do anything you like with the files and folders you find there, just as though you're actually seated in front of that Mac.

All other disks and folders on the Mac, including the System and Application folders, are invisible to you.

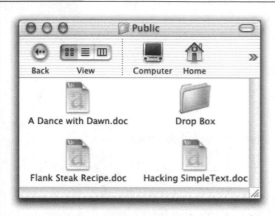

Figure 12-8:
Suppose that Frank has put three files into his Public folder. (Every person's Home folder contains a Public folder that's available for everybody else to access.) When you connect to his Mac, you'll see whatever is in his Public folder—in this case, his Drop Box plus those three files. You can't put anything in Frank's window, but you can open the three files he's left there for you to see.

If You're an Administrator

When you connect to a Mac OS X machine as a guest or normal user, you never even see the name of the hard drive on that machine; as illustrated in Figure 12-7, you see only the names of the users who have accounts on that machine (so that you can get to their Drop Boxes and Public folders).

But if you've been designated an *administrator,* you get to see both those user folders as well as the hard drive itself to which you're connecting. In fact, you even get to see the names of any other disks connected to that Mac.

If you, O lucky administrator, open the hard drive, you'll discover that you have not only the same freedoms as a Normal account holder (described above), but also the freedom to see and manipulate the contents of these folders:

- Applications
- Developer (if it's been installed; see page 246)
- Desktop folder
- Library (and the System→Library folder, but nothing else in the System folder)
- Users→Shared folder (page 287)
- The other disks connected to the Mac OS X machine

Note: There's actually one more kind of account, of course, as described in the previous chapter—the *root user.* Whoever holds this account has complete freedom to move or delete *any file or folder anywhere,* including critical system files that could disable your Mac, which is why this feature comes turned off from the factory. Page 290 has details.

It's easy to figure out why neither Normal nor Administrator account holders are allowed to see what's in the System folder or in other people's folders: it's all about stability and security. Mac OS X is extremely protective of its System folder. To make Mac OS X remain as solid and stable as the day you installed it, human beings, whether visiting over the network or not, are not allowed to play with it.

The reason for the other users' Home folders being off-limits should also be self-evident: that's part of Mac OS X's security feature. Each person who uses a Mac OS X machine has an individual account to which she alone has access. More on this topic in Chapter 11.

POWER USERS' CLINIC

Other Kinds of Servers

A Mac for which you've turned on File Sharing is known in the business as a *file server*—a computer designed to "serve up" files to other computers over the network. But Macs aren't the only file servers you may encounter.

If your network includes other computers running Unix, whatever smart person set up the network may have set up NFS (network file system) servers: folders or disks that have been set up so that you can see them from across the network. You don't even use the Connect To command to bring these folders and disks onto your screen; instead, you choose Go→Computer and double-click the Network icon you find there. In the resulting window, you'll see the icons of the shared Unix disks and folders, which you can just double-click as though they're sitting right there on your hard drive.

Your iDisk, a 20-MB, free storage shoebox provided to you by Apple on the Internet, is also a file server. The easiest way to bring its icon onto the screen is, of course, to choose Go→iDisk—but you could also type, into the Connect to Server dialog box shown here, *afp://idisk.mac.com.*

If your Mac has a permanent (static) IP address, you can connect to it from anywhere in the world via the Internet, using exactly the same technique. Details on this procedure begin on page 505.

Disconnecting Yourself

When you're finished using a shared disk or folder, drag its icon to the Trash (whose icon changes as you drag), highlight its icon and choose File→Eject, or Control-click its icon and choose Eject from the contextual menu. You also disconnect from a shared folder or disk when you shut down your Mac, or if it's a laptop, put it to sleep.

Disconnecting Others

In Mac OS X, no visual clue lets you know that other people on the network are accessing *your* Mac. (In previous versions of the Mac OS, the File Sharing control panel showed you a tidy list of who was doing what on your Mac from across the network.)

Maybe that's because there's nothing to worry about. You certainly have nothing to fear from a security standpoint, because remember that people from across the network are allowed to access only their own folders. Nor will you experience much computer slowdown as you work (another traditional drawback of having people access your hard drive from across the network), thanks to Mac OS X's prodigious multitasking features.

Still, if you're feeling particularly antisocial, you can slam shut the door to your Mac just by turning off the File Sharing feature. (Click System Preferences on the Dock, click the File Sharing icon, and click Stop.)

If anybody is, in fact, connected to your Mac at the time, you see the dialog box shown in Figure 12-9. If not, your Mac instantly becomes an island once again.

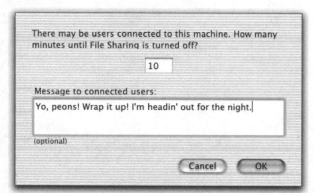

Figure 12-9:
This dialog box asks you how much notice you want to give your co-workers that they're about to be disconnected—10 minutes to finish up what they're doing, for example. If you're feeling rushed or rude, type a zero. Doing so disconnects that person instantly, without warning. Then click OK. (When you disconnect people by closing your laptop lid, having a system crash, or unplugging the network wires, your co-workers get no notice at all. A message appears on their screens that says, "The server has unexpectedly shut down.")

GEM IN THE ROUGH

Instant Network Messaging

As figure 12-9 makes clear, turning off File Sharing gives you the opportunity to send a little message to everyone who is currently connected to your Mac via network. But you don't have to turn off File Sharing just to gain the opportunity to send little instant messages to your buddies. The dialog box shown in Figure 12-9 is suitable for warning your network buddies that the boss is coming, for example, or to request that they get you a beverage.

To do so, open System Preferences, click File Sharing, and click the Stop button. Type your message into the box that

appears, and click OK. Your message pops up on the screens of everyone who's connected to you.

Technically, you also just began the File Sharing shutdown process—now you should cancel that. After sending a message, you'll find that you're now staring straight at the Cancel button on the Sharing panel. Clicking it cancels the shutdown of File Sharing. (It also sends yet another message to your network comrades' screens, to the effect that File Sharing is no longer going to be cut off—a small price to pay for having learned about the secret Mac OS X instant-messaging system.)

Advanced Control

If you're used to file sharing the pre–Mac OS X way, you may have noticed that the new operating system adopts a fairly rigid scheme of permissions (access privileges). Most people on the network are allowed to see only their own folders (and what's in other people's Public folders) when they connect to a Mac OS X machine.

But consider these possibilities:

- You want your co-workers to be able to access other folders.

- You'd rather not have your Public folder be quite that public.

- You work in a corporation where every machine has a full-time, high-speed connection to the Internet, which makes you worry even about that Drop Box. If somebody figures out your Mac's IP address, it's conceivable that they could dump unsavory files into your Drop Box anonymously over the Internet.

- You find it annoying that Normal account holders can't access the other disks attached to your Mac from across the network.

Fortunately, Mac OS X's very restrictive folder-permission scheme is just a suggestion. It's perfectly possible to make individual folders either better protected or less protected, as you see fit—a bit technically hairy, but possible.

Tip: In Mac OS X, you can even control how much access people have to an individual *file*—not just an entire folder, as in Mac OS 9 and earlier. Keep that useful fact in mind as you read the following discussion.

Changing access permissions for a file or folder

To begin, highlight a file or folder on your hard drive. It has to be one that you've created yourself, perhaps on the desktop or in your Home folder. (You're never allowed to mess with other people's folders.)

Choose File→Show Info (or press ⌘-I). When the Show Info dialog box appears, choose Privileges from the pop-up menu at the top of the window (see Figure 12-10).

Tip: You can also change the permissions for many folders at once. Just highlight all of them before choosing File→Show Info.

Now you see three pop-up menus: Owner, Group, and Everyone. More on these designations in a moment. For now, note that the three pop-up menus contain identical commands. They let you specify what you, the other people in your work group, and the entire network community can do with this document or folder:

- If you choose **None,** then you're a network tease—your co-workers may be able to see the folder, but its name and icon will be dimmed and unavailable.

• Choose **Write only (Drop Box)** if you want your network co-workers to be able to see the folder, but not open it; all they can do is copy files into it. (Your own Drop Box—which Mac OS X creates automatically in your Home→Public folder—works this way, too.) It's great for setting up a place where people can put documents that are intended for your eyes only. (Think students turning in homework, underlings turning in quarterly reports, and so on.)

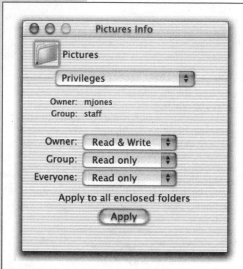

Figure 12-10:
This window lets you establish who's allowed to see or use the contents of a particular folder or disk. Using the triple pop-up menus, you can specify how much access you, the Owner, a selected group, and everyone else has.

• The **Read only** option lets visitors open the folder, open the files inside, or copy the files inside to their own hard drives—but they can't put anything new into the folder, nor save changes to files they find there. Set up a folder like this as a distribution point for newsletters, standard logos, or other company information.

• Finally, choose **Read & Write** if you'd like your networked colleagues to have full access to the folder. They can do anything they want with the files inside, including trashing them.

Note: Whenever you adjust the permissions for a folder like this, remember to take into account the permissions of the folder it's *in* (that is, its parent folder). No matter how exquisitely you set up a drop box folder, for example, nobody will even know it's there unless it's inside a folder for which you've turned on at least "Read only" access.

Fortunately, you can assign these different levels of freedom to different subsets of people on your network. That's why there are three different pop-up menus:

• **Owner.** That's you. Of course, ordinarily, you have full access (Read & Write) to all of your folders. You can put anything into them, take anything out of them, and do whatever you like with them. But if you feel the need to protect yourself from your own destructive instincts, or if you have a habit of leaving your Mac unattended when you wander away without logging out first, you can actually limit your own access to certain folders. For example, you can turn one into a drop box using this pop-up menu, as described below.

- **Group.** In pre–Mac OS X systems, you could put every person in your office into certain groups, such as Marketing, Accounting, or Temps. Mac OS X itself, however, offers no easy mechanism for setting up such groups. (There is a complicated way, however, which is described beginning on page 312.)

  But Mac OS X does come with a whole bunch of canned, prefab groups, to which it automatically assigns everyone on the network. If you're an administrator (page 275), for example, you belong to the *admin* group, among others; if you're a mere peon, a Normal account holder, you're part of the *staff* group.

  When you change this pop-up menu, you're specifying how much access everyone else *in your group* will have to this file or folder.

- **Everyone.** This pop-up menu specifies how much freedom everybody else in the network will have to the selected file or folder, including guests. Needless to say, if security is an issue where you work, you may not want to set the Everyone pop-up menu to permit full access.

  You can't give "Everyone" more access to the folder than you gave the Group people—only the same degree of freedom, or less. For example, you can't give Read & Write access to a folder to Everyone, but give your own administrator group only drop-box access.

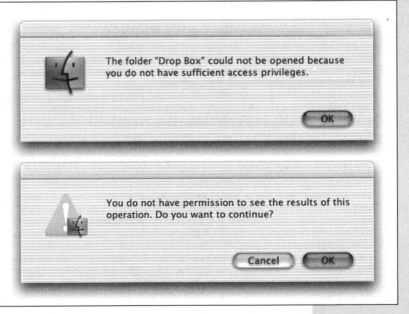

Figure 12-11:
In Mac OS X, you're perfectly free to open up a folder that's been defined as a "drop box"—as long as it's empty. Once something's inside, however, you get the message shown here at top if you try to open it, and the message shown at bottom if you try to put something inside it.

The folder "Drop Box" could not be opened because you do not have sufficient access privileges.

OK

You do not have permission to see the results of this operation. Do you want to continue?

Cancel   OK

Click Apply Now to make your changes take effect. (Careful—making this kind of change to a folder also affects *all the folders inside it* in the same way.)

While Show Info is still on the screen, feel free to click other folders to change their privileges, too. The Show Info window changes to reflect the status of each folder you click in turn. You don't have to close and reopen it.

Making other disks available over the network

Ordinarily, you can only see the primary hard drive of the Mac OS X machine from across the network. Only administrators are allowed to access any other disks connected to it. Especially if you (or your Normal account holders) work on a small network, such as a home network, that extra security precaution can seem like so much red tape.

You can give Normal account holders access to secondary hard drives or other disks associated with your Mac; the process involves creating a new group, adding to it the names of people you want to be able to access these disks, and finally assigning that group to the disk in question. This routine isn't as easy as flipping a switch, by any means, but it's not as hard as brain surgery, either. Instructions begin on the next page.

Tip: This chapter describes the *visual* way to connect from across the network—a system of dialog boxes, menus, and nice clickable buttons.

If you're willing to forego all of that Mac-like stuff, a second, highly regarded system of connecting to your Mac from across the network—or from across the Internet—awaits: a Unix program called *SSH (Secure Shell).* If you're still game, page 506 offers the details.

Networking with Windows

Microsoft Windows may dominate the corporate market, but there *are* Macs in the offices of America. Mac OS X makes it easier than ever for Macs and Windows machines to coexist on a single network. In fact, there are several ways to go about it.

The Built-in, One-Way Way: SMB

Mac OS X version 10.1 and later can automatically connect to shared files on Windows machines. No special software has to run on the Windows PCs—nor on your Mac OS X machine. You'll find step-by-step instructions on page 151.

The Two-Way Way: Dave

Even though you can see what's on the other *Windows* PCs using Mac OS X, you still need add-on software if you want them to see *your* machine.

Once you've installed Dave 3.1 or later *(www.thursby.com),* for example, Mac OS X and Windows speak the same networking language. On your Mac, you connect to Windows machines on your network using the Connect To command, exactly as though you were connecting to other Macs. Similarly, people seated in front of the Windows computers can access files and folders on your Mac OS X machine just as they would connect to any other Windows computers.

The One-Way Way: Web Serving

As described in Chapter 21, Mac OS X's Apache software turns your Mac into a living Web site. And the beauty of the Web, of course, is that it doesn't care what kind of computer you're using. The contents of the Web site are dished up exactly the same way to Macs, Windows machines, Unix machines, and so on.

All of this gives you a great way to distribute files to other people on the network—even people who are using less enlightened operating systems. You can simply list files for distribution on a simple Web page, to which other people on the network can connect.

Chapter 21 offers the full details of setting up such a system—but in the context of making your Mac available to anyone on the Internet. The point to note here is that other people on your office network can access your Mac in exactly the same way, just by typing *http://192.168.1.5/~shortname/* (or whatever; see page 500) into the address bar of their Web browsers.

The FTP Way

You can think of an *FTP server* as something like a Web site designed specifically as a holding tank for files that you want to distribute or accept. Chapter 21 has complete details. Here again, though, it's worth remembering that you can use the Mac OS X built-in FTP server to distribute and accept files on your local network, not just over the Internet. The Windows PC user, using only a Web browser, will be able to download any files in the folder that you've set up for such transactions, exactly as described in Chapter 21. (And using an *FTP client* program—the Windows equivalent of Fetch, for example—that person can copy files to *and* from the folder.)

Managing Groups

As noted earlier in this chapter, the circuitry of Mac OS X's file-sharing software seems to lack one feature that was present in earlier versions of the Mac OS: the ability to create and manipulate *groups*. As your networking setup becomes more complex, being able to work with subsets of the people on your network can be a great timesaver.

For example, you might create groups called Marketing, Temps, and Executives. Later, you can permit an entire group of these people access to a particular file, folder, or disk in one fell swoop. (And, as noted earlier in the chapter, groups are also the key to letting Normal account holders on your network see and access secondary *drives* on your Mac OS X computer.)

You can still perform this function in Mac OS X, but (at least in Mac OS X 10.1.1) the process is vastly more technical than it was in Mac OS 9, where a simple Users & Groups control panel let you create and manage groups.

Phase 1 involves creating and naming the groups you want. It requires NetInfo Manager, an advanced utility program that comes with Mac OS X.

Phase 2 involves assigning those groups to individual disks, files, or folders on your system. You can go about this task in either of two ways. One involves downloading a shareware program—and dipping your little toe into the world of Unix. The other involves using a built-in Mac OS X utility program, stripping down to your underwear, and diving into the *deep* end of Unix.

The following pages take you through both methods.

Phase 1: Creating Groups

To set up groups, start by opening NetInfo Manager, which is in your Applications→Utilities folder (Figure 12-12).

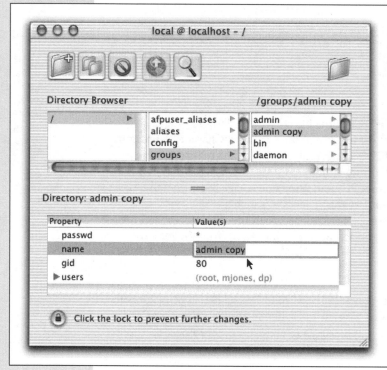

Figure 12-12:
Consider yourself warned: NetInfo is an extremely technical program designed for network administrators with years of training and full employee benefits somewhere in corporate America. Not only do you need an administrator's account to play with it (see page 275), but veering off the instructional path specified in the following pages could, in theory, get your Mac in trouble.

Defining and naming the group

Here's how you might go about creating a new group called Executives and then adding the names of three employees to it. (These steps assume that you've already created accounts for these people, as described in Chapter 11.)

1. **In NetInfo Manager, click the tiny padlock in the lower-left corner.**

   A dialog box appears, prompting you for an administrator's name and password.

The Mac is just checking to make sure that somebody with a clue is at the helm. This is just the kind of surgical activity you don't want most high school students, 10-year-olds in your family, or other Normal account holders performing.

2. **Type the name and password of an administrator (page 275), and then click OK.**

   Now you get to see a staggering array of network-related variables. In the second column, you'll see that one of them is called *groups*.

3. **Click *groups*.**

   In the next column to the right, you'll see a list of all the canned groups that come installed with Mac OS X: *admin, bin, daemon, kmem,* and so on. These terms aren't especially closely related to English, but then again, Unix was designed primarily for efficiency in typing.

   You're ready to add a new group to this list. The easiest way is to duplicate one of the existing groups.

4. **Click *admin* in the list of groups, and then click the Duplicate Selected Directory button (the double-folder icon at the top of the window). Click Duplicate in the confirmation message.**

   You wind up with a new group in the list, called *admin copy*. Note that it's highlighted, and a few morsels of information about it appear at the bottom of the window. One of them—in the Property column—says *name* (see Figure 12-12).

5. **Double-click *admin copy* at the bottom of the window (in the Value(s) column, as shown in Figure 12-12). Type the new name for your group, and then press Enter.**

   You've just created and named a new group. To help Mac OS X keep this one separate from the others, you'll also need to give it a new group ID number, abbreviated *gid* in Unix-ese:

6. **If the *gid* value (in the third row at the bottom of the window) isn't already highlighted, double-click it. Then type *200* and press Enter.**

   The ID number doesn't especially matter except that it can't be the same as any the other folders' group IDs. The existing ones are all under 100, so you should be in good shape.

At the moment, your new group lists the names of all administrator accounts (because you began this process by duplicating the *admin* group). Now you need to make sure that the right people belong to this group.

Adding people to the new group

The adding-people-to-group process takes place in the bottom half of the window.

1. **Click the *users* row at the bottom of the window. Choose Directory→Insert Value (or press Option-⌘-I).**

As shown in Figure 12-12, the *users* row now expands, showing individual rows for each account holder that already belongs to this group. A *new_value* box waits for you to type in the name of somebody for whom you've created an account. (Sorry, efficiency fans, there's no simple pop-up list of the accounts on your Mac; NetInfo Manager assumes that you can remember the precise name and capitalization of every account.)

2. **Type the *short* account name (page 277) of the person you want to add to this group, and then press Enter.**

   If you want to add another person, choose Directory→Insert Value again, and then type in another name. (You can also delete someone from this group by highlighting the appropriate row and then choosing Directory→Delete Value.)

3. **When you're finished adding people, save your changes (Domain→Save), and click "Update this copy" in the confirmation dialog box.**

   If you have more groups to create, you can start over at step 4 on the previous page. Otherwise, quit NetInfo Manager.

At the moment, you've got yourself a properly defined group, but this information is just kicking around in Mac OS X's head without any practical value. The next step is to tell Mac OS X which folders are the private stomping grounds of this group.

Assigning Groups: The Easy, Shareware Method

As noted at the beginning of this section, you can assign groups to files, folders, or disks in either of two ways. The method described here lets you avoid mucking around in Unix commands.

If that's just fine with you, read on. (If you belong to the "no pain, no gain for your brain" camp, on the other hand, check the next page for more on using the Unix method.)

You'll need a piece of shareware called SuperGetInfo. You can download it from, for example, the software page of *www.missingmanuals.com.*

Drag the icon of a disk, file, or folder directly onto the SuperGetInfo icon. The small window shown in Figure 12-13 appears—a more elaborate version of the standard Show Info dialog box. Click the Permissions tab.

Specifying what group has access to this folder is as easy as choosing its name from the Group pop-up menu.

People who are in the group can interact with the disk, file, or folder according to the status of the Group checkboxes in this window. (*Read* means that group members can open and look at whatever is. *Write* means that they can also make changes to it. *Execute* has no effect in the Finder; for its meaning to Unix, see page 403.)

The key point here is that anybody that you didn't specifically put into this group has *no* access to this file, disk, or folder from across the network.

Once you've made your changes, click Apply. Prove that you're a card-carrying administrator (or have access to one) by entering the name and password of an Administrator account. The deed is done.

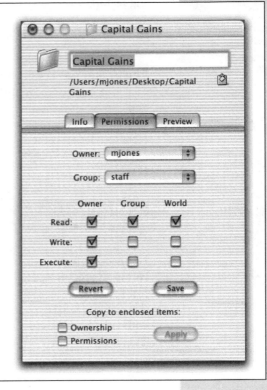

Figure 12-13:
The shareware program SuperGetInfo simplifies the process of applying group ownership to a particular icon. It can get you out of all kinds of binds, especially when "you do not have sufficient access privileges" or other ownership-related error messages appear.

Assigning Groups: The Grisly, Unix Method

Plenty of Mac fans, many of them recent converts from Unix, would scoff at the notion of downloading a shareware program just to change the group access to a few files and folders. You can do exactly the same thing using Terminal, Mac OS X's rabbit hole into the world of Unix commands. The average Macintosh fan will certainly consider this method insanely opaque, user-hostile, and counterintuitive. The average Unix fan will love it.

You'll find an overview on page 407.

Dialing in from the Road

If you are one of the several million lucky people who have full-time Internet connections—in other words, cable modem or DSL accounts—a special thrill awaits. You can connect to your Mac from anywhere in the world via the Internet. If you have a laptop, you don't need to worry when you discover you've left a critical file on your desktop Mac at home.

Mac OS X offers several ways to connect to your Mac from a distant location. Chapter 21 has the details, but here's a summary of the possibilities:

- **Connecting from another Mac:** *Use File Sharing over the Internet.* The file-sharing feature described earlier in this chapter makes absolutely no distinction between connections made on the local network and connections made from across the entire Internet. You can use all the security features and access-privilege features of standard file sharing.

  There's only one key difference. Suppose you're sitting with your laptop in a hotel room, thousands of miles away from the Mac OS X machine at home. When you choose Go→Connect To Server (if your laptop runs Mac OS X) or open the Chooser (if not), you won't see a tidy listing of the Macs on your network. You have to type, into the Address box (or on pre–Mac OS X Macs, in the box that appears when you click Server IP Address), the *IP address* of your home-based Mac.

Note: If you've installed some *firewall* software, as described on page 439, your home-base Mac is much more secure, but connecting from the road requires more configuration.

- **Connecting from a Unix or Windows machine:** *Use FTP.* This feature lets you connect to files in your Home folder (or special account folder that you've set up just for FTP connections) via the Internet. The great thing about this method is that you don't need a Mac to get your stuff from across the Internet—Windows, Unix, or any other computer—will work. Complete instructions are in Chapter 21.

- **Connecting the Unix way:** *Use SSH.* The Unix program called Secure Shell (*SSH)* offers yet another way to connect. Of course, you must be using a Unix terminal of some kind (such as Mac OS X's Terminal or a real Unix box) from the dialing end. Otherwise, however, connecting to your home machine works just the same way across the Internet as it does across your home-base office network. See page 506 for details.

Note: There's no longer any built-in way for you to dial directly over a phone line, Mac to Mac, as there was in Mac OS 9. All of the methods described here involved connecting from across the Internet.

Forgettable Passwords: The Keychain

The information explosion of the computer age may translate into bargains, power, and efficiency, but it carries with it a colossal annoyance: the proliferation of *passwords* we have to memorize. Shared folders on the network, Web sites, your iDisk, FTP sites—each requires another password to remember. We're not even allowed to use the same password over and over again, because each Web page, file server, FTP site, or protected file requires a different *form* of password—"five to seven digits, which must include both letters and numbers"; "six characters or more, beginning with a letter"; and so on.

Apple has done the world a mighty favor by inventing the *Keychain.* The concept is brilliant: Whenever you log into Mac OS X and type in your password, you've typed the master code that tells the computer, "It's really me. I'm at my computer now." The Mac responds by *automatically* filling in every password blank you encounter in your networking exploits. You can safely forget all of the passwords required for accessing the various other Macs on your network.

If you're used to the Keychain feature of Mac OS 9, you'll be pleasantly surprised by the simplified version in Mac OS X. Because it's on all the time and memorizes most passwords automatically, it winds up being invisible for many people. Just go about your business, tapping into other Macs on the network as described earlier in this chapter, connecting to your iDisk, and so on. Behind the scenes, the Mac quietly collects the various passwords so that you won't have to enter them again.

Note: Unfortunately, when it comes to password proliferation, we're not out of the woods yet. The Keychain can't store passwords in programs that haven't been rewritten to be *Keychain-aware.* Notable among programs that ignore the Keychain is Internet Explorer (version 5.1). In other words, the Keychain doesn't store passwords for secure Web pages, such as those for your bank and online-brokerage accounts, that you type into Internet Explorer. (On the other hand, Internet Explorer has its own built-in password-memorizing feature. It's not as convenient as the master Keychain password, but it's better than nothing.)

The highly regarded Web browser called OmniWeb, however, is Keychain-aware, and does memorize many kinds of Web site passwords. This Web browser is available from the software page of *www.missingmanuals.com,* for example.

Locking and Unlocking the Keychain

When your Keychain is unlocked, you can open your password-protected FTP sites, iDisk, Web sites, and so on, without ever having to enter a password. Technically, you're supposed to enter a name and master password to "unlock" the Keychain every time you sit down in front of your Mac, thereby turning on this automatic-password feature. But Apple figured: "Hey, you've *already* entered a name and master password—when you logged into the Mac. That's good enough for us." If you work alone, the Keychain therefore becomes automatic, invisible, and generally wonderful.

But if you work in an office where someone else might sit down at your Mac while you're getting a candy bar, you might want to *lock* the Keychain when you wander away. (Locking it requires no password.) Mac OS X will no longer fill in your passwords—until you return to your desk and *unlock* the Keychain again.

You can lock the Keychain in any of several ways, each of which involves the Keychain Access program (in your Applications→Utilities folder):

• **Lock the Keychain manually.** Click the Lock button at the upper-right corner of the Keychain Access window (see Figure 12-14).

• **Lock the Keychain automatically.** In the Keychain Access program, choose Edit→[your name] Settings. As shown in Figure 12-14, you can set up the Keychain to lock itself, say, five minutes after the last time you used your Mac, or whenever the Mac goes to sleep. When you return to the Mac, you'll be asked to re-enter your account password in order to unlock the Keychain, restoring your automatic-password feature.

Note: As noted above, you unlock your Keychain using the same password you used to log into Mac OS X. But that's just a convenience. If you're really worried about security, you can click Change Passphrase (see Figure 12-14) and thereby establish a *different* password for your Keychain. Of course, doing so also turns off the automatic-Keychain-unlocking-when-you-log-in feature.

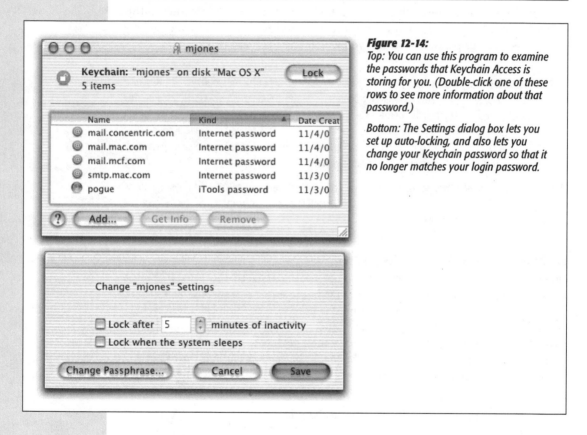

Figure 12-14:
Top: You can use this program to examine the passwords that Keychain Access is storing for you. (Double-click one of these rows to see more information about that password.)

Bottom: The Settings dialog box lets you set up auto-locking, and also lets you change your Keychain password so that it no longer matches your login password.

Managing Keychains

To take a look at your Keychain, open the Keychain Access program (Figure 12-14). By double-clicking one of the password rows shown here, you open the special information box shown in Figure 12-15. At this point, you can click View Password to see the actual password it's storing.

You can also choose Access Control from the Show menu, which gives you even more control over the security settings (see Figure 12-15).

Tip: The primary purpose of the Keychain is, of course, to type in passwords for you automatically. But it's also an excellent place to record all kinds of private information just for your own reference: credit card numbers, ATM numbers, and so on. Just click the Add button shown in Figure 12-15, and proceed as illustrated there.

No, the Mac won't type them in for you automatically anywhere. But it does maintain them in one central location that is, itself, password-protected.

Figure 12-15:
Top: This dialog box lists the programs that are allowed to "see" this password—which gives you yet another degree of security. Still another degree of protection comes in the form of the "Allow access to this item without warning" checkbox. If you turn it off, Mac OS X will ask you for permission before filling in a password for you automatically.

Bottom: You can also store credit card numbers and other secret information in the Keychain Access program.

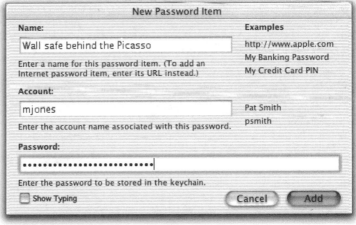

Multiple Keychains

By choosing File→New Keychain, you can create more than one Keychain, each with its own master password. On one hand, this might defeat the simplicity goal of the Keychain. On the other hand, it's (faintly) conceivable that you might want to encrypt all of your business documents with one master password, and all of your personal stuff with another, for example.

Keychain Files

Keychains are represented by separate files in your Home folder→Library→ Keychains→[your name] folder. Knowing that can be handy in several circumstances:

- **Deleting a Keychain.** You can delete a Keychain easily enough—just drag a Keychain file out of this folder and into the Trash.

- **Copying a Keychain.** You can copy one of your keychain files into the corresponding location on another computer, such as your laptop. It carries with it all the password information for the networks and Web sites of your life.

Graphics, Fonts, and Printing

M acintosh may be only the five-percent solution in the mainstream business world, but in the graphics and printing industries, it's the 800-pound gorilla. You'd better believe that when Apple designed Mac OS X, it worked very hard to keep its graphics and printing fans happy.

This chapter tackles all printing, fonts, graphics, and ColorSync. It also covers PDF (Acrobat) files, which Mac OS X uses as an everyday exchange format—which is one of the biggest perks in Mac OS X.

Mac Meets Printer

One of the biggest complaints about the original Mac OS X was that at the outset, not many printer companies had rewritten their *printer drivers*—the software that controls various printer models—for Mac OS X.

Fortunately, the situation has improved: today's Mac OS X comes preinstalled with hundreds of printer drivers. All the major printer companies—Epson, HP, Canon, and so on—are on the case, working to develop drivers for current and future printer models. Even so, millions of older printers are incompatible with Mac OS X. The moral: investigate the situation before you buy the printer (or before you upgrade to Mac OS X).

When you're ready to hook up your printer, follow this guide:

1. **Install the printer software.**

If you bought the printer relatively recently, its software CD-ROM may already contain the necessary drivers for Mac OS X. If it's an older printer, you'll probably have to search the printer company's Web site for Mac OS X drivers.

Tip: You may be able to skip this step. Mac OS X 10.1 and later comes preloaded with the software drivers for dozens of recent printer models. Open your hard drive→Library→Printers folder. Examine the printer-manufacturer folders inside. If you find files bearing your printer's model number, skip ahead to step 2.

On the other hand, if you have an Administrator account, you can save a lot of disk space by throwing away the driver icons for printer models you don't own.

You need to sign in with an Administrator account (page 275) to install printer drivers. If you're trying to hook up a PostScript laser printer, its installer puts something called a *PPD* (PostScript Printer Description) file into your Library→Printers→PPDs folder. And if you're hooking up any other kind of printer, such as a color inkjet, its driver software winds up in the Library→Printers folder, usually in a folder named for the company (like Epson or Canon).

2. **Connect the printer to the Mac.**

Inkjet printers usually connect to your USB jack. Laser printers generally hook up to your Ethernet connector. (If you're on an office network, the laser printer may already be connected somewhere else on the network, saving you this step; if you're hooking the printer straight into your Mac's Ethernet jack, you'll need a Ethernet *crossover cable* to connect it, rather than a standard Ethernet cable.)

Note: Most Ethernet- or network-connected laser printers communicate with your Mac using a language called AppleTalk. If you have such a printer, here is step 2.5: open the Network pane of System Preferences. Click the AppleTalk tab. Turn on Make AppleTalk Active, and then click Apply Now. (If you omit this step, Print Center will nag you about it in step 5.)

3. **Open Print Center.**

Print Center is Mac OS X's printing program. This single program incorporates the functions of a broad array of software you may have known in Mac OS 9, including the Chooser, desktop printer icons, and PrintMonitor.

You'll find it in your Applications→Utilities folder. You might want to consider dragging it onto your Dock for quicker access the next time.

Tip: You can also open Print Center at the actual moment of printing. In the Print dialog box illustrated in Figure 13-3, you'll see a pop-up menu called Saved Settings. If you choose Edit Printer List from this menu, Print Center opens automatically.

If you haven't already set up a printer, you see the dialog box shown in Figure 13-1.

4. Click Add.

Now a strange little window called Directory Services appears (shown at bottom in Figure 13-1). If you work in a corporation, where some highly paid network expert has already configured some network printers (using technical tools like NetInfo or LDAP databases), you'll see these printers listed here. Click the one you want to use, and then click Add.

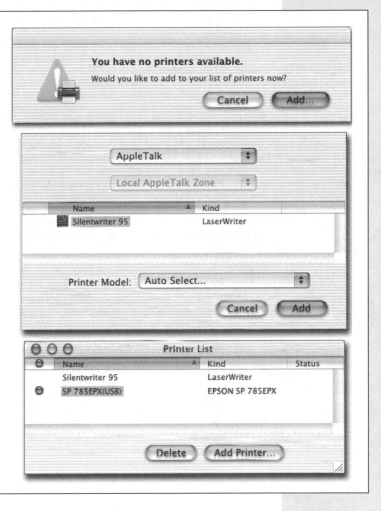

Figure 13-1:
Top: If you've never before hooked up a printer to your Mac, Print Center may show you this message. (If you're trying to hook up an additional printer, on the other hand, begin by choosing Printers→Add Printer.)

Middle: If you choose the right connection method from the pop-up menu, your Mac should automatically "see" any printers that are hooked up and turned on.

Bottom: If you've set up more than one printer in this way, you'll see all of them listed in the Printer List. The one marked by a colored dot is the currently selected one—the one destined to produce your next printout.

But if you don't work on a corporate network, you'll find the Directory Services window empty. You need to tell Print Center where to look to find its new printer.

5. From the pop-up menu, choose *USB, AppleTalk,* or *LPR Printers using IP*.

In other words, tell Print Center how the printer is connected to the Mac. Your selection here should mirror your actions in step 2. For example, choose USB if you've connected an inkjet printer to your USB port. Choose AppleTalk if you've hooked up a laser printer through your Ethernet jack.

Most Mac fans are unfamiliar with LPR (Line Printer) printers, which are most often found on corporate networks (and are therefore connected to your Mac's Ethernet jack). If you and your company's network nerd determine that the printer you want to use is, in fact, an LPR printer, choose "LPR Printers using IP" from the pop-up menu and fill in the appropriate IP address and other settings, as directed by your cheerful network administrator.

After a moment, the names of any printers that are turned on and connected appear in the printer list. For most people, that means just one printer, but that's all you need.

Note: You may need to take one of two detours here. First, if you're on a really huge corporate network, the printer list may show you the names of several different network *zones* (network subdivisions). You may need to choose the appropriate zone, using the pop-up menu that miraculously appears, before you see the names of the printers in it.

Second, you may occasionally need to use the Printer Model pop-up menu. Most of the time, the Auto Select setting works just fine. If you find yourself having trouble printing, however, consider choosing a specific printer model from this pop-up menu. (And if you don't see it listed, then something might have gone wrong with your software installation. Call the printer company for help.)

---

6. Click the name of the printer you want to use, and then click Add.

After a moment, you return to the main printer list window, where your printer now appears. You're ready to print.

If you're lucky enough to own several printers, by the way, you'll have to repeat the steps above for each one. Eventually, you'll have introduced the Mac to all the printers available to it, and all of their names will show up in the printer list.

Whenever you want to switch from one printer to the other, you *can* return to Print Center and click the new printer's name. There's a much easier way, however: use the Printer pop-up menu that appears in the actual Print dialog box (Figure 13-3).

Tip: The color dot beside the name of one printer denotes the *default* printer—the one that the Mac will use unless you explicitly choose a different one for a particular printout. To specify a different default printer, click its name in Print Center and then choose Printers→Make Default (⌘-D).

Making the Printout

You print documents from within the programs you used to create them, exactly as in previous versions of the Mac OS. The options for printing should feel distinctly familiar.

Page Setup

The experience of printing depends on the printer you're using—laser printer, color inkjet, or whatever. In every case, however, all the printing options hide behind two commands: File→Page Setup, which you need to adjust only occasionally, and File→Print, which you generally use every time you print. You'll find these two commands in the File menus of almost every Macintosh program.

The pop-up menu at the top of the Page Setup dialog box offers a command called Summary, which simply displays a textual description of the printout you're about to make (orientation, paper dimensions, and so on). It sometimes offers a command specific to the program you're using. For example, in Microsoft Word, the Settings pop-up menu→Microsoft Word offers a screenful of custom page-size and margin settings.

But the real action is in the dialog box that appears when you choose Page Attributes from this pop-up menu. Here, for example, are the controls you need to print a document rotated sideways on the page, so that it prints "the long way." The Scale control lets you reduce or enlarge your document, which can be handy if the program you're using doesn't offer such a control. And the Paper pop-up menu, of course, specifies what size paper you're printing on—US Letter, US Legal, or one of the standard European paper sizes (A4 and B5).

Tip: Don't be confused by the "small" variants listed here (such as US Letter Small); these paper dimensions are identical to the non-small versions. The only difference is the margin: if you turn on the Small option, the laser printer chops off any part of the printout closer than half an inch to the edge of the page. (The non-small page sizes can get to within a quarter of an inch.)

The remaining choices vary; the Page Setup options for an Epson inkjet, for example, differ dramatically from those for a laser printer. Only your printer's user manual can tell you exactly what these choices do.

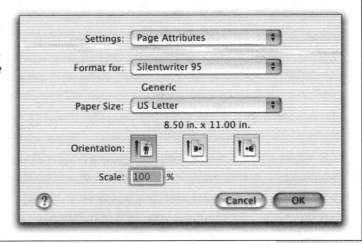

Figure 13-2:
The options included in this dialog box depend on the printer model you're using. Sometimes, as when printing on a laser printer, the pop-up menu at the top lets you switch among different screens full of choices. Unfortunately for whimsy fans, the little animal known as the Dogcow no longer illustrates the effect of each printing option.

The Print Command

Although you can grow to a ripe old age without ever seeing the Page Setup dialog box, you can't miss the Print dialog box. It appears, like it or not, whenever you choose File→Print in one of your programs.

Once again, the options you encounter depend on the printer you're using. You're always offered a few standard options on the Copies & Pages screen, however, including these:

- **Printer.** One cool thing about Mac OS X is that if you have more than one printer connected to your Mac, you can indicate which you want to use for a particular printout just by choosing its name from this pop-up menu.

- **Saved Settings.** Here's a way to preserve, and call up again with one click, your favorite print settings. Once you've proceeded through this dialog box, specifying the number of copies, which printer trays you want the paper taken from, and so on, you can choose Save Custom Setting from the pop-up menu shown in Figure 13-3. Thereafter, you'll be able to re-create that elaborate suite of settings just by choosing Custom from this pop-up menu.

  You can't actually create *numerous* sets of settings. Think of this feature instead as a way to recall the *one* configuration that you use most often.

- **Copies.** Type the number of copies you want printed. The Collated checkbox controls the printing order for the various pages. For example, if you print two copies of a three-page document, the Mac will generally print the pages in this order: 1, 2, 3; 1, 2, 3. If you turn off Collated, on the other hand, you'll get printouts of pages 1, 1, 2, 2, 3, and 3.

- **Pages.** You don't have to print an entire document—you can print, say, only pages 2 through 15. You can use commas and hyphens to spell out exactly the pages you want. Typing *1, 3-6, 9* will give you pages 1, 3, 4, 5, 6, and 9.

Tip: You don't have to type numbers into both the *From* and *to* boxes. If you leave the first box blank, the Mac assumes that you mean "from page 1." If you leave the second box blank, the Mac understands you to mean "to the end." To print only the first three pages, in other words, leave the first box blank, and type *3* into the second box. (These page numbers refer to the physical pages you're printing, not to any fancy numbering you've set up in your word processor. As far as the Print dialog box is concerned, the first printed page is page 1, even if you've told your word processor to label it page 455.)

If you examine the unnamed pop-up menu just below the Saved Settings pop-up menu, you'll find that you have dozens of additional options. For example:

- **Layout.** As shown in Figure 13-3, you can save paper and ink or toner cartridges by printing several miniature "pages" on a single sheet of paper.

- **Output Options.** If you turn on "Save as File," you won't get a paper printout at all. Instead, using the Format pop-up menu, you can turn your printout into a file on your hard drive. This file contains a complete, self-contained computer-language description of your printout, suitable for sending to a print shop, or, indeed, anyone with a computer. They'll be able to open and print your document without requiring the program you used to create it—or even the document itself.

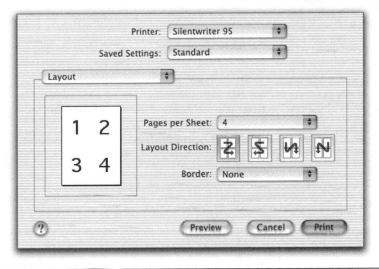

Figure 13-3:
By asking the Mac to print several pages per sheet of paper, you can compare various designs, look over an overall newsletter layout, and so on. Using the Border pop-up menu, you can also request a fine border around each miniature page. Some printers even offer a Print on Both Sides option here, so that you can print little booklets.

Use the Format pop-up menu to specify whether you want a standard PostScript file, which you can send to print shops or import into page-layout programs, or a *PDF* file. That means an Adobe Acrobat document—a file that any Mac, Windows, Linux, or Unix user can view, read, and print using the free Acrobat Reader program included with every Mac and PC. (Much more on PDF files on page 330.)

Once you've made your selection, you can click either Preview (to see what the file will look like) or Save (to save the actual PostScript or PDF document onto your hard drive).

- **Paper Feed.** If you chose the correct PPD file for your printer (page 322), then this screen "knows about" your printer's various paper trays. Here's where you specify which pages you want to come from which paper tray. (By far the most popular use for this feature is printing the first page of a letter on company letterhead, and the following pages on regular blank paper from a second tray.)

- **Mode/quality settings** or **Print Settings** (inkjet printers only). Here's where you specify what print quality you want, what kind of paper you're printing on, and so on.

- **Error Handling.** Using these controls, you can specify that you want a technical message to print out when the laser printer reports a PostScript error (when your document is too complex for the printer's memory, for example). Depending on your printer, you may also be able to specify what should happen if the paper tray you've specified runs out of paper.

- **[Program Name].** Whatever program you're using—Internet Explorer, Word, AppleWorks, or anything else—may offer its own special printing options on this screen.

- **Summary.** This command summons a text summary all of your settings so far.

- **Save Custom Setting.** As noted above, you can make Mac OS X memorize your favorite printing settings just by choosing this command. (The dialog box itself doesn't change when you choose this option.) Thereafter, you can save yourself the hassle of making all the settings just by choosing Custom from the Save Settings pop-up menu at the top of the window.

Previewing and Printing

When all of your settings look good, click Print (or press Enter) to send your printout to the printer.

It's worth pointing out, however, the Preview button in this dialog box. In effect, it provides a print-preview function to every Mac OS X program on earth, which, in the course of your life, could save huge swaths of the Brazilian rain forest and a swimming pool's worth of ink in wasted printouts.

Technically, the Preview button sends your printout to the Mac OS X program called Preview (which sits in your Applications folder). As described on page 216, Preview lets you zoom in or zoom out, rotate, or otherwise process your preview. When

---

DON'T PANIC

Background Printing

Where's the Background Printing control? I used to like turning background printing off when I was in a hurry, or leaving it on if I wanted to keep working while printing.

In the beginning, the Mac simply locked you out whenever it was printing. You couldn't do anything with the Mac except stare at the "now printing" message.

With the invention of background printing, your options became more interesting. Background printing lets you keep using your Mac while the printing takes place. As a result, the printout takes longer—but you can keep working in the meantime.

There's no longer a background printing control in Mac OS X, for one very good reason: it would be completely unnecessary. Background printing is turned on all the time in Mac OS X—you can't turn it off.

As you may have realized by now, Mac OS X is the king of multitasking. Managing printouts in the background is a trivial task for this mighty beast. It has to spend about as much of its attention thinking about printing as you do thinking about what you'll have for breakfast next Wednesday.

---

you're satisfied with the way it will look, you can either print it (File→Print), cancel it (File→Close), or turn it into an Acrobat file (File→Save as PDF). This final option, which is a very big deal, is described on the next page.

Managing Printouts

The real fun of printing begins only after you've used the Print command. Once you've done so, the Mac hands off the printing tasks to the Print Center program.

At this point, you can manage the printouts-in-waiting in a number of ways—ways that are useful primarily for people who do a lot of printing, have connections to a lot of printers, or share printers with a lot of other people.

Start by opening Print Center. In the list of printers, the Status column shows you which printers are busy. Double-click a printer's name to see something like Figure 13-4: the printouts that will soon be sliding out of your printer appear in a tidy list.

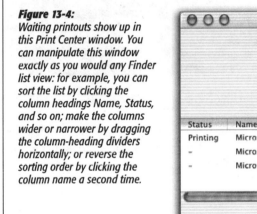
Figure 13-4:
Waiting printouts show up in this Print Center window. You can manipulate this window exactly as you would any Finder list view: for example, you can sort the list by clicking the column headings Name, Status, and so on; make the columns wider or narrower by dragging the column-heading dividers horizontally; or reverse the sorting order by clicking the column name a second time.

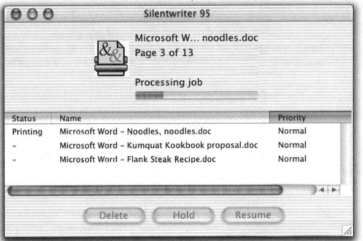

Here are some of the ways in which you can control these waiting printouts, which Apple collectively calls the *print queue:*

- **Delete them.** By clicking an icon, or ⌘-clicking several, and then clicking the Delete button at the bottom of the window, you remove items from the list of waiting printouts. Now they won't print.

- **Put in more paper.** By highlighting a printout and then clicking the Hold button, you pause that printout. It won't print out until you highlight it again and click the Resume button. This pausing business could be useful when, for example, you need time to check or refill the printer.

• **Halt them all.** You can stop all printouts for a specific printer by highlighting its name in the main printer list and choosing Queue→Stop Queue. (Choose Queue→Start Queue to re-enable printing on this printer.)

Note: As of Mac OS X version 10.1, you can't rearrange printouts by dragging them up or down in the queue lists, nor drag printouts between these lists, as you could in Mac OS 9.

UP TO SPEED

Printing from Classic Programs

If you imagine Mac OS X as an intervening layer between the Classic programs (see Chapter 5) and Macintosh circuitry itself, you won't find it so surprising that making printouts from within Classic programs isn't, shall we say, one of the highlights of the Mac OS X experience.

Many older printers (that use the so-called QuickDraw technology), including the ImageWriter, StyleWriter, and many in the Personal LaserWriter line, can't print at all from within

Classic programs. If you want to use these printers, you must restart in Mac OS 9, as described on page 140.

Some USB inkjet printers work within Classic, and some don't. (Most PostScript laser printers, fortunately, work fine.)

In any case, you need to treat Classic as though it's a separate Macintosh. That is, even if you've already installed your printer's software under Mac OS X, you must install it again while running Classic.

PDF Files

Sooner or later, almost everyone with a personal computer encounters PDF (portable document format) files. Many a software manual, Read Me file, and downloadable "white paper" comes in this format. Until recently, you needed the free program called Acrobat Reader (page 206) if you hoped to open or print these files. In fact, Windows users still do.

But PDF files are one of Mac OS X's common forms of currency. In fact, you can turn *any document* (in any program with a Print command) into a PDF file—a trick that once required the $250 program called Adobe Acrobat Distiller. (Maybe Apple should advertise: "Buy Acrobat Distiller for $250, get Mac OS X free—and $120 cash back!")

And why would you want to do so? What's the big deal about PDF in Mac OS X? Consider these advantages:

• **Other people see your layout.** When you distribute PDF files to other people, they see precisely the same fonts, colors, page design, and other elements that you did in your original document. And here's the kicker: they get to see all of this even if they don't *have* the fonts or the software you used to create the document. (Contrast with the alternative: Sending somebody, for example, a Microsoft Word document. If your correspondents don't have precisely the same fonts you have, then they'll see a screwy layout. And if they don't have Microsoft Word, they'll see nothing at all.)

- **It's universal.** PDF files are very common in the Macintosh, Windows, and even Unix/Linux worlds. When you create a PDF file, you can distribute it (by email, for example) without even having to think about what kind of computers your correspondents are using.

- **It has very high-resolution.** PDF files print at the maximum quality of any printer. A single PDF file prints great on both cheapo inkjets and on high-quality image-setting gear at professional print shops. (You're looking at a PDF file right now, in fact, which was later printed at a publishing plant.)

- **You can search it.** Although you may be tempted to think of a PDF file as something like a captured graphic of the original document, it has several key differences. Behind the scenes, its text is still text. You can search it using a Find command—an especially handy feature when you work with electronic software manuals in PDF format.

Opening PDF Files

There's nothing to opening up a PDF file: double-click it. The Mac OS X version of Acrobat Reader (page 206) takes over from there, and opens the PDF file on your screen.

Creating PDF Files

Opening, schmopening—what's really exciting in Mac OS X is the ability to create your *own* PDF files. You can do so in any of several ways:

- **The File→Save as PDF method.** Not all programs offer a File→Save as PDF command. But the ones that do give you by far the easiest method of creating a PDF file. A Save dialog box appears (see page 109). All you have to do is type a name for the file and save it. It's then ready for distribution, backing up, or whatever.

- **The Preview method.** The standard Print dialog box offers a Preview button (Figure 13-3). When you click it, your printout-to-be opens up in the Preview program. From here, just choose File→Save as PDF.

WORKAROUND WORKSHOP

When PDF Doesn't Match the Original

Once you've created a PDF file, you can email it to someone, put it in another user's Drop Box folder (page 303), back it up—or print it (after opening it in Preview or Acrobat Reader).

Note, however, that in certain situations, the document another person sees and prints may not always be 100 percent identical to the original. One key reason: the characteristics of the currently selected printer affect things like letter spacing and margins (of any document, not just PDF files).

For example, if an inkjet printer was selected in Print Center at the moment you created the PDF file, the layout may be slightly out of whack when printed on laser printer. There's not much you can do to prevent this problem except to try to anticipate the kind of printer that your audience will use when printing.

• **The Save as File method.** If that business of opening up a virtual printout in Preview strikes you as too roundabout, you can also choose File→Print. In the Print dialog box (Figure 13-3), choose Output Options from the unnamed pop-up menu. Turn on Save as File, and choose PDF from the Format menu. Finally, click Save.

Fonts in Mac OS X

Over the years, Macintosh fonts have improved considerably. No longer do you have to pray to the printer gods that your beautiful flyer won't come out with jagged-looking type because you chose the wrong font *type,* one that doesn't have smooth edges.

Up until Mac OS 9, a family of typefaces called *bitmapped fonts* was still kicking around, a holdover from the jagged-printing days of the original 1984 Macintosh. But Mac OS X can't even use such fonts. Only always-smooth font formats work in Mac OS X: namely, TrueType, PostScript Type 1, and OpenType. (OpenType is a font format developed by Microsoft and Adobe that's already common on Windows machines.)

In short, Mac OS X brings us fully into the era of type that is *all smooth, all the time.* Fonts always look smooth on the screen, no matter what the point size, and always look smooth in printouts, no matter what kind of printer you use. Never again will you spend money on programs like Adobe Type Manager just to make your type look smooth.

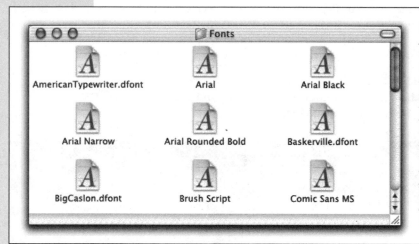

Figure 13-5:
Apple giveth, and Apple taketh away. In Mac OS X, all kinds of fonts are represented by a single icon apiece—a single font suitcase. PostScript fonts no longer require separate files for printer display and screen display. On the other hand, you can no longer double-click a font suitcase to see a preview of what its characters look like, as you could in Mac OS 9.

Where Fonts Live

As noted in Figure 13-5, the font-management situation in Mac OS X is both better and worse than it was in Mac OS 9. One of the most confusing changes is that there is no longer one single Fonts folder for your Mac. There are now *five* Fonts folders. The fonts you actually see listed in the Fonts menus of your programs are combinations of these Fonts folders' contents:

- **Your private fonts (your Home folder→Library→Fonts).** This Fonts folder sits right inside your own Home folder. You're free to add your own custom fonts to this folder. Go wild: It's your font collection and yours alone. Nobody else who uses the Mac will be able to use these fonts, and will never even know that you have them.

- **Main font collection (Library→Fonts).** This, for all intents and purposes, is the equivalent of the traditional Fonts folder. Any fonts in this folder are available to everyone to use in every program. (As with most features that affect everybody who shares your Macintosh, however, only people with Administrator accounts are allowed to change the contents of this folder.)

- **Network fonts (Network→Library→Fonts).** In certain corporations, a network administrator may have set up a central font collection on another computer on the network, to which your Mac and others can "subscribe." The beauty of this system, of course, is that everybody on the network will be able to rely on a consistent set of fonts. (In this case, the Network "folder" is represented by the Network icon in your Go→Computer window.)

- **Essential system fonts (System→Library→Fonts).** This folder contains the fonts that the Mac itself needs: the typefaces you see in your menus, dialog boxes, icons, and so on. You can open this folder to *see* these font suitcases, but you can't do anything with them, such as opening, moving, or adding to them. Remember that, for stability reasons, the System folder is sealed under glass forever. Only the *superuser* (page 290) can touch these files—and even that person would be foolish to do so.

- **Classic fonts (Mac OS 9 System Folder→Fonts).** Mac OS X automatically notices and incorporates any fonts in the System Folder that you've designated for use by the Classic environment (Chapter 5). This folder is also, of course, the source of fonts that appear in the Font menus of your Classic programs.

Note: With up to five folders containing fonts, you might wonder what happens in the case of *conflicts*. For example, suppose you have two slightly different fonts, both called Optima, which came from different type companies, and are housed in different Fonts folders on your system. Which font will you actually get when you use it in your documents?

The scheme is actually fairly simple: Mac OS X proceeds down the list of Fonts folders in the order shown above, beginning with your own home Fonts folder. It only acknowledges the existence of the *first* duplicated font it finds.

Installing Fonts

One of the biggest perks of Mac OS X is its preinstalled collection of over 50 great-looking fonts—"over $1000 worth," according to Apple, which licensed many of them from type companies. In short, fewer Mac users than ever before will wind up buying and installing new fonts.

But when you do buy or download new fonts, you're in luck. There's no longer any limit to the number of fonts you can install. Furthermore, installing them is a simple matter of dragging the new font files into the appropriate Fonts folder. (As in older versions of the Mac OS, newly installed fonts don't appear in the Font menus of programs that are already open. You have to quit and reopen them.)

Note: When you install new fonts in Classic, you must not only quit your open Classic programs—you must actually restart *Classic itself* to make the new fonts show up in your menus.

To remove a certain font, of course, you (or an administrator) must drag its corresponding icon out of *all five* Fonts folders. You don't have to quit your open programs first, although you may get confused by the fact that the font's name remains, now orphaned, in their Font menus.

The Font Panel

As noted in Chapter 4, some existing Mac programs have simply been touched up—Carbonized, in the lingo—to be Mac OS X-compatible. Choosing fonts in these programs works exactly like it always has on the Mac: You choose a typeface name from the Font menu or a formatting palette.

Things get much more interesting when you use programs that have been written from scratch expressly for Mac OS X. These so-called Cocoa programs, which include TextEdit and Mail, offer a new, standard Mac OS X feature called the Font panel. If you're seated in front of your Mac OS X machine now, fire up TextEdit and follow along.

Choosing fonts from the Font panel

Suppose you've just highlighted a headline in TextEdit. Now you want to choose a really good typeface for it.

In TextEdit, you open the Font panel (Figure 13-6) by choosing Format→Font→Font Panel (⌘-T). See how the Font panel is divided into columns (if the window is wide enough)? The first column, Collections, contains the names of font-list subsets, such as Fun or Modern, which make it easier to find the kind of font you're looking for. (*PDF* represents a set of standard fonts used in PDF files. *Web* lists fonts you're safe using on Web pages—that is, fonts that are very likely to be installed on the Macs or Windows PCs of your Web visitors).

The second column, Family, shows the names of the actual fonts in your system. The third, Typeface, shows the various style variations—Bold, Italic, Condensed, and so on—available in that type family. (Oblique and Italic are roughly the same thing. So are Bold and Black.)

Note: Unfortunately, not all fonts offer all these styles. Some, in fact, offer no style variations at all.

This silver lining here is that these are "real" styles. Desktop publishers will never again wind up with a phony, onscreen bold effect that winds up printing out standard non-bold characters—an expensive and wasteful discovery.

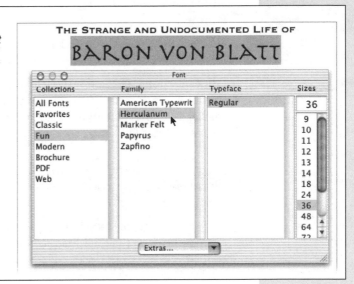

Figure 13-6:
The Font panel, available for the most part only in Cocoa programs, contains some of the genetic material of old-style programs like Suitcase and Font Juggler. By clicking the name of a collection in the far left column, you can summon subsets of your fonts that make it much easier to home in on what you're looking for.

The last column shows a sampling of point sizes. Of course, you can actually use any point size you want—type any number into the box at the top of the Sizes list; these common sizes are just listed to save you a little typing.

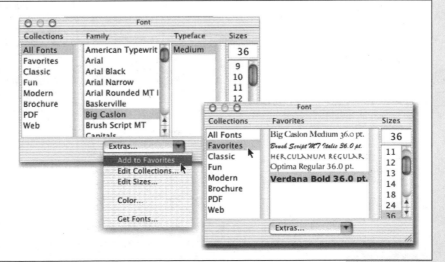

Figure 13-7:
Left: To designate a font as one of your favorites, specify a font, style, and size by clicking in the appropriate columns of the Font panel. Then, from the Extras pop-up menu, choose Add to Favorites.

Right: Thereafter, the specific typefaces you specified are easily available.

Designing collections and favorites

At the bottom of the Font panel is a small pop-up menu labeled Extras. It offers a few useful tools for customizing the standard Font panel:

- **Add to Favorites.** In the Collections column of the Font panel, the category called Favorites represents the first of several tools Apple has given you to manage unwieldy font collections. Figure 13-7 shows you how to designate a font as a favorite.

  For now on, whenever you click Favorites in the Collections column, you'll see a list of the specific typefaces you've specified (at right in Figure 13-7).

- **Edit Collections.** This command lets you add to the Collections column. Maybe you want to put certain fonts in groups called Headline or Sans Serif, creating smaller groupings of fonts for easier selection in your everyday work. Either way, the instructions in Figure 13-8 show how you do it.

Tip: Each time you create a new font collection, Mac OS X records its name and contents in a little file in your Home folder→Library→FontCollections folder. (A font collection called Fun, for example, shows up as an icon named *Fun.fcache.*)

By copying these files into the Shared folder (see page 287), you can make them available to anyone who uses the Mac. If your sister, for example, copies one of these files into her own Home folder→Library→FontCollections folder, she'll see the name of your collection in her own Font panel, the better to benefit from the effort and care you put into its creation.

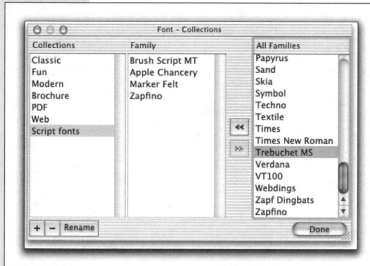

Figure 13-8:
When you choose Edit Collections from the Extras pop-up menu, you get this display. Click the + button to create a new entry in the Collections column, whose name you can edit. Click the name of a font, and then click the << button, to add this font's name to your collection. (To remove it from your collection, click its name in the Family column and then click >>.) Each font can be in as many different collections as you want. When you're finished, click Done.

- **Edit Sizes.** As noted on page 335, the point sizes listed in the Font panel are just suggestions. You can actually type in any point size you want.

By choosing this command, in fact, you can edit this list, so that the sizes you use most often are only a click away. As shown in Figure 13-9, you can even replace the entire column of numbers with a point-size *slider* that makes your highlighted text grow or shrink in real time as you drag it—a spectacular effect that almost single-handedly justifies your installation of Mac OS X.

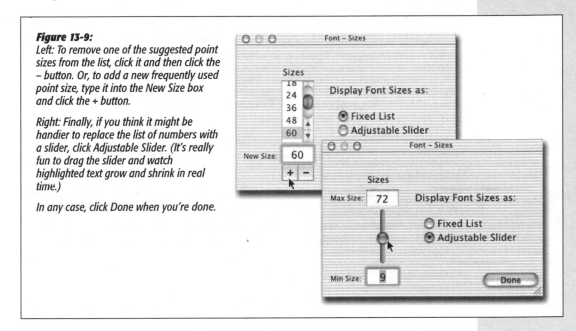

Figure 13-9:
Left: To remove one of the suggested point sizes from the list, click it and then click the – button. Or, to add a new frequently used point size, type it into the New Size box and click the + button.

Right: Finally, if you think it might be handier to replace the list of numbers with a slider, click Adjustable Slider. (It's really fun to drag the slider and watch highlighted text grow and shrink in real time.)

In any case, click Done when you're done.

Font Fuzziness on the Screen

As noted earlier in this chapter, *printed* type generated by Mac OS X always looks smooth and terrific, at all sizes and on any printer.

On the screen, however, some people describe the type in Mac OS X as remarkably smooth—and others describe it as fuzzy. There's a lot of confusion about Mac OS X's jaggies-eliminating technology, which is technically referred to as *antialiasing*.

Mac OS X's success in making screen type look great depends on primarily on size of the type. Fortunately, beginning in version 10.1, Apple has made it easy for you to control at least half of this equation. If you find that very small type is too fuzzy for comfort, open System Preferences, click the General icon, and choose a higher number from the "Turn off text smoothing for font sizes __ and smaller" pop-up menu. This setting you make here affects type in every program, including the Finder.

By all means experiment with this control. You'll probably discover, however, that the smoothing actually helps more than it hurts in most cases.

Tip: You can't make Mac OS X apply antialiasing to eight-point type or smaller—at least not without the help of TinkerTool, a shareware program you can download from the software page at *www.missingmanuals.com.*

ColorSync

As you may have read elsewhere in this book—or discovered through painful experience—computers aren't great with color. Every device you use to create and print digital images "sees" color a little bit differently, which explains why the deep amber captured by your scanner may be rendered as chalky brown on your monitor, but come out as a fiery orange on your Epson inkjet printer. Since every gadget defines and renders color in its own way, colors are often inconsistent as a print job moves from design to proof to press.

ColorSync attempts to sort out this mess, serving as a translator between all the different pieces of hardware in your workflow. For this to work, each device (scanner, monitor, printer, digital camera, copier, proofer, and so on) has to be calibrated with a unique *ColorSync profile*—a little file that tells your Mac exactly how your particular monitor (or scanner, or printer, or digital camera) defines colors. Armed with the knowledge contained within the profiles, the ColorSync software can make on-the-fly color corrections, compensating for the various quirks of the different devices.

Most of the people who lose sleep over color fidelity are those who do commercial color scanning and printing, where "off" colors are a big deal—after all, a customer might return a product after discovering, for example, that the actual product color doesn't match the photo on a company's Web site.

Getting ColorSync Profiles

ColorSync profiles for most Apple color printers, scanners, and monitors come built into Mac OS X. When you buy equipment or software from, say, Kodak, Agfa, or Pantone, you may get additional profiles. If your equipment didn't come with a ColorSync profile, visit Profile Central *(www.chromix.com),* where hundreds of model-specific profiles are available for downloading. Put new profiles into the Library→ColorSync→Profiles folder.

Even if your particular color appliance doesn't have a ColorSync module, you should still use the ColorSync profiles you *do* have for the other elements of your system. Every little bit helps.

On the other hand, use a ColorSync profile only if it's an exact match for your particular monitor, scanner, or other piece of hardware. If you don't have the right profile selected for each device, the color consistency could end up being worse than not using ColorSync at all.

Choosing Your System's Profiles

You specify which equipment you're using by opening the ColorSync panel of System Preferences. Here you'll find four pop-up menus: one each for Input (scanner or digital camera), Display (that is, the monitor you're using), Output (printer), and Proof (the printer you use for test copies).

Tip: In your Applications→Utilities folder, you'll find a program called Display Calibrator. It's designed to create a profile for your particular monitor in your particular office lighting—all you have to do is answer a few fun questions on the screen and drag a few sliders.

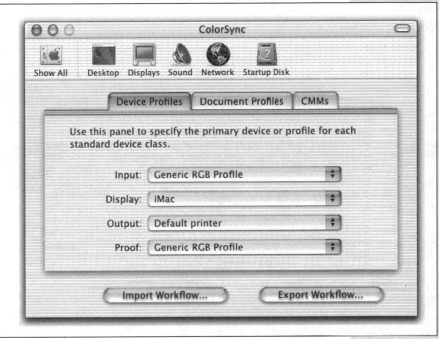

Figure 13-10:
Tell the Macintosh what scanner and printer you intend to use. The Document Profiles pane lets you choose which profile you want to use in rendering images created in different color modes.

Workflow Switching

Fortunately, you're not condemned to using the same scanner and printer forever. Nor are you forced to switch the ColorSync panel settings every time you switch printers or scanners.

Instead, you can save a "snapshot" of the current ColorSync settings into a configuration called a *workflow*. To do so, click Export Workflow at the bottom of the System Preferences screen. A Save dialog box appears, in which you can name and save the currently selected Workflow configuration. (You're free to distribute the resulting file, of course; you could put it into your Users→Shared folder for use by other people who use your Mac.)

Then, to switch from (for example) your Agfa Scanner/Kodak Printer configuration to your Kodak Camera/Proofer configuration, just click the Import Workflow button at the bottom of the System Preferences window. Find and open the workflow document you saved earlier.

More on ColorSync

There's quite a bit more you can learn about ColorSync. For example, some programs embed ColorSync profiles right into the documents themselves. If your program doesn't, use the Document Profiles tab of the ColorSync System Preferences panel to specify what color settings your documents should use by default. Clearly, knowing what settings to apply here requires a certain understanding of *color spaces* (color-description algorithms like RGB and CMYK).

If you find yourself wishing you could get deeper into ColorSync, you won't find much in the online help for Mac OS X. Instead, your quest should begin on the Web. At *www.apple.com/colorsync,* for example, you'll find articles, tutorials, and—perhaps most important of all—a link to an email discussion group where you can pose questions and read other people's answers. Going to a search site like *www.google.com* and searching for *ColorSync* is also a fruitful exercise.

POWER USERS' CLINIC

AppleScript and ColorSync

Using AppleScript, described in Chapter 7, you can harness ColorSync in elaborate ways. Just by dragging document icons onto AppleScript icons, for example, you can embed ColorSync profiles, modify the already incorporated profiles, remove profiles, review the profile information embedded in a graphic, and much more. Better yet, you don't even have to know AppleScript to perform these functions—you can use the built-in AppleScripts that come with Mac OS X.

To find them, open the Library→ColorSync→Scripts folder. Unfortunately, you don't get any instructions for using these eighteen ready-made AppleScripts. Nonetheless, Apple's real hope is that these example scripts will give you a leg up on creating your own AppleScripts. One day, Apple hopes, you, the print shop operator, will be able to automate your entire color processing routine using AppleScript and ColorSync.

Graphics in Mac OS X

Now you're talking. If you want to see dilated pupils and sweaty palms, just say "graphics" to any Mac OS X junkie.

Yes, graphics is one of the big deals with Mac OS X, thanks to its extremely sophisticated Quartz graphics-processing technology. Everywhere you look in Mac OS X, you'll find sophisticated visual effects that would make any other operating system think about early retirement. For example, how many of these effects have you noticed?

- Menus don't roll up when you release them—they fade away like the Invisible Man.

- Menus are slightly transparent.

- You can set the bars in Excel graphs to be slightly transparent, so that they don't block other bars in 3-D graphs.

- When you paste files or folders into windows in icon view (page 29), their icons fade into view.

- When you open an especially long or heavily formatted message in Mail, its text, too, fades in from white.

Graphics Formats in Mac OS X

Mac OS X understands and opens many of the same graphics file formats as Mac OS 9 or even Windows. Better yet, its Preview program (page 216) can open such graphics and then export them in a different format, making Preview an excellent file-conversion program.

You can confidently double-click graphics files—from a digital camera, scanner, or a Web download, for example—in any of these formats:

- **PICT files.** For almost 20 years, the PICT file was the graphics format Mac fans were most familiar with. It was the graphics format used by the Macintosh Clipboard, and it was the format created by the ⌘-Shift-3 keystroke (see page 343).

  Unfortunately, no other kinds of computers could open these files, and PICT files gave conniption fits to the equipment at printing shops. Mac OS X acknowledges the existence of PICT files, and can open them just fine; the Preview program can even export them. Otherwise, however, Mac OS X dramatically plays down the importance of PICT files, which will soon ride into the sunset.

- **TIFF files.** The TIFF file format is a high-density *bitmap*—that is, the Mac has memorized the color of every single tiny dot in the file. Trying to enlarge one is like trying to enlarge a fax: make it too big, and the image starts to break down into visible dots.

  Nonetheless, TIFF files are very popular in the printing industry—all the graphics in this book, for example, were stored as TIFF files. They print beautifully, work very nicely in page-layout programs, and are understood by both Macs and Windows machines. In fact, TIFF files are what Mac OS X creates when you press the ⌘-Shift-3 keystroke (see page 343).

- **JPEG files.** This graphics format is one of the most popular on the Web, particularly for photos or other high-quality, full-color artwork. You'll also see JPEG files by the thousands on America Online and elsewhere online, ready for downloading.

What makes JPEG files ideal for online use is that they've been compressed using a program like Photoshop; just enough of the color data has been thrown out from the original file to make the image a quick download. (Just be careful not to open a JPEG file, edit it, and then save it *again* as a JPEG file. In effect, you'll be throwing away another half of the color data, sometimes making the resulting photo look pretty blotchy.)

- **GIF files.** GIF stands for *graphics interchange format.* Today, GIF files are used almost exclusively on the Web, usually for solid-colored graphics like cartoons, headlines, and logos. (A GIF file can have a maximum of 256 colors, which is not even close to the photorealism of, say, JPEG. That's what makes GIF files inappropriate for photographs.)

- **PNG files.** As it turns out, the algorithms used by GIF files are, technically speaking, the property of a company called Unisys, which threatened to sue everybody who was creating GIF files. No problem, said the World Wide Web consortium—we'll just come up with our own replacement, a file format that has no legal strings attached. What they came up with was PNG (for Portable Network Graphics). It's already in the file-format lists of AppleWorks and Preview, and every modern Web browser understands it.

  PNG files aren't limited to 256 colors, as GIF files are, and don't lose quality when compressed, as JPEG files do. On the other hand, PNG files don't animate, as GIF files do. And when it comes to photos, they don't offer as good a size/quality balance as JPEG.

- **PDF (Acrobat) files.** You can read all about these files on page 330. There you'll find out that PDF files offer some spectacular features, especially when it comes to distributing documents built of both text and graphics. You'll also be delighted to find out that Mac OS X traffics effortlessly in PDF files, meaning that you can distribute documents you create to almost anyone, confident that they'll be able to open and print your stuff regardless of what kind of computer, fonts, and programs they have.

- **Photoshop files.** If you're a graphic designer or Webmeister, this one is kind of neat: Mac OS X can open (and its Preview program can even export) actual Photoshop files, the kind that you could once create only by using Adobe Photoshop. In practical terms, the fact that Mac OS X can open and display these files means that you could use a Photoshop masterpiece, complete with layers and transparency, as, for example, a desktop background (page 183).

- **BMP.** You can think of this graphics format as the PICT files of the Windows world. It's nice that Mac OS X can open (and Preview can export) them, especially because you may occasionally find .bmp files on the Web or attached to email messages.

- **Silicon Graphics, MacPaint, Targ.** Talk about obscure—you could go through your whole life without ever seeing a graphic in one of these formats. Silicon Graphics is, of course, the format created by Silicon Graphics computers. MacPaint is a black and white-only, 8-by-10-inch maximum, ancient Macintosh graphics format that disappeared from the scene in about 1987. And Targ (Targa) is the file format once used by products from the Truevision Corporation.

Screen-Capture Keystrokes

If you're reading a chapter about printing and graphics, you may someday be interested in creating *screenshots*—printable illustrations of the Mac screen.

Screenshots are a staple of articles, tutorials, and books about the Mac (including this one). Mac OS X (10.1 and later) has a secret built-in feature that lets you make them.

Press Shift-⌘-3 to create a picture file on your desktop, in TIFF format, that depicts the entire screen image. A satisfying camera-shutter sound tells you that you were successful.

The file is called *Picture 1* (or *Picture 1.tiff.*, if you have chosen to reveal file name extensions as described on page 103). Each time you press Shift-⌘-3, you get another file, called Picture 2, Picture 3, and so on. You can open these files into Preview, AppleWorks, or another graphics program, in readiness for editing or printing (see Figure 13-11 for a variation).

Tip: These screen-capture screenshots don't have to generate TIFF files; if you prefer, they can produce JPEG, PNG, or even PICT files.

You have to make the change using a Unix command in Terminal, however (see Chapter 15). Once in Terminal, type this: *defaults write NSGlobalDomain AppleScreenShotFormat JPEG* (but substitute the file format you want in place of *JPEG:* TIFF, PNG, or PICT). Press Enter, quit Terminal, and then log out. When you log back in, your change will be in effect.

Figure 13-11:
If you're interested in capturing only part of the screen, press Shift-⌘-4 to turn your cursor into a tiny + symbol. Now drag diagonally across the screen to capture only a rectangular chunk of it, as illustrated here.

When you release the mouse, you hear the camera-click sound, and the Picture 1 file appears on your desktop as usual.

Unfortunately, Mac OS X doesn't offer all the variations on these techniques that Mac OS 9 did, such as adding Caps Lock to neatly clip out a particular window, or Control to copy the resulting image to the Clipboard. It does come with Grab (Chapter 9), which at least offers a timer option that lets you set up the screen before it takes the shot.

But if you're really serious about capturing screenshots, you should opt instead for Snapz Pro X *(www.ambrosiasw.com),* which can capture virtually anything on the screen—even movies of onscreen procedures, along with your narration—and save it into your choice of graphics format.

Sound, Movies, and Speech

For years, as other computer companies whipped themselves into a frenzy attempting to market one multimedia computer or another, Mac fans just smiled. Macs have been capable of displaying sound and graphics—no add-on sound, graphics, or video boards required—from day one, years before the word *multimedia* was even coined.

The Mac's superiority at handling sound and video continues in Mac OS X. QuickTime, for example, is software that lets you play digital movies on your screen and watch live "streaming" broadcasts from the Internet. This chapter covers both creative pursuits: creating and using sound, and playing and editing movies.

As a bonus, this chapter also covers Mac OS X's speech features: how to command your Mac by voice, as well as making your Mac talk back.

Playing Sounds

You can have a lot of fun with digital sounds if you know where to find them, where to put them, and how to edit them. You can play almost any kind of digitized sound files, even MP3 files, right in the Finder—if you put its window into column view (page 40). But that's just the beginning.

Controlling the Volume

Adjusting the volume of your Mac's speakers couldn't be easier: add the tiny speaker menu on your menu bar, as directed in Figure 14-1. That illustration also shows the Sound panel of System Preferences, which offers another way to go about it.

Tip: Actually, all current Macs offer an even more direct way to control the speaker volume: speaker-control keys right on the keyboard. (The key to their left is the Mute button, which instantaneously cuts off all the Mac's sound—a wonderful feature when you find yourself trying to use the Mac surreptitiously in the library or in church.)

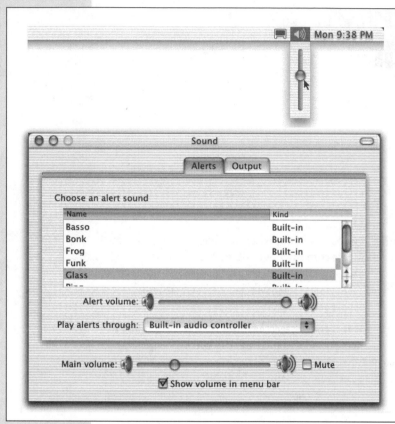

Figure 14-1:
Top: The tiny speaker silhouette in the upper-right corner of your screen turns into a volume slider when you click it. To make this sound menulet appear, open the Sound pane of System Preferences (bottom) and turn on "Show volume in menu bar."

Bottom: Another way to adjust the overall speaker volume is to drag the "Main volume" slider in System Preferences.

The Output tab of this panel, by the way, is designed to let you adjust the left-to-right balance of your stereo speakers, if you have them. The stereo speakers on most Macs that have them (iMacs, PowerBook) are already perfectly centered, so you'll have little need to adjust this slider unless you generally list to one side in your chair. (You may find additional controls here if you have extra audio gear—an iSub subwoofer system, for example.)

Alert Beeps and You

In the first decades of the Macintosh experience, everybody knew what an error beep was: the little quack, simple beep, or trumpet blast that said, "You can't click here." For example, in Mac OS 9, choosing File→Print and then clicking anywhere outside of the Print dialog box produced a beep.

In Mac OS X, a lot of the beeping goes away. Dialog boxes very rarely commandeer your screen as they did in Mac OS 9. These days, if you try to click outside the Print dialog box, you just switch into whatever window or program you clicked.

Nonetheless, you still hear error beeps occasionally. (Try typing letters into a dialog box where a program expects numbers, for example.)

Choosing an alert beep

To choose one that suits your own personal taste, open the Sound panel of System Preferences (Figure 14-1, bottom). The Alerts screen offers a canned choice of thirteen witty and interesting sound snippets for use as error beeps. Press the up and down arrow keys to "walk" through them, listening to each. Whatever is highlighted when you close the window becomes the new error beep.

You can also drag the "Alert volume" slider to adjust the error beep volume relative to your Mac's overall speaker setting.

Adding new alert beeps

Mac OS X's error beeps are actually AIFF sound files (see the sidebar box below). As it does with fonts, Mac OS X builds the list of error beeps that you see in the Sound panel of System Preferences from several folder sources:

- **System→Library→Sounds folder.** This folder contains the basic Mac OS X set. Because it's in the System folder, it's off-limits to manipulation by us meddlesome human beings. You can't delete one of the original Mac OS X error beeps, nor add to this collection (unless you take the drastic step of logging in as the root account holder [page 290] or restarting the computer in Mac OS 9).

UP TO SPEED

AIFF Files

Until the dawn of Mac OS X, the standard sound-file format for the Macintosh was something called System 7 format. All error beeps were stored in this format.

What made these files especially wonderful was that you didn't need any particular program to play them. Just double-clicking a System 7 file made it play, right there on the desktop. Millions of Mac fans delighted in putting System 7 files into the System→Startup Items folder ("Kirk to Enterprise!") or in the Shutdown Items folder ("He's dead, Jim").

As part of its trend to abandon Macintosh-only file formats like PICT files (Chapter 13), however, Apple has now left behind System 7 sound files. The standard sound format

in Mac OS X is the AIFF file, a popular Mac/Windows/Internet sound format. (The abbreviation stands for *audio interchange file format.*)

The bad news is that you can no longer double-click one of these files to play it. Instead, double-clicking one opens it up in QuickTime Player (described later in this chapter), where you must press the Space bar to begin or end playback.

The good news is that you can exchange these files with both Mac and Windows fans, download them from Web sites without worrying that your Mac won't be able to play them, and so on.

- **Home folder→Library→Sounds folder.** Fortunately, it's easy enough to add sounds for your own use, however—just add them to this folder.

- **Library→Sounds folder.** If you, an administrator, want to make a sound file available to all account holders on your Mac (if there's more than one), create a new Sounds folder in the main hard drive window's Library folder. Any sound files you put there show up in every account holder's list of alert sounds.

The sound files you put into these folders must be in AIFF format (see the sidebar box below). Stranger yet, their names must end with the extension *.aiff*. If the file's name ends with a simple .aif, which is the usual extension on Windows computers, System Preferences won't recognize it. This is all the more confusing because when you export a sound file from Apple's own QuickTime Player Pro, it insists that *.aif* is the correct extension!

Note: Any changes you make to these Sounds folders don't show up until you've quit and reopened System Preferences.

Recording Sound

Somebody at Apple doesn't think much of the Mac's traditional sound-recording features. The microphone-input jacks have begun disappearing from most Mac models; Apple instead suggests that customers who want to record their own sounds buy USB microphones.

Now, in Mac OS X, even the *software* for recording sounds is gone. Mac OS 9 offered two different recording programs: SimpleSound and the traditional Sound control panel. But in Mac OS X 10.1, it's all gone.

You can work around both problems—the vanishing microphone and the vanishing software—but it'll cost you.

Macs and Mikes

If you hope to record new sounds, of course, you'll need a microphone. Your microphone situation depends on the kind of Mac you have:

- **iMac, PowerBook, 2001 iBook.** You have a built-in microphone, usually a tiny hole just above the screen. This microphone couldn't be more convenient: it's always with you, and always turned on.

- **Original iBook, Cube, recent Power Macs.** You can plug in an external USB microphone (the Apple Products Guide at *www.guide.apple.com* offers a list) or use an adapter (such as the iMic, *www.griffintechnology.com*) that accommodates a standard microphone.

- **Older Power Macs.** These models came with a gray, half-cone-shaped microphone called the PlainTalk microphone. You'll find a corresponding miniplug jack for it on the back. Note, however, that the PlainTalk mike's pin is slightly longer than a standard miniplug. Standard microphones don't work in a Mac without an adapter like the NE Mic from *www.griffintechnology.com*.

Tip: You may have discovered that the Sound panel of System Preferences doesn't offer a pop-up menu that lets you choose which sound source you want the Mac to listen to. Mac OS X automatically "listens to" your microphones, if you have more than one, in this order: external USB microphone, external analog microphone (that is, something plugged into the microphone or Line In jacks of older Macs), built-in microphone.

Making the Recording

Once you've got your microphone situation taken care of, you need to get your hands on some sound-recording software.

The iMovie method

There is, in fact, one piece of sound-recording software that comes with Mac OS X, although you might never suspect it: iMovie 2, which lurks in your Applications folder. iMovie's primary purpose, of course, is to let you edit your own camcorder footage. But as it turns out, iMovie's voice-over narration feature makes a convenient sound-recording studio.

In a new, arbitrarily named movie file, click the Audio button shown in Figure 14-2. Click Record Voice and begin to speak; click Stop to complete the recording.

Figure 14-2:
Top: To summon the Record Voice controls, click the Audio button. If your microphone is correctly hooked up, the Record Voice button is available. (Otherwise, it's dimmed.) Just above the button is a live "VU" level meter. Test your setup by speaking into the microphone; if this meter twitches in response, you're ready to record.

Bottom: Your recording takes the form of an orange bar at the bottom of the screen. (Click the clock icon tab if you don't see it.)

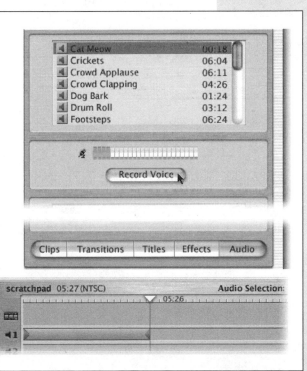

Now a new stripe appears in the upper sound track, orange and highlighted, like the one shown in Figure 14-2. Drag the playhead to the left—to the beginning of the new recording—and then press the Space bar to listen to your voice-over work. If the narration wasn't everything you hoped for, it's easy enough to record another "take." Just click the stripe representing your recording and then press Delete to get rid of it. Then repeat the process.

When you're satisfied with the recording, there's nothing left to do except to save it as a sound file. Unfortunately, iMovie can't directly export files in the AIFF file format for use as an error beep. The best you can do is to choose File→Export Movie, choose To QuickTime from the pop-up menu, and save the file as a QuickTime movie that has no video component.

At that point, you need either QuickTime Pro (page 352) or one of the programs described next to extract the sound and convert it into an AIFF file.

The shareware method

If you're willing to spend a few dollars, you can buy a shareware program that puts iMovie, as a sound studio, to shame. Some of the most useful, economical, and powerful include Sound Studio for OS X ($35) and Amadeus II ($25). You can download 14-day trial versions of both programs from *www.missingmanuals.com*, among other places.

These programs make terrific sound recorders. Better yet, they make great editors, too. If there's excess silence at one end of the clip, or a few too many "uh"s and "um"s in the middle, you can edit them out just by dragging through the appropriate section of the scrolling sound-wave map (Figure 14-3) and pressing Delete.

These programs can open almost any kind of sound files, including tracks from your music CDs, and convert them to any other kind—including AIFF format.

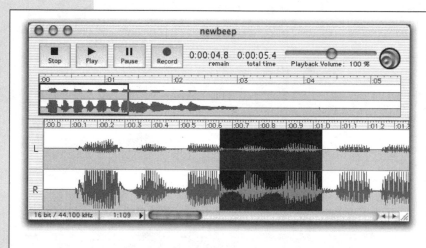

Figure 14-3:
In Sound Studio, you can see the entire sound file in one window; you can drag across a section of sound waves to highlight the piece of sound, in preparation for deleting, copying, or applying one of the many special effects. The program is shareware; it's fully functional for two weeks, whereupon the honor system suggests that you send the programmer $35 for his efforts.

QuickTime Movies

A QuickTime movie is a digital movie—a file on your hard drive, on a CD-ROM, or on the Internet, that flashes many individual frames (photos) per second before your eyes, while also playing a synchronized sound track.

Movies on the Desktop

As noted on page 40, you don't need any special software to play QuickTime movies. Just view their windows in column view, and then proceed as shown in Figure 14-4.

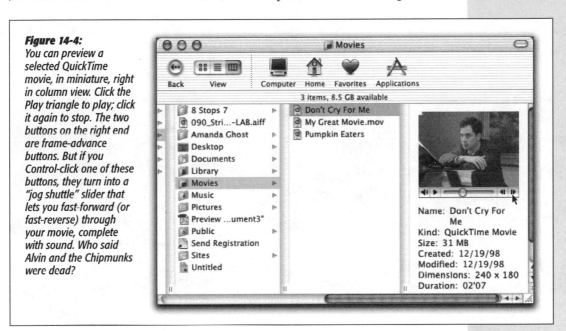

Figure 14-4:
You can preview a selected QuickTime movie, in miniature, right in column view. Click the Play triangle to play; click it again to stop. The two buttons on the right end are frame-advance buttons. But if you Control-click one of these buttons, they turn into a "jog shuttle" slider that lets you fast-forward (or fast-reverse) through your movie, complete with sound. Who said Alvin and the Chipmunks were dead?

QuickTime Player

Dozens of Mac OS X programs can open QuickTime movies, play them back, and sometimes even incorporate them into documents: Word, FileMaker, AppleWorks, PowerPoint, Internet Explorer, America Online, and so on.

But the cornerstone of Mac OS X's movie-playback software is QuickTime Player, which sits in your Applications→QuickTime folder (and even comes factory installed on the Dock). It does exactly what it's designed to do: show pictures, play movies, and play sounds.

Tip: Like Preview, another basic Mac OS X utility program, QuickTime Player can also open many graphics files—such as JPEG, GIF, TIFF, PICT, and even native Photoshop documents. You can either drag these graphics files onto the QuickTime Player icon, or—from within QuickTime Player—choose File→Open Movie in New Player.

Playing movies with QuickTime Player

You can open a movie file either by dragging it onto the QuickTime Player icon or by launching QuickTime Player and then choosing File→Open Movie in New Player (⌘-N). As shown in Figure 14-5, a number of controls help you govern the movie's playback:

- **Audio level meters.** This little graph dances to indicate the relative strength of various frequencies in the sound track, like the VU meters on a stereo. If you don't see any dancing going on, then you've opened a movie that doesn't have a sound track.

- **TV.** Click this peculiar button to fill your "movie screen" with the icons of Web sites that provide video feeds, as described below.

- **Resize handle.** Drag diagonally to make the window bigger or smaller.

FREQUENTLY ASKED QUESTION

QuickTime Player vs. QuickTime Player Pro

Every time I launch QuickTime Player, I get this stupid ad about upgrading to QuickTime 5 Pro. How can I get rid of it?

Easy one. Quit QuickTime Player. Open System Preferences; click Date & Time. Reset your Mac to a date far beyond its obsolescence point—the year 2020, for example. (Turn off "Use a network time server" on the Network Time tab first, if it's on.) Close the window.

The next time Quick-Time Player shows its ad (which it does only once a day), click the Later button for the very last time. Quit the program, reset your clock to the correct date, and enjoy the fact that you've played a little trick on the program's calendar-watching feature. You'll never see the ad again (at least, not until 2020).

All of these shenanigans are only necessary, of course, if you've decided not to upgrade to QuickTime Player Pro, whose additional editing playback and exporting features are documented in this chapter.

For $30, Apple will sell you a password that turns your copy of QuickTime Player into something called QuickTime Player Pro. (To obtain this password, call 888-295-0648, or click the Upgrade to QuickTime 5 Pro Now button to go online to *www.apple.com/quicktime/buy.*)

To record your password, choose QuickTime Player→ Preferences→Registration. Your password gets stored in your Home folder→ Library→Preferences folder, in a file called QuickTime Prefer-ences; remember that when you upgrade to a new Mac.

Once you've up-graded, you gain several immediate benefits—not the least of which is the permanent disappearance of the "upgrade now" advertisement. Now QuickTime Player is QuickTime Player Pro, and is capable of editing your movies, as described later in this chapter. It can also import many more sound and graphics formats, and—via the File→Export command—convert sounds, movies, and graphics into other formats.

Create Internet-ready audio & video.

QuickTime

Why Go Pro?   Get QuickTime 5 Pro Now   Later

Tip: When you drag the resize handle, QuickTime Player strives to maintain the same *aspect ratio* (relative dimensions) of the original movie, so that you don't accidentally squish it. If you want to squish it, however—perhaps for the special effect of seeing your loved ones as they would look with different sets of horizontal and vertical genes—press the Shift key as you drag.

If you press the Option key while dragging, meanwhile, you'll discover that the movie frame grows or shrinks in sudden jumping factors of two—twice as big, four times as big, and so on. On slower Macs, keeping a movie at an even multiple of its original size in this way ensures smoother playback.

- **Scroll bar.** Drag the diamond to jump to a different spot in the movie.

Tip: You can also press the right and left arrow keys to step through the movie one frame at a time. If you press *Option*-right and -left arrow, you jump to the beginning or end of the movie. In the Pro version, Option-arrow also jumps to the beginning or ending of the selected stretch of movie, if any.

- **Play/Stop button.** Click once to start, and again to stop. You can also press the Space bar, Return key, or ⌘-right arrow, for this purpose. (Or avoid the buttons altogether and double-click the movie itself to start or stop playback.)

Tip: You can make any movie play automatically when opened, so that you don't have to click the Play button. To do so, choose QuickTime Player→Preferences→Player Preferences, and turn on "Automatically play movies when opened."

Figure 14-5:
Some of the controls you see here are available only in the Pro version of QuickTime Player—they appear as soon as you type in your registration code (which you get when you pay $30).

Counter · Volume · Playhead · Audio level meters · QuickTime TV window · Resize handle · Rewind to start · Selection handle · Play/Stop · Scroll bar · Jump to end

Don't Cry For Me.mov · 00:01:25

- **Selection handles.** These tiny black triangles appear only in the $30 Pro version; you use them to select, or highlight, stretches of footage.

- **Volume.** If you like, you can make the soundtrack louder or softer by dragging this slider with your mouse or clicking in its "track." You may find it easier, however, to press the up or down arrow keys.

Tip: To mute the sound, click the little speaker icon, or press Option-down arrow. Press Option-up arrow to make the volume slider jump to full-blast position.

- **Counter.** In "hours: minutes: seconds" format, this display shows how far your diamond cursor has moved into the movie.

  If you have QuickTime Pro, the counter shows the position of whichever selection handle you've most recently clicked (if any).

- **Rewind, Fast Forward.** When you click one of these buttons and keep the mouse button pressed, you get to speed through your movie, backward and forward, respectively, complete with sound. This is a terrific way to navigate your movie quickly, regardless of whether you're using QuickTime Player or QuickTime Player Pro.

- **Jump to Start, Jump to End.** These buttons do exactly what they say: scroll to the beginning or end of your movie. In the Pro version, they can also jump to the beginning and ending of the selected portion of the movie, if any. All of this, in other words, is exactly the same as pressing the Option-left arrow or -right arrow keys.

Tip: Try minimizing a QuickTime Player window while a movie is playing. It shrinks to the Dock—and *keeps on playing.* Do this enough times, and you'll know what it's like to be Steve Jobs on stage.

Hidden controls

Don't miss the Movie→Show Video Controls and Movie→Show Sound Controls commands. As shown in Figure 14-6, they let you fine-tune the audio and video you're experiencing.

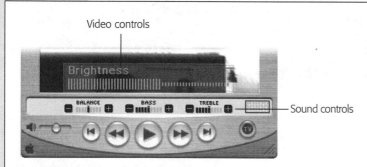

Video controls

Sound controls

Figure 14-6:
Click the word Brightness to summon the Contrast or Tint slider; drag your mouse across the vertical bars to adjust the picture accordingly. The Sound controls replace the scroll bar. When you're finished adjusting the balance, bass, or treble, click the light gray grid at the right edge to bring the scroll bar back.

Tip: Clicking the tiny, grayed-out grid to the right of the scroll bar is a quicker alternative to choosing Movie→Show Audio Controls.

Fancy playback tricks

Nobody knows for sure what Apple was thinking when it created some of these additional features—exactly how often do you want your movie to play backward?—but here they are. Some of these features are available only in the unlocked Pro version of the QuickTime Player, as indicated below.

- **Change the screen size.** Using the Movie menu commands, such as Double Size and Fill Screen, you can enlarge or reduce the actual "movie screen" window. Making the window larger also makes the movie coarser, because QuickTime Player simply doubles the size of every dot that was present in the original. Still, when you want to show a movie to a group of people more than a few feet back from the screen, these larger sizes are perfectly effective.

- **Play more than one movie.** You can open several movies at once and then run them simultaneously. (Of course, the more movies you try to play at once, the jerkier the playback gets.)

  As a sanity preserver, QuickTime Player plays only one soundtrack—that of the movie you most currently clicked. If you really want to hear the cacophony of all the sound tracks being played simultaneously, choose QuickTime Player→Preferences→Player Preferences, and turn off "Play sound in frontmost player only." (The related checkbox here, "Play sound when application is in background," controls what happens when you switch out of QuickTime Player into another program.)

Tip: If you have Player Pro, you can use the Movie→Play All Movies command to begin playback of all open movies at the same instant.

- **Play the movie backward.** You can play the movie backward—but not always smoothly—by pressing ⌘-left arrow, or by Shift-double-clicking the movie itself. (You must keep the Shift button pressed to make the backward playback continue.) There's no better way to listen for secret subliminal messages.

- **Loop the movie.** When you choose Movie→Loop and then click Play, the movie plays endlessly from beginning to end, repeating until you make it stop.

- **Play a selection (Pro only).** When you choose Movie→Loop Back and Forth and then click Play, the movie plays to the end—and then plays backward, from end to beginning. It repeats this cycle until you make it stop.

- **Play every frame (Pro only).** If you try to play a very large movie that incorporates a high frame rate (many frames per second) on a slow Mac, QuickTime Player skips individual frames of the movie. In other words, it sacrifices smooth motion in order to maintain synchronization with the soundtrack.

But if you choose Movie→Play All Frames and then play the movie, QuickTime Player says, "OK, forget the soundtrack—I'll show you every single frame of the movie, even if it isn't at full speed." You get no sound at all, but you do get to see each frame of the movie.

QuickTime TV (Internet Streaming)

QuickTime TV got a few raised eyebrows when Steve Jobs announced it in 1998, but few Mac fans have even noticed it since. That's too bad—it's a clever and well-implemented feature that lets you watch "Internet slide shows," watch a couple of live TV stations, or listen to the radio, as you work on your Mac—at no charge.

Streaming video from your browser

With ever-increasing frequency, modern Web sites advertise *streaming video* events, such as Steve Jobs keynote speeches and the occasional live rock-group performance. You'll find a note on a Web page that says, for example: "Watch the live debate by clicking here on October 15 at 9:00 p.m. EST."

If you do so, you'll find yourself transported once again into QuickTime Player, which connects to the appropriate Internet "station" and plays the video in its window. (You can also choose File→Open URL in New Player from within QuickTime Player to type in the Web address.)

Note: You don't have much control when watching a live broadcast. You generally can't rewind, and you certainly can't fast forward. You may be able to pause the broadcast, but when you un-pause, you wind up at the current broadcast moment—not where you stopped.

Streaming video in QuickTime Player

Fortunately, if you're eager to experience the early-technology thrill of watching live Internet video, you don't have to wait until you stumble onto a broadcast advertised on a Web page. Thanks to Apple's QuickTime TV initiative, a number of TV and radio broadcasts are going on at this very moment—24 hours a day. A list of them is built right into QuickTime Player.

To access these "channels," click the little TV button (or choose QTV→QuickTime TV→Show QuickTime TV Channels). Icons for the installed channels replace the video image, as shown in Figure 14-7.

When you click one of these channel buttons, your Mac connects to the Internet and, after a while, begins to play the corresponding channel in all its flickering glory. As you'll soon discover, some of these channels are more useful than others. They fall into these categories:

• **Live TV.** You might expect that this format would be the standard for QuickTime TV—it's certainly the most exciting. Unfortunately, only a few channels, such as BBC News, use this approach, actually showing you a live TV broadcast, 24 hours a day.

- **Canned videos.** Most of the channels work like this: when you click the channel icon, you summon a "billboard" that offers several buttons, each of which plays one short video clip. The VH-1, HBO, Rolling Stone, Weather Channel, Disney, and Warner Records channels take this sometimes self-promotional approach. (So do the CNN and Fox News channels, but at least these videos are updated almost every day.)

Figure 14-7:
The QuickTime TV tab contains icons for various Web sites that offer streaming audio and video. Click one to have a look or listen—but be prepared to wait.

- **Live radio.** These channels let you listen to the radio while you work. They include the ESPN, WGBH radio, and NPR channels. (You don't get any video with these channels. Furthermore, note that iTunes [Chapter 10] offers a much better selection of stations.)

- **Web-site buttons.** Some channels provide little more than links to the corresponding Web sites, which then open in your Web browser.

Tip: You can find a list of additional QuickTime TV channels at *www.apple.com/quicktime/qtv.*

While you're there, don't miss the links on this page, which direct you to over 100 more radio stations, rock-videos, and other Internet QuickTime sources that aren't actually QuickTime TV channels. But they're live, streaming audio and video sources that can become QuickTime TV channels—that is, icons on your Favorites tab—as soon as you choose the QTV→Favorites→Add Movie As Favorite command (⌘-D; also see Figure 14-8).

Manipulating your Favorites
When you click the little heart-shaped tab, you see a second screen full of icons known as Favorites.

Although few people have use for this feature, it's possible to add the icons of your own QuickTime movies to the Favorites panel—not QuickTime TV channels, but actual movies on your hard drive. To do so, you can use any of these methods:

- Drag the icon of a QuickTime movie, picture file, or sound clipping directly off of your desktop and into the QuickTime Player window—onto an empty slot in the Favorites tab.

- Open a movie, picture, or sound, and then choose QTV→Favorites→Add Movie As Favorite.

- Open a movie or picture, and then drag its image out of the QuickTime Player movie screen and onto a Favorites drawer slot.

- Drag the icon of the QuickTime TV source (on the main QuickTime TV page) onto the heart-icon tab itself.

No matter which method you use, an icon for that movie, sound, or picture now appears on the Favorites drawer. You can then manipulate, delete, or rename them as shown in Figure 14-8.

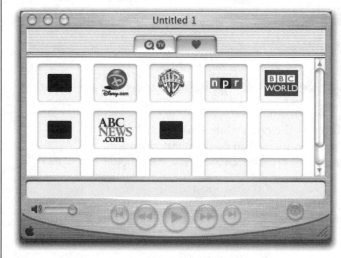

Figure 14-8:
To delete one of your "favorites," drag its icon directly out of this window and onto the Trash can. (No confirmation box appears.) You can also reorganize the locations of the Favorites icons just by dragging them around. Unfortunately, you can't drag one on top of another in hopes of switching their locations–you wind up wiping one of them out. You must drag these icons only onto empty slots if you hope to preserve the full collection.

QuickTime Player Pro

If you've spent the $30 to upgrade your free copy of QuickTime Player to the Pro version, you've unlocked a number of useful features. For example:

- Your Movie menu contains additional playback options, such as those described in "Fancy playback tricks," above.

- When you find a QuickTime movie on a Web page, you can usually save it to your hard drive. (Click on the movie; hold down the mouse button until a pop-up menu appears; choose Save Movie to Disk, or the equivalent in your browser.)

- Using the commands in the Edit menu, you can view, turn on and off, add, or delete the individual tracks in a particular movie. (Most movies have nothing but a video track and a soundtrack. But a few specialized movies may also contain a text track, an animation track, alternate sound tracks, and so on.)

- The Movie→Present Movie command is extremely useful. It's the best possible way to view a QuickTime movie on your screen, in fact. When you use this command, QuickTime Player blacks out the screen and devotes all the Mac's processing power to playing the movie smoothly. (To interrupt the movie, press Esc or ⌘-period.)

Tip: The dialog box that appears when you choose File→Present Movie gives you a few other options, such as Full Screen. These movie-enlarging features are terrific when you want to show a group of people a movie, but remember that an enlarged QuickTime movie is also a jerkier and grainier one.

By far the most powerful feature you gain in the Pro version, however, is its ability to *edit* QuickTime movies. You can rearrange scenes, eliminate others, and save the result as a new movie with its own name. (Even QuickTime Player Pro doesn't let you *create* live-action QuickTime movies with your camcorder; for that, you need iMovie—or a more complex editing program, such as Final Cut. QuickTime Player Pro simply lets you edit existing movies.)

Selecting footage

Before you can cut, copy, or paste footage, QuickTime Player needs to provide a way for you to specify *what* footage you want to manipulate. Its solution: the two tiny black triangles that start out at the left end of the horizontal scroll bar, as shown in Figure 14-5. These are the "in" and "out" points; by dragging these triangles, you're supposed to enclose the scene you want to cut or copy.

Tip: You can gain more precise control over the selection procedure by clicking one of the black triangles and then pressing the right or left arrow key. Doing so expands or contracts the selected chunk of footage by one frame at a time.

You may also prefer to select a piece of footage by Shift-clicking the Play button. As long as you hold down the Shift key, you continue to select footage; when you release the Shift key, you stop the playback, and the selected passage appears in gray on the scroll bar.

Once you've highlighted a passage of footage, you can proceed as follows:

- Jump to the beginning or end of the selected footage by pressing Option-right arrow or -left arrow key.

- Deselect the footage by dragging the two triangles together again.

- Play only the selected passage by choosing Movie→Play Selection Only. (The other Movie menu commands, such as Loop, apply only to the selection at this point.)

- Drag the movie picture out of the Player window and onto the desktop, where it becomes a movie clipping that you can double-click to view.

- Cut, copy, or clear the highlighted material using the commands in the Edit menu.

Tip: If you paste some *text* directly into QuickTime Player Pro, you get a two-second title (such as an opening credit), professionally displayed as white type against a black background, at the location of the scroll bar playhead. QuickTime Player automatically uses the font, size, and style of the text that was in the text clipping. You can paste a graphic image, too; once again, you get a two-second "slide" of that still image.

If you find it easier, you can also drag a text or picture clipping file directly from the desktop into the QuickTime Player window; once again, you get a two-second insert.

Pasting footage

After cutting or copying footage, you can move it elsewhere in the movie. Specify where you want the pasted material to go by first clicking or dragging in the horizontal scroll bar, so that the black diamond marks the spot; then choose Edit→Paste. The selection triangles (and their accompanying gray scroll-bar section) appear to show you where the new footage has appeared. (That makes it easy for you to promptly choose Edit→Cut, for example, if you change your mind.)

By pressing some secret keys, moreover, you gain two clever variations of the Paste command. They work like this:

- If you highlight some footage before pasting, and then press Shift, you'll find that the Edit→Paste command has changed to become Edit→Replace; whatever footage is on your clipboard now *replaces* the selected stretch of movie.

- If you press Option, the Edit→Clear command changes to read Trim. It eliminates the outer parts of the movie—the pieces that *aren't* selected. All that remains is the part you first highlighted.

- If you highlight some footage, and then press Option, the Paste command changes to read Add. This command adds whatever's on the Clipboard so that it plays *simultaneously* with the selected footage—a feature that's especially useful when you're adding a different *kind* of material to the movie (see Figure 14-9).

- If you highlight some footage and then press Shift-Option, the Edit→Paste command changes to say Add Scaled. Whatever you're pasting gets stretched or compressed in time so that it fits the highlighted region, speeding up or slowing down both audio and video. The effect can be powerful, comical, or just weird.

Tip: You can edit sounds exactly as you edit movies, using precisely the same commands and shortcuts. Use the File→Open Movie in New Player command in QuickTime Player Pro to locate a sound file to open. It opens exactly like a QuickTime movie, except with only a scroll bar, no picture.

Figure 14-9:
QuickTime Player Pro has a little-known subtitling feature, complete with freedom of type style. Copy some formatted text from a word processor; highlight a slice of footage in QuickTime Player; press Option; and choose Edit→Add. The copied text appears as a subtitle on a black band, beneath the picture, as shown here.

Saving the finished movie

After you've finished working on your sound or movie, you can send it back out into the world in any of several ways. If you choose Edit→Save As, for example, you can specify a new name for your edited masterpiece. You must also choose one of these two options:

- **Save normally.** The term "normally" is a red herring—in fact, you'll almost never want to use this option, which produces a very tiny QuickTime file that contains no footage at all. Instead, it's something like an alias of the movie you edited—the "Save normally" edited file works only as long as the original, unedited movie remains on your hard drive. If you try to email the newly saved file, your unhappy recipient won't see anything at all.

- **Make movie self-contained.** This option produces a new QuickTime movie—the one you've just finished editing. Although it consumes more disk space, it has none of the drawbacks of the "save normally" file described above.

Exporting the finished work

Instead of using the File→Save As command, you can also use the File→Export command. The resulting dialog box offers two pop-up menus that can be very useful in tailoring your finished work for specific purposes:

- **Export.** Using this pop-up menu, you can convert your movie to AVI (Windows movie) format, DV Stream (for use as a clip in digital-video editing programs like iMovie and Final Cut), Image Sequence (which produces a very large collec-

---

GEM IN THE ROUGH

QuickTime Virtual Reality

If they live to be 100, most Mac users will probably never encounter a *QuickTime VR* movie. Yet this kind of "panorama movie" technology is built into every Mac.

The trick is *finding* a QuickTime VR movie; your best bet is, as usual, the Web. (The best starting point is Apple's own QuickTime VR page, *www.apple.com/ quicktime/qtvr.*)

When you open a QuickTime VR movie, you might think at first that you've simply opened a still photo; there's no scroll bar, for example. The trick is to *drag* your cursor around inside the photo. Doing so rotates the "camera," permitting you to look around you in all directions.

Then try pressing the Shift key, to zoom in (move forward) as much as you like. If you go too far, the image gets too grainy. Press the Control key to zoom out (move backwards).

And if you really want to blow your mind, try one of the *cubic* VR movies posted on that Web page. It lets you rotate your view not just side to side, but also up to the sky and down to your feet.

Using the free and commercial tools listed on the Apple Web site, you can even make your own QuickTime VR movies—provided you've got a camera, tripod, and a good deal of patience.

---

tion of individual still frames), and so on. This pop-up menu also lets you convert a sound you've been working on to AIFF, System 7, Wave (Windows), and other formats.

• **Use.** This pop-up menu lets you establish your preferences for the export format you've just specified above. For example, if you're exporting your movie as individual still frames, you can use this pop-up menu to specify the format for those individual still frames—BMP (Windows format), JPEG, and so on. If you're exporting your work as a QuickTime movie, you can specify how much QuickTime Player should compress it. (Compression makes a file much smaller, but decreases the video quality.) For example, if you intend to let people watch this movie over the Internet, you should use one of the Streaming options, which makes the movie extremely small and extremely cruddy-looking. If you plan to burn your movie onto a CD-ROM, use one of the "CD-ROM" options at the bottom of the pop-up menu.

Compression and special effects

One of QuickTime Player's most powerful features is hidden in the Export dialog box, in a place where you might never find it. If none of the canned compression settings appeals to you, you can click the Options button in this dialog box. In the Settings dialog box that appears (see Figure 14-10), QuickTime Player Pro offers a staggering degree of control over the movie you're exporting.

Figure 14-10:
If you're used to standard moviemaking software, such as Adobe Premiere or Final Cut, you may have wondered where QuickTime Player hides its compression settings. They're here, in the Options dialog box (left) and the Settings boxes that spring from within it (right).

Hint: For smooth playback, use 15 frames per second or above; for best quality but small file size, use the Sorenson 3 Video Compressor; for the smallest possible file size—at more picture-quality sacrifice—use the Cinepak compressor.

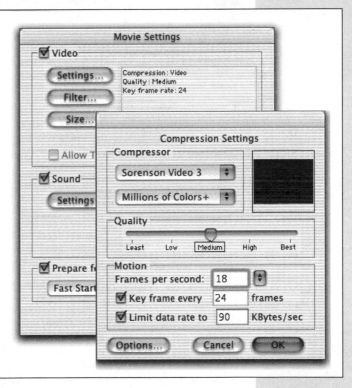

When exporting a movie, for example, here's where you can specify what *compression format* you want to use, how many frames per second you want, and (by clicking Size) what dimensions you want the finished movie to have. As a bonus, you even get a Filter button that offers fourteen special video effects. They let you blur or sharpen your movie, adjust the brightness or contrast, fiddle with the color balance, and so on.

Similarly, when you're exporting a sound file, the Options button lets you specify what sound quality you want, what compression method, and so on—all various ways of manipulating the trade-off between file size and sound quality.

Speech Recognition

Although it comes as a surprise to many Mac users, the Mac is quite talented when it comes to speech. Its abilities fall into two categories: reading text aloud, using a synthesized voice; and taking commands from your voice.

The Apple marketing machine may have been working too hard when it called this feature "speech recognition"—the Mac OS feature called PlainTalk doesn't take dictation, typing out what you say. (For that, you need a program like IBM ViaVoice for Mac OS X, *www.ibm.com*.)

Instead, PlainTalk is what's known as a *command-and-control* program. It lets you open programs, trigger AppleScripts, and click menu items by speaking their names.

Few people use PlainTalk speech recognition. But if your Mac has a microphone, as described on page 348, PlainTalk is worth at least a 15-minute test drive; it may become a part of your work routine forever.

Your First Conversation with the Mac

The on/off switch for speech recognition in Mac OS X is the Speech panel of System Preferences (Figure 14-12). Where you see "Apple Speakable Items is," click On. (The first time you do this, a small instructions window appears. Read it if you like, and then click Continue. If you ever want to see these tips again, click the Helpful Tips button on this pane.)

The Feedback window

Check out the right side of your screen: a small, round, microphone-ish floating window now appears (Figure 14-11). The word *Esc* in its center indicates the "listen" key—the key you're supposed to hold down when you want the Mac to respond to your voice. (You wouldn't want the Mac listening all the time—even when you said, for example, "Hey, it's cold in here. *Close the window.*" Therefore, the Mac comes ready to listen to you only when you're pressing that key.)

You can specify a different key, if you wish, or eliminate the requirement to press a key altogether, as described in the next section.

When you start talking, you'll also see the Mac's interpretation of what you said written out in a yellow balloon just over the Feedback window.

Tip: The Feedback window lacks the standard Close and Minimize buttons. If it's in your way, just double-click it (or say "minimize speech window") to shrink it onto your Dock.

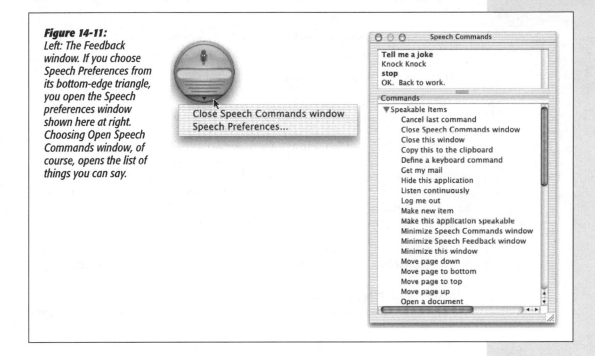

Figure 14-11:
Left: The Feedback window. If you choose Speech Preferences from its bottom-edge triangle, you open the Speech preferences window shown here at right. Choosing Open Speech Commands window, of course, opens the list of things you can say.

The Speakable Commands window

Here's the most important single fact to understand about PlainTalk speech recognition: the only commands it understands are what's listed in the Speakable Commands window, which generally appears automatically when you turn on speech recognition.

Especially when you're first using PlainTalk, the Speakable Commands window is handy: it offers a complete list of everything your Mac understands. As you can see, some of them represent shortcuts that would take several steps if you had to perform them manually.

To open this list if it's not open, click the tiny arrow at the bottom of the Feedback window and choose Open Speech Commands Window from the commands that appear. Here are a few examples of what you'll find in the list:

- **Open Sherlock.** Launches the Sherlock file-finding program, as described in Chapter 20, saving you the trouble of using a menu or keystroke to open it.

- **Close this window.** Closes the frontmost window instantly.

- **Empty the trash.** This one works only when you're in the Finder.

- **Switch to AppleWorks.** Actually, you can say "switch to" and the name of *any* running or recently used program.

- **Quit all applications.** Saves you the trouble of switching into each program and choosing Quit.

- **Open the Speech Commands window** or **Show me what to say.** Opens the Speech Commands window, of course.

- **What day is it?** Tells you the date.

- **Tell me a joke.** Begins a pathetic/funny knock-knock joke. You've got to play along, providing the "who's there?" and "so-and-so *who?*" answers.

Through all of this, Mac OS X updates the listing in the Speech Commands window in real time, according to the context. When you switch from one program to another, you see a list of the local commands that work in the new program. You'll discover that when you use the "Tell me a joke" command, for example, you don't necessarily have to say, "Who's there?" You can also say "Stop," "Go away," or "Stop with the jokes!" (It must really be fun to work at Apple.)

The commands listed in this window aren't the only ones you can speak, of course. You'll find out how to create new commands of your own later in this section.

Speaking to the Mac

When you decide you're ready to try talking to your computer, position the microphone between one and three feet from your mouth. If it's a headset, make sure it's plugged in. If it's built in, speech recognition may not be as accurate.

In any case, finish up by opening the Speech panel of System Preferences. Click the Listening tab, and use the Microphone pop-up menu to specify which microphone you'll be using (if you have a choice).

Now you're ready to begin. While pressing the Esc key (if that's still the one identified in the Feedback window), begin speaking. Speak normally; don't exaggerate or shout. Try one of the commands in the Speakable Commands list—perhaps "What time is it?" If the Feedback window doesn't show animated sound waves, indicating that the Mac is hearing you, something's wrong with your microphone setup. Open the Speech panel again, and confirm that the correct microphone is selected.

You'll probably find that speech recognition has come a long way in Mac OS X. Even on slower machines, recognition is snappy, and commands are executed faster.

Customizing Speech Recognition

You can tailor the speech recognition feature in two ways—by adjusting the way it looks and operates, and by adding new commands to its vocabulary.

Changing when the Mac listens

Early experimentation quickly showed Apple's speech engineers that having the microphone "open," listening full-time, was an invitation for disaster. Everyday phone conversations, office chatter, and throat clearings completely bewildered the software, triggering random commands.

Therefore, you must explicitly *tell* the Mac when you're addressing it. When you first turn on the speech recognition feature, the Mac expects you to get its attention by pressing a key when you speak, such as the Esc key.

Tip: To change the key you hold down when you want the Mac to listen, visit the Speech panel of System Preferences; click the Listening tab, and then click Change Key. A little message prompts you to press the keyboard key you'd prefer to use. Your choices are Esc, tilde (~), Delete, F5 through F15 (not including the Eject key), or the keys on your numeric keypad—with or without the Shift, Control, or Option keys.

If you'd rather not have to press some key whenever you want the computer's attention, click the other option in this box, "Key toggles listening on and off" (see Figure 14-12). Now you must get the computer's attention by speaking its name—which you type into the Name box—before each command. For example, you might say, "Computer, open AppleWorks," or "Hal, what day is it?"

The name you specify appears in the middle of the round Feedback window.

Note: This method of getting the computer's attention is less reliable than the push-a-key-to-talk system. *Especially* if you name the computer Hal; although that's hilarious in theory, polysyllabic names work better in practice.

Using the "Name is" pop-up menu, meanwhile, you can specify how big your window of opportunity is:

- **Optional before each command.** If you work alone in a quiet room, this is the choice for you. It means that you don't have to press a key *or* say the Mac's name when issuing a voice command. *Everything you say* is considered a command.

- **Required before each command.** When this option is selected, nothing you say is interpreted as a command unless you say the computer's name first, as in, "*Macintosh,* switch to Microsoft Word."

- **Required 15 seconds after last command, Required 30 seconds after last command.** Sometimes you want to issue several commands in a row, and would feel foolish saying, "Computer, close all windows. Computer, empty the trash. Computer, switch to AppleWorks." When you turn on this option, you can say the computer's name just once; all commands that you issue in the next 15 or 30 seconds "belong to" that first salutation. The push-to-talk key and the spoken name, in this case, serve as a master on/off switch for the Mac's listening mode.

Tip: If you're not using the push-to-talk method, you can still turn speech recognition off temporarily by saying, "Turn on push to talk." (Now the Mac listens to you only when you're pressing the designated key.) When you want to return to listening-all-the-time mode, say, "Listen continuously."

Finally, note that the Speech pane also lets you turn off recognition completely. On the On/Off tab, click Off (see Figure 14-12). On the other hand, if you really love the speech feature, you can save yourself the trouble of visiting this control panel each morning by turning on "Open Speakable Items at login." (Never mind the wording of this button. It doesn't actually open your Speakable Items folder; it simply means that speech recognition will be turned on and "listening" as soon as you log in.)

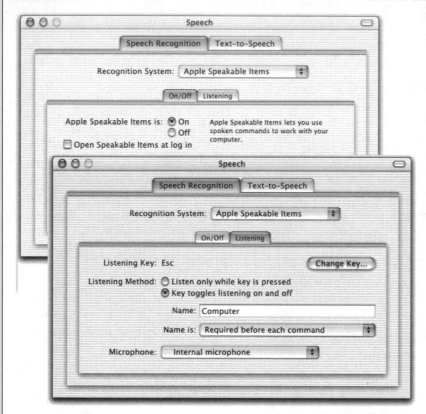

Figure 14-12:
Top: Turn off listening altogether using the On/Off tab.

Bottom: If you turn on "Key toggle listening on and off," then you don't have to press a key to make the Mac listen. (Instead, pressing the designated key turns the speech recognition feature on or off completely.) In the Name blank, type the name you want the Mac to listen for as it monitors the sound from your mike.

Changing the feedback

Another set of options in the Speech panel governs what the Mac does when it understands something that you've said. For example:

- **Speak text feedback.** Sometimes the Speech Feedback window shows you a message of its own—when you use the "Empty the trash" command, for example, text in the Feedback window may inform you that a locked item prevents the emptying. The Mac generally reads this text aloud to you; turn this checkbox off if you'd rather have the Mac be silent.

- **Play sound when recognized.** The Mac generally makes a sound whenever it recognizes something you've said. Use this pop-up menu to control which of your built-in your beeps you want it to use—or choose None.

Note: Looking for the cute little cartoon characters in the Feedback window that, in Mac OS 9, reacted to the things you said? Forget about it—Apple got much more serious in Mac OS X.

Improving the PlainTalk vocabulary

As you'll soon discover, PlainTalk has an extremely limited vocabulary—in fact, it understands *only* the names of the icons in your Home folder→Library→Speakable Items folder. Behind the scenes, all PlainTalk can ever really do is *open* things.

At first, you might imagine that this limitation means that PlainTalk can do little more than open programs or documents—"Open AppleWorks," "Open Internet Explorer," and so on. And indeed, that's one of PlainTalk's primary functions. By putting an alias of the favorite document, folder, disk, or program into the Speakable Items folder, you've just taught PlainTalk to recognize its name, and to open it for you on command. (You can name these icons anything you want. You can also rename the starter set that Apple provides. You'll have the best luck with multi-word or polysyllabic names—"Microsoft Word," not just "Word.")

But one kind of icon PlainTalk can open is an *AppleScript* icon, of the sort you create by following the instructions in Chapter 7. If you open your Home folder→Library→Speech→Speakable Items, you'll discover that most of the built-in speakable-item icons are, in fact, AppleScript icons. The point is that you can make PlainTalk do almost anything you want, especially in the Finder, simply by creating AppleScripts and putting them into the Speakable Items folder.

Tip: You can trigger any menu command in any program by voice—as long as it has a keyboard equivalent listed in the menu. To set this up, just say, "Define a keyboard command." When the "Press the keys" dialog box appears, press the keyboard combination you want (⌘-S, for example). Click OK; in the next dialog box, type the phrase you'll want to trigger that command (and use the "Use command in" controls to specify whether it should be a global command or one that works only in the current program). Click Save. Your new "spoken keystroke" is ready to use.

Application-specific commands

Most of the preinstalled PlainTalk commands work in any program. You can say, for example, "Open Sherlock" to launch Sherlock from within any program.

However, you can also create commands that work only in a specific program. They sit in your Speakable Items→Application Speakable Items folder, inside individual application-name folders. For example, Mac OS X comes with commands for Internet Explorer that include Go Back, Go Forward, and Page Down.

If you get good at AppleScript, you can create your own application-command folders in the Speakable Items→Application Speakable Items folder. Follow these steps:

1. **Launch the program for which you want to create special commands.**

    Make sure PlainTalk is on and listening.

---

2. Say, "Make this application speakable."

   The Mac creates a folder for the program in the Speakable Items folder.

3. Drag the AppleScripts you've created into the newly created Speakable Items→[application name] folder.

Of course, not every program is equally suitable to being voice-controlled—since PlainTalk is based on AppleScript, only programs that are AppleScriptable (Chapter 7) thrive with this treatment.

Tip: If you give an application-specific icon the exact same name as one of the global commands, the Mac executes the application-specific one—if that program is running.

PlainTalk tips, tricks, and troubleshooting

When you're creating new commands, keep this advice in mind:

- Favor longer icon names. "Save the file" works better than "Save."

- If the name of an icon includes an acronym (such as *FTP)*, put spaces between the letters (F T P), if you'll be pronouncing them as individual letters.

- You can precede the name of something in your Speakable Items folder with the word "Open." PlainTalk doesn't care—"open Excel" and "Excel" do the same thing.

If you can't seem to make the speech recognition feature work, consider this checklist:

- If the stripes on the bottom half of the Feedback window don't change color when you're speaking, something's wrong with your microphone arrangement. Revisit the Speech panel of System Preferences, and make sure you've selected the correct microphone. Also make sure you've plugged the microphone into the correct jack on the back or side of the computer.

- Make sure you're pressing the correct key (if you're using the push-to-talk method), or speaking the name of the computer before each command (if not).

- Make sure you're saying the name of the working command, as listed either in the Speakable Commands window (which appears when you say "Show me what to say") or the Speech Commands list.

The Mac Talks Back

So far in this chapter, you've read about the Mac's listening ability. But the conversation doesn't have to be one-way. It's even easier to make the Mac talk.

In fact, the Mac can read almost anything that appears on the screen, using your choice of eighteen synthesizer voices. The Mac's voice comes out of its speakers, reading with a twangy, charmingly Norwegian accent.

Setting Up the Mac's Voice

To configure the way the Mac talks, revisit the Speech panel of System Preferences. Click the Text-to-Speech tab at the top of the window. As you can see in Figure 14-13, you can control which of the Mac's eighteen voices you want your computer to use, as well as how fast it should speak.

As with the other aspects of Mac OS speech, this one is filled with whimsical touches. Four of the voices, as it turns out, *sing* rather than speaking. (They're Good News, which sings to the tune of "Pomp and Circumstance," otherwise known as the Graduation March; Bad News, which sings to the tune of the Chopin Prelude in C minor, better known as the Funeral March; Cellos, which sings to the tune of Grieg's "Peer Gynt" suite; and Pipe Organ, which sings to the tune of the Alfred Hitchcock TV theme.)

In other words, these voices sing whatever words you type to those melodies. (To hear the melody in its entirety, don't use any punctuation.)

Where to Use Text-to-Speech

In the old days of Mac OS 9, quite a few programs had, buried in their Preferences commands, options to make them speak the text on the screen: AppleWorks, America Online, Microsoft Word, FileMaker Pro, and so on. Unfortunately, the Mac OS X versions of many of these programs lack this feature. But here are a few that are still chatty:

Figure 14-13:
For 15 minutes of hilarious fun, try clicking the Mac's voices in turn (or press the up and down arrow keys) to hear a sample sentence spoken in that voice. Drag the slider to affect how fast he or she speaks. (Clearly, Apple's programmers had some fun with this assignment.)

Mail

It's easy to make Mac OS X's email program (Chapter 19) read your messages aloud. Just Control-click inside a message window. From the pop-up menu, choose Speech→Start Speaking. (Choose Speech→Stop Speaking when you've heard enough.)

AppleWorks 6

To add the Speak Text button to your button bar, choose Edit→Preferences→Button Bar. In the Customize Button Bars dialog box, scroll down to the Word Processing triangle; click it. Scroll down even more, until you see the Speak Text button. Drag it out of the dialog box and onto the button bar. Click Done.

The icon you clicked now appears on the button bar whenever a word processing document is open. Click it to hear your Mac speak any highlighted piece of text, once again using the voice you've selected in the Speech preference panel.

FileMaker Pro

You can use the Speak script command to build speech features into a FileMaker database. You can read about this script command in FileMaker's built-in help; it's worth noting, however, that you can have it speak either a canned phrase or the contents of a database field. You can also specify which voice you want to use.

GEM IN THE ROUGH

Talking to Chess

If your friends and co-workers are, for some reason, still unimpressed by Mac OS X and your mastery of it, invite them over to watch you play a game of chess with your Mac—by *talking* to it.

Open the Chess program (which is described on page 208). Unless you've turned it off (in Chess→Preferences), the game's speech recognition feature is already turned on. When it's on, the round Feedback window should be visible on the screen.

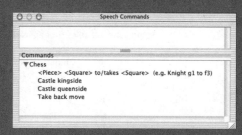

To learn how to speak commands in a way that Chess will understand, click the small gray triangle at the bottom of the Speech Feedback panel to open the Speech Commands window. As usual, it lists all the commands that Chess can comprehend.

You specify the location of pieces using the grid of numbers and letters that appear along the edges of the chessboard. The White King, for example, starts on square e1 because he's in the first row (1) and the fifth column (e). To move the King forward by one square, you'd say: "King e1 to e2."

Actually, although it doesn't, for some reason, seem quite as satisfying, you can leave off the name of the piece you want to move (Pawn, Knight, and so on). It's perfectly OK to call out the square locations only ("g3 to f5").

As the Speech Commands window should make clear, a few other commands are at your disposal. "Take back move" is one of the most useful. When you're ready to close in for the kill, the syntax is: "Pawn e5 takes f6."

And smile when you say that.

Terminal:
The Unix Window

A s you're certainly aware by now, Mac OS X's resemblance to the traditional
Mac operating system is only superficial. The engine underneath the pretty
skin is utterly different. In fact, it's Unix, one of the oldest and most re-
spected operating systems in use today.

The first time you see it, you'd swear that Unix has about as much in common with
the traditional Mac OS as a Jeep does to a melon (see Figure 15-1).

Figure 15-1:
*Top: What most people think of
when they think "Macintosh" is a
graphic interface: one that you
control with a mouse, using menus
and icons to represent files and
commands.*

*Bottom: Terminal offers a second
way to control Mac OS X: a
command line interface, meaning
you operate it by typing out
programming codes.*

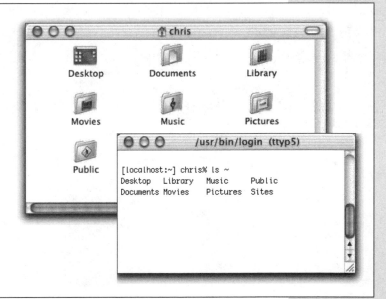

What the illustration at the bottom of Figure 15-1 shows, of course, is a *command line interface:* a place where you can type out instructions to the computer itself. This is a world without icons, menus, or dialog boxes; even the mouse is almost useless.

Surely you can appreciate the irony: The brilliance of the original 1984 Macintosh was that it *eliminated* the command line interface that was still the ruling party on the computers of the day (like Apple II and DOS machines). Most non-geeks sighed with relief, delighted that they'd never have to memorize commands again. Yet here's Mac OS X, Apple's supposedly ultramodern operating system, complete with a command line! What's going on?

UP TO SPEED

Mac OS X's Unix Roots

In 1969, Bell Labs programmer Ken Thompson found himself with some spare time after his main project, an operating system called Multics, was canceled. Bell Labs had withdrawn from the expensive project, disappointed with the results after four years of work.

But Thompson still thought the project—an OS that worked well as a cooperative software-development environment—was a good idea. Eventually, he and colleague Dennis Ritchie came up with the OS that would soon be called Unix (a pun on Multics). Bell Labs saw the value of Unix, agreed to support further development, and became the first corporate users.

In the age when Thompson and Ritchie started their work on Unix, most programmers wrote code that would work on only one kind of computer (or even one computer *model*). Unix, however, was one of the first *portable* operating systems: its programs could run on different kinds of computers without being rewritten. That's because Thompson and Ritchie wrote Unix using a new programming language of their own invention called *C.*

Programmers need only write their code once, in a language like C. After that, a software Cuisinart called a *compiler* can convert the newly hatched software into the form a particular computer model can understand.

Unix soon found its way into labs and, thanks to AT&T's low academic licensing fees, universities around the world. Programmers all over the world added to the source code,

fixed bugs, and then passed those modifications around.

In the mid-1970s, the University of California at Berkeley became the site of especially intense Unix development. Students and faculty there improved the Unix *kernel* (the central, essential part of the OS), added features to the OS, and wrote new Unix applications. By 1977, they had enough additional software to release their own version of Unix, the first of what would be several *Berkeley Software Distribution* (BSD) versions.

As it happened, the government's Defense Advanced Research Projects Agency (DARPA) was looking for a uniform, portable OS to use for their growing wide-area network, originally called ARPAnet (and now called the Internet).

DARPA liked Unix and agreed to sponsor further research at Berkeley. In January 1983, DARPA changed ARPAnet's networking protocol to TCP/IP—and the Internet was born, running mostly on Unix machines.

In 1985, Steve Jobs left Apple to start NeXT Computer, whose NextStep operating system was based on BSD Unix. When Apple bought NeXT in 1996, Jobs, NextStep (eventually renamed OpenStep), and its Terminal program came along with it. The Unix that beats within Mac OS X's heart is just the latest resting place for the OS Jobs's team developed at NeXT.

The next time you hear Apple talk about its "new" operating system, in other words, remember that its underlying technology is actually over 30 years old.

Actually, the command line never went away. At universities and corporations worldwide, professional computer nerds kept right on pounding away at the little *C:* or *%* prompts, appreciating the efficiency and power such direct computer control gave them.

You're to be forgiven if your reaction to the concept of learning Unix is, "For goodness' sake—can't I finish learning one way to control my new operating system before I have to learn yet another one?"

Absolutely. You never *have* to use Mac OS X's command line. In fact, Apple has swept it far under the rug, obviously expecting that most people will use the beautiful icons and menus of the regular desktop.

But for intermediate or advanced Mac fans with a little time and curiosity, the command line opens up a world of possibilities. It lets you access corners of Mac OS X that you can't get to from the regular desktop. It lets you perform certain tasks with much greater speed and efficiency than you'd get by clicking and dragging icons. And it gives you a fascinating glimpse into the minds and moods of people who live and breathe computers.

If you've ever fooled around with ResEdit, experimented with AppleScript, or set up a Mac on a network, you already know the technical level of the material you're about to read. The Unix command line may be *unfamiliar,* but it doesn't have to be especially technical, particularly if you have some "recipes" to follow like the ones in this chapter and the next.

Note: Unix is, of course, an entire operating system unto itself. This chapter is designed to help you find your footing and decide whether or not you like the feel of Unix. If you get bit by the bug, see Appendix E for some sources of additional Unix info.

Terminal

The keyhole into Mac OS X's Unix innards is a program called Terminal, which sits in your Applications→Utilities folder (see Figure 15-2). Terminal is named after the terminals (computers that consist of only a monitor and keyboard) that tap into the mainframe computers at universities and corporations. In the same way, Terminal is just a window that passes along messages to and from the Mac's brain.

The first time you open Terminal, there's not much in its window except its *command line prompt* (Figure 15-2). For user-friendliness fans, Terminal doesn't get off to a very good start; this prompt looks about as technical as computers get. It breaks down like this:

- **localhost:** is the name of your Mac (at least, as Unix thinks of it). Don't worry that it doesn't match the name you gave your hard drive. Just rest assured that almost everyone sees the phrase *[localhost:~]* at the beginning of the prompt.

- ~ indicates what folder you're "in" (see Figure 15-2). It denotes the *working directory*—that is, the current folder. Remember, there are no icons in Unix. This notation tells you where you are as you navigate your machine.

As you may remember from page 378, the tilde symbol (~) is shorthand for "your own Home folder." It's what you see the first time you start up Terminal, but you'll soon be seeing the names of other folders here—*[localhost /Users]* or *[localhost /System/Library]*, for example. (More on this slash notation on page 378.)

Note: Before Apple came up with the user-friendly term *folder* to represent an electronic holding tank for files, folders were called *directories.* (Yes, they mean the same thing.) But in this chapter and the next, you'll encounter the term *directory* almost exclusively. In any discussion of Unix, "directory" is simply the correct term.

And besides, using a term like "working *folder"* within earshot of Unix geeks is likely to get you lynched.

- **chris%** begins with your short user name (page 277). It reflects whoever's logged into the shell, which is usually whoever's logged into the Mac at the moment. As for the % sign: think of it as a colon. In fact, think of the whole prompt shown in Figure 15-2 as Unix's way of asking, "OK, Chris, I'm listening. What's your pleasure?"

Unless you've fiddled with Terminal's preferences, the insertion point looks like a block, a tall rectangle at the end of the command line. It trots along to the right as you type.

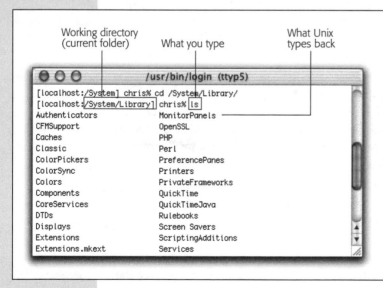

Working directory (current folder)   What you type   What Unix types back

Figure 15-2:
On the Web, Mac OS X's Terminal is one of the most often discussed elements of Mac OS X. Dozens of step-by-step tutorials for performing certain tasks circulate online, usually without much annotation as to why you're typing what you're typing.

As you read this chapter, remember that capitalization matters in Terminal, even though it doesn't in the Finder. As far as Unix commands are concerned, Hello *and* hello *are two very different things.*

Unix Programs

An enormous number of programs have been written for Unix. And thanks to thousands of open-source developers—programmers all over the world who collaborate and make their work available for the next round of modification—much of this software is freely available to all, including Mac OS X users.

Each Unix command generally calls up a single application (or *process*, as geeks call it) that launches, performs a task, and closes. Many of the best known such applications come with Mac OS X.

Here's a fun one: Just type *uptime* and press Enter or Return. (That's how you run a Unix program: just type its name and press Enter). On the next line, Terminal shows you how long your Mac has been turned on continuously. It shows you something like: "6:00PM up 8 days, 15:04, 1 user, load averages: 1.24, 1.37, 1.45"—meaning your Mac has been running for 8 days, 15 hours nonstop.

You're finished running the *uptime* program. The % prompt returns, suggesting that Terminal is ready for whatever you throw at it next.

Try this one: Type *cal* at the prompt, and then press Enter. Unix promptly spits out a calendar of the current month:

```
[localhost:~] chris% cal
      September 2002
 S  M Tu  W Th  F  S
 1  2  3  4  5  6  7
 8  9 10 11 12 13 14
15 16 17 18 19 20 21
22 23 24 25 26 27 28
29 30
[localhost:~] chris%
```

POWER USERS' CLINIC

Of Terminal and Shells

One Unix program runs automatically when you open a Terminal window: *tcsh* (pronounced "T.C. Shell").

Technically, a *shell* is a Unix program that interprets the commands you've typed, passes them to the *kernel* (the operating system's brain), and then shows you the kernel's response.

But more practically, the shell is the Unix Finder. It's the program that lets you navigate the contents of your hard drive, see what's inside certain folders, launch programs and documents, and so on. (There are actually several different shells available in Unix, each with slightly different command syntax. A few others—like sh, zsh, and csh—come with Mac OS X, but Terminal comes set to use tcsh.)

You can open additional Terminal windows (31 max) by choosing Shell→New. Each window runs independently of any others. For proof, try opening several windows and then running the *cal* command in each.

This time, try typing *cal 11 2002, cal -y,* or *cal -yj.* These three commands make Unix generate a calendar of November 2002, a calendar of the current year, and a *Julian* calendar of the current year, respectively.

Tip: The mouse isn't very useful at the command line. You generally move the cursor only with the left and right arrow keys. (The Delete key works as it always does.)

You *can* use the mouse, however, to select text from anywhere in the window (or other programs) and paste it in at the prompt. You can also use the mouse to drag an icon off your desktop into the Terminal window, as shown in Figure 15-3. And in the Terminal→Preferences→Emulation dialog box, you'll find an option that lets you Option-click in a command line to plant the insertion point there.

Navigating in Unix

If you can't see any icons for your files and folders, how are you supposed to work with them?

You have no choice but to ask Unix to tell you what folder you're looking at (using the *pwd* command), what's in it (using the *ls* command), and what folder you want to switch to (using the *cd* command), as described in the following pages.

pwd (print working directory, or "Where am I?")

Here's one of the most basic navigation commands: *pwd,* which stands for *print working directory.* The *pwd* command doesn't actually print anything on your printer; instead, the *pwd* command types out, on the screen, the *path* of the folder Unix thinks you're in (the working directory).

Try typing *pwd* and pressing Enter. On the next line, Terminal may show you something like this:

Pathnames 101

In some ways, Unix is just like the Finder: Its System folder encloses a bunch of other folders, which in turn contain other folders.

In this chapter and the next, you'll be asked to specify a certain file or folder in this tree of folders. But you can't see their icons from the command line. So how are you supposed to identify the file or folder you want?

By typing its *pathname.* The pathname is a string of folder names, something like a map, that takes you from the *root*

level to the next nested folder, to the next, and so on. (The root level is, for learning-Unix purposes, the equivalent of your main hard drive window. It's represented in Unix by a single slash. The phrase */Users,* in other words, means "the Users folder in my hard drive window"—or, in other terms, "the Users directory at the root level.")

To refer to the Documents folder in your own Home folder, for example, you could type */Users/chris/Documents* (if your name is Chris, that is).

MAC OS X: THE MISSING MANUAL

```
/Users/chris/Movies
```

Terminal is showing you the working directory's *path*—a list of folders-in-folders, separated by slashes, that specifies a folder's location on your hard drive. */Users/chris/Movies* pinpoints the Movies folder in Chris's Home folder (which, like all Home folders, is in the Users directory).

Tip: Capitalization counts in Unix. Command names are almost always all lowercase (like *cal* and *pwd*). But when you type the names of folders, be sure to capitalize correctly.

---

ls (list, or "What's in here?")

The *ls* command, short for *list*, makes Terminal type out the names of all the files and folders in the folder you're in (that is, your working directory). You can try it right now: just type *ls* and then press Enter. Terminal responds by showing you the names of the files and folders inside in a horizontal list, like this:

```
Desktop Documents Library Movies Music  Pictures Public Sites
```

In other words, you see a list of the icons that, in the Finder, you'd see in your Home folder.

Note: Terminal respects the limits of the various Mac OS X accounts (Chapter 11); in other words, a Normal or Administrator account holder isn't generally allowed to peek into someone else's Home folder. If you try, you'll be told: "Permission denied."

You can also make Terminal list what's in any other directory (one that's *not* the working directory) just by adding its pathname as an *argument*. An argument tells the command *what* to work on. (Remember the Calendar example? When you wanted the November 2002 calendar, you typed *cal 11 2002*. The "11 2002" part was the argument.)

If you want to see a list of the files in your Documents directory, then, you could just type *ls /Users/chris/Documents*. Better yet, because the ~ symbol is short for "my home directory," you could save typing with *ls ~/Documents*. The pathname "~/Documents" is an argument that you've fed the *ls* command.

Tip: Pressing the Tab key at any prompt is another quick way to see what's in the working folder. You don't even have to type *ls*.

About flags

Between a command and its arguments, you can sometimes insert *option flags* (also called *switches*)—short modifying phrases that affect how the command works. In the Calendar example, for example, you can type *cal -y* to see a full-year calendar; the *-y* part is an option flag.

Option flags are almost always preceded by a hyphen (-), although you can usually run several flags together following just one hyphen, like this: *ls -ai* (that is, both the *-a* and *-i* flags are in effect).

Here are some useful options for the *ls* command:

- **-a.** The *ls* command even shows you the names of *invisible* files and folders—at least by the Finder's definition. The Unix shell uses its own system of denoting invisible files and folders, and ignores the Finder's. That doesn't mean you're seeing everything; files that are invisible by the Unix definition still don't show up.

  You can use one of the *ls* command's flags, however, to force even Unix-invisible files to show up. Just add the *-a* flag. In other words, type this: *ls -a.* When you press Enter, you might see something like this:

  ```
  .       Desktop         Movies      Public
  ..      Documents       Music       Sites
  .       CFUserTextEncoding Library  Pictures
  ```

- **-F.** As you see, the names of invisible Unix files all begin with a period (Unix folk call them *dot files*). But are these files or folders? To find out, use *ls* with the *-F* option (capitalization counts), like this: *ls -aF Movies.* You're shown something like this:

  ```
  ./ Picnic Movie 1 Yosemite/     Reviews.doc
  ../  Picnic Movie 2 Tahoe/
  ```

  The names of the items themselves haven't changed, but the *-F* flag makes slashes appear on directory (folder) names. This example shows that there are four directories and one file in *~/Movies* (that is, the *Movies* folder in your home directory).

- **-R.** The -R flag produces a *recursive* listing—one that shows you the directories *within* the directories in the list. If you type *ls -R,* for example, you might get something like this:

  ```
  Bad Reviews.doc  Old Tahoe Footage 2 Picnic Movie 2
  Reviews.doc

  ./Old Tahoe Footage 2:
  Tahoe 1.mov    Tahoe 3.mov    Tahoe Project File
  Tahoe 2.mov    Tahoe 4.mov

  ./Picnic Movie 2:
  Icon?       Media       Picnic Movie 2 Project

  ./Picnic Movie 2/Media:
  Picnic Movie 1 Picnic Movie 3 Picnic Movie 5
  Picnic Movie 2 Picnic Movie 4 Picnic Movie 6
  ```

Tip: As you can tell by the *cal* and *ls* examples, Unix commands are very short. The reason has partly to do with conserving the limited memory of early computers and partly to do with efficiency: most programmers would just as soon type as little as possible to get things done. User-friendly it ain't, but as you find yourself having to type these commands over and over again over the months, you'll eventually be grateful for the keystroke savings.

cd (change directory, or "Let me see another folder")

Now you know how to find out what directory you're in, and how to see what's in it, all without double-clicking any icons. That's great information, but it's just information. How do you *do* something in your command-line Finder—like switching to a different directory?

To change your working directory, use the *cd* command, followed by the path of the directory you want to switch to. Want to see what's in the Movies directory of your home directory? Type *cd /Users/chris/Movies* and press Enter. The [localhost] prompt shows you what it considers to be the directory you're in now (the new working directory). If you perform an *ls* command at this point, Terminal will show you the contents of your Movies directory.

That's a lot of typing, of course. Fortunately, instead of typing out that whole path (the *absolute* path, as it's called), you can simply specify what directory you want to see *relative* to the directory you're already in.

TROUBLESHOOTING MOMENT

When You Get Stuck

When you're first learning Unix, it's easy to become frustrated. Here are some common ways you might find yourself derailed, and ways to get back on track.

You mistyped a command: Use the left and right arrow keys to move the cursor around the command line, or Option-click in the command line to move your cursor to that point. Use the Delete key as necessary and then re-type.

You get an error message: Error messages usually indicate a mistyped command. Just carefully enter the command again at the new prompt.

There is no new prompt, the shell seems to hang, or lines of text scroll continuously: Chances are you've inadvertently started a lengthy or chain-reaction process that requires a *break signal* to stop. Press ⌘-period or Ctrl-C to send that signal.

Terminal says "OK? ...?": The *tcsh* shell's built-in spelling checker is asking if it can make a correction. The command name after *OK?* is the one closest in spelling to what you typed. If the spelling checker has correctly guessed what you meant, type *y* for yes; if not, press Enter again.

You keep getting error messages when you type a command that includes a pathname: The pathname probably contains a space, slash, or another character that has a special meaning to Terminal. In that case, you have to enclose the pathname in single or double quotes (for example, *ls "New Files"*), or the command won't work.

"Permission denied" or "Operation not permitted": You're trying to use a command that requires an administrator or superuser's account (or just somebody else's account), as described in Chapter 11.

For example, if your Home folder is the working directory, the relative pathname of the Trailers directory inside the Movies directory would be *Movies/Trailers*. That's a lot shorter than typing out the full, absolute pathname (*/Users/chris/Movies/Trailers*).

If your brain isn't already leaking from the stress, here's a summary of three different ways you could switch from ~/ *(your home directory)* to ~/*Movies*:

- **cd /Users/chris/Movies.** That's the long way—the absolute pathname. It works no matter what your working directory is.

- **cd ~/Movies.** This, too, is an absolute pathname that you could type from anywhere. It relies on the ~ shorthand (which always means "my home directory").

- **cd Movies.** This streamlined *relative* path capitalizes on the fact that you're already in your home directory.

Tip: Actually, there's a fourth way to specify a directory that involves no typing at all: *drag the icon* of the directory you want to specify, directly into the Terminal window. Figure 15-3 should make this clear.

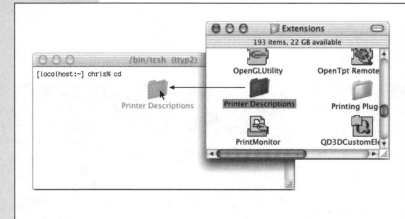

Figure 15-3:
This may be the quickest way of all to identify a directory or file you want to manipulate: don't type anything at all. You can drag icons directly from the desktop into a terminal window. The icon's pathname appears automatically at the insertion point. Terminal even adds backslashes to any special characters in these pathnames for you (a necessary step known as escaping the special characters).

. and .. (*dot* and *dot-dot,* or "Back me out")

So now you've burrowed into your Movies directory. How do you back out?

Sure, you could type out the full pathname of the directory that encloses Movies—if you had all afternoon. But there's a shortcut: you can type a period (.) or a double period (..) in any pathname. These shortcuts represent the *current directory* and its *parent directory* (the directory that contains it), respectively.

To go from your home directory up to */Users*, for example, you could just type *cd ..* (that is, *cd* followed by a space and two periods).

You can also use the dot-dot shortcut *repeatedly* to climb multiple directories at once, like this: *cd ../..*, which would mean "switch the working directory to the direc-

---

tory two layers out." If you were in your Movies directory, ../.. would change the working directory to the Users directory.

Another trick: You can mix the .. shortcut with actual directory names. For example, suppose your Movies directory contains two directories: Trailers and Shorts. Trailers is the current directory, but you want to switch to the Shorts directory. All you'd have to do is type *cd ../Shorts*, as illustrated in Figure 15-4.

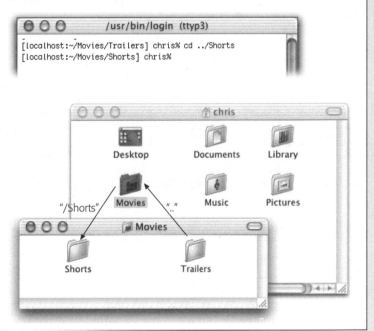

Figure 15-4:
The double dot tells Unix to switch its attention to the Movies directory (walking upward *through the directory tree); the rest tells it to walk* down *the Movies directory into the Shorts directory. Note that the prompt always identifies the current working directory.*

Keystroke-Saving Features

By now, you might be thinking that clicking icons would still be faster than doing all this typing. Here's where the typing shortcuts of the *tcsh* shell come in.

Tab completion

You know how you can highlight a file in a Finder window by typing the first few characters of its name? The tab-completion feature works much the same way. Over time, it can save you miles of finger movement.

It kicks in whenever you're about to type a pathname. Start by typing the first letter or two of the path you want, and then press Tab; Terminal instantly fleshes out the rest of the directory's name. As shown in Figure 15-5, you can repeat this process to specify the next directory-name chunk of the path.

Some tips for tab completion:

- Capitalization counts.

- Terminal will add backslashes automatically if your directory names include spaces, $ signs, or other special characters. But you still have to insert your own backslashes when you type the "hint" characters that tip off tab completion.

- If it can't find a match for what you typed, Terminal beeps.

  If it finds *several* files or directories that match what you typed, Terminal shows you a list of them. To specify the one you really wanted, type the next letter or two and then press Tab again.

Figure 15-5:
Top: You type cd /U *and then press Tab.*

Second from top: Terminal finishes the directory name Users *for you.*

Third from top: You type c *and then press Tab.*

Bottom: Terminal finishes the home-directory name chris.

You can also use tab completion to specify file names, as when you type ls -l Movies/R *and then press Tab; Terminal finishes the name* Reviews.doc.

Using the history
You may find yourself at some point needing to run a previously entered command and not enjoying the prospect of having to enter the whole command again. Retyping a command, however, is never necessary. Terminal (or, rather, the shell it's running) remembers the last 150 commands you entered. At any prompt, instead of typing, just press the up or down arrow keys to walk through the various commands in the shell's memory. They flicker by, one at a time, right there on the same line, at the % prompt.

Wildcards
Wildcards are special characters that represent other characters—and they're huge timesavers.

The most popular wildcard is the asterisk (*), which means "any text can go here." For example, if you wanted to see a list of the files in the working directory that end with the letters *te,* you could type *ls *te.* Terminal would show you files named

Yosemite, BudLite, Brigitte, and so on—and hide all other files in the list.

Likewise, to see which files and directories begin with "Old," you could type *ls Old** and press Enter. You'd be shown only the names of icons in the working directory called Old Yeller, Old Tahoe Footage, Olduvai Software, and so on.

If you add the asterisk before *and* after the search phrase, you find items with that phrase *anywhere* in their names. Typing *ls *jo** will show you the files named Johnson, Mojo, Major Disaster, and so on.

Tip: Using * by itself means "show me everything." To see a list of what's in a directory *and* in the directories *inside it* (as though you'd highlighted all the folders in a Finder list view and then pressed ⌘-right arrow), just type *ls **.

Directory switching

A hyphen (-) after the *cd* command means, "take me back to the previous working directory." For example, if you changed your working directory from *~/Movies/Movie 1* to *~/Documents/Letters*, simply enter *cd -* to change back to *~/Movies/Movie 1*. Use *cd -* a second time to return to *~/Documents/Letters*. (Note the space between *cd* and the hyphen.)

WORKAROUND WORKSHOP

No Spaces Allowed

Terminal doesn't see a space as a space. It thinks that a space means, for example, "I've just typed a command, and what follows is an argument." If you want to see what's in your Short Films directory, therefore, don't bother trying to type *ls ~/Movies/Short Films*. You'll get nothing but a "No such file or directory" error message. (See the space in the Short Films directory name?)

Similarly, $ signs have a special meaning in Unix. If you try to type one in a pathname (because a directory name contains $, for example), you'll have nothing but trouble.

Fortunately, you can work around this quirk by using a third reserved, or special, character: the backslash (\). It says, "Ignore the special meaning of the next character—a space, for example. I'm not using it for some special Unix meaning. I'm using the following space as, well, a space." (And if it's at a Unix user-group meeting, it might also say, "I'm *escaping* the space character.")

The correct way to see what's in your Short Films directory, then, would be *ls ~/Movies/Short\ Films*. (See how the backslash just before the space means, "This is just a space—keep it moving, folks"?)

Of course, if you have to enter a lot of text with spaces, it'd be a real pain to have to remember to type the backslash before every single one. Fortunately, you can instead enclose the whole mess with single quotation marks instead of using backslashes. That is, instead of typing this:

cd /Users/chris/My\ Documents/Letters\ to\ finish/Letter\ to\ Craig.doc

... you could just type this:

cd '/Users/chris/My Documents/Letters to finish/Letter to Craig.doc'.

It gets even more complicated—what if there's a single quote *in* the path? (Answer: protect *it* with double quotes.) But you have years of study ahead of you, grasshoppa.

Tip: On the other hand, if you're doing a lot of switching between directories, you should probably just open and switch between two Terminal windows, each with a different working directory.

The ~ shortcut

You already know that the tilde (~) character is a shortcut to your home directory. But you can also use it as a shortcut to somebody else's home directory—just tack on that person's account name. For example, to change to Miho's home directory, use *cd ~Miho*.

Special keys

The tcsh shell offers dozens of special keystroke shortcuts for navigation. You may recognize many of them as useful undocumented shortcuts that work in any Cocoa application (see page 116); but even more are available (and useful) in Terminal:

Keystroke	Effect
Ctrl-U	Erases the entire command line you're working on.
Ctrl-A	Moves the insertion point to the beginning of the line.
Ctrl-E	Moves the insertion point to the end of the line.
Ctrl-T	Transposes the previous two characters.
Esc-F	Moves the insertion point to the beginning of the next word.
Esc-B	Moves the insertion point to the beginning of the previous word.
Esc-Delete	Erases the previous word (defined as "anything that ends with a space, slash, or most other punctuation marks, periods and asterisks not included"). You have to press and release the Esc key and *then* the Delete key; repeat for each word.
Esc-D	Erases the word following the insertion point.
Esc-C	Capitalizes the word following the insertion point.
Esc-U	Changes the next word to all uppercase letters.
Esc-L	Changes the next word to all lowercase letters.

Working with Files and Directories

The previous pages show you how to navigate your directories using Unix commands. Just perusing your directories isn't particularly productive, however. Fortunately, this section shows you how to *do* something with the files you see listed: copy, move, create, and delete directories and files.

Tip: You're entering Serious Power territory, where it's theoretically possible to delete a whole directory of stuff with a single typo. As a precaution, consider working through this section with administrator privileges turned off for your account, so that you won't be able to change anything outside your home directory.

To do so, quit Terminal. Open the Users pane of System Preferences. Select your account name, click Edit, and then turn off the "Allow user to administer this machine" checkbox. Finally, click OK. (One Mac OS X account, on the other hand, must always have administrator privileges, so you may first have to create another Administrator account as described on page 275.)

cp (copy)

Using the Unix command *cp*, you can copy and rename a file in one move. (Try *that* in the Finder!)

The basic command goes like this: *cp path1 path2*, where the *path* placeholders represent the original file and the copy, respectively.

Copying in place

To duplicate a file called Thesis.doc, you would type *cp Thesis.doc Thesis2.doc.* (That's just a space between the names.) You don't have to call the copy *Thesis2*—you could call it anything you like; the point is that you wind up with two identical files in the same directory. Just remember to add a backslash before a space if you want to name the copy with two words (*Thesis\ Backup*, for example).

Tip: If this command doesn't seem to work for you, remember that you must type the *full* names of the files you're moving—including their file name suffixes like .doc or .gif, which Mac OS X usually hides. Using the *ls* command before a copy may help you find out what the correct, full file names should be, or you may just want to use the tab-completion feature, making Terminal type in the whole name for you.

Copying and renaming

To copy the same file into, say, your Documents folder at the same time, you'd just change the last phrase so that it specifies the path, like this: *cp Reviews.doc ~/Documents/ Reviews2.doc.*

Tip: Note that *cp* replaces identically named files without warning. Use the *-i* flag (that is, *cp -i*) if you want to be warned before *cp* replaces a file like this.

Copying without renaming

To copy something into another directory without changing its name, just use a pathname (without a file name) as the final phrase. So to copy Reviews.doc into your Documents folder, you could type *cp Reviews.doc ~/Documents.*

FREQUENTLY ASKED QUESTION

The Slash and the Colon

OK, I'm so confused. You say that slashes denote nested directories. But in Mac OS 9, I always read that colons (:) denote the Mac's internal folder notation, and that's why I can't use colons in the names of my icons. What's the story?

At the desktop, the Mac still uses colons as path separators instead of the slash. Therefore, you *are* allowed to use slashes in file names in the Finder, but not a colon. Conversely, in

Terminal, you can use colons in file names but not slashes!

Behind the scenes, Mac OS X automatically converts one form of punctuation to the other, as necessary. For example, a file named *Letter 6/21/2001* in Aqua shows up as *Letter 6:21:2001* in Terminal. Likewise, a directory named *Attn: Jon* in Terminal appears with the name *Attn/ Jon* in the Finder. Weird—and fun!

Tip: You can use the "." directory shortcut (which stands for the current working directory) to copy files from another directory *into* the working directory, like this: *% cp ~/Documents/Reviews.doc .* (notice the space and the period after *Reviews.doc*).

Multiple files

You can even move several files or directories at once. Where you'd normally specify the source file, just list their pathnames separated by spaces, as shown in Figure 15-6.

```
cp Tahoe1.mov Tahoe2.mov ../FinishedMovies
```

Figure 15-6:
The first argument of this command lists two different files. The final clause always specifies where you want all of these files moved to (in this case, the Finished directory).

You can also use the * wildcard to copy several files at once. For example, suppose you've got these files in your iMovie Projects directory: Tahoe 1.mov, Tahoe 2.mov, Tahoe 3.mov, Tahoe 4.mov, Script.doc, and Tahoe Project File. Now suppose you want to copy *only* the QuickTime movies into a directory called FinishedMovies. All you'd have to do is type *cp *mov ../FinishedMovies* and press Enter; Mac OS X instantly performs the copy.

If you wanted to copy *all* of those files to another directory, you'd use the * by itself, like this: *cp * ../Finished Movies.*

Unfortunately, if the iMovie Projects directory contained other *directories* and not just files, that command would give you an error message; the Unix *cp* command doesn't copy directories within directories unless you explicitly tell it to, using the *-R* option flag. Here's the finished command that copies everything in the current directory—both files and directories—into FinishedMovies: *cp -R * ../FinishedMovies.*

Here's one more example: a command that copies everything (files and directories) whose names contain *Tahoe* into someone else's Drop Box directory: *cp -R *Tahoe* ~miho/Public/Drop\ Box.*

Tip: The Finder generally copies files faster than the *cp* command. The speed difference is negligible when copying small amounts of data; however, you'll save time by doing it in the Finder when copying more than a few hundred megabytes of data.

mv: Moving and Renaming Files and Directories

Now you know how to copy files; when you want to move or rename them, you use the Unix command *mv.* You use it almost exactly the same way you'd use *cp* (except that it always moves directories inside of directories you're moving—you don't have to type *-R*).

The syntax looks like this: *mv oldname newname*. For example, to change your Movies directory's name to Films, you'd type *mv Movies Films*. You can rename both files and directories this way.

WORKAROUND WORKSHOP

When Forks Collide: Copying Applications with CpMac

If you could inspect certain traditional Macintosh files with the software equivalent of a CAT scanner, you'd see that its single icon might actually house two chunks of computer code, which the geeks call the *data fork* and the *resource fork*. (Data refers to, well, data—stuff you type, or the programming code that makes up an application. Resources are programming components like icons, windows, toolbars, and other pieces of your applications.)

This fork business is news to Unix, however. When you use the *cp* command to copy a file, Unix moves only the data fork—the one it knows about. The effect on the copy could be minor or disastrous, depending on the type of file. Most non-Cocoa programs (AppleWorks, Word, and so on), for example, will be rendered useless, having lost many of their essential resources.

To address this problem, Apple came up with a command line application called *CpMac,* which is just like *cp* except that it copies all forks of any file it copies. The standard Mac OS X installation doesn't include it, however; it's available only if you install the Developer Tools (see page 246).

Once you've done that, you can run CpMac by invoking it at the % prompt. Unfortunately, because CpMac is an add-on Unix program, you have to refer to it using its entire path notation, like this: */Developer/Tools/CpMac.* A typical command might therefore look like this: */Developer/Tools/CpMac -r MacWrite\ Folder ~/Applications.* (You can set things up so that typing the pathname isn't necessary, but that's another book.)

You can replace *cp* with *CpMac* in any of the examples in this chapter. There's just one difference: *CpMac* uses a lowercase *r* for its recursive copying option instead of a capital R.

Moving files and directories

To rename a file and move it to a different directory simultaneously, just replace the last portion of the command with a pathname. To move the Tahoe1 movie file into your Documents directory—and rename it LakeTahoe at the same time—you'd type this: *mv Tahoe1.mov ~/Documents/LakeTahoe.mov.*

All the usual shortcuts apply, including the wildcard. Here's how you'd move everything containing the word *Tahoe* in your working directory (files and directories) into your Documents directory: *mv *Tahoe* ~/Documents.*

Option flags

You can follow the *mv* command with either of two options:

- **-i.** Makes Terminal ask you permission before replacing a file with one of the same name.

- **-f.** Overwrites like-named files without asking you first. (Actually, this is how *mv* works if you don't specify otherwise.)

Note: This command never replaces one directory with an identically named one (or an identically named *file*). If there is such an item among multiple source items, only those named differently from any subdirectories in the target directory will be moved.

mkdir: Creating New Directories

In the Finder, you make a new folder by choosing File→New Folder. In Terminal, you create one using the *mkdir* command (for *make directory*).

Follow the command with the name you want to give the new directory, like this: *mkdir 'Early iMovie Attempts'* (the single quotes in this example let you avoid having to precede each space with a backslash).

The *mkdir* command creates the new directory in the current working directory, but you can just as easily create it anywhere else. Just add the pathname to your argument. To make a new directory in your Documents→Finished directory, for example, you'd type *mkdir '~/Documents/Finished/Early iMovie Attempts'*.

Tip: If there *is* no directory called Finished in your Documents directory, you'll just get an error message—unless you use the *-p* option, which creates as many new directories as necessary to match your command. For example, *mkdir -p '~/Documents/Finished/Early iMovie Attempts'* would create *both* a Finished directory and an Early iMovie Attempts directory inside of it.

touch: Creating Empty Files

To create a new, empty file, type *touch filename*. For example, to create the file *practice.txt* in your working directory, use *touch practice.txt*.

And why would you bother? For the moment, you'd use such new, empty files primarily as targets for practicing the next command.

rm: Removing Files and Directories

Unix provides an extremely efficient way to trash files and directories. With a single command, *rm*, you can delete any file or directory—or *all of them* that you're allowed to access with your account type (page 275).

The dangers of this setup should be obvious, especially in light of the fact that *deletions are immediate* in Unix. There is no Undo, no Empty Trash command, no "Are you sure?" dialog box. In Unix, all sales are final.

The command *rm* stands for "remove," but could also stand for "respect me." Pause for a moment whenever you're about to invoke it. For the purpose of this introduction to *rm*, make sure once more that administration privileges are turned off for your account.

To use this command, just type *rm,* a space, and the exact name of the file you want to delete from the working directory. To remove the file *practice.txt* you created with the *touch* command, for example, you'd just type *rm practice.txt*.

To remove a directory and everything in it, add the *-r* flag, like this: *rm -r PracticeFolder.*

If you're feeling particularly powerful (and you like taking risks), you can even use wildcards with the *rm* command. Now, many experienced Unix users make it a rule to *never* use *rm* with wildcards while logged in as an administrator, because one false keystroke can wipe out everything in a directory. But here, for study purposes only, is the atomic bomb of command lines, the one that deletes *everything* in the working directory: *rm -r *.*

Tip: Be doubly cautious when using wildcards in *rm* command lines, and triply cautious when using them while logged in as an administrator.

Just after the letters rm, you can insert options like these:

- **-d** deletes any empty directories it finds, in addition to files. (Otherwise, empty directories will trigger an error message.)

- **-i** (for *interactive*) makes the Mac ask you for confirmation before nuking each file or directory.

Tip: If you use both the -f (see page 389) and -i options, which appear to contradict each other, the last command (farthest to the right) wins.

- **-P** performs a "secure delete," scrubbing the file's location on the hard drive three times so that nothing, not even Norton Utilities or the CIA, will know what was there.

echo: The Safety Net

You can take a lot of danger out of the *rm* command by prefacing it with the *echo* command. It makes Terminal type out the command a second time, this time with a handy list of exactly what you're about to obliterate. If you've used wildcards, you'll see the names of the files that will be affected by the * character. If you type *echo rm -r **, for example (which, without the *echo* part, would normally mean "delete everything in this directory"), you might see a list like this:

```
rm -r Reviews.doc  Tahoe Footage  Picnic Movie  Contract.doc
```

Once you've looked over the list and approved what Terminal is about to do, *then* you can retype the command without the *echo* portion.

Note: The *rm* doesn't work on file or directory names that begin with a hyphen (-). To delete these items from your working directory, preface their names with a dot slash (./), like this: *rm ./-Recipes.doc.*

Online Help

Mac OS X comes with hundreds of Unix programs like the ones described in this chapter. How many? Try pressing Control-X, releasing both keys, and pressing Tab. You see a gigantic list of all of the programs at your disposal in Terminal (including *cd, ls, rm,* and all the rest). How are you supposed to learn what they all do?

Fortunately, almost every Unix program comes with its own little help file. It may not appear within an elegant Aqua window—in fact, it's pretty darned plain—but it offers much more material than the regular Mac Help Center.

These help files are called user-manual pages, or *manpages*, which hold descriptions of virtually every command and program available. Mac OS X, in fact, comes with manpages on about 1,800 topics—about 3,000 printed pages' worth.

Unfortunately, manpages rarely have the clarity of writing or the learner-focused approach you'll find in the Mac Help Center. They're generally terse, just-the-facts descriptions. You'll probably find yourself needing to reread certain sections again and again. The information they contain, however, is invaluable to new and experienced users alike, and the effort spent mining them is usually worthwhile.

Using *man*

To access the manpage for a given command, type *man* followed by the name of the command you're researching. For example, to view the manpage for the *ls* command, enter: *man ls.*

Tip: The *-k* option flag lets you search by keyword. For example, *man -k appletalk* produces a list of all manpages that refer to AppleTalk, whereupon you can pick one of the names in the list and *man* that page name.

Now the manual appears, one screen at a time, as shown in Figure 15-7.

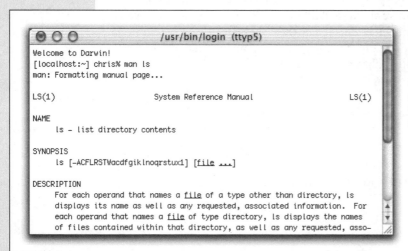

Figure 15-7:
To move on to the next man *screen, press the Space bar. To go back, you can either use the Terminal window's scroll bar or press B. To close the manual and return to a prompt, press Q.*

A typical manpage begins with these sections:

- **Name.** The name and a brief definition of the command.

- **Synopsis.** Presents the syntax of the command, including all possible options and arguments, in a concise formula. For example, the synopsis for *du* (disk usage) is: *du [-H | -L | -P] [-a | -s] [-ckrx] [file ...].*

  This shows all the flags available for the *du* command and how to use them.

  Brackets ([ ]) surround the *optional* arguments. (*All* of the arguments for *du* are optional.)

  Vertical bars called *pipes* (|) indicate that you can use only one item (of the group separated by pipes) at a time. For example, when choosing options to use with *du*, you can use *either* -H, -L, or -P—not two or all three at once.

  The word *file* in the synopsis means "type a pathname here." The ellipsis (...) following it indicates that you're allowed to type more than one pathname.

- **Description.** Explains in more detail what the command does and how it works. Also included in the description is the complete list of that command's option flags.

For more information on using *man,* view its *own* manpage by entering—what else?—*man man.*

Tip: The free program ManOpen, available for download at *www.missingmanuals.com,* is a Cocoa manual-pages reader that provides a nice looking, easier to control window for reading *man* pages.

Other Online Help

Sometimes Terminal shoves a little bit of user-manual right under your nose—when it thinks you're having trouble. For example, if you use the *mkdir* command without specifying a pathname, *mkdir* interrupts the proceedings by displaying its own synopsis as a friendly reminder (subtext: "Um, this is how you're *supposed* to use me"), like this: *usage: mkdir [-p] [-m mode] dirname ...*

Terminal Preferences

Like most applications, Terminal has a Preferences command (see Figure 15-8). If you spend endless hours staring at the Terminal screen, as most Unix junkies do, you'll eventually be grateful for the preference settings that let you control how Terminal looks and acts.

Tip: Changes you make in the Preferences window affect *all subsequent* Terminal windows you open. The Inspector window (⌘-I), on the other hand, lets you make the same kinds of changes to each open window independently.

Most of the options here are self-explanatory, but here are a few worth noticing.

General

- **Window Size** affects the width in characters (columns) and height in lines (rows) of new Terminal windows. (Of course, you can always resize an existing window by dragging its lower-right corner; as you drag, the title bar shows you the window's current dimensions.)

- **When Shell Exits.** When you're finished fooling around in Terminal, you end your session either by closing the window or by typing *exit* (or pressing Control-D) at the prompt. This setting determines what happens in the latter case.

- **Font.** No matter what font you choose for your future Terminal sessions, note that the characters in successive rows of text will line up with each other, monospaced as though they're all Monaco or Courier.

Tip: You can change the Terminal window's background by using the Preferences window, but here's a more fun way. Choose Fonts→Show Colors; in the Colors dialog box, choose the color you want. Finally, drag the color square (lower-left) into any empty area of the Terminal window. Boom! It changes color to match. (You can even drag the color swatch onto some text in the Terminal window to change your font color.)

Figure 15-8:
To access the Preferences panel, choose Terminal→Preferences. The Terminal prefs box is designed to look like System Preferences; click an icon at the top of the window to see the corresponding category of settings.

Startup

- **Startup File.** If you choose to use a startup file (see the sidebar box on page 395), enter its full path here.

Shell

- **Shell.** As noted on page 377, the default shell for Mac OS X is *tcsh*, as indicated by */bin/tcsh* in the Shell dialog box. If you get really good at Unix and want to switch to a different shell (with the understanding that many of the examples in these chapters won't work properly except in tcsh), you can specify its path here.

Display

- **Scrollback Buffer.** As your command line activity fills the terminal window with text, older lines at top disappear from view. So that you can get back to these previous lines for viewing, copying, or printing, Terminal offers this *Scrollback Buffer,* which sets aside a certain amount of memory—and adds a scroll bar—so that you can do so.

Tip: Although it may be tempting to set the buffer to *Unlimited,* hold back; that will increase Terminal's memory use. The default setting—10,000 lines—should be plenty.

POWER USERS' CLINIC

Startup Files

Once you've got a few windows open—your main Terminal window, a couple of *man* (user-manual) windows, a *top* window showing all the running programs (page 413), and so on, you may get dizzy just looking at the seas of black-on-white type. One easy solution is to customize the colors, fonts, and positions of these favorite windows—and then make Terminal take a snapshot of that configuration.

A Terminal *startup file* stores the size, location, and visible/invisible status of all windows that are open when you create the startup file. It also stores each window's preference settings, including its Font, Title Bar, and Colors settings. (It doesn't store any text in these windows.) Once you've saved a startup file, you can open it again anytime to replicate your saved window layout in Terminal.

To create a startup file, first set up the Preferences dialog box the way you like it. Then open and arrange Terminal windows the way you like *them.* Press ⌘-I, if you like, to open the Inspector window, which you can use to make different preference settings for different windows.

Next, choose Shell→Save. Use the pop-up menu in the Save dialog box to choose whether to save the settings for only the Main window (the active window) or for all windows. You can also choose in this dialog box to have the saved startup file opened when Terminal launches. (If so, the settings stored with the startup file overrides any settings you've made in the Preferences window.)

The best place to store them is in a directory called Terminal in your home directory's Library/Application Support/Terminal folder. (You may have to create this directory yourself.)

Finally, give the startup file a descriptive name and save it into that Terminal directory. Terminal appends the *.term* file name extension.

Title Bar

- **Include these Elements.** Turn on the elements that you'd like Terminal to display in each window's title bar. It's possible to set the preferences differently for each Terminal window; you might therefore want the windows' title bars to identify the differences. You can incorporate any combination of these tidbits into the windows' titles: shell path, device name (an identifying terminal number), filename (the startup file the window consulted upon opening), size, and a custom element you type into the Custom Title field.

Activity

Shell commands can often take some time to complete. If you close a Terminal window before its work is finished, you'll cancel the process and lose your work. In the Activity preferences pane, you can configure Terminal to monitor such active processes, and warn you if closing the window (or quitting) will make you lose that kind of ground.

Note: As you survey these options, you'll encounter the terms *clean* and *busy*. Windows with running processes that Terminal deems worthy of monitoring are termed *busy;* those with no running processes, or processes Terminal determines don't need monitoring, are *clean*.

Terminal Tips and Tricks

This is a list you'll probably want to come back to after you've used Terminal for a while, since some of these tips might not be applicable to a new user.

Setting Window Opaqueness

Not only can you change the background color of your Terminal windows, but you can then make the windows translucent, a sure way to make Linux users stare at you with jealousy.

The Unix program that lets you change default settings like this is *defaults*. For example, to make your window 85 percent opaque, enter this command at the prompt and press Enter:

```
defaults write com.apple.terminal TerminalOpaqueness .85
```

Actually, you can substitute any decimal number you want between 0 and 1, which is how you specify how transparent you want the window to be. For example, .5 makes the Terminal window 50 percent transparent. (The effect is visible only in subsequent Terminal windows that you open by choosing Shell→New. Also note that you can't see Classic programs through your translucent window.)

Is this really useful? You'd have to do quite a bit of stretching to imagine how. Still, the effect is really neat, especially when you consider the drop shadows and other lighting effects that are still visible at the window edges.

Tip: This effect looks especially cool if you make the Terminal window black with white writing before issuing the command. You do that by choosing Terminal→Preferences→Colors. This change, too, doesn't kick in until you make a new Terminal window.

Switching Windows

You can switch among your various Terminal windows by pressing ⌘-1, ⌘-2, and so on (up to ⌘-5). Technically, you're referring to your Terminal windows by their *tty* identifying numbers, which you can see displayed in their title bars.

Default Startup File

After you've changed Terminal's preferences, it's not easy to get the default settings back—unless you first save them in a startup file.

If you've already made changes to your Terminal's preferences, quit Terminal and temporarily remove its *property list* file, called *com.apple.Terminal.plist*, from your Home folder→Library→Preferences folder. (Drag it out of the Finder window to the desktop, for example.)

Next, reopen the Terminal, where you'll find that all original settings have been restored. Save this window as a startup file named Default (see page 395). Finally, quit Terminal and replace the newly created property list file (com.apple.Terminal.plist) with the one you removed initially. When you next open Terminal, you'll have your old preferences back and a new Default item in your Library menu that will always open a factory-fresh Terminal window. (You may want to consider locking the Default startup file [see page 66].)

Fun with Terminal

Chapter 15 shows you the basics of using the command line instead of the Finder for getting around and manipulating files and directories. So far, however, you haven't seen many examples of tasks you can perform *only* at the command line.

This chapter offers guided tutorials for performing more specialized tasks, most of which you *can't* do in the Finder. These procedures, and the commands you need to perform them, are also new starting points for further learning.

Note: This chapter assumes that you're already familiar with the Unix commands introduced in Chapter 15.

Moving Unmovable Files and Directories

Sooner or later, it happens to almost everyone who uses Mac OS X: the system tells you that you're not allowed to trash or even move certain files or directories. As you'll find out in this section, any of several problems may be responsible—but Terminal can help you can get around all of them.

Permissions Errors

If you get the dialog box shown in Figure 16-1, you've got yourself a *permissions error.* Maybe you have a Normal account, but you're trying to trash something that only administrators are allowed to manipulate. Or maybe you're an administrator, but that's still not high enough clearance to delete a certain directory (such as the orphaned home directory of a deleted account, described on page 281).

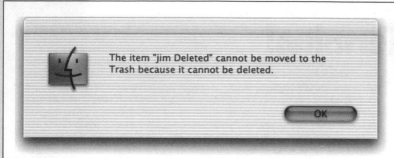

The item "jim Deleted" cannot be moved to the Trash because it cannot be deleted.

OK

Figure 16-1:
The Finder reports an item cannot be moved to the Trash. In this case, it's because Mac OS X itself (root or system) "owns" the folder in question.

To find out what's going on with a directory's permissions, highlight it and choose File→Show Info (see Figure 16-2).

To view the same information within Terminal, use the *ls* command like this: *ls -al / Users.*

The *-l flag* gives you a *long list*—an expanded display. The *-a* flag tells the Unix shell (page 377) to list invisible files, too (those whose names begin with a period). That's handy in this example, because the "." directory refers to the directory you want to examine (Users), and the ". ." directory indicates *its* parent directory (in this case, the root directory [page 378], which is represented by a simple slash).

Figure 16-2:
Suppose you're trying to trash a folder called "jim Deleted." Start by examining the Users folder (which contains it). Highlight the folder's icon and choose File→Show Info. In this dialog box, choose Show→Privileges. As you can see, only the user named "System" can modify ("Write") the contents of the Users folder.

Now you see something like this:

```
total 0
drwxr-xr-x  5 root  wheel   264 Jun 20 20:07 .
drwxrwxr-t 39 root  admin  1282 Jun 21 18:10 ..
drwxrwxrwt  2 root  wheel   264 Feb 25 00:04 Shared
drwxr-xr-x 29 chris staff   942 Jun 19 12:57 chris
drwxr-xr-x 11 chris staff   330 Jan 30 15:17 jim Deleted
```

Thanks to the -*l* option, the first line shows the grand total size of all the files in the directory. Since there are no *files* in the Users directory—only more directories—the total size is 0.

Next you see the names of everything in the Users directory, one line apiece. In this case, aside from the dot directories (page 382), there are only the three directories in Users: *shared, chris,* and *jim Deleted*. But what on earth is *drwxrwxrwt*? Is Terminal having a meltdown?

Not at all; you're just seeing still more Unix shorthand, listed in what are supposed to be helpful columns. Figure 16-3 breaks down the meaning of each clump of text.

- **Type.** The first character of the line indicates the *file type*—usually **d** (a directory), a **hyphen** (a file), or **l** (a *symbolic link*—the Unix version of aliases).

- **File Mode.** Rammed together with the type is a string of nine characters. They indicate, in a coded format, the actual access permissions for that item, as described in the next section.

- **Owner.** The account name of whoever owns this file or directory, which is usually whoever created it. Remember that *root* means that Mac OS X itself owns it. That's why even administrators aren't allowed to delete directories that bear "root" ownership.

Note: In the Finder's Show Info windows, you may see ownership listed as *System.* That's Apple's kinder, gentler term for *root.* Both terms mean the same thing: that you're looking at a file or folder that only the root account holder (page 290) can fiddle with.

- **Group.** The name of the *group* that owns this file or directory. "Wheel," as in "big wheel," indicates the group with the highest powers; "staff" is usually everybody else. (See page 312 for much more on groups.)

- **Pathname.** The path of this file or directory (page 378).

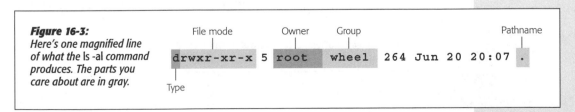

Figure 16-3:
Here's one magnified line of what the ls -al *command produces. The parts you care about are in gray.*

File mode | Owner | Group | Pathname

`drwxr-xr-x 5 root   wheel   264 Jun 20 20:07 .`

Type

File Mode Code

To understand the coded nine-character file mode section, you need a good grasp of the topics covered in Chapter 11. There you'll find out that the whole business of *access privileges* should interest anyone who shares a Mac, either over a network or over time (by sharing a Mac with other citizens of a family, school, or workplace).

There you'll also find out that as you create new files and directories, you can specify who else is allowed to see or make changes to them. In fact, you can specify these permissions for three different categories of people: the owner (usually yourself), your group (page 312), and everyone else.

The file mode column is made of three subcolumns (Figure 16-4), which correspond to those three categories of people: *owner, group,* and *everybody else.*

Within each sequence, three characters describe the *read (r), write (w),* and *execute (x)* permissions this person has to this file or directory. A hyphen (-) means, "Nope, this person isn't allowed this kind of access." In Figure 16-4, you can see that you, the owner of this file, can do everything you want to it—no hyphens!

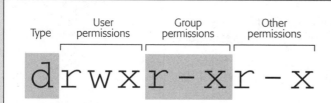

Figure 16-4:
If you look very closely and move your nose right up against the screen, you'll see that the file mode column isn't just a string of random letters—it's four distinct sets of information that tells you who's allowed to do what.

But the other people in your group can't make changes to it; there's no *w* in the Group column. In fact, there's no *w* in the final ("everyone else") column, either.

The three forms of access—read, write, and execute—have slightly different meanings when applied to files and directories:

- **Read access** to a *file* means that someone can open and read it. Read access to a *directory* (folder), on the other hand, just means that someone using Terminal can see a list of its contents using a command like *ls.*

- **Write access** to a *file* means that someone can modify and save changes to it. Write access to a *directory* means that someone can add, remove, and rename any item the folder contains (but not necessarily the items within its subdirectories).

Note: Turning off write access to a certain file doesn't protect it from deletion. If write access is turned on for the folder it's in, the file is still trashable.

To protect a certain file from deletion, in other words, worry about the access settings of the *folder* that encloses it.

• **Execute access,** when applied to applications, means that people can run that particular program. (In fact, Unix distinguishes applications from ordinary files by checking the status of this setting.) Execute access to a *directory,* on the other hand, means that someone can *cd* to it (make it the working directory) when working in Terminal, or list the attributes of its contents using the *ls* command.

Solving Permissions Problems

Back to the "can't delete this directory" problem: The reason you can't delete the "jim Deleted" folder is that its *parent* folder, Users, is supposedly owned by *root.* No wonder you're not allowed to trash "jim Deleted"—you don't have the root account.

Now check the group for the Users directory: it's *wheel.* Even if you're in the wheel group, you still wouldn't be allowed to trash "jim Deleted," because there's a hyphen instead of a *w* in the group permissions code of the folder that contains it.

Besides—are you even *in* the wheel group? To find out, type *groups* and press Enter. On the next line, Terminal types out a list of the groups to which you belong—*staff wheel admin,* for example.

Now you know why even administrators are never allowed to move directories out of the Users directory. Sure enough, administrators are members of the group that owns Users (*wheel*). But the Users directory's group permissions still don't allow writing, and therefore don't permit trashing any of its contents by *wheel* group members.

So how do you solve the problem? The most obvious approach would be to simply change the permissions of the directory—but only the owner of the item can do that, and you're not the owner. Even if you were, it's not a great idea to fool around with permissions that Mac OS X itself has set up.

Another possibility: You could always log into Mac OS X as the owner—turning on the root account as described on page 290—thereby obtaining the permission you need to modify the directory. But that's a lot of time and hassle.

Fortunately, there's a quick, easy, and effective third possibility, which explains its popularity in Unix circles: the *sudo* command.

sudo

sudo is a great command name. Technically, it's short for *superuser do,* which means that you'll be allowed to execute any command as though you had logged in with the root (superuser) account—but without actually needing to know the password for the root account, and without actually having to log out and log in again. (See page 290 for more on the root account.)

It's also a great command name because it looks as though it would be pronounced "pseudo," as in, "I'm just *pretending* to be the root user for a moment. I'm here under a pseudonym." (In fact, you pronounce it "SOO-doo," because it comes from *superuser do.* But in the privacy of your own brain, you can pronounce it however you like.)

Note: Only people with Administrator accounts can use the *sudo* command.

If you have the root account—or can simulate having it using *sudo*—you can override any permissions settings, including the ones that prevent you from moving items out of the Users directory.

Finally, you're ready to remove that recalcitrant "jim Deleted" directory. To use *sudo*, you preface an entire command line with *sudo* and a space. Type this:

```
sudo rm -r /Users/jim\ Deleted
```

Taken slowly, this command breaks down as follows:

- *sudo.* "Give me the power to do whatever I want."

- *rm.* "Trash the directory name I'm about to give you…"

- *-r.* "…*and* all the directories inside it…"

- */Users/jim\ Deleted.* "The directory I want to delete is "jim Deleted," inside Users."

The first time you run *sudo*, you're treated to the characteristic deadpan humor of programmers worldwide: "We trust you have received the usual lecture from the local System Administrator. It usually boils down to these two things: 1) Respect the privacy of others. 2) Think before you type."

UP TO SPEED

Beware the Dread Typo

Use *sudo* with caution, especially with the *rm* command. Even a single typing error in a *sudo rm* command can be disastrous.

Suppose, for example, that you intended to type this:

sudo rm -ri /Users/jim\ Deleted

—but you accidentally inserted a space after the first slash, like this:

sudo rm -ri / Users/jim\ Deleted

You've just told Terminal to delete *all data on all drives!*

Because of the extra space, the *rm* command sees its first pathname argument as being only /, the root directory (page 378). The -r flag means "and all directories inside it."

Good thing you added the *-i* flag, which makes Mac OS X ask you for confirmation before deleting each directory. It's almost always a good idea to include *-i* whenever you use *sudo* with *rm*.

History buffs—and Unix fans—may remember that first Apple's iTunes 2 installer, released in October 2001, contained a tiny bug: It had a tendency to erase people's hard drives. (Oops.) Apple hastily withdrew the installer and replaced it with a fixed one. But behind the scenes, an improperly formed *rm* command was the culprit.)

In other words, *sudo* is a powerful tool that lets you tromp unfettered across delicate parts of Mac OS X, and you should proceed with caution. At the outset, at least, you should use it only when you've been given specific steps to follow, as in this chapter.

Now *sudo* asks you for your usual login password, just to make sure that you're not some seventh-grader up to no good. If you are indeed an administrator, and your password checks out, *sudo* gives you a five-minute window in which, by prefacing each command with *sudo*, you can tromp around as though you're the all-high, master root account holder. (After five minutes, you have to input your password again.)

Tip: Mac OS X comes preinstalled with dozens of printer drivers—most of which, of course, are just taking up space. (After all, you probably own only one or two printers.) Since the root account technically owns them, you can use *sudo* to delete them.

Start by making the Printers directory the working directory *(cd /Library/Printers).* Now type *sudo rm -r EPSON,* or *sudo rm -r Canon,* or whatever. When you press Enter, those useless drivers are gone. The disk space you reclaim could be your own.

The Sticky Bit Error

Suppose your Mac has a handful of administrators, you and your incompetent boss Jim among them. Want to know how annoying he is? He creates a folder called Jim's Digipix right there in the hard drive window.

A few weeks later, Jim leaves the company—"to pursue other interests."

After he's gone, you, with relief, decide to get rid of his silly pictures folder. But when you try to delete it, boom: "The operation cannot be completed because this item is owned by Jim." Uh-oh.

You, a shrewd Mac OS X guru, immediately question the access privileges—not of the Jim's Digipix folder, but of its *parent,* the folder that contains it. In this case, its parent is the hard drive window itself—the *root directory* (see Figure 16-5).

You do a File→Show Info→Privileges on the hard drive icon. Sure enough, "Read & Write" is turned on for your Group (because you're part of the Admin group). According to this dialog box, administrators *should* be allowed to trash anything in the main hard drive window.

"Maybe Jim protected the Jim's Digipix folder itself," somebody suggests. But lo and behold, Jim had even turned on Read & Write privileges for *that* folder, perhaps hoping that other administrators would put their own digital photos in that folder.

If both a folder and its parent have given you Write privileges, you should be able to trash it, no matter who owns it.

Clearly, there's some other factor at play here.

Off you go into Terminal to check out the permissions for the relevant directories. You switch to the root directory (by typing *cd /*) and call up a list of what's at the root level by typing *ls -al* (page 379). You'd see these entries, among many others:

```
drwxrwxr-t 41 root admin   1350 Jun 25 20:41 .
drwxrwxrwx  2 jim admin     24 Jun 25 20:26 Jim's Digipix
```

Sure enough, according to the access codes (*rwxrwxrwx)* of the root directory, you and your fellow group members have full access to do whatever you want to the Jim's Digipix directory inside it.

But look more closely at the permissions in the first line, which refers to the root directory itself. See the *-t?* This *t* sits where the *execute* file mode for "everyone else" normally belongs. It tells you that this directory's *sticky bit* is turned on.

The sticky bit means: "I don't care *what* the group permissions say; only my owner (and the superuser) can mess with me." A directory whose sticky bit is set is therefore something like a drop box: Anyone with write access can put icons into that directory, but only its owner can remove items from inside it, no matter what the group settings are.

So who owns the root directory? Why, Mac OS X itself (or *root,* as circled in Figure 16-5).

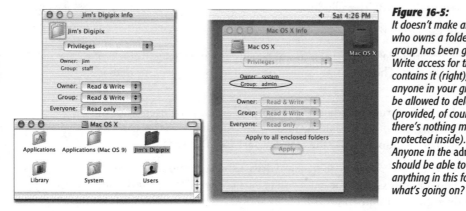

Figure 16-5:
It doesn't make any difference who owns a folder. If your group has been given Read & Write access for the folder that contains it (right), then anyone in your group should be allowed to delete it (provided, of course, that there's nothing more protected inside). Circled: Anyone in the admin *group should be able to move anything in this folder. So what's going on?*

As a precautionary measure, the Mac OS X installer turns on the sticky bit for the root directory (and, by the way, the Users→Shared folder). That's why administrators can put things *into* folders like Applications and Users, but even they aren't allowed to drag these folders *out* of the hard drive window.

When Jim created the Jim's Digipix folder, he wound up creating, in effect, a new member of this protected directory class. Mac OS X is treating Jim's Digipix as though it's every bit as important as System, Users, or Applications.

You could, of course, just turn off the root directory's sticky bit; here again, though, it's not nice to go changing permissions set by Mac OS X.

Instead, the best solution would be to make *yourself* the owner of the Jim's Digipix directory. At that point, the sticky bit won't affect you. The sticky bit never blocks a file or folder's *owner*.

To change the ownership of an item, you use the *chown* (for "change owner") command followed by its two arguments: the new owner's account name and the pathname of the directory you want to reassign. Since Jim currently "owns" Jim's Digipix, you'll have to use *sudo* with *chown*, like this:

```
sudo chown -R chris /jim's\ Digipix/
```

(The *-R* flag means *recursive:* that is, "make all folders *inside* this folder mine, too." Oh, and substitute your own account name for *chris*.)

That's all there is to it. Jim's Digipix now belongs to you. Once you're back in the Finder, you're free to drag it wherever you please—like into the Trash.

Tip: There's also a command called *chgrp* that lets you change an icon's *group* owner. For example, to change the Library→Fonts directory's group owner from *admin* to *staff*, you would type *sudo chgrp staff /Library/Fonts*.

Of course, you know from Chapter 12 that Super GetInfo offers a far simpler way to perform this kind of ownership reassignment. But learning about the Unix way builds character.

Protecting Files En Masse

It could happen to you. You've got yourself a folder filled with hundreds of files—downloaded photos from your digital camera, for example. Most are pretty crummy, but the ones you took in Tahoe (and therefore have Tahoe in their file names) are spectacular. You want to protect those files from deletion without having to turn on the Locked checkbox (page 66) of every file individually.

When you turn on a file's Locked checkbox, Mac OS X turns on an invisible switch known to Unix veterans as the *user immutable flag*. Not even the superuser is allowed to change, move, or delete a file whose user immutable flag is turned on. In other words, a file is much more "locked" in Mac OS X than in Mac OS 9.

The command you need to change such flags is *chflags*—short for *change flags*, of course. You can always read its *man* manual (see page 392) to find out all the different flags it can change; for now, though, all you care about is the user immutable flag.

You can follow the *chflags* command with three arguments: its own option flags, the file flags, and the pathname of the file whose flags are being changed. In this case, the command you care about is called *uchg* (short for *user changeable*—in other words, this is the immutable flag).

To protect all of the Tahoe shots in one fell swoop, then, here's what you'd type at the prompt:

```
chflags uchg ~/Pictures/*Tahoe*
```

The asterisks, of course, are wildcards that mean, "all files containing the word Tahoe in their names." So in English, you've just said: "Change the immutable flag (the Locked checkbox setting) for all the Tahoe files in my Pictures folder to 'locked.'"

Tip: To *unlock* a file, thus turning off its *uchg* flag, you just add the word "no," like this: *chflags nouchg ~/Pictures/*tahoe*.*

To see the results of your handiwork, you could always switch to the Finder, where you'd see that the Tahoe files now have their Locked checkboxes turned on. Or, to confirm your work right in Terminal, issue this command: *ls -lo ~/Pictures* (or any other path to a folder containing locked items). That's the familiar *ls* (list) command that shows you what's in a certain directory, followed by an *-l* flag for a more complete listing and an *-o* flag that produces a "flags" column in the resulting table.

In any case, Terminal might spit out something like this:

```
total 830064
-rw-r--r-- 1 chris   staff   -       158280000  Jun 16 20:05 Sunset.jpg
-rw-r--r-- 1 chris   staff   uchg     58560000  Jun 16 20:05 NewMoon.jpg
-rw-r--r-- 1 chris   staff   uchg 107520000  Jun 16 20:05 Tahoe.jpg
-rw-r--r-- 1 chris   staff   uchg 100560000  Jun 16 20:05 Buddy.jpg
```

The fifth column, the product of the *-o* flag, lists any file flags that have been set for each file. In this case, three of the files are listed with ***uchg***, which represents the user immutable (locked) flag. (The hyphen for the first listed file means "no flags"—not locked.)

Enabling the Root Account

Only one person is allowed to clomp through any Mac OS X directory, unfettered and unrestricted: whoever holds the *root* (superuser) account. There are two ways to turn on this usually hidden account: the easy way (see page 291) and the Unix way.

To enable the root account in Terminal, all you have to do is make up a password for the dormant account using the *passwd* command.

Normal account holders can use *passwd* to change their own passwords (although the Users pane of System Preferences strikes most people as a more direct way to do so). To change your own password, for example, just type *passwd* and press Enter. You'll be asked to type your old password, and then the new one twice.

Note: As you type your old and new password, no typing appears on the screen. That's a safeguard against people peeking over your shoulder as you type.

The superuser, on the other hand, can change *anyone's* password—including the root account's password. Fortunately, so can an administrator using *sudo,* like this:

```
sudo passwd root
```

At this point, *sudo* will prompt you for *your* password, to confirm that you're actually an administrator. After you've entered it, the *passwd* utility will prompt you to enter a new password for the root account. Make it a good one: no spaces, four to eight letters and numbers long.

Tip: If you ever lose the root-account password, you can set up a new one by starting up the Mac from the Mac OS X installer CD; from the Installer menu, choose Reset Password.

Once the root account has a password, you can use it to log in with the user name *root,* exactly as described on page 290. When you do, you'll find that the root account's Home folder isn't in the Users folder like everyone else's; instead, it's in the private→var folder. You'll also find, of course, that you have complete freedom to modify, move, or change access privileges for any file and folder on your system.

Note: Not only is your system at risk of inadvertent damage when you log in as root, but some applications may behave oddly when run by the root account. Therefore, you should log in to Mac OS X as the superuser only when you have a specific job to do, and log out as soon as you've completed the task.

Eight Useful Unix Utilities

So far, you've read about only a handful of the hundreds of Unix programs that are built into Mac OS X and ready to run. Yes, *ls* and *sudo* are very useful tools, but they're only the beginning. Here's a rundown of some more cool (and very safe to try) programs that await your experimentation.

Tip: If you don't wind up back at the % prompt after using one of these commands, type *q* or, in some cases, *quit,* and hit Enter.

---

bc

Mac OS 9 and Windows aren't the only operating systems that come with a basic calculator accessory; Unix is well equipped in this regard, too.

When you type *bc* and hit Enter, you get a copyright notice and then—nothing. Just type the equation you want to solve, such as *2+2,* or *95+97+456+2-65,* or *(2*3)+165-95*(2.5*2.5),* and then press Enter. On the next line, *bc* instantly shows you the result of your calculation.

(In computerland, * designates multiplication, and / represents division. Note, too, that *bc* solves equations correctly: multiplication and division before addition and subtraction, inner parentheses working toward the outer ones. For more *bc* tricks and tips, type *man bc* at the prompt.)

kill

Mac OS X offers no shortage of ways to cut the cord on a program that seems to be locked up. You can force quit it (page 94), use Process Viewer (page 246)—or use *kill.*

The *kill* program in Terminal simply force quits a program, as though by remote control. (It even works when you telnet or SSH into your Mac from a remote location, as described in Chapter 21.) All you have to do is follow the *kill* command with the ID number of the program you want to terminate. (And how do you know its ID number? You start by running *top*—described in a moment—whose first column shows the PID [process ID] of every running program.)

Tip: Unless you also use *sudo,* you can *kill* only programs that you "own"–that are running under your account. (The operating system itself–*root*–is always running programs of its own, and it's technically possible that other people, dialing in from the road, are running programs of their own even while you're using the Mac!)

When you hear Unix fans talk about *kill* online, they often indicate a number flag after the command, like this: *kill -9.* This flag is an "non-catchable, non-ignorable kill"—in other words, it's an industrial-strength assassin that accepts no pleas for mercy from the program you're killing.

If you check *top* and find out that BeeKeeper Pro's process ID is 753, then, you'd abort it by typing *kill -9 753* and then pressing Enter.

Tip: Try this one when you need a laugh. At the prompt, simply type *bill gates* and press Enter. Does the Galactic Unix Oversight committee know about this use of the *kill* command?

---

open

What operating system would be complete without a way to launch programs? In Unix, the command is easy enough: *open,* as in *open /Applications/Chess.app.* You can even specify which document you want to open into that program by adding a space and then the document's name, like this: *open /Applications/Preview.app MyGraphic.tif.*

Tip: Also, the -e flag opens any text document in TextEdit, like this: *open -e MyTextDoc.txt.* This shortcut saves you having to specify the pathname of TextEdit itself.

Of course, there may not be much real utility in simply *launching* programs and documents this way. But you can see how useful *open* can be when you're writing automated scripts for your Mac, like those used by the *cron* auto-launcher program.

ps

The *ps* (process status) command is another way to get a quick look at all the programs running on your Mac, even the usually invisible ones, complete with their ID numbers. (For the most helpful results, use the *-a, -u, -x,* and *-w* flags like this: *ps -auxw.* For a complete description of these and other flags, type *man ps* and hit Enter.)

shutdown

It's perfectly easy to shut down your Mac from the menu. But using *shutdown* in Terminal has its advantages. For one thing, you can control *when* the shutdown occurs, using one of these three flags:

- **Now.** You can safely shut down by typing *shutdown now.* (Actually, only the root user is allowed to use *shutdown,* so you'd really type *sudo shutdown now* and then type in your administrator's password when asked.)

- **Later today.** The *-h* flag means, "shut down at the time I specify." Typing *sudo shutdown -h 2330,* for example, shuts down your machine at 11:30 p.m. today (because *2330* is military-time notation for 11:30 p.m.).

- **Any time in the next 100 years.** To make the machine shut down at 5:00 p.m. on November 5, 2003, for example, you could type *sudo shutdown 0311051700.* (That number code is in year:month:date:hour:minute format. So 0204051700 means 2002, April 5, 5:00 p.m.)

Tip: Once you set the auto-shutdown robot in motion, you can't stop it easily. You have to use the *kill* command described above to terminate the *shutdown* process itself. To find out *shutdown's* ID number in order to terminate it, use the *top* or *ps* command.

Nor are those the only useful flags. For example:

- The *-r* flag means "restart instead of just shutting down," as in *sudo shutdown -r now.*

- You can use *shutdown* to knock all connected network users off your machine without actually shutting down. Use the *-k* flag, like this: *sudo shutdown -k now.*

Finally, note that one of the most powerful uses of *shutdown* is turning off Macs by remote control, either from across the network or across the world via Internet. That is, you can use telnet or SSH (both described in Chapter 21) to issue this command.

tar, gzip

You don't encounter StuffIt files much in the Unix world; they're a Macintosh convention. You're much more likely to run across *tar* (for combining) and *gzip* (for compression) files.

Terminal lets you stuff and combine files in these formats with the greatest of ease. To compress a file, just type *gzip*, a space, and then the pathname of the file you want to compress (or drag the file or folder directly from the desktop into the Terminal window). When you press Enter, Mac OS X compresses the file.

Tarring a folder (combining its contents into a single file) is only slightly more complicated; you have to specify both the resulting file's name, followed by the actual directory pathname, like this: *tar -cf Memos.tar /Users/chris/Memos*. Add the *-z* flag to tar *and* compress the folder: *tar -czf Memos.tar.gz /Users/chris/Memos*.

Either way, if you switch to the Finder, you'll see that the file or folder you specified is now compressed (with the suffix *.gz*) or combined (with the suffix *.tar)*.

Tip: The *gzip* command deletes the original file after gzipping it. The *tar* command, on the other hand, "stuffs" the folder but leaves the original alone.

---

top

When you type *top* and press Enter, you get a handy table that lists every program that's currently running on your Mac, including the obscure background ones you may not even know are alive (Figure 16-6). (Actually, you get the top 20; make the window taller to see the rest.)

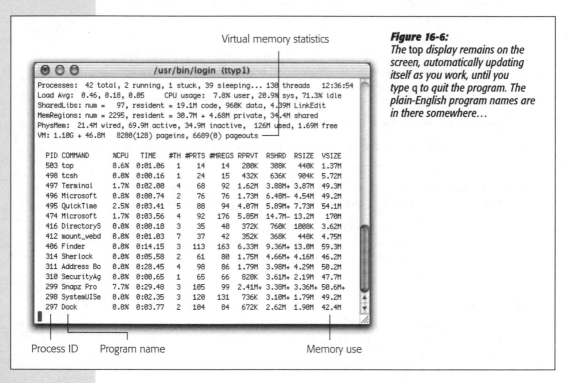

Virtual memory statistics

Figure 16-6:
The top *display remains on the screen, automatically updating itself as you work, until you type q to quit the program. The plain-English program names are in there somewhere...*

Process ID   Program name   Memory use

You also get statistics that tell you how much memory and speed (CPU power) they're sucking down. In this regard, *top* is similar to Process Viewer, described on page 246.

Tip: If you type *top -u,* you get a list sorted by CPU usage—that is, the power-hungry programs are listed first. If your Mac ever seems to act sluggish, checking *top -u* to see what's tying things up is a good instinct.

Where to Go from Here

This crash course in Unix should give you a first helping of guidance—enough to perform some genuinely useful tasks in Mac OS X, and to get a feeling for how Unix commands work.

There's a lot more to learn, however. As you peruse beginner-level Unix books and Web sites (see Appendix E), for example, you'll gradually become familiar with terms and tools like these:

Aliases

Don't be confused: Aliases in Unix have nothing to do with traditional Macintosh icon aliases. Instead, Unix aliases are more like text macros: longish commands that you can trigger by typing a much shorter abbreviation.

For example, remember the command for unlocking all the files in a folder? Probably not. (It was *sudo chflags -R nouchg [pathname].* To unlock everything in your account's Trash, for example, you'd type *sudo chflags -R nouchg ~/.trash.)*

POWER USERS' CLINIC

Secrets of Virtual Memory

The *top* command's table offers a fascinating look at the way Mac OS X manages memory. At the end of the "Processes" section above the table, for example, you'll see current statistics for *pageins* and *pageouts*—that is, how many times the virtual-memory system has had to "set down" software code for a moment as it juggles your open programs in actual memory. (These numbers are pointed out in Figure 16-6.)

The pageins and pageouts statistics are made of two different numbers, like this: *45451(0) pageins, 42946(0) pageouts.* The big number tells you how many times your Mac has had to shuffle data in and out of memory since the Mac started up. The number in parentheses indicates how much of this shuffling it's had to do within the *last second.*

This is the number to worry about. If it stays above zero for

a while, your Mac is gasping for RAM (as the hard-drive thrashing sounds and program-switching delays are probably also telling you).

In the listing of individual programs, the last four columns give details about the memory usage of each listed program. The one you care about is the RPRVT (Resident Private) column, which shows how much memory each program is actually using at the moment. (If you remember the About This Macintosh memory graph of Mac OS 9, then you probably remember the filled portion of the memory bars. That's what this number tells you: how much memory each program is actually using.) This number goes up and down as you work, and that's the miracle of Mac OS X: programs don't just grab a chunk of memory and sit with it. They put RAM back in the pot when they don't need it.

But using the *alias* command, you can create a much shorter command (*unlock,* for example) that has the same effect. (The *alias* command takes two arguments: the alias name you want, and the command it's supposed to type out, like this: *alias unlock sudo chflags -R nouchg ~/.trash.*)

Aliases you create this way, however, linger in Terminal's memory only while you're still in the original Terminal window. As soon as you close it, you lose your aliases. When you get better at Unix, therefore, you can learn to create an *aliases.mine* file that permanently stores all your command aliases.

pico, emacs, vi

One way to create and edit text files containing aliases (and to perform other command-related tasks) is to use *pico,* one of the most popular text processors (see Figure 16-7).

As you'll discover just by typing *pico* and pressing Enter, *pico* is a *full-screen* Unix application. You enter text in *pico* much as you do in TextEdit or SimpleText. But *pico* is filled with features that are especially tailored to working with Unix tasks and commands.

Nor is that the only text editor that's built into the Unix under Mac OS X. Some Unix fans prefer *vi* or *emacs,* in the same way that some people prefer AppleWorks to Microsoft Word.

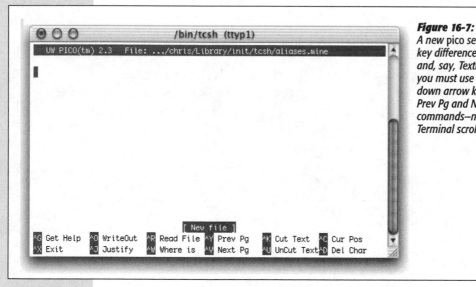

Figure 16-7:
A new pico *session. One key difference between* pico *and, say, TextEdit: to scroll, you must use the up and down arrow keys, or the Prev Pg and Next Pg commands—not the Terminal scroll bar.*

du

du is the Unix *disk usage* program. When you type it, you get to see the amount of space occupied on disk by whatever directory or directories you identify. If you type *du -ak ~,* for example (which adds the *a* flag to make sure both files and directories are listed, and the *k* flag for reporting in kilobytes), you might get this listing for your home directory:

```
4          /Users/chris/.CFUserTextEncoding
8          /Users/chris/.DS_Store
16         /Users/chris/Desktop/.DS_Store
4          /Users/chris/Desktop/Desktop (Mac OS 9)
4          /Users/chris/Desktop/Desktop Folder
24         /Users/chris/Desktop
8          /Users/chris/Documents/.DS_Store
4          /Users/chris/Documents/Tahoe Movie 1/ Tahoe 1 Project
4          /Users/chris/Documents/ Tahoe Movie 1/Icon
35660      /Users/chris/Documents/ Tahoe Movie 1/Media/Clip 01
28392      /Users/chris/Documents/ Tahoe Movie 1/Media/Clip 02
...
433808     /Users/chris
```

The last line tallies the grand total of disk space used by all items in the specified directory.

grep

The grep program is a *filter,* a powerful program designed to search data fed to it on a quest for text that matches a specified pattern. It can pass on the processed result to another program, a file, or the command line itself.

You specify the text pattern you want *grep* to search using a notation called *regular expressions.* For example, the regular expression *dis[ck]* will search for either *disk* or *disc.* Another example: to search for lines containing the file names *Yosemite1.mov,* *Yosemite2.mov,* and *Yosemite3.mov,* you could tell *grep* that you're looking for *Yosemite[1-3]\.mov.*

But *grep* can search much more than just file and directory names. Its search material can be part of any file, especially plain text files. The text files on your Mac include HTML files, log files, and—possibly juiciest of all—your email mailbox files. Using *grep,* for example, you could search all your Mail mail for messages matching certain criteria with great efficiency.

awk

awk (named for its creators Aho, Weinberger, and Kernighan) is a versatile Unix application that scans and processes lines of text as directed by instructions written in the *awk* programming language. Like *grep,* *awk* can search text for precisely specified strings, but *awk* then lets you extract and restructure the data into any conceivable format.

cron

This little Unix program can trigger certain commands according to a specified schedule, even when you're not logged in. People use *cron* to trigger daily backups or monthly maintenance, for example. You program your unattended software robot in simple text files called *crontabs*.

Mac OS X comes set up to run *cron* automatically. (If you open the Process Viewer program in your Applications→Utilities folder, you'll see them listed among the programs that your Mac is running all the time.)

In fact, it comes with three under-the-hood Unix maintenance tasks already scheduled; there's a daily *cron*, a weekly *cron*, and a monthly *cron*. They come set to run at 3:15 a.m., 4:30 a.m., and 5:30 a.m., however. If your Mac isn't generally turned on in the middle of the night, these healthy *cron* jobs may never get run.

You can either leave your Mac on overnight every now and then or, if you're feeling ambitious, change the time for them to be run; a glance at *man 5 crontab* shows you how. (Hint: It involves using *sudo pico* and editing the crontab file.)

telnet, ftp

Telnet and FTP aren't exclusively Unix commands, of course; techies from all walks of operating-system life have used telnet for years whenever they want to tap into another computer from afar, and FTP to deliver and download software files. Details on both are in Chapter 21.

Putting It Together

Suppose you wanted to know how much disk space is used by all the QuickTime movies in your Home folder. How would you go about it? Well, you'd probably open Sherlock (Chapter 20) and, using the Custom screen, set up a search for QuickTime files, restricted to the Home folder. But Sherlock lists the file size of *each* found file; it doesn't show the total.

If you were especially clever, you might remember that iTunes can catalog movie files as well as sound files—and it *does* show the total. You could select all the items in Sherlock's results list and drag them over into a new playlist window in iTunes to see the total size displayed at the bottom of the iTunes window.

And you'd wish there were a better way.

To use Mac OS X's Unix engine, you could just launch Terminal and type this:

```
du -ak ~ | grep -i '\.mov$' | awk '{total += $1 }; END {print
total, "KB"}'
```

Even after two chapters of Unix basics, you still may not understand every portion of this command. But pieces of it should now look familiar:

- **du -ak ~ |**. *du* is the disk usage program, and *-ak* are some of the option flags that tell it how to behave. And the ~ tells it to analyze your own home directory. Then comes the *pipe* (the vertical bar), which you can use to direct the results (output) of one command into the input of another.

- **grep -i \.mov$ |.** The *du* command sends two columns of text to *grep*: a number (the file size) and a pathname of an item in your home directory. Now *grep* searches these lines for pathnames containing the suffix *.mov* (that is, QuickTime movies), in effect screening out everything but movie files. Once it's done, it passes on some text—each line of which looks like "21512 /Users/chris/Documents/Finished Movies/Tahoe 1.mov" (a file size and a matching file's path)—to the *awk* program for processing.

  awk '{total += $1 }; END {print total, "KB"}'. *Awk* commands take the form of little pieces of programming; this one creates a variable called *total*, adds up the first column of the text sent to it by *grep* (in other words, the file sizes), and then *prints* (that is, sends to your screen) the total, followed by the letters "KB" to remind you that you're dealing with kilobytes.

When you press Return or Enter after that command, Mac OS X scans all the directories inside your Home directory, rounds up QuickTime movie files (.mov), adds up the amount of disk space used by each file, and displays the total on the Terminal screen before you: *7532 KB*.

Once you've gained some experience with Unix commands and programs like these, you'll find it fairly easy to adapt them to tasks of your own. For example, this command finds the total disk usage of PDF files that are larger than a megabyte in all home directories, and shows you the total size, in megabytes:

```
sudo du -ak /Users | grep -iE '^[0-9]{4,}.*\.pdf$' | awk
'{total += $1 } ; END {print total/1000, "MB"}'
```

It may look complex, but it's actually a variation on the same QuickTime-movie example described above.

With just a few more keystrokes, you could modify that command to produce a list of all those movies' names and sizes, send the list to someone else by email, or convert the list to HTML and upload it to your Web site. You could even automate this command to run at any scheduled time, day of the week, or interval using *cron*, as described on page 416. With the command line tools included with OS X (and others that are freely available), the possibilities are limitless.

For some guidance in picking up your Unix career from here, see Appendix E.

Tip: Many a programming toolkit helps you spot missing parentheses and quotes. For example, if you enclose a word in a command with only an open quote but forget to add the close quote, the error message might read, "Unmatched '."

But that message takes on a whole new meaning when you type, at the % prompt: *What's my skill at chess?*

Hacking Mac OS X

If you were to list the customization features of Mac OS 9 and Mac OS X side-by-side, the Mac OS 9 column would be much longer. The truth is that Mac OS X offers only a subset of the tweakable features Mac fans have grown used to. You can no longer record sounds, change the fonts used in the Finder, make the basic text-editor talk, and so on.

Apple was certainly right to focus on making the less fluffy features that remain work extremely well. On the other hand, customizing the Mac has always been one of life's most enjoyable time killers.

Fortunately, you can still fool around with the look and behavior of Mac OS X; Chapter 8, for example, shows you how to customize your desktop picture and screen saver. For anything more, though, you need some of Mac OS X's less obvious tools, or even free downloadable customizing software. Either way, this chapter is your guide to performing visual and behavioral surgery on your copy of Mac OS X, from changing the startup screen image to replacing the "poof" that appears when you drag something off the Dock with a new animation of your own.

Some are frivolous. Some are actually functional and useful. None is officially sanctioned by Apple, although all are perfectly safe.

Note: History has shown that Apple considers Mac OS X a work in progress. A huge number of the fun little hacks that worked in Mac OS X versions 10 through 10.0.4 stopped working in 10.1. All of the tricks in this chapter work in 10.1.1, but may well "break" in subsequent versions of Mac OS X. The Errata page for this book at *www.missingmanuals.com* will keep you up to date.

TinkerTool: Customization 101

If you poke around the Mac OS X Web sites and newsgroups long enough, you'll find little bits of Unix code being passed around. One of them purports to let you change the genie animation that you see when you minimize a window to the Dock. Another eliminates the drop shadow behind icon names on your desktop. Yet another lets you change the transparency of the Terminal window (Chapter 15)—a cool, although not especially practical, effect.

If you really want to fool around with these bits of Unix code, go for it. You'll find most of these tidbits at Web sites like *www.macosxhints.com*.

The truth is, however, that there's no good reason for you to subject yourself to the painstaking effort of typing out Unix commands when easy-to-use, push-button programs are available to do the same thing.

TinkerTool 2, for example, is a free utility that shows up as a new icon in System Preferences (Figure 17-1). It offers an amazing degree of control over the fonts, desktop, Dock, scroll bar arrows, and other aspects of the Mac OS X environment. (You can download it from the software page of *www.missingmanuals.com*, among other places.)

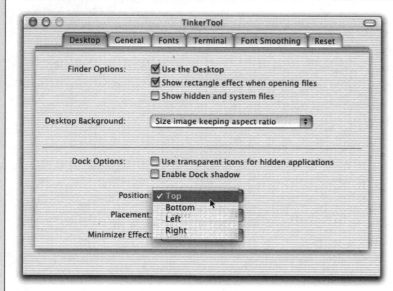

Figure 17-1:
Iconoclasts, take note: TinkerTool (shown here open) even lets you choose to put the Dock against the top edge of your screen. Its Desktop Background pop-up menu restores some of the flexibility Mac OS 9's Appearance control panel offered when it comes to positioning a graphic as your desktop background.

Here are some of the highlights:

- **Zooming rectangles.** When you open any icon, you see an animated expanding-rectangle effect to simulate the expansion of that icon into a window. It's nice, but it takes time. Using TinkerTool, you can turn off this effect.

- **The desktop picture.** As noted on page 192, the Displays panel of System Preferences lets you apply a digital photo of your choice to the backdrop of your screen. But only TinkerTool lets you specify what should happen if your background graphic isn't exactly the same *size* as the screen—whether you want the photo centered on the screen, resized to fit the screen, and so on.

- **Dock.** TinkerTool also lets you turn the Dock's drop shadow on or off, make hidden programs show up with transparent icons on the Dock, and specify the Dock's position on the screen (see Figure 17-1). TinkerTool even unlocks a third option for the animation of windows collapsing onto the Dock; in addition to the standard Mac OS X choices (Genie and Scale), you also get something called Suck (no comment).

- **Scroll bars.** TinkerTool gives you greater control over the placement of Mac OS X's scroll-bar arrows—together at one end of the scroll bar, duplicated at both ends of the scroll bar, and so on.

- **Language.** A pop-up menu lets you specify what language Mac OS X starts up in.

- **Fonts.** TinkerTool lets you change the default fonts that show up in the dialog boxes of your programs, such as the names of the icons in System Preferences. (Even TinkerTool doesn't let you change the menu bar font or the fonts used by desktop icons, however.)

- **Terminal.** Yes, this is the slider that lets you control the transparency of the Terminal window.

- **Font Smoothing.** You can read more about Mac OS X's font-smoothing feature on page 337. The important thing here is that TinkerTool can turn off this feature altogether, or set a point-sized threshold for its kicking in.

What's great about TinkerTool is that it's completely safe. It's nothing more than a front end for a number of perfectly legitimate Unix settings that Apple simply opted not to make available in the regular Finder. Furthermore, the changes you make using TinkerTool are stored in your own Home folder→Library folder—that is, they

---

POWER USERS' CLINIC

Moving Your Virtual Memory

It was the hit tip of the Mac OS X online community: By moving your virtual memory *swap file* to a different disk, you could accelerate Mac OS X by 20 percent!

Before getting excited about the prospect, however, consider these bits of news, just in. First, those benchmarks are based on Mac OS X 10.0.4. Version 10.1 was considerably accelerated, which mostly wipes out the speed benefits of moving virtual memory to another disk.

Second, the process of moving the swap file itself is very technical (it's surgery you perform with Unix commands in Terminal)—and, if you're not careful, dangerous.

If you're still interested in experimenting with this advanced technique, you'll find instructions at, for example, *www.macosxhints.com* (search for "virtual memory") or *http://homepage.mac.com/gdif/virtmem.html.*

---

affect only your account. Whatever changes you make don't affect the Mac experience for anyone else using your machine.

Tip: OSXSettings is an older, less refined shareware program that duplicates many of the functions of TinkerTool. Many of its functions don't work in Mac OS X 10.1 and later, but a few of its settings—including the ability to turn off the drop shadow effect that appears behind desktop icons—still work and aren't available in TinkerTool.

Redefining Keystrokes

If ⌘-S has never made sense to you as the keystroke for Save, or if some program you use has a menu command that lacks a keyboard equivalent altogether, this one is for you. Using the *defaults* command in Terminal (Chapter 15), you can easily massage whatever keystrokes you like—at least in any Cocoa program (page 116).

Launch Terminal and type this command carefully, including the punctuation, (precisely as shown here), taking care to substitute appropriate commands for those shown here in bold:

```
defaults write com.apple.Mail NSUserKeyEquivalents '{"Activity
Viewer"="*A";}'
```

Here's what to put in place of the bold elements above:

- **Mail.** Type the name of the Cocoa program containing the menu command you want to change. (Mac OS X's Cocoa programs include Stickies, Mail, Address Book, and TextEdit.)

- **Activity Viewer.** Replace this with the wording of the command as it now exists in the program.

- ***A.** Replace these two characters with the keystroke you'll want to trigger the menu command from now on. Instead of the asterisk (*), however, type @ for the ⌘ key, $ for the Shift key, ~ for the Option key, and ^ for the Control key. Follow these modifier stand-ins with the letter key you want. In other words, if you type $~D, you've just changed the keyboard equivalent of the menu command to Shift-Option-D.

If you've typed the command correctly, then when you press Enter you'll get no reaction from Terminal except another % prompt. Launch the program you modified and check out the results for yourself.

What's great about this procedure is that it affects only your own Library folder, which means that the keyboard equivalent has changed only for your account. When other people log in and use the same program, they'll see it the way it was before you went to work changing keystrokes.

Tip: You use this same procedure both when changing an existing keystroke assignment and when as-signing a new one.

Redoing Mac OS X's Graphics

The professional interface artists at Apple use Photoshop, just like professional art-ists everywhere else. But in Mac OS X, they've made very little effort to cover their tracks. Almost every element of the famous Aqua interface is nothing more than a Photoshop-generated PDF file.

The great thing about PDF files, of course, is that you can edit them. Maybe you just want to adjust the colors. Maybe you found a replacement graphic online, or maybe you actually want to draw a new graphic from scratch. In each of these cases, using a program like Photoshop, you can dress up your own desktop your own way.

Note: Unfortunately, the delightful shareware program GraphicConverter can't edit PDF files, so it won't work for most of these hacks.

A Dock Makeover

Have you had quite enough of the lightly shaded pinstripes that lie behind the Dock? Then by all means—change them.

1. **Restart the Mac in Mac OS 9.**

   You'll find this instruction—restarting in Mac OS 9—to be a running theme in this chapter. Doing so bypasses the objections you'll get from Mac OS X itself as you try to hack the system. (There is an alternative, however: logging into Mac OS X as the *root user,* as described on page 290. But for many people, simply restarting in Mac OS 9 is a less intimidating routine.)

GEM IN THE ROUGH

200 MB—Yours Absolutely Free

Mac OS X is extremely world-friendly. You can switch it into any of dozens of languages.

But what if, like almost everyone, you do most of your work in a single language? The other language software modules are taking up about 200 MB of your hard drive at this very moment.

The quickest way to get rid of them is to restart in Mac OS 9. Use Sherlock to search for folders whose names contain the letters *.lproj.* From the list that it finds, you can throw away all the folders—there will be many duplicates—of the languages that don't interest you: French, Dutch, Spanish, Portuguese, Italian, or whatever. When you reboot in Mac OS X, you'll discover that you have a lot more disk space to play with.

---

2. **In the Finder, open the System→Library→CoreServices folder. Control-click the Dock.app icon; choose Show Package Contents from the contextual menu. In the Dock.app window, open the Contents→Resources folder.**

Inside you'll find quite a number of files. The three you care about are the graphics files that constitute the Dock. They're called *left.pdf, middle.pdf,* and *right.pdf.*

You'll probably notice right away that these are tiny files, only a few pixels square. Mac OS X creates the Dock's background by tiling them over and over.

Tip: If you think you may want to go back to the Dock's original look after your experiment, make a safety copy of these PDF files before proceeding.

---

3. **Drag the three PDF files to the desktop. Switch into Photoshop, open them using the File→Open command, and edit them.**

The left and right files are only very narrow "bookends" for the Dock itself. Most of what you see is the middle file. If you decide to keep these files at their original sizes, you can't do much beyond changing their color or pattern. But if you decide to resize the middle graphic and paste in an entirely new image, the sky's the limit (see Figure 17-2).

4. **Save your changes, put the edited PDF files back where you found them (Resources folder), and restart in Mac OS X.**

The deed is done. You now have the most remarkable Dock on the block.

Figure 17-2:
Top: The middle file—called middle.pdf—can be almost any size you like. For best results, set the width to the maximum width of your monitor, and height to about 100 pixels. Bottom: The result offers some fascinating possibilities for a redesigned Dock.

POWER USERS' CLINIC

Goodbye Dock

When you start up Mac OS X, the system automatically launches Dock.app in your System→Library→CoreServices folder. If, like many people, you become addicted to a Dock replacement like DragThing (shareware), no big deal: Restart in Mac OS 9 and move Dock.app to a different folder.

Then start up in Mac OS X again. Using the Login panel of System Preferences, set up DragThing to open automatically at login time. Now every time you sign in, you'll get DragThing instead of the Dock. (To reinstate the original Dock, just put Dock.app back where it came from.)

Replacing the Poof

When you drag an icon off the Dock, it disappears with a literal puff of smoke—a cute, cartoon-like animation that Apple has been trying to work into its operating systems ever since the days of the Newton palmtop. Most people find this tiny, one-second display of interface magic charming and witty, but others argue that it demeans the dignity of the otherwise professional-looking Mac OS X.

If you follow that latter camp, you can replace the animation with either of two alternatives:

• **A professionally designed replacement animation.** You can download a number of them from *www.resexcellence.com/user_poofs.shtml*. Each takes the form of a specially formatted PDF file. After restarting in Mac OS 9, put the PDF file into your System→Library→CoreServices→Dock.app→Contents→Resources folder. (To open Dock.app, Control-click its "application" icon and choose Show Package Contents from the contextual menu.)

• **A new animation that you've created yourself.** The process isn't a short one by any means—it involves 28 steps, Adobe Photoshop, and the step-by-step instructions of Poof-meister Patrick Gerrity. His complete, illustrated instructions (Figure 17-3) are available on the software page of *www.missingmanuals.com*.

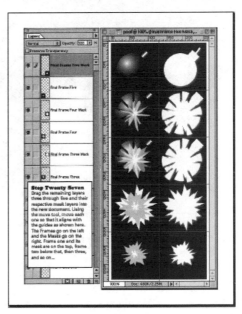

Figure 17-3:
You can replace the cartoon puff of smoke with any little animation you can dream up. All you need is the illustrated instructions created by Patrick Gerrity for the benefit of this book's readers. (Photoshop is required, especially because many of the steps involve editing transparent layers of the graphic.)

The Startup and Login Screens

Yeah, yeah, sure, Mac OS X makes it easy to change the desktop picture. But what about the boring Mac OS X, blue-Apple-logo picture that appears during startup process? And what about the default swirling blue desktop picture that appears be-hind the sign-in screen?

Fortunately, you can make these look like anything you want. Restart in Mac OS 9 and then proceed like this:

- **The "Welcome to Mac OS X" image** is a JPEG graphic, called Aqua Blue.jpg, in the Library→Desktop Pictures folder. You can just edit this file—or replace it with another graphic having the same name and file format. At the next startup, you'll enjoy your new background.

- **The sign-in screen graphic** is only a little bit harder to change. Using Photoshop, choose File→Open. Navigate to and open System→Library→CoreServices→SystemStarter→QuartzDisplay.bundle→Resources→BootPanel.pdf. As always, you can edit this file to your heart's content. When you save changes and then restart, you'll find your new graphic in place (Figure 17-4).

Figure 17-4:
Photoshop can directly edit the PDF files that constitute much of the Mac OS X interface. Of course, you can always create your own PDF files from any programPalm OS 2 or later

That's a handy thing to remember when you want to edit Mac OS X interface elements like the startup screen.

A Better Clock

Why should you send away $20 apiece for cheapo company-logo watches for your employees? Stamp your logo right onto the face of Mac OS X's own Clock program!

As always, restart the Mac in Mac OS 9. Choose File→Open from within Photoshop (or, this time, almost any graphics program, including AppleWorks and GraphicConverter). Navigate to the Applications→Clock→Contents→Resources folder of your Mac OS X disk.

To modify the analog clock face (Figure 17-5), open and edit the file called *Clock02.tif.* (Back up the original first, if you think you'll ever want to go back.) To change the digital clock/calendar, on the other hand, operate on the file called *background.tif.* In either case, save your changes when you're done.

The result is something you can call your own, no matter what.

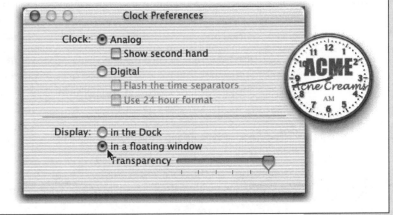

Figure 17-5:
To see the results of your editing (right), be sure to choose Clock→Preferences and turn on "Display in a floating window" (left). If the new clock face isn't stark enough, drag the Transparency slider to the right.

Colorizing Menulets

You can colorize the little menu-bar symbols fondly called *menulets* (see page 87), or even redesign their graphics completely. Like many other Mac OS X screen elements, these are nothing more than little tiny graphics saved in PDF format.

You can edit them, as usual, by restarting the Mac in Mac OS 9 and launching Photoshop. Choose File→Open; navigate to the System→Library→CoreServices→ Menu Extras→*AirPort.menu*→Contents→Resources folder.

You'll find that the Menu Extras folder contains individual folders for every possible menulet: Battery, Clock, Displays, and so on. Open whichever one you want to customize, substituting its name for the italicized folder above.

Inside the Resources folder are a number of TIFF files that represent the various forms your menulet might take: the Volume icon, for example, seems to emit different numbers of sound waves depending on your volume setting. Edit each of the graphics as you see fit. (The ones whose names are tagged with an *s* or *w* represent the inverted *highlighted* graphic, the one you see when you actually click the menulet.)

Tip: In Photoshop 6, you can keep the background transparent by choosing File→Preferences→Saving Files; turn on the checkbox for advanced TIFF saving options. Now, when you export your TIFF file, you'll be offered the option to keep the background transparent, so that the gray Mac OS X pinstripes still show through.

Rewriting the Words

Mac OS X stores the text and settings of its menus, dialog boxes, and other elements in special text files called *plist* (for Property List) files. They sit in one of the three Library folders (in your Home folder, the System folder, or the hard drive window).

The easiest way to edit them is to use Apple's PropertyList Editor, a program that came on your Mac OS X Developer CD. Once you've installed your developer tools as described on page 246, you'll find PropertyList Editor in Developer→Applications.

There are hundreds of plist files, so some experimentation and patience is required. Most of the cool changes you can make to your plists can be made much more easily using TinkerTool, described at the beginning of this chapter. Here, however, is an example of the smaller kind of change you can make this way.

Renaming the Trash

It's called Trash, but in Mac OS X, it looks more like an office wastebasket. When inspiration on the work you're *supposed* to be doing runs dry, consider patching this discrepancy by changing the name of the Trash icon to anything you like.

In PropertyList Editor, choose File→Open. Navigate to System→Library→ CoreServices→Dock.app→Contents→Resources→English.lproj→InfoPlist.strings.

After a moment, you see the display shown in Figure 17-6. Click the Root triangle to see and edit the three settings, as directed in the figure.

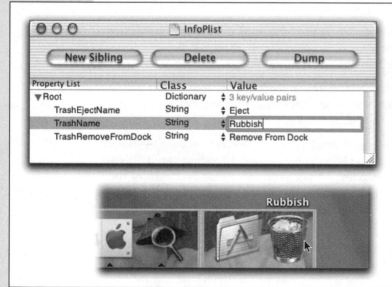

Figure 17-6:
Top: This simple file contains the name of the Trash icon on the Dock—and the name of the Eject icon that replaces it when you're dragging a disk. By double-clicking the text in the Value column, you can edit these descriptions to change the corresponding names.

Bottom: The resulting Trash has a very different name.

Once you're finished making the change, choose File→Save As, and save your edited plist document to the desktop. You can't simply save changes to the original, because Mac OS X is extremely protective of its System folder. Instead, you must now replace the original document (after making a safety copy, if you like) with your edited version. To do that, you must dodge Mac OS X's system-software security in one of these ways:

- Restart in Mac OS 9.

- Log in as the *root user* (a somewhat hairier route for the novice, as described on page 290).

- Log in as *>console,* a technique described on page 559. (This deposits you at a command line interface, and is therefore best for Unix aficionados; use the *sudo* command to do your dirty deeds).

In any case, the next time you log in, you'll see your new name on the Trash.

Rewording the Dock

Using the same routine described in the previous paragraphs, you can edit all of the commands that pertain to the Dock—both its commands in the menu (Dock Preferences, Turn Magnification On, and so on) and the contextual menus that pop out of the Dock icons themselves. These wordings are in System→Library→ CoreServices→Dock.app→Contents→Resources→English.lproj→DockMenus.plist; click the flippy triangles to see the various commands you can rewrite.

5

Part Five:
Mac OS X Online

Internet Setup, iDisk, and iTools

A s Apple's programmers slogged away over the months on the massive Mac OS X project, there was one spot where they must have felt like they were happily gliding on ice: networking and the Internet. The Internet already runs, for the most part, on Unix, and hundreds of extremely polished tools and software chunks were already available.

Most people connect to the Internet using a modem that dials out over ordinary phone lines. But a rapidly growing minority connects over higher-speed wires, using connections that are always on: cable modems, DSL, or corporate networks. This chapter shows you how to set up each one (and how to use any of them with a wireless Apple AirPort system).

This chapter also describes some of Mac OS X's offbeat Internet featurettes: the iDisk, a free 20 MB backup or transfer disk that Apple gives to every Mac fan (via the Internet); the other Apple iTools, including HomePage (which lets you publish your own Web pages); and the system-wide Internet bookmarks known as *Internet location files*.

The Best News You've Heard All Day

If you installed Mac OS X onto a Mac that was already set up to get online in Mac OS 9, breathe easy. Mac OS X was kind enough to pick up your networking and Internet settings from your Mac OS 9 System Folder. The moment you first see the Mac OS X desktop, you're ready to use the Internet (and skip the next two pages).

Read on, however, if you're setting up a new Mac, a new Internet account, or otherwise need to plug in the Internet settings manually.

Connecting by Dial-up Modem

Mac OS X doesn't come with an Assistant that walks you through the creation of an Internet account. Instead, signing up for one of these $20-a-month service providers is up to you; companies like EarthLink and AT&T WorldNet are some popular Internet-access services.

To set up your account, you have to plug in a series of settings into the Network pane of System Preferences. This process may require the assistance of your Internet service provider (ISP)—in the form of its Web page, the little instruction sheets that came with your account, or a help-desk agent on the phone.

Phase 1: The TCP/IP Tab

Start by opening System Preferences and clicking the Network tab. (You might suppose that the Internet tab would be the right place to start. But as described in Chapter 8, you use that control panel simply to specify your favorite Web browser, email program, and so on.)

When you choose Internal Modem from the Show pop-up menu, you see a Configure pop-up menu and two text boxes. Your main mission here is to fill in the Domain Name Server numbers provided by your ISP—at least if you hope to get onto the Web. If Using PPP is selected in the Configure pop-up menu, you can move on to Phase 2. (If you find yourself unable to get online, however, contact your ISP on the off chance that some unusual settings are required here.)

Phase 2: The PPP Tab

Now click the PPP tab (Figure 18-1) and fill in the blanks like this:

- **Service Provider.** Type in the name of your ISP, if you like (*EarthLink*, for example).

- **Telephone Number.** This, of course, is the local access number that your modem is supposed to dial to connect to your ISP.

Tip: If you need your Mac to dial a 9 or an 8 for an outside line (as you would from within a hotel), add it to the beginning of the phone number followed by a comma. The comma means "pause for two seconds," which you can also put to good use when typing in the dialing sequence for a calling-card number.

- **Alternate Number.** This blank lets you type in a number to dial if the first one is busy.

- **Account Name.** This is one of the most important pieces of information yet: your account name, as assigned by the ISP. If you're BillG@earthlink.net, for example, type *BillG* here.

- **Password.** Specify your ISP account password here. Turn on "Save password" if you'd rather not have to retype it every time you connect.

- **PPP Options.** Click this button to bring up a special Options dialog box, filled with checkboxes that control your online sessions. Here, for example, you can specify how long the Mac waits before hanging up the phone line after your last online activity, and how many times the Mac should dial if the ISP phone number is busy.

Tip: In the Session Options, one checkbox you'll almost certainly want to turn on is "Connect automatically when starting TCP/IP applications." It makes your Mac dial the Internet automatically whenever you check your email or open your Web browser. (Otherwise, you'd have to establish the Internet call manually, using the Internet Connect program described on page 436; only then could you check your email or open your Web browser.)

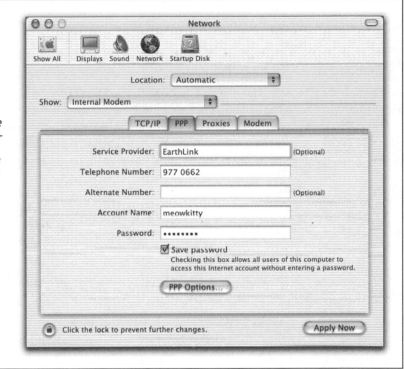

Figure 18-1:
Even if several user accounts (Chapter 11) are set up on your Mac, they all share the same Internet connection settings. Only an administrator can make changes to the Internet dial-up settings, therefore. That's why the little padlock appears in the lower-left corner of the dialog box. When you're finished making your settings, either close the window or click Apply Now.

Phase 3: The Proxies Tab

Most people can ignore this tab altogether. (Proxy servers are computers used primarily in corporations to accelerate or filter the delivery of Internet information. Of course, if you work in a corporation, you probably don't connect to the Internet with a dial-up modem anyway. If you are that rare exception, ask your network administrator to show you how to set up this screen.)

Phase 4: The Modem Tab

This is where you specify what kind of modem you have. Most Mac OS X-compatible Macs have built-in Apple modems, which is why the pop-up menu already says "Apple Internal 56K Modem (v.90)." If you, the heretic, have some other kind of modem, choose its name from the pop-up menu.

Tip: This list of modems corresponds to configuration files in your Library→Modem Scripts folder. You can save some disk space and simplify your life by throwing away the scripts for all of the modems except the one you actually use.

Some of the other settings that can be handy:

- **Sound.** By clicking Off, you make your Mac dial the Internet silently, sparing sleeping family members or dorm roommates from having to listen to your modem shriek as it connects.

- **Dialing.** Specify what kind of phone service you have—Tone or, in a few rural locations, Pulse.

- **Wait for dial tone before dialing.** This is for you, North American laptop owners. The dial tones in certain foreign countries sound weird to the Mac, which therefore won't dial; it's still listening for that good old North American dial tone. In that case, turning off this checkbox makes the Mac dial bravely even though it hasn't heard the sound it's listening for.

Going Online

That's all there is to it. If you turned on "Connect automatically when starting TCP/IP applications," your Mac dials and connects to the Internet automatically whenever an Internet-related program tries to connect (a Web browser or email program, for example).

If you didn't turn on that option, then you make your Mac dial the Internet in one of these ways:

- **Using Internet Connect.** This little program is in your Applications folder. The main item of interest here is the Connect button, which makes the Mac dial. Once the indicators show that you're online, open your Web browser, email program, or other Internet software and get surfing.

  By clicking the black triangle button next to the Configuration pop-up menu, you can collapse the Internet Connect window so that it takes up much less screen space. You hide everything, in fact, but the pop-up menu and the Connect/Disconnect button.

  If you're smart, however, you'll turn on the "Show modem status on menu bar" checkbox. It adds a tiny telephone icon to the upper-right corner of your screen (Figure 18-2), which lets you bypass Internet Connect completely the next time you want to go online.

• **Use the menu-bar icon.** Just click that little telephone icon on the menu bar and choose Connect from the pop-up menu. Your Mac dials without even blocking your desktop picture with a dialog box.

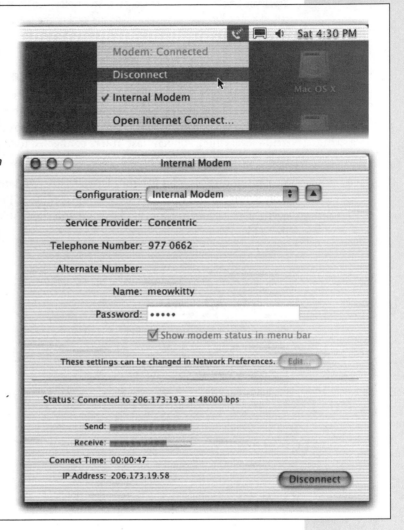

Figure 18-2:
Going online automatically (by launching an Internet program) is by far the most convenient method, but you can also go online on command, in one of these two ways.

Top: The quick way is to choose Connect from this menulet (which doesn't appear until you turn on "Show modem status on menu bar" on the Internet Connect screen).

Bottom: You can also go online manually the long way (using Internet Connect, shown here in its expanded form).

Disconnecting

The Mac automatically drops the phone line 15 minutes after your last activity online (or whatever interval you specified in the PPP Options dialog box). In fact, if other people have accounts on your Mac (Chapter 11), the Mac doesn't even hang up when you log out. It maintains the connection so that the next person can Net-surf without having to redial.

Of course, if other people in your household are screaming for you to get off the line so that they can make a call, you can also disconnect manually. Either choose Disconnect from the Internet menulet or click Disconnect in the Internet Connect window (both shown in Figure 18-2).

Tip: If you travel between two locations with your laptop, don't miss the Location feature. It lets you switch sets of dial-up modem settings—including the local phone number—with a simple menu selection. It's described on page 441.

Connecting Via Cable Modem, DSL, or Office Network

If one of these terms—"cable modem, DSL, or office network"—sounds familiar, you're one of the lucky ones. You have a high-speed connection to the Internet that's always available, always on. You never have to wait to dial, to disconnect, or to download—everything happens fast. You're connected to the Net via your Mac's Ethernet jack, leaving its built-in modem pretty much benched.

You set up your account like this: Open System Preferences; then click the Network icon. From the Show pop-up menu, choose Built-in Ethernet (or the name of whatever Ethernet card is connected to your Internet equipment). Now, you see something like Figure 18-3.

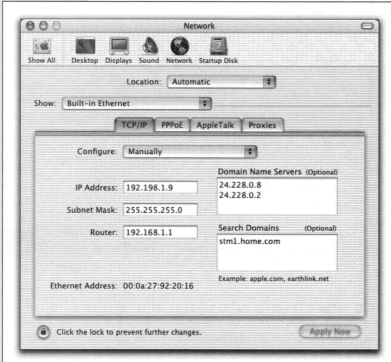

Figure 18-3:
Don't be alarmed by the morass of numbers and periods—it's all in good fun. (If you find TCP/IP fun, that is.) In this illustration, you've got a cable-modem account with a static IP address, which means you have to type in all of these numbers yourself, as guided by the cable company. The alternative is a DHCP server account, which fills most of it in automatically.

The next step is to make a selection from the Configure pop-up menu. Only your Internet service provider (cable TV company or phone company, for example) can tell you exactly what settings to use, but you'll generally choose one of these options:

- **Manually.** Your cable or phone company will tell you precisely what *IP address* (Internet address) to type in here. The bad news is that you'll also have to fill in all the other boxes here—Subnet Mask, Router, and so on—with cryptic numbers separated by periods.

  On the other hand, look at the bright side: You've just been given a *static IP address,* an Internet address that is all your own and that won't change. Because your Mac has this one, reliable address, several cool Mac OS X features are available to you. For example, you'll be able to access your files from anywhere in the world, as described on page 505.

- **Using DHCP.** This acronym means *dynamic host configuration protocol,* the operative word being *dynamic.* If your Internet company tells you to use this option, then it intends to assign your Mac a different IP address every time it turns on.

  The good news is that this option saves you from having to fill in any of the other boxes in this control panel. All the settings will come to you, over the Internet. (The one occasional exception: the Domain Name Servers box.)

  The bad news is that you don't have a single, unchanging IP address, which can make it more difficult to use the remote-control features of Mac OS X, like dialing in from the road. (There is a workaround, however; see page 498.)

That's all the setup—click Apply Now. If your settings are correct, you're online, now and forever. You never have to worry about connecting or disconnecting.

You may, however, want to worry about installing *firewall software.* Because you're connected to the Internet at all times, it's theoretically possible for some hacker to use automated hacking software to blast you—flood you with email or take control of your machine. Shareware programs like BrickHouse and Firewalk (available for download from *www.missingmanuals.com)* can block them.

POWER USERS' CLINIC

PPoE and DSL

If you have DSL service, you may be directed to click the PPoE tab (which is also in the Network pane of System Preferences). It stands for *PPP over Ethernet,* meaning that although your DSL "modem" is connected to your Ethernet port, you still have to make and break your Internet connections manually, as though you had a dial-up modem.

In other words, you're not online full-time.

Fill in the PPoE tab as directed by your ISP (usually just your account name and password). From here on in, you start and end your Internet connections exactly as though you had a dial-up modem, as described on page 436.

Tip: If you have more than one Mac, you can share a single cable modem or DSL box among them, no matter what your phone or cable company tells you. The trick is to buy a *router*: a box that intercepts the signal from the cable modem or DSL box and shares it with all the different Macs you've plugged into it. (Many of these routers double as Ethernet hubs, providing four or eight jacks into which you can plug the Macs.) As a bonus, many of these routers act as firewalls to keep out hackers.

AirPort Networks

AirPort is Apple's term for its wireless networking technology. If you have it, you'd remember having paid $100 for an AirPort card, which lets any modern Mac model communicate, like a cordless phone, with an AirPort base station up to 100 feet away. Doing so lets you surf the Web from your laptop in the TV room, for example, or share files with someone across the building from you.

The base station can either be the $300 AirPort Base Station (which looks like a small silver flying saucer); a non-Apple brand of the same thing (page 295); or another AirPort-equipped Mac that you've configured, using the AirPort Setup Assistant for Mac OS 9, to serve as a *software-based* base station. You can plug the base station into an Ethernet hub, thus permitting 10 or 20 airport-equipped Macs to join an existing Ethernet network without wiring.

For the easiest AirPort network setup, begin by configuring your Mac so that it can go online the wired way, as described on the previous pages. Once it's capable of connecting to the Internet via wires, you can then use the Airport Setup Assistant (in your Applications→Utilities folder) to transmit those Internet settings wirelessly to the base station itself. From then on, the *base station's* modem or Ethernet jack—not your Mac's—will do the connecting to the Internet.

At that point, you can do all the controlling you like from the Airport menulet (Figure 18-4).

Figure 18-4:
Once your AirPort system is working, you can use the menu-bar icon to turn off your AirPort card (for battery savings in a laptop), to switch from one AirPort network to another (in schools or companies that have more than one), and to check your wireless signal strength (by counting the "waves" coming out of the icon on your menu bar).

Switching Locations

If you travel with a laptop, you know the drill. You're constantly opening up System Preferences→Network so that you can switch between Internet settings: Ethernet at the office, dial-up at home. Or maybe you simply go on trips to another branch office from time to time, and you're getting tired of having to change the local access number for your ISP each time you leave home (and return home again).

The simple solution is the ⌘→Location submenu. As Figure 18-5 shows, all you have to do is tell it where you are. Mac OS X handles the details of switching to the correct Internet connection and phone number.

Figure 18-5:
The Location feature lets you switch from one "location" to another just by choosing its name—either from the ⌘ menu (top) or from this pop-up menu in System Preferences (bottom). The Automatic location just means "the standard, default one you originally set up." (Don't be fooled: Despite its name, Automatic isn't the only location that offers multihoming, *which is described later in this chapter.)*

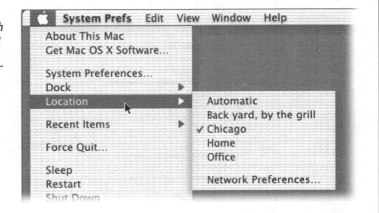

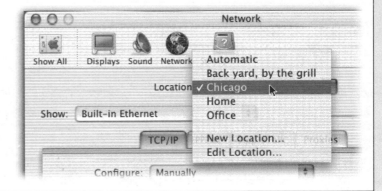

Creating a New Location

To create a *Location*, which is nothing more than a set of memorized settings, open System Preferences, click Network, and choose New Location from the Location pop-up menu. You'll be asked to provide a name for your new location, such as *Chicago Office* or *Dining Room Floor.*

When you click OK, you return to the Network panel, which is now blank. You're supposed to take this opportunity to set up the kind of Internet connection you use at the corresponding location, just as described on the first pages of this chapter. If you travel regularly, in fact, you can use Location Manager to build a long list of city locations, each of which "knows" the local phone number for your Internet access company (because you've entered it on the PPP tab).

Tip: If you use nothing but a cable modem when you're at home, create a location in which you've turned off the built-in modem, as described in the following numbered steps. Conversely, if your laptop uses nothing but its dial-up modem when on the road, create a location in which you've turned off the Ethernet port. You'll save a few seconds each time you try to go online, because your Mac won't bother hunting for an Internet connection that doesn't exist (see "Multihoming," below).

Making the Switch

Once you've set up your various locations, you can switch among them using either the Location pop-up menu (in System Preferences→Network) or the →Location submenu, as shown in Figure 18-5. As soon as you do so, your Mac is automatically set to dial the new phone number, or to connect using the different method.

Tip: If you have a laptop, create a connection called Offline. From the Show pop-up menu, choose Active Network Ports; turn off *all* the connection methods you see in the list. When you're finished, you've got yourself a laptop that will *never* attempt to go online, saving you the occasional interruption of a program that tries to dial but takes three minutes to discover you're on Flight 800 to Miami and have no phone line available.

WORKAROUND WORKSHOP

The Internet Via Classic

You may remember that the Classic environment (Chapter 5) may look and feel like Mac OS 9, but is actually just a simulation. You're still running Mac OS X. Signals that Classic programs try to send directly to the hardware of your Mac—its modem, for instance—must then pass through the Mac OS X software layer.

In many cases, that's no big deal. If you inspect your TCP/IP control panel in Classic, you'll see that Apple has shrewdly rigged it to inherit the Internet settings you've established for Mac OS X. (Don't fiddle with them, either.) If you're connected to the Internet via your Ethernet jack (cable modem, DSL), your Classic programs can get online without a hiccup.

There are some glitches, however. If you connect to the Internet via dial-up modem, you may find that Classic programs don't automatically dial when you run them. The solution: Connect to the Internet manually in Mac OS X (using the Internet Connect program, for example) before switching to the Classic program and going online.

The other problem is America Online. It tries to "talk to" your modem directly, unaware that Mac OS X is standing in the way. As a result, the Mac OS 9 version of the AOL software can't get online at all when you're running Mac OS X.

You have only two choices: Restart the Mac in Mac OS 9 when you need to use AOL, or install the Mac OS X version of AOL when it becomes available.

Multihoming

Speaking of different ways to get online, Mac OS X offers one of the coolest features known to Internet-loving mankind: *multihoming*. That's the ability to auto-detect which Internet connections methods are available—and to switch to the fastest one available, automatically.

This feature is especially ideal for laptops. When you open your Web browser, your laptop might first check to see if it's at the office, plugged into a cable modem via Ethernet—the fastest possible connection. If not, it automatically looks for an AirPort network. Finally, if it draws a blank there, the laptop reluctantly dials the modem. It may not be the fastest Internet connection, but it's all you've got at the moment.

In short, for each location you create, you can specify which network connections the Mac should look for, and in which order. You can even turn off some connections entirely; for example, if you have a desktop Mac that's always connected to a cable modem, you may never want your Mac to dial using its built-in modem. In that case, you could turn off the modem entirely.

Here's how to go about using this multihoming feature:

1. **Open System Preferences. Click the Network icon.**

   Make sure the appropriate location is selected in the Location pop-up menu.

2. **From the Show pop-up menu, choose Active Network Ports.**

   Now you see the display shown in Figure 18-6. It lists all the different ways your Mac knows how to go online, or onto an office network.

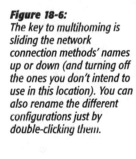
Figure 18-6:
The key to multihoming is sliding the network connection methods' names up or down (and turning off the ones you don't intend to use in this location). You can also rename the different configurations just by double-clicking them.

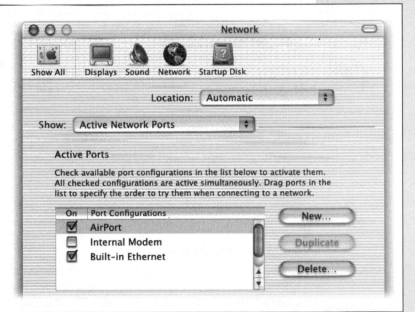

3. **Drag the items up and down in the list into priority order.**

If you have a cable modem, DSL, or office network connection, for example, you might want to drag Built-in Ethernet to the top of the list, because that's almost always the fastest way to get online.

At this point, you can also *turn off* any connections you don't want your Mac to use when it's in this location—the internal modem, for example.

4. **Click Apply Now.**

That's all there is to it. Your Mac will actually switch connections—not just each time you go online, but even in real time, during a single Internet session. If lightning takes out your cable modem in the middle of your Web surfing, your Mac will seamlessly switch to your AirPort network—or, if necessary, dial using the modem—to keep your session alive.

iTools @ Apple.com

In January 2000, Apple CEO Steve Jobs explained to the Macworld Expo crowds that he and his team had had a mighty brainstorm: Apple controls *both ends* of the connection between a Mac and the Apple Web site. As a result, he went on, Apple ought to be able to come up with some pretty clever Internet-based features as a reward to loyal Mac fans. And sure enough, later that same day, the Apple Web site appeared with its completely new look (see Figure 18-7).

Figure 18-7:
The Apple Web site features special tabs across the top. For example, the iCards feature lets you send attractively designed electronic greeting cards by email to anyone on the Internet. Email and HomePage are the other second-tier features. The big one, however, is iDisk.

What iTools Gets You

For most people, the crown jewel of these free services is iDisk, which creates a 20 MB hard-drive icon on your desktop. Anything you drag into the folders on this gets copied—apparently onto this miniature hard drive, but actually to Apple's secure servers on the Internet.

In other words, iDisk is a free backup disk. It's the perfect solution for people whose Macs don't have floppy drives or Zip drives—and even a good idea for those who do, because this backup disk is off-site. If a fire or thief destroys your office *and* your backup disks, your iDisk is still safe.

Furthermore, you can pull the iDisk onto *any* computer's screen—at your office, at your home, at your friend's house, Mac or Windows (page 448)—so you don't have to carry around a physical disk to transport important files.

Best of all, the iDisk is extremely well integrated into Mac OS X. For example, when you're saving a document from within a program, you can save it directly onto your iDisk.

The iDisk isn't the only iTools feature, however. Signing up for an iTools account also gives you goodies called iCards, HomePage, and Email. In the following pages, you'll find out how to use each of these features.

Signing Up for iTools

Mac OS X makes it easier than ever to sign up for an iTools account. Open System Preferences. When you click Internet, the iTools tab is staring you in the face. Click Sign Up.

Now you go online, and your Web browser opens up to the iTools sign-up screen. Fill in your name and address, make up an account name and password, and, if you like, turn off the checkbox that invites you to get junk mail.

You're also asked to make up a question and answer (such as, "First-grade teacher's name?" and "Smithers"). If you ever forget your password, the iTools software will help you—but only if it knows that you're you when you answer this question correctly. Click Continue.

An account summary screen now appears (print it or save it). On the next screen, the system offers to send an email message to your friends letting them know about your new email address (which is *whatever-name-you-chose@mac.com*).

The final step is to return to the Internet pane of System Preferences. On the iTools tab, fill in the account name and password you just composed. You're ready to use iTools.

iDisk

As noted above, iDisk is a free 20 MB virtual disk that behaves as though it's an external (and very slow) hard drive attached to your Mac. (You can pay for a larger disk, if you need it; details are on the Apple Web page.)

You can pull the iDisk onto your screen in any of several ways:

- Choose Go→iDisk (or press Shift-⌘-I).

- Click the iDisk icon on the toolbar of any Finder window. (If it's not there, see page 84.)

- From within any program, choose File→Save As or File→Open. In the Save or Open dialog box, choose iDisk from the Where pop-up menu (see Figure 18-8).

- Double-click an alias you made of your iDisk the last time it was on the screen.

- Choose Go→Connect to Server. At the bottom of the resulting dialog box, type *afp://idisk.mac.com* and press Enter. In the next dialog box, type your iTools name and password, and then click Connect. (This is the quickest approach if you're using somebody else's Mac OS X machine.)

- Visit *http://itools.mac.com* and click the iDisk icon. Type in your name and password, and then click Enter. Finally, click Open Your iDisk. (Clearly, this is a lot more work than the one-click methods described above. Use this technique when you're using a Mac OS 9 machine far from home, for example.)

At this point, using iDisk is exactly like using a very slow—but very safe—floppy disk or Zip disk. You can drag files or folders from your hard drive into one of the folders that appear on the iDisk.

Note: You can't create your own folders on the iDisk. You must put your files and folders into one of the folders *already on the iDisk,* such as Documents or Pictures. If you try to drag an icon directly into the iDisk window, or onto the iDisk icon, for example, you'll get an error message.

Thereafter, you can retrieve or open whatever you copied to the iDisk. Open one of the folders on it; you can now open, rename, trash, or copy (to your hard drive) whatever you find inside. (The Software folder is a special case, as described below.)

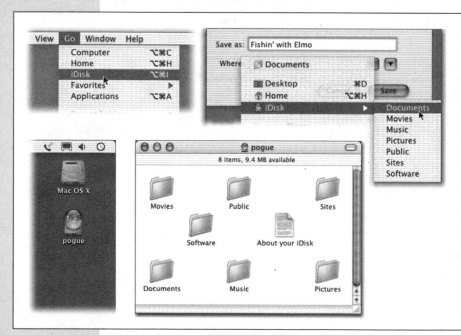

Figure 18-8:
Choose Go→iDisk (top left) or, from within a Save dialog box, pick Where→iDisk (top right). When the iDisk finally appears (bottom left, double-click it—and wait—to see its contents (bottom right). Note that you can't create your own folders on this special disk— you must drag your files directly into one of the folders shown here.

The permanence of the iDisk

In Mac OS X (10.1 and later), you can leave the iDisk's icon on the screen for as long as you like. (In previous operating systems, you were logged out after about an hour. The new permanence of the iDisk is a side benefit of the so-called *WebDAV* technology that's built into Mac OS X 10.1 and later.)

If you have a full-time Internet connection, great: you can consider the iDisk a permanent fixture of your Macintosh. But even if you have a dial-up Internet account, you can leave the iDisk on your screen. Whenever you double-click it or save something onto it, your modem automatically dials the Internet and opens the pipes you need to feed your iDisk.

The Public folder

In general, whatever you put onto your iDisk is private. Without your password, nobody can see what you've stored there. There's one exception, however: Anything you put into the *Public* folder on every iDisk can be seen, opened, and copied out by any other iTools member. All they need is your member name, not your password. (You can think of the iDisk Public folder as the twin of the Public folder in your own Home folder.)

The Public folder is terrific for storing family photos where anyone who's interested can look at them. It's also handy when you're collaborating; you can post the latest drafts of your work in the Public folder for your co-workers to review.

Tip: To view someone else's Public folder, choose Go→Connect to Server. At the bottom of the dialog box, type *http://idisk.mac.com/*yourname*/Public*. Click Connect or press Enter.

After a minute or so, a new iDisk icon appears on your desktop, bearing that member's name. Double-click it to view the contents of that person's Public folder. You can copy these files to your hard drive, or double-click them to open them directly.

Checking your free disk space

To see how much room is left on your iDisk, summon its status bar as you would in any Finder window: by choosing View→Show Status Bar.

Your free software stash

Now *this* is cool: Apple has filled up your iDisk with Mac OS X programs! Just open the Software→Mac OS X Software folder on your iDisk. Inside, you'll find dozens of shareware programs, utilities, games, drivers for scanners and printers, and much more (Figure 18-9).

Email

Apple offers a free email account to any Mac OS X user. Of course, anyone who's able to *get* to the Apple Web site probably already *has* an email account, provided by whoever is providing the Internet service. Furthermore, the Apple Web site feature offers no way to read or write email—this particular iTool offers you only an email *address* (account). You're still expected to use a program like Entourage, Eudora, or Mail to get and send your Mac.com email.

So why bother? The first advantage is the simple address: *YourName@mac.com*. Furthermore, because iTools is a Mac OS X-only service, un-trafficked by 200 million Windows users, the odds are good that you'll be able to claim the name you want. No longer must you be known as *bgates28514@earthlink.net*.

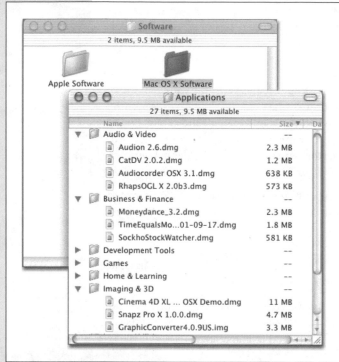

Figure 18-9:
You have a whole software collection you didn't even know you had: the Software folder on your iDisk. After looking over these programs, drag the software you want to your hard drive or your desktop. You can open or install the software from there.

In fact, there's a second stash inside Software→Apple Software→Mac OS X. This folder has all the latest versions of Apple programs like AppleWorks, iMovie, and iTunes. (Fortunately, none of this eats into your 20 MB limit.)

POWER USERS' CLINIC

The iDisk from Windows

In the old days, you could only get to your iDisk from a Macintosh—and it had to be running Mac OS 9 or later, at that. These days, you can bring your iDisk onto the screen of any computer, even one running Windows or Linux.

The procedure varies by operating system, but the general idea is the same: you're going to create a new "network place" that uses the address *http://idisk.mac.com/yourname*, where *yourname* is your iTools account name.

In Windows 2000, Me, or XP, there's a quick way to do that. Choose File→Open from within Internet Explorer. Turn on the "Open as Web Folder" checkbox, and then type your iDisk's address (http://idisk.mac.com/yourname). Enter your name and password when you're asked for it! When it's all over, your iDisk window appears on the screen exactly as though it's a very slow hard drive.

Thereafter, you can summon your iDisk by double-clicking its icon in the Network Places folder.

Second, Mac.com addresses are smoothly integrated into the Mail program that comes with Mac OS X, as you can find out in the next chapter.

Finally, the Apple Web site gives you two additional features that help you process your email. First, it offers a Forward function that can route any incoming Mac.com email to another address of your choice. Second, you can set up your Mac.com account to send automatic "I'm out-of-town" replies to anyone who emails you. You still get your email—or if you really *are* out-of-town, it piles up until you return—but each incoming message gets the generic response you've created.

HomePage

Creating a Web page (an HTML document) isn't difficult. Using a program like Dreamweaver, Netscape Composer, or even AppleWorks, you can design the text and graphics for a simple Web page in an afternoon. It's much more difficult, however, to figure out how to *post* that Web page—to hang it on the Internet where the world can see it. To do that, you need special software, several passwords and codes, and a lot of help from your ISP.

The iTools HomePage feature eliminates all that hassle. All you have to do is drag your Web-page documents and graphics into the Sites folder on your iDisk (described in the previous section). Your Web page is instantly available for viewing by the 300 million people on the Internet.

Creating a Web page using your own tools

If you already know how to design Web pages, great; put the HTML documents and graphics you've created into the Sites folder of your iDisk.

Tip: Remember Image Capture, described on page 211? One of its best stunts is turning photos downloaded from your digital camera into a Web page. After it has done so, drag the resulting HTML documents and image folders into the Sites folder—and presto, you've got yourself a photo-gallery Web page.

Then tell your friends its Web address. Suppose that the Web page you designed is called *index.html,* and that your iTools member name is SkiBunny. In that case, your custom-designed Web address is *http://homepage.mac.com/skibunny/index.html.*

Creating a simple Web page using HomePage

If you have no experience designing Web pages, you can use iTools itself to create gorgeous, if simple, Web pages. Sign into the Apple Web site's iTools screen; click HomePage. Click one of the "created page" tabs on the welcome screen. They offer you a number of standard Web page templates:

• **Photo Album.** Your Web page will look like a beautifully designed page full of slides, each showing a miniature version of one of the pictures you've selected. Your visitors can click one of the slides to view the picture at full size.

If this is the kind of Web page you want, prepare by saving your photos as *JPEG files.* Copy them into the Pictures folder of your iDisk before using this template.

- **Movies.** Prepare for this project by saving your QuickTime movies in a Web-friendly format—with a small window size and a low frames-per-second rate. If you're using iMovie, choose File→Export Movie, and then choose "Web Movie (small)." (Making your movies small in this way isn't just thoughtful for your Web site visitors, who must wait for the movie to download; it also acknowledges that your iDisk is only 20 MB in size, and bigger movies might not fit.)

  Put the movies in the Movies folder of your iDisk before using this template.

- **Resume.** This template may owe its existence to the high-turnover job market in Silicon Valley, where Apple is based; in any case, it lets you post your résumé online for all headhunters to see.

- **Personal.** Newsletters in various designs are available here.

- **Baby.** You're offered a choice of Boy or Girl announcements.

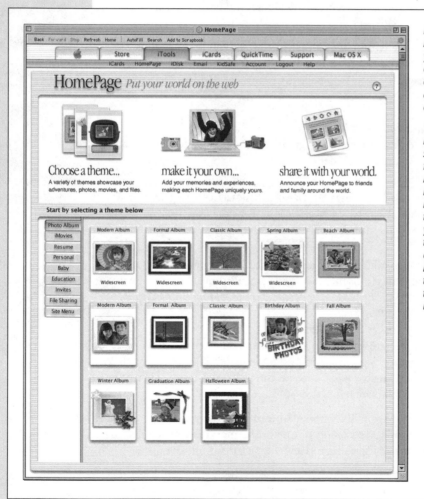

Figure 18-10:
Making a Web page of your own is as easy as clicking one of the category tabs (lower left) and then choosing a canned design template.

Where a picture or movie is called for, you'll be shown a list of any folders in the Pictures or Movies folders of your iDisk (and lists of the individual files inside those folders). (With luck, you remembered to put them there before embarking on your Web-building adventure.) Pick the folder that contains the pix or flix you want to use.

- **Education.** Find play tickets, homework sheets, newsletters, and similar templates.

- **Invites.** Use this option for Web-based invitations to parties and other events.

- **File Sharing.** This Web page format lists the contents of your Public folder, with a Download button for each. The result is an extremely easy way for you to share files with anyone using any kind of computer. Just dump Word files, JPEG files, HTML files, or whatever into your Public folder, and then give your collaborators the Web address. They can click Download for the files they want.

- **Site Menu.** This button takes you to a summary page that shows all of the Web pages you have created so far—or, if you haven't created any yet, it shows four templates for creating menu pages for multipage sites.

After you've selected one of these tabs (Figure 18-10), click the miniature image of the design you want. Finally, you arrive at a full-size mock-up of the finished Web page; click Edit at the top of the page to change the chunks of dummy text. Click Preview to see how the Web page will look.

When you finally click the Publish button at the top of the screen, new Web page (HTML) documents appear in the Sites folder of your iDisk; if you know how to use a Web-design program like Dreamweaver, you can edit these documents. Now the URL (Web address) for your page appears on your screen, which you can copy and then email to anyone who'd be interested. (Unfortunately, it's not particularly catchy: it's along the lines of *http://homepage.mac.com/YourMemberName/baby.html*).

Finally, your Web page is now available for anyone on the Internet to see. Corporations and professional Web designers may sniff at the simplicity of the result—but it takes *them* a lot longer than ten minutes, and more than $0, to do their thing.

Tip: You can create as many Web pages as you want. When you return to the HomePage screen, a list of your existing Web pages appears (complete with Edit Page and Delete Page buttons).

Internet Location Files

One of the least convenient aspects of using the Internet is having to remember the often cumbersome addresses for various Internet features. The Mac offers a clever way to manage and memorize these addresses: *Internet location files*. Figure 18-11 shows the procedure for creating one of these special clipping files.

Figure 18-11:
To create an Internet location file, highlight an Internet address in any drag-and-droppable program (such as TextEdit or Stickies). Drag the highlighted text to your desktop, where it becomes an Internet location file.

The idea is simple: When you double-click an Internet location file, your Web browser opens automatically to that page, or your email program launches and generates a new, blank, preaddressed outgoing message.

In other words, an Internet location file is like a system-wide Bookmarks feature. You might consider gathering together the location files for Web sites you frequently visit, put them into a folder, and put that folder into the Dock. Do the same with addresses to which you frequently send email. Thereafter, you save a step every time you want to jump to a particular Web page or send email to a particular person—just choose the appropriate name from the Dock folder's pop-up menu.

Tip: Rename your Internet location files. Doing so doesn't affect their original programming–they still take you to the same Web pages or email addresses–but it lets you substitute plain English names ("Bob Smith" instead of bsmith@earthlink.net, for example).

Although Web and email addresses are by far the most popular uses of the Internet location file feature, they're not the only ones. You can also create location files for the addresses of newsgroup addresses (*news://news.apple.com*), FTP sites (*ftp:// ftp.apple.com*), AppleShare servers (*afp://at/Engineering:IL5 3rd Floor*), AppleTalk zones (*at://IL5 2nd Floor*), and even Web pages stored on your Mac (*file://Macintosh HD/Website Stuff/home.html*).

Tip: As far as your Mac is concerned, an Internet location file and a Favorite (or bookmark), as defined by Internet Explorer, are the same thing. As Figure 18-12 illustrates, you can create one from the other just by dragging.

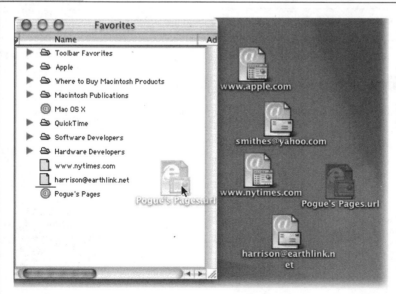

Figure 18-12:
In Internet Explorer, choose Favorites→Organize Favorites. Now, impressively enough, you can drag Internet location files from the desktop directly into your bookmarks list. Oddly, this trick even works with email location files: if you add one to your Favorites menu, then choosing it (from within Internet Explorer) launches your email program and pre-addresses an outgoing message.

Mail

Email is a fast, cheap, convenient communication medium; it's almost embarrassing these days to admit that you don't have an email address. To spare you that humiliation, Mac OS X includes Mail, a program that lets you get and send email messages. It's a surprisingly complete, refreshingly attractive program that's filled with shortcuts and surprises—and it's free.

Setting Up Mail

The first time you open Mail (by clicking its icon on the Dock, for example, or from your Applications folder), interview screens appear to walk you through the setup process.

If you've signed up for a Mac.com account (and typed its name into System Preferences as described on page 199), you're all ready to go. You've just saved yourself several minutes of typing and fiddling. Skip ahead to "Checking Your Mail."

If you're using a regular Internet service provider (ISP) account instead, you see the dialog box shown in Figure 19-1, where you're supposed to input the various settings to specify your email account. (Some of this information may require the help of your ISP's phone representative.) Here's the rundown:

- **Your Name** will appear in the "From" field of the email you send. Type it just the way you'd like it to appear.

- **Email Address.** This is the address you were assigned when you signed up for Internet services, such as *billg@microsoft.com*.

- **Incoming Mail Server, Mail Server Type, Outgoing (SMTP) Mail Server.** Enter the information your ISP gave you about its mail servers: the type of server, the name of the incoming mail server, and the name of the outgoing mail server. Most of the time, the incoming server is a *POP3 server* and its name is connected to the name of your ISP, such as *popmail.mindspring.com.* The outgoing mail server (also called the *SMTP server*) looks something like *mail.mindspring.com.*

- **User Account ID, Password.** Enter the name and password provided by your ISP.

Click OK when you're finished.

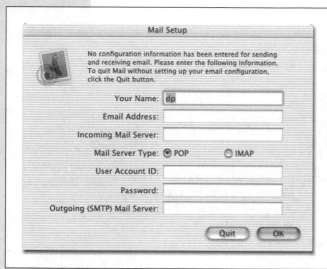

Figure 19-1:
This dialog box lets you plug in the email settings provided by your ISP. If you want to add a second email account later, choose Mail→Preferences and then click Create Account, which opens up a duplicate of this dialog box. (Mail collects all of your email in a single set of "mailbox" folders. If you'd rather see a separate set of Inbox, Outbox, and other folders for each account, choose Mail→ Preferences; click Accounts; and turn on "Show this account separately in mailboxes drawer.")

Figure 19-2:
Top: If you click Yes, Mail will offer to import your old email collection from whatever program you used before you switched to Mac OS X (bottom left). You can even specify which email folders you want to import (bottom right); when the importing process is finished—which can take quite awhile—you'll find precisely the same folders already set up in Mail.

Now Mail offers to import your email collection from whatever email program you used before your Mac OS X adventure began—Entourage, Outlook Express, Claris Emailer, Netscape, or Eudora. Importing is a tremendous help in making a smooth transition between your old email world and your new one. Figure 19-2 has the details.

Checking Your Mail

You get new mail and send mail you've written using the Get Mail command. You can trigger it in any of several ways:

- Click Get Mail on the Toolbar.

- Choose Mailbox→Get New Mail. (If you have several accounts, you can check only one of them by choosing from the Mailbox→Get New Mail In Account submenu.)

- Press Shift-⌘-N.

UP TO SPEED

POP, IMAP, and Web-based Mail

When it comes to email, there are three flavors of accounts (not counting America Online mail, which is a mutant breed and not something that Mail can talk to): *POP* (also known as POP3), *IMAP* (also known as IMAP4), and *Web-based*. Each has its own distinct feeling, with different strengths and weaknesses.

POP accounts are the most common kind. A POP server transfers your incoming mail to your hard drive before you read it, which works fine as long as you're only using one computer to access your email.

If you want to take your email world along with you on the road, you have to copy the Mail folder in your Home folder →Library folder—into the corresponding location on your laptop's hard drive; when you run Mail on the laptop, you'll find your messages and attachments already in place.

IMAP servers are newer than, and have more features than, POP servers, but as a result they don't enjoy as much popularity or support. IMAP servers are Internet computers that store all of your mail for you, rather than making you download it each time you connect; you can access the same mail regardless of the computer you use. IMAP servers remember which messages you've read and sent, too. (Your Mac.com account is an IMAP account, which is why you can access the mail in your Inbox repeatedly from any Mac in the world.)

One downside to this approach, of course, is that you can't work with your email except when you're online, because all of your mail is on an Internet server, not on your hard drive. Another is that if you don't conscientiously manually delete mail after you've read it, your online mailbox eventually overflows. Sooner or later, the system starts bouncing fresh messages back to their senders, annoying your friends and depriving you of the chance to read what they had to say.

Free, Web-based servers like Hotmail also store your mail on the Internet; you can use a Web browser on any computer to read and send messages. They're also slower and more cumbersome to use than "regular" email accounts; Mail can't check these accounts at all.

- Be patient. Mail comes set to check your email every few minutes automatically. To adjust its timing or turn it off completely, choose Mail→Preferences; choose a time interval from the "Check accounts for new mail" pop-up menu.

Now Mail contacts the mail servers listed in the account list, retrieving new messages and downloading any files attached to those messages. It also *sends* any outgoing messages and their attachments.

Tip: The Activity window gives you a Stop button, progress bars, and other useful information. Summon it by choosing Window→Activity Viewer—or just by double-clicking the little rotating arrows that appear in the upper-right corner of the Mail window when the program is checking for new messages.

The Mailbox Drawer

Mail organizes your email into folders that Apple calls *mailboxes* at one side of the screen, in a sliding pane that looks and acts like a drawer (Figure 19-3). The Mailbox icon on the toolbar opens and closes it. Yours are probably listed under the heading

---

POWER USERS' CLINIC

The Mighty Morphing Interface

You don't have to be content with the factory-installed design of the Mail screen; you can control almost every aspect of its look and layout.

For example, you can control the main window's information columns exactly as you would in a Finder list view window—that is, you can make a column narrower or wider by dragging the right edge of its column heading, rearrange the columns by dragging their titles, and so on. You can also control which columns appear using the Hide and Show commands in the View menu. Similarly, you can *sort* your email by clicking these column headings, exactly as in the Finder (click a second time to reverse the sorting).

The various panels of the main window are also under your control. For example, you can drag the divider bar—between the list of messages and the Preview pane (where you see what's actually in a message)—up or down to adjust the relative proportions, as shown here. In fact, you can get rid of the Preview pane altogether just by double-clicking the divider line, double-clicking just above the vertical scroll bar, or dragging the divider line's handle all the

way to the bottom of the screen. (Bring it back by dragging the divider line back up from the bottom.)

You can also control the mailbox's *drawer*. Drag its outer edge inward or outward to make the drawer wider or narrower, for example. You can even make the drawer disappear or reappear completely by clicking the Mailbox icon on the toolbar.

If you'd like to swap the drawer to the other side of the main window, *drag a message* in the main message list horizontally, toward the side where you want the drawer to appear.

Finally, you have full control over the toolbar, which works exactly like the Finder toolbar. You can rearrange or remove the icon buttons by ⌘-dragging them; add interesting new buttons to the toolbar (choose View→Customize Toolbar); change its display to show *just* text labels or *just* icons (again, choose View→Customize Toolbar); or hide the toolbar entirely by clicking the white button in the upper-right corner (or by using the View→Hide Toolbar command). Chapter 3 offers full details on Mac OS X toolbar customization.

Personal Mailboxes; if you have a Mac.com address, it gets a heading of its own, called iTools. Under these headings, sometimes hidden by the "flippy triangles," you may find these mailbox folders:

- **Inbox** holds mail you've received.

- **Outbox** holds mail you've written but haven't yet sent.

- **Sent Mail** holds copies of messages you've sent.

- **Deleted Messages** works a lot like the Trash, in that messages you put there don't actually disappear. They remain in the Deleted Messages folder, awaiting rescue on the day you decide that you'd like to retrieve them.

- **Drafts** holds messages you've started but haven't yet finished, and don't want to send just yet.

To see what's in one of these folders, click it once. The list of its messages appears in the top half of the main window; when you click a message name, the message itself appears in the bottom half of the main window.

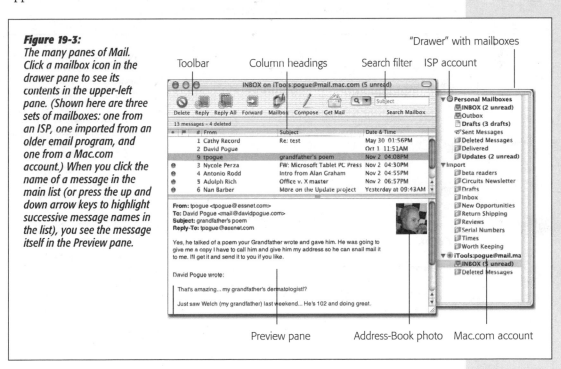

Figure 19-3:
The many panes of Mail. Click a mailbox icon in the drawer pane to see its contents in the upper-left pane. (Shown here are three sets of mailboxes: one from an ISP, one imported from an older email program, and one from a Mac.com account.) When you click the name of a message in the main list (or press the up and down arrow keys to highlight successive message names in the list), you see the message itself in the Preview pane.

"Drawer" with mailboxes

Toolbar   Column headings   Search filter   ISP account

Preview pane   Address-Book photo   Mac.com account

Writing Messages

To send email to a recipient, click the Compose icon on the toolbar. The New Message form, shown in Figure 19-4, opens so you can begin creating the message.

Here's how you go about writing a message:

1. **Type the email address of the recipient into the To field.**

   If you want to send this message to more than one person, separate their addresses with commas: *bob@earthlink.net, billg@microsoft.com, steve@apple.com.*

   You don't have to remember and type those addresses, either. If somebody is in your address book (page 476), just type the first couple letters of his name; Mail automatically completes the address. (If the first guess is wrong, just type another letter or two until Mail revises its proposal.)

   As in most dialog boxes, you can jump from blank to blank (from the To field to the CC field, for example) by pressing the Tab key.

2. **To send a copy of the message to other recipients, enter the email address(es) in the CC field.**

   CC stands for *carbon copy.* Getting an email message where your name is in the CC line implies: "I sent you a copy because I thought you'd want to know about this correspondence, but I'm not expecting you to reply."

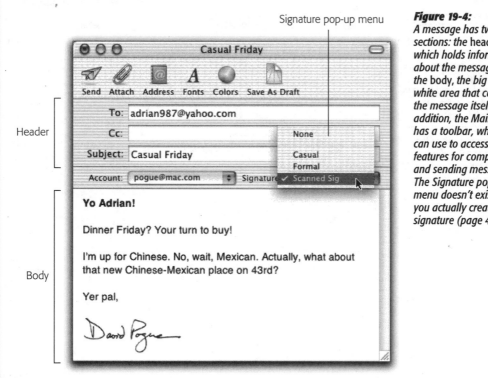

Signature pop-up menu

Figure 19-4:
A message has two sections: the header, *which holds information about the message; and the* body, *the big empty white area that contains the message itself. In addition, the Mail window has a toolbar, which you can use to access other features for composing and sending messages. The Signature pop-up menu doesn't exist until you actually create a signature (page 461).*

3. **Type the topic of the message in the Subject field.**

It's courteous to put some thought into the Subject line (use "Change in plans for next week" instead of "Hi," for example).

4. **Specify an email format.**

There are two kinds of email: *plain text* and *formatted* (HTML or, in Mail's case, what Apple calls Rich Text). Plain text messages are faster to send and open, are universally compatible with the world's email programs, and are greatly preferred by many veteran computer fans. (You can still attach pictures and other files.)

Formatted messages sometimes open slowly, and in some email programs (such as Claris Emailer), the formatting won't come through at all.

To control which kind of mail you send on a message-by-message basis, choose, from the Format menu, either Make Plain Text or Make Rich Text. To change the factory setting for new outgoing messages, choose Mail→Preferences; click the Composing icon; and use the "Default message format" pop-up menu.

Tip: Remember that your recipients won't see the fonts you've specified unless their machines have the same ones installed. Bottom line: For email to Mac and Windows fans alike, stick to Arial, Times, Courier, and similarly universal choices.

---

5. **Enter the message in the message box.**

You can use all the standard editing techniques, including text drag-and-drop, the Copy and Paste commands, and so on. If you selected the Rich Text style of email, you can even use word processor-like formatting (see Figure 19-5).

As you type, Mail checks your spelling, using a dotted underline to mark questionable words (also shown in Figure 19-5). To check for alternative spellings for a suspect word, Control-click the underlined word; a list of suggestions appears in the contextual menu. Click the word you really intended, or choose Learn Spelling to add the word to the Mac OS X dictionary.

(To turn off automatic spell check, choose Edit→Spelling→Check Spelling As You Type so that the checkmark disappears. If you want to spell-check a message all at once, choose Edit→Spelling→Check Spelling [⌘-;] after composing it.)

Tip: If you're composing a long email message, or if it's one you don't want to send until later, click the Save as Draft button, press ⌘-S, or choose File→Save As Draft. You've just saved the message in your Drafts folder. To reopen a saved draft later, click the Drafts icon in the mailbox drawer, and then click the draft that you want to work on.

---

6. **Click Send (or press Shift-⌘-D).**

If you're not already online, your modem dials, squeals, connects to the Internet, and sends the message.

Tip: If you'd rather have Mail place each message you write in the Outbox folder instead of connecting to the Net when you click Send, choose Mailbox→Go Offline. While you're offline, Mail will refrain from trying to connect, which is a great feature when you're working on a laptop at 39,000 feet. (Choose Mailbox→Go Online to reverse the procedure.)

Figure 19-5:
If you really want to use formatting, click the Fonts icon on the toolbar to open the Font panel described on page 334, or the Colors icon to open the Color Picker described on page 115. In fact, the Format menu contains even more controls—paragraph alignment (left, right, or justify), and even Copy and Paste Style commands that let you transfer formatting from one block of text to another.

Blind Carbon Copies

A *blind carbon copy* is a secret copy. This feature lets you send a copy of a message to somebody secretly, without any of the other recipients knowing that you did so. To view this field when composing a message, choose Message→Add Bcc Header.

You can use the BCC field to quietly signal a third party that a message has been sent. For example, if you send your co-worker a message that says, "Chris, it bothers me that you've been cheating the customers," you could BCC your boss or supervisor to clue her in without getting into trouble with Chris.

The BCC box is useful in other ways, too. Many people send email messages (containing jokes, for example) to a long list of recipients. You, the recipient, have to scroll through a very long list of names the sender placed in the To or CC field.

But if the sender used the BCC field to hold all the recipients' email addresses, you, the recipient, won't see any names but your own at the top of the email. (Unfortunately, spammers, those awful people who send you junk mail, have also learned this trick.)

Attaching Files to Messages

Sending little text messages is fine, but it's not much help when you want to send somebody a photograph, a sound, or a Word document. To attach a file to a message you've written, use one of these methods:

- Drag the icons you want to attach directly off the desktop (or out of a folder window) into the New Message window. There your attachments appear with their own hyperlinked icons (Figure 19-5), meaning that your recipient can simply click to open them.

- Click the Attach icon on the New Message toolbar, choose Message→Attach File, or press Shift-⌘-A. The standard Open File dialog box now appears, so that you can navigate to and select the files you want to include.

Tip: You can choose multiple files simultaneously in this dialog box. Just ⌘-click or Shift-click the individual files you want, just as though you were selecting them in a Finder column-view window (page 40).

Once you've selected them, click Open (or press Enter). You return to the New Message window, where the attachments' icons show up, ready to ride along when you send the message.

To remove an attachment, drag across its icon to highlight it, and then press the Delete key. (You can also drag an attachment icon clear out of the window onto your Dock's Trash, or choose Message→Remove Attachments.)

If you have a high-speed connection like a cable modem, by the way, have pity on your recipient. A big picture or movie file might take you only seconds to send, but tie up your correspondent's modem for hours.

Note: Mail automatically uses the MIME/Base64 encoding scheme for sending attachments. As a result, your Mac- and Windows-using correspondents will generally have no problem opening files you send.

You can't, however, choose a different encoding scheme. Nor does Mail offer automatic compression (using StuffIt, for example); if you want to compress your files before sending them, do so using DropStuff, which you can download as part of the shareware StuffIt Lite package from *www.aladdinsys.com*.

Signatures

Signatures are bits of text that get stamped at the bottom of your outgoing email messages. A signature may contain a name, postal address, a pithy quote, or (in Mail) even a scan of your *real* signature, as shown in Figure 19-4.

To create a signature, choose Mail→Preferences, and then click the Signatures icon (Figure 19-6). You can create any number of signatures by clicking the Create Signature button, which opens an editing window in which you can type your new signature (and define a name for it).

Once you've created a signature, or several, you can tack it onto your outgoing mail either always or on a message-by-message basis.

• **Always append a signature.** On the Signatures preference screen (Figure 19-6, top), choose the signature that you'd like to have at the bottom of every email message. (You can always override this choice on a message-by-message basis.)

Tip: If you choose Randomly or Sequentially, Mail will choose a different one of these gems to grace the bottom of every email message that you send out. This is the way to rotate your quotes from, say, Monty Python, without seeming repetitive to your correspondents.

• **Message by message.** On the Signatures preference screen, turn on "Choose signature when composing email." From now on, a Signature pop-up menu appears just above the message-body area on every outgoing email note. When you choose from it, Mail pastes the signature at the bottom of the message.

Keeping a Copy

Once the message has been sent, it disappears from your Outbox. Fortunately, asking Mail to keep a copy in your Sent Messages folder is easy enough. Just choose

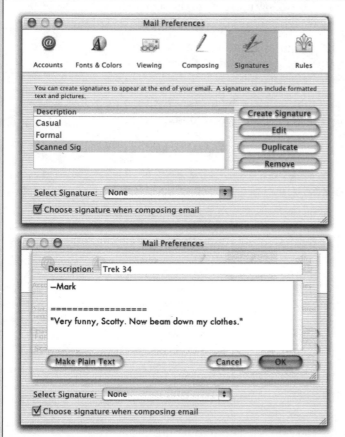

Figure 19-6:
Top: Your list of signatures, and the doorway to the signature-creation box.

Bottom: After typing some signature material, don't miss the Format menu, which you can use to dress up your signature with colors and other formatting. You can even drag or paste a picture into the signature box. Click OK when you're finished. (You'll be able to use formatted signatures only if you're sending Rich Text messages, of course.)

Mail→Preferences; click the Composing icon. From the "Save sent mail in" pop-up menu, just choose the name of your Sent Messages mailbox, and then close the window. (You may first have to *create* a Sent Messages folder, if you don't see one already in your Mailboxes drawer. See page 467 for instructions on creating folders.)

Reading Email

Mail puts all the email you get into your Inbox; the statistic in parentheses after the word *Inbox* lets you know how many of its messages you haven't yet read. New messages are also denoted by colorful, liquidy dots in the main list.

Tip: The Mail icon in the Dock also shows you how many new messages you have waiting—it's the number in the red circle, as shown in Figure 19-7.

Click the Inbox folder to see a list of received messages. If it's a long list, press Control-Page Up and Control-Page Down to scroll. Click the name of a message once to read it in the Preview pane, or double-click a message to open it into a separate window.

Tip: Instead of reading your mail, you might prefer to have Mac OS X read it *to* you, as you sit back in your chair and sip your strawberry daiquiri. Just Control-click inside the Preview pane and choose Speech→Start Speaking from the contextual menu. You'll hear the message read out loud, in the voice you've selected on the Speech pane of System Preferences (Chapter 8).

To stop the insanity, choose Speech→Stop Speaking from the same contextual menu.

Once you've viewed a message, you can respond to it, delete it, print it, file it, and so on. The following pages should get you started.

GEM IN THE ROUGH

All the Little Symbols

The first column of the main email list shows little symbols that let you know at a glance how you've processed certain messages. The most common one is, of course, the gelatinous blue dot ( ), which means "new message." (After reading a message, you can mark it once again as an *unread* message by choosing Message→Mark As Unread—or Control-click the message's name and choose Mark As Unread from the contextual menu.)

You might also see these symbols, which represent messages that you've replied to ( ), forwarded ( ), redirected ( ), or flagged ( ).

Incidentally, you may have noticed that, by default, Mail marks a message as having been read the moment you click it. You can change it back to unread, of course, by Control-clicking it—but there's also a more permanent workaround. Just double-click the divider bar above the Preview pane, which hides the Preview pane itself. Once the Preview pane is gone, Mail no longer marks messages "read" just because you clicked one in the list. (You can bring back the Preview pane by double-clicking just above the vertical scroll bar, or by dragging the divider bar back up from the bottom.)

Adding the Sender to Your Address Book

Mail offers a time-saving feature: The Message→Add Sender To Address Book command. Whenever you choose it, Mail memorizes the email address of the person whose message is on the screen. In fact, you can highlight a huge number of messages and add them all simultaneously using this technique.

Thereafter, you'll be able to write new messages to this person just by typing the first couple letters of the name.

Opening Attachments

Just as you can attach files to a message, so people often send files to you. Sometimes they don't even bother to type a message; you wind up receiving an empty email message with a file attached. Only the presence of the file's icon in the message body tells you that there's something attached.

Tip: Mail doesn't ordinarily indicate the presence of attachments in the main mail list. It can do so, however. Just choose View→Show Contents Column. A new column appears in the email list—at the far right—where you'll see a paper-clip icon and the number of file attachments listed for each message.

Mail doesn't store downloaded files as normal file icons on your hard drive. They're actually encoded right into the *.mbox* mailbox databases described on page 475. To extract an attached file from this mass of software, you must proceed in one of these ways:

- Drag the attachment icon out of the message window and onto any visible portion of your desktop, as shown in Figure 19-7.

Figure 19-7:
Dragging an attachment's icon onto your desktop takes the file out of the Mail world and into your standard desktop world, where you can file it, trash it, open it, or manipulate it as you would any file.

From: Ted Wilcox <twilcox@apple.com>
Date: Fri Apr 02, 2002 08:56:59 PM US/Eastern
To: steve@apple.com, david@pogueman.com
Subject: Apple prototypes for 2002

Here are the specs for our upcoming handheld, desktop, and laptop devices. Please, please, DO NOT DISTRIBUTE. You especially, Pogue. Make sure this note doesn't, you know, get pictured in one of your books like last time.

Apple 2002 Product Matrix CONFIDENTIAL (14.5KB)

Apple 2002 Product Matrix CONFIDENTIAL

- Double-click the attachment's icon in the message. If you were sent a document (such as a photo, Word file, Excel file, and so on), it now opens in the corresponding program (Preview, Word, Excel, or whatever).

Warning: After the attachment is open, *use the File→Save As command* to save the file into a folder of your choice. Otherwise, any changes you make won't be visible in the file except when you open it from within Mail.

When attachments don't open

Several factors may be at work if you're unable to open a file attachment. For starters, your correspondent's email program may have *compressed* or *encoded* the file to make it take less time to send. If you're having trouble getting a file to open, therefore, your first step should be to drag the attachment's icon onto that of StuffIt Expander, which is in your Applications→Utilities folder. This little program can gracefully re-expand just about any geeky Internet file. (Real Mac OS X masters simplify their lives by parking Expander on the Dock for easy drag-and-drop access.)

If the file still won't open, then you may be dealing with a file from a Windows PC that requires a little more effort to open. For example:

- **.exe** denotes an *executable* file—in other words, a Windows program. By itself, your Mac can't run Windows programs, just as Windows computers can't run Macintosh programs.

- **.html.** A file whose name ends in .html or .htm is a Web page. In the beginning, Web pages hung out only on the Internet. These days, however, you're increasingly likely to find that you've downloaded one to your Mac's hard drive (it may be a software manual for some shareware, for example). You can open it just by double-clicking; Mac OS X comes set to open all .htm and .html files into Internet Explorer.

- **.vcf.** A "business-card" file; see page 478.

If you were sent a file with a three-letter code not listed here, you may well have yourself a file that can be opened only by a Windows program that you don't actu-

---

FREQUENTLY ASKED QUESTION

The Resend Command

Hey, what happened to the Resend command? What if I want to resend a message, or send it to somebody new after I've already sent it once?

No problem. Just Option-double-click the message in your Sent Messages folder. Mail dutifully opens up a brand-new duplicate, ready for you to edit, readdress if you like, and then send again.

(The prescribed Apple route is to highlight the message and then choose File→Restore from Draft, but that's a lot more trouble.)

---

ally own. You might consider asking your correspondent to resend it in one of the more universal formats, such as the graphics formats JPEG and TIFF, and the text formats RTF, TXT, and PDF. (Mac OS X opens all of these formats easily.)

Replying to a Message

To answer a message, click the Reply button on the message toolbar (or choose Message→Reply To Sender, or just press ⌘-R). If the message was originally addressed to multiple recipients, you can send your reply to everyone simultaneously by clicking the Reply to All button instead.

A new message window opens, already addressed. As a courtesy to your correspondent, Mail places the original message at the bottom of the window, denoted by brackets or a vertical bar, as shown in Figure 19-8.

Tip: If you highlight some text before clicking Reply, Mail pastes only that portion of the original message into your reply. That's a great convenience to your correspondent, who now knows exactly which part of the message you're responding to.

At this point, you can add or delete recipients, edit the Subject line or the original message, attach a file, and so on.

Figure 19-8:
In Rich Text formatted Mail messages (not to be confused with RTF [Rich Text Format] word processing format, which is very different), a reply includes the original message, marked in a special color (which you can change in Mail→ Preferences) and with a special vertical bar to differentiate it from the text of your reply. (In plain-text messages, each line of the reply is >denoted >with >brackets, although only your recipient will see them.) The original sender's name is automatically placed in the To field. The subject is the same as the original subject with the addition of Re (shorthand for Regarding). You're ready to type your response.

Tip: Use the Return key to create blank lines in the original message. Using this method, you can splice your own comments into the paragraphs of the original message, replying point by point. The brackets preceding each line of the original message help your correspondent keep straight what's yours and what's hers.

When you're finished, click Send. (If you click Reply to All in the message window, your message goes to everyone who received the original note, *even* if you began the reply process by clicking Reply. Mac OS X, in other words, gives you a second chance to address your reply to everyone.)

Forwarding Messages

Instead of replying to the person who sent you a message, you may sometimes want to pass the note on to a third person.

To do so, click the Forward toolbar button (or choose Message→Forward Message, or press Shift-⌘-F). A new message opens, looking a lot like the one that appears when you reply. You may wish to precede the original message with a comment of your own, along the lines of: "Frank: I thought you'd be interested in this joke about Congress."

Finally, address it as you would any outgoing piece of mail.

Redirecting Messages

A redirected message is similar to a forwarded message, with one extremely useful difference. When you *forward* a message, your recipient sees that it came from you. When you *redirect* it, your recipient sees the *original* writer's name as the sender; the message bears no trace of your involvement (unless the recipient thinks to choose View→Show All Headers). In other words, a redirected message uses you as a low-profile relay station between two other people.

Treasure this feature. Plenty of email programs, including Outlook and Outlook Express for Windows, don't offer a Redirect command at all. You can use it to transfer messages from one of your own accounts to another, or to pass along a message that came to you by mistake.

To redirect a message, choose Message→Redirect, or press ⌘-Option-J. You get an outgoing copy of the message—this time without any quoting marks. (You can't edit redirected messages; they're supposed to end up at their destination intact.)

Printing Messages

Sometimes there's no substitute for a printout. Choose File→Print, or press ⌘-P; the Print dialog box appears as usual.

Filing Messages

Mail lets you create new mailboxes in the drawer. You might create one for important messages, another for all order confirmations from Web shopping, still another

---

for friends and family, and so on. You can even create mailboxes *inside* these mailboxes, a feature beloved by the hopelessly organized.

To create a new mailbox folder, begin by clicking the mailbox in the drawer that will *contain* it. For example, click Personal Mailboxes if you want to create a new mailbox within it, or click Inbox if you want to create folders inside *it*. Now choose Mailbox→New Mailbox. The Mac asks you to title the new mailbox; once you've done so, a new icon appears in the mailbox drawer, ready for use.

Tip: The Mailbox menu also contains the commands you need to rename or delete an existing mailbox. You can also drag the mailbox icons up and down in the drawer to place one inside of another. To move a mailbox *out* of the one it's in, drag it all the way up onto its heading (Personal Mailboxes, for example).

You can move a message (or group of messages) into a mailbox in any of three ways:

- Drag it out of the list pane onto the mailbox icon (Figure 19-9).

- Highlight a message in the list pane, or several, and then choose from the Message→Transfer submenu, which lists all your mailboxes.

- Control-click a message (or one of several that you've highlighted): From the resulting contextual menu, choose Transfer, and then choose the mailbox you want from the submenu.

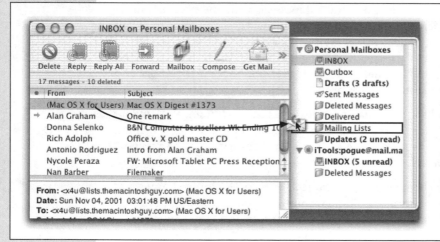

Figure 19-9:
You can use any part of a message's "row" in the list as a handle; the little envelope cursor tells you that Mail knows what's happening. You can also drag messages en masse onto a folder. If you Option-drag a message into a folder, you make a copy, leaving the original message where it was.

Flagging Messages

Sometimes you'll receive email that prompts you to some sort of action, but you may not have the time (or the fortitude) to face the task at the moment. ("Hi there… it's me, your accountant. Would you mind rounding up your expenses for 1993 through 2001 and sending me a list by email?")

That's why Mail lets you *flag* a message, summoning a little flag icon in a new column next to a message's name. These indicators can mean anything you like; they simply call attention to certain messages. You can sort your mail list so that all your flagged messages are listed first (click the flag at the top of the column heading), for example.

To flag a message in this way, select the message (or several messages) and choose Message→Mark As Flagged, or press Option-⌘-G, or Control-click the message's name in the list and choose Mark As Flagged from the contextual menu. (To clear the flags, repeat the procedure, but use the Mark As Unflagged commands instead.)

Finding Messages

As noted earlier in this chapter, you can sort the columns in your main email list just by clicking the headings (From, Subject, Date & Time, and so on).

But when you deal with masses of email, you may find it easier to process your messages using any of Mail's three message-finding methods.

Finding messages within a mailbox

See the little text box in the upper-right corner of your main mail window? You can use it to hide all but certain messages, as shown in Figure 19-10.

Canning Spam

Help! I'm awash in junk email!

While there's no instant cure for spam (junk email), you can take certain steps to protect yourself from it.

1. If you have more than one email account, consider using one just for online shopping, Website and software registration, and newsgroup posting. Spammers have automated software robots that scour every *public* Internet message and Web page, recording email addresses they find. These are the primary sources of spam, so at least you're now restricting the junk mail to one, secondary mail account. (Reserve a separate email account for person-to-person email.)

2. When filling out forms online, turn off the checkboxes that say, "Yes, send me exciting offers and news from our partners."

3. When posting messages in a newsgroup, insert the letters NOSPAM somewhere into your email address. Anyone replying to you via email must delete the NOSPAM from your email address, which is a slight hassle; but meanwhile, the spammers' software robots will lift a bogus email address from your newsgroup posts.

4. Create *message rules* filtering out messages containing typical advertising words such as *casino, guaranteed, loan,* and so forth. (You'll find instructions in this chapter.)

5. Get a new email address. Give it to people you trust; use the old address only for junk mail, and check it for messages only infrequently.

Finally, don't miss the Message→Bounce to Sender command. This juicy Mail bonus sends a junk message back to the sender, coded as though it had reached a non-working email address. Not only are the spammers inconvenienced, but they take your name off their lists so they won't waste their time the next time around.

Tip: You can also set up Mail to show you only certain messages that you've *manually* selected, hiding all others in the list. To do so, highlight the messages you want, using the techniques described on page 57. Then choose View→Focus On Selected Messages. (To see all of them again, choose View→Show All Messages.)

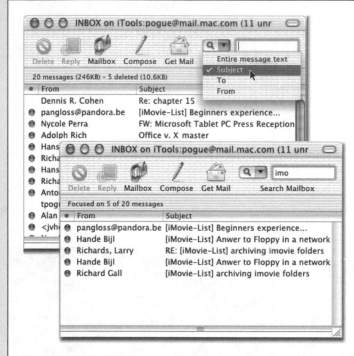

Figure 19-10:
Top: Use the magnifying glass pop-up menu to specify how you want to filter your email list: message body, subject, recipient, or sender. Type the text you're looking for in the Subject box.

Bottom: As you type, Mail shrinks the list of email messages in real time, so that you're looking at only the ones matching what you typed (in this case, messages with the word iMovie in the subject line).

Finding text within an open message

You can also choose Edit→Find (or press ⌘-F) to bring up the Find panel shown in Figure 19-11, which lets you search for certain text within a single message.

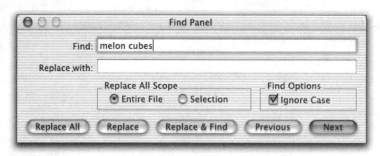

Figure 19-11:
The Find panel works just as it might in a word processor, except that the Replace function works only on messages that you have written yourself—Mail doesn't let you change the words of mail you've received.

Deleting Messages

Sometimes it's junk mail; sometimes you're just done with it. Either way, it's a snap to delete a selected message, several selected messages, or a message that's currently before you on the screen. Use any of these methods:

- Press the Delete key.

- Click the Delete button on the toolbar.

- Choose Message→Delete.

- Drag a message (or several selected messages) out of the list window and into your Deleted Messages mailbox—or even onto the Dock's Trash icon.

Tip: If you delete a message by accident, the Undo command (Edit→Undo or ⌘-Z) works to restore it.

These commands move the messages to the Deleted Items folder, which works like the Finder's Trash folder. If you like, you can click this icon to view a list of the messages you've deleted. You can even rescue some by dragging them into any other mailbox (such as right back into the Inbox).

Emptying the Deleted Items folder

Mail doesn't vaporize messages in the Deleted Items folder until you "empty the trash." You can empty it in any of several ways:

- Click a message, or a folder, within the Deleted Items folder list and then click the Delete icon on the toolbar (or press the Delete key). Now it's really gone.

- Choose Mailboxes→Empty Deleted Message (⌘-K).

- Wait. Mail will permanently delete these messages automatically after a week.

  You can change this interval by choosing Mail→Preferences, clicking the Viewing icon, and using the "Erase deleted mail when" pop-up menu. It offers choices like "Never," "One day old," "One week old," "One month old," and "Quitting Mail" (which makes the program delete your deleted messages every time you quit the program).

Method 2: Deleted mail turns invisible

Mail offers a second, very unusual method of deleting messages that doesn't involve the Deleted Messages folder at all. Using this method, pressing the Delete key, or clicking the Delete toolbar button, simply hides the selected message in the list. Hidden messages remain that way forever—or at least until you use the Rebuild Mailbox command described in the sidebar box on page 478.

If this arrangement sounds useful to you, choose Mail→Preferences. Click the Viewing icon. Turn off the checkbox called "Move deleted mail to a folder named." From now on, messages you delete simply vanish from the list.

They're not really gone, however. You can bring them back, at least in ghostly form, by choosing View→Show Deleted Messages (or pressing ⌘-L). Figure 19-12 shows the idea.

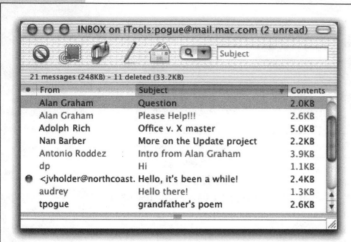

Figure 19-12:
The gray-looking type indicates deleted messages. You can bring any of them back from the world of the dead by selecting them and then choosing Message→Undelete (or just press ⌘-U). The gray type turns to black, and the message is alive and well once again.

Using this system, in other words, you never truly delete messages; you just hide them. At first, you might be concerned about the disk space and database size involved in keeping your old messages around forever like this. The truth is, however, that Mac OS X is perfectly capable of maintaining many thousands of messages in its mailbox databases. Meanwhile, there's a huge benefit to this arrangement: Almost everyone, sooner or later, wishes they could resurrect one deleted message or another—maybe months later, maybe years later. Using the hidden-deleted-message system, your old messages are always around for reference.

On the other hand, when you do want to purge these messages for good, you can always return to the Mail→Preferences dialog box and turn the "Move deleted mail to a folder named" checkbox back on.

Using Message Rules

Once you know how to create folders, the next step in managing your email is to set up a series of *message rules* (filters) that file, answer, or delete incoming messages *automatically* based on their contents, such as subject, address, or size. Message rules require you to think like the distant relative of a programmer, but the mental effort can reward you many times over; message rules turn Mail into a surprisingly smart and efficient secretary.

Setting up message rules

Here's how to set one up:

1. **Choose Mail→Preferences. In the Preferences dialog box, click the Rules icon.**

   The Rules dialog box appears, as shown at top in Figure 19-13.

2. **Click Create Rule.**

   Now a formidable dialog box appears (shown at bottom in Figure 19-13).

3. **Use the Criteria options to specify how Mail should select messages to process.**

   For example, if you'd like the program to watch out for messages from a particular person, you would set up the first two pop-up menus to say "From" and "Contains," respectively.

   To flag messages containing *loan, $$$$, XXXX, !!!!,* and so on, set the pop-up menus to say "Subject" and "Contains."

4. **Specify *which* words or people you want the message rule to watch out for.**

   In the text box to the right of the two pop-up menus, type the word, address, name, or phrase you want Mail to watch out for—a person's name, or *XXXX*, in the previous examples.

5. **In the lower half of the box, specify what you want to happen to messages that match the criteria.**

   If, in Steps 1 and 2, you've told your rule to watch for junk mail containing *$$$$* in the Subject line, here's where you can tell Mail to delete it or move it into, say, a Spam folder.

TROUBLESHOOTING MOMENT

Secrets of the Mbox Files

Mail keeps all of its messages in a series of mailbox database files (with file name extensions *.mbox)* in your Home folder→Library→Mail folder.

Knowing this permits you to perform a number of interesting tricks. For example, now you know what files to back up for safekeeping.

Second, you now have yourself a beautiful monthly (or yearly) archiving system. Each month, create a new mailbox folder in Mail, named for a certain month. Drag into it all the mail you want to archive, and then back up just that mailbox file ("June2002.mbox") from your hard drive—instant archiving system! (If you ever want to work with these messages again, just drag that .mbox file back into your Home folder→Library→Mail folder before opening Mail.)

Third, now you know which files to copy to your laptop when you travel if you want to maintain email continuity.

With a little imagination, you'll see how the options in this pop-up menu can do absolutely amazing things with your incoming email. Mail can colorize, delete, move, redirect, or forward messages, or even play a sound when you get a certain message. (Consider, for example, what happens when you go on a trip. By setting up the controls as shown in Figure 19-13, you have specified that only messages from your boss, Chris Herbert, are to be redirected to your vacation email address, *feelio@yahoo.com*. The rest of the mail will just have to wait until you're home again.)

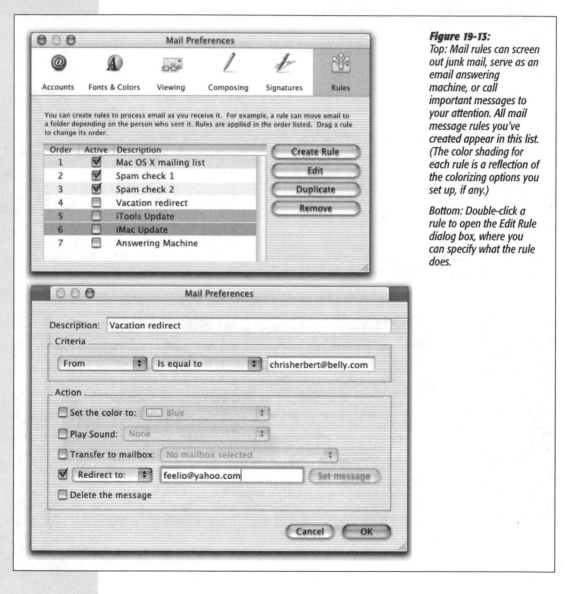

Figure 19-13:
Top: Mail rules can screen out junk mail, serve as an email answering machine, or call important messages to your attention. All mail message rules you've created appear in this list. (The color shading for each rule is a reflection of the colorizing options you set up, if any.)

Bottom: Double-click a rule to open the Edit Rule dialog box, where you can specify what the rule does.

6. **In the very top box, name your mail rule. Click OK.**

Now the Rules dialog box appears (Figure 19-13, top). Here, you can choose a sequence for the rules you've created by dragging them up and down. Here, too, you can turn off the ones you won't be needing at the moment, but may use again one day.

Tip: Mail applies rules as they appear, from top to bottom, in the list. If a rule doesn't seem to be working properly, it may be that an earlier rule is intercepting and processing the message before the "broken" rule even sees it. To fix this, try dragging the rule up or down in the list.

Two sneaky message-rule tricks

You can use message rules for many different purposes. But here are two of the best:

- **Create a spam filter.** When spammers send out junk email, they usually put your address on the BCC (blind carbon copy) line, so that you can't see who else got the message. This characteristic makes it easy for you to screen out such mail. First create a rule that puts messages where "To or Cc" contains your email address into the Inbox as usual.

  But then create another message rule that puts *all* messages into a folder called Possible Spam. (How do you create a rule that affects all incoming messages? Make the pop-up menus say "From" and "Does not contain," and then type something improbable into the text box, like *kwyjibo*.)

  Because the second rule doesn't kick in until *after* the first one has done its duty, the second rule affects only messages in which your name appears on the BCC line (which is almost always spam). Once a week, you can look through the Possible Spam mailbox in case a legitimate message found its way there.

TROUBLESHOOTING MOMENT

Rebuilding Your Mail Databases

As noted earlier in this chapter, Mail keeps your messages in a series of mailbox database files in your Home folder→Library→Mail folder.

Over time, you add and delete hundreds of messages from these database files; over time, some digital sawdust gets left behind, resulting in peculiarities when addressing messages, or general Mail sluggishness. You also wind up with *massive* message files hidden on your hard drive, which can consume hundreds of megabytes of disk space. That's a particular bummer if you like to copy your message

databases to your laptop when you go on a trip.

Fortunately, it's easy enough to *rebuild the message databases*. Doing so cleanses, repairs, and purges your message files. As a result, you wind up with a much more compact and healthy database.

To rebuild an email database, highlight it in the mailboxes "drawer" in Mail. (Highlight several, if you like.) Then choose Mailbox→Rebuild Mailbox. Mac OS X takes several minutes (or hours, depending on the sizes of your mailboxes) to repair and compact your database.

Note: If you subscribe to mailing lists that put your address in the BCC line, create *another* mail rule that intercepts them, filing them in any folder you like. Drag this "mailing list" rule so that it takes effect before the Possible Spam rule does.

- **The email answering machine.** If you're going to be on vacation, you can turn Mail into an email answering machine that sends a canned "I'm away until the 15th" message to everyone who writes you. To do so, set the pop-up menus so that they say "To or Cc" and "Contains"; put your own email address in the text box. In the bottom half of the dialog box, turn on the Reply checkbox. Click "Set message" and type your boilerplate reply in the resulting box.

Tip: Here again, if you subscribe to mailing lists, set up another mail rule that intercepts and files them *before* your answering-machine rule kicks in. Otherwise, you'll incur the wrath of the other Internet citizens by littering their email discussion groups with copies of your auto-reply message.

Address Book

You'll find Mac OS X's little-black-book program in your Applications folder, or you can open it from within Mail by choosing Windows→Address Book (or clicking the Address toolbar icon when you're composing a message).

Tip: The Address Book toolbar works exactly like the Mail or Finder window toolbars. You can hide it by clicking the upper-right white button, move its icons around (or delete them) by ⌘-dragging them, Control-click it and choose Customize Toolbar from the contextual menu, and so on.

Adding and Looking Up Names

One way to add somebody to the list is to click New and then fill in the blanks, as shown in Figure 19-14. (Press Tab to jump from blank to blank.)

Of course, a much easier method is simply to choose Message→Add Sender To Address Book (⌘-Y), as described on page 464.

In any case, once you've collected a few names, you can pluck one of your contacts' needles out of the haystack by typing a few letters of the name into the Search blank (Figure 19-14, bottom). The more letters you type, the shorter the visible list becomes.

You can put the Address Book to use in any of several ways:

- Click somebody's name and then click the Mail icon. Mail starts up and automatically opens a preaddressed outgoing message.

- In Mail, start typing somebody's name. If that person is in the address book, Mail completes the full email address for you. (You can also drag names out of the Address Book and into the CC field—but not, for some reason, into the To field.)

- Import an address book you've exported from another program, such as your former email program or Palm Desktop.

- Choose File→New Group. A window appears, in which you can name, describe, and populate an email group (by dragging addresses from the address list into the main box). From now on, when addressing an outgoing message, you can type this group name instead of having to painstakingly fill in the addresses of everybody who's supposed to get this note—a godsend if you send out periodic newsletters, jokes, or baby pictures to your family.

Figure 19-14:
Top: Fill in the blanks. Press ⌘-N each time you want to create another new entry. If you click the down-arrow button just above the Save button, you expand the window to include a massive array of additional fields—just the ticket when somebody you know has a pager, fax, cell phone, instant-message address, home phone, and work phone.

Bottom: Pinpoint matching names in the master list by typing a few letters into the Search box.

Jabber

Um, one of the field labels in the pop-up menus for the phone-number blanks for each Address Book person is Jabber. Am I supposed to know what Jabber is?

It's an instant-message program, along the lines of AOL Instant Messenger (AIM), although much less popular. You can read more about it at *www.jabber.org*.

Don't ask why Apple built in a field for it in Address Book. Maybe the guy who wrote Address Book is a Jabber fan.

Tip: vCard is short for *virtual business card.* More and more email programs send and receive these electronic business cards.

If you ever receive an email to which a *vCard file* is attached, drag it into your address book window to create an instant entry with a complete set of contact information. You can create vCards of your own, too: just drag anyone's name out of your Address Book and onto the desktop (or into a piece of outgoing mail).

Pictures

You can dress up each address book entry not only with textual information, but also with a photo. Whenever you're editing somebody's address book card, just drag or paste a digital photo—preferably 64 pixels square—into the "picture well" at the right side, as shown in Figure 19-14. From now on, if you receive an email from that person, the photo shows up right in the email message. (You don't necessarily need an actual photo of that person. You can add a graphic of your choice that you want to represent someone, even if it's a Bart Simpson face or skull and crossbones.)

It will be years before this feature gets the momentum it really deserves—but wow, do we have a lot to look forward to.

Sherlock

Sherlock is Mac OS X's Find command. It can quickly find three kinds of things:

- **Icons.** Sherlock can look for a particular file or folder based on its description—by its name, size, date stamp, and so on.

- **Words.** Sherlock can also look for words *inside* your files. That's a powerful feature if you remember having typed or read something, but can't remember the file's name.

- **Web sites.** Most intriguingly of all, Sherlock can look for words that appear on Web pages, exactly like such search engines as Yahoo.com or Google.com. In fact, Sherlock can harness the power of several Internet search engines simultaneously—all right from your desktop, without even having to open your Web browser. It can even compare prices on shopping Web sites and track bids on auction Web sites.

This chapter covers these three searching systems in sequence.

Finding Icons

Most people, most of the time, use Sherlock to search for files by name. Here's how the process works:

Preparing to Search

To open Sherlock in readiness for searching for icons, click its Sherlock hat icon on the Dock. Or, if you're already in the Finder, choose File→Find (or press ⌘-F).

The window that appears is enormous, filled with unlabeled icons and blanks (see Figure 20-1). The list in the middle of the window lets you specify *where* you want Sherlock to do its searching. Every disk attached to your Mac at the moment—your hard drive, a Zip disk, a CD, a networked disk you've mounted (see Chapter 12), and so on—shows up here with its own checkbox, along with a special checkbox for your own Home folder. Most of the time, you just want to search your primary hard drive. Ensure that a checkmark appears next to its name (or press ⌘-T to select or deselect all of them), and then proceed.

Tip: This window acts like a Finder list view: You can drag the dividers between the column names to make the columns wider or narrower, and you can click the name of a column to sort the list by that criterion. (For details on what the Index Status column represents, see "Finding Words" later in this chapter.)

It's worth noting, however, that you can greatly speed up the searching by telling Sherlock which specific *folders* you want it to search. Figure 20-1 shows how to do that.

Figure 20-1:
To limit (and thereby speed up) Sherlock's search, you can drag a folder, or set of folders, directly off the desktop and into the list of disks. (Alternatively, choose Find→Add Folder.) Their names appear there, marked with checkboxes that you can turn on or off. In fact, they'll still be listed here the next time, and every time, you open Sherlock—until you drag them out of the window to the Trash can, or highlight them and then choose Find→ Remove Folder.

To find a file whose name you know, just type a few letters of its name into the blank. (Capitalization doesn't matter, and neither does the position of the letters you type— if you type *John,* Sherlock will find files with names Johnson, Peterjohn, and DiJohnson.) Finally, click the magnifying glass icon or press Return.

While the searching is going on, the green magnifying glass icon turns reddish. To interrupt the search in progress, click the red button. (On the other hand, if a search is taking a long time, you're free to switch into another program. Sherlock keeps working in the background.)

A couple of seconds after you've clicked the magnifying glass icon, the Sherlock screen changes. In place of the disk list, you now see a list of files whose names contain what you typed in the blank. (Figure 20-2 shows this list.)

Note: If you share your Mac with other people, as described in Chapter 11, you'll see only the files that belong to you. Sherlock ignores the files and folders that other people have created (unless, of course, they're files and folders that have been explicitly put into the Public or Shared folders, as described in Chapter 11).

POWER USERS' CLINIC

Searching by File Name Extension

It's important to note that Sherlock doesn't consider *hidden* file name extensions part of your files' names. If you're trying to round up all your Word documents, for example, searching for *.doc* in the file name won't work.

Of course, you can always *un-hide* your file name extensions. (To do so, click the desktop, choose Finder→

Preferences, and then turn on "Always show file extensions.")

Now the file name suffixes appear on all your documents, system-wide, so that you can use Sherlock to hunt for documents based on their file name extensions. That's a great way to round up, for example, all Word files (*.doc*).

You can manipulate this list much the way you'd approach a list of files in a standard Finder list view window. You can move up or down the list by pressing the arrow keys, scroll a "page" at a time with the Page Up and Page Down keys, and so on. You can also jump from place to place in the Sherlock window—from the list of found items to the folder map below them, and back to the blank at the top of the window—by pressing the Tab key. You can also highlight multiple icons simultaneously, exactly as you would in a Finder list view: Highlight all of them by choosing Edit→Select All, highlight individual items by ⌘-clicking them, drag diagonally to enclose a cluster of found items, and so on.

At this point, you can proceed in many different ways:

Find out where something is

If you click *once* on any item in the results list, the bottom half of the window becomes a folder map that shows you where that item is. For example, in Figure 20-2, the notation in the bottom half of the window (read from bottom to top) means: "The Report icon you found is in Harold's Home folder, which is in the Users folder, which is on the hard drive called Macintosh HD."

If you want to get your hands on the actual icon, choose File→Open Enclosing Folder (⌘-E). Sherlock instantly retreats to the background, as the Finder highlights the actual icon in question, sitting there in its window wherever it happens to be on your hard drive.

Open the file (or open one of the folders it's in)

If one of the found files is the one you were looking for, double-click it to open it (or highlight it and press ⌘-O). In many cases, you'll never even know or care *where* the file was—you just want to get into it.

You can also double-click to open any of the folders that appear in the folder map in the bottom half of the window. For example, in Figure 20-2, you could double-click the Harold icon to open it, or the Users folder to open *it,* and so on.

Figure 20-2:
In the top half of the window: the file Sherlock found. In the bottom half: the path, or map, that shows you exactly where the highlighted found icon is filed. You can drag the horizontal divider between the halves of this window upward or downward to adjust the relative sizes of the panes. (You can also drag the lower-right corner of the window to make it bigger or smaller.)

Move or delete the file

You can drag an item directly out of Sherlock's found-files list and into a different folder, window, or disk. The folder map at the bottom of the window updates itself to reflect the file's new location.

Print or Trash

After highlighting an icon (or icons) in the list of found files, you can use the commands in the File menu, including Print Item and Move to Trash. (If you want to Show Info for a highlighted icon, press ⌘-E, ⌘-I in succession.)

Adjust the list

By clicking the column headings, you can sort the list of found files in various ways: by name, size, date, and so on. (You can reverse the order by clicking the same heading a second time.) You can also make the window bigger by dragging the lower-right corner handle, adjust the relative widths of the columns by dragging the column-name dividers, or rearrange the columns horizontally by dragging their names. All of this works exactly as it does in a Finder list view window.

Make an alias

You can make an alias for one of the found items exactly the way you'd do in a Finder window: drag it out of the window while pressing ⌘-Option. The alias appears wherever you release the mouse (on the desktop, for example).

Search for similar files

By choosing Find→Find Similar Files, Sherlock does its best to round up other files on your hard drive that resemble the one you highlighted. (It tries to find files that contain similar words, have a similar name, have the same type and creator codes, and so on.) In general, Sherlock's fuzzy logic in performing this kind of search may be a bit fuzzier than you'd like—it can pull up some genuinely bizarre documents. But every now and then, the program will surprise you with its accuracy.

Save the search setup

By choosing File→Save Search Criteria (or by pressing ⌘-S), you can immortalize the search you've just set up. You might use this feature if you perform the same search each day—if, for example, you like to scan the Internet each morning for newly posted articles on Conan O'Brien, or round up all the documents you created yesterday for backing up.

The Save File dialog box appears, so that you can name (and choose a location for) the Save Find File document you're about to create. (If you've elected to make file name extensions visible [page 103], this one has the suffix *.find.*)

This file describes the search you've set up—what text was in the box at the top of the window, what kind of search it was, and even which disks or folders were involved in the search.

The next time you want to repeat that search, just double-click the .find document you created. Sherlock launches automatically, instantly fills in the saved search criteria, and begins searching.

Do another search

To start over with another search, choose Channels→Files, press ⌘-F, or click the hard drive button at the upper-left corner of the window. The list of found files disappears, and the original Sherlock screen (showing your list of disks) reappears.

Searching by Date, Size, and More

Searching for a file by typing in a few letters of its name is by far the most frequently used Sherlock function. But in certain circumstances, you may not remember the name you gave a file, or you may want to narrow the search by confining it to, say, only Microsoft Word files. Using the More Options dialog box—which opens when you choose Find→More Options, or choose Edit from the Custom pop-up menu (Figure 20-3)—you can limit your search to files that were created before or after a certain date, that are larger or smaller than a certain size, that were created by a specific program, and so forth. Figure 20-3 shows exactly how detailed this kind of search can be.

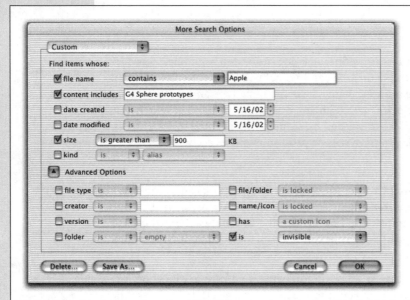

Figure 20-3:
By choosing Edit from the Custom pop-up menu on the Sherlock screen, you open this massive dialog box (shown here after clicking the Advanced Options button to expand the box). Turn on the checkboxes of as many criteria as you'd like; each additional checkbox further narrows the search. This example would find invisible files larger than 900 K whose file names contain the word Apple and whose text (inside the document) includes the phrase "G4 Sphere prototypes."

More Options—the basics

The checkboxes refer to the following details about your files:

- **File name.** When you turn on this checkbox, the pop-up menu becomes available—and you suddenly realize how this file-name search differs from the one on the main Sherlock screen. This time, Sherlock won't just find files whose names *contain* the letters you type—it can find files whose names *begin* with those letters, *end* with those letters, *don't* contain those letters, and so on.

- **Content includes.** This box lets you search for words within files, as described in the next section.

- **Date created, date modified.** These options, along with the options in the corresponding pop-up menus, let you search for files according to when you first created them or when you last saved them. Some of the fuzzy-logic commands on these pop-up menus are particularly useful: options like "is within 1 month of" are exactly what you need when you only vaguely remember when you last worked with the file.

- **Size.** Using this control, and its "is less than"/"is greater than" pop-up menu, you can restrict your search to files of a certain size. (Remember that there are 1,024 kilobytes per megabyte; this field requires a number in kilobytes, or K.)

- **Kind.** These two pop-up menus let you search for everything that is, or isn't, a certain kind of file—an alias, folder, extension, stationery file, and so on. Some of these items, such as "control panel" and "desktop printer," are clearly holdovers from the Mac OS 9 days and have no equivalents on a Mac OS X system (except for the Mac OS 9 System Folder still on board, of course).

More Options–advanced

If you click the Advanced Options button, the window expands, revealing an additional set of file criteria:

- **File type, creator.** The *type and creator codes* associate every file on your hard drive with the programs that can open it; see page 101 for details. Technical as this option may sound, it's actually among the most useful in this entire box—by searching for a creator code, for example, you can tell Sherlock to find all documents that belong to a particular program, such as all AppleWorks files. (Remember, however, that many Mac OS X programs create *file name extensions,* not type and creator codes, to indicate documents' parenthood.)

- **Version.** If you inspect the Show Info window of the programs on your hard drive, you'll discover that almost every application has a version number. This option lets you search for applications that have a particular version number. (You would do this to find out if you have the latest version of an application; then you can delete the outdated one.)

Note: Documents don't have built-in version numbers, so don't turn this checkbox on except when looking for applications (or Mac OS X *frameworks*). If you specify a version number when searching for documents, Sherlock will come up empty-handed every time.

- **File/folder is locked/is unlocked.** Use this option to find all files that you've locked using the File→Show Info command.

- **Folder is/is not empty/shared/mounted.** It feels good, every now and then, to round up all empty folders on your hard drive and throw them away.

   Shared folders are those you've made available to other people on the network using the File Sharing feature (see Chapter 11). *Mounted folders* are those on other Macs on the network that you've brought onto your screen using that same File Sharing feature.

- **File/folder is locked/is unlocked.** This option lets you find files you've locked using the File→Show Info command. (In Mac OS X, you can't lock a *folder*, but you can in Mac OS 9, in order to prevent other people on the network from messing with this particular folder. Sherlock can even find locked Mac OS 9 folders.)

- **Name/icon is locked/is not locked.** Under Mac OS 9, the system locked the names and icons of certain system folders (Appearance, Apple Menu Items, Extensions, and so on) so that you couldn't rename them or give them new, custom icons. You can use this option to round them up. (Mac OS X's equivalent feature doesn't work the same way.)

- **Has a custom icon/no custom icon.** A *custom icon* is a replacement graphic that you've pasted onto one of your icons, as described on page 59.

- **Is invisible/visible.** Your hard drive is teeming with invisible files. Thousands of files, for example, constitute the Unix operating system—all hidden. Using this command, you can take a look at them. (Don't move or throw away invisible files, however; Apple made them invisible expressly so you wouldn't tamper with them.)

Note: Unfortunately, you can no longer search for the text you've entered in the Comments field of your files' Show Info boxes, as you could in Mac OS 9.

How to specify all this information in half a second

Some of the information in this More Search Options window is easy to specify—such as the Kind of file you're looking for. Other bits of information, particularly the file and creator codes, are normally hidden from view. If you want to round up all documents created by, say, BeeKeeper Pro, how are you supposed to know what type codes to type?

By *showing* Sherlock. You can drag any icon directly from your desktop or any Finder window right on top of the More Search Options window. Sherlock responds by filling in *all* of the blanks described above—the ones whose checkboxes you've turned on, anyway—with the information that describes the file you dragged: its size, kind, label, type code, and so on, turning the More Search Options window into the world's largest Show Info window. This doesn't mean that you must now search for documents matching all of these criteria; just turn on the checkboxes of the criteria you *do* want to match when searching.

Saving searches

After spending an hour or two inside the More Search Options dialog box setting up elaborate search criteria, you may be relieved to learn that you can save a snapshot of this search setup. When you need to search for this kind of file again, you'll be able to restore this setup using a single pop-up menu. Figure 20-4 shows the steps. (Behind the scenes, the Mac stores your saved criteria as individual search documents in the Users→[your Home folder]→Library→Internet Search Sites→Files folder.)

Saving a More Search Options setup in this way isn't quite the same as using the File→Save Search Criteria command on the main Sherlock screen, as described earlier in this chapter. This Save As button produces a saved search that (a) doesn't have a *.find* file name extension, and (b) shows up in the Custom pop-up menu. But both create stand-alone files that, when double-clicked, launch Sherlock and begin searching.

Figure 20-4:
Top: After setting a search in the More Search Options dialog box, click Save As. You'll be asked to provide a short name for the search you're preserving, such as "Empty folders" or "Created in the last week."

Bottom: When you click Save again, you're returned to the main Sherlock window, where your new search label shows up in the pop-up menu next to the Edit button. (Several Apple-created custom searches already appear in this pop-up menu to show you the idea. To retire any searches you don't find useful in this pop-up menu, click the Delete button shown in Figure 20-3.) Note how Sherlock always summarizes the nature of your search at the very bottom of the window.

Actually performing the search

After you've specified your complex search options, click OK. You return to the main Sherlock window, where the Custom button now appears selected. More important, the bottom of the window shows, in plain English, what you're looking for: "Find items whose name contains 'fish', date created is within 2 months of 7/4/2002, file/folder is locked," for example.

Tip: By typing into the text box at the top of the Sherlock window, you can specify letters to look for in your file names *in addition* to whatever criteria you've selected using the Custom menu. For example, suppose you've used the Custom pop-up menu to choose Applications (one of the preinstalled examples). By typing *Apple* into the text box above it, you can limit your search to applications whose name contains *Apple*.

At last you're ready to perform the search—by pressing Return or clicking the magnifying glass button.

Finding Text in Your Files

Sooner or later, it happens to everyone: a file's name doesn't match what's inside it. Maybe a marauding toddler pressed the keys while playing KidPix, inadvertently renaming your doctoral thesis "xggrjpO#$5%////." Maybe, in a Saturday afternoon organizing binge, your spouse helpfully changed the name of your "ATM Instructions" document to "Cash Machine Info," little realizing that it was a help file for Adobe Type Manager. Or maybe you just can't remember what you called something.

For this purpose, Sherlock offers a powerful Contents button that lets you search for words *inside* your files, regardless of their names. It performs this kind of search with amazing speed, and has saved thousands of Mac fans hours of frustrated searching by hand.

The Indexing Catch

Left unaided, however, the Mac would take almost as long as *you* would to search your files for a particular phrase. To eliminate that delay, Apple programmed Sherlock to do something ingenious: Like a kid cramming for an exam, Sherlock reads, takes notes on, and memorizes the contents of all of your files.

After having indexed your hard drive, however, Sherlock can produce search results in seconds.

Indexing a hard drive

When you first get your Mac, the hard drive has never been indexed. When you open the Sherlock window for the first time, the Index Status column in the list of hard drives tells you as much.

The first time you index your hard drive, Sherlock may require 20 minutes to an hour or so, during which you can continue working. In Mac OS 9, your Mac feels drugged while the indexing is going on; in fact, Sherlock in Mac OS 9 offered an elaborate set of features for setting up unattended, automatically scheduled indexing.

None of that is necessary in Mac OS X, which is perfectly capable of indexing away in the microseconds between your keystrokes and mouse clicks in other programs, producing no measurable slowdown. To index a disk, just click its name in the Sherlock list and then choose Find→Index Now.

Note: You can't index the main hard drive in its entirety; the only folder you'll see indexed automatically on your hard drive is your own Home folder. As the note in its Index Status tells you, you can force other folders to get indexed by dragging them directly into the Sherlock window.

After the first indexing is over, Sherlock needs only a few minutes per day to update its miniature card catalog of your hard drive, to bone up on any new documents you've written. All you have to do is open the Sherlock program itself; the updating is automatic.

Tip: In Mac OS X, there's no longer a single, invisible Sherlock index file on the hard drive. Now *every folder* has its own invisible index file (called *.FBCIndex).* (If you use Sherlock's advanced options to find invisible files [page 486], you'll see these files by the hundreds.) The beauty of this system is that folders remain indexed even when copied to other disks—because the invisible index travels along with them.

What gets indexed

Sherlock is smart enough to ignore files on your hard drive that don't actually contain *words,* such as applications, pictures, movies, system files, and so on. What it does index includes word processing files, text files, clipping files, HTML (Web page) documents, Acrobat (.pdf) files, and sometimes email, depending on the program you use.

Sherlock can't index CDs or other hard drives on the network. And, as noted earlier, if you share your Mac with other people, Sherlock indexes only *your stuff.*

Tip: Choose Sherlock→Preferences. Click Languages, and turn off the checkboxes of every language except the ones you use in your documents. (Chances are, the factory-installed set of languages to be indexed—Afrikaans, Catalan, Norwegian, and so on—is more inclusive than you actually need.) Now the indexing will go much faster.

And if you don't search for words within files very often at all, you can turn off indexing completely, too, to save a few seconds and a few megabytes. Choose Sherlock→Preferences and turn off "Automatically index folders when they're added to the Files channel."

How to Search for Text

After you've indexed your hard drive, you can begin to enjoy the payoff—searching for words inside your files. Just click the Contents button to prepare for a content search.

Now type the word or phrase you seek. Click the magnifying glass icon (or press Return). Sherlock quickly produces a list of results, ranked by *relevance,* as shown in Figure 20-5.

After the list appears, you can open, print, move, make an alias of, or otherwise handle the resulting files exactly as described in "The Search Results," earlier in this chapter.

When Sherlock Fails

If you find yourself frustrated by Sherlock's ability to find words inside your files, it helps to understand the way it searches. For example:

- Sherlock indexes only the first 2,000 different words in each file. That's why Sherlock might miss your book manuscript if the search term occurs late in the document.

• Sherlock tries to find files containing *any* of the words you type into the search blank. If you search for *Steve Jobs,* you'll turn up every document that contains the word Steve, *and* every document that contains the word jobs. You can't tell Sherlock to a search for a specific pair of words that occur together (as you can, using quotation marks or + signs, when using most Internet search pages).

Figure 20-5:
When you search for the words inside your files, Sherlock adds a column called Relevance to the found-files list. Longer bars indicate more relevance; relevance is defined as "how many times the search term appears relative to the whole document's length." In other words, a four-word file containing the search term "lizard" twice has higher relevance than one containing "lizard" three times in a 500-word essay.

• Sherlock sometimes even tries to find files containing *pieces* of what you searched for. If you search for *Steven,* Sherlock's roundup includes files containing just the word Steve. That phenomenon partly explains why Sherlock sometimes finds files that don't seem to contain the search term at all.

• It bears repeating: On a Mac on which several people have accounts (Chapter 1), Sherlock can find only *your files.*

Searching the Internet

Any old computer can search for the files on its own hard drive. Sherlock's special twist, however, is that it lets you use exactly the same program to search for information on the World Wide Web (if your Mac has an Internet account).

You put Sherlock into search-the-Internet mode by choosing Find→Search Internet (⌘-K), by choosing from the Channels menu, or by clicking one of the icons at the top of the window. These icons represent different kinds of Web sites that Sherlock can search (see Figure 20-6). When you click one, the screen changes to show a list of checkboxes, each corresponding to a particular Web site that you can search.

Here's what these *channel buttons* (as Apple calls them) represent. (To identify one of these icons by name, point to it without clicking; a pop-up label appears.)

- **Internet.** When you click this channel button, you see a list of checkboxes. Each represents a popular *search engine*—a Web site, like Yahoo.com or AltaVista.com, that searches part of the Internet. The benefits of having them listed in Sherlock are that, first, you can search more than one simultaneously; and second, you can perform this kind of search without actually having to launch your Web browser.

Tip: One of the most valuable entries here is VersionTracker, which lets you keep current on which programs have been made available for Mac OS X.

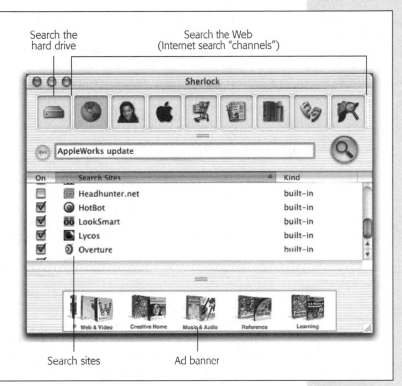

Figure 20-6:
The "channels" (buttons) at the top of the Sherlock screen control which Web sites you include in the search. Each button summons a different list of Web-site search checkboxes, which behave exactly like the list of hard drives that appears when you're searching your own hard drive for files. You can move a site to a different channel by dragging its name onto the appropriate icon at the top of the screen.

Search the hard drive

Search the Web (Internet search "channels")

Search sites

Ad banner

- **People.** This tantalizing option (⌘-J) lets you type in somebody's name. Sherlock then consults any of several "White Pages" Web sites in an attempt to track down that person's email address and telephone number.

Unfortunately, the technology gods don't always smile on this feature. You may get many listings for a certain name, several of which are out of date. On the other hand, you may be surprised at how often one of those listings is, indeed, the person you're stalking. (Make that "seeking." Sorry.)

- **Apple.** Using the checkboxes, you can search the Apple Macintosh Products Guide, a database of 14,000 programs for the Mac (to find out if there's an interior design program for the Mac, for example). You can also search the Apple Tech Info Library, a huge collection of answers, troubleshooting tips, and feature explanations for every Mac model ever made; and Apple.com (the rest of the Apple site, including press releases, developer tools, news blurbs, and so on).

- **Shopping.** Now we're talking. The checkboxes on this screen represent shopping and auction Web sites, such as Amazon, eBay, and Barnes & Noble. When you search these sites, you type in the name of a product; Sherlock shows you a list of matching items from those Web sites, sorted by price and including shipping-delay information.

  Unless you don't buy anything on the Internet much beyond books, flowers, and CDs, the included plug-ins for this screen may not seem very useful. But as you add new plug-ins, as described later this chapter, the Shopping channel could emerge as a powerful comparison-shopping feature.

- **News.** These checkboxes let you search various Internet-based news, sports, and financial-news services.

- **Reference.** The three checkboxes on this screen may look sparse, but they represent a delicious Mac feature: what amounts to a built-in dictionary, thesaurus, and encyclopedia. Type the term you're looking for, click the appropriate checkboxes, and let Sherlock retrieve the definition, encyclopedia entry, or list of synonyms from the corresponding Web sites.

- **Entertainment.** One-stop clicking for movie, music, and showbiz fans. Of special note is the Internet Movie Database, an invaluable source of information on the cast, crew, and release information on every movie anyone's ever heard of, complete with user reviews (so you don't rent any more turkeys).

- **My Channel.** When you click this Sherlock Holmes-cap icon, you get an empty space where the checkboxes usually appear. This is *your* channel—actually, the first of many that you can create—which is an empty screen to be filled with your own personal selection of checkboxes. To add a checkbox to this screen, switch to one of the *other* screens (by clicking a different top-row icon) and then drag a checkbox directly onto the Holmes-cap icon.

  More on creating your own channels, and managing plug-ins, in the next section.

Performing a Search

Searching the Web sites listed in one of the channel screens works just like searching your own Mac disks for particular files. Begin by switching to the appropriate channel, either by clicking one of the icons or by using the commands in the Channels menu. Turn on the checkboxes of the Web sites you want to search, type the text you wish to find, and then click the magnifying glass icon (or press Return).

Tip: You can save a canned search setup when using the Internet search features, exactly as you can with other kinds of searches (see page 483). When you double-click the saved search file, Sherlock launches, connects to the Internet, and performs the predetermined search automatically.

If you're not already online, Sherlock now dials the Internet, sends your search request to the selected Web sites and, after a moment, shows you the results of its search. Instead of seeing a list of files, however, this time Sherlock shows you a list of Web pages containing the text you typed. Figure 20-7 shows the idea.

Figure 20-7:
When you search the Internet, you get a list of Web pages that contain the text you seek. As with find-by-content searches, many of these results are sorted by relevance. When you're searching the Web, the Sherlock window sprouts a new element: the advertising banner at the bottom of the screen—a concession to the various Web-search pages, such as Excite and Lycos, whose Web-page ads are invisible to people using Sherlock.

Here's what you can do with one of these results:

- **Read the first paragraph.** Click one of the Web pages listed in the search results; as shown in Figure 20-7, Sherlock shows you, just above the advertising panel, the first paragraph or so of text that appears on that Web page. This blurb is a very useful preview, one that can save you the effort of opening that Web page only to find that it's not what you were looking for.

- **Go to the Web page.** Double-click one of the listings to launch your Web browser and actually visit the corresponding page. If you double-click a name you found using one of the People channels, your email program opens, and a new outgoing message appears—preaddressed.

Tip: If your Web browser is already open, you can drag one of the Sherlock results directly into its window to switch to the corresponding new page.

- **Create an Internet location file.** If you think you might like to visit one of these Web sites later, you can drag it out of the list and onto your desktop, where it becomes an Internet location file (see page 452). You can also drag it directly into the Internet Explorer Favorites list, where it becomes a bookmark for that browser.

- **Repeat the search.** Click the same channel button again to restore your original search setup—to correct a typo, for example. Or click a different channel button to search a different kind of Web page—or even your hard drive.

When Sherlock Fails on the Internet

If you find the Web pages that Sherlock locates inconsistent in quality, you're not alone. Remember that, first of all, it's not Sherlock doing the searching—it's the Web-search pages whose checkboxes you've selected. To understand what's going on with Sherlock, you must understand what's going on with Internet search pages.

For example: Web pages sometimes turn up in Sherlock that don't, in fact, appear to contain any of the words you searched for. When this happens, it's probably because the creator of that Web page buried your search words invisibly on the page—in its HTML *keyword list,* for example, exactly in hopes of being found by search engines like yours. That technique may seem dishonest, but it's very popular on the Internet— and you're likely to encounter it if you're searching for commonly sought terms.

Each Web-search page has different conventions, too, concerning punctuation marks in your search phrase. For example, search engines like Yahoo rely on quotation marks ("like this") to indicate words that must be found together; otherwise, it turns up all Web pages containing *either* word, not necessarily together. Other Web sites accept punctuation like + and -, the words *and* and *or,* the excluding term *not,* and so on. There's no way to find out exactly how to punctuate your search request for a particular Web-search page except to visit that Web page and read its Help screen.

Of Channels and Plug-ins

By downloading additional plug-ins—which are free—you can take Sherlock's Internet searching abilities far beyond Lycos and Amazon.com. You can create and manage your own channels, stocked with your own plug-ins, simply by understanding how Mac OS X organizes these files in the System folder.

Tip: By studying a little bit of HTML (Web page coding), you can actually create plug-ins of your own. If you know how to write HTML code, visit Apple's "how to make Sherlock plug-ins" page at *http:// developer.apple.com/macos/sherlock.html.*

Getting more plug-ins

You can find additional Sherlock plug-ins all over the Internet. For example:

- **SearchStandard.com.** Here you'll find about 350 plug-ins ready to go, all in one downloadable collection, including those for Time Daily (Time magazine), Onelist (a list of email-based discussion groups), MacCentral (Macintosh news and opinion), MP3.com (music files to download), Adobe, Deal Mac (a roundup of discount offers on Macs and related products), US Government, eToys, and so on. *www.searchstandard.com.*

- **Sherlock international plug-ins.** These plug-ins are specifically geared toward searching international-information databases: the U.S. State Department, Central Europe Online, Kennedy School of Government, and so on, plus French and Spanish versions of the Lycos search engine. *www.xenophone.com/sherlock.*

Installing plug-ins

When properly decompressed, a plug-in's name generally ends in the letters *.src* (for "Sherlock resource"). You can install a new plug-in by dragging it:

- Directly onto one of the channel buttons. Sherlock installs the plug-in onto that channel "page."
- Straight into the list of plug-in/sites on any channel page.

To move a site plug-in to a different channel, drag its checkbox onto one of the channel icons at the top of the Sherlock screen. And to remove one of these new checkbox items from your Sherlock screen, drag its icon directly out of Sherlock—onto the desktop, for example, or into the Trash.

Tip: To become a Sherlock master, try deleting, adding, or moving plug-in files around the manual way. Open your Home folder→Library→Internet Search Sites folder. Inside, you'll find a folder corresponding to each of your channels; inside each of these folders is the set of plug-ins that appears on that page. By dragging these icons around, you can assign them to different channels, delete them, and so on.

Managing channels

To create a new channel, choose Channels→New Channel. In the resulting dialog box (see Figure 20-8), type a name for the channel, a description, if you like, and then choose an icon from the scrolling list at the right side of the dialog box.

Figure 20-8:
Use this dialog box to set up a new channel, or to edit an old one (but not Apple's canned channels). You can choose an icon for the channel either by using the scrolling arrows at right, or by dragging a graphics file off the desktop and directly onto the icon box shown here. (You can also drag a graphic directly onto a channel icon in the main Sherlock window—but again, you can't change Apple's channel icons.)

You can return to this channel-customizing dialog box at any time: Just click one of your custom channels and then choose Channel→Edit Channel. (You can't, alas, edit any of the channels that come built into Sherlock. Despite the availability of several other people-heads in the list of available icons, your People channel is stuck with the twenty-something brunette forever.)

You can also rearrange your channel icons: just drag them into any blank slots in the channel palette. Doing so is easiest, of course, if there *are* some blank slots; you can make blank ones show up by dragging downward the "grip strip" handle—centered just below the channel icons.

FREQUENTLY ASKED QUESTION

It's Not Nice to Fool Mother Apple

I keep trying to delete the People channel, which doesn't really work anyway. But it keeps coming back!

You're welcome to play around in the Home folder→ Library→Internet Search Sites folder. Inside, each folder represents one of your channels, and each plug-in inside these folders represents the checkbox on the corresponding channel page. You can rename a channel by renaming its folder, delete the channel by deleting its folder, reas-

sign a checkbox by dragging it to a different channel folder, and so on.

You'll soon discover, however, that Apple doesn't want you disturbing its original channel lineup—People, Shopping, and so on. If you drag one of these folders out of the Internet Search Sites folder, Sherlock will re-create it automatically. You'll have lost the individual plug-ins in that channel, but the icon will still be there at the top of the Sherlock window.

Web Sharing, FTP, and Remote Access

E mail and Web surfing may be the most popular Internet activities, but the world's most gigantic network has many other uses. The general idea is always the same, though: letting one computer reach out and touch another.

Mac OS X offers a few features that embrace the more literal aspects of that notion. For example, you can turn your Mac into a *Web server*—an actual living Web site that anyone on the Internet can visit. This chapter also explores various ways to manipulate your own Mac from the road, using such *remote access* technologies as long-distance file sharing, FTP, and SSH.

Tip: These technologies are designed for full-time Internet connections (cable modem or DSL, for example). If you have a dial-up modem, these features work only when you're actually online. Still, they may occasionally be useful even then. You could always call up a friend and say, "Check out my Web site right now—here's the current IP address" or call someone back home to say, "I have to grab a file off my hard drive. Could you make the Mac on my desk go online?"

Web Sharing

Using the Sharing panel of System Preferences, you can turn your Mac into a Web site (or *server*), accessible from the Web browsers of people on your office network, the Internet at large, or both.

This feature assumes, of course, that you've already created some Web pages. For this purpose, you can use Web-design programs (Macromedia Dreamweaver, for example, or the free Netscape Composer) or the File→Save as Web Page command of a program like Microsoft Word. Or you could let Mac OS X build Web pages for you using Image Capture (page 211).

After you provide your friends and co-workers with your Mac's Web site address, they can view your Web pages, graphics, and documents in their own Web browsers. And whenever you're online, your Web site is also available to anyone on the Internet—but you don't have to pay a penny to a Web-hosting company.

Tip: Web Sharing is also an easy and efficient way to share your Mac files with Windows PCs, either those on your office network or those on the Internet. No special software or translation is required, and posting your files on the Web page avoids all the usual complexities of sending files by email.

Don't mistake Mac OS X's Web Sharing feature, by the way, with the relatively feeble equivalent feature in Mac OS 9 or Windows, which was designed to handle only a handful of visitors at a time (and couldn't handle anything fancy like CGI scripts). Inside Mac OS X is *Apache*, one of the strongest and most popular Unix Web server programs—precisely the same one that drives 60 percent of the Internet's commercial Web sites (including Apple.com).

UP TO SPEED

IP Addresses and You

Every computer connected to the Internet, even temporarily, has its own exclusive *IP address* (IP stands for Internet Protocol). What's yours? Open the Sharing pane of System Preferences to find out (see Figure 21-1). As you'll see, an IP address is always made up of four numbers separated by periods.

Some Macs with high-speed Internet connections (cable modem, DSL) have a permanent, unchanging address called a *fixed* or *static* IP address. Clearly, life is simpler if you have a fixed IP address, because other computers will always know where you find you.

Other Macs get assigned a new address each time they connect (a *dynamic* IP address); that's always the case, for example, when you connect using a dial-up modem. (If you can't figure out whether your Mac has a static or fixed address, ask your Internet service provider.)

You might suppose that Mac fans with dynamic addresses can't use any of the remote-connection technologies described in this chapter. After all, your Mac's Web address *changes* every time you connect, making it impossible to provide a single, permanent address to your friends and co-workers.

The answer is a *dynamic DNS service* that gives your Mac a name, not a number. Whenever you're online, these free services automatically update the IP address associated with the name you've chosen (such as *macmania.dyndns.org*), so that your friends and colleagues can memorize a single address for your machine.

To sign up for one of these services, just go to their Web sites—*www.dyndns.org, www.dhs.org, www.dtdns.com, www.hn.org, www.no-ip.com,* and so on.

Once you've got a fixed DNS name associated with your Mac, you'll be able to access it from elsewhere (provided it's online at the time), via File Sharing (Chapter 12), the screen-sharing program called Timbuktu, the Web Sharing and FTP features described in this chapter, and so on.

(If you have a fixed address, you can also pay a few dollars a year to register your own *domain name*, a bona fide address like *www.yournamehere.com.* To register one [or to find out if the name you want is taken], visit a site like *www.networksolutions.com.*)

The bottom line: If you build it, they won't necessarily come. But at least you'll have the capacity to handle them if they do.

Firing Up Personal Web Sharing

Here's how you turn your Mac into a low-budget Web site:

1. **Put the HTML documents, graphics, and files you want to publish into your Home→Sites folder.**

   Everyone with an account on your Mac has a Sites folder, and therefore the Mac can actually serve up lots of Web sites at once.

   Your Web site's home page, by the way, must be named *index.html*. (Apple has already put an *index.html* document into your Sites folder, just to give you the idea; feel free to replace it.)

2. **Open System Preferences; click Sharing (Figure 21-1).**

   You open System Preferences by clicking its Dock icon or by choosing its name from the menu.

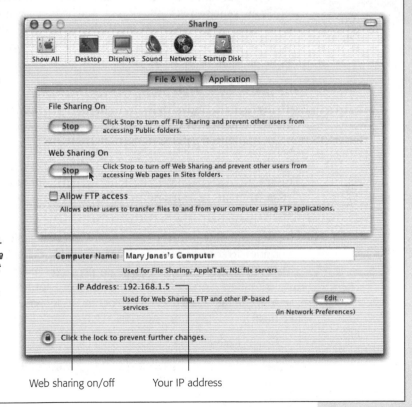

Figure 21-1:
Use the Web Sharing System Preferences pane to make designated folders on your hard drive available to anyone on the Internet. Note your Mac's IP address, indicated here. It's the basis for all of the fun Mac-sharing-over-the-Internet features described in this chapter.

Note: Once you're online, remember that you've just provided a rabbit hole into your Mac for the hackers on the Internet. If you plan to leave your Web site "up" full-time, consider installing some firewall software, if you don't already have a router that provides this function. (More on this topic on page 439.)

Web sharing on/off   Your IP address

3. **Where it says Web Sharing, click Start.**

You've just made the contents of your Web Pages folder available to anyone who can connect to your Mac.

4. **Note your IP address.**

In general, your Mac's Web address is based on its IP address, the string of numbers separated by periods that appears at the bottom of the Sharing pane.

Tip: If you connect to the Internet via dial-up modem, you may not see an IP address here until you're actually online.

---

5. **Email your new Web address to your friends and co-workers.**

In this example, your address is *http://111.222.3.44/~chris/* (the number is your IP address, and the name should be your short user name). Don't forget the final slash. Tell your friends to bookmark it so they won't have to remember this address, or use one of the DNS naming services described on page 498.

You've just put your folder-based Web page on the Internet for all to see—that is, all who know your secret Web address. Maybe you'll want to distribute the address only to other people on your office network, using your tiny Web site as a distribution source for documents. Or maybe you'll want to go whole-hog, hosting an e-commerce Web site (read on).

The Mac's Own Web Site

The instructions above show you how to create a Web site in your Home→Sites folder. In other words, they guide you through creating your *personal* Web site.

But if you have an Administrator account (Chapter 11), you can also put your Web pages into the main hard drive window's Library→WebServer→Documents folder. This is your Mac's *main* Web site folder, and its address is simply *http://111.222.3.44/* —that is, it's just your IP address (or domain name, if you have one), no user name needed.

Working with this primary Web site folder is only slightly different from the personal ones described above. Because you're now working inside an official Mac OS X system folder, you have to mind your *privileges* (page 307). Using the File→Show Info command, you should set up the permissions of any folders and documents *inside* the Library→WebServer→Documents folder (an Images folder, for example) like this:

• **Owner:** Read & Write

• **Group:** Read & Write (or Read Only, if you don't want other administrators to have access)

• **Everyone:** Read Only

You've just ensured that your visitors will be allowed to see your Web documents—but that random Internet citizens can't make any changes to them.

Note: This step is especially important if you've copied HTML documents over from another Mac, or even from Mac OS 9. The Mac automatically gives Read permissions only to their owner (meaning only the owner can open them). It's up to you to permit the rest of the Group—and Everyone else—to see them.

The Easiest Way to Distribute Files

Here's a handy secret: If there isn't a document called *index.html* in your Sites folder (or Library→WebServer→Documents folder), visitors see, in their browsers, a handy list of the files that *are* in that folder (see Figure 21-2).

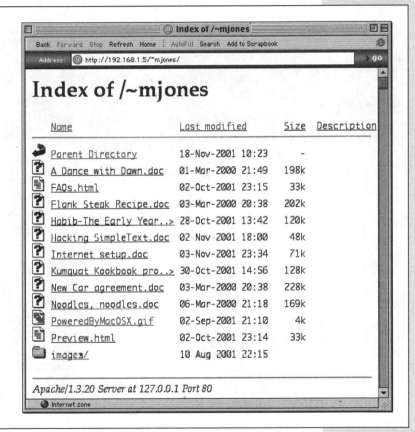

Figure 21-2:
Here's a great way to make available files to other people on your network or collaborators across the Internet. Just put your files into the Sites or Library→WebServer→Documents folder and make sure nothing is named index.html. The Parent Directory link takes you to the folder that contains this one—if you've been given access to it, that is.

Index of /~mjones

Address: http://192.168.1.5/~mjones/

Name	Last modified	Size	Description
Parent Directory	18-Nov-2001 10:23	-	
A Dance with Dawn.doc	01-Mar-2000 21:49	198k	
FAQs.html	02-Oct-2001 23:15	33k	
Flank Steak Recipe.doc	03-Mar-2000 20:38	202k	
Habib-The Early Year..>	28-Oct-2001 13:42	120k	
Hacking SimpleText.doc	02-Nov-2001 18:00	48k	
Internet setup.doc	03-Nov-2001 23:34	71k	
Kumquat Kookbook pro..>	30-Oct-2001 14:56	128k	
New Car agreement.doc	03-Mar-2000 20:38	228k	
Noodles, noodles.doc	06-Mar-2000 21:18	169k	
PoweredByMacOSX.gif	02-Sep-2001 21:10	4k	
Preview.html	02-Oct-2001 23:14	33k	
images/	10 Aug 2001 22:15		

Apache/1.3.20 Server at 127.0.0.1 Port 80

This is a terrific convenience: It offers a quick, simple way for you to make a bunch of documents available for downloading. All your visitors have to do is click one of these file names. It downloads immediately, no matter what kind of computer your Web visitor is using.

Tip: If people are having trouble downloading your files, here are some tips. First of all, if one of the files listed is a graphic, like a JPEG or GIF file, it appears right in the browser window. Tell your visitors to Alt-click or Option-click the link to download it instead. Second, if a file doesn't download properly, you may have to compress it using StuffIt Deluxe or StuffIt Lite (a free download from *www.aladdinsys.com*) first.

Browser Navigation of Your Own Mac

Once you've turned on Web Sharing, you can navigate the folders of your own machine right from within a browser—just use *localhost* as the "Web address."

To see what's in your own Sites folder, for example, type *http://localhost/~chris/* (or whatever your short account name is) into your browser's address bar. Or to see what's in the Library→WebServer→Documents folder, the address is even shorter: *http://localhost/* is all you need.

POWER USERS' CLINIC

Adding CGI Scripts

A CGI script (computer gateway interface) is a program, written in a language like Perl, AppleScript, or Java, that runs right on your Web page. You've seen these on many a Web page: Web counters, interactive polls, shopping forms, and so on.

If you've got a CGI script of your own that you'd like to incorporate into your Web page, copy it into your Library→WebServer→CGI-Executables folder (this means you, administrators). The script's Web address becomes *http:// 111.222.3.44/cgi-bin/scriptname*. (Substitute your actual IP address and the real name of the script file, of course.)

Unfortunately, you won't get far testing out your CGI script—or even one of the two sample scripts Apple provides in the CGI-Executables folder—because they come with their "execute" permissions turned *off*. To turn them on again, you need to use the *chmod* (change mode) command.

The easy way is to drag them onto the icon of SuperGetInfo, a shareware program you can download from *www.missingmanuals.com*. Just drag the CGI script's icon onto SuperGetInfo, click the Permissions tab, and turn on the top three checkboxes, as shown here.

To do this work in Terminal instead, at the % prompt, switch the Mac's attention to the proper folder like this:

```
cd /Library/WebServer/CGI-
Executables
```

Press Enter. At the next prompt, type:

```
sudo chmod 755 test-cgi
```

The *chmod* command is a quick way to change access privileges—including Execute permission, which isn't available in the File→Show Info window.

The *755* business is a long story, which you can read at any Terminal prompt by typing *man chmod* and hitting Enter. In short, however, this code is shorthand for "Change the permissions so that everyone can read and execute (but not make changes to) this file"—just what you'd want for a CGI script.

After hitting Enter, you're ready to proceed. As you know from page 403, *sudo* now asks for your administrator's password. Once you've entered it, press Enter; the deed is done. You can test your script either on the same Mac *(http://localhost/cgi-bin/test-cgi)* or on another one across the network or across the Internet *(http://111.222.3.44/ cgi-bin/test-cgi)*.

Tip: In any address that involves the word *localhost* (like the previous examples), you can leave out the word *localhost* to save a little typing. But keep all the slashes that were once around it. For example, *http:///* is enough to see the list of documents in your Mac's main Web-pages folder.

But why stop at HTML documents? You can see the contents of *any* folder on your Mac, just by typing its folder pathname. For example, to see what's in your Documents folder, type: *file:///Users/chris/Documents/* into your browser's Address bar. You get a tidy list like the one shown in Figure 21-2, listing what's in that folder. Click a link to open it.

More on Apache

As noted above, Apache is the most popular Web-serving software in the world. As you can well imagine, it's powerful, reliable—and very technical. It is, after all, a Unix program.

You can read more at any of these sources:

- **The Apache manual.** To open it up, type *http://localhost/manual/* into your browser's address bar. You won't get far reading this thing without having spent some time enrolled at a technical college, but at least you'll know what you're up against.

- *Apache: The Definitive Guide.* A book from O'Reilly.

- **MacOSX Hints.** Dozens of Mac OS X fans have posted specific Apache-tweaking tips and ticks at *www.macosxhints.com.*

Note, too, that $300 will buy you a graphic front end for the various Apache settings, in the form of Tenon's iTools program (no relation to Apple's iTools service). It still requires an understanding of the technical aspects of Web hosting, but at least it spares you from having to type out Unix commands to make your changes.

FTP

FTP sites (file transfer protocol) store pieces of software that can be accessed from the Internet. If you've heard of FTP at all, it was probably under one of two circumstances—either you've downloaded software from an Internet FTP site, or you've created and maintained your own Web site.

To hook into an FTP site, you need an FTP *client program* that runs on the kind of computer you use (Mac, Windows, or whatever). On the Mac, the most popular FTP client programs are the shareware programs Fetch and Interarchy.

Using these programs, Web designers, for example, can view a list of all the text and graphics documents, sitting there on some Internet-connected computer somewhere, that make up their Web pages. When they want to update one of those pages, they add it to this list; to delete a Web page, they remove it from this list.

Becoming an FTP Server

Thanks to Mac OS X and its Wonder Unix, you can turn your own Mac into an FTP site. Once again, the key is the Sharing pane of System Preferences; this time, just turn on "Allow FTP access."

Once again, the key to your own Mac is its IP address, as shown at the bottom of the System Preferences pane. At this point, you (or other people you trust) can connect to your FTP server by running an FTP program like Fetch (see Figure 21-3).

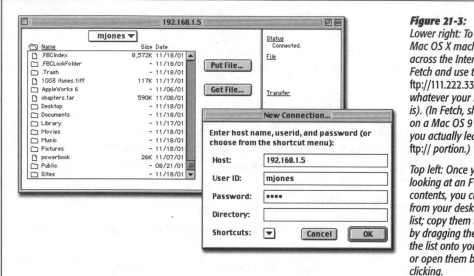

Figure 21-3:
Lower right: To access your Mac OS X machine from across the Internet, fire up Fetch and use the address ftp://111.222.33.4 (or whatever your IP address is). (In Fetch, shown here on a Mac OS 9 machine, you actually leave off the ftp:// portion.)

Top left: Once you're looking at an FTP server's contents, you can drag files from your desktop into the list; copy them to your Mac by dragging them out of the list onto your desktop, or open them by double-clicking.

In fact, if you're just going to *look at* and *download* files (but not upload or delete any), you don't even need a special FTP program like Fetch. Any old Web browser will work. Just type *ftp://111.222.3.44* (or whatever your IP address is) into the address bar. A dialog box asks for an account name and password; once you're in, you see a list of everything in your Home folder, displayed much like the list shown in Figure 21-2.

Note: FTP isn't a very hacker-proof system. On the other hand, there's no need to grow paranoid; hackers would have to figure out your password before being able to do anything sneaky. Still, for maximum safety, turn off this FTP master switch whenever possible, especially if you don't use a firewall (page 439).

Visiting Other FTP Sites

The previous instructions show you how to turn your Mac into an FTP server. But you can also visit *other* FTP sites.

The easiest way is simply to type the FTP address into the address bar of a Web browser like Internet Explorer, like this: *ftp://ftp.apple.com*. Of course, you can also download a true FTP *client program* like Fetch or Interarchy (visit *www.versiontracker.com*) to get the latest. Each offers a simple way to access other people's FTP sites.

Connecting from the Road

You can also connect to your Mac's regular File Sharing feature (Chapter 12) from over the Internet. This feature is a blessing to anyone who travels, whether with a laptop or to a branch office, because you'll never be up the creek without a paddle if you discover that you need to look at a file you accidentally left at home.

To connect over the Internet, make sure that you've set up the home-base Mac for file sharing, as directed in Chapter 12. Then, once you're on the road, hook up your laptop to an Internet connection, go online, and proceed like this:

1. **Choose Go→Connect to Server.**

   The Connect to Server dialog box appears, as shown in Figure 21-4.

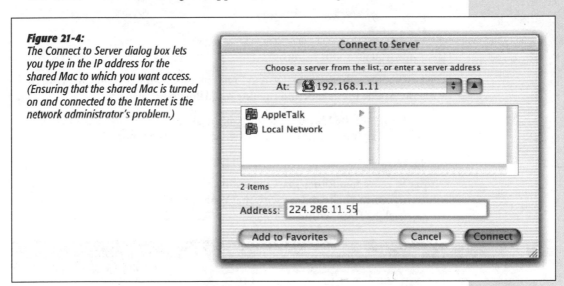

Figure 21-4:
The Connect to Server dialog box lets you type in the IP address for the shared Mac to which you want access. (Ensuring that the shared Mac is turned on and connected to the Internet is the network administrator's problem.)

2. **Type in the IP address (or domain name) of the Mac to which you want to connect, and then click Connect (or press Enter).**

   If you don't know the shared Mac's IP address, pick up the phone and call somebody in the office there. That person can find out the shared Mac's IP address by opening the Network pane of System Preferences.

   And if you've signed up for a DNS naming service as described on page 498, you can type your Mac's domain name instead.

3. **Continue with step 3 on page 300.**

This kind of connection is slower than an Ethernet hookup in the same building. But when you're in Hong Kong and need a document from your Mac in Minneapolis, you may not care.

Remote Access with SSH

Are you a geek? Take this simple test at home. Do you get excited about Mac OS X's ability to permit SSH access?

If you answered "What's SSH?" or "I'm *already* being quiet," then the following discussion of Unix remote control may not interest you. To be sure, SSH is not a program with a graphic user interface (icons and menus); you operate it from within a program like Terminal by typing commands, exactly as described in Chapter 15.

If you're willing to overlook that little peccadillo, though, SSH (Secure Shell) is an extremely powerful tool. It lets you connect to your Mac from anywhere—from across the network or across the Internet—and take control of it, copying files, running commands, rearranging folders, or even shutting it down, all by remote control.

Getting In

Here's how you go about using SSH:

1. **Set up your Mac by opening System Preferences; clicking the Sharing icon; clicking the Applications tab; and turning on "Allow remote login."**

   You've just told the Mac it's OK for you (or other people with accounts on your machine) to connect from the road. Quit System Preferences.

2. **Go away.**

   You can move to another machine on the network, or another computer on the Internet. Once you're online with that other machine, you contact your home-base machine from within a program like Terminal.

FREQUENTLY ASKED QUESTION

Where Did Telnet Go?

How do I telnet into my Mac OS X machine?

Telnet and SSH are very similar in concept. But the problem with telnet is that it's fairly susceptible to hackers.

The SSH networking program, on the other hand, is extremely secure, immune to all kinds of the hacker attacks you may have read about: IP spoofing, IP source writing, DNS spoofing, and so on. That's why Apple replaced its telnet feature with SSH beginning in Mac OS X 10.1.

Apple also hopes that Unix-savvy Mac fans will recognize SSH to be a superior replacement for such remote control Unix programs as *rlogin, rsh,* and *rcp,* for that matter.

Tip: It doesn't have to be Terminal, and it doesn't have to be a Mac. You can get *SSH client* programs for almost any kind of computer, including Windows and Mac OS 9.

For pre–Mac OS X Macs, for example, you can try MacSSH or NiftyTelnet SSH, both of which you can download from *www.missingmanuals.com.* To find SSH programs for Windows, visit *www.versiontracker* *.com,* click the Windows tab, and search for *SSH.*

3. **At the % prompt, type *ssh -l chris 111.222.3.44.* Press Enter.**

   Instead of *chris,* type your actual short account name (as you're known on the Mac you're tapping into), and replace the phony IP address shown here with your real one. (If your Mac back home has a domain name unto itself, such as *macmania.com,* you can type that instead of the IP address.)

   If all goes well, the *ssh* command acknowledges your first successful connection by displaying a message like this: "The authenticity of host '172.24.30.189 (172.24.30.189)' can't be established. RSA key fingerprint is d9:f4:11:b0:27:1a:f1: 14:c3:cd:25:85:2b:78:4d:e7. Are you sure you want to continue connecting (yes/no)?" (You won't see this message on subsequent connections. You're seeing SSH's security features at work.)

4. **Type *yes* and press Enter.**

   Now you see one more note ("Warning: Permanently added '172.24.30.189' (RSA) to the list of known hosts"). You're then asked for your account password.

5. **Type your account password and press Enter.**

   You're in. Issue whatever commands you want. You can conduct a full Unix Terminal session exactly as described in Chapters 15 and 16—but by remote control.

Tip: For a list of options you can use in SSH, type *ssh* at the prompt (nothing more) and press Enter.

Remote Control Program Killing

One of the most common uses of SSH is quitting a stuck program. Maybe it's a program that doesn't respond to the usual Force Quit commands—maybe even the Finder or Terminal. Or maybe, having just arrived in Accounting on the fifth floor, you realize that you accidentally left your Web browser, open to Dilbert.com, up on your screen in clear view of passersby.

In any case, you'd fire up Terminal and proceed like this. (What you type is shown in bold. The responses you see are in normal type.)

```
[localhost:~] chris% ssh 172.24.30.182
The authenticity of host '172.24.30.182 (172.24.30.182)' can't
be established. RSA key fingerprint is
d9:f4:11:b0:27:1a:f1:14:c3:cd:25:85:2b:78:4d:e7.
```

```
Are you sure you want to continue connecting (yes/no)? yes
Warning: Permanently added '172.24.30.182' (RSA) to the list of
known hosts.
chris@172.24.30.189's password: fisheggs
Welcome to Darwin!
[dhcp-172-24-30-182:~] chris% top
```

The *top* command, as described in Chapter 15, shows you a list of running programs. After a block of memory statistics, you might see a list like this:

```
387 top        10.0%  0:07.39  1  14  14  200K    248K   440K   1.37M
382 tcsh        0.0%  0:00.21  1  24  15  444K    568K   904K   5.72M
381 Terminal   12.5%  0:07.76  5  91 164  3.03M+  6.34M  7.02M+ 54.0M
377 klist       0.0%  0:00.21  1  20  20  264K    964K   832K   5.62M
376 tcsh        0.0%  0:00.01  1   9  14   36K    776K   172K   5.72M
375 CCacheServ  2.5%  0:03.72  1  21  20  288K    948K   880K   5.36M
371 Finder      0.0%  0:04.85  3  91 210  9.20M   7.32M  10.8M  58.2M
358 Sherlock    0.0%  0:05.15  1  63  81  1.98M   5.71M  5.04M  47.4M
```

As you can see, the Finder is program #371. If that's the stuck program, then, you could quit it like this:

```
[dhcp-172-24-30-182:~] chris% kill 371
```

The Finder promptly quits (and relaunches in, you hope, a healthier incarnation). You could also, at this point, type *shutdown now* to make your Mac, elsewhere on the network, shut down. Type *exit* to complete your SSH session.

Tip: If you're intrigued by the notion of accessing your Mac from across the Net, try out Memora Server, which lets you—or selected family and friends—listen to music, open photos, or watch movies stored on your Mac OS X machine, from any Web browser on any machine. A three-week trial is available at *www.memora.com*.

6

Part Six: Appendixes

The "Where'd It Go?" Dictionary

This one's for you, veteran Mac fans. Even if you ultimately conclude that Mac OS X's stability, good looks, and security make it worth the switch, you'll do quite a bit of fumbling at first to find your way around.

Here's your complete guide to which of the classic Mac features live on into Mac OS X, which have moved around to confuse you—and which have bit the dust.

Tip: Some commands are listed under the names of the menus in which they appear. Applications, System Folder folders, and control panels are all listed under their own names.

~ATM control panel

You won't find Adobe Type Manager (ATM) in Mac OS X. The ability to smooth out jagged edges on PostScript fonts is built in and no longer requires this separate control panel. See Chapter 13 for more on fonts.

Appearance control panel

There's no longer a control panel called Appearance, but the best of its features are still around. Here's the rundown:

- **Themes tab.** Gone.

- **Appearance tab.** You'll find the equivalent pop-up menus (for text highlight color, etc.) in Mac OS X's System Preferences→General pane.

- **Fonts tab.** Gone. You can't change the system fonts used by Mac OS X (at least not without TinkerTool, described at the beginning of Chapter 17).

- **Desktop tab.** Now you apply a picture to your desktop by opening the System Preferences→Desktop tab.

- **Sound tab.** Eliminated. Mouse clicks, scrolling, and other desktop activity are conducted in silence now.

- **Options.** The Smart Scrolling option is now in the System Preferences→General pane. There's no longer a "double-click title bar to windowshade the window" option, because the equivalent effect is always on in Mac OS X. (Double-clicking a title bar minimizes the window.)

Apple DVD Player

It's now called DVD Player, and (if your Mac does, in fact, have a compatible DVD player built in) it's in the Applications folder.

Apple Extras

There's no longer an Apple Extras folder, but several of the items that used to be in this folder live on in new locations:

- The **AppleScript** folder is now in the Applications folder.

- **Digital Color Meter**, which used to be in the Monitor Extras folder, is now located in Applications→Utilities. See Chapter 9.

- The **Font Extras** folder, which contained the FontSync control panel, is gone, but FontSync itself is alive and well. The AppleScripts that let you use FontSync sit in the hard drive's Library→Scripts→FontSync Scripts folder.

- The **Mac OS Runtime for Java** folder is gone, but the Apple Applet Runner, which was inside that folder, has been replaced with the Applet Launcher in Applications→Utilities.

Most of the other Apple Extras items—miscellaneous folders like FireWire, Iomega, and Apple LaserWriter Software—have disappeared because they've been incorporated into Mac OS X itself.

Apple menu

The menu is still in Mac OS X, but it's no longer customizable. Instead, it lists several useful commands that you'll want to access no matter what program you're using: Sleep, Restart, Shut Down, and so on. The menu's quick-access icon launching features have now been taken over by the Dock (Chapter 3).

- **About This Computer.** This command's functions have been scattered across Mac OS X. To find out your Mac's system-software version, total installed memory, and processor type, choose →About This Mac. For memory stats on running programs, go to Applications→Utilities and open Process Viewer. It shows you, perhaps, a little more information than you need, but the memory consumption listings are still there, updated in real time (because Mac OS X programs don't use one fixed amount of RAM; they constantly adjust as needed).

- **Apple System Profiler.** Still in Mac OS X, better than ever—but now found in Applications→Utilities.

- **Calculator.** Cosmetically revamped and moved to your Applications folder.

- **Chooser.** Eliminated. Its two primary functions—choosing a printer and connecting to a network—have been moved to Print Center (in Applications→Utilities) and the Go→Connect to Server command, respectively.

- **Control Panels.** It's now called System Preferences (Chapter 8). You can get to it by clicking its Dock icon or by choosing →System Preferences.

- **Favorites.** In Mac OS X, your favorites are now listed as a submenu of the Go→Favorites command in the Finder.

- **Key Caps.** Better than ever. Now in the Applications→Utilities folder.

- **Network Browser.** Eliminated. Use the Go→Connect to Server command at the desktop instead; it works almost exactly the same.

- **Recent Applications, Recent Documents, Recent Servers.** Recent Applications and Recent Documents are now submenus of the →Recent Items command. To see networked disks (servers) to which you've recently connected, choose either Go→Recent Folders or, for a network-only list, Go→Connect to Server. In the Connect to Server dialog box, the pop-up menu lists recently accessed servers.

- **Remote Access Status.** It's now called Internet Connect, and it's in your Applications folder (see page 434).

- **Scrapbook.** Eliminated. The closest equivalent is Stickies (in your Applications folder), which can now accept graphics, sounds, and movies.

- **Sherlock 2.** Sherlock is still the Mac's search engine, but now you launch it by choosing File→Find (⌘-F) or by just clicking the Sherlock icon on the Dock. (You can always double-click it in the Applications folder, but that takes longer.)

- **Speakable Items.** To get the list of speakable commands that your Mac can understand, first turn on Speakable Items using System Preferences→Speech→Speech Recognition→On/Off. The round Speech Feedback panel appears on your screen. Click the small black triangle at the bottom of the panel and choose the Open Speech Commands window (see page 365).

- **Stickies.** Stickies got a major update in Mac OS X, as described in Chapter 9. (It's in the Applications folder.)

Apple Menu Options control panel

Gone, because there are no menu options in Mac OS X. The menu isn't customizable or configurable.

AppleCD Audio Player

Replaced by the vastly superior iTunes (in the Applications folder). See Chapter 10.

AppleScript

Apple's built-in scripting language for the Mac works in Mac OS X, but the Mac OS X 10.1 Finder isn't *recordable*, so you can't create Finder scripts simply by having Script Editor record your actions, step by step. To write your own scripts, you'll actually have to type some code (Chapter 7). Find the Script Editor in the Applications→AppleScripts folder.

AppleTalk control panel

These networking controls are now in the System Preferences→Network panel.

Application menu

Gone. You now use the Dock to see which programs you have running (they're the icons with little blank triangles beneath them) and to switch between those programs. As noted in Chapter 4, however, you can still use the Dock for many of the tricks the Application menu used to play.

The Hide application and Hide Others commands, meanwhile, are now at the *left* end of the menu bar in the *new* Application menu—the one that bears the current application's name.

Audio CD AutoPlay

This option—once a part of the QuickTime Settings control panel—is now available though the iTunes program. In the iTunes Preferences window, go to the General panel and choose Insert→Begin Playing from the CD.

Balloon Help

Balloon Help is officially defunct.

Battery Level

The status of the battery in your PowerBook or iBook used to be displayed in the Control Strip. In Mac OS X, this indicator appears on the menu bar—immediately after you open System Preferences→Energy Saver→Options and turn it on.

Button View

Gone—to the great disappointment of the six people who ever used it.

Chooser

Replaced by Print Center and the Go→Connect to Server command. See the menu entry above for more information.

Clean Up command

Just where it always was, good as ever.

Click-and-a-half

Mac OS X folders are not spring-loaded, so they don't pop open automatically when you hover over them after a "click-and-a-half"—when you double-click, then do another half-click, so that the mouse button stays down. (Sound complicated? Maybe that's why Apple killed it.)

CloseView

This control panel, which produced a magnified view of the Mac screen for visually impaired users, is no longer available. (There are some close approximations of it, however, as described on page 192.)

⌘-Drag to scroll an icon-view window

Now you hold down Option *and* ⌘ to achieve this function.

⌘-Shift-3, ⌘-Shift-4

These keystrokes still take pictures of your screen, although Mac OS X offers several superior alternatives (page 343).

Collapse box

Windows don't collapse with a "window shade" action in Mac OS X, but you can *minimize* them, reducing them to icons that stay parked in the Dock until you need them. Click the yellow button on the left side of a window's title bar, or press ⌘-M, to minimize it.

ColorSync control panel

ColorSync color management settings are now set in System Preferences→ColorSync. You can also get information about your ColorSync profiles using the ColorSync Utility, located in Applications→Utilities.

Control panels

There are no control panels in Mac OS X. Instead, there's a program called System Preferences that handles the various hardware and software settings formerly configured with control panels. Choose →System Preferences, or click the System Preferences icon on the Dock. (System Preferences is also in the Applications folder.)

Control Strip control panel

The Control Strip is gone. However, several of its traditional features survive in the form of *menulets*—icon/pop-up menus in your menu bar that let you monitor and control dial-up settings, monitor resolution, color depth, sound volume, and battery levels, as well as the date and time. You make these menulets appear using checkboxes in the corresponding panes of System Preferences (such as Displays, Sound, Energy Saver, and Date & Time), and the Internet Connect application.

Contextual Menu Items folder

Mac OS X makes extensive use of contextual pop-up menus, but there's no longer a folder into which you can drop expansion modules to add new contextual menu commands.

Date & Time control panel

Replaced by the Date & Time panel in System Preferences.

Desktop clippings

Text and picture clippings produced by dragging selected text and images to the desktop work just as they did in Mac OS 9.

Desktop printers

Desktop icons no longer represent each printer configured to work with your Mac. To see what printers you have available, or to configure a new printer, use Print Center (in Applications→Utilities).

Disk First Aid

Disk First Aid is now a part of Disk Utility, located in the Applications→Utilities folder. Launch Disk Utility and click the First Aid tab.

Dial Assist control panel

Eliminated. Enter dialing information for dial-up modem connections in the PPP pane of the System Preferences→Network panel.

Disk icons

Disk icons still appear on the desktop, but a checkbox in Finder→Preferences now gives you the option of *not* having hard disks, network volumes, CDs, or other removable disks appear on the desktop.

Draggable window edges

Gone. You can drag a Mac OS X window only by its title bar, not the side edges or bottom.

Drive Setup

Drive Setup is now a part of Disk Utility, in the Applications→Utilities folder. Launch Disk Utility and go to the Erase and Partition panes.

Edit menu

This Finder menu is alive and well.

Eject

Now located in the Finder's File menu instead of the now-defunct Special menu.

Empty Trash

Moved to the Finder application menu. You can also access the Empty Trash command by clicking and holding down the mouse button when pointing to the Trash icon in the Dock, or by pressing Shift-⌘-Delete.

Encrypt

You can no longer encrypt and lock individual files. Then again, why bother? Thanks to Mac OS X's accounts feature (Chapter 11), you can keep your *entire Mac* password-protected.

Energy Saver control panel

Now located in the Energy Saver panel of System Preferences.

Erase Disk

Erase Disk is no longer a Finder command. To erase a disk (or reformat it), use the Erase panel of the Disk Utility program, which is in the Applications→Utilities folder.

Extensions

Extensions don't exist in Mac OS X. Neither do extension *conflicts*—the number one cause of crashes, freezes, and hangs on traditional Macs. This is a good thing.

Extensions Manager control panel

No extensions means no Extensions Manager.

Favorites

Moved from the menu to the Finder's Go menu. Favorites also has its own dedicated keyboard shortcut: Option-⌘-F.

File Exchange control panel

Eliminated. Mac OS X now understands and remembers the three-letter file extensions PCs use to recognize file types for better Mac/PC file compatibility. Still, if you want to remap a certain document so that it opens in a different program (a primary function of the old File Exchange program), proceed like this: Highlight its icon, choose File→Show Info, choose "Open with application" from the pop-up menu, choose a new program from the "pop-up icon," and then click the Change All button.

File menu

Most of the Finder's File menu has stayed the same, with the following exceptions:

- A New Finder Window command (⌘-N) has been added.
- The New Folder command has a new keyboard shortcut: Shift-⌘-N.
- Get Info is now Show Info.
- The Encrypt command is gone.

- The Eject command has migrated over from the Special menu.

- Burn Disc was added.

File Sharing control panel

Replaced by the Sharing panel of System Preferences.

File Synchronization control panel

Eliminated. Use a program like Iomega's QuickSync to keep a folder automatically backed up instead.

Find Similar Files

This contextual menu item is no longer available, but the command is available in Sherlock's Find menu when you have selected items in the Items Found window.

Finder (the application)

Mac OS X still has an actual Finder program, living in System→Library→ CoreServices. You can't do anything to the file, of course, other than take note of where it lives.

Finder Preferences

Moved from the Edit menu to Finder→Preferences. Many of the Finder Preferences of Mac OS 9 are gone, however, including Simple Finder, spring-loaded folders, grid-spacing controls, and icon labels.

Fonts folder

Mac OS X doesn't have a Fonts folder—it has at least *four* of them, as described on page 332.

FontSync

The control panel, which was hidden away in the Apple Extras folder under Mac OS 9, is obsolete. The AppleScripts that allow you to create FontSync profiles are found in your Library→Scripts→FontSync Scripts folder.

Force quitting

You can still press Option-⌘-Esc to quit a locked-up program, but it's much easier and safer to do so in Mac OS X (page 94).

General Controls control panel

The control panel is gone, and so are the various options it offered. In Mac OS X, you can't change the insertion-point blinking rate, nor the number of times a menu command flashes when you select it. (Of course, you can still launch General Controls when you're using the Classic environment, as described in Chapter 5.)

Get Info

Now called Show Info. A few changes are worth noting: The Memory panel is gone, because you no longer have to manually adjust the amount of memory needed for each program. Also, the Sharing panel is now called Privileges, a new Name & Extension panel is available (page 103), and an "Open with application" panel (documents only) lets you decide which program opens when you double-click a certain document (or kind of document).

Graphing Calculator

No longer included with Mac OS X.

Grid Spacing

Finder Preferences no longer offers the choice between Tight and Wide grid-spacing for icon views.

Help menu

A trimmed-down Help menu retains its position in the Finder menu bar. It now contains a single item, Mac Help, which launches the Mac OS X Help system.

Hide commands

Commands for hiding the active program, or hiding everything else *but* the active program, have moved from the old Application menu (on the far right of the menu bar) to the new Application menu (the one on the left next to the menu) that bears the name of the frontmost program. Hiding the current program also now has an official keyboard shortcut: ⌘-H.

Info Strip

The Info Strip at the top of Finder windows is now called the Status Bar. Choose View→Show Status Bar to display your available disk space and each folder's item count.

Infrared control panel

Gone. Infrared networking doesn't work in Mac OS X.

Internet control panel

Replaced by System Preferences→Internet panel.

Internet Utilities

No longer included. Some of the programs that used to be stored in this folder under Mac OS 9—such as StuffIt Expander—are now in the Applications→Utilities folder.

iTunes

An updated version of iTunes is in the Applications folder.

Key Caps

The new Mac OS X version is in the Applications→Utilities folder.

Keyboard control panel

The functions of this old control panel are split between two System Preferences panels. You can find the Key Repeat and Delay Until Repeat controls in the System Preferences→Keyboard panel. Switch keyboard layouts (for use with other languages) in the Keyboard Menu pane of the System Preferences→International panel.

The Function Keys feature of the Mac OS 9 Keyboard control panel isn't in Mac OS X; you can no longer open selected files or programs by pressing the Fkeys at the top of your keyboard. (You can, however, now operate menus, open Dock icons, and navigate dialog boxes from the keyboard, as described on page 106.)

Keychain Access control panel

Replaced by the Keychain Access program, located in Applications→Utilities.

Label command

Obliterated. You can't apply color or text labels to icons in Mac OS X. Some people manage by typing identifying phrases into the Comments boxes of their icons (highlight an icon, choose File→Show Info).

Launcher control panel

Replaced by the far superior Dock.

Location Manager

The control panel is gone. But in System Preferences→Network, you can save various dialing and networking settings on a location-by-location basis using the Location pop-up menu. Thereafter, you can switch settings using the →Locations submenu. (Locations no longer store printer, volume, clock, and other settings.)

Locked

You can still lock any file on your Mac by selecting its icon, choosing File→Show Info (formerly Get Info) and turning on the "Locked" checkbox in the Info window.

Mac Help

Apple's help system is still accessible from the Help menu in the Finder's menu bar.

Mac OS Runtime for Java

The old Apple Applet Runner has been replaced by Applet Launcher, which is in the Applications→Utilities folder. See Chapter 9 for details.

Map control panel

Eliminated. You can set your Mac's location/time zone using the Time Zone pane of System Preferences→Date & Time. But without the venerable Map control panel, there's no longer any way to calculate the *distance* between two cities.

Memory control panel

Gone. Memory management in Mac OS X is a hands-off affair, as the system simply gives each running program as much memory as it needs without you having to adjust settings.

Modem control panel

Replaced by the Modem pane in System Preferences→Network panel.

Monitors control panel

Replaced by System Preferences→Displays.

Mouse control panel

Replaced by System Preferences→Mouse.

Multiple Users control panel

Replaced, in a much more industrial-strength form, by System Preferences→Users (Chapter 11). Some login options that used to be handled by the Multiple Users control panel are in System Preferences→Login→Login Window.

New Folder command

It's still in the File menu, but the keyboard shortcut has changed from ⌘-N (which now opens a new Finder window) to Shift-⌘-N.

Note Pad

Gone. Use the new, improved Stickies to jot down quick notes.

Numbers control panel

Replaced by System Preferences→International panel→Numbers pane.

Open Transport

Open Transport networking is built into Mac OS X, but there's no Open Transport extension, and nothing for you to turn on, toggle, or trigger. Configure your network settings using the System Preferences→Network panel.

Picture 1, Picture 2…

You can still capture pictures of your Mac screen by pressing ⌘-Shift-3 (for a full-screen grab) or ⌘-Shift-4 (to grab a selected portion of the screen). However, the resulting image files, called Picture 1, Picture 2, and so on, now appear on the desktop instead of in the hard drive window—and in the more universal TIFF format instead of PICT.

Pop-up windows

To create the Mac OS X equivalent of a pop-up window, just drag a folder or disk icon onto the Dock. From now on, when you click-and-hold (or Control-click) its docked icon, a list of its contents sprouts upward, for your perusal pleasure.

Preferences folder

Mac OS X stashes away its own preference files in numerous hidden locations, but the folder that contains *your* application preference settings is in the Users→[your Home folder]→Library→Preferences folder. Preference files of this type (known in geek circles as *plist*, or property list, files) are even easier to identify in Mac OS X, because they clearly bear the application's name.

PrintMonitor

Obsolete. With Mac OS X, you monitor the queue of jobs waiting to be printed using Print Center, which is in Applications→Utilities. Launch Print Center, select a printer from the list of available printers and choose Printers→Show Queue.

Put Away command

It's gone. To eject Zip disks, CDs, and other removable disks, use the Eject command (or the Eject key on your keyboard). To put away files you've dragged to the desktop, you must drag them back to their original locations manually (or use the Edit→Undo command, if you remember to do so promptly).

QuickTime Settings control panel

Replaced by the System Preferences→QuickTime panel.

Quit command

It's not in the File menu of your programs any more—it's in the Application menu (the one bearing the program's name).

Remote Access

Replaced by Internet Connect, in the Applications folder.

Reset Column Positions

Gone. If you scramble the order and size of columns in a list view, there's no one-shot way to undo the mess.

Restart

Moved to the menu.

Script Editor

A Mac OS X version of this AppleScript authoring program is now located in Applications→AppleScript.

Scripting Additions

Five scripting additions, which can add special functions to AppleScripts, are included with Mac OS X. They're now in System→Library→Scripting Additions.

Search Internet

The Search Internet command in the Finder's File menu is gone. Instead, you launch Sherlock by choosing File→Find (⌘-F). Then click the globe icon, or press ⌘-K, to search the Internet

Security

Under Mac OS 9, the Security folder was the home of two programs, Apple File Security and Apple Verifier, which were used to encrypt and lock files using the Finder's Encrypt command. Both security applications are gone, having been replaced by the vault-like Unix accounts system described in Chapter 11.

Select New Original

Still lets you hook up aliases to new original files, but the Get Info window in which this button appears is now called the Show Info window.

Set to Standard Views

This option, in Mac OS 9's View Options window, lets you apply a set of standard view settings simultaneously (as defined in Finder Preferences→Views) to any folder window. In Mac OS X, you accomplish the same thing in the View Options window by switching the top option from "This window only" to "Global."

Sherlock

There's a new Mac OS X version in the Applications folder. You can launch it from there, or by choosing File→Find (⌘-F) in the Finder.

Show All

Works just like in Mac OS 9—that is, it brings all hidden windows into sight—but has been moved from the old Application menu (on the far right of the menu bar) to the new Application menu, which bears the name of the program you're using.

Show Clipboard

Unchanged from Mac OS 9.

Show warning before emptying Trash

This option is now in Finder→Preferences instead of the Trash's Show Info window.

Shutdown Items

There's no longer a Shutdown Items folder. In Mac OS X, there's no easy way to make certain icons open automatically when you shut down the machine.

Shut Down

Moved to the menu.

Simple Finder

The Simple Finder option is gone. Few are likely to notice.

SimpleSound

Apple no longer includes this sound-recording program with Mac OS X.

SimpleText

Replaced by the much better TextEdit program, in the Applications folder.

Size box

The button that lets you resize a window by dragging is still in the lower-right corner.

Sleep

The Sleep command has moved to the menu.

Smart scrolling

Relocated from the Options pane of the Mac OS 9 Appearance control panel to System Preferences→General panel. The radio buttons in the middle of the panel control the placement of scroll arrows and the behavior of scroll bars.

Software Update control panel

Replaced by System Preferences→Software Update.

Sorting triangle

This tiny triangle, which indicates whether columns in list views are sorted in ascending or descending order, no longer appears atop each window's vertical scroll bar. Instead, you reverse the sorting order for lists of information (such as Mail messages or Finder list view items) by clicking a column heading (such as Name or Date).

Sound control panel

Replaced by System Preferences→Sound. But the new Sound preferences don't allow you to record new Alert sounds or select an audio input source for your Mac. See Chapter 8 for more information.

Special menu

Gone. This was the only Finder menu that was completely removed in Mac OS X. Most of the Special menu's commands now live in the File or menus.

Speech control panel

Replaced by System Preferences→Speech.

Spring-loaded folders

Mac OS X folders are not spring-loaded; they don't pop open automatically when you drag icons over them. As noted in Chapter 1, you can achieve a similar effect using column view.

Stationery pad

Works just as it did in Mac OS 9 and earlier. The Stationery Pad checkbox is in each file's Show Info window (the former Get Info window).

Startup Disk control panel

Go to the System Preferences→Startup Disk panel to choose the *disk* and *System folder*—either Mac OS X or Mac OS 9—from which your Mac will start up next.

Startup Items

The Startup Items folder is gone, but you can still set up programs to launch automatically at startup. Just include those applications in the list of Login Items in the System Preferences→Login panel.

Stickies

A dramatically improved version of Stickies is in the Applications folder.

System Folder

Mac OS X's System Folder is simply called System, and it sits in your main hard drive window. There's a big difference, however: in Mac OS X, you're forbidden to add, remove, or change anything inside.

(You still have a System Folder, too—the home of the Mac OS 9 system software needed by your Mac to run Classic applications.)

System file

You can't open it, modify it or move it, but Mac OS X *does* have a System file, just like earlier Mac versions. You'll find it in System→Library→CoreServices.

TCP/IP control panel

Replaced by System Preferences→Network panel, which has a TCP/IP pane for configuring these settings.

TCP/IP, AppleTalk

Configure your TCP/IP and AppleTalk settings in System Preferences→Network panel.

Text control panel

Replaced by the System Preferences→International panel→Language pane. Choose the language you need from the Languages list box.

Trackpad

Replaced by a tab in the System Preferences→Mouse panel.

USB Printer Sharing

Not used in Mac OS X. Set up shared printers using Print Center, located in Applications→Utilities.

View menu

The "as Columns" view replaces the "as Buttons" view, and there are new commands for displaying and customizing the Finder toolbar. Otherwise, the View menu hasn't changed much (see Chapter 1).

View Options

You still open View Options from the Finder's View menu. You'll find only a few changes: In list views, Mac OS X offers a choice of two icon sizes instead of three. On the other hand, in icon views, Mac OS X gives you total control over the size of icons, which you can adjust using the Icon Size slider.

Warn before emptying

This option is now called "Show warning before emptying Trash" and is located in Finder→Preferences.

Web Pages folder

There's no longer a Web Pages folder to store the Web page files you publish using Personal Web Sharing. Instead, your public Web pages go in your Home→Sites folder or the Library→WebServer→Documents folder, as described in Chapter 21.

Web Sharing control panel

Replaced by System Preferences→Sharing panel→File & Web pane.

Window collapsing

See "Collapse box."

Zoom box

Windows no longer have a zoom box; they have a green zoom *button,* which makes a desktop window just large enough to show you all of the icons inside it.

Mac OS X, Menu by Menu

T he menus of Mac OS X are translucent, beautiful, and easy to read, and they stay open as long as you like with a single click. They're also utterly undocumented in Apple's online help.

Here's a plain-English rundown of the Mac OS X Finder's menu commands.

Apple (🍎) Menu

The 🍎 menu icon no longer displays the six colored stripes of the original Apple logo. In function, however, it still does what it did in 1984: serves as the North Star of menus, a reliable and permanent listing that never varies, no matter what program you're using.

About This Mac

The first command in the 🍎 menu is About This Mac (a return to its roots after the strangely generic About This Computer wording of the last several years). It no longer produces a memory graph, as in the days of Mac OS 9; instead, the small resulting dialog box simply shows you what version of Mac OS X you're using, how much installed memory your Mac has, and what processor is inside (see Figure B-1).

Get Mac OS X Software

This command takes you online, if you're not already, and opens your Web browser to an Apple Web page that offers downloads of Mac OS X-compatible programs.

System Preferences

This item gives you direct access to the System Preferences program described in Chapter 8. (The System Preferences icon is also on your Dock, of course, but Apple put it here, too, in case you accidentally [or purposely] dragged it off the Dock.)

Figure B-1:
Ironically, the About This Computer window spent years not telling you anything actually about this computer, such as its model name or processor specs. In Mac OS X, it actually gives you a few relevant facts.

Dock

These commands are shortcuts to the settings in the Dock pane of System Preferences. That is, they let you tweak the Dock.

- **Turn Magnification On/Turn Magnification Off.** *Magnification* refers to the peculiar animated, wave-like effect in which Dock icons swell in size as your cursor passes over them. When there's a lot of stuff packed onto your Dock, forcing the icons to become fairly tiny, magnification can be a useful visual aid.

- **Turn Hiding On/Turn Hiding Off.** When Dock hiding is turned on, the Dock retreats, relinquishing the screen space it was using. To bring it back, just move your mouse to the edge of the screen where the Dock used to be—or, even quicker, press Option-⌘-D. (That's the keystroke for both hiding and showing the Dock. If you learn it, you'll never need the Turn Hiding On/Off command.)

Note: The Dock-hiding keystroke doesn't work when a Classic program is frontmost—a pity, because that's precisely when you need the Dock out of the way.

- **Position on Left, Position on Bottom, Position on Right.** As noted in Chapter 3, the bottom of the screen isn't actually such a great place for the Dock. Most screens have more horizontal area to spare than vertical area. These commands let you specify which edge of the screen you want to harbor the Dock.

- **Dock Preferences** opens the Dock pane of System Preferences, where you can make a few other adjustments to the Dock's behavior. For example, using a slider, you can specify *how* big the Dock icons get when magnified.

Location

A *Location* is a canned set of network settings. You might have a high-speed Internet connection at the office, but have to use a plain old dial-up modem at home. Once you've set up a location for each (page 441), you can use this menu to switch among them, making this primarily a command for laptop owners.

- **Automatic** refers to the standard network settings, the ones you use if you don't, in fact, ever use the Locations feature.

- **Backyard, Upstairs, Office....** Next comes a list of the Locations you've set up.

- **Network Preferences** opens the System Preferences program to the Network pane, where you can create new Locations.

Recent Items

As you open and close your various programs and files, Mac OS X tracks them. It maintains a list of the most recent programs and documents you've used in the submenu of this command. (The permanently dimmed "commands" called "Recent Applications" and "Recent Documents" serve to differentiate these two portions of the menu.) By choosing its name, you can launch one of these files without having to hunt down the actual icon on your hard drive.

Tip: You control how *many* programs Mac OS X tracks using the General pane of System Preferences. There's no downside to increasing this number—many power users let the Recent Applications command track the most recently used 30 or 40 programs, turning the command into a launching bay for every application on the hard drive.

The Clear Menu command, by the way, makes Mac OS X "forget" its current list—an effective means of wiping your tracks.

Force Quit

This command offers one way to open the Force Quit dialog box described on page 94. It lets you manually terminate a frozen or locked-up program.

Sleep

Puts your Mac into Sleep mode, darkening the screen and putting the computer into a low-power, dormant state. Press a key, or click the mouse, to wake it up again.

Restart

Turns the Mac off, then on again. You won't have to do nearly as much restarting in Mac OS X as you did in Mac OS 9, but restarting may occasionally be required after you've installed a new software or hardware component.

Shut Down

Turns the Mac off, quitting all running programs (and asking you to save any unsaved work) in the process.

Logout

Leaves the computer on, but exits your *account*—your personalized desktop world of settings, files, and folders (Chapter 11). Logging out simultaneously locks away *your* stuff and summons the Login screen, so that somebody else can sign into the machine.

Finder

In Mac OS X, every program now has a menu bearing its name (but generically called the Application menu), and the Finder is no exception.

About the Finder

Every Mac OS X program's Application menu begins with an About command. It usually summons a dialog box that identifies the software version number you're using.

Preferences

Opens the Finder Preferences dialog box, as shown in Figure A-2. This dialog box offers a number of controls that make a big difference in the way the Finder works:

- **Show these items on the Desktop.** For years, Mac fans have enjoyed seeing the icons of their disks right on the desktop. In Mac OS X, seeing the hard drive icon on the desktop is less useful, because it doesn't contain anything but reserved System folders. (As noted in Chapter 2, what *you* care about are the Applications and Home folders.) These checkboxes let you control what kinds of disks, if any,

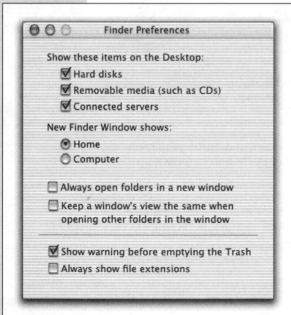

Figure B-2:
The Finder→Preferences command summons this dialog box. Use the controls to adjust several miscellaneous Finder-related settings, most of which have to do with icons and window behavior.

show up on the screen. (No matter what you choose here, you can always see all your disks by choosing Go→Computer.)

- **New Finder Window shows.** When you choose File→New Finder Window, what should appear in the resulting window: the Computer window (showing all installed disks) or your own Home folder?

    For most people, the Home folder is far more useful, making this a good setting to change on Day One.

- **Always open folders in a new window.** In Mac OS X, double-clicking a folder in a window doesn't actually open another window. Every time you double-click a folder in an open window, its contents *replace* whatever was previously in the window.

    If you prefer the traditional Mac behavior, in which double-clicking a folder or disk always opens into a new, additional window, turn this checkbox on.

- **Keep a window's view the same.** This useful checkbox ensures that double-clicking a folder will open its window into the same *view* (icon, list, or column—see page 49) as its parent.

- **Always show file extensions.** Forces the Mac to show the file name suffixes, , which are ordinarily hidden, on all of your documents (Letter.*doc,* Budget.*xls,* and so on). For much more on this topic, see page 103.

Empty Trash
Deletes the icons you've dragged onto the Trash can icon.

Services
See page 120 for details on this universal set of Mac OS X commands. They generally work only in Cocoa programs (which the Finder is not).

Hide Finder
Hides all open Finder windows.

Hide Others
Hides all windows of all *other* open programs, giving you a clearer shot at whatever desktop manipulation you're doing.

Show All
Brings back all hidden windows.

File Menu

Almost every productivity program has a File menu—and now the Finder does, too.

New Finder Window

As noted above, Mac OS X comes set to show you only a single window at all times; when you double-click a folder in it, its contents fill the frame of the single window that remains on the screen. Choosing this command is one way to create another, independent window (so that you can copy files from one to another, for example).

New Folder

Creates a new folder, called *untitled folder,* inside the open window (or, if no window is open, on the desktop). Beware the changed keyboard equivalent, which is now Shift-⌘-N.

Open

Opens a highlighted document, program, folder, or disk, exactly as though you had double-clicked its icon.

Close Window

Closes the active (frontmost) window, exactly as though you had clicked the red close button in its upper-left corner.

Show Info

Opens the Info window for the highlighted icon, as described on page 68.

Duplicate

Makes a copy of the highlighted icon, exactly as though you had Option-dragged it into a different window. The Mac adds the word "copy" to the end of the file's name to distinguish it from the original.

Make Alias

An alias is a duplicate of a file's *icon*—not the file itself—which you can double-click to open the original, in effect permitting you to have one file in more than one place on your hard drive. This command creates an alias of a highlighted icon, exactly as though you had Option-⌘-dragged it.

Show Original

This command is available only if you've highlighted an alias. It highlights the original icon, the one from which you made the alias, in whichever window happens to contain it.

Add to Favorites

Creates, in your Home→Library→Favorites folder, an alias of whatever icon you've highlighted. That icon's name instantly appears, as a result, in the File→Favorites submenu for quick launching. For details on this feature, see page 64.

Move to Trash

Puts the highlighted file icon (or icons) into the Trash. The Mac is now ready to delete it forever (when you choose Finder→Empty Trash).

Eject

Available only if you've first highlighted a disk icon that is, in fact, removable. This command makes the Mac spit the disk out.

Burn Disc

Available only if you've highlighted an erasable CD icon. (You can't erase the disk you started up from, a CD-ROM, or a DVD-ROM.) Sets about recording the disk with whatever icons you've dragged onto it, as described on page 255.

Find

This command summons Sherlock, the file- and Internet-searching program described in Chapter 20. When the program opens, it's ready to search for the names of files on your hard drive.

Edit Menu

For years, the Edit menu's standard commands—its Cut, Copy, and Paste commands—weren't very useful. But in Mac OS X, you can actually copy and paste icons into a different window, and the Undo command can "take back" whatever you last did, even if that was just dragging an icon.

Undo

This command reverses your last desktop action: moving an icon, renaming a folder, and so on. It can also undo typing or pasting while editing an icon's name.

Cut, Copy, Paste

You can copy and paste files from one window to another, just as you can, for example, in Microsoft Windows.

These commands are also operational when you're editing file names, which is sometimes useful—for example, if you're renaming a long list of icons *Case History 12*, *Case History 13*, and so on, you could save yourself a lot of typing by pasting "Case History" and then manually typing the numbers.

Finally, you can also use these commands when replacing a file's icon (by using the Show Info window as described on page 59).

Tip: The Clear command is similar to Cut—in that it removes a selected chunk of text or graphics—but it doesn't put the removed material on the invisible Clipboard, as Cut would. In other words, you can't then paste what you've Cleared.

Select All

Highlights all of the icons in the open window (or, if no window is open, on the desktop).

If you're editing an icon's name, and your cursor is blinking in the renaming rectangle, this command highlights the entire file name instead.

Show Clipboard

Opens a window that reveals whatever material you've most recently cut or copied.

View Menu

These commands affect how the icons in a Finder window appear, for your organizational pleasure.

As Icons, As List, As Columns

These commands let you view the files in a window as *icons* (which you move by dragging freely), as a *list* (a neat list view that's automatically sorted), or as *columns* (a multipaned, horizontally scrolling window that lets you burrow from folder to folder in a single window). Chapter 1 contains complete descriptions of these three views and their relative advantages.

Cleanup, Arrange by Name

These commands, too, are described in Chapter 1; they're both useful for tidying a window filled with randomly spaced icons. (They're unavailable in list views.)

Hide Toolbar

Hides the Finder toolbar that generally appears at the top of every Finder window. (Clicking the white capsule-shaped button in the upper-right corner of a window does the same thing.) Also puts that window into "Old Finder Mode," described on page 25.

Customize Toolbar

Opens the Customize window described on page 83, where you can add new functions and buttons to the standard Finder toolbar, or rearrange and delete the ones that are there.

Show Status Bar/Hide Status Bar

Summons or dismisses the thin Status bar near the top of a Finder window, which provides an icon count for the window and shows how much space remains on the disk.

Show View Options

Opens the View Options dialog box. Its offerings depend on which view the open window was in (list or icon—there are no options for column view), but the point is the same: to let you adjust icon sizes, column selection, automatic grid positioning, and so on, for the current window.

Go Menu

This menu, new to Mac OS X, gives you direct navigational access to the folders you're most likely to use.

Computer

Opens the Computer window shown in Figure B-3, providing quick access to any disk connected to the Mac. (It's especially useful if you've chosen not to show disk icons on the desktop.)

Figure B-3:
The Mac's new Computer window holds the icons for all the disks connected to your machine—the hard drive, a CD that you've inserted, an iPod, another external hard drive, and so on—as well as an icon called Network, which is primarily useful in Mac OS X Server networks.

Home

For most people, the Home folder is one of the most important places on the Mac. It's where your entire Mac world lives: your documents, settings, fonts, sounds, pictures, personally installed programs, and so on.

The long way to get there is to open the hard drive→Users→[Your Name] folder. The short way is to choose this command, or press Option-⌘-H .

iDisk

This command connects to the Internet and summons the icon of your iDisk, a 20-megabyte "virtual hard drive" that Apple provides to every customer. Chapter 18 contains much more detail.

Favorites

The Add to Favorites command (in the File menu) places the names of icons you've highlighted into this command's submenu. The Favorites scheme, therefore, is yet another mechanism that lists your favorite files, folders, and programs for quick access—much like the Dock and the Finder toolbar.

Every time you use the Add to Favorites command, the Mac puts an alias of the highlighted icon into your Home→Library→Favorites folder. This behind-the-scenes transaction is worth knowing about, if only because it offers the sole method of *removing or renaming* something from the Go→Favorites listing. That is, choose Go→Favorites to open the Favorites window; throw away or rename any of the aliases in it; and then close the window. The Go→Favorites submenu updates itself instantly.

Applications

Opens the Applications folder, bringing before you the icons of your Mac's primary programs list.

Recent Folders

This handy command lists the folders and disks you've most recently opened. After all, the odds are pretty good that you may need to open them again.

Tip: This submenu also lists the *disks* you've had open recently, which is especially convenient if you're on a network. It provides one-click access to other Macs' hard drives that you'd otherwise have to summon using the Go→Connect to Server command.

Go to Folder

Opens a simple window into which you can type the *pathname* for any folder or disk on your Mac. The pathname is a "this folder within that folder" expression separated by slashes, using a slash to represent your startup hard drive. To jump to the Documents folder in your Home folder, therefore, you could type */Users/chris/ Documents* (if your name is Chris). Actually, you wouldn't have to type anywhere near that much, thanks to the many shortcuts available in this dialog box (page 378).

Back

As in a Web browser, returns you to the window you last had open.

Connect to Server

Opens a window that displays an icon for every computer in every zone of the network (page 299).

To access the contents of the computers that show up, just double-click icon after icon, burrowing ever closer, until the folder or hard drive you seek appears on your desktop. Along the way, you may be asked for your name and password, thus proving that you're authorized to meddle with the contents of the computer you're breaking into. Finally, an icon for the actual shared hard drive or folder appears, which you can double-click to open. (For more detail on networking and sharing files, see Chapter 12.)

Window Menu

In this menu, you'll find all things window-related.

Zoom Window

Resizes the window so that it's just large enough to show you all of its contents (or as close as it can get, given your screen size). Of course, clicking the green round button at the upper-left corner of a Mac OS X window does the same thing with one less mouse click, but this command is here if you forget.

Minimize Window

Takes the frontmost window off the screen, collapsing it instead into a Dock icon, just as though you'd clicked the yellow button at the upper-left corner of the window. Details on page 22.

Bring All to Front

As noted on page 99, Mac OS X makes possible, for the first time on the Macintosh, the concept of *layered* windows—a front-to-back shuffling of windows belonging to different programs. That is, in the old Mac OS, all windows belonging to, say, your Web browser were frontmost; behind them were all the windows of your word processor; and so on. In Mac OS X, these windows may wind up intermingled.

If you find yourself in a program that seems to have a few AWOL windows, use this command to bring *all* of the program's windows in front of all other programs' windows.

[Window Names]

Finally, at the bottom of the Window menu, you'll find the names of the actual desktop windows that are currently open. Choose a window's name to bring it to the front—a handy trick if your screen is awash in overlapping windows.

Help Menu

Apple, perhaps in a show of support for computer-book authors, cut way back on its online help efforts in Mac OS X. All you get is a single command, Mac Help, that opens the fairly sparse list of Mac help topics. Details on using this browser-like help system are on page 46.

Installing Mac OS X

I f you bought your Mac after July 2001, you probably found Mac OS X already
installed—deactivated, but there on your hard drive. The machine may have
started up in Mac OS 9, but the newer, second operating system was there.

You're one of the lucky ones. All you have to do is restart your Mac in Mac OS X
(page 142) and run through the Setup Assistant program described later in this
appendix. Mac OS X is even smart enough to pick up your Internet settings from
the Mac OS 9 System Folder you already have in service.

Tip: There's a downside to the preinstalled copy of Mac OS X, however: it doesn't come with the Developer Tools CD that accompanies the store-bought Mac OS X boxes. (To find out what you're missing, see
page 246.) On the other hand, you can download the programs that are on it from Apple's Web site at no
charge; you just have to sign up for a free developer account.

If your Mac didn't come with Mac OS X preinstalled, you have a little bit more
homework to do.

Getting Ready to Install

For starters, you need to make sure that you and your Mac have what it takes to
handle Mac OS X—specifically this:

- **A Macintosh that came with a G3 or G4 processor.** In other words, a Power Mac
  G3, Power Mac G4, iMac, PowerBook G4, PowerBook G3 (except the very first

---

model, the one bearing a six-color Apple logo), or iBook. See the sidebar on page 542, however. (According to Apple, Macs with G3 or G4 upgrade cards don't qualify.)

- **Plenty of free hard disk space.** You need 1.5 GB free to install Mac OS X.

- **A lot of memory.** Remember that when you use Mac OS X, you'll often be running Mac OS 9 (in the form of the Classic simulator) simultaneously. One modern operating system takes a lot of RAM—two of them require even more. Apple recommends 128 MB of memory, but Mac OS X absolutely *loves* memory. For the greatest speed, install 256 MB or more if you can afford it (and these days, you probably can).

- **The latest version of Mac OS 9.** Once again, Mac OS X and Mac OS 9 will be coexisting on the same computer. Mac OS X version 10.1 requires Mac OS 9.2.1 or later. You'll have the best luck if you upgrade your copy of Mac OS 9 *before* installing Mac OS X.

- **The latest firmware.** *Firmware* describes the hard-coded, burned-in software that controls the actual circuitry of your Mac. Every now and then, Apple updates it for certain Mac models, and it's very important that your Mac has the absolute latest. The Software Update control panel of Mac OS 9 is supposed to alert you automatically when such updates become available, but the Utilities→Firmware Updates on your Mac OS X CD also contains a set of the very latest. Open the folder bearing your Mac model's name and run the updater inside before diving into Mac OS X. (These updaters are also available for download from the Support area of the Apple Web site, of course.)

All that, believe it or not, is the easy part. The more difficult part is assessing whether or not you'll actually be *happy* in Mac OS X. Are the programs you use available in Mac OS X versions? Will your scanner and printer work? As noted in Chapter 5, you want to minimize returning to Mac OS 9 just to run some program or piece of add-on equipment that hasn't yet been adapted for Mac OS X.

The Partitioning Question

In the coming months and years, you'll save yourself a lot of trouble and time if you keep Mac OS 9 and Mac OS X on two different drives. This kind of setup offers several advantages:

- It's much easier to switch between the two operating systems at startup time. (You may hear this feature called *dual booting*.)

- Life is much easier if you ever decide to remove or freshly install Mac OS X, as described later in this chapter.

- Troubleshooting Mac OS 9 *or* Mac OS X is much easier.

- You don't have to see, and try to distinguish, your Mac OS 9 and Mac OS X folders all mixed together in the single hard drive window (two Applications folders, two System folders, and so on).

The easy and expensive way to achieve this happiness is, of course, to install Mac OS X on a second hard drive.

Fortunately, there's also a free method: *partitioning* your Mac's main hard drive—dividing its surface so that it shows up on your desktop with two different icons and two different names. You can keep Mac OS 9 on one of them, and Mac OS X on the other. Now you can live like a king, enjoying all the advantages of people who have two separate hard drives.

Unfortunately, partitioning your hard drive requires first *erasing it completely.* And that, of course, involves copying all of your files and programs onto some kind of backup disk first—and then copying them back onto the hard drive when the process is over. Ponder this compromise, weighing it against the advantages of partitioning.

If you decide that all that backing up, erasing, and copying is too much hassle to merit the payoff, no harm done. It's perfectly OK to install Mac OS X right onto your Mac OS 9 hard drive. You'll find instructions for both methods in the coming pages.

Note: You may *have* to partition your hard drive if you have certain older Mac models: a PowerBook that lacks USB jacks, a beige Power Mac G3, or an iMac with a CD tray. If your Mac model is one of these, here's the strange little footnote to the installation instructions: you must install Mac OS X onto a partition that's "within" the first 8 GB of the disk. If your hard drive is smaller than 8 GB as it is, never mind—you don't have to partition. If it's larger, however, run Disk Utility as described below to create smaller partitions.

How to Partition

If you decide to partition your drive, on the other hand, here's how to do it:

1. **Back up everything worth preserving.**

   Burn it onto CDs, copy it onto another Mac over the network, email it to yourself, whatever it takes—just remember that you're about to erase the hard drive completely.

2. **Insert the Mac OS X CD. Double-click the Install Mac OS X icon. Click the Restart button.**

   Your Mac restarts, booting up from the Mac OS X CD. After a moment, the Installer screen appears—but you *don't* want to install Mac OS X just now, so don't click Continue.

3. **Choose Installer→Open Disk Utility.**

   The Disk Utility program opens.

4. **Click the Partition tab. Partition your hard drive as shown in Figure 9-15 (which appears on page 239).**

   Actually, you can create more than two partitions, if you see any value in it.

Tip: How do you decide how big to make the partitions? If you expect to use your Mac OS 9 System Folder primarily as the basis of your Classic environment (see Chapter 5), its partition can be fairly small, maybe 2 GB or so. The same advice applies if you're an iMovie fan; give the Mac OS X partition as much space as you can, so your DV files will have somewhere to go.

If you expect to restart your Mac in Mac OS 9 quite a bit, however, you may want to divide the hard drive roughly in half, so that you'll have plenty of room no matter which operating system you're using.

5. **Click OK. In the warning box, click Partition.**

Now you've done it. Disk Utility erases your hard drive and divides it into the number of partitions you've specified. When the progress bar disappears, choose Disk Utility→Quit Disk Utility. You arrive at the first Mac OS X installer screen; skip to step 3, below.

The OS X Installer, Step by Step

The installation process takes about 45 minutes, but for the sake of your own psyche, you'll probably want to set aside a whole afternoon. Once the installation is over, you'll want to play around, organize your files, and learn the lay of the land.

Phase 1: The Installer

Here's how the installation goes:

1. **Insert the Mac OS X CD.**

What you see in its main window differs depending on the version of Mac OS X you have, but there's always a Read Me document worth looking over before you begin.

WORKAROUND WORKSHOP

Installing Mac OS X on Forbidden Macs

Apple says that you can't install Mac OS X except on models with G3 or G4 processors. The truth is a little bit more complicated: The Mac OS X *installer* doesn't run on any models except those, but Mac OS X itself can indeed be made to work. All you need is a patch to make the installer work, and a few pieces of software in the System folder.

That's exactly the point of the Unsupported UtilityX, a free software program that lets Mac OS X operate on certain pre–G3 Macintosh models, including these: Macintosh 7300, 7500, 7600, 8500, 8600, 9500, 9600, and certain clones (Umax S900 and J700; and Power Computing PowerWave and PowerTower Pro).

There are a few glitches along the way—floppy drives don't work in this configuration, and you can't reboot into Mac OS 9.2.1 (although you can use it for Classic). For rebooting purposes, pretty much the only solution is to keep a separate partition with Mac OS 9.1 on it.

Even so, if your Mac has enough speed and memory, there's no reason why you shouldn't be able to enjoy Mac OS X and all the cool new programs that run only on it. Just don't call Apple asking for technical support.

You can download Unsupported UtilityX (and get your questions answered) at *http://eshop.macsales.com/ OSXCenter*.

2. **Double-click the Install Mac OS X icon. When the Restart button appears, click it.**

The Mac starts up from the CD and takes you directly to the first Installer screen.

Note: If you're installing a Mac OS X updater and not a fresh copy, you'll be asked for an Administrator's password (see Chapter 11). Installing new versions of the operating system is something that only competent people are allowed to do.

The installer will soon fall into a pattern: Read the instructions, make a couple choices, and click Continue to advance to the next screen.

As you go, the list on the left side of the screen shows where you are in the overall procedure.

Tip: You can back out of the installation at any time before step 6, just by choosing Installer→Quit. When the Restart button appears, click it. Then eject the Mac OS X CD, either by holding down the mouse button while the computer restarts or, if you have a tray-loading CD drive, pushing its eject button during the moment of darkness during the restart.

---

3. **Click your way through the Select Language, Welcome, Important Information, and Software License Agreement screens.**

Important Information duplicates the Read Me file; the Software License Agreement requires you to click a button confirming that you agree with whatever Apple's lawyers say.

4. **On the Select Destination screen, click the disk or partition on which you want to install Mac OS X.**

Icons for all of your disks (or partitions) appear on the screen, but ones that are off-limits to Mac OS X (like CDs and USB hard drives) appear dimmed. Click the icon of the drive—or the drive *partition,* if you've created one to hold Mac OS X—that will be your new main startup drive.

The "Erase destination" checkbox is an important one. In times of trouble, after backing up all of your files and programs, you can turn on this box in order to perform a clean installation, as described later in this appendix. Needless to say, it wipes out everything on the selected drive before installing Mac OS X. (From the pop-up menu, choose Mac OS Extended. The other choice, UNIX File System, is exclusively for people who want to write UNIX programs or require a case-sensitive directory system.)

5. **Click Continue Installation.**

You arrive at the Installation Type screen. The easiest way to proceed here is to click Continue. But you can save a few hundred megabytes of disk space if you take the time to click Customize.

The Installer shows you a list of the various chunks that constitute Mac OS X. A few of them are easily dispensable.

You can start by turning off the Localized Files checkboxes for Japanese, German, French, and any other languages you don't speak. With each language you turn off, you save about 22 MB of disk space. While you're at it, turn off Additional Print Drivers if you don't use an inkjet printer from Canon, Epson, or Hewlett-Packard. You save another 111 MB.

6. **Click Continue.**

Now you're in for a 25-minute wait as the Installer copies software onto your hard drive. When the installer's finished, you see a message indicating that your Mac will restart in 30 seconds. If you haven't wandered off to watch TV, click the Restart button to end the countdown and get on with it.

Mac OS X is now installed on your Mac—but you're not quite ready to use it yet.

Phase 2: The Setup Assistant

When the Mac "comes to" after restarting, the first thing you experience is some arty, liquid visual effects, some jazzy music, and an animated stream of Welcome messages in various languages. Once Apple has finished showing off its multimedia prowess, you arrive at a Welcome screen.

Once again, you're in for a click-through-the-screens experience, this time with the aim of setting up your Mac's various settings. After answering the questions on each screen, click Continue.

1. **Choose your area of the country.**

If you chose English as your primary language during the installation phase, for example, you're now asked which particular regional form of English you speak: United States, Australia, Canada, or United Kingdom. Select the appropriate one and click Continue.

2. **Choose a keyboard layout.**

Page 188 describes the purpose of keyboard layouts. Most people can click right past this screen.

3. **Fill in the Registration Information screen, if you like.**

This is your chance to become a grain of sand on the great beach of the Apple database. Click Continue.

Tip: If you're not interested in providing your personal information to Apple, or if you've already done so during a previous installation, press ⌘-Q. A message offers you Skip, Shut Down, and Cancel buttons. If you click Skip, you jump straight ahead to step 5.

---

4. **Answer "A Few More Questions."**

This window includes two pop-up menus that let you tell Apple where your computer will be used (Home, Home Business, and so on) and what you do for a living. You'll also find buttons that let you accept or decline some exciting new junk mail from Apple and its partners. Click Continue.

The "Thank You" screen now appears, telling you that the information you've just supplied will be sent to Apple as soon as you connect to the Internet. Click Continue.

5. **Create your Administrator account (Figure C-1).**

Most of the steps up to this point have been pretty inconsequential, but this is a big moment. You're about to create your *account*—your Administrator account, in fact, as described in Chapter 11.

All you have to do is make up a name, short variation of your name (eight characters or fewer—no spaces), and password (same deal). Choose carefully; you can't easily change your account name later.

As noted in Figure C-1, this is the only chance you'll ever have to create an Administrator account with no password at all. If you're the only one who uses your Mac, it's perfectly OK to leave the password blank empty.

What you come up with here is extremely important, however, if several different people use this Mac at different times, or if other people connect to it on a network. See page 278 for details on creating a password and a hint that will help you remember it.

Click Continue.

Note: The rest of the setup process involves the creation of an Internet account. If your Mac was already connected to the Internet under Mac OS 9, Mac OS X is kind enough to absorb those settings and take you straight to the final screen. In other words, you may not encounter the screens described in steps 6, 7, 8, and 9.

---

6. **Specify how you want to connect to the Internet.**

You can tell the setup program that you don't want to set up an Internet account right now. Otherwise, the buttons on this screen let you sign up for an EarthLink Internet account (which will wind up costing about $20 per month) or indicate that you already have an Internet service.

Click Continue. (For the purposes of these instructions, let's say that you decided not to sign up for an EarthLink account, which would introduce a detour in the setup process.)

7. Indicate how your Mac is connected to the Internet.

Your choices are "Telephone modem" (your Mac's built-in dial-up modem); "local area network (LAN)" (either an office network or a *router* connected to your cable modem or DSL); "Cable modem" (a cable modem connected directly to your Mac); "DSL (Digital Subscriber Line)" (one that's connected directly to your Mac); and, if you have an AirPort card, "AirPort wireless."

When you click Continue, you may be asked for the specific information—the local access number, account name and password, and so on—for your Internet account. See Chapter 18 for advice on filling in these settings. Click Continue.

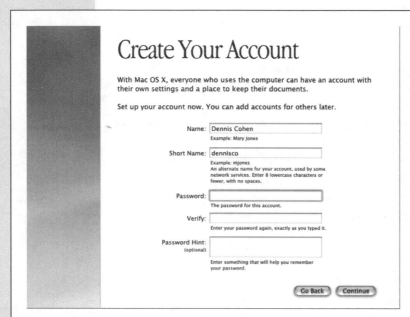

Create Your Account

With Mac OS X, everyone who uses the computer can have an account with their own settings and a place to keep their documents.

Set up your account now. You can add accounts for others later.

Name: Dennis Cohen
Example: Mary Jones

Short Name: dennisco
Example: mjones
An alternate name for your account, used by some network services. Enter 8 lowercase characters or fewer, with no spaces.

Password:
The password for this account.

Verify:
Enter your password again, exactly as you typed it.

Password Hint:
(optional)
Enter something that will help you remember your password.

Go Back   Continue

Figure C-1:
If you are the only person who uses your Mac—if it's your personal laptop, for example—none of this information is especially important. You'll never have to remember any of it. In fact, if security isn't an issue for you, you might want to consider leaving the Password field empty. (The Mac will warn you that this isn't a particularly secure scenario if you work on an office network, but you don't care. Having no password will make it easier for you to hook up your Mac to another one, as described in Chapter 12.)

8. Sign up for an iTools account, if you don't already have one.

You can read all about the advantages of a free iTools account in Chapter 18. The crown jewel, of course, is a free, 20 MB, Internet-based backup hard drive called an iDisk. If you already have an iTools account, click the appropriate button and fill in your account name and password. If not, click the iTools button; you're offered the opportunity to make up an iTools name and password.

9. Go online.

When you click Continue, you wind up at the Now You're Ready to Connect screen. If you click Continue, your Mac attempts to connect to the Internet and send your registration information to Apple, as three blue blobs juggle themselves to entertain you.

When the registration is complete, you're offered the opportunity to set up your email account. If you've just been through the iTools business, your account information—that is, your *yourname@mac.com* email account information—is already filled in. To set up a different email account, click "Add my existing email account" and fill in the information on the right side of the screen. (Advice on what to fill in here appears on page 453.) When you're done, click Continue.

10. **Set the time zone, date, and time.**

These final screens help to set your Mac's built-in clock—a surprisingly important step, because it determines how the files you create will know whether they are older or newer than other versions.

When you click Continue, the final screen asks you to enjoy your Apple computer—and when you click Done, you wind up at the Mac OS X desktop, just as described in Chapter 1.

Uninstalling Mac OS X

There isn't any easy way to remove Mac OS X if you decide that you don't like it.

The chief problem is that thousands of its pieces are invisible. Even if you start up the Mac in Mac OS 9 and then drag all the visible Mac OS X folders to the Trash, you'll leave behind many megabytes of Mac OS X software crumbs that you can't see.

Here and there, in books and on Web sites, you'll find conflicting lists of these invisible files, along with elaborate steps for making them visible and then throwing them away. The truth is, however, that you'll probably save time by simply backing up the data that's worth preserving—your Home folder, Applications folder, Library folder, and whatever folders you use in Mac OS 9—and then erasing the hard drive or partition, using the Drive Setup program on your Mac OS 9 CD.

At this point, your hard drive will be clean, fresh, and ready for an up-to-date installation of Mac OS 9.

Reinstalling Mac OS X—and the Clean Install

In the days of Mac OS 9 and earlier operating systems, the *clean install* was considered an essential troubleshooting technique. It entailed installing a second System Folder—a fresh one, uncontaminated by the detritus left behind by you and your software programs.

But in general, you and your software *can't* invade the Mac OS X System folder. The kind of gradual corruption that could occur in the old Mac OS is impossible in Mac OS X, and therefore the need to perform a clean install is nearly eliminated.

That's not to say that you might not want to reinstall Mac OS X, perhaps to reinstate some software components that you've thrown away or chose not to install the first time around. See page 557 for details on this process.

But if every cell in your body is still screaming that a clean install is absolutely necessary, the only sure and remotely easy way to do it is to back up your important stuff—your Home folder, whatever folders you use in Mac OS 9, and so on. Then run the Mac OS X installer anew, being sure to turn on the "Erase destination" checkbox described on page 543.

Then reinstall any Mac OS X updaters (to 10.0.1, for example) that Apple may have released since you got your Mac OS X CD. Finally, copy your stuff back into place.

At that point, you'll be confident that your Mac OS X installation is clean, fresh, and ready for action.

Troubleshooting Mac OS X

Whether it's a car engine or an operating system, anything with several thousand parts can develop the occasional technical hiccup. Mac OS X is far more resilient than its predecessors, but it's still a complex system with the potential for occasional glitches.

Beware, however: very few pages of the traditional Macintosh troubleshooting workbook apply to Mac OS X. Except when troubleshooting programs in Classic (Chapter 5), you can forget about all the conventional rituals, including:

- **Giving a program more memory.** There's virtually no such thing as "out of memory" messages in Mac OS X, which gives memory to programs *as they need it,* changing their memory allotment from instant to instant.

- **Turning off system extensions.** There are no system extensions in Mac OS X, so there's nothing to turn off.

- **Rebuilding the desktop.** Mac OS X stores your icons and file names using a completely different system, so that old business of pressing Option-⌘ at startup is obsolete.

In short, Mac OS X is a whole new world when it comes to troubleshooting.

It's safe to say that you'll have to do *less* troubleshooting in Mac OS X than in Mac OS 9, especially considering that most freaky little glitches go away if you just try these two steps one at a time:

- Quit and restart the wayward program

- Log out and log back in again..

It's the *other* problems that will drive you batty. Ladies and gentlemen, here it is: the *new* Macintosh troubleshooting curriculum.

Five Problems That Aren't Problems

Before you panic, accept the possibility that whatever is frustrating you is a Mac OS X *difference,* not a Mac OS X *problem.* Plenty of "problems" turn out simply to be quirks of the way Mac OS X works. For example:

- **Can't empty the Trash.** You'll find a complete discussion of this problem on page 66, but start by checking to see if there's a locked file in the Trash. (Pressing Option as you choose the Empty Trash command no longer overrides locked files in the Trash, which is why this one catches so many Mac veterans by surprise.)

- **System Preferences controls are dimmed.** As noted in Chapter 8, many of Mac OS X's control panels are off-limits to standard account holders. That is, only people with Administrator accounts are allowed to make changes, as indicated by the padlock icon at the lower-left corner of such panels.

- **"I can't log in! I'm in an endless login loop!"** If the standard Login screen never seems to appear, it's because somebody has turned on the automatic login feature described on page 283. The Login screen won't appear, and give you a chance to sign in with your own account, until somebody either turns off automatic login or chooses →Log Out.

- **Can't move or open a folder.** Like it or not, Mac OS X is Unix, and Unix has a very strict sense of who, among the people who share a Mac over time, *owns* certain files and folders. For starters, people who don't have Administrator accounts (page 275) aren't allowed to move, or even open, certain important folders. Page 554 has much more on this topic.

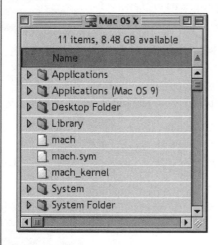

Figure D-1:
What are these things? They're invisible files when you're actually seated at your Mac. But when viewed from across the network (from a Mac OS 9 machine, in this case), they can certainly be disorienting. Learn to ignore them.

- **My hard drive is filled with weird-looking files.** If you inspect your Mac OS X computer from across the network, you may well be appalled: Its main hard drive window is filled with icons called *mach, mach.sym,* and *mach_kernel* that you've never seen when seated at your Mac in person (see Figure D-1). These are only a few of the thousands of Unix files that constitute Mac OS X—and are generally hidden from view. You can generally see them only from across the network. Ignore them.

If whatever problem you're having doesn't fall into one of those five categories, then maybe something truly has gone wrong; read on.

Minor Eccentric Behavior

Mac OS X itself is generally about as unstable as Mount Everest. It's the *programs* that most often cause you grief.

All kinds of glitches may befall you. Maybe Mail has sprouted new mailboxes, or your Freehand palettes won't stay put, or the Dock leaves remnants of its "puff of smoke" animation on the screen.

When a single program is acting up like this, try the following steps, in this sequence:

First Resort: Restart the Program

If a program starts acting up, the first and easiest step to take is simply to quit the program and start it up again.

Remember that in Mac OS X, every program lives and dies in solitude, in its own stainless-steel memory bubble. Jettisoning a confused program doesn't affect other running programs in the least. Restarting the flaky program lets it load from scratch, having forgotten all about its previous problems.

Second Resort: Toss the Prefs File

Here we are in the age of Mac OS X, and we're still throwing away preference files?

Absolutely. A corrupted preference file can bewilder the program that depends on it just as badly as it did in Mac OS 9.

Before you go on a dumpfest, however, take this simple test. Log in using a different account (perhaps a dummy account that you create just for testing purposes). Run the problem program. Is the problem gone? If so, then the glitch exists only when *you* are logged in—which means it's a problem with *your* copy of the program's preferences.

Return to your own account. Open your Home folder→Library→Preferences folder, where you'll find neatly labeled preference files for all of the programs you use. Each ends with the file name suffix *.plist*. For example, com.apple.finder.plist is the Finder's preference file, com.apple.dock.plist is the Dock's, and so on.

Put the suspected preference file into the Trash, but don't empty it. The next time you run the recalcitrant program, it will build itself a brand-new preference file that, if you're lucky, lacks whatever corruption was causing your problems.

If not, quit the program. You can reinstate its original .plist file from the Trash, if you'd find that helpful as you pursue your troubleshooting agenda.

Remember, however, that you actually have *three* Preferences folders. In addition to your own Home folder's stash, there's a second one in the Library folder in the main hard drive window (which administrators are allowed to trash), and a third in the System→Library folder in the main hard drive window (which nobody is allowed to trash).

The only way to throw away the .plist files from this most deep-seated source (inside the System folder) is to use one of the usual security-bypass methods described in the sidebar box on page 554.

In any case, the next time you log in, the Mac will create fresh, virginal preference files.

Third Resort: Log Out

Sometimes you can give Mac OS X or its programs a swift kick by logging out (→Log Out) and logging back in again. It's an inconvenient step, but not nearly as time-consuming as restarting the computer.

Last Resort: Trash and Reinstall the Program

Sometimes reinstalling the problem program clears up whatever the glitch was.

First, however, throw away all traces of it. Fortunately, trashing a program is much easier in Mac OS X than in Mac OS 9, thanks to its *application package* structure (page 96). Just open the Applications folder and drag the program's icon (or its folder) to the Trash. In most cases, the only remaining piece to discard is its .plist file in your Home→Library→Preferences folder.

Then reinstall the program from its original CD or installer—after first checking the company's Web site to see if there's an updated version, of course.

Frozen Programs (Force Quitting)

The occasional unresponsive application has become such a part of Mac OS X life that, among the Mac cognoscenti online, the dreaded, endless "please wait" cursor has been given its own acronym: SBOD (Spinning Beachball of Death). When the SBOD strikes, no amount of mouse clicking and keyboard pounding will get you out of the recalcitrant program.

Here are the different ways you can go about *force quitting* a stuck program, in increasing order of desperation:

- **Use the Dock.** If you can't use the program's regularly scheduled File→Quit command, try Control-clicking its Dock icon and choosing Quit from the pop-up menu.

- **Force quit the usual way.** Choose →Force Quit to terminate the stuck program, or use one of the other force-quit methods described on page 94.

- **Force quit the sneaky way.** Some programs, including the Dock, don't show up at all in the usual Force Quit dialog box. Your next attempt, therefore, should be to open the Process Viewer program (in Applications→Utilities), which shows *everything* that's running. Double-click a program to force quit it. (If you're a Unix hound, you can also use the *kill* command in Terminal, as described on page 410.)

Tip: *If you find yourself having to quit the Dock more than once, here's an easier way: make yourself a little AppleScript (Chapter 7) consisting of a single line:* tell application "Dock" to quit. *Save it as an application. Whenever you feel that the Dock needs a good kick in the rear, double-click your little Apple-Script.*

- **Force quit remotely.** If the Finder itself has locked up, you can't very well get to Process Viewer. At this point, you may have to abort the locked program from another computer across the network, if you're on one, by using the *SSH* (secure shell) command. The end of Chapter 21 offers a blow-by-blow description of how you might terminate a program by remote control in this way, either from elsewhere on the office network or even from across the Internet.

Tip: *If all of this seems like a lot to remember, you can always force-restart the Mac. On desktop Macs, press the left-pointing triangle button on the front or side of the computer; on laptops, you press Control-⌘-power button.*

The Wrong Program Opens

As noted in Chapter 4, the way documents are linked to the programs that can open them is very different in Mac OS X than it was before. Some documents have invisible, four-letter type and creator codes that tell them which programs they "belong to," just as in Mac OS 9. Other documents lack these codes, and open up in whichever program recognizes its file name extension (.doc or .txt, for example).

Page 101 shows you how to choose which program opens a certain document (or kind of document). But that's not much help when you double-click a SimpleText document and have to sit there while SimpleText opens up—*in Classic,* mandating a 45-second wait.

The simple rule to remember here is that *creator codes override file name extensions.* In other words, a file called Contract.txt generally opens in Mac OS X's TextEdit—*if* it doesn't have a four-letter creator code behind the scenes. If that same file has

SimpleText's creator code (ttxt), however, it opens in SimpleText (and Classic) no matter what its file name is.

In the SimpleText case, the quick solution is to install the Carbonized (that is, Mac OS X-compatible) version of SimpleText. It's on the Mac OS X Developer CD (see page 246).

In other cases, the quickest solution may be to *strip away* the type and creator codes. You can do that by dragging the troubled files' icons onto a program like Wipe Creator (available from the software page of *www.missingmanuals.com*). At that point, Mac OS X has only the document's file name extension to go on when choosing a program to open it.

WORKAROUND WORKSHOP

Fixing Permissions Problems

Sooner or later, when you try to move or delete a certain file or folder, you may get an error message like this—"The folder 'Junk' could not be opened because you do not have sufficient access privileges"—or this: "The operation could not be completed because this item is owned by Chris" (or by *root,* which means by Mac OS X itself).

Both kinds of messages, with their awkward passive-voice construction, clank on the trained English-speaking ear. However, what they're trying to say is, you've run into a *permissions* problem.

As noted in Chapter 11, Mac OS X is designed to accommodate a number of different people who share the same Mac over time. Nobody is allowed to meddle with other people's files or folders. But even if you're the solo operator of your Mac, you still share it with Mac OS X itself (which the error messages may refer to as *root* or *system*).

In any case, if you're confident that whatever you're trying to do isn't some kind of nihilistic, self-destructive act like trashing the Applications folder, it's easy enough to get past these limitations.

One way is to restart the Mac in Mac OS 9, which doesn't recognize Mac OS X's permissions system, and makes all Mac OS X files susceptible to whatever you want to do with them.

Another way is to log in with the *root* or *superuser* account, as described on page 290.

A third method is to drag the recalcitrant file or folder onto the icon of SuperGetInfo (a shareware program described on page 314). In its window, you'll find a pop-up menu that lets you reassign ownership of any icon to, for example, yourself, as shown here.

A fourth method—the Unix lovers' way—is to fire up Terminal and use the *chown* command (for "change owner"), followed by its two arguments: the new owner's account name and the pathname of the directory you want to reassign. If you're Chris, and somebody else currently "owns" ObnoxiousFolder, you'd type this:

```
sudo chown -R chris /StuckFolder/
```

A more detailed discussion of the *chown* command and its syntax appears in Chapter 16.

Can't Empty the Trash

For some reason, the can't-empty-the-trash problem seems to be far more prevalent in Mac OS X than in Mac OS 9. One reason: pressing Option as you choose Finder→Empty Trash no longer wipes out any *locked* files in the Trash, as it once did.

First Resort: Bypass the Lock

As noted in Chapter 2, the solution is to press Option as you click and hold on *the Trash icon itself*. Now, when you choose Empty Trash from the pop-up menu, Mac OS X empties the Trash without complaint, locked files and all.

Alternately, you could simply unlock all of the locked files at once, as described on page 68. Or, if you're a Unix fiend, use the *chflags -R nouchg* command described on page 408 to unlock them from Terminal.

Last Resort: Check the Permissions

If emptying the Trash gives you "Could not be completed because this item is owned by Marge," you're trying to move or delete another Mac account holder's stuff. As you know, that's a big no-no in Mac OS X.

If the file or folder's original owner is no longer in your life (or house, or office), however, then you can blow past such permissions problems either by using the *rm* (remove) command in Terminal (see page 390) or by designating *yourself* as the file or folder's new owner, as described on the sidebar box on the facing page.

Can't Move or Rename an Icon

If you're not allowed to drag an icon somewhere, the error message that appears almost always hits the nail on the head: You're trying to move a file or folder that *isn't yours*. The sidebar box on page 554 explains the many solutions to this problem.

Application Won't Open

If a program won't open (if its icon bounces merrily in the Dock for a few seconds, for instance, but then nothing happens), begin by trashing its preference file, as described on page 551. If that doesn't solve it, reinstalling the program usually does.

Program Icons Turn to Folders

You may remember from page 96 that in Mac OS X, every application, behind the scenes, is actually a folder. All you see (and double-click to open) is one icon called Mail, for example, but inside are dozens of folders, icons, and chunks of software code. The only way you'd ever know that a Mac OS X "application icon" is an optical illusion would be to Control-click the application (in icon view) and, from the pop-up menu, choose Show Package Contents.

Every now and then, though—most often after a power failure—Mac OS X puts on a much more showy display of this feature than perhaps you'd like: Suddenly *all* applications show up as folders, whose names bear the suffix *.app*. All very educational, of course, but now you have no way to actually *run* those programs, because the icon to double-click has disappeared.

First Resort: Trash the Three Prefs

Most of the time, the generic-folders problem stems from the corruption of three particular preference files in your Home→Library→Preferences folder: *LSApplications, LSClaimedTypes,* and *LSSchemes.* Throw them away, and then log out. When you log back in, your applications should all have been restored to their rightful conditions.

Note: Unfortunately, tossing these preference files also discards any document-to-application relationships you've established as described on page 101.

Second Resort: Check the Disk

Sometimes your NetInfo database itself—the massive, central database of all accounts, programs, network connections, and just about everything Mac OS X knows about its world—gets confused. Running Disk Utility or *fsck,* its Unix equivalent, should clear it up (page 559).

Last Resort: Make it Your Own

Finally, it's conceivable that the permissions for your own Home folder have become hosed, meaning that Mac OS X believes that somebody else owns your Home folder.

Check its access privileges by highlighting your Home folder's icon and choosing File→Show Info. If *you* aren't identified as the "owner," see "Fixing Permissions Problems" on page 554.

Startup Problems

Not every problem you encounter is related to running applications. Sometimes trouble strikes before you even get that far. For example:

Kernel Panic

When random text gibberish starts superimposing itself on your startup screen, you've got yourself a *kernel panic*—a Unix nervous breakdown. (In such situations, *user panic* might be the more applicable term, but that's programmers for you.)

Kernel panics were rare to begin with, but in Mac OS X 10.1 and later they're becoming increasingly unusual. If you see one at all, it's likely to be the result of a hardware glitch: some memory board, accelerator card, graphics card, SCSI gear, or USB hub that Mac OS X doesn't like, for example.

If restarting doesn't solve the problem, detach every shred of gear that didn't come from Apple. Restore these components to the Mac one at a time until you find out which one was causing Mac OS X's bad hair day. If you're able to pinpoint the culprit, seek its manufacturer (or its Web site) on a quest for updated drivers, or at least try to find out for sure whether the add-on is compatible with Mac OS X.

Tip: This advice goes for your Macintosh itself. Apple periodically updates the Mac's *own* "drivers" in the form of a *firmware update.* You download these updaters from the Support area of Apple's Web site (if indeed Mac OS X's own Software Update mechanism doesn't alert you to its existence).

There's one other cause for kernel panics, by the way, and that's moving, renaming, or changing the access privileges for Mac OS X's essential system files and folders—the Applications or System folder, for example. (You can do so only by restarting the Mac in Mac OS 9 or by signing in with the root account.) This cause isn't even worth mentioning, of course, because nobody would be that foolish.

Freezes During Startup

If the Mac locks up during the startup process, you need to run Mac OS X's disk-repair program, as described on page 558.

Gray Screen During Startup

Confirm that your Mac has the latest firmware, as described in the previous Tip. Detach and test all your non-Apple add-ons, also as described in the previous paragraphs. Finally, perform a disk check (see page 558).

Blue Screen During Startup

Most of the troubleshooting steps for this problem (which is usually accompanied by the Spinning Beachball of Death cursor) are the same as those described under "Kernel Panic," above. But there's one other cause to examine: a corrupted font file in your *Mac OS 9* System Folder.

TROUBLESHOOTING MOMENT

The Reinstall

When some component is missing, your troubleshooting steps have failed, and Mac OS X continues to act up, consider reinstalling Mac OS X.

That's not a big deal at all. It involves inserting the Mac OS X CD, restarting the Mac, pressing the C key as the computer starts up, and proceeding with the installer as described in Appendix C.

The good news is that reinstalling Mac OS X *doesn't touch your files, folders, or settings.* It simply patches whatever holes have opened up in the Unix undercarriage of your operating system—which, every now and then, does you a world of good.

The bad news is that that's not all there is to it. Apple continues to hone Mac OS X with successive versions—10.1.1, 10.1.2, whatever. If you've installed downloaded updates since you've installed your CD-based version of Mac OS X, you may be out of luck. Reinstalling an earlier version of Mac OS X over a later version is always asking for trouble.

To test for this problem, restart the Mac in Mac OS 9, open its System Folder (that's the folder called System Folder, not just System), and drag the Fonts folder to the desktop. Restart in Mac OS X. If the startup proceeds smoothly, you know you've got a damaged font file in that Fonts folder.

Forgotten Password

If you or one of the other people who use your Mac have forgotten the corresponding account password, no worries: just read the sidebar box on page 286.

Fixing the Disk

As noted in the introduction of this book, the beauty of Mac OS X's design is that the operating system itself is frozen in its perfect, pristine state, impervious to conflicting system extensions, clueless Mac users, and other sources of disaster.

That's the theory, anyway. But what happens if something goes wrong with the complex software that operates the hard drive itself?

Fortunately, Mac OS X comes with its own disk-repair program. In the familiar Mac universe of icons and menus, it takes the form of a program in Applications→Utilities called Disk Utility. In the barren world of Terminal and the command line interface, there's a utility that works just as well but bears a different name: *fsck* (for file system check).

In any case, running Disk Utility or its alter ego *fsck* is a powerful and useful troubleshooting tool that can cure all kinds of strange ills, including these problems, among others:

- Your Mac freezes during startup, either before or after the Login screen.

- The startup process interrupts itself with the appearance of the text-only command line.

- You get the "applications showing up as folders" problem (see page 555).

Method 1: Disk Utility

The easiest way to check your disk is to use the Disk Utility program. Use this method if your Mac can, indeed, start up. (See Method 2 if you can't even get that far.)

Unlike its Mac OS 9 equivalent Disk First Aid, Disk Utility can't check the disk it's *on*. That's why you have to restart the computer from the Mac OS X CD-ROM (or another startup disk), and run Disk Utility from there. The process goes like this:

1. **Start up the Mac from the Mac OS X CD.**

   The best way to do that is to insert the CD and then restart the Mac while holding down the C key.

   You wind up, after some time, at the Mac OS X Installer screen. Don't be fooled—installing Mac OS X is *not* what you want to do here. Don't click Continue!

2. **Choose Installer→Open Disk Utility.**

   That's the unexpected step. After a moment, the Disk Utility screen appears.

3. **Click the First Aid tab.**

   The program now looks like the illustration in Figure D-2.

4. **Click the disk or disk partition you want to fix, and then click Repair.**

   The Mac whirls into action, checking a list of very technical disk-formatting parameters.

If you see the message, "The volume 'Macintosh HD' appears to be OK," that's meant to be *good* news. Believe it or not, that cautious statement is as definitive an affirmation as Disk Utility is capable of making about the health of your disk.

Note: Don't be alarmed. The message's last line says "Repair completed" whether or not any repairing was done at all.

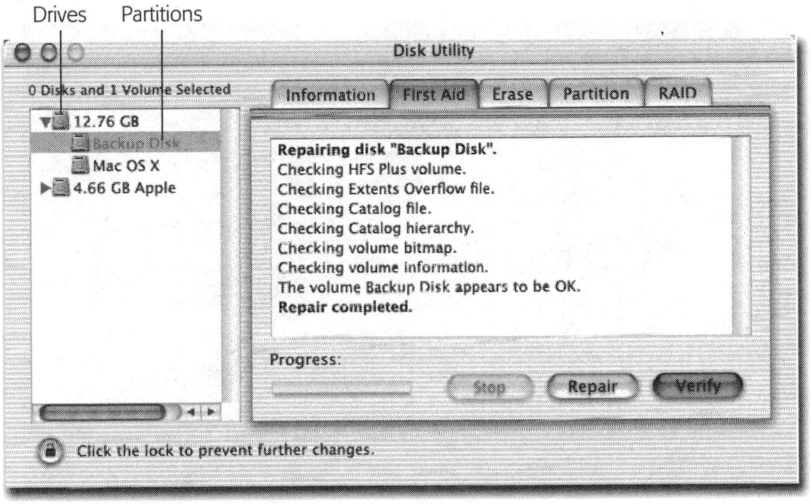

Figure D-2:
Disk Utility is the Mac OS X version of the old Disk First Aid program. When your hard drive is acting up, don't waste your time with the Verify button. It's exclusively for use on disks that you can't repair, like CD-ROMs and the startup disk— disks you just want to have a look at.

Disk Utility may also tell you that the disk is damaged, but that it can't help you. In that case, you need a more heavy-duty disk-repair program like Drive 10 (*www.micromat.com*).

Method 2: *fsck* at the Console

Disk Utility isn't of much use when you can't find the Mac OS X CD, when your CD drive isn't working, or when you're in a hurry to get past the startup problems that are plaguing your machine. In these cases, you'll be glad that you can boot into the Mac's raw Unix underlayer to perform some diagnostic (and healing) commands.

Specifically, you'll be glad that you can run the Unix program *fsck,* for which Disk Utility is little more than a pretty faceplate.

Like any Unix program, *fsck* runs at the command line. You launch it from the all-text, black Unix screen by typing the command and pressing Enter.

Single-user mode (⌘-S at startup)

The Terminal program is the best known form of Mac OS X's command line, but it's not the only one. In fact, there are several other ways to get there.

In general, you don't hear them mentioned except in the context of troubleshooting, because the Terminal program offers many more convenient features for doing the same thing, and, because it's contained in a Mac OS X–style window, Terminal is not so disorienting as the three methods you're about to read.

All of these techniques take you into *console mode,* shown in Figure D-3. In console mode, Unix takes over your screen completely, white type against black, no windows or icons in sight. Abandon the mouse, all ye who enter; in console mode, you can't do anything but type commands.

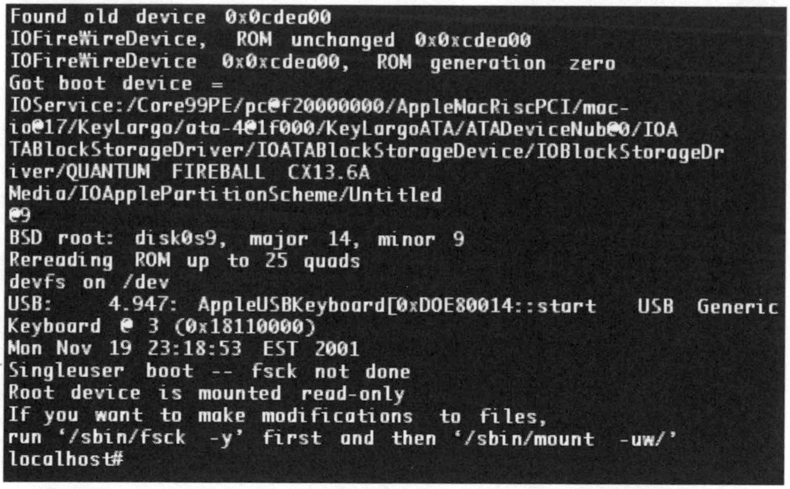

```
Found old device 0x0cdea00
IOFireWireDevice,   ROM unchanged 0x0xcdea00
IOFireWireDevice  0x0xcdea00,   ROM generation  zero
Got boot device =
IOService:/Core99PE/pc@f20000000/AppleMacRiscPCI/mac-
io@17/KeyLargo/ata-4@1f000/KeyLargoATA/ATADeviceNub@0/IOA
TABlockStorageDriver/IOATABlockStorageDevice/IOBlockStorageDr
iver/QUANTUM  FIREBALL  CX13.6A
Media/IOApplePartitionScheme/Untitled
@9
BSD root: disk0s9, major 14, minor 9
Rereading  ROM up to 25 quads
devfs on /dev
USB:    4.947: AppleUSBKeyboard[0xDOE80014::start    USB Generic
Keyboard @ 3 (0x18110000)
Mon Nov 19 23:18:53 EST 2001
Singleuser boot -- fsck not done
Root device is mounted read-only
If you want to make modifications  to files,
run '/sbin/fsck  -y' first and then '/sbin/mount  -uw/'
localhost#
```

Figure D-3:
In Console mode, your entire screen is a command line interface. Unix jockeys can go to town here. Everyone else can timidly type fsck -y *after the* localhost # *prompt—see this prompt on the very last line?—and hope for the best.*

To get there in times of startup troubleshooting, press ⌘-S while the Mac is starting up. (If you're stuck at the frozen remnants of a previous startup attempt, you may first have to force-restart your Mac; see page 553.)

Instead of arriving at the usual desktop, you see technical-looking text scrolling up a black screen as the Mac runs its various startup routines. When it finally stops at the *localhost #* prompt, you're ready to type commands. You're now in what's called *single-user mode,* meaning that the Unix multiple-accounts software has yet to load. You won't be asked to log in.

At the *localhost #* prompt, type *fsck -y* (note the space before the hyphen) and press Enter. (The *y* means "yes," as in "yes, I want you to fix any problems automatically.")

Tip: You've probably gone to this trouble for the sake of running *fsck,* the Unix disk-checking program. But you can also use *ls, cd, rm,* or any of the other Unix commands described in Chapters 15 and 16.

Now the file system check program takes over, running through five sets of tests. When it's complete, you'll see one of two messages:

- **The volume Macintosh HD appears to be OK.** All is well. Type *reboot* and press Return to proceed to the usual Login screen and desktop.

- **File system was modified.** A good sign, but just a beginning. You need to run the program again. One *fsck* pass often repairs only one layer of problems, leaving another to be patched in the next pass. Type *fsck -y* a second time, a third time, and so on, until you finally arrive at a "disk appears to be OK" message.

Other ways to get to the console

Pressing ⌘-S at startup isn't the only way to get to the console (command line). You can also:

- **Log in as >*console*.** Add the "Other" option to the Login screen (see page 284 for instructions). Then, when you sign in, click the Other option, type >*console* as your user name, and leave the password field blank. When you click Log In, you arrive at the usual black console screen.

- **Parachute out of Terminal.** From within Terminal (see Chapter 15), type *sudo shutdown now*. Once again, you arrive in console mode—black screen, no windows, ready to accept your Unix commands.

For most Mac fans, however, the primary reason to use console mode is to run *fsck*, and the best way to do *that* is by pressing ⌘-S at startup.

Tip: In all cases, typing *reboot* at the prompt and pressing Return is how you get back to the familiar Aqua world of icons and windows.

Where to Get Troubleshooting Help

If the basic steps described in this chapter haven't helped, the universe is crawling with additional help sources.

Help Online

These Internet sites contain nothing but troubleshooting discussions, tools, and help:

- **MacFixIt** *(www.macfixit.com).* The world's one-stop resource for troubleshooting advice.

- **Mac newsgroups** (such as *comp.system.mac*). A newsgroup is an Internet bulletin board, which you can access using a program like Microsoft Entourage or Thoth (*www.thothsw.com*). If you're polite and concise, you can post questions to the multitudes here and get more replies to them than you'll know what to do with.

- **Other Apple support resources** (*apple.com/support*). Apple's help Web site also includes downloadable manuals, software updates, frequently asked questions, and many other resources.

The mother of all troubleshooting resources, however, is Apple's own Knowledge Base. This is the collection of 50,000 individual technical articles, organized in a searchable database, that the Apple technicians themselves consult when you call for help.

If you like, you can visit this library using your Web browser; the address is *http:// kbase.info.apple.com*. You can search it either by typing in keywords or by using pop-up menus of question categories. (You'll have to sign up for a free AppleCare ID first.)

Help by Telephone

Finally, consider contacting whoever sold you the component that's making your life miserable: the printer company, scanner company, software company, or whatever.

If it's a Mac OS 9 problem, you can call Apple at 800-275-2273 (that's 800-APL-CARE). For the first 90 days following your purchase of Mac OS X (which, as far as Apple knows, is the date of your first call), the technicians will answer your questions for free.

After that, unless you've paid for AppleCare for your Mac (a three-year extended warranty program), Apple will charge you to answer your questions—unless the problem turns out to be Apple's fault, in which case they won't charge you.

FREQUENTLY ASKED QUESTION

Viruses? What viruses?

One great thing about the old Mac OS was that there were hardly any viruses to worry about—all of the nasties seemed to be written for Windows. But now that we're using Unix, which has been around for 30 years and has a huge user base, is it time to worry again?

Nope. There are even fewer viruses for Unix than for the Mac OS.

You still need to be careful with Word and Excel macro viruses, of course. If you open a Word or Excel attachment sent by email from someone else, and a big fat dialog box warns you that it contains macros, simply click Disable Macros and get on with your life.

Otherwise, you have little to worry about. Sleep well.

Where to Go From Here

I f read in a comfortable chair with good lighting, this book can be the foundation of a sturdy Mac OS X education. But particularly when it comes to mastering the Unix side of this operating system, years of study may await you still.

Web Sites

The Web is the salvation of the Mac OS X fan, especially considering the information vacuum that dominated Mac OS X's early days. The Internet was the only place where could people find out what the heck was going on with their beloved Macs. Here are the most notable Web sites for learning the finer points of Mac OS X:

Mac OS X

- *www.versiontracker.com*. A massive database that tracks, and provides links to, all the latest software for Mac OS X.

- *www.macosxhints.com.* A gold mine of tips, tricks, and hints.

- *www.resexcellence.com*. Another rich resource of hacks and information on the underpinnings of X.

- *www.apple.com/developer*. Even if you aren't a developer, joining the Developer Connection (Apple's programmers' club) gets you an email newsletter, and the discussion boards are a great place for hearing Mac news first—all for free. (Pay $500 a year to become a Select member, and you get CDs mailed to you containing upcoming versions of Mac OS X.)

- *www.macobserver.com.* A good source for news and commentary about the Mac and related products.

- *www.macworld.com.* The discussion boards are an ideal place to find solutions for problems. When a bug pops up, the posts here are a great place to start.

- *www.macaddict.com.* Another great location for discussion boards.

- *www.macfixit.com.* The ultimate Mac troubleshooting Web site, complete with a hotbed of Mac OS X discussion.

- *www.geekculture.com.* A hilarious satire site, dedicated to lampooning our tech addiction—especially Apple tech. Perhaps best known for creating the David Pogue's Head icon for Mac OS X (*www.geekculture.com/joyoftech/joyarchives /254.html*). Or perhaps not.

Mac OS X–Style Unix Lessons and Reference

- *www.westwind.com/reference/OS-X/commandline.* A command reference of *cd, ls, rm,* and all the other commands you can use in Terminal or the console.

- *www.ee.surrey.ac.uk/Teaching/Unix.* A convenient, free Web-based course in Unix for beginners, focused on the tcsh shell—that is, the same dialect found in Mac OS X.

Tip: Typing *unix for beginners* into a search page like Google.com nets dozens of superb help, tutorial, and reference Web sites. If possible, stick to those that feature the tcsh shell; that way, everything you learn online should be perfectly applicable to navigating Mac OS X via Terminal.

Advanced Books

By a happy coincidence, this book is printed and distributed by O'Reilly & Associates, the industry's leading source of books for programmers. And a big chunk of O'Reilly's catalog is dedicated to teaching Unix, especially intermediate and advanced Unix. If this book—particularly Chapters 7, 15, and 16—have given you the programming bug or the Unix bug, here are some titles that apply:

Writing Software for Mac OS X

- *Learning Cocoa* by Apple Computer, Inc. Eases you into the experience of writing Cocoa programs.

- *Learning Carbon* by Apple Computer, Inc. Gives you a head start in writing Carbon programs.

- *AppleScript In a Nutshell* by Bruce W. Perry. The first modern reference to AppleScript, including its use in Mac OS X.

Unix Essentials

- *Learning the Unix Operating System,* 5th Edition, by Jerry Peek. A good primer for Mac users who want to know a little more about Unix.

- *Learning GNU Emacs,* 2nd Edition, by Debra Cameron, Bill Rosenblatt, & Eric Raymond. A comprehensive guide to the GNU Emacs editor, one of the most widely used and powerful Unix text editors.

- *Learning the vi Editor,* 6th Edition, by Linda Lamb & Arnold Robbins. A complete guide to editing with vi, the text editor available on nearly every Unix system.

- *Unix in a Nutshell: System V Edition,* 3rd Edition, by Arnold Robbins. A complete Unix reference, containing all commands and options, with descriptions and examples that put the commands in context.

- *Unix Power Tools,* 2nd Edition, by Jerry Peek, Tim O'Reilly, & Mike Loukides. Practical advice about most every aspect of advanced Unix: POSIX utilities, GNU versions, detailed bash and tcsh shell coverage, a strong emphasis on Perl, and a CD-ROM that contains the best freeware available.

OS X Administration

- *Apache: The Definitive Guide,* 2nd Edition, by Ben Laurie & Peter Laurie. Describes how to set up, and secure the Apache Web-server software.

- *Essential System Administration,* 2nd Edition, by Aileen Frisch. A compact, manageable introduction to the tasks faced by everyone responsible for a Unix system.

Index

X

Y

Z

Colophon

Due to an annoying and permanent wrist ailment, the author wrote this book by voice, using Dragon Naturally Speaking on a generic Windows PC. To avoid further contamination, the Microsoft Word files were then transferred as quickly as possible to a Power Mac G4, where they were edited and transmitted to the book's editors and technical reviewers.

The screenshots were captured with Ambrosia Software's Snapz Pro X *(www. ambrosiasw.com)* on Mac OS X–equipped iMac DV, PowerBook G4, and 2001 iBook machines. Adobe Photoshop and Macromedia Freehand *(www.adobe.com)* were called in as required for touching them up.

The book was designed and laid out in Adobe PageMaker 6.5 on a PowerBook G3 and Power Mac G4. The fonts used include Formata (as the sans-serif family) and Minion (as the serif body face). To provide the and ⌘ symbols, a custom font was created using Macromedia Fontographer.

The book was generated as an Adobe Acrobat PDF file for proofreading and indexing, and finally transmitted to the printing plant in the form of PostScript files.

Oh, and about the sailboat on the cover—*Dock,* get it?

More Titles from Pogue Press/O'Reilly

The Missing Manuals

Mac OS 9: The Missing Manual

By David Pogue
1st Edition March 2000
472 pages, ISBN 1-56592-857-1

The latest system software for the resurgent Macintosh platform is Mac OS 9, which includes over 50 new features. However, Apple ships Mac OS 9 without one of the most important features of all: a manual. O'Reilly/Pogue Press comes to the rescue with *Mac OS 9: The Missing Manual*. Award-winning author David Pogue brings his humor and expertise to Mac OS 9 for the first time in this lucid, impeccably written guide. Readers will appreciate the step-by-step guides to setting up small networks, the tutorials on Mac OS 9's new Multiple Users control panel, and the coverage of Mac OS 9's speech-recognition, color printing, digital video, and self-updating software features.

AppleWorks 6: The Missing Manual

By Jim Elferdink & David Reynolds
1st First Edition May 2000
450 pages, ISBN 1-56592-858-X

AppleWorks, the integrated application that arrives in 4 million homes, schools, and offices a year, includes everything—except a printed manual. In *AppleWorks 6: The Missing Manual*, authors Jim Elferdink and David Reynolds guide the reader through both the basics and the hidden talents of the new AppleWorks, placing special emphasis on version 6's enhanced word processing, Internet, and presentation features. As a Missing Manual title, the book is friendly, authoritative, and complete, rich with clever workarounds, examples, and step-by-step tutorials.

iMovie 2: The Missing Manual

By David Pogue
1st Edition January 2001
420 pages, ISBN 0-596-00104-5

iMovie 2: The Missing Manual covers every step of iMovie video production, from choosing and using a digital camcorder to burning the finished work onto CDs. Far deeper and more detailed than the meager set of online help screens included with iMovie, the book helps iMovie 2 users realize the software's potential as a breakthrough in overcoming the cost, complexity, and difficulty of desktop video production.

Dreamweaver 4: The Missing Manual

By Dave McFarland
1st Edition July 2001
480 pages, ISBN 0-596-00097-9

Dreamweaver 4: The Missing Manual is the ideal companion to this complex software. Following an anatomical tour of a web page to orient new users, author Dave McFarland walks you through the process of creating and designing a complete web site. Armed with this handbook, both first-time and experienced web designers can easily use Dreamweaver to bring stunning, interactive web sites to life.

Office 2001 for Macintosh: The Missing Manual

By Nan Barber & David Reynolds
1st Edition May 2001
648 pages, ISBN 0-596-00081-2

Office 2001 for Macintosh: The Missing Manual tackles each of the primary Office applications with depth, humor, and clarity, and provides relief for the hapless Mac user who'd rather read professionally written printed instructions than hunt through a maze of personality-free help screens. This book is a must-read for any Mac Office 2001 user.

POGUE PRESS™
O'REILLY®

TO ORDER: **800-998-9938** • *order@oreilly.com* • *www.oreilly.com*
O'REILLY BOOKS ARE AVAILABLE AT MOST BOOKSTORES.
ONLINE EDITIONS OF MOST O'REILLY TITLES ARE AVAILABLE BY SUBSCRIPTION AT **safari.oreilly.com**

How to stay in touch with O'Reilly

1. Visit Our Award-Winning Web Site

http://www.oreilly.com/

★ "Top 100 Sites on the Web" —PC Magazine
★ "Top 5% Web sites" —Point Communications
★ "3-Star site" —The McKinley Group

Our web site contains a library of comprehensive product information (including book excerpts and tables of contents), downloadable software, background articles, interviews with technology leaders, links to relevant sites, book cover art, and more. File us in your Bookmarks or Hotlist!

2. Join Our Email Mailing Lists

New Product Releases

To receive automatic email with brief descriptions of all new O'Reilly products as they are released, send email to:
ora-news-subscribe@lists.oreilly.com
Put the following information in the first line of your message (not in the Subject field):
subscribe ora-news

O'Reilly Events

If you'd also like us to send information about trade show events, special promotions, and other O'Reilly events, send email to:
ora-news-subscribe@lists.oreilly.com
Put the following information in the first line of your message (not in the Subject field):
subscribe ora-events

3. Get Examples from Our Books via FTP

There are two ways to access an archive of example files from our books:

Regular FTP

- ftp to:
  ftp.oreilly.com
  (login: anonymous
  password: your email address)
- Point your web browser to:
  ftp://ftp.oreilly.com/

FTPMAIL

- Send an email message to:
  ftpmail@online.oreilly.com
  (Write "help" in the message body)

4. Contact Us via Email

order@oreilly.com
To place a book or software order online. Good for North American and international customers.

subscriptions@oreilly.com
To place an order for any of our newsletters or periodicals.

books@oreilly.com
General questions about any of our books.

cs@oreilly.com
For answers to problems regarding your order or our products.

booktech@oreilly.com
For book content technical questions or corrections.

proposals@oreilly.com
To submit new book or software proposals to our editors and product managers.

international@oreilly.com
For information about our international distributors or translation queries. For a list of our distributors outside of North America check out:
http://www.oreilly.com/distributors.html

5. Work with Us

Check out our website for current employment opportunites:
http://jobs.oreilly.com/

O'Reilly & Associates, Inc.
1005 Gravenstein Hwy North
Sebastopol, CA 95472 USA
TEL 707-829-0515 or 800-998-9938
    (6am to 5pm PST)
FAX 707-829-0104

Titles from O'Reilly

O'REILLY®

TO ORDER: **800-998-9938** • **order@oreilly.com** • **www.oreilly.com**
ONLINE EDITIONS OF MOST O'REILLY TITLES ARE AVAILABLE BY SUBSCRIPTION AT **safari.oreilly.com**
ALSO AVAILABLE AT MOST RETAIL AND ONLINE BOOKSTORES

International Distributors

http://international.oreilly.com/distributors.html • international@oreilly.com

UK, EUROPE, MIDDLE EAST, AND AFRICA (EXCEPT FRANCE, GERMANY, AUSTRIA, SWITZERLAND, LUXEMBOURG, AND LIECHTENSTEIN)

INQUIRIES

O'Reilly UK Limited
4 Castle Street
Farnham
Surrey, GU9 7HS
United Kingdom
Telephone: 44-1252-711776
Fax: 44-1252-734211
Email: information@oreilly.co.uk

ORDERS

Wiley Distribution Services Ltd.
1 Oldlands Way
Bognor Regis
West Sussex PO22 9SA
United Kingdom
Telephone: 44-1243-843294
UK Freephone: 0800-243207
Fax: 44-1243-843302 (Europe/EU orders)
or 44-1243-843274 (Middle East/Africa)
Email: cs-books@wiley.co.uk

FRANCE

INQUIRIES & ORDERS

Éditions O'Reilly
18 rue Séguier
75006 Paris, France
Tel: 33-1-40-51-71-89
Fax: 33-1-40-51-72-26
Email: france@oreilly.fr

GERMANY, SWITZERLAND, AUSTRIA, LUXEMBOURG, AND LIECHTENSTEIN

INQUIRIES & ORDERS

O'Reilly Verlag
Balthasarstr. 81
D-50670 Köln, Germany
Telephone: 49-221-973160-91
Fax: 49-221-973160-8
Email: anfragen@oreilly.de (inquiries)
Email: order@oreilly.de (orders)

CANADA

(FRENCH LANGUAGE BOOKS)
Les Éditions Flammarion ltée
375, Avenue Laurier Ouest
Montréal (Québec) H2V 2K3
Tel: 1-514-277-8807
Fax: 1-514-278-2085
Email: info@flammarion.qc.ca

HONG KONG

City Discount Subscription Service, Ltd.
Unit A, 6th Floor, Yan's Tower
27 Wong Chuk Hang Road
Aberdeen, Hong Kong
Tel: 852-2580-3539
Fax: 852-2580-6463
Email: citydis@ppn.com.hk

KOREA

Hanbit Media, Inc.
Chungmu Bldg. 210
Yonnam-dong 568-33
Mapo-gu
Seoul, Korea
Tel: 822-325-0397
Fax: 822-325-9697
Email: hant93@chollian.dacom.co.kr

PHILIPPINES

Global Publishing
G/F Benavides Garden
1186 Benavides Street
Manila, Philippines
Tel: 632-254-8949/632-252-2582
Fax: 632-734-5060/632-252-2733
Email: globalp@pacific.net.ph

TAIWAN

O'Reilly Taiwan
1st Floor, No. 21, Lane 295
Section 1, Fu-Shing South Road
Taipei, 106 Taiwan
Tel: 886-2-27099669
Fax: 886-2-27038802
Email: mori@oreilly.com

INDIA

Shroff Publishers & Distributors Pvt. Ltd.
12, "Roseland", 2nd Floor
180, Waterfield Road, Bandra (West)
Mumbai 400 050
Tel: 91-22-641-1800/643-9910
Fax: 91-22-643-2422
Email: spd@vsnl.com

CHINA

O'Reilly Beijing
SIGMA Building, Suite B809
No. 49 Zhichun Road
Haidian District
Beijing, China PR 100080
Tel: 86-10-8809-7475
Fax: 86-10-8809-7463
Email: beijing@oreilly.com

JAPAN

O'Reilly Japan, Inc.
Yotsuya Y's Building
7 Banch 6, Honshio-cho
Shinjuku-ku
Tokyo 160-0003 Japan
Tel: 81-3-3356-5227
Fax: 81-3-3356-5261
Email: japan@oreilly.com

SINGAPORE, INDONESIA, MALAYSIA, AND THAILAND

TransQuest Publishers Pte Ltd
30 Old Toh Tuck Road #05-02
Sembawang Kimtrans Logistics Centre
Singapore 597654
Tel: 65-4623112
Fax: 65-4625761
Email: wendiw@transquest.com.sg

AUSTRALIA

Woodslane Pty., Ltd.
7/5 Vuko Place
Warriewood NSW 2102
Australia
Tel: 61-2-9970-5111
Fax: 61-2-9970-5002
Email: info@woodslane.com.au

NEW ZEALAND

Woodslane New Zealand, Ltd.
21 Cooks Street (P.O. Box 575)
Waganui, New Zealand
Tel: 64-6-347-6543
Fax: 64-6-345-4840
Email: info@woodslane.com.au

ARGENTINA

Distribuidora Cuspide
Suipacha 764
1008 Buenos Aires
Argentina
Phone: 54-11-4322-8868
Fax: 54-11-4322-3456
Email: libros@cuspide.com

ALL OTHER COUNTRIES

O'Reilly & Associates, Inc.
1005 Gravenstein Hwy North
Sebastopol, CA 95472 USA
Tel: 707-829-0515
Fax: 707-829-0104
Email: order@oreilly.com

O'REILLY®

TO ORDER: **800-998-9938** • **order@oreilly.com** • **www.oreilly.com**
ONLINE EDITIONS OF MOST O'REILLY TITLES ARE AVAILABLE BY SUBSCRIPTION AT **safari.oreilly.com**
ALSO AVAILABLE AT MOST RETAIL AND ONLINE BOOKSTORES